FAMILY DEVELOPMENT

FAMILY DEVELOPMENT

FOURTH EDITION

Evelyn Millis Duvall, Ph.D.

Family Life Consultant

J. B. Lippincott Company

Philadelphia, New York, Toronto

THIRD PRINTING

ISBN-O-397-47238-2

Library of Congress
Catalog Card Number:
78-124987

Printed in the
United States of America

Cover and interior
design by Peter Bertolami

Charts drawn by
Martin L. May, Jr.

PREFACE

This book is designed to equip the preprofessional worker with conceptual tools useful in his or her work with families, and to help the experienced worker get a sharper cutting edge on the tools of his or her profession: teaching, public health work, extension work, social agency programs, community development, social work, family life education, counseling and research, or whatever involves working with and for families and family members.

The thesis of the book is that families grow through predictable stages of development that can be understood in terms of the development of the individual family members and of the family as a whole. It deals with concepts that have been in the process of formulation for many years, with hundreds of persons contributing to their development.

The Developmental Task Concept—A Personal History

When I returned to the University of Chicago in 1941–1942 to complete my residency for a Ph.D. in human development, I was fresh from seven years' active community work with teenage youth and their parents. At that time "impulses" and "drives" were popular ways of interpreting adolescent behavior. Such concepts appeared to remove responsibility for their behavior from young people, and to make it seem to them and to those who worked with them that adolescents were, as one writer in a book for youth put it, "human puppets on an invisible string." Such a point of view interpreting human behavior in terms mainly of biological drives was inacceptable to me.

Another concept that had gained considerable acceptance was that of "needs." This had the advantage of recognizing that people, like all other growing organisms, have needs that must be met if they are to grow satisfactorily. It had the disadvantage of being ambiguous. Even more serious from my point of view was that so often "the needs of youth" were discussed in terms of the limitations and inadequacies of schools, families, and community agencies in meeting these seemingly inexhaustible requirements. Youth was too often seen as an empty cup impatiently waiting for someone or something to fill it. Problems were seen as reflecting unmet needs. Growth of young people was likened to that of a tomato plant, which, given the proper amounts and kinds of nutrients, sunshine, moisture, and other requirements, would flower and bear fruit in due time. Again, the person himself had little responsibility for his behavior, development, or destiny.

It was with this immediate background that I found members of the Committee on Human Development exploring the possibilities of the concept of the developmental task. Work in classes, seminars, and professional workshops with Daniel Prescott, director of the Division of Child Study of the Commission on Teacher Education of the American Council on Education, and a member of the faculty of the University of Chicago, first introduced me to the developmental task concept. Study with Robert J. Havighurst, who had just come to the University of Chicago as chairman of the Committee on Human Development, acquainted me with the history of the developmental task concept to that time. He credits Lawrence K. Frank with first using the term in his hearing about 1935, at one of the many meetings of the staff of the Progressive Education Association's "Adolescent Study" under the direction of Caroline Zachry.[1] It is probable that the original idea came from Frankwood Williams, who several years earlier had published essays stressing what youth must do to work through his developmental problems.[2]

Peter Blos of the Adolescent Study Staff referred briefly to adolescent adjustment problems as "tasks" in his book that appeared in 1941[3] as one of several volumes published by members of the staff in which adolescence was increasingly recognized as a time of life in which certain essential tasks must be mastered if the young person is to emerge into effective adulthood.

The first published work giving a central place to the developmental task concept was a chapter written collaboratively by Robert J. Havighurst, Daniel Prescott, and Fritz Redl for the North Central Association's *General Education in the American High School* in 1942.[4]

The developmental task concept satisfied my search for a frame of reference that dealt dynamically with the challenges of human development, keeping responsibility in the hands of the developing persons, and still allowing room for the helping and assisting roles that family members, school personnel, and community workers might play. It satisfactorily met the objections raised in the use of "impulse," "drive," and "needs," and yet covered the realities implied in each of these concepts. Further, it seemed adequate to cover not only the developmental sequence of the teen years,

---

[1] Robert J. Havighurst, *Human Development and Education* (New York: Longmans, Green and Company, 1953), p. 328.

[2] Frankwood Williams, *Adolescence-Studies in Mental Hygiene* (New York: Farrar and Rinehart, 1930).

[3] Peter Blos, *The Adolescent Personality* (New York: Appleton-Century, 1941), p. 275. (This reference was mainly illustrative, with developmental task still to be recognized as a key concept.)

[4] B. L. Johnson, ed., *General Education in the American High School* (Chicago: Scott, Foresman, 1942), chap. 4.

but appeared to be quite as effective throughout the entire life cycle.

In 1943, the American Council on Education undertook, through a committee chaired by T. R. McConnell, to prepare an outline of objectives and courses in general education that would be appropriate for members of the armed forces. Ernest W. Burgess of the University of Chicago chaired the subcommittee, of which Reuben Hill, Oliver Ohmann, and myself were members, commissioned to draw up an outline of a course in marriage and family adjustment.[5]

As a result of this assignment Reuben Hill and I were appointed by the United States Armed Forces Institute to prepare a workbook on marriage and the family for the use of members of the armed services. This eventuated in the text *When You Marry*,[6] the first to be written functionally to satisfy student interests and readinesses, from "first date through last baby." It was during this collaboration that the life cycle approach, well known among sociologists, and the developmental task concept, emerging in human development, began to be seen as a series of developmental tasks through the life cycle.

In 1947, Reuben Hill and I were asked to work together in the preparation of background papers for the forthcoming National Conference on Family Life held in Washington in May, 1948. As cochairmen of the Committee on the Dynamics of Family Interaction, Dr. Hill and I prepared a two-dimensional outline for plotting the developmental tasks of children, and of parents, for each stage of the family life cycle with implications for services arising out of the challenges, hazards, and problems involved in the achievement of each developmental task in our culture. Eight subcommittees of specialists at the various developmental levels were appointed by the cochairmen to prepare reports on the various life cycle stages, as noted in chapters 7 through 15.

In referring to this committee's work, Dr. Havighurst credits it with creatively contributing to the development of the concept:

> This committee made a step forward in the use of the concept by showing how each member of the younger, middle, and older generations in the family has his own developmental tasks, and how the successful achievement of one person's tasks is dependent on and contributory to the successful achievement by others in the family of their appropriate tasks.[7]

The work of the Committee on the Dynamics of Family Interaction appeared in several hundred pages of mimeographed working papers used as background study

---

[5] American Council on Education, *A Design for General Education* (Washington, D.C.: American Council on Education, 1944), pp. 74–84.

[6] Evelyn Millis Duvall and Reuben Hill, *When You Marry* (Boston: D. C. Heath and Company; New York: Association Press, 1945).

[7] Havighurst, *Human Development and Education*, p. 331.

for the National Conference on Family Life.[8] Many years have come and gone since the report first appeared. In that interval, faculty members of several university centers have generously shared criticisms, questions, and further elaborations of the original materials that have helped bring it to the present state of development.

Family Development Tasks—Conceptual Origins

The idea of developmental tasks of the family as a whole emerged out of the first interdisciplinary workshop on marriage and family research at the University of Chicago during the summer of 1950, which, as executive for the National Council on Family Relations, I called and directed. One of the subgroups of that workshop set itself the task of carving out a multidisciplinary way of studying families that would have creative possibilities for research in family development. This 1950 Work Group in Family Development research was the first to formulate the concept of family developmental tasks as such. In its report it defined family developmental tasks as "those which must be accomplished by a family in a way that will satisfy (a) biological requirements, (b) cultural imperatives,

and (c) personal aspirations and values, if the family is to continue and grow as a unit."[9] Using the structure-function approach, this work group compiled an outline of family developmental tasks for stage one of the family life cycle. Since then, this outline has been greatly elaborated and extended to cover the entire family life cycle and developed into this book. Earlier editions attempted to do full justice to the contributions of the many family specialists who helped carve out the first basic outlines of how families develop through the family life cycle.

Now, new census and vital statistics data and projections, breakthroughs in research and theory in human development, and pioneer longitudinal family studies make it possible to take the next step in providing further substance to the structural outlines of the framework, which continues with refinements that have emerged over the years.

This edition of *Family Development* is in four parts. Part 1, "Growing Families in the Modern World," starts with a treatment of the functions of present-day families and reviews the types of family study contributing to the family development approach. This is followed by two chapters on how families differ by social status, and how families adapt to changing times in the modern world. Upon this is built a con-

---

[8] Evelyn Millis Duvall and Reuben Hill, "Report of the Committee on the Dynamics of Family Interaction," mimeographed (Washington, D.C.: National Conference on Family Life, 1948).

[9] Quoted by Reuben Hill in his report of the workshop—Reuben Hill, "Interdisciplinary Workshop on Marriage and Family Research," *Marriage and Family Living* 13, no. 1 (February 1951): 21–22.

sideration of the types and trends of family values as seen in child-rearing practices and policies. At this point, the reader is taken through the life cycle of the typical American man and wife in a series of stages in the family life cycle from its establishment by the original pair to the death of them both. There is explicit recognition of a generation overlap in that even though individual family members die, the family continues through one family life cycle after another in the generation spiral. Part 1 concludes with a basic orientation into the developmental tasks of families and of their members that readies the reader for the rest of the book that lies ahead.

Part 2, "Expanding Families," takes the family from its inception at the marriage of husband and wife through the period of expansion with the coming and rearing of children until they are about to be launched into lives of their own. Part 3, "Contracting Families," starts with the launching of the first young adult "child" from the family and follows the family through its middle and later years, with a final chapter on aging family members in modern society.

Part 4, "Developmental Prognoses and Prospects," points to the relative vulnerability of families at each stage of the family life cycle, with glimpses of what reliably may be expected throughout the years of a family's history. The book concludes with implications for personal, family, and social policies conducive to family development based upon known problems and potentials in family development. Woven through these policy recommendations are suggestions for explicit programs designed to facilitate developing families in attaining their potentialities as the building blocks of a free society. A glossary of terms and concepts is appended to help students in any one profession to get a quick working definition of terminology used in other disciplines whose work touches family development in one or more ways.

Each chapter is designed to put into the hands of the reader effective tools for a professional attitude toward families. Consequently, throughout the book there are outlines and detailed analyses for meeting the problems that arise in the family life cycle, such as child-proofing the home for the rearing of children, checking a child's readiness for school, gathering information on how to prepare a child for a new baby brother or sister, building in safety features in the home during the middle and later years, learning to live with in-laws, adjusting to bereavement.

Readings are more extensive than is usual in a book of this kind so that they may (1) stimulate the student of the family and (2) functionally serve the professional worker who is currently concerned with the problems of families and family members.

Suggested activities offer a variety of methods, materials, and resources for a multifaceted approach to teaching and learning in family development. These become, in essence, built-in teachers' guides, with proposals for papers, projects, and questions for open-book examinations, as well as designs for self-appraisal, at strategic points throughout the text.

Considerable advance in family theory and research in recent years has made possible extensive updating and upgrading throughout this edition. I am grateful to the busy professional specialists who gave time from full schedules to read this work critically and who, in every instance, added something of their own wisdom and expert knowledge to particular chapters. It should be clear that a book such as this is the work of no single author alone; it represents the thinking of the most creative minds in professions holding central concerns in family living. It would be inadequate to merely acknowledge these contributors, but it is appropriate to recognize them as the collaborators they all are in the development of this work.

EVELYN MILLIS DUVALL, PH.D.

Sarasota, Florida
November, 1970

CONTENTS

LIST OF CHARTS

LIST OF TABLES

PART 1

GROWING FAMILIES IN THE MODERN WORLD

1

FAMILY DEVELOPMENT—
A WAY OF SEEING FAMILIES

The family is the nucleus of civilization. Will Durant

When you think of families, do you think of your own? The one in which you grew up? The one you are a member of now? One you will establish some day? If you do, you are seeing families as most people do, through the experience you have had as a family member. Your own family and others you have known personally over the years are your base line for recognizing the dynamics of family life. Such an egocentric view of families is understandable, and to be expected. But it is limited to your own kind of family in your special setting, at your particular time in history. It does not take into account the many families unlike your own, nor does it recognize the form and function your family of the future may take.

Families in the mass media are portrayed as mother-father-young children combinations with monotonous regularity. Television commercials and situation comedies beam in on middle-class, middle-sized mediocrity with few exceptions. Church literature and religious materials of the various faiths and denominations deal with little beyond the families of their church school children, with but infrequent attention to the unmarried, the childless cou-

ple, of the parents without partners in the community. Family-of-the-year awards rarely go to any but the freshly washed, prosperous, intact family that is seen as the backbone of the society. Business makes "family rates" available for mother, father, and minor children in transportation, movies, and restaurants, with little concession made for aging family members or others in need of special consideration. Housing developments, insurance programs, nutritional and preventive health campaigns are rightly designed for families with small children, even though they represent but a minority of all families.

Families in the news are by definition atypical; otherwise they would not be newsworthy. Few newspapers or magazines are sold on the appeal of ordinary families doing everyday things. The families headlined on the front pages of our papers are involved in some tragedy, accident, crime, or achievement that is beyond readers' usual experience. Such things happen in every country and culture, and it is the job of the reporter to get them into the news coverage as quickly and prominently as possible. But they are hardly an accurate gauge of the health and well-being of families in general.

Typical actions and interactions of family members are but rarely reported publicly. The milestones of a family's experience are memorable to its own members, but are of little general interest. So, listed on the back pages of the daily paper, and but seldom in the so-called "family magazines" are the births, confirmations, graduations, marriages, retirements, and deaths of family members—of someone else's family usually. Yet these are the punctuation points of family development—the stuff of life itself.

Why Study Families?

If everyone "knows" about family life from his own experience, why is family study needed? The answer is tenfold: (1) to get a broader view of family life than has been afforded by the experience of growing up in any one family; (2) to correct the fallacies and distortions that prevail in a society about the intimate areas of life that center in personal and family living; (3) to focus on the normal aspects of family living in contradistinction to the atypical, abnormal forms more often reported; (4) to test objectively what "everybody knows," which in many instances is untrue; (5) to recognize the family as the hub of society around which all other institutions and groups revolve—in every society and subculture known to man through all of history; (6) to learn more of the foundations of human

development that lie in family life; (7) to keep up with the changes in families resulting from their adaptation to changing social conditions; (8) to see and foresee the predictable problems and potentialities that arise from time to time in all families as they change in form and function over the years; (9) to attain reliable bases for individual and family decisions that occur and recur throughout the life-span; and (10) to adopt valid plans and policies for future family situations in a given home, community, or nation.

MODERN FAMILY FUNCTIONS

Critics of American families make much of the fact that most modern families no longer perform many of the old functions that used to prevail. No longer do women "slave over a hot stove," preparing meals from foodstuffs they have grown and processed. Few family members today wear "homemade" garments as used to be typical. The health and medical care of family members is largely the responsibility of professionals in clinics, hospitals, medical centers, and nursing homes, rather than relying on home remedies as once was the case. Formal education of children is no longer in the hands of parents, having long since been turned over to professionally trained educators. Children's play is supervised by child care center personnel, youth-serving agency staffs, and paid baby-sitters now that parents are often away from home to an extent unheard of at an earlier time. Family protection is no longer dependent upon the rifle over the fireplace and the water bucket in the well, but rather is the duty of police and fire departments in most communities. What functions are left to the family itself? What, indeed, but the most important tasks of all—those of producing human beings capable of living creatively in a world their fathers never knew. Social changes through the twentieth century require families to respond to new needs, conditions, and challenges, as well as to create fresh images of who they are and what they must do to adapt creatively in today's world.

The modern family "is more specialized than before, but not in a general sense less important, because the society is dependent *more* exclusively for the performance of *certain* of its vital functions," says Talcott Parsons.[1] The new image of family life is that of the nurturing center for human development.

Men and women as fathers and mothers today are engaged in childbearing and rearing with conscious intent upon socializing the child, transforming him or her from an immature human organism into a participating member of society, capable of creative contribution and personal integrity in a complicated, explosive world situation. Parents themselves recognize that they too must continue to develop if they are to find personal happiness and be of some good to others. The garden for human development, both child and adult, continues to be the family, in which the emotional soil and the spiritual climate for human growth originate.

A family is, therefore, the matrix of personality which emerges as the idiomatic patterns of functioning, of habits, ideas, beliefs, values, assumptions, and, above all, of emotional reactions and persistent feelings as each child learns to live within his particular family in his or her own individual way.

Families are still the primary agents for health: in the selection and preparation of food for adequate nutrition in family meals; in the establishment of attitudes conducive to healthful eating, eliminating, resting, working, and being, as well as in the endless tasks of housecleaning, laundering, dishwashing, and all the other functions that cannot be performed by doctors or outside medical agencies, but must be provided for in the home.

Families are the primary agents for basic mental health, which cannot be brought about solely by psychiatrists, psychologists, or social workers. Only the family can protect and conserve the mental health of individuals through the quality of interpersonal relationships, the provision of reassurance and comfort, the release and encouragement that each person needs to keep on

---

[1] Talcott Parsons and Robert F. Bales, *Family, Socialization and Interaction Process* (Glencoe, Ill.: Free Press, 1955), pp. 9–10.

FAMILY DEVELOPMENT

striving for fulfillment. Love itself, the prime necessity for mental health, has its genesis in the intimate, everyday warmth that husbands and wives, parents and children find in and with each other.

The family is a unity of interacting persons related by ties of marriage, birth, or adoption, whose central purpose is to create and maintain a common culture which promotes the physical, mental, emotional, and social development of each of its members.[2] Modern families fulfill the promise of this definition through at least six emergent, nontraditional functions: (1) affection between husband and wife, parents and children, and among the generations; (2) personal security and acceptance of each family member for the unique individual he is and for the potential he represents; (3) satisfaction and a sense of purpose; (4) continuity of companionship and association; (5) social placement and socialization; (6) controls and a sense of what is right.

Affection is a product of family living. Men and women marry for love and usually beget their children as an expression of their love for one another. Their children literally have to have love in order to survive and thrive in an emotional climate of ongoing affection. The family unit stays together through the years not because it has to, but because the members want to,

out of their love for one another. Marital and family happiness are gauged by the strength of the love that family members have for one another. The majority of wives feel that their families are more closely knit than "most other families" they know, thereby attesting to the depth of affection they feel and generate in their homes.[3] Modern man looks for love and affection in his home, where it can be found in normal, legitimate, healthy forms not generally available so freely elsewhere. A man's love for his sons and daughters is an extension of the affection he and his wife share. Ideally, both parents and children grow in a climate of mutual affection that assures them of optimal development. Families, therefore, do more than regulate the sex drive and reproduce the members of the next generation; they bear and rear their young in an ongoing, nurturing setting that is essential for the attainment of full human potential.

Personal security and acceptance are important for every member of society. It is to the family that most persons look for the security and acceptance they need to live lives of dignity and worth. Home is a haven in the sense that "if you have to go there, they have to take you in." Families fill the needs for food and clothing, shelter and sustaining care. But more, the family

---

[2] For a fuller discussion see Ernest W. Burgess and Harvey J. Locke, *The Family*, 2d ed. (New York: American Book Company, 1953), pp. 7–8.

[3] Robert O. Blood, Jr., *Impact of Urbanization on American Family Structure and Functioning* (Ann Arbor: Center for Research on Social Organization, 1964), pp. 8–9.

is the primary source of mental and emotional health for its members. It is in the family that individuals may make mistakes within an atmosphere of protection and have the opportunity to learn from their mistakes in a climate of security. The family is among the few remaining places where complementary, rather than competitive, relationships can be learned and enjoyed. It thus affords a stable and continuing home base in which all its members may grow and develop, each in his own way, each at his own pace.

Satisfaction and sense of purpose are basic needs modern families fulfill in an industrial age. Job satisfactions for the unskilled worker are infrequent, and at higher levels of employment are mixed with anxiety, conflict, and struggle. In the modern age a man's basic satisfactions are found in his family, at the same time that a woman's sense of purpose and reason for being lie in her family roles, more often than not. It is the family that functions to give modern man a sense of basic satisfaction and worth in ways the industrial world only occasionally provides. It is in the family that adults and children enjoy life and each other—in family gatherings, around the family table, in family rituals, on family trips and vacations, in front of the television set, and in myriad other ways in which family members find satisfaction and pleasure.

Continuity of companionship and association is assured by families more than any other institution or group. There is an expectation of permanence in his family that means much to modern man. Friends, neighbors, work associates, teachers, religious leaders, and others may not be close more than a few years. A man expects to change his work from time to time over the years. Family moves from place to place occur with predictable regularity. Only family associations continue for most people, most of the time. It is as families that persons attend religious services, are expected at community events, and spend an evening with friends. Companionship means a chance to relate the happenings of the day, to share the disappointments and satisfactions as they occur in ways difficult outside the family. Who but members of one's family can join so fully in the flush of success, or share so completely the burden of disappointment? It is companionship that over the years ranks high as a function of family life.

Social placement and socialization are essential family functions in any society. In the complexity of the modern age they are imperative. At his birth a child is placed in the status of his family within the genetic, physical, ethnic, national, religious, cultural, economic, political, and educational heritage unique to his parents and their kin. The family functions as the transmitter of the cultural heritage of the race from one generation to the next. It serves as an ongoing interpreter to all its members of the meanings of the many situations of which they are a part. The elder family members serve as role models for the younger ones, as the boys identify with their fathers, and the girls with their mothers through the formative years of personality development.

It is also generally recognized that lifelong patterns of behavior, values, goals, and attitudes of children are strongly associated with the characteristics of their parents, especially as these are expressed in child-rearing and family life styles. Although later experiences outside the home also have important influences on the developing child, the availability of these experiences to him and the ways in which he uses them . . . are strongly affected by what he has learned in his home.[4]

Establishing limits and inculcating a sense of what is right are twin functions of the family. It is in the family that individuals learn the rules and rights, the obligations and the responsibilities essential for the survival of a society. Family members keep an eye on one another and feel free to encourage or to criticize, to suggest or to order, to praise or to blame, to reward or to punish, to entice or to threaten each other in ways that are unthinkable elsewhere. "In all these ways, the family is an instrument or agent of the larger society; its failure to perform adequately means that the goals of the larger society may not

CAMERA PRESS — PIX

Little girls identify with their mothers through the formative years of personality development.

be attained effectively."[5] The early sense of right or wrong learned in what a child was praised or punished for in his earliest years carries over into adulthood in a person's moral values and definitions of the good, the right, and the worthy. The family acts as "the choosing agency" between many ways of life, and so serves as the primary source of human values that spread outward into society as a whole.

[4] Catherine S. Chilman, *Growing Up Poor*, Welfare Administration Publication, no. 13 (Washington, D.C., 1966), p. 2.

[5] William J. Goode, *The Family* (Englewood Cliffs, N.J.: Prentice-Hall, 1964), p. 5.

Family life is here to stay because it serves society in urgently needed ways and because it meets basic needs of individuals better than any other group or institution now known. Families are expected to bear and rear responsible citizens capable of carrying the responsibilities of today's complex society. "Without a family unit to deal with the idiosyncracies of aged parents, the emotional needs of adults, or the insecurities of children, very likely not enough adequately functioning people would be produced to man the industrial system."[6]

Family Interaction

Families function through the continuing interaction of their members. Family interaction is the process by which a family relates to life outside itself, and through which one member's action is stimulated by the behavior of other members within the family.[7] Family interaction is the sum total of all the family roles being played within a given family. Family roles are *reciprocal*, in that the roles played by each family member are related directly to roles played by others in the family. Each of these roles is defined by *norms*[8] which both the family and the larger society expect of the person occupying a given position. The *position* a family member holds is a location in the family associated with a set of social norms. A family, then, can be seen as composed of a number of positions related to each other in dyads, i.e., paired positions of "father" and "child," "husband" and "wife." Thus one family member can occupy two (or more) positions: both husband and father (as well as son, brother, etc.).

A *role* is a part of a social position consisting of a more or less integrated or related set of social norms distinguishable from other sets of norms forming the same position. For instance, father plays many roles in the family—that of breadwinner, teacher, disciplinarian, companion, and so forth. These concurrent roles may be thought of as a *role cluster*.

Although a role is defined by the expectations the group has for it (social norms), it is rarely played in exactly the same way. The manner in which a person actually plays a given role may be termed *role behavior*, i.e., a given father's actual performance as provider. When the role behavior deviates too greatly from the norms, negative *sanctions* in the form of punishment are applied to press the person to

---

[6] Ibid., p. 109.

[7] See Robert F. Bales, *Interaction Process Analysis* (Cambridge, Mass.: Addison-Wesley Press, 1950); and George C. Homans, *The Human Group* (New York: Harcourt, Brace and Company, 1950).

[8] For a discussion of the concepts norm, position, and role, as they are used here, see Frederick L. Bates, "Position, Role, and Status: A Reformulation of Concepts," *Social Forces* 34, no. 4 (May 1956): 313–321.

meet group expectations. A person's role behavior that conforms to the norms may bring forth positive sanctions as rewards from the group.

Throughout his lifetime each person is a developing and changing organism—biologically, intellectually, and socially. As a person develops, he is expected to take on new roles and to abandon old ones. That is, the role content of the positions he holds over time changes. If the individual is to be an acceptable member of the family, he must play those roles expected of him by virtue of his position in the group. If he does not, or is incapable of doing so for one reason or another, his adjustment in the group, and hence his personal adjustment, will suffer, as does also the adjustment of the family group.

TYPES OF FAMILY STUDY

Families lend themselves to a variety of types of research. Families can be seen from many points of view, each one providing a different aspect of the reality to be found in family contexts. Since families are the laboratories of life, as most people live it, they are important testing grounds for all kinds of theories, programs, and evaluative studies. Because families put into operation the recommendations of the various professional disciplines, they must be understood well enough to provide viable access for the helping agents of the society. Each discipline limits itself to those facets of family life that have some bearing upon its theoretical interests explorable with the tools and methods of its profession.

The discussion that follows deliberately omits certain areas of professional study of and interest in families. Biology, with its many family foci in genetic studies, metabolic rates, energy levels, reproductive cycles, and organic functioning, is not explicitly dealt with; nor are the many medical, surgical, and therapeutic practices involving families and family members. Housing, architecture, community planning, urban renewal, public and private developments of single and multi-unit dwellings are all concerned with family living and could gain much by knowledge of family development; yet they belong largely outside the scope of this discussion. Food and fiber production and distribution and the channeling of the many products of industry to families as ultimate consumers are tangential to the focus of this treatment.

Family study, as herein considered, is an ongoing activity of the several behavioral sciences and disciplines. Listed alphabetically in table 1–1 is a series of fifteen of the social sciences and disciplines conducting research in one or more aspects of family life. The illustrative studies are not all-inclusive, but serve to indicate kinds of studies that have been undertaken in a given category. The listing of representative researchers is only that, necessarily

Table 1–1. *Behavioral Sciences and Disciplines Involved in Family Study*

Disciplines	Illustrative studies	Representative researchers*
Anthropology Cultural anthropology Social anthropology Ethnology	Cultural and subcultural family forms and functions Cross-cultural comparative family patterns Ethnic, racial, and social status family differences Families in primitive, developing, and industrial societies	Ruth Benedict Allison Davis Clyde Kluckhohn Oscar Lewis Ralph Linton Helen and Robert Lynd Margaret Mead George Murdock W. Lloyd Warner
Counseling Counseling theory Clinical practice Evaluation	Dynamics of interpersonal relationships in marriage and family Methods and results of individual, marriage, and family counseling	Rollo May Emily Hartshorne Mudd James K. Peterson Carl Rogers
Demography	Census and vital statistics on many facets of family life Cross-sectional, longitudinal, and record-linkage surveys Differential birth rates Family planning and population control	Donald Bogue Hugh Carter Harold Christensen Ronald Freedman Paul Glick Philip Hauser P. K. Whelpton
Economics	Consumer behavior, marketing, and motivation research Insurance, pensions, and welfare needs of families Standards of living, wage scales, socioeconomic status	Robert C. Angell Howard Bigelow Milton Friedman John Kenneth Galbraith John Morgan Margaret Reid
Education Early childhood Early elementary Secondary College Parent Professional	Child-rearing methods Developmental patterns Educational methods and evaluation Family life education Motivation and learning Preparation for marriage Sex education	Orville Brim Catherine Chilman Cyril Houle Harold Lief Nevitt Sanford Ralph Tyler James Walters
History	Historical roots of modern family Origins of family patterns Predictions of the future of families Social influences on the family Social trends and adaptations	Arthur Calhoun Franklin Frazier Bernard Stern Edward Westermarck Carle Zimmerman

Disciplines	Illustrative studies	Representative researchers*
Home economics	Evaluation of practices and measurement of	Muriel Brown
Family relationships	educational results	Irma Gross
Home economics education	Family food habits and nutrition	Paulena Nickell
Home management	Home management practices	Evelyn Spindler
Nutrition	Relationships between family members	Alice Thorpe
Human development	Character development	Nancy Bayley
Child development	Child growth and development	Urie Bronfenbrenner
Adolescent development	Developmental norms and differences	Erik Erikson
Middle age and aging	Nature of cognitive learning	Dale Harris
	Cross-cultural variations	Robert Havighurst
	Personality development	Lois Barclay Murphy
	Social roles of aging	Bernice Neugarten
		Jean Piaget
Law	Adoption and child protection	Paul Alexander
	Child care and welfare	John Bradway
	Marriage and family law	Harriet Daggett
	Divorce and marital dissolution	Marie Kargman
	Sexual controls and behavior	Harriet Pilpel
	Parental rights and responsibilities	Max Rheinstein
Psychoanalysis	Abnormal and normal behavior	Nathan Ackerman
	Clinical diagnosis and therapy	Erik Erikson
	Foundations of personality	John Flugel
	Stages of development	Irene Josselyn
	Treatment of mental illness	Harry Stack Sullivan
Psychology	Aspirations and self-concepts	Rosalind Dymond
Clinical	Drives, needs, and hungers	Gerald Gurin
Developmental	Dynamics of interpersonal interaction	Robert Hess
Social	Learning theory	Eleanore Luckey
	Mental health	Frederick Stodtbeck
	Therapeutic intervention	John Whiting
Public health	Epidemiology and immunization	Cecelia Deschin
	Family health and preventive medicine	Nicholson Eastman
	Maternal and infant health	Earl L. Koos
	Noxious materials research	Niles Newton
	Pediatric health education	Clark Vincent
	Venereal disease	
Religion	Church policies on marriage and family	Stanley Brav
	Families of various religions	Roy Fairchild
	Interfaith marriage	Seward Hiltner
	Love, sex, marriage, divorce, and family in	John L. Thomas
	religious contexts	John C. Wynn

Table 1–1. *Behavioral Sciences and Disciplines Involved in Family Study—Continued*

Disciplines	*Illustrative studies*	*Representative researchers**
Social work	Appraising family need	Dorothy F. Beck
Family casework	Devising constructive programs for family	L. L. Geismar
Group work	assistance	James Hardy
Social welfare	Measuring family functioning	Charlotte Towle
Sociology	Courtship and mate selection	Ernest W. Burgess
	Family formation and functioning	Ruth S. Cavan
	Effects of social change on families	Harold Christensen
	Family crises and dissolution	Reuben Hill
	Prediction of family success	Judson Landis
	Social class influence on families	Marvin Sussman

* Illustrative of those research workers whose published findings may be available to students of the family in various disciplines; not an all-inclusive listing.

omitting many productive scholars whose work is acknowledged elsewhere. The table serves to give scope to the discussion of the types of family research a student of whatever discipline may encounter in his study of families and their members.

INTERDISCIPLINARY APPROACHES TO FAMILY STUDY

Beyond the research initiated and carried out by the separate professions are areas of family study conducted collaboratively by workers from two or more disciplines. Scholars developing family theory and re-search find interdisciplinary approaches fruitful in making more than one vantage point available at a time. The specialized concepts of the combined disciplines provide a variety of lenses, giving depth of field as each discipline sheds light on some aspect of family life.

Specialists in family theory recognize a number of conceptual frameworks being employed in family research. They view a conceptual framework as a group of related concepts that tells a scholar where to focus his attention in studying some facet of family life. Since each of the behavioral sciences has its own basic assumptions, concepts, and methods of study, conceptual frameworks using the interdisciplinary approach give a multifaceted view of the problem being investigated. Interdisciplinary family research may be discussed under five approaches:[9] (1) the institutional-historical approach, (2) the structure-function approach, (3) the interactional approach, (4) the situational approach, and (5) the family development approach.

The institutional-historical approach combines history and sociology in family study. It grew out of eighteenth-century anthropological studies of families in various cultures, and still deals largely with cross-cultural, historical, and evolutionary aspects of family study. The institutional-historical approach sees families as institutions active and reactive to other social, material, and cultural components within a society. Research by such scholars as William Fielding Ogburn, John Sirjamaki, and Carle C. Zimmerman exemplifies this approach in studying American families. As a conceptual framework, it functions best in tracing family change over long periods of time, but it does not attempt to deal with interpersonal interaction or with the behavior of families and their members.

The structure-function approach comes from anthropology and sociology. It views the family as a social system within the community and the larger society. It sees the family interacting with other social systems, like the school, or functioning in small groups, such as the husband-wife dyad. Family studies by Kingsley Davis, William J. Goode, Robert Merton, Talcott Parsons, W. Lloyd Warner, and others are illustrative of the structure-function approach in the United States. Enjoying a strong theoretical development in recent years, it copes well with the interaction of the family with other institutions in society, but it does not deal with change.

The interactional approach has developed in sociology and social psychology as an outgrowth of the work of George Herbert Mead and his followers at the University of Chicago. As early as 1928, Ernest W. Burgess defined the family as "an arena of interacting personalities." Among many American research scholars using the interactional approach are Ruth Shonle Cavan, Leonard S. Cottrell, Gerald Handel, Robert Hess, Reuben Hill, Mirra Komarovsky, Willard Waller, and Paul Wallin. The interactional approach sees the family as a relatively closed system of interaction. It is especially fruitful in studying processes of communication, conflict, decision-making, problem-solving, and reaction to crisis. It tends to focus upon the family members in

---

[9] Fuller discussion of conceptual frameworks in family research may be found in Reuben Hill and Donald A. Hansen, "The Identification of Conceptual Frameworks Utilized in Family Study," *Marriage and Family Living* 22, no. 4 (November 1960): 299–311; Harold T. Christensen, ed., *Handbook of Marriage and the Family* (Chicago: Rand McNally and Company, 1964), pt. 1, pp. 3–211; F. Ivan Nye and Felix M. Berardo, eds., *Emerging Conceptual Frameworks in Family Analysis* (New York: Macmillan Company, 1966); and Reuben Hill, with chapters in collaboration with Nelson Foote, Joan Aldous, Robert Carlson, and Robert Macdonald, *Family Development in Three Generations* (Cambridge, Mass.: Schenkman Publishing Company, 1970), chap. 1.

given groups of families rather than upon cultural patterns or institutional aspects of family life.

The situational approach has roots in both psychology and sociology. It is able to freeze time so as to catch a given situation in sharp focus. It is helpful in exploring the related elements in a given situation within a family or other group. Family researchers employing the situational approach include Robert O. Blood, Jr., Eleanor S. Boll and James H. S. Bossard, Oscar Lewis, W. I. Thomas, and others. The situational approach has strength in analyzing family interaction and the two-way interplay of family members with the family as a whole. Since it relies on observation and interviewing methods, there is little attempt to capture changes in families over long periods of time, or to study the ways in which families interact with other groups and institutions in the society.

The family development approach is highly interdisciplinary in its combination of concepts, insights, and methods from the fields of biology, cultural anthropology, demography, developmental psychology, home economics (especially child development and family relationships and home management), human development (infant, child, adolescent, as well as young, middle-aged, and aging adult), several branches of medicine, psychology, and sociology. Researchers using this approach have been most notably Robert J. Havighurst and colleagues over the years, Harold Feldman, Wells Goodrich, Reuben Hill, Rhona Rapoport, Roy Rodgers, Marvin Sussman, and others.

USING THE FAMILY DEVELOPMENT APPROACH

Family development borrows its lenses from a number of disciplines. From rural sociology comes the generational sweep of the family life cycle. From human development comes awareness of developmental tasks, critical periods of development seen as developmental crises, and their teachable moments. From sociology come the insights of social change, social class, and other invaluable filters. From anthropology comes the vision of cultural influences that shape and are shaped by families. From psychology are the contributions of learning theory and of interaction processes. From home economics the foci of child development and family relationships, home management, housing, and nutritional aspects of family practices are utilized. Family development is an intricate complex that offers much to family study.[10]

---

[10] For a diagrammatic treatment see Clifford Kirkpatrick, "Familial Development, Selective Needs, and Predictive Theory," *Journal of Marriage and the Family* 29, no. 2 (May 1967): 229–236; and Carlfred B. Broderick, "Reaction to 'Familial Development, Selective Needs, and Predictive Theory,'" *Journal of Marriage and the Family* 29, no. 2 (May 1967): 237–240.

Table 1–2. *Properties of the Developmental Approach*

Social time:

Copes well with action and interaction, as well as with change and process over time. The time span is the life cycle of the nuclear family, the basic time units are stages demarcated by spurts of growth and development.

Social space:

1. Area: Emphasizes changing internal structure and development of family. May cope with family systems and collateral systems and with the personality system of members.

2. Environment: Cultural imperatives and demands.

3. Peripheral: Agencies outside the family; members' outside activities, physical elements.

4. Residual: Not determinable. Potentially can cope with full array of social and cultural elements with which the family has contact, including the social system (in structure-function terms).

Structure:

1. Units of study: Family group (basic); interacting individuals, individual.

2. Configuration: Basically life cycle and stages, family tempos and rhythms.

3. Cohesion: Basically developmental tasks (interrelating stages with one another) and roles and functions (interrelating individuals within stages).

Bridges:

1. Conditions: Basically teachable moment (physical maturation, cultural prerequisites, communication) and psychological elements such as perception, identity formation, and motivation.

2. Mechanisms: Little development apparent. Can probably borrow heavily from interactional and micro-functional approaches.

Overt behavior:

1. Transactional: Treatment of transactional be-

havior only now beginning; only limited development shown.

2. Interactional: Strong development likely. Can cope with individual interacts as well as process within a stage; stages and development allow treatment of long-range changes and process over time.

3. Actional: Little added development to date but leans on psychology of child development for identification of stages of individual growth and development.

Source: Reuben Hill and Donald A. Hansen, "The Identification of Conceptual Frameworks Utilized in Family Study," *Marriage and Family Living* 22, no. 4 (November 1960): 308, used with permission.

Family development sees family members in paired positions such as husband-wife, father-son, mother-daughter, brother-sister, grandmother-grandchild, and so forth. In using the family development approach, the family can be traced through a predictable history beginning with the newly married husband and wife whose family comes into being with the arrival of their children, enlarges to accommodate their sons and daughters as they appear, and then contracts as the children grow up and leave home for work and homes of their own.

The family development approach sees the orderly sequential changes to be expected in growth, development, and dissolution or decline within families throughout the entire family life cycle. In recognizing that there is an unbroken flow from one generation to the next, the family development approach envisages family life cycles overlapping one another in intergenerational interaction in predictable ways.

"Family development theory may be said to encompass the entire range of family behaviors which are stimulated and constrained by the changing age and sex composition of nuclear or extended families over the family life span."[11]

Simply summarized, family development (1) keeps the family in focus throughout its history, (2) sees each family member in interaction with all other members, (3) watches how individuals affect the family unit, and the ways the family influences individual development, (4) catches what a given family is going through at a particular time in its life and at a given point in history, (5) highlights critical periods of personal and family growth and development, (6) views both the universals and the differences among families, (7) beams in on the ways in which the culture influences family life, and how families make themselves felt, and (8) provides a predictive glass through which it is possible to forecast what a given family will be going through at any period in its life-span.

Ways of anticipating what to expect are inherent in family development. Knock on any door, and what will you find within? No one can tell you exactly, because each family differs in many ways from any other. But, generally, you can predict somewhat reliably the overall pattern of a family's activities if you know these three things: (1) where the family is in time (in history, year, season, day, and hour) and in its life

cycle; (2) the number, age, and relatedness of the family members in the household; (3) how the family rates in the community, as seen in its ethnic, religious, and social class status. When you know these three things before you meet a given family, you know what significant elements to look for and what forces you may expect to find in action within the family and its members.

Concepts in Family Development

As the most interdisciplinary of all approaches to family study, the family development approach sometimes suffers from semantic failure. The tendency is for each discipline to develop its own specialized language of words and terms which tend to be unintelligible to outsiders or to translate poorly from one scientist to another in a different discipline. Collaboration of workers from a number of professional backgrounds involves developing a common set of meanings to facilitate the necessary communication.

Concepts are more than words and phrases. In a real sense, they are tools to think with, ways of making sense of multitudes of particulars. Concepts are universal in human experience, wherever language is used. One speaks of "green," and listeners see the color; one reads of "roundness," and the shape is perceived. In the professions—education, law, medicine, sociology, and the others—concepts are developed, names are given them, and advances are made in distinguishing characteristics, pro-

---

[11] Hill, *Family Development in Three Generations,* chap. 13.

FAMILY DEVELOPMENT

cesses, cause and effect relationships, the universals and idiosyncratic phenomena. These achievements would be impossible without the clarification afforded by conceptual development.

Family development, as an interdisciplinary way of seeing families, represents a number of technical theories and areas of specialty. So, some familiarity with its major concepts, taken from a variety of disciplines, is essential for any student of whatever background. Those trained in home economics must become familiar with concepts used by sociologists; social science majors can benefit from familiarity with home economics conceptual terminology; and both from an orientation in child, adolescent, and adult phases of human development.

One step toward a broad-based interdisciplinary approach to family development is clarification of the assumptions, concepts, and generalizations a given discipline has already formulated.[12] The necessity for interdisciplinary exchange in the social sciences is widely recognized. An editorial in the *New York Times* for August 7, 1969, said in part:

> Social science—which embraces such disciplines as anthropology, economics, politics, psychology and sociology—is not

ever likely to attain the spectacular power of physics. But it can nevertheless be exceedingly useful in identifying emergent social problems and in providing time needed to devise public policies for their solution.

There is no dearth of social science research . . . but individual researchers seldom move beyond the confines of their specialties and communication between the disciplines is poor. These shortcomings would be remedied by a proposal set forth by a National Science Foundation panel. It calls for the establishment of interdisciplinary institutes that would bring to bear varieties of knowledge on specific social problems. . . .

A detailed glossary of terms and concepts used in family development appears at the end of this text. Many of these definitions are obviously simple to persons trained in one of the related fields. To those in other professional disciplines, and to students interested in interdisciplinary study, such a semantic foundation must be attained.

Growing Edges of the Family Development Approach

One of the newest of all approaches to family study, the family development approach has not yet achieved a fully developed theoretical base thoroughly tested by research. Functioning best in longitudinal research,

[12] A national project sponsored by the U.S. Office of Education has identified basic concepts and generalizations in home economics; see American Home Economics Association, "Report of a National Project," in *Concepts and Generalizations* (Washington, D.C.: American Home Economics Association, 1967), pp. 25–28.

it encounters a number of problems that smaller, shorter-term, horizontally designed studies do not have. Data from families over their entire life-spans are hard to gather, largely because families outlive the research team, as well as its commitment, its financing, and its authority to continue. Keeping in touch with the same families over many months and years is made difficult by changes in their residence, configurations, and interest in the project over a considerable period of time. Ways around these research problems are being developed in ingenious ways as the family development approach is explored. Still lacking to date, however, are adequate cross-cultural and subcultural studies in family development.

There are limitations in the family development approach in what it does not do while it is doing something else. While studying normal, intact families, it may lose track of deviant families involved in premature dissolution, divorce, remarriage, parents without partners, stepparents, and the many combinations of "his children, her children, and their children." Family development depends upon a number of divisions through the decades of the life-span to provide units small enough to conceptualize and to study in their critical periods of development. Breaking the family life cycle into too large units blurs an otherwise clear focus on the characteristics of a given period of life. Cutting up the family life cycle into too many stages yields too many units to cope with effectively.

Some compromise must be made as to how and when to break into the flow of family experience in such a way that meaningful study may be facilitated.

No one knows better than those who use the family development approach the many problems it presents. Nevertheless, there has been growing interest in this way of seeing and studying families ever since it was first designed in preparation for the first National Conference on Family Life in Washington, D.C., in 1948. Year by year it is making progress through the accretions of longitudinal research coming out of child development centers, human development programs, and most recently family study centers in major universities across the United States.

LONGITUDINAL RESEARCH

Longitudinal research studies a given population over time. It differs from the survey or horizontal study that explores aspects of a cross section of a population at any given moment. Longitudinal research is especially fruitful in that it: (1) keeps each participant in the study in focus, so that developmental patterns and individual differences emerge with clarity; (2) provides a time dimension in which developing individuals, families, interrelationships, recurrent crises, and growth plateaus may be

Table 1–3. *Representative Longitudinal Studies in Human Development*

Research center	Chief researchers	Illustrative published work
Brush Foundation Study of Child Development	E. Ebert K. Simmons	*Society for Research in Child Development,* vol. 8, no. 2 (1943).
Clinic of Child Development, Yale University	Arnold Gesell Frances Ilg	*Infant and Child in the Culture of Today; The Child from Five to Ten; Youth: The Years from Ten to Fifteen.*
Fels Research Institute for the Study of Human Development	Lester W. Sontag Charles T. Baker Virginia L. Nelson	"Mental Growth and Personality Development: A Longitudinal Study," *Society for Research in Child Development,* vol. 23, no. 68 (1958).
Harvard University Growth Study	W. F. Dearborn J. W. M. Rothney	*Predicting the Child's Development* (1941).
Menninger Foundation	Lois Barclay Murphy Sibylle Escalona Grace Heider	*Prediction and Outcome* (1959); *The Widening World of Childhood* (1962); *Methods in the Longitudinal Study of Children* (1963).
Stanford University	Lewis M. Terman	*The Gifted Child Grows Up* (1947); *The Gifted Group at Mid-life: Thirty-five Years' Follow-up of the Superior Child* (1959).
University of California Berkeley Growth Study	Nancy Bayley Harold E. Jones	"The Berkeley Growth Study," *Child Development,* vol. 12 (1941).
	Jean W. Macfarlane Lucile Allen Marjorie P. Honzik	*A Developmental Study of the Behavior Problems of Normal Children between Twenty-one Months and Fourteen Years* (1954).
University of Chicago Chicago Study	Frank Freeman C. D. Flory	"Growth in Intellectual Ability as Measured by Repeated Tests," *Society for Research in Child Development,* vol. 2, no. 2 (1937).
Committee on Human Development	Robert J. Havighurst Bernice Neugarten	*Growing Up in River City* (1962); *Middle Age and Aging* (1968).
University of Iowa	B. T. Baldwin	*The Physical Growth of Children from Birth to Maturity* (1921).
University of Minnesota	John E. Anderson	*Experience and Behavior in Early Childhood and the Adjustment of the Same Persons as Adults* (1963).

73- 551

seen; (3) gives a basis for comparing different patterns of development among the individuals or the families in the study; (4) makes it possible to describe the tendencies and trends that appear to be general within a population. For instance, from such norms and general patterns, early-developers and late-maturers at puberty can be spotted.

Longitudinal studies of infant, child, adolescent, and adult development have been under way over fifty years, in a number of research centers, under a variety of auspices, and by a far-flung constellation of scholars. Representative longitudinal studies in human development, most of which extended over ten or more years each, are listed in table 1-3, along with their chief investigators and titles of illustrative published work.

There is a search for reliable bases for prediction in these various investigations. In these and in other longitudinal studies of human development, the family life of the individual is kept in focus as a major influence in his development. Largely unheralded for their contributions to family development are ongoing longitudinal studies of persons as they grow and develop, each in his own way, in his own family, through the years, the decades, or, in a few instances, into the second and third generation. Longitudinal studies in human development parallel longitudinal family studies through the same decades of this century.

Family Studies with Longitudinal Depth

Men can study generations of fruit flies in a matter of months. Human families tend to outlive their researchers, and hence ways must be found to telescope the generations of family development within the lifetime of a research project. This has been done in five different ways in as many longitudinal marriage and family studies, brief descriptions of which follow.

1. The University of Chicago marriage prediction studies began in the early 1930s with intensive interviews of one thousand engaged couples in the greater Chicago area, by Ernest W. Burgess and Leonard Cottrell, whose book *Predicting Success or Failure in Marriage* (New York: Prentice-Hall, 1939) is a landmark. Fourteen years later, when most of these engaged pairs had been married for some time, Ernest Burgess and Paul Wallin reported a follow-up study of 666 of the original couples, now married. Their rationale was:

. . . it presents findings on the pairing of couples from their first dating experiences through the stages of going together, keeping steady company, engagement, and the first three to five years of marriage. In their interviews with engaged men and women the authors found out their relationships with their parents and brothers and sisters in childhood and adolescence. These data are utilized in analyzing the significance of family backgrounds for success in marriage.

This book is also unique in that it reports the use of data secured from a large group of couples *before* marriage to predict their success in marriage. Obviously in a strictly scientific study of marital success a sharp line must be drawn between the factors predictive of success in any given activity and the measurement of success in that activity. This is guaranteed only if replies on predictive items are secured from couples before marriage. Then the findings are not subject to criticism made of previous studies of the errors arising because background and other predictive data were obtained after marriage, and that consequently the information given by husbands and wives have been influenced by their happiness or unhappiness in marriage.[13]

The third wave of interviewing in what was called the "Middle Years of Marriage Study" was conducted when the original couples had been married up to twenty years. The summary and discussion of findings of this step in the longitudinal research reports:

> Data from the Burgess-Wallin longitudinal study of marriage indicate that a process of gradually reducing marital satisfaction or euphoria typically characterizes the marriages studied. It is further found that this loss of marital adjustment is not accompanied by equal loss of personal adjustment. Finally, different rates of disenchantment are found to characterize those who have married and those who subsequently divorced.

Viewing marriages in a processual sense, in which change is emphasized, offers a fruitful addition to the static view, which regards marital adjustment, for example, as a contemporary configuration of a limited number of attitudes and background factors.[14]

More recently, data from the first two waves of the Burgess-Wallin longitudinal study of marriage were reviewed with the focus of attention on three questions:

1. Do husbands and wives grow more alike with time?
2. Do women make more adjustments in marriage than men?
3. What are the determinants of rates of change in behavior and attitude shown by married men and women?[15]

The report concludes with the observation that as the developmental aspects of marriage and family continue to interest professional educators, theorists, and researchers, further longitudinal studies of

---

[13] Ernest W. Burgess and Paul Wallin, *Engagement and Marriage* (Chicago: J. B. Lippincott Company, 1953), p. viii.

[14] Peter C. Pineo, "Disenchantment in the Later Years of Marriage," *Marriage and Family Living* 23, no. 1 (February 1961): 11.

[15] Peter C. Pineo, "Development Patterns in Marriage," *Family Coordinator* 18, no. 2 (April 1969): 135.

families are needed to test their ideas and hypotheses.

2. In their study of 909 families interviewed in the Detroit Area Study, under the auspices of the University of Michigan, Robert O. Blood, Jr., and Donald M. Wolfe brought in a longitudinal focus by using stage of the family life cycle as one dimension of their treatment of the various facets of marital adjustment. The authors define their goals as follows:

> Our primary purpose is to understand the dynamics of American marriage, by systematically analyzing our empirical evidence. The general question is: what factors determine how husbands and wives interact and what are the effects of varying interaction patterns on the general welfare of the husband, the wife, and the family as a whole?

> In order to find meaningful answers to this question, we shall delve into the impact, on the husband-wife relationship, of various characteristics of the nuclear family (such as, number of children and stage in the family life cycle); the effects of the family's position and experience in the larger society (the church, the occupational system, etc.); the effects of their past experience and training (education, nationality background, social mobility, etc.); and at times, the role of the personal needs and desires of the husband and wife.[16]

3. Professor Harold Feldman of Cornell University combined cross-sectional and short-term longitudinal approaches with controls in his study of 852 families in an upstate New York urban area. Choosing every third dwelling in selected census tracts in the city, the research team conducted closed-end inventories in an attempt to map aspects of the husband-wife relationship over the life cycle of the marriage.

Some overall trends in the relationship over this period of time were noted as were the characteristics of couples at several points along the developmental path. In addition, data were presented about five other questions. These were:

a. characteristic patterns of the husband-wife relationship for the total sample

b. development of statistically sophisticated variables to measure dimensions of the marital relationship

c. differences in the marital relationship attributable to selected demographic variables

d. sex differences and similarities in perception about the marriage

e. development of the marital relationship over its life cycle

f. the effect of the presence of a child or children in the home on the marital relationship.[17]

---

[16] Robert O. Blood, Jr., and Donald M. Wolfe, *Husbands and Wives: The Dynamics of Married Living* (Glencoe, Ill.: Free Press, 1960), p. 4.

[17] Harold Feldman, "Development of the Husband-Wife Relationship: A Research Report," mimeographed (Ithaca, N.Y.: Cornell University, 1965), p. 156.

4. Helene Borke has intensively explored members of three generations of a single family selected according to the following criteria: "(1) the family should be intact and have at least three school-age children; (2) all family members should be adequately handling their primary life tasks at school, at work, and at home; (3) the grandparents on both sides should be living; and (4) each of the parents should have at least one married sister or brother with school-age children who could participate in the study."[18]

A total of twenty-five persons representing all three generations participated in the study through tape-recorded interviews. These provided observations of actual behavioral transactions between the couples, and also information on how the adults in the family perceived themselves and other family members. In addition, parents and children of each nuclear family entered into interaction situations involving dinner with the investigator and four structured family tasks: (1) selecting three out of five Thematic Apperception Test pictures and arriving at a group story for each; (2) deciding as a family what to do with an unexpected inheritance of $1,000; (3) cooperatively building an agreed-upon structure out of a selected construction set; and (4) selecting one gift from a group of objects differing in their attractiveness for various family members. Continuity in interaction and relationship patterns was found to occur from one generation to the next, at the same time that differences among individuals and generations were clear.

5. Reuben Hill and his colleagues have been involved for some years in the "Three Generation Family Study" at the University of Minnesota. Each of 312 related families stretching over three generations participated in intensive interviewing for more than twelve hours extending over several months. The major focus of the investigation was long-term financial planning, decision-making, and consumption. The initial questions explored were:

a. Do families follow similar patterns in the acquisition of durable goods and automobiles as in acquiring children, negotiating residential moves or making changes in the family's financial portfolio?

b. What are the predominant styles of problem-solving behavior for the generations?

c. Do these styles run in families?

d. How planful are families in the major areas of decision-making?

e. What are some of the outcomes of different types of planning and non-planning?

f. Who are the most successful planners?[19]

[18] Helene Borke, "A Family over Three Generations: The Transmission of Interacting and Relating Patterns," *Journal of Marriage and the Family* 29, no. 4 (November 1967): 639.

[19] Hill, *Family Development in Three Generations*, preface.

Beyond the major objectives of the study fulfilled in the report are data on intergenerational continuity, similarities and differences in education, income, religious activities, childbearing practices, roles of husband and wife, conflict resolution, help patterns between the generations, visiting among members of the extended families, sources of help in family and personal crises, variation in the family life cycle in the three generations, family mobility patterns over the years, time for equipping the home in grandparents', parents', and young marrieds' time, value orientations of the three generations, and many other aspects of family development. This three-generation family study takes a giant step forward in family theory and research design, and as such makes a significant contribution to family development.

It is upon data available from longitudinal family studies and official government census figures and projections, as well as other research findings from many sources, that *Family Development* draws to put flesh on the skeleton of its conceptual framework in the chapters that follow.

SUMMARY

After recognizing that each reader starts from his own family experience and orientation, a tenfold rationale for family study is presented. Discussion of modern family functions that continue to be urgently needed by an industrial society serves to introduce six emergent nontraditional family functions that center in the development and interaction of family members. Types of family study coming from fifteen behavioral sciences and disciplines are listed along with illustrative studies and representative researchers. Familiarity with concepts coming from relevant disciplines is recommended as necessary in the study of family development with interdisciplinary scope and longitudinal depth. Interdisciplinary family research is illustrated in five conceptual frameworks, of which one is the family development approach. Using the family development approach has both promises and problems that are considered. Longitudinal research in human development is seen as paralleling and supporting studies in family development. The chapter closes with brief descriptions of five different studies of marriage and the family with longitudinal depth.

SUGGESTED ACTIVITIES

1. Make a friend of one of the book-length reports of marriage and family research with longitudinal features, listed in your readings (Blood and Wolfe, Feldman, or Hill, for instance), and begin an intensive study of its methods and findings as an avenue to understanding the chapters to come in the text.

2. Conduct a vocabulary review with other students in your class, taking as a point of departure the glossary of terms and concepts. Discuss the various ways in which you and your fellow students have been accustomed to defining some of these terms. Suggest other definitions that better reflect your present understanding of the concepts. Make notations in your class notebook.

3. Start a personal journal of your own reactions to the week-by-week study of *Family Development*. In it talk back to the text; add ideas and second thoughts beyond those that come out in discussion; and jot down your questions for further study and reflection.

4. Compare the five interdisciplinary approaches to family study treated in this chapter by reading two of the basic references on emerging conceptual frameworks for family study listed in your readings (Christensen, Hill and Hansen, or Nye and Berardo). Outline their similarities and differences, as well as the strengths and weaknesses of each frame of reference, documenting your treatment in detail.

5. Review any six texts on marriage and the family in your library in terms of their inclusion or omission of a family development orientation, either explicitly or implicitly. Prepare a comparative review in the form of a well-documented paper.

6. Interview some older member of a family known to you for personally observed similarities and differences among members of the three or more generations in his or her family. Consult Helene Borke's methods of study listed in your readings, as a guide to preparing for your interview by structuring your questions in ways that may elicit maximum family developmental content. Conclude your write-up of your interview with a statement of the ways in which your approach differs from well-designed three-generation study of large numbers of families.

7. Write a letter to your best friend telling him or her why you feel it is important to study family life. Include any of the points in this chapter you consider persuasive along with any of your own. Develop as convincing a rationale as you wish, or be a devil's advocate and present the argument that family study is irrelevant to the modern situations you face, now and in the foreseeable future.

8. Draft a comparative chart of both the traditional and the emergent nontraditional functions of families and of other structures in modern society. Star each that appears to be an essential family function in an industrialized society like the United States. Footnote from professional sources.

READINGS

American Home Economics Association. "Report of a National Project." In *Concepts and Generalizations*, pp. 25–28. Washington, D.C.: American Home Economics Association, 1967.

Bates, Frederick L. "Position, Role, and Status: A Reformulation of Concepts."

Social Forces 34, no. 4 (May 1956): 313–321.

Bell, Norman W., and Ezra F. Vogel. *A Modern Introduction to the Family.* Glencoe, Ill.: Free Press, 1960. Esp. "Functions of the Nuclear Family," pp. 6 ff.

Blood, Robert O., Jr., and Donald M. Wolfe. *Husbands and Wives: The Dynamics of Married Living.* Glencoe, Ill.: Free Press, 1960.

Borke, Helene. "A Family over Three Generations: The Transmission of Interacting and Relating Patterns." *Journal of Marriage and the Family* 29, no. 4 (November 1967): 638–655.

Broderick, Carlfred B. "Reaction to 'Familial Development, Selective Needs, and Predictive Theory.'" *Journal of Marriage and the Family* 29, no. 2 (May 1967): 237–240.

Cavan, Ruth Shonle. *The American Family.* 4th ed. New York: Thomas Y. Crowell Company, 1969.

Christensen, Harold T., ed. *Handbook of Marriage and the Family.* Chicago: Rand McNally and Company, 1964.

Feldman, Harold. "Development of the Husband-Wife Relationship: A Research Report." Mimeographed. Ithaca, N.Y.: Cornell University, 1965.

Godfrey, Eleanor. "A Construction of Family Typologies and Their Initial Verification." Ph.D. dissertation, Radcliffe College, 1951.

Goode, William J. *The Family.* Englewood Cliffs, N.J.: Prentice-Hall, 1964.

Handel, Gerald. "Psychological Studies of Whole Families." *Psychological Bulletin* 63, no. 1 (1965): 19–44.

Hill, Reuben. "Interdisciplinary Workshop on Marriage and Family Research." *Marriage and Family Living* 13, no. 1 (February 1951): 13–28.

Hill, Reuben, with chapters in collaboration with Nelson Foote, Joan Aldous, Robert Carlson, and Robert Macdonald. *Family Development in Three Generations.* Cambridge, Mass.: Schenkman Publishing Company, 1970.

Hill, Reuben, and Donald A. Hansen. "The Identification of Conceptual Frameworks Utilized in Family Study." *Marriage and Family Living* 22, no. 4 (November 1960): 299–311.

Hill, Reuben, and Roy H. Rodgers. "The Developmental Approach." Chap. 5 in *Handbook of Marriage and the Family,* edited by Harold T. Christensen, pp. 171–211. Chicago: Rand McNally and Company, 1964.

King, Raymond J. R., ed. *Family Relations: Concepts and Theories.* Berkeley, Calif.: Glendessary Press, 1969.

Kirkpatrick, Clifford. "Familial Development, Selective Needs, and Predictive Theory." *Journal of Marriage and the Family* 29, no. 2 (May 1967): 229–236.

Neugarten, Bernice, Joan W. Moore, and John C. Lowe. "Age Norms, Age Constraints, and Adult Socialization." *Amer-*

ican *Journal of Sociology* 70 (1965): 710–717.

Nye, F. Ivan, and Felix M. Berardo, eds. *Emerging Conceptual Frameworks in Family Analysis.* New York: Macmillan Company, 1966.

Rowe, George P. "The Developmental Conceptual Framework to the Study of the Family." Chap. 9 in *Emerging Conceptual Frameworks in Family Analysis,* edited by F. Ivan Nye and Felix M. Berardo, pp. 198–222. New York: Macmillan Company, 1966.

Zetterberg, Hans L. *On Theory and Verification.* 3d ed. Totowa, N.J.: Bedminster Press, 1965.

2 FAMILY STOCK AND STATUS

*Inferiors revolt in order that they may be equal,
and equals that they may be superior.*   Aristotle

*I have to live for others and not for myself;
That's middle-class morality.*   George Bernard Shaw

American families spring from varied racial, ethnic, national, and religious roots. They come from many nations and make their homes in many neighborhoods, regions, and conditions in this country. They differ in status, standard of living, and life style. There are strong, stable families and others that weaken or break under strain. Each family lives through its own time with its own way of doing things that are characteristic of it. There is no such thing as *the* American family, but there are family patterns and norms within each of the several subcultures of the United States. Racial, national, religious, and social class identification allows some measure of prediction as to how each subculture differs from the others, in what respects, and to what degree. It is to this dimension of family study that this chapter turns.

NATIONAL, RELIGIOUS, AND RACIAL SOLIDARITIES

The slain Kennedy brothers were Irish-American, but they found themselves in the mainstream of life and influence in the United States. Fiorello La Guardia and many other Italian-Americans have long been appreciated for the quality of leadership they gave to their country. Walter Lippmann and Elie Abel have been read and listened to for their astute comments on the current scene, without thought of the family stock from which they came. Jackie Robinson and many other Negro athletes carved places for themselves in the sports world, and hosts of other nonwhite men and women have been applauded as talented artists, musicians, entertainers, teachers, scientists, and statesmen by Americans of every color. The people of the United States come from families that immigrated here from other parts of the world in the near or distant past. In time most of them develop their talents and make their contribution to American life.

There are other families that do not assimilate. They remain lumps in the melting pot for one of three or more reasons: (1) family pride; (2) apartness by cultural preference; and (3) involuntarily separate and unequal. Pride in a family line going back through the generations accounts for the solidarity of many an old family that makes its home in the United States but resists being absorbed by it. Apartness by preference is seen in the orthodox Jewish family, the Amish, the Mennonites and the other "plain people," and to some extent in the new communes, separatists' movements, and solidarities that appear in the current scene.[1]

What America is witnessing is a new kind of clustering together of ethnic groups, who are perhaps frightened of being isolated from that which is familiar and reassuring. In a society that seems to be spinning apart, one's own special identity becomes essential to survival.[2]

Left behind in the progress made by other families in American life are many from the West Indies, Puerto Rico, Latin America, the Philippines, Africa, Asia, American Indians, whose quality of life on the reservation has declined over time, and American Negroes. Economically, educationally, culturally, and politically many of these families have been disadvantaged in a land where others found and took advantage of opportunities to develop. Recent migrants have come at a time in the history of the nation's economy when work for the unskilled was limited. American Indians have lost much of their tribal strength along with the prairies and forests in which they lived when the white man came. Many nonwhite families have been successful in developing with the country; others have been caught in "pockets of poverty" where high concentrations of American Negroes live.

The Negro American family has been a focal point of national concern in recent years. It is the hub of the wheel from which many action programs sprout like spokes: the fight for civil rights and racial justice; demands for equality and riots in the inner city; the "war on poverty" and the battle for fair employment practices. The widely discussed Moynihan report pointed to the Negro family as the very heart of deterioration of the black community when it reported, "the Negro family

---

[1] "The Commune Comes to America," *Life* 67, no. 3 (July 18, 1969): 16b–22.

[2] Paul Jacobs and Saul Landau, "To Serve the Devil," *Center Magazine* 2, no. 2 (March 1969): 48.

in the urban ghettos is crumbling."[3] The bases for this conclusion are amply documented in a series of sections that announce, one after another, "Nearly a quarter of urban Negro marriages are dissolved." "Nearly one-quarter of Negro births are now illegitimate." "Almost one-fourth of Negro families are headed by females." The breakdown of the Negro family has led to a startling increase in welfare dependency."[4]

The problems of Negro Americans "are compounded by the present extraordinary growth in Negro population," in which Negro women start their childbearing earlier and bear more children than do whites. "This population growth must inevitably lead to an unconcealable crisis in Negro unemployment," already higher than it is among white workers. "So long as this situation persists, the cycle of poverty and disadvantage will continue to repeat itself."[5]

The Negro husband and father with a full-time job has a significantly smaller family income than do whites, age for age, through the working years, as is seen in table 2–1.

More than half of all nonwhite children under eighteen in this country (59 percent) live in poverty, as compared with 15 per-

Table 2–1. *Median Family Income of Negro Male Family Heads in the Full-time Labor Force*

Age of husband-father	Family income	Percentage of white median family income
Under 25	$4,400	72%
25-44 years	6,200	71
45-54 years	6,550	67
55-64 years	5,300	59
Average	$5,950	68%

Source: U.S. Department of Labor, Bureau of Labor Statistics, *Social and Economic Conditions of Negroes in the United States,* Bureau of Labor Statistics Report, no. 332 (Washington, D.C., 1967), VIII, IX, pp. 13–25; as reported in *Marital and Family Characteristics of Workers,* Special Labor Force Report, no. 94 (Washington, D.C.: U.S. Department of Labor, 1967), p. 21.

Note: "Existing income disparities between white and Negro families mirror white and Negro imbalances in occupational distribution, educational attainment, job opportunities, incidence of unemployment, residence, and other factors."

cent of all white children, making the proportion of nonwhite children in poverty four times that of white children. However, since the white population is nearly eight times as large as the nonwhite population, the number of white children classified as poor is larger than the number of nonwhite children (9 million as compared with 6 million, approximately). The paradox of numbers versus proportions sometimes obscures the fact that white children in poverty outnumber the nonwhite, as shown in chart 2–1.[6]

This tangle of social and family problems is proving difficult to unravel. Understanding the interwoven roots of the situation is demanding. Racism and prejudicial treat-

[3] Daniel P. Moynihan, *The Negro Family: The Case for National Action* (Washington, D.C.: U.S. Department of Labor, Office of Policy Planning and Research, 1965), introduction.

[4] Ibid., chap. 2, "The Negro American Family."

[5] Ibid. See also Lee Rainwater and William L. Yancey, *The Moynihan Report and the Politics of Controversy* (Cambridge, Mass.: M.I.T. Press, 1967), p. 43.

[6] Elizabeth Herzog and Catharine Richards, eds., *The Nation's Youth,* Children's Bureau Publication, no. 460 (Washington, D.C., 1968), chart 11.

FAMILY DEVELOPMENT

Chart 2-1. *The Majority of Nonwhite Children Are Poor,*
and the Majority of Poor Children Are White

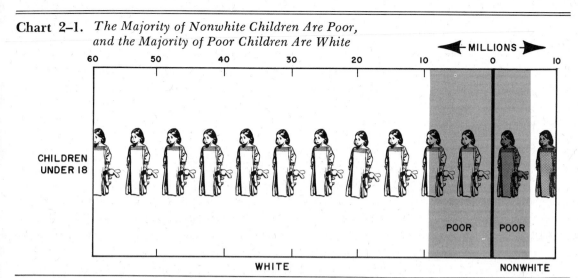

Source: Elizabeth Herzog and Catharine Richards, eds., *The Nation's Youth*, Children's Bureau Publication, no. 460 (Washington, D.C., 1968), chart 11.

ment are part of the picture, as are also resistance to change, reluctance to assume responsibility, and reaction to continuing low status within the social class system. Social class position is conferred by families, and it influences every facet of family life. Few other factors are so potent in determining where a family lives and on what, where it goes to work and play, how much education its members have, and how it fares, generally.

FAMILY STATUS AND SOCIAL CLASS

A child at birth is placed within society according to the social status of his parents. He may live out his life within the family status into which he was born, or he may move up or down the social ladder as he "betters himself" or "is no credit to his family." Such things are generally recognized; in recent years they have been studied intensively.[7]

A family generally is aware of its status within the community. Others are seen as "our kind of folks," or "better than we are," or "not the kind of people we want to associate with," as families identify those of similar status, those of higher, and those of lower status, respectively. Families who

[7] See, for instance, such comprehensive volumes as: Pitirim A. Sorokin, *Social and Cultural Mobility* (Glencoe, Ill.: Free Press, 1959); Leonard Reissman, *Class in American Society* (Glencoe, Ill.: Free Press, 1959); Reinhard Bendix and Seymour Martin Lipset, eds., *Class, Status, and Power: A Reader in Social Stratification* (Glencoe, Ill.: Free Press, 1959); W. Lloyd Warner and Paul S. Lunt, *The Social Life of a Modern Community*, vol. 1 of Yankee City Series (New Haven: Yale University Press, 1941); and other references listed at the end of this chapter.

have social access to each other are generally considered to be of the same general social class.

A community may be predominantly of one social class, or it may consist of several discernible status groups. A factory town may be made up of working-class families; a suburban community of middle-class people; while the wealthy upper class tends to cluster in the exurban areas that ring the great metropolitan areas.[8] Most modern communities have several social classes that range all the way from the families "across the tracks" to those who live in mansions "on the hill." Although definitions of, and patterns of, social stratification differ, studies of many kinds and sizes of communities in various parts of the country find at least six social classes that may be seen as a continuum from top to bottom of the social ladder.

Social Classes in America

There are no classless societies, and this country is no exception. The United States as a whole has six well-defined social classes that may be characterized as follows. The *upper-upper* class consists of the established old families who live in the most exclusive sections of the community in homes built by their ancestors. Upper-upper families live upon inherited wealth and upon the

income of the heads of the household, who are usually professional men or business executives. Members of upper-upper families tend to associate with each other in exclusive clubs, to send their children to private schools, to marry within their social class, and to maintain a strong feeling of family solidarity.

The *lower-upper* class is made up of the well-to-do families whose wealth has been too recently acquired for them to be completely accepted socially by the old established families in the best sections of town. Members of the lower-upper classes belong to the less exclusive "good" clubs, send their children to the best colleges, and live as much as they can like the upper-uppers.

The *upper-middle* class consists of the families who are "the backbone of the community." These families live in the better, but not the most exclusive sections of the community. They earn a comfortable living by professional service or business activity. They send their children to college and encourage them to make friends with "nice people" (of their own or higher status) and make a "good marriage," preferably with a member of the upper class. Upper-middle-class families are active in social service organizations and churches, and they do what they can to improve standards of living for themselves and others.

The *lower-middle* class is made up of skilled workmen, clerks, small shopkeepers, and some professional men and women who live in respectable sections of town in nice, comfortable homes. Lower-middle-

---

[8] A. C. Spectorsky, *The Exurbanites* (Philadelphia: J. B. Lippincott Company, 1955).

class parents try to give their children a good education and some of the advantages of life that they may have lacked. They work hard and put great stress on honesty, fair dealing, and decency.

The *upper-lower* class, with the lower-middle class just described, is "the level of the common man." Families in the upper-lower class live in rented houses or apartments or simple family dwellings not very far from the slums. The father and sometimes the mother and/or grown children earn the family income as semiskilled workers in factories, mills, mines, or in civil service jobs. These families work hard to keep up a respectable, independent life that is not to be confused with that at the bottom of the social ladder.

The *lower-lower* class is made up of families who live in the least desirable parts of town, in slums or slumlike dwellings. The family income comes from wages earned by the father and, usually, the mother at unskilled jobs that alternate with unemployment and being on relief. There is not always enough money to go around, and the family lives from day to day. Children of lower-lower-class families drop out of school earlier than do members of other classes and are sooner in the labor force.

COURTESY OF THE LIBRARY OF CONGRESS

Middle-class families live in the better, but not the most exclusive, sections of the community, in good-sized homes that are in good condition.

There are differences in the proportions of the various social classes by communities and by regions in this country. In general, the number and percentage of families in the middle classes are increasing rapidly with the higher levels of income and education that American families enjoy today.

How a Family's Social Class Is Determined

Research studies tell us that a family's social class is determined by a number of factors: occupation, source of income, neighborhood, and type of house lived in. The Index of Status Characteristics, popularly known as the I.S.C., has been developed as a way of objectively determining the social class of a given family. The ratings have been derived from social science research findings of actual families in a number of communities. The simplified version in table 2–2 generally applies.

Putting the scoring device for determining social class into practice, let us take family *A* as an example. Mr. *A* manages the local plant (score 8), and has earned his present wealth (score 6). The *A*s live in a

COURTESY OF THE LIBRARY OF CONGRESS

Lower-class families live in the less desirable parts of town, in simple family dwellings or slumlike apartments that are apt to be crowded.

Table 2–2. *Table for Determining Social Class*

Characteristics	Score
Occupation	
Professionals and proprietors of large businesses (such as doctors and factory owners)	4
Semiprofessionals and smaller officials of large businesses (such as lab technicians or managers)	8
Clerks and similar workers (secretaries, bookkeepers, etc.)	12
Skilled workers (bakers, carpenters, etc.)	16
Proprietors of small businesses (owners of small groceries, restaurants, etc.)	20
Semiskilled workers (bus drivers, cannery workers, etc.)	24
Unskilled workers (such as warehousemen or ditchdiggers)	28
Source of income	
Inherited wealth	3
Earned wealth	6
Profits and fees	9
Salary	12
Wages	15
Private relief	18
Public relief and "nonrespectable" incomes (e.g., gambling)	21
House type	
Large houses in good condition	3
Large houses in medium condition; medium-sized houses in good condition	6
Large houses in bad condition	9
Medium-sized houses in medium condition; apartments in regular apartment buildings	12
Small houses in good condition; small houses in medium condition; dwellings over stores	15
Medium-sized houses in bad condition; small houses in bad condition	18

Characteristics	Score
All houses in very bad condition; dwellings in structures not originally intended for homes	21
Area lived in	
Very exclusive; Gold Coast, etc.	2
The better suburbs and apartment house areas, houses with spacious yards, etc.	4
Above average; areas all residential, larger than average space around house; apartment areas in good condition, etc.	6
Average; residential neighborhoods, no deterioration in the area	8
Below average; area not quite holding its own, beginning to deteriorate, business entering, etc.	10
Low; considerably deteriorated, run-down, and semislum	12
Very low; slum	14

Scoring

Social class	Total score
Upper class	12–17
Upper class probably, with some possibility of upper-middle class	18–22
Indeterminate: either upper or upper-middle class	23–24
Upper-middle class	25–33
Indeterminate: either upper-middle or lower-middle class	34–37
Lower-middle class	38–50
Indeterminate: either lower-middle or upper-lower class	51–53
Upper-lower class	54–62
Indeterminate: either upper-lower or lower-lower class	63–66
Lower-lower class probably, with some possibility of upper-lower class	67–69
Lower-lower class	70–84

Source: W. Lloyd Warner and Mildred Hall Warner, *What You Should Know about Social Class* (Chicago: Science Research Associates, 1953), pp. 22, 25.

medium-sized house in good condition (score 6), in an above-average residential community (score 6). The total I.S.C. score is 26, which puts the *A* family into the upper part of the upper-middle class. Family *B,* on the other hand, lives in an apartment building (score 12) in an area that is rapidly changing and not quite holding its own (score 10). The *Bs'* income is derived entirely from profits (score 9) from their fruit store (score 20). Totaling their score, we get 51, an indeterminate score between lower-middle and upper-lower social classes, which means the *Bs* could be either, depending upon how their neighbors rate them.

Social status is on a continuum. The indeterminate scores between each of the six social classes indicate that there are no rigid categories into which all families must fit, but rather, as Cuber and Kenkel[9] suggest, we have a continuum of social status from the bottom to the top of the social ladder. In this continuum, some characteristics loom larger than others in the minds of people. Among the items used in the I.S.C. scale, occupation is felt to be most important by the people studied. Source of income and type of house lived in rank second in people's thinking, with the area of the community lived in falling into fourth place. Other factors, such as the amount and type of education, church attended, style of clothing worn, clubs belonged to, and activities participated in, are all part of the status reputation a family member or a family as a whole enjoys.

Family Income and Work Differentials

There are about 100,000 millionaires in the United States. Not quite two hundred American families are worth a hundred times that much, a dozen of whom measure their wealth in billions.[10] A few of the very wealthy squander their substance in riotous living, but more try to have their money work for them in wise investments that require supervision. Some, like the Rockefellers, give of themselves and their resources to public life. A very rich man worth millions may work twelve- and fourteen-hour days in the entertainment world, professional life, or the family business.

Wives and mothers of very wealthy families are not necessarily "the idle rich," as they entertain lavishly with few domestic servants available, keep inherited family homes in several elite areas, sponsor a variety of charities, and possibly pursue personal or professional interests as well. Upper-class mothers prepare their children for the roles they must play in society by finding suitable nurses, governesses, and tutors; escorting the children on frequent trips and wide travel; enrolling them in the "right" schools; supervising their learning

[9] John F. Cuber and William F. Kenkel, *Social Stratification in the United States* (New York: Appleton-Century-Crofts, 1954).

[10] Ruth West, "The Care and Feeding of the Very Rich," *McCall's,* August 1969, pp. 57, 109–110, 112, quoting recent census data.

of second and third languages; inculcating good taste in music, art, cuisine, and personal grooming; and seeing to it that their children develop skills in a variety of sports and social graces. At the proper time, upper-class parents introduce their debutante daughters into society and help their sons find themselves in the family interests or in some other position worthy of the family name.

Not all upper-crust families are wealthy. Many have to "put on a front" to maintain the family status with dwindling resources, high taxes, and the perpetual problem of being property-poor. Being upper class is not measured by annual income figures, but rather in the elevated status the family has in the community through inherited and acquired privileges.

At the other end of the scale are the families who subsist below the poverty line. These are the disadvantaged migrant workers, the Negro, Spanish-American and Indian families, and those of any stock who try to eke out a living in depressed areas. Families headed by women and families of nonwhites are four times more vulnerable to poverty than white families and those headed by men, as seen in the percentages of children classified as poor in the United States, chart 2–2.

Inequalities in family income are declining somewhat. The percentage share of the aggregate income received by the poorest fifth of the nation increased by 5 percent between the mid-1950s and 1967. Persons below the poverty level declined proportionally from 22 percent of the total popu-

Chart 2–2. *Most Vulnerable to Poverty: Farm Families, Nonwhite Families, and Families Headed by a Woman*

PERCENT OF CHILDREN CLASSIFIED AS POOR

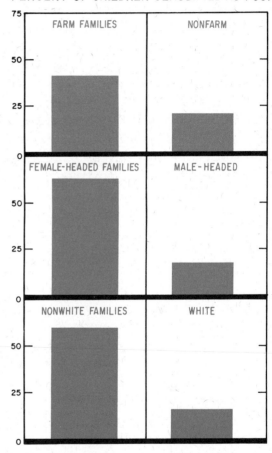

Source: Elizabeth Herzog and Catharine Richards, eds., *The Nation's Youth,* Children's Bureau Publication, no. 460 (Washington, D.C., 1968), from original data in Mollie Orshansky, "Recounting the Poor: A Five-year Review," *Social Security Review* 29, April 1966, table 3, p. 25.

lation in 1959 to 13 percent in 1967. During the same decade, the total income received by the richest 5 percent of America's families dropped from about 17 percent in 1960 to approximately 15 percent in 1967.[11]

Not all lower-class people are poor; the crime syndicate boss and the gambler may have "money to burn," and yet have a low status in the community. Most lower-class families have incomes dependent upon social security, relief checks, and wages for unskilled labor.[12] Currently, unskilled women work in laundries, factory jobs, and as cleaning women. Unskilled jobs for men have fallen off with the wide use of heavy machinery that digs the ditches and lays the roads that once gave any man willing to work at least occasional day labor. Unemployment is highest among unskilled workers in lower-class families. During the depression of the 1930s, 26 percent of the unemployment and 46 percent of the part-time employment were among lower-lower class workers, in contrast to 6 percent unemployed and 94 percent with full employment among lower-upper workers. In this period, 34 percent of the lower-lower class, 10 percent of the upper-lower, 4 percent of the lower-middle, and less than 1 percent of the upper-middle class were on relief.[13]

Traditionally, the poorly paid father's wages were supplemented by the earnings of his adolescent and young adult children. Now, more often it is the mother's income that keeps a lower-class family above the poverty line, whether she is the family head or not. In a 1965 survey of working mothers with children under fourteen years of age, 86 percent gave as their reason for working the need for more money for their families.[14]

In nations made up of masses of the very poor, topped with a thin layer of the very wealthy, there is chronic poverty and underdevelopment. Only when a strong middle class emerges does one find massive personal, social, and economic progress. The large and growing American middle class has been denigrated in the recent struggle for equal opportunity and civil rights. "The Establishment," target of many a militant, is largely middle-class in the United States and in other relatively well-developed countries. It is the middle class whose vision and industry brought forth economic progress, the scientific achievements on earth and in outer space, and the many aspects of the society that modern man thinks of as personal and national development.

The middle class is the burden-bearer of the culture. Middle-class men and women build, maintain, and man the nation's schools, churches, youth-serving agencies, helping professions, legal institutions, and to a large extent the art and culture in theater, concert hall, opera house, art gallery, museum, and library.

[11] "The Changing Income Distribution," *Family Economics Review*, June 1969, p. 13.

[12] Warner and Lunt, *The Social Life of a Modern Community*, p. 261.

[13] Ibid., pp. 277–279.

[14] Vera C. Perrella and Elizabeth Waldman, *Marital and Family Characteristics of Workers in March 1965*, U.S. Department of Labor, Bureau of Labor Statistics, Special Labor Force Report, no. 64 (1966), table J, p. A-17.

The contribution members of the middle class make to society does not insure them against the weaknesses of all men. "White-collar crimes," such as swindling, pork-barreling, and other "respectable delinquencies" reported in the daily press, are middle-class forms of the illegal behavior that exists at all class levels. In spite of the moral injunctions heard at their mothers' knee, in the classroom, and at church, middle-class businessmen charge "all the law allows," split fees they did not earn, figure ways to avoid taxes, and beat the other fellow at the red light or in a canny deal, with predictable regularity. While scolding Junior for hitting his brother, his parents may engage in cutthroat competition in their business and support extremist groups at home and aggression on a foreign front. Struggling to become middle-class calls for a certain amount of competitive drive that does not cease when the goal is won, and "keeping up with the Joneses" is no longer necessary. Having an investment in one's home and the way of life it represents calls for a kind of conservatism that is anathema to those who want to radically change things.

Splinter groups of middle-class alienated youth[15] occasionally break from what they

[15] Kenneth Keniston, *Young Radicals: Notes on Committed Youth* (New York: Harcourt, Brace and World, 1968).

Chart 2–3. *The Majority of Children Live in Middle- or Upper-income Families*

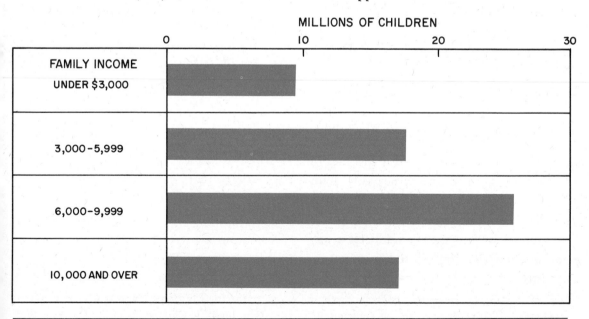

Source: Elizabeth Herzog and Catharine Richards, eds., *The Nation's Youth,* Children's Bureau Publication, no. 460 (Washington, D.C., 1968), chart 11.

see as middle-class arrogance, intolerance, materialism, and hypocrisy. Student groups protest the military policies of the country and demand immediate solutions to age-old problems of poverty, prejudice, and unequal power that disenfranchises the disadvantaged. There is little that is really new in "the generation gap" today. There have been student uprisings through the centuries and around the world.[16] Currently, a small minority of American middle-class youth rebel to the extent of repudiating the society to which they belong, but the overwhelming tendency is for the nation's young to continue in the way of life they have learned in their families. Middle-class norms and values continue in the oncoming generations.

The great majority of tomorrow's citizens are already middle-class. Most of the children in the United States are growing up in middle- or upper-income families. Over 60 percent of America's children under the age of eighteen lived in families with annual incomes of $6,000 or more in 1965. Another 25 percent of the nation's children were in families with incomes of $10,000 or more in the same year. This 85 percent of the next generation is mainly middle-class in its orientation.

With all its faults, the middle-class way has proven itself to be effective in an urban, industrialized society. The middle class has built the system and, in turn, has been shaped and reinforced by it. Such middle-class values as (1) commitment to long-term goals, (2) high aspiration for self and children, (3) achievement-orientation and pride in accomplishment, (4) eagerness for learning and satisfaction in growth, (5) problem-solving based upon rational cause-and-effect premises, (6) self-restraint and the willingness to postpone present pleasure for future purposes, and (7) the basic attitude that man can cope with his world rather than have to accept or to fight it blindly—all these and other qualities have been central in the development of the complex way of life known as American. This highly organized, productive society makes demands on its members to continue the values and behavior that are necessary for its survival. This tends to "reinforce a middle-class way as the way of success."[17] The demand for education is felt more in certain segments of society than in others.

EDUCATION RUNS IN FAMILIES

Schooling is directly related to social class, with children of the higher classes getting more years of formal education than lower-

[16] Lewis S. Feuer, *The Conflict of Generations: The Character and Significance of Student Movements* (New York: Basic Books, 1969).

[17] Catherine S. Chilman, *Growing Up Poor*, Welfare Administration Publication, no. 13 (Washington, D.C., 1966), p. 23.

class children. Social class differences in school attendance are apparent from the beginning. Children from the lower social classes attend preschool in significantly smaller percentages than do those from the middle and upper social classes: A study of parents of five social classes (Warner, Meeker, and Eels classification) whose children were in school or were to enter first grade in the fall shows marked differences by social class in the preschool attendance of the children:

> Results showed that a child's chances of attending preschool decrease as one goes down the social ladder; almost 100 percent of uppers and upper-middles send their children to preschool, while only 14 percent of lower-lowers send theirs. Results cannot be explained solely in terms of the economic factor but may be due to differences in the way in which different social classes regard the school.[18]

School dropouts during the elementary and high school years show sharp social class differences. An extensive study of the social class system in one midwestern community[19] through the 1940s found that three-fourths of the children at the lowest social class level and more than half of the upper-lower class did not finish the ninth grade. Poor family heritage in terms of slum neighborhoods, broken homes, and low and sporadic family income are causes for many lower-class children never finishing high school.

College doors open to many students willing to work their way through to more education than their parents ever had in their time. Whereas in the 1930s colleges were made up largely of upper-middle-class students, now less than a third of college students are from upper-middle-class families. With increasing numbers of local community colleges, more and more students from working-class families go to college. Extensive studies in one midwestern city found more lower-middle-class students than any other going to college. The greater size of the working-class population means that about 20 percent of its students go to college, while 75 percent of the high status students do, even though the numbers of students from the two social classes are similar. The lower-lower-class family sends no girls to college and almost no boys.[20]

Studies of able young people who do not go to college find that they are disproportionately from families of lower social status, did less well in high school, have lower achievement drive and lower scores on personality adjustment tests. Even though they

---

[18] Celia Burns Stendler, "Social Class Differences in Parental Attitude toward School at Grade I Level," *Child Development* 22, no. 1 (March 1951): 45.

[19] August B. Hollingshead, *Elmtown's Youth* (New York: John Wiley and Sons, 1949).

[20] Robert J. Havighurst, Paul Hoover Bowman, Gordon P. Liddle, Charles V. Matthews, and James V. Pierce, *Growing Up in River City* (New York: John Wiley and Sons, 1962), chap. 8.

rank in the upper quarter of their class in intellectual ability, their low family status proves to be a disadvantage in providing the incentives and the resources for going on with their education.[21]

A student's parents' education, his father's and mother's work, and the family income are all related to the education he receives. In one recent year, 64 percent of high school graduates from white-collar families and only 37 percent of graduates whose parents were manual or service workers went on to college. Of the high school graduates whose fathers had graduated from college, 82 percent went to college, compared with 54 percent of the graduates whose fathers had not gone beyond high school and 22 percent of those whose fathers had not finished elementary school. Mother's education is similarly related to how far a family's children go in school, with a straight-line trend—the more education the mother had, the more likely her children are to become educated themselves (table 2–3).

A number of interrelated factors account for the differentials between educational attainments of children from different social classes. Family beliefs, values, aspirations, and expectations either encourage or discourage its children educationally. The child of a working-class family may receive little help or encouragement at home. At the same time, he may feel rejected by his teacher, who, being middle-

class, may not understand or accept the behavior of the lower-class child. Dr. Allison Davis, after many years of study of this problem, concludes that "the middle-class . . . family's insistent pressure upon them for early and rapid attainment, and for conscientious work habits, makes middle-class children work much harder in school.

Table 2–3. *College Attendance by Parents' Education, 1967*

Father's and mother's education	Percentage of high school graduates	
	Attended college	Did not go to college
Father's and mother's education		
Mother no college	40.8	59.2
Father no college	38.6	61.4
Father some college	60.5	39.5
Mother some college	82.2	17.8
Father some college	86.4	13.6
Mother's education		
Less than 8 years	19.1	80.9
3 years high school	33.1	66.9
4 years high school	53.1	46.9
College:		
1 to 3 years	82.7	17.3
4 years or more	81.3	18.7
Father's education		
Less than 8 years	22.2	77.8
3 years high school	35.0	65.0
4 years high school	53.6	46.4
College:		
1 to 3 years	62.5	37.5
4 years or more	82.4	17.6

Source: U.S. Bureau of the Census, "Factors Related to High School Graduation and College Attendance: 1967," *Population Characteristics,* Current Population Reports, series P-20, no. 185 (July 11, 1969), table 7, p. 6.

[21] Ibid.

Thus they please the teacher much more than do lower-class children. . . ."[22]

Lower-class children are not as socially acceptable as are their middle-class classmates. Children from lower-class families are less often wanted as friends (even by children of their own social class), while children of middle-class families are desired as friends by children of all social levels represented in the fifth and sixth grades of a school studied. These middle-class children are considered better-looking than their lower-class fellow students in significant percentages.[23] Such differences between children from families of various social status and racial stock continue throughout the second decade of life and influence the boy-girl relationships of teenagers.

DIFFERENTIALS IN DATING AND COURTSHIP

Teenagers from lower-class families have fewer social opportunities and are less socially acceptable than young people from higher social levels. Their lack of acceptability and of conduct and appearance generally considered appropriate limit their friendships and boy-girl relationships to those of their own social strata. Their parents' reputation in the community and their own limited plans restrict many to association with young people of similar background and aspirations.

Hollingshead's classic study of the high school students of Elmtown, population 7,000, found from 49 to 70 percent of all friendships were within the same social class.[24] One-third of the boys and girls with close associations in a class other than their own have them with members of a social class adjacent to their own in the status hierarchy. Bridging over more than one social class position is infrequent in friendships and in dating; the social distance is much too great.

Dating partner patterns of Elmtown's high school students show interesting sex differences in interclass dating. When a boy crosses a social class line, the chances are two to one that he dates a girl from a class below himself. A girl, conversely, usually dates above herself when she steps out of her own social class. Note that in table 2–4 not one upper-class girl dated a lower-class boy; nor did any upper-class boy date a girl from the lower-lower class. In the current mood among youth, rebelling from conventional expectations and demanding more personal equality among those of dif-

---

[22] Allison Davis, "Socio-Economic Influences upon Children's Learning," *School Life* 33, no. 6 (March 1951): 87.

[23] Bernice L. Neugarten, "The Relation between Family Social Position and the Social Development of the Child" (Doctoral dissertation, University of Chicago, 1943).

[24] Hollingshead, *Elmtown's Youth*, p. 213.

Table 2–4. *Dating Partners of High School Students, by Social Class*

	Boys			
Social class of girl dated	Upper and upper-middle	Lower-middle	Upper-lower	Lower-lower
Upper and upper-middle	54%	38%	8%	—
Lower-middle	18	53	27	2%
Upper-lower	3	11	79	7
Lower-lower	—	2	28	70
	Girls			
Social class of boy dated	Upper and upper-middle	Lower-middle	Upper-lower	Lower-lower
Upper and upper-middle	50%	35%	15%	—
Lower-middle	15	58	27	—
Upper-lower	4	16	74	6%
Lower-lower	—	9	33	58

Source: August B. Hollingshead, *Elmtown's Youth* (New York: John Wiley and Sons, 1949), p. 231, excerpts from chart I, used with permission.

fering socioeconomic status, there has been some modification of these trends in some communities, but the tendency to date within the same or a similar social class continues, in the main.

Boys and girls at the higher social class levels have more friendships, but perhaps few more dates than do teenagers at the lower social class levels. This is not because they are not more popular, but often because high school students with aspirations for getting into and succeeding in a good college or university prefer not to get involved in ways that might take too much time from their studies or cut short their educational plans. Similarly, there are many able, attractive students who frown upon going steady as a regular practice because of the possible emotional and sexual involvements that might result.

Young people from lower-class families, with fewer plans for the future and less pressure from their parents, tend to be more direct in expressing their sexual impulses and less accepting of extended petting than are young people from middle-class families.[25] The more education a young person aspires to, and the better the education he has, the less premarital sexual experience he or she has. This association of educational level (anticipated or achieved) to incidence of premarital sex experience is in a straight-line relationship age for age and grade for grade. The predominant tendency is for the greatest incidence of genital experience to occur at the lower educational levels, as is clear in table 2–5. The simplest explanation of this phenomenon is that the youngster with little to look forward to in his future, growing up in a lower-class culture that has emphasized the importance of getting what one can in the present, has no reason to wait and little experience in self-restraint. The middle-class teenager has future goals to which he

---

25 Alfred C. Kinsey, Wardell B. Pomeroy, and Clyde E. Martin, *Sexual Behavior in the Human Male* (Philadelphia: W. B. Saunders Company, 1948), chap. 10; and Alfred C. Kinsey, Wardell B. Pomeroy, Clyde E. Martin, and Paul H. Gebhard, *Sexual Behavior in the Human Female* (Philadelphia: W. B. Saunders Company, 1953), chap. 8.

Table 2–5. *Premarital Sex Relations by Educational Level Experienced by Girls and Boys in Age Group 16–20*

Educational level	Girls	Boys
Grade school	38%	85%
High school	32	76
College and graduate school	17–19	42

Source: Alfred C. Kinsey, Wardell B. Pomeroy, Clyde E. Martin, and Paul H. Gebhard, *Sexual Behavior in the Human Female* (Philadelphia: W. B. Saunders Company, 1953), p. 331.

is committed, family expectations that do not include immediate gratification of sexual impulses, and quite possibly religious ties that further restrain him from full sexual experience before he or she is educationally, occupationally, and morally ready for it.

Recent longitudinal studies of college students find about the same percentages of college girls without sex experience as Kinsey and his staff found twenty years ago. It is generally agreed among scholars of the question that there has been no "sexual revolution" in recent decades beyond more openness in attitudes and discussion.[26]

26 Winston W. Ehrmann, "Influence of Comparative Social Class of Companion upon Premarital Heterosexual Behavior," *Marriage and Family Living* 17, no. 1 (February 1955): 48–53; Winston W. Ehrmann, *Premarital Dating Behavior* (New York: Henry Holt and Company, 1959); Ira L. Reiss, *Premarital Sexual Standards in America* (Glencoe, Ill.: Free Press, 1960); Evelyn Millis Duvall, *Why Wait Till Marriage?* (New York: Association Press, 1965); and Mervin B. Freedman, "The Sexual Behavior of American College Women," *Merrill-Palmer Quarterly* 11, no. 1 (January 1965): 33–48.

MARRIAGE AND DIVORCE PATTERNS BY FAMILY STATUS

Young people tend to marry within their own social class. This generally holds true of men and women of all status groups and is known as the principle of *homogamy*, the tendency for like to marry like. Over recent decades, when members of both sexes have enjoyed more freedom and mobility than formerly, most of them continue to marry within their own social class.[27] Interracial marriage is widely publicized but not generally practiced. Of the forty million couples in the United States in 1960, only 163,800 (four-tenths of 1 percent) were interracial pairs. Of these, 51,400 were Negro-white couples, and 21,700 were white husbands married to Japanese wives.[28]

Persons of foreign stock assimilate rapidly in the United States. Half again as large a proportion of first-generation Americans (62 percent) as second-generation (39 percent) married a person of the same foreign stock as themselves. Some nationalities

27 Simon Dinitz, Franklin Banks, and Benjamin Pasamanick, "Mate Selection and Social Class: Changes during the Past Quarter Century," *Marriage and Family Living* 22, no. 4 (November 1960): 348–351.

28 Paul C. Glick, "Marriage, Socio-economic Status, and Health," *World Views of Population Problems* (Budapest, 1968), p. 130.

"marry out" (*heterogamy*, marrying outside one's culture) more than do others. In general, individuals from English-speaking countries and from Germany have high rates of intermarriage with mates from other countries, while persons from Poland, Italy, and Russia much less often marry those of other national stock.[29]

There is a tendency for young people to marry within their own religious faith. Those who marry outside their national or ethnic group still tend to marry within their own faith.[30] In one recent year, 94 percent of the married couples were both Protestant, both Catholic, or both Jewish. Marriage of a Protestant to a person of another faith occurred 15 percent as often as random marriage. Marriage of a Catholic to someone of another faith occurred 16 percent of random; and of Jewish faith to some other only 4 percent of random.[31]

Those who plan to marry either during or very soon after high school are predominantly from low-income and low-education-level homes. These young people see themselves as leaving school and going to work, into military service (boys), or into home-making (girls) immediately following graduation.[32]

More young people of lower-class families marry earlier than do those from families of higher status. Lower-class students are usually out of school in their middle teens, and so miss out on what family life education is offered in their high schools.[33] Members of lower-class families are more active in direct sex expression, are burdened less with social pressures for supporting the sex code and by urgent reasons for postponing pregnancy and marriage such as restrain more members of the middle-class families. Aspirations and achievement drives are weak in lower-class youth. Their homes are crowded; their parents are tired of trying to make ends meet. Early marriage follows as the inevitable next step for the majority of lower-class youth.

"People with the poorest chance of making a good marriage are most likely to marry early," is the conclusion of a University of Chicago research team, after studying all the boys and girls growing up in River City from the time they were in the sixth grade until they were nineteen years old. The young people who marry early tend to be of lower intelligence, have poorer school records, more often are high

[29] Ibid., p. 130.

[30] Ruby J. Kennedy, "Single or Triple Melting Pot? Intermarriage Trends in New Haven, 1870–1940," *American Journal of Sociology* 49 (1944): 331–339; August B. Hollingshead, "Cultural Factors in the Selection of Marriage Mates," *American Sociological Review* 15, no. 5 (October 1950): 619–627.

[31] Glick, "Marriage, Socio-economic Status, and Health," pp. 130–131.

[32] Harold Christensen, "Lifetime Family and Occupational Role Projections of High School Students," *Marriage and Family Living* 23, no. 2 (May 1961): 181–183.

[33] Robert J. Havighurst, "Social Class Differences and Family Life Education at the Secondary Level," *Marriage and Family Living* 12, no. 4 (Fall 1950): 133–135.

school dropouts, are less well adjusted, come from the lower social classes, and have little contact with the church—all of which augurs against their succeeding in marriage.[34]

Divorce and separation are more frequent among lower-class families than among more affluent couples. The 1960 census devoted "much attention to social and economic analysis of the patterns of marriage and dissolution of marriage among men 45 to 54 years old, a group that has reached its peak earning capacity and among whom few additional marriages will occur. There was one and a half million ever-married white men in this age group with incomes less than $3,000, and more than two million with incomes of $10,000 or more. Fully 29 percent of the poor men, but only 16 percent of the affluent men, were no longer living with their first wives at the time of the census. The corresponding relationship was even more striking among nonwhites than it was for whites."[35]

Rainwater's study of the very poor points to some of the dynamics of instability in the lower-class marriage. He finds that low-income wives tend to see men as dominant, unpredictable, and powerful, while their husbands see themselves as powerless in an unpredictable world. The psychological distance between the sexes in lower-class culture is marked by wives' resignation and hopelessness and husbands' distrustful hostility. Their impulsive, unplanned marriage plunges both members of the pair into circumstances not anticipated and gives them little companionship, satisfaction, or security. Even sex is often used in hostile, punitive ways in lower-class marriage.[36]

UNEVEN DISTRIBUTION OF HEALTH AND HAPPINESS

Marriage is good for one's health, especially if one is a man. An analysis of census and vital statistics data concludes that being married is twice as advantageous to men as to women in terms of continued survival. Men apparently benefit from having wives help them take care of themselves, something most women do very well for themselves as well as for their mates. Married men have fewer disabling health problems, less nervous strain, are less likely to be institutionalized, and in many other ways have better health than do bachelors.[37]

---

[34] Havighurst, Bowman, Liddle, Matthews, and Pierce, *Growing Up in River City*, chap. 9, "Marriage," pp. 119–130; quote from p. 130.

[35] Robert Parke, Jr., and Paul C. Glick, "Prospective Changes in Marriage and the Family," *Journal of Marriage and the Family* 29, no. 2 (May 1967): 254.

[36] Lee Rainwater and Karol K. Weinstein, *And the Poor Get Children: Sex, Contraception, and Family Planning in the Working Class* (Chicago: Quadrangle Books, 1960).

[37] Glick, "Marriage, Socio-economic Status, and Health," pp. 134–135.

Some families have better health than do others. An intensive study of some 2,168 illnesses[38] reported by 1,256 persons in an upstate New York community found markedly different patterns of health and sickness, health care, and use of medical facilities among the social classes. The members of the middle and upper classes know more of the dynamics of illness and health and are more aware of the resources to be tapped for prevention and treatment of sickness. They live in a climate of social acceptance of the services of physicians, specialists (gynecologists, obstetricians, pediatricians, psychiatrists, and the rest), dentists, orthodontists, plastic surgeons, and the other professions whose services make life safer and more pleasant for human beings. The men and women of the lower classes, on the contrary, are not as aware of the nature of sickness and health. They do not feel that the health resources and facilities of a community are for "our kind of folks," so they tend to live in a heritage of bravely "getting along and making do." Self-medication and the use of nonmedical personnel are patterns that are transmitted to the children as the thing to do in everyday family living. This attitude is represented in such statements as the following: "We take H—— Tonic (alcohol 16 percent) all the time during the winter when we aren't outdoors much. It keeps us fit; we don't have hardly any sickness since we've been doing this for three years now." "I

Always take S—— Compound every fall. It thickens my blood, and gets me ready for cold weather."[39]

Families in the higher social strata feel better emotionally as well as physically. A national study of mental health found, "The percentage of persons having more good feelings and fewer bad feelings increases as one moves from less education to more education, from low income to high income, and from age to youth age groups."[40] This and other studies have found less anxiety among the better-educated and the more affluent than among those less well off. There is a sense of security in some families measured not only by a thicker financial cushion, but also in visiting friends and relatives, meeting new people, traveling, eating out of the home, and belonging to organized groups in the community.[41]

SECURITY AND INSECURITY IN AMERICAN FAMILIES

Families differ by the social class level they occupy in the number of crises they go through, what they consider a family crisis, the severity of their reaction to family troubles, and in the ways in which they weather

[38] Earl Lomon Koos, *The Health of Regionville* (New York: Columbia University Press, 1954).

[39] Ibid., pp. 89–90, 122.

[40] Norman M. Bradburn, *In Pursuit of Happiness* (Chicago: University of Chicago, National Opinion Research Center, 1963), p. 5.

[41] Ibid., p. 6.

family crises. In his review of his own and others' investigations of family crises, Earl Koos concluded that "middle-class families more often react more severely to crisis than do low-income families, but they recover their earlier interaction patterns more readily, and . . . they are more likely to come out of the crisis with some benefit to themselves . . . the middle-class family has far more to lose in the way of morals than does its counterpart in the low-income group; in general too, it has much more opportunity, and much more with which to re-establish itself after the crisis is over."[42]

Upper-class family ties bind the members of a large network of kinfolk in joint holdings in a family business and in the properties they hold in common. Their many relatives can be counted on for emotional support, family loyalty, concerned counsel, and financial help in times of personal or family stress. Underneath is the cushion of inherited wealth that even in the "poor but proud" upper-class family is a source of security.

The middle-class family gets its security from its high levels of education and its reliance on its wits and willingness to work. With expanding industrialization, business and professional men find openings across the country and around the world, sure of their skills and technical competence, and secure in the hope that the company will protect its valuable workers in time of crisis. The middle-class wife typically has the education, training, and previous work experience to make her income a valuable source of security. Protection against future contingencies through insurance coverage, savings, investments, and rational planning more than offsets accumulated debts and time payments in many a middle-class family.

Lower-class families have few margins of security in hand-to-mouth living. Many lower-class family members get along with the help of welfare checks, pension funds, aid-to-dependent-children monies, old-age assistance, unemployment guarantees, and various other public, company, union, and

COURTESY OF DOROTHEA LANGE: "FAMILY OF MAN"

The lower-class family has few resources for meeting its crises and often suffers permanent damage as each recurring trouble leaves the family unit more vulnerable and less well integrated.

---

42 Earl L. Koos, "Class Differences in Family Reactions to Crisis," *Marriage and Family Living* 12, no. 3 (Summer 1950): 78.

private sources. Low levels of education, few job skills, high birth rates, high unemployment, and low wages, plus the general policy of pursuing present pleasures rather than worrying about tomorrow make insecurity a recurrent problem in many lower-class families.

Relatives are a basic source of security for families at all social class levels. Intergenerational study through recent decades finds mutual assistance generally among American families. There may be differences in the amount of financial aid received by family members from their kinfolk in the various socioeconomic strata, but there are few differences in the proportion of families who give, receive, or exchange help in some form from members of their extended families.[43]

SOCIAL MOBILITY

A person is born into the social class of his family, but whether or not he remains in the status of his family of orientation depends upon many factors. An individual

may conform to his or her family standards and patterns as a "chip off the old block," remaining in the same social status all his life. Or, he or she may, by any of many available means (education, occupational success, sports, beauty, "a good marriage," fortunate investment of earned or inherited money, special talents, etc.), move up out of the social status in which he or she was born, so that his family of procreation established upon marriage is a notch or so higher than the family of orientation in which he or she grew up. This is called upward mobility. Downward mobility occurs when the person slips down the social ladder through some aspect of educational inadequacy, dissipation, ill fortune, delinquency, incompetence, or whatever—losing his place in the social scene for one farther down the scale.

It is estimated that one of every four or five persons moves upward at least one social class level during his lifetime in the United States.[44] The greatest amount of upward mobility occurs in the lower-middle and the upper-lower class levels, with nearly 30 percent mobility from the status below reported at these levels. The lowest percentage of upward mobility is found at the upper-class levels, in which there is less than 8 percent mobility from the class below. The great American dream of "doing better than your parents did" is

[43] Marvin B. Sussman, "Relationships of Adult Children with Their Parents in the United States," chap. 4 in Ethel Shanas and Gordon F. Streib, eds., *Social Structure and the Family: Generational Relations* (Englewood Cliffs, N.J.: Prentice-Hall, 1965), p. 68; see also Joan Aldous, "Intergenerational Visiting Patterns," *Family Process*, vol. 6, September 1967; and Reuben Hill, *Family Development in Three Generations* (Cambridge, Mass.: Schenkman Publishing Company, 1970), chap. 3.

[44] Carson McGuire, "Social Stratification and Mobility Patterns," *American Sociological Review* 15, no. 2 (April 1950): 195–204.

possible for the boy or girl from a lower-class family who gets an education, learns a salable skill, makes a good marriage, and establishes a nice home in a good neighborhood. The part of the promise that says "there is plenty of room at the top" is realized by few of those who strive for upper-class status. It takes time to accumulate the necessary wealth, to gain acceptance into upper-class circles, and to achieve the reputation needed for upper-class placement, as many a social climber has learned the hard way. Families oriented toward upward mobility tend to carry their children along with them and to encourage their young people to climb, while more static families, in which mother and father accept the way of life that is theirs, tend to have nonmobile children (85 percent).[45]

Women generally tend to rise in social status more than do men, especially in the later decades of life.[46] A person of either sex who spends his teens in a large community is more apt to be upward mobile than is an individual who grows up in a small community.[47] The rising standard of living, the increase in the assimilation of ethnic groups, the differential birth rate that creates a middle-class vacuum to be filled with lower-class children, the high valuation of education, the growth of labor unions—all seem to be associated with upward social mobility in the United States generally. A study of adults between the ages of forty and sixty in Kansas City, Missouri, reveals more than a third as upwardly mobile (33.6 percent) and 12.5 percent downwardly mobile, yielding a net upward mobility of 21.1 percent.[48]

Here, then, we have a picture of the open social class system in the United States: a pyramid of status levels with the lower classes claiming the greatest number of poor families, with a large and growing middle class, and with a small but influential upper class. Each social class has distinguishing characteristics that tend to be general for the families within it. Whatever a family's social class and its mobility pattern, they greatly affect the life of every member of the family and determine in large measure its strivings and values, practices and policies.

SUMMARY

Family stock and status affect every aspect of living. National, religious, and racial solidarities keep some groups apart from the whole of society, either by choice

[45] Carson McGuire, "Conforming, Mobile, and Divergent Families," *Marriage and Family Living* 14, no. 2 (May 1952): 109–115.

[46] Robert J. Havighurst and Ruth Albrecht, *Older People* (New York: Longmans, Green and Company, 1953), chap. 19.

[47] Seymour Martin Lipset, "Social Mobility and Urbanization," *Rural Sociology* 20, nos. 3–4 (September-December 1955): 220–228.

[48] Richard Coleman, research paper on social mobility for the Committee on Human Development, University of Chicago, May 1956, p. 2.

or by chance. Negro families exemplify the disadvantages of minority group status, especially in urban ghettos and marginal farmlands. There are well-defined social classes in the United States, determined by objective scales. Family incomes vary greatly by social class, type of employment, and other factors, such as education. Education tends to run in families, with expectations of a good education highest in the upper levels and lowest among low-status families. Dating, courtship, and sexual behavior, as well as marriage and divorce patterns, differ by social class, with the most stability and satisfaction at the higher levels of society. Health and happiness are unevenly distributed, with the economically disadvantaged impoverished psychologically too. Security is found differently in the various social classes, except that families, regardless of status, tend to find comfort and assistance in their kin networks, upon which they depend in everyday problems and serious crises.

SUGGESTED ACTIVITIES

1. Write a paper making proposals for how to combat poverty in this country. Base your recommendations on a critical review of the literature, including such research-oriented materials as: Catherine S. Chilman, *Growing Up Poor*; Daniel P. Moynihan, *The Negro Family: The Case for National Action*; Lee Rainwater and Karol K. Weinstein, *And the Poor Get Children*; any of Oscar Lewis's recent reports on the culture of poverty; relevant data from the United States Bureau of the Census, and other well-documented reports.

2. Review one of the following works of fiction, identifying (1) the social class level of the principal family portrayed, (2) the extent of the social mobility exhibited by the main character, (3) the stage(s) of the family life cycle in which the action takes place. Document your decisions on all three points with direct quotations from the book and primary research sources for the criteria you employ.

Farrell, James T., *Father and Son* (New York: Vanguard Press, 1940).
Fitzgerald, F. Scott, *The Great Gatsby* (New York: Charles Scribner's Sons, 1925).
Gilbreth, Frank B., and Ernestine Carey, *Cheaper by the Dozen* (New York: Thomas Y. Crowell Company, 1948).
Lewis, Sinclair, *Babbitt* (New York: Harcourt, Brace and Company, 1922).
MacDonald, Betty, *Onions in the Stew* (Philadelphia: J. B. Lippincott Company, 1954).
Marquand, John P., *The Late George Apley* (New York: P. F. Collier and Son, 1936).
Morley, Christopher, *Kitty Foyle* (Philadelphia: J. B. Lippincott Company, 1939).
Schulberg, Budd, *What Makes Sammy Run?* (New York: Random House, 1941).
Smith, Betty, *A Tree Grows in Brooklyn* (New York: Harper and Brothers, 1943).

Streeter, Edward, *Father of the Bride* (New York: Simon and Schuster, 1948).

Wouk, Herman, *Marjorie Morningstar* (New York: Doubleday and Company, 1955).

3. Plot on an area map of your locality the residences of the families mentioned in the society columns of one of your local papers for the period of one week. Discuss your findings in the light of what you know about social class and membership of families in the "social set."

4. Using the simplified version of the Index of Status Characteristics (table 2–2) given early in this chapter, determine your own social class placement, as seen in your family of orientation and in your plans for your family of procreation. Discuss the mobility evidences apparent in any discrepancies between the two scores, with indications of their possible sources in your developmental experience.

5. Write a paper on the social class origins of the men who are the controlling voices in large industrial organizations in contemporary America using as your primary source the material found in the analysis by W. Lloyd Warner and James Abegglen in *Big Business Leaders in America* (New York: Harper and Brothers, 1955).

6. Make a simple survey of the school dropouts in your community for the past year. Try to find out from the school authorities which children dropped out (in terms of occupation and income of the

father, area lived in, probable social class placement, etc.), percentages of children leaving school by grade levels, and attitudes of representative teachers toward the boys and girls who have left school.

7. Graph the divorces granted in your area during the past year by income and occupation of the man and by the section of the community the couples had lived in just prior to the granting of their divorce. To what extent do these findings corroborate those on the national level that divorce is more frequent among the unskilled and low-income families than among the more privileged and skilled?

8. Review Moss Hart, *Act One: An Autobiography* (New York: Random House, 1959), emphasizing particularly the social class placement of Mr. Hart's family of orientation as compared with his family of procreation. Discuss the means by which his mobility was achieved step by step through his career. Conclude with your appraisal of how typical this mobility pattern is in modern American life, and the other ways by which a young person can improve his family's status today.

READINGS

Aldous, Joan. "Wives' Employment Status and Lower-Class Men as Husband-Fathers: Support for the Moynihan Thesis." *Journal of Marriage and the Family* 31, no. 3 (August 1969): 469–476.

Bernard, Jessie. *Marriage and Family among Negroes.* Englewood Cliffs, N.J.: Prentice-Hall, 1966.

Carter, Hugh, and Paul C. Glick. *Marriage and Divorce: A Social and Economic Study.* Cambridge, Mass.: Harvard University Press, 1970.

Cavan, Ruth Shonle. *The American Family.* 4th ed. New York: Thomas Y. Crowell Company, 1969. Pt. 2, "Social and Cultural Configurations of the American Family," pp. 71–228.

Chilman, Catherine S. *Growing Up Poor.* Welfare Administration Publication, no. 13. Washington, D.C., 1966.

Cuber, John F., and Peggy B. Harroff. *The Significant Americans.* New York: Appleton-Century-Crofts, 1965.

Dinitz, Simon, Franklin Banks, and Benjamin Pasamanick. "Mate Selection and Social Class: Changes during the Past Quarter Century." *Marriage and Family Living* 22, no. 4 (November 1960): 348–351.

Eshleman, J. Ross, and Chester L. Hunt. *Social Class Factors in the College Adjustment of Married Students.* Kalamazoo, Mich.: Western Michigan University, 1965.

Gass, Gertrude Zemon, William C. Nichols, Jr., and Aaron L. Rutledge. "Family Problems in Upgrading the Hardcore." *Family Coordinator* 18, no. 2 (April 1969): 99–106.

Goldscheider, Calvin, and Sidney Goldstein. "Generational Changes in Jewish Family Structure." *Journal of Marriage and the Family* 29, no. 2 (May 1967): 267–276.

Herzog, Elizabeth. "Is There a 'Breakdown' of the Negro Family?" *Social Work* 2, no. 1 (January 1966).

Herzog, Elizabeth, and Catharine Richards, eds. *The Nation's Youth.* Children's Bureau Publication, no. 460. Washington, D.C., 1968.

Hill, Reuben. *Family Development in Three Generations.* Cambridge, Mass.: Schenkman Publishing Company, 1970.

Kaplan, Max. *Leisure in America: A Social Inquiry.* New York: John Wiley and Sons, 1960.

Kohn, Melvin L. "Social Class and Parent-Child Relationships: An Interpretation." *American Journal of Sociology* 68, no. 4 (January 1963): 471–480.

Komarovsky, Mirra. *Blue-collar Marriage.* New York: Random House, 1964.

Koos, Earl L. "Class Differences in Family Reactions to Crisis." *Marriage and Family Living* 12, no. 3 (Summer 1950): 77–78, 99.

Koos, Earl Lomon. *The Health of Regionville.* New York: Columbia University Press, 1954.

Kriesberg, Louis. *Mothers in Poverty: A Study of Fatherless Families.* Chicago: Aldine Publishing Company, 1970.

Lalli, Michael. "The Italian-American Family: Assimilation and Change, 1900–1965." *Family Coordinator* 18, no. 1 (January 1969): 44–48.

McGuire, Carson. "Family Life in Lower and Middle Class Homes." *Marriage and Family Living* 14, no. 1 (February 1952): 1–6.

Mayer, John E. *The Disclosure of Marital Problems: An Exploratory Study of Lower and Middle Class Wives.* New York: Community Service Society of New York, 1966.

Moynihan, Daniel P. *The Negro Family: The Case for National Action.* Washington, D.C.: U.S. Department of Labor, Office of Policy Planning and Research, 1965.

Olsen, Marvin E. "Distribution of Family Responsibilities and Social Stratification." *Marriage and Family Living* 22, no. 1 (February 1960): 60–65.

Parke, Robert, Jr., and Paul C. Glick. "Prospective Changes in Marriage and the Family." *Journal of Marriage and the Family* 29, no. 2 (May 1967): 249–256.

Rainwater, Lee, and Karol K. Weinstein. *And the Poor Get Children: Sex, Contraception, and Family Planning in the Working Class.* Chicago: Quadrangle Books, 1960.

Rainwater, Lee, and William L. Yancey. *The Moynihan Report and the Politics of Controversy* (including the text of Daniel P. Moynihan, *The Negro Family: The Case for National Action*). Cambridge, Mass.: M.I.T. Press, 1967.

Schulz, David A. *Coming Up Black.* Englewood Cliffs, N.J.: Prentice-Hall, 1969.

Seeley, John, Alexander Sim, and Elizabeth Loosley. *Crestwood Heights.* New York: Basic Books, 1956.

Sorokin, Pitirim A. *Social and Cultural Mobility.* Glencoe, Ill.: Free Press, 1959.

Staples, Robert E. "Research on the Negro Family: A Source for Family Practitioners." *Family Coordinator* 18, no. 3 (July 1969): 202–209.

U.S. Department of Agriculture, Federal Extension Service. *Low Income Families.* Washington, D.C.: U.S. Department of Agriculture, 1963.

Warner, W. Lloyd. *American Life: Dream and Reality.* Chicago: University of Chicago Press, 1953.

West, Ruth. "The Care and Feeding of the Very Rich." *McCall's*, August 1969, pp. 57, 109–110, 112.

3 FAMILIES FIT THE TIMES

And step by step, since time began,
I see the steady gain of man. John Greenleaf Whittier

Families are found in all cultures throughout human history, partly because of their remarkable ability to adapt to social change. In a hunting era, families moved with the game they used to meet their needs. In an agricultural economy, families settled on farms and raised most of their food and fiber. Now, in a complex industrial period, families initiate new forms, functions, purposes, and potentials in response to the pressures and promises they face.

American families today are markedly different in many respects from those of two or more generations ago. Within the memory of men now living, family life has shifted from one way of life to another. The world grandfather knew at the turn of the century is no more. Families now have new demands made upon them that the old-fashioned family never knew. Family members are moving rapidly today from a familiar past to an unknown and uncertain future.

HOW FAMILIES ARE CHANGING

Keeping up with the nature of changing families in today's world is not an easy task. Reliable data are often harder to obtain than exaggerated distortions of the facts. The seeming paradoxes in modern family trends are many. For instance, how can one account for more divorces and more marriages, more resources and greater debts, fewer farms and more farm surpluses, more freedom and greater insecurity, smaller families and an expanding population? It is to these intriguing dimensions of modern life that this chapter turns.

Nearly All Americans Marry Nowadays

Ninety-seven percent of the men and women now in their late twenties are either married already or will marry before they become middle-aged.[1] This is in sharp contrast to earlier decades of this century. At the turn of the century, a man typically left school at fourteen and worked a dozen years before he married, usually a girl considerably younger than himself. Young peo-

---

[1] Current data and projections are from Robert Parke, Jr., and Paul C. Glick, "Prospective Changes in Marriage and the Family," *Journal of Marriage and the Family* 29, no. 2 (May 1967): 249–256, based on March 1966 Current Population Survey, U.S. Bureau of the Census.

ple are more inclined today than formerly to marry within a fairly narrow range, usually in their early twenties. Teenage marriages, so popular in the 1950s, have declined in numbers and percentages since. Only 15 percent of the eighteen- and nineteen-year-old girls in 1967 were married by the time they reached their eighteenth year. One reason for the decline in teenage marriages was the temporary shortage of men of marriage age among young people born during the postwar baby boom. The sex ratio is currently about even again. By delaying marriage until the twenties, young people of both sexes have time for more education, some work experience, and possible travel in or out of military service. There is wide recognition of the instability of teenage marriages, which break up twice as often as those established by persons at least in their twenties.

Most Marriages Last through the Years

Viewers with alarm talk of a spiraling divorce rate in the United States. Official

Chart 3–1. *Divorce Rates: United States, 1920–1967*

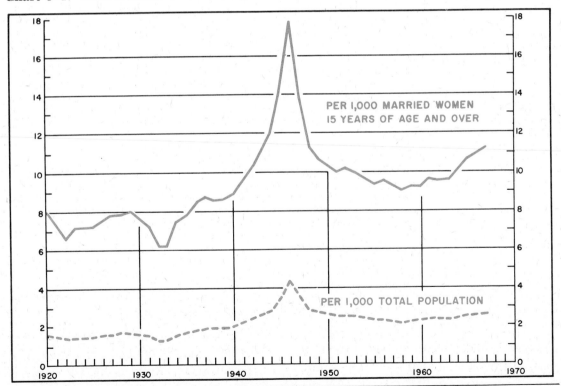

PER 1,000 MARRIED WOMEN
15 YEARS OF AGE AND OVER

PER 1,000 TOTAL POPULATION

Source: U.S. Department of Health, Education, and Welfare, Public Health Service, *Monthly Vital Statistics Report* 18, no. 1, supp. (April 16, 1969): 1.

Table 3–1. *Marital Status by Number of Times Married, Years Since First Marriage, and Race, for Men Ever Married Fourteen to Sixty-nine Years Old: United States, 1967*

Number of times married and marital status at survey date	All races, 14 to 69 years old (Numbers in thousands)				White, 14 to 69		Negro, 14 to 69	
	Total	Years since first marriage			Total	20+ years since first marriage	Total	20+ years since first marriage
		Under 10	10–19	20+				
Total men ever married	43,657	10,631	11,566	21,461	39,507	19,537	3,727	1,748
Percent	100.0	100.0	100.0	100.0	100.0	100.0	100.0	100.0
Married once	86.5	96.3	88.5	80.6	87.3	81.9	77.8	64.9
Married twice	12.2	3.6	10.7	17.2	11.5	16.1	19.8	30.1
Married three times or more	1.3	0.1	0.8	2.2	1.2	2.0	2.4	5.0
Married once	37,766	10,239	10,236	17,291	34,494	16,006	2,898	1,135
Percent now:								
Married	93.9	95.4	94.5	92.5	94.8	93.7	83.4	76.3
Widowed	1.8	0.1	0.6	3.4	1.6	3.0	4.0	9.0
Divorced	4.4	4.4	4.8	4.1	3.7	3.3	12.6	14.7
Married twice	5,319	384	1,240	3,695	4,531	3,142	738	526
Percent now:								
Married	92.2	95.6	94.4	91.1	92.7	91.9	88.5	86.1
Widowed	2.0	1.0	0.1	2.7	1.9	2.6	2.7	3.6
Divorced	5.8	3.4	5.6	6.1	5.4	5.5	8.8	10.3
Married three times or more	573	8	90	475	482	388	91	87
Percent now:								
Married	82.4	*	80.0	82.7	83.6	84.0	75.8	77.0
Widowed	3.7	*	0.0	4.4	3.5	4.4	4.4	4.6
Divorced	13.8	*	20.0	12.8	12.9	11.6	19.8	18.4

Source: U.S. Bureau of the Census, unpublished data from the 1967 Survey of Economic Opportunity, presented by Paul C. Glick and Arthur J. Norton, "Probabilities of Marriage, Divorce, Widowhood, and Remarriage," at the annual meeting of the Population Association of America, Atlanta, Ga., April 16–18, 1970, mimeographed, fig. 3.
* Base extremely small.

government figures provide a more valid basis for evaluating family stability through the century. Chart 3–1 shows some increase in divorce since 1920. In the past fifty years, the divorce rate has risen from something less than two to less than three divorces per thousand population. Using the measure of number of divorces per thousand married women over fifteen years of age, the upper line of the graph indicates an increase from eight in 1920 to 11.2 in recent years. Even at current levels of divorce, 99 percent of the couples who are married today will escape divorce within

58

the year. Experts in the interpretation of the United States Bureau of the Census data remind us that increases in the percentages of divorced persons "do not necessarily imply the existence of a rising divorce rate. . . . A stable divorce rate may produce an increasing accumulation of divorced persons in the population unless remarriage is universal and instantaneous. This it is not. . . ."[2]

A nationwide survey by the United States Bureau of the Census in 1967 found 86.5 percent of all men between fourteen and sixty-nine years of age married but once; 12.2 percent married twice; and 1.3 percent married three times or more (table 3–1).

Divorces are more numerous in some periods than in others. Divorce rates declined during the depression, as is strikingly seen in the slump in divorce rate curves in 1932–1933. The number of divorces increased during the World War II years, and again since 1960, when economic and military conditions have been similar. The relationship between marital instability and economic prosperity is complex. When times are good, some couples who do not get along divorce and support themselves separately. When jobs are scarce and family incomes drop, a husband and wife may stay together because they cannot afford two separate households. On the other hand, there is clear evidence that both separation and divorce are less extensive among the affluent than among the poor. The reduction of poverty and the improvement of America's health may be expected to increase the proportion of those who marry, those who remarry, and those who stay married.[3] Even now, nine out of ten families include both husband and wife.

Divorces are more frequent among some groups than others. In general, the data point in these directions:[4]

Divorces more frequent

Among city families
In states with lenient divorce laws
In interfaith marriages
In Protestant marriages
Among working-class families
Among less-educated people
Among teenage marriages
In first years of marriage
In childless marriages

---

[2] Parke and Glick, "Prospective Changes in Marriage and the Family," p. 254.

[3] Hugh Carter and Paul C. Glick, *Marriage and Divorce: A Social and Economic Study* (Cambridge, Mass.: Harvard University Press, 1970).

[4] Paul H. Jacobson, *American Marriage and Divorce* (New York: Rinehart and Company, 1959); and summary of research in Jessie Bernard, "Divorce and Remarriage—Research Related to Policy," chap. 6 in Evelyn M. Duvall and Sylvanus M. Duvall, eds., *Sex Ways—in Fact and Faith: Bases for Christian Family Policy* (New York: Association Press, 1961), pp. 93–111.

Among farm families
In states with strict divorce laws
In marriages within same faith
In Roman Catholic marriages
Among professional families
Among better-educated men and women
Among those who marry at more mature
   ages
In later years of marriage
In marriages with children

The reasons for the increase in family instability are many. The factors involved in understanding who gets divorced and why are complex. There is no question but what the revolutionary social changes of recent decades have blasted relatively stable families out of their old ways that had persisted for many hundreds of years, into new forms and functions with far-reaching repercussions. The eminent historian Arnold Toynbee feels that, "The vital revolution of our time is the emancipation of women, workingmen, and 'natives'. . . . The women are the most important contingent of the three because, in the long run, their emancipation is going to affect everybody's life. Above all, it is going to demand an immense and disturbing psychological adjustment on the part of the men, because it implies a revolutionary change in the traditional relations between the sexes."[5]

[5] Arnold J. Toynbee, "We Must Pay for Freedom," *Woman's Home Companion*, March 1955, pp. 52–53, 133–136.

Individual Family Members Have More Freedom

Traditionally, each family member was subordinate to the group. The very survival of the family and its members depended upon family and community solidarity. With the greater resources of our modern way of life has come an increase in individuation. The individual man, woman, and child today expects to be happy. He is encouraged to develop himself and to work out his own problems in his own way. If his marriage is not happy, he can dissolve it. Or, better still, he is encouraged to select the kind of partner whom he can love, who will be good for him to live with, and to prepare with her for their life together from early in their courtship. Children now exist not for what they can do to help the family, but rather for themselves as growing persons with rights, privileges, and values recognized as uniquely theirs. A child no longer is expected to follow in his father's footsteps, but rather to find his own interests and talents and choose a vocation that is meaningful to him.

Even the nature of the family is chosen today by its individual members. A couple may or may not have children. They may live much as their grandparents did, or they may establish their own unique family patterns. They may make the old rambling family homestead their home, or, more likely, they may choose compact efficiency in a new little suburban dwelling or a city apartment. They may remain close to the place where they grew up or set out into the world calling any number of places "home" for a while. Both may work and jointly run the household, or he may be the sole breadwinner, or she may support them both during intervals of his military training or further education. They may live for a while with his parents or with her parents. They may share their home with relatives, or they may live by themselves while institutions care for their dependent relatives.

They may pour everything they have into living it up as they go along, or save all they can spare for the future; or they may budget for satisfactions both in the present and the near and distant future. They may bring up their children in traditional ways, or according to any of the fads or fancies proposed in our age, or try to gear into the developmental patterns that are emerging for child-rearing. Any of these and numerous other possibilities are open to families today. They may choose what they will, both as families and as persons, and few there are who will either reward or punish them for their choices.

With so much freedom, is it any wonder today's families are confused and bewildered? When family tasks change so rapidly, it takes time and effort to become familiar with new expectations and to assume appropriate new roles. For members of transition generations this means a period of uneasiness and instability, of innovations and exploration of new possibilities, until

we can become more completely at home in these new families of ours.

Few Families Remain on Farms

American families have moved off farms and into the cities, towns, and suburbs at a rapid rate. In 1890, 64 percent of America's families lived on farms. In the decades that followed there was a steady migration off the farms and into more heavily populated areas. With the coming of the 1970s only 5 percent of all households in the United States were those of farmers.[6]

Two related social forces brought about the decline in farm families. One was the rapid industrialization that attracted workers to the factories concentrated in and around urban areas. The second was the increased efficiency of farm operation. Farming has become mechanized, chemically fortified and enhanced, so that fewer workers produce huge surpluses year after year. "Agriculture in all its phases is now in the process of 'industrialization.' It has taken on such characteristics of nonfarm industry as specialization, standardization of product, and separation of functions of ownership, management, and labor. Nearly all technological change is pressing in this direction. The 1970's will see a continuation of the process."[7]

[6] "Families Then and Now," *Family Economics Review*, March 1968, pp. 3–4.
[7] From an address by John H. Southern, Economic Research Service, U.S. Department of Agriculture, "Rural Change—Perspective for the 1970's," *Family Economics Review*, June 1969, pp. 17–18.

U.S. DEPARTMENT OF AGRICULTURE

There was a time when raising many children was an economic advantage.

Small Families Are Typical Now

There was a time when raising many children was an economic advantage. In the old farm family, the more "hands" a family had, the more acres they could till, and the more stock they could raise. Now, when the vast majority of families live and work in city and suburb, children have become an economic liability, so it is not surprising that American family size has declined sharply over the years. In 1700, the average mother by the age of forty-five had borne 7.4 children. By 1910, the number had dropped to 4.7; by 1940 to 2.9; and by 1950 to 2.5 children.[8] The 1955 Growth of American Families Study reported that nearly all couples had some limitation on their fertility. Some 70 percent had used some method of contraception; another 9 percent expected to; and most of the remaining couples were those who were below normal in their capacity to reproduce.[9]

In spite of urbanization and contraception, American families remain about the same size in terms of how many relatives live in the same house or apartment. There has been only a slight decline in the number of adults per family, which is now close to the minimum husband-wife pair. The number of children under eighteen living in their parental home is expected to be in 1985 what it now is, an average of 1.4 per family. Most families now have only one or two children, as seen in chart 3–2. More than twenty million families now have no children under eighteen in the home, but about nine out of every ten of these fami-

[8] Reuben Hill, "The American Family Today," in Eli Ginsberg, ed., *The Nation's Children*, vol. 1, *The Family and Social Change* (New York: Columbia University Press, 1960), p. 88.

[9] Arthur A. Campbell, "Population Dynamics and Family Planning," *Journal of Marriage and the Family* 30, no. 2 (May 1968): 204.

Table 3–2. *Persons per Family in the United States, 1940–1966, and Projections for 1985*

Year	All ages	Under 18	18 and over
1940	3.8	1.2	2.5
1950	3.5	1.2	2.4
1960	3.7	1.4	2.3
1966	3.7	1.4	2.3
1985	3.5	1.4	2.2

Source: Robert Parke, Jr., and Paul C. Glick, "Prospective Changes in Marriage and the Family," *Journal of Marriage and the Family* 29, no. 2 (May 1967): 254.

Chart 3–2. *Most Families Are Small*

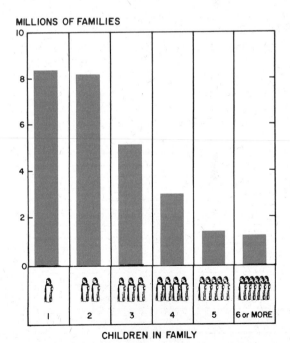

MILLIONS OF FAMILIES

CHILDREN IN FAMILY

Source: Elizabeth Herzog and Catharine Richards, eds., *The Nation's Youth*, Children's Bureau Publication, no. 460 (Washington, D.C., 1968), chart 7.

lies either have had children who have left home or will have children later. Four out of five families today have no more than three children.[10]

There Are More Dependents in the Population

Proportionally there are more children and more aging family members in the population than at the turn of the century. Chart 3–3 shows population pyramids for 1900, 1960, and projections for 1980, with population distributions by age and sex for each of the three periods. Low birth rates dur-

ing the depression of the 1930s and sharp increases in numbers of children born during the postwar period have resulted in a current situation in which a smaller proportion of men and women in the most productive age groups now support larger percentages of potential dependents at the early and late decades of life.

About half of the total population is under twenty-five years of age. Why should there be more children when families tend to be smaller? Because there are more family units now than there used to be, and because nearly 40 percent of the nation's children live in 11 percent of America's families, having four or more children. As individuals of the baby boom of the postwar years marry and have their children, the nation's child population will increase still further.

[10] U.S. Bureau of the Census, "Household and Family Characteristics: March 1966," *Population Characteristics*, Current Population Reports, series P-20, no. 164 (April 12, 1967), table D, p. 3.

Chart 3–3. *Population Patterns Have Changed—More Children and More Old People*

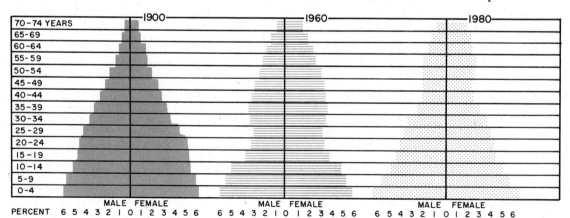

Source: 1960 White House Conference on Children and Youth, *Children in a Changing World* (New York: Columbia University Press, 1960), p. 4, from original data supplied by U.S. Bureau of the Census.

Chart 3–4. *Percentage of Workers in the United States by Age, Sex, and Marital Status*

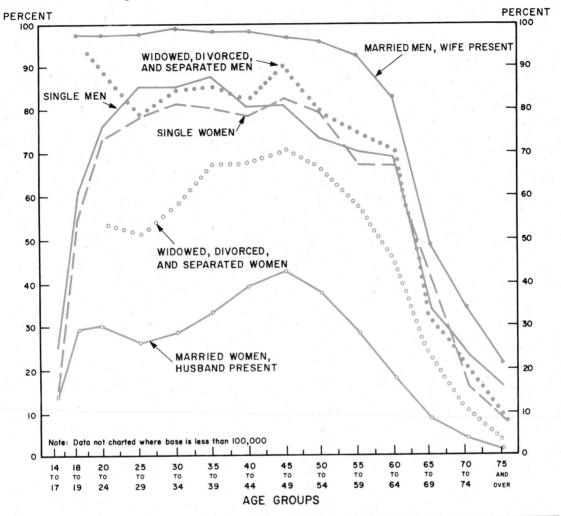

PERCENT

MARRIED MEN, WIFE PRESENT

WIDOWED, DIVORCED, AND SEPARATED MEN

SINGLE MEN

SINGLE WOMEN

WIDOWED, DIVORCED, AND SEPARATED WOMEN

MARRIED WOMEN, HUSBAND PRESENT

Note: Data not charted where base is less than 100,000

| 14 TO 17 | 18 TO 19 | 20 TO 24 | 25 TO 29 | 30 TO 34 | 35 TO 39 | 40 TO 44 | 45 TO 49 | 50 TO 54 | 55 TO 59 | 60 TO 64 | 65 TO 69 | 70 TO 74 | 75 AND OVER |

AGE GROUPS

Source: Jacob Schiffman, *Marital and Family Characteristics of Workers, March 1960*, Special Labor Force Report, no. 13 (Washington, D.C.: U.S. Department of Labor, Bureau of Labor Statistics), from the *Monthly Labor Review*, April 1961.

Now, when more persons live out their life-span, aging family members increase in number. At the turn of the century it was not unusual for a mother to die before her last child was grown. Now a man and wife typically live to see their children married, their grandchildren off to a good start, and not unusually to know one or more of their great-grandchildren before their marriage is broken by death.

More Women Work outside the Home

At the turn of the century practically half of American women never entered paid employment. Now, at least nine out of ten women work outside their homes sometime in the course of their lives.[11] Some of these women workers are single, widowed, divorced, or separated, as chart 3–4 shows.

More married women are employed now than formerly. In 1890, seven out of every ten working women were single. Six of every ten women now working are married, and three or four out of every ten married women are employed.[12] The general tendency is for the young wife to work for a while after she marries, until her first child comes, when she may leave employment or take a diminished schedule until her children demand less care. By the time they reach adolescence and near the launching stage, she may return to work. More married women in their forties and fifties work than at any other time in their marriages (chart 3–4).

Whether a married woman plans to work or not depends upon many factors: (1) the age of her children, (2) her replacement in the home, (3) her husband's income, (4) her husband's attitude toward his wife's work-ing, (5) her interests and salable skills, and (6) other personal and family factors.[13] The question of the effect of the mother's working upon her marriage, her family life, and her children has been widely studied. The evidence to date all points in the same direction—that the fact of her working is in itself not a significant factor in her marriage and family adjustment or in the development of the children in the home.[14] Whether a wife's working helps or hurts appears to depend upon many personal and family factors rather than on the working itself.

Family Members Are Better Educated

More Americans go farther in school now than formerly, and the trend is likely to continue through the twentieth century. Chart 3–5 graphically shows the increase in school enrollment to be more rapid than

[11] National Manpower Council, *Womanpower* (New York: Columbia University Press, 1957), p. 10.

[12] National Manpower Council, *Womanpower*, p. 10.

[13] See, for instance, National Manpower Council, *Work in the Lives of Married Women* (New York: Columbia University Press, 1958); Robert O. Blood, Jr., and Donald M. Wolfe, *Husbands and Wives: The Dynamics of Married Living* (Glencoe, Ill.: Free Press, 1960), chap. 4; Charlotte Montgomery, "Can Working Wives Make It Pay?" *Better Homes and Gardens*, November 1957, pp. 68, 137–138; Mildred W. Weil, "An Analysis of the Factors Influencing Married Women's Actual or Planned Work Participation," *American Sociological Review* 26, no. 1 (February 1961): 91–96.

[14] For a review of more than fifty studies, see Lois H. Meek Stolz, "Effects of Maternal Employment on Children: Evidence from Research," *Child Development* 31, no. 4 (December 1960): 749–782.

Chart 3–5. *Percentage Growth of Population, School Enrollment, Households, and Labor Force: 1960–1985 (1965 = 100)*

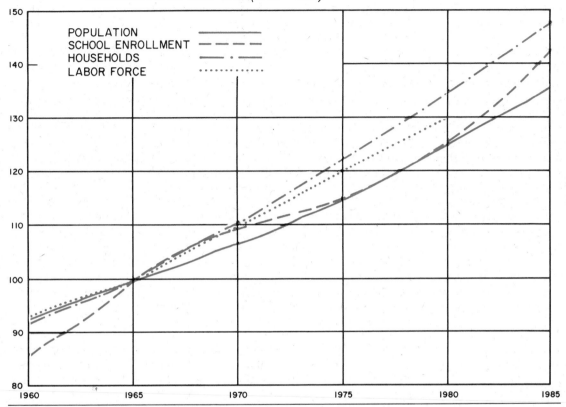

POPULATION
SCHOOL ENROLLMENT
HOUSEHOLDS
LABOR FORCE

Source: U.S. Bureau of the Census, "Summary of Demographic Projections," *Population Estimates,* Current Population Reports, series P-25, no. 388 (March 14, 1968), fig. 1, cover.

the increase in population for the twenty-five years between 1960 and 1985. By 1985, practically all young people between seven and seventeen years of age will be in school. By that time the proportion of eighteen- to twenty-one-year-olds in school will have increased by 80 percent since 1960. The proportion of students in college has risen every year since 1951, and between 1965 and 1985 will increase 66 percent, proportionally more than any other age group. High school enrollment will be up 26 per-

cent, and grade school by 31 percent in the same quarter-century. Total school enrollment will reach seventy-two million by 1985.[15]

_____

[15] U.S. Bureau of the Census, "Projections of School and College Enrollment in the United States to 1985," *Population Estimates,* Current Population Reports, series P-25, no. 338 (May 31, 1966), table 1 (series B-2), p. 4; and U.S. Bureau of the Census, "Revised Projections of School and College Enrollment in the United States to 1985," *Population Estimates,* Current Population Reports, series P-25, no. 365 (May 5, 1967), table A, p. 9.

Through the 1960s and 1970s practically all elementary-age pupils between seven and thirteen are in school, and approximately nine out of ten teenagers between fourteen and seventeen are enrolled. Education runs in families. College attendance varies widely by family income and parents' education. In one recent year, fewer than one-fourth (22 percent) of the high school graduates entering college had fathers with less than eighth-grade education, in contrast with 82 percent of those whose fathers were college graduates.[16]

The trend toward each generation having more education than former ones is illustrated in data for three-generation families' actual experience, table 3-3.

In these three-generation families, the grandfathers typically had less than seven

[16] U.S. Bureau of the Census, "Factors Related to High School Graduation and College Attendance: 1967," *Population Characteristics,* Current Population Reports, series P-20, no. 185 (July 11, 1969), pp. 1–2.

years of school; the fathers more likely graduated from elementary school; and the married sons tended at least to finish high school. The trend for women to have more education in the younger generations is quite as striking: 82 percent of the grandmothers, 32 percent of the mothers, and only 1 percent of the youngest generation of wives left school at the eighth grade or earlier.

Now, when our complex society calls for better-educated citizens, when children's labor is not needed at home, and when money is more readily available, families fit the times by encouraging their children to get as much education as is feasible.

Families Have More Money

The more education a man has, the higher his income decade by decade during his working years. This is true in general for most periods of our economy. In prosper-

Table 3–3. *Education of Husbands and Wives in Three Generations*

Years of school	Grandparents		Parents		Married children		All three generations	
	H	*W*	*H*	*W*	*H*	*W*	*H*	*W*
7 or less	56%	49%	16%	6%	—	—	23%	17%
8	28	33	31	26	6%	1%	21	19
9–11	7	10	21	25	20	24	16	20
12	4	5	23	35	44	55	24	32
13–15	5	3	8	8	15	16	9	9
16–17 or more	—	—	2	1	15	6	6	2
Total	100%	100%	100%*	100%*	100%	100%*	100%*	100%*

Source: Reuben Hill, *Family Development in Three Generations* (Cambridge, Mass.: Schenkman Publishing Company, 1970), chap. 2, table 2.03.
* Due to rounding of figures, the columns may not total 100%.

Chart 3–6. *Income in 1967 of Families in the United States*

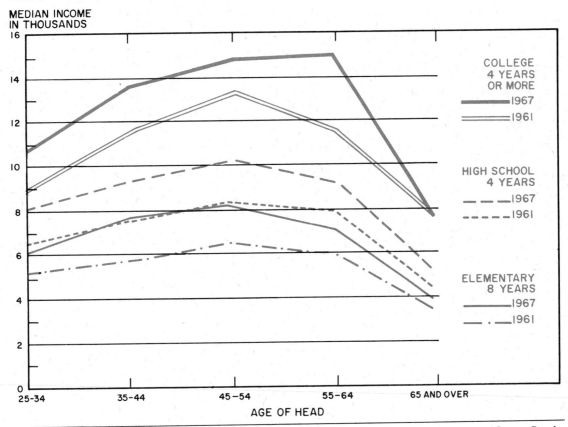

MEDIAN INCOME
IN THOUSANDS

COLLEGE
4 YEARS
OR MORE
——— 1967
——— 1961

HIGH SCHOOL
4 YEARS
– – – 1967
- - - - 1961

ELEMENTARY
8 YEARS
——— 1967
—·—— 1961

AGE OF HEAD

Source: U.S. Bureau of the Census, "Income in 1967 of Families in the United States," *Consumer Income*, Current Population Reports, series P-60, no. 59 (April 18, 1969), p. 1.

ous periods, such as prevailed in the late 1960s, workers of all educational levels had higher incomes than in 1961, as is shown graphically in chart 3–6. Typically, a man's income increases between his twenty-fifth and fifty-fourth years of age, with better-educated family heads' incomes rising more sharply than those of family heads with less education. A college graduate's income is at its peak when he retires in his mid-sixties, in contrast to the worker who dropped out of school after a high school or grade school education, whose income peak comes a full ten years or more earlier, when he is between forty-five and fifty-four years old. Education is an asset that is amply rewarded in an industrial economy, in ever-increasing amounts.

In a rapidly expanding economy, family incomes rise sharply in all three educational levels, as is seen in comparisons of 1967 with 1961 family incomes in chart 3–6. When times are good, a man with only an eighth-grade education earns more at every decade of his working years than was typical six years earlier. At the same time, college-educated workers' incomes rise even more sharply.

Family incomes increased throughout the twentieth century, as is seen in table 3–4. In the immediate postwar period of 1947, some 57 percent of American families had incomes under $5,000 a year; by 1967 only 26 percent were this low; and by 1985 only 12 percent are estimated below the $5,000 annual income level. At the other end of the income scale, some 9 percent of American families received over $15,000 annual incomes in 1947; by 1985, 44 percent will be getting at least this much.

The trend toward higher incomes is illustrated in the responses of members of three-generation families. The married-child generation reports more adequate family incomes than either their parents or grandparents. Whereas 28 percent of the grandparents do without many needed things, only 4.7 percent of the parents and 1.2 percent of the married children do. On the item, "Have the things we need and a few of the extras," 30.5 percent of the grandparents, 61 percent of the parents, and 76 percent of the married children respond affirmatively. It is clear that "family development over the life span shows not only upgrading in performance from the oldest to the youngest generation in all spheres of economic activity but there is an acceleration in this process from generation to generation."[17]

[17] Reuben Hill, *Family Development in Three Generations* (Cambridge, Mass.: Schenkman Publishing Company, 1970), chap. 2, table 2.09, and chap. 13.

Table 3–4. *Median Family Income, 1947–1985*

1967 dollars	1947 $4,531	1957 $5,889	1967 $7,974	1985 $13,800
Under $3,000	27%	20%	13%	6%
$3,000 to $4,999	30	19	13	6
$5,000 to $6,999	21	24	16	8
$7,000 to $9,999	14	22	24	12
$10,000 to $14,999		11	22	25
$15,000 and over	9	4	12	44
Total	100%*	100%	100%	100%*

Source: "The Changing Income Distribution," *Family Economics Review*, June 1969, p. 14.
* Due to rounding of figures, the columns may not total 100 percent.

Housing and Equipment Are Acquired Sooner

Practically all married couples over twenty years of age have their own households (98 percent in 1965, 99 percent by 1985).[18] The younger generation today has better housing than the older, in a progressive improvement in which each generation is better housed than its parents or grandparents. The married-child generation today not only is more adequately housed, but sooner than its forebears in the same families.[19]

Families today have equipment unknown to "the old-fashioned family" at the turn of the century. Many grandparents who married in the first decade of the twentieth century never have acquired what young people start out with today. Grandparents, most of whom have celebrated their golden wedding anniversary, had been married forty years or more before they acquired their first electric coffee maker, electric frypan, food freezer, gas or electric clothes dryer, garbage disposer, dishwasher, electric blanket, air conditioner, or television set. All of these items had been acquired by the young generation married only five years, on the average. The generation between, married during the depression, did better than the old folks, but fell short of their married children in the speed at which they equipped and furnished their homes. During the year the three-generation study was being made, the differential rate of household acquisitions continued. The grandparents that year acquired fifty-two new pieces of equipment (seven refrigerators, five gas ranges, five electric frypans, five electric blankets, and sundry other items) to increase their household inventories by 5 percent. The parents increased their family inventories by 9 percent with the acquisition of fourteen radios, fourteen television sets, thirteen electric frypans, and a variety of other items their married children had since they were first married. That same year, the youngest generation further outstripped its parents and grandparents with 132 new pieces of equipment (twelve television sets, eleven wall-to-wall carpeting, eleven vacuum cleaners, and other items) to upgrade their household inventories by 12 percent.[20]

In the early years of the century, when most families lived on farms, and the economy was yet to commence its rapid development through industrialization, a couple learned to do without, or "to make do." Those husbands and wives who married during the depression of the 1930s knew deprivation too, and only after World War II did they begin to have many of the

---

[18] Parke and Glick, "Prospective Changes in Marriage and the Family," p. 255.

[19] Hill, *Family Development in Three Generations*, chap. 5.

[20] Ibid., chap. 7.

things their children were to take for granted when they married. Couples marrying now have more to begin with, expect more, and acquire more faster in ways that keep the industrial machine going at peak levels.

Families fit the times, then as now. Before modern factories took over the tasks of processing and preparing foods, clothing, and all the other things that people need and want, families made them in their own homes. Now, in a modern industrial age, most of the things a family uses are mass-produced in an economy that depends on selling its products to ever larger markets. So families have shifted from production to consumption in the lifetimes of members now living, in ways appropriate to family functioning in a rapidly expanding industrial society.

FAMILIES CHANGE AS THEIR WORLD CHANGES

Times are changing so fast that no one today can expect to live out his life in the world in which he was born, nor will many die in the world in which they matured. Change in itself is neither good nor bad, but it makes demands upon families and family members. Social changes through this century have brought families face to face with new conditions, possibilities, problems, promises, and challenges. That families have responded so well and adapted so quickly to the new situations and potentials they have met is an evidence of the amazing flexibility and creative capacity of families. There was a time when family members spent most of their time together. They worked side by side on the old home place. They played together or with their closest neighbors from nearby farms. Today family members are scattered, and their work and play activities are more individual than family-based.

The roles of family members have become more complex and flexible. Men, women, and children worked hard on the old family farm in bygone years. But they knew what was expected of them, and they had been prepared rather specifically for the roles they played. A woman had to be a good cook, since her family would depend upon her food throughout its lifetime. A man had to be a good, steady provider, as it was not possible for his wife to get a job to supplement his earnings. Both men and women had learned their roles in their own homes before they married. Children had their place in the scheme of things and knew what was expected of them from the beginning. The whole neighborhood agreed on what was man's work and what was woman's work and what was to be expected of a child. The family lived according to relatively rigid rules traditionally established and maintained by social and moral pressures of the entire society.

Today both men and women expect a wide variety of roles of each other. These expectations differ from couple to couple and from family to family. In one home a woman is expected to work outside; in another her place is seen to be in the home. In one family a man is expected to be a companion to his wife and children; in another his roles are more traditionally defined. In general, the trend is for both husbands and wives to expect more of each other in the intangible roles of understanding companion, stimulating colleague, and loving, sympathetic parent than formerly.

The challenge of democratic interaction between family members—husband and wife, parent and child, close and extended family members—imposes new tasks and responsibilities upon all members of the family. Now that the authority of the father-head in many families has been taken over by family discussion, decisions are not as quick, nor plans as easily made. Now, when the social pressures of church and neighborhood have declined, every member of every family faces innumerable choices and possibilities.

Seeing home as a place good for people to grow up in is life at a much deeper level than seeing it as a "roof over our heads." Its potentialities are tremendous, but its problems, especially for transitional generations, are felt in the very warp and woof of family living. The family, freed at last from the burden of producing things, faces as its primary task today the development of sturdy, wholesome personalities. But such a shift does not come all at once. Every step in the new direction is taken slowly, some with pain, others only after real effort, as every member of the family learns his new roles and practices the innovations that are appropriate in today's family.

It is much harder to learn how to raise a child according to sound child development principles than it used to be when anyone with any "common sense" knew what was good for a child. Being a warmly sympathetic and companionable spouse is more difficult than baking a light biscuit or mending the harness. Such arts and skills of human interaction as are expected of family members today open new social and emotional frontiers where few have been adequately prepared by previous experience. Today's family becomes a laboratory at work on the most challenging worldwide problem—how to live together in creative peace, build harmony out of difference, and make democracy work.

Today's American families have a level of conscious aspiration unknown to other times and places. The big change in family life in recent decades is in family dreams and aspirations. It is no longer enough to make ends meet, or to feed and clothe a child. Present-day families in ever-increasing numbers seek a quality of life for all their members that is truly something new in the history of mankind.

SUMMARY

Rapid industrialization through the twentieth century has been accompanied by remarkable changes in American family life, many of which can be expected to continue into the foreseeable future: (1) nearly everyone gets married; (2) most marriages last through the years; (3) family members have more freedom; (4) few families remain on farms; (5) small families are typical now; (6) there are more dependent children and elderly family members proportionally; (7) more women work outside the home; (8) family members are better educated; (9) families have larger incomes; (10) housing and equipment are acquired sooner. Families change as the world around them changes, in ways that are appropriate to their times. Before industry produced the goods people need, families were the units of production. Now that most goods are mass-produced, families have become units of consumption. Families have moved from one way of life to another with flexibility. In the process of adapting in appropriate ways to the new conditions of the modern world, the roles of family members have become more complex, varied, and interchangeable. Today's family, freed from the drudgery of producing things, aspires to a quality of life that is something new under the sun. How successful a family becomes in the pursuit of its goals depends upon its values and policies, to be discussed in the next chapter.

SUGGESTED ACTIVITIES

1. Make a checklist of the furnishings and equipment you now have, or plan to have in your own home. Interview a couple married less than five years, a couple married between twenty-five and thirty years, and another married at least fifty years. Note when each of these three families first acquired each item on your household inventory of anticipated items. Compare your findings with the three-generation data found in Reuben Hill, *Family Development in Three Generations*. See if you can explain any wide discrepancies with possible differences in social status, as discussed in chapter 2 of this book. Write a paper on your findings and interpretation.

2. Develop Toynbee's thesis ("We Must Pay for Freedom," *Woman's Home Companion*, March, 1955) in an essay dealing with the strains and stresses in the relationships between men and women, between the generations, and between the family and the larger community, that come with emancipation.

3. View the film *Our Changing Family Life* (McGraw-Hill Book Company, New York, twenty-two minutes, sound) contrasting a three-generation farm family of the 1880s with today's urban family. List the explicit and implied changes in family living over the decades.

4. Select situations from Clarence Day's *Life with Father* portraying interaction

between father and mother, and parents and children, as it was at the turn of the century. Role-play parallel current family situations known to you in a series of impromptu "then and now" skits. Discuss the reasons why family interaction has changed in the evident directions through the twentieth century.

5. Document Peter Drucker's articles "America's Next Twenty Years," *Harper's Magazine*, March, April, May, and June, 1955, with current data from primary sources, and discuss how the trends he predicted have, have not, and may or may not continue, and why.

6. Collect evidence on the effect of a mother's employment outside the home on her family life, using such research reports as those listed in your readings by the National Manpower Council, Lois Meek Stolz, and Mildred W. Weil. Develop it into a carefully documented summary of what is known about the problems and promises of working wives and mothers in the modern scene.

7. Write a critical review of Evelyn Duvall, *Faith in Families* (Chicago: Rand McNally, 1970), documenting your critique with evidence from your reading and study.

===

READINGS

Allen, Frederick Lewis. *Only Yesterday*. New York: Harper and Brothers, 1931.

Allen, Frederick Lewis. *Since Yesterday*. New York: Harper and Brothers, 1939.

Allen, Frederick Lewis. *The Big Change*. New York: Harper and Brothers, 1952.

Allen, Frederick Lewis. "The Big Change: The Coming—and Disciplining—of Industrialism," *Harper's Magazine*, October 1950, pp. 145–160.

Burgess, Ernest W., and Harvey J. Locke. *The Family: From Institution to Companionship*. New York: American Book Company, 1953. Chap. 16, "The Family in Transition," pp. 447–482.

Calhoun, Arthur W. *A Social History of the American Family from Colonial Times to the Present*. Cleveland: Arthur H. Clark Company, 1917–1919.

Carter, Hugh, and Paul C. Glick. *Marriage and Divorce: A Social and Economic Study*. Cambridge, Mass.: Harvard University Press, 1970.

Cavan, Ruth Shonle, ed. *Marriage and Family in the Modern World: A Book of Readings*. 3d ed. New York: Thomas Y. Crowell Company, 1969. Chap. 2, "From Colonial Family to the Family of the Future," pp. 22–38.

Drucker, Peter F. "America's Next Twenty Years." *Harper's Magazine*, March 1955, pp. 27–32; April 1955, pp. 41–47; May 1955, pp. 39–44; June 1955, pp. 52–59.

Duvall, Evelyn Millis. *Faith in Families*. Chicago: Rand McNally and Company, 1970.

Ginsberg, Eli, ed. *The Nation's Children*, vol. 1, *The Family and Social Change*. New York: Columbia University Press, 1960.

Herzog, Elizabeth, and Catharine Richards, eds. *The Nation's Youth*. Children's Bureau Publication, no. 460. Washington, D.C., 1968.

Hill, Reuben. *Family Development in Three Generations*. Cambridge, Mass.: Schenkman Publishing Company, 1970.

Kirkpatrick, Clifford. *The Family as Process and Institution*. 2d ed. New York: Ronald Press Company, 1963. Pt. 2, "Social Changes and the Family," pp. 99–174.

National Manpower Council. *Womanpower*. New York: Columbia University Press, 1957.

National Manpower Council. *Work in the Lives of Married Women*. New York: Columbia University Press, 1958.

Nye, F. Ivan, and Lois W. Hoffman. *The Employed Mother in America*. Chicago: Rand McNally and Company, 1963.

Ogburn, William Fielding, and Meyer Nimkoff. *Technology and the Changing Family*. New York: Houghton Mifflin Company, 1955.

Parke, Robert, Jr., and Paul C. Glick. "Prospective Changes in Marriage and the Family." *Journal of Marriage and the Family* 29, no. 2 (May 1967): 249–256.

Sirjamaki, John. *The American Family in the Twentieth Century*. Cambridge, Mass.: Harvard University Press, 1953.

Stolz, Lois H. Meek. "Effects of Maternal Employment on Children: Evidence from Research." *Child Development* 31, no. 4 (December 1960): 749–782.

Wattenberg, Ben J., and Richard M. Scammon. *This U.S.A.* Garden City, N.Y.: Doubleday and Company, 1965.

Yinger, J. Milton. "The Changing Family in a Changing Society." *Journal of Social Case Work* 40, no. 8 (October 1959): 419–428.

4 FAMILY VALUES IN CHILD-REARING — TYPES AND TRENDS

The hickory stick is obsolete
Discipline has long been on the skids
Everything in the modern home
Is controlled by a switch—but the kids! Author Unknown

He who stops being better
*   stops being good.* Oliver Cromwell

Values are qualities having worth in themselves, in popular parlance. They are the acts, customs, and institutions regarded in an especially favorable way by a given people, to use the language of behavioral science. Family values are found in the system of ideas, attitudes, and beliefs that bind together the members of a family in a common culture. They are the characteristic ends in themselves that a family tries to protect, increase, and attain. Family values are the conceptions of the desirable shared by members of a family. "A value is a conception, explicit or implicit, distinctive of an individual or characteristic of a group, of the desirable which influences the selection from available modes, means, and ends of action."[1]

Family values are the overriding purposes that express a family's life-style. They arise out of a family's orientation and reflect its social class, its mobility drives, and the family's view of itself in perspective. Family values are closely related to the family's philosophy of life at a particular time. Changing conditions, continually growing family members, and the developing family itself call for refinements in the philosophy of life from stage to stage through the family life cycle. As the philosophy of life of a given family changes to fit new conditions, family values may be expected to be somewhat modified. But since a family's life-style remains relatively constant, family values tend to be more permanent than

[1] Clyde Kluckhohn, "Values and Value Orientations," in Talcott Parsons and Edward A. Shills, eds., *Toward a General Theory of Action* (Cambridge, Mass.: Harvard University Press, 1951), p. 395.

either its short-term aspirations or the stage-oriented goals that motivate a family. Family values may be seen as giving a sense of direction to the aspirations and goals of a family.

Out of its values emerge the direction, the goals, and the types of behavior that characterize a given family. Family values, ambitions, aspirations, and philosophy of life are all rooted in family orientation. A family's orientation arises from the family heritage and individual self-conceptions that a husband and wife bring to marriage and redefine throughout their life together. In essence, family orientation is the image of itself by which a family lives. It is the collective sense of identity the members of a family share—the image of itself by which a family is oriented.

TYPES OF VALUE ORIENTATIONS

A family's value orientations arise out of the issues of life it faces. In studying families of mentally retarded children, Farber finds three types of family orientation:[2] (1) *child-oriented* in which both parents structure their family life around the needs and demands of the children. In the child-oriented family husband-wife roles are sharply defined, economic security is highly valued, and community participation is very important; (2) *home-oriented*, in which both parents concentrate on congenial interpersonal relations in the home, the husband-wife roles tend to overlap, and community participation is of little importance; and (3) *parent-oriented*, in which husband and wife concentrate on his career advancement, and their family life is built around achievement, personal development, and the acquisition of social skills in their children and themselves.

Analyzing the psychological and social processes in family interaction, Hess and Handel find a variety of family themes which express the dominant concerns of individual family members.[3] A family theme arises out of some significant issue in the life of one or more family members and has consequences for the personalities of all the members of a given family. A parent's unresolved psychological issue thus becomes a concern for the children as well. For instance, the family theme of one family, seen to be avoidance of emotional and economic catastrophe, is understood to arise from the lack of stability in the childhood experience of the parents. In another family the dominant theme is desire for companionship and cooperation in family

[2] Bernard Farber, *Family Organization and Crisis: Maintenance of Integration in Families with a Severely Mentally Retarded Child*, monograph of the Society for Research in Child Development, serial no. 75, vol. 25, no. 1 (1960), pp. 39–63.

[3] Robert D. Hess and Gerald Handel, *Family Worlds: A Psychosocial Approach to Family Life* (Chicago: University of Chicago Press, 1959).

FAMILY DEVELOPMENT

interaction, which is seen to help meet the parents' need for warding off feelings of incompetence. Such family themes are idiosyncratic, highly individual, and helpful in understanding the dynamics of interaction within a given family.

Families vary by the amount of connectedness and separateness characterizing their basic family patterns. This dimension is seen in what they do together and how they feel about their family ties. Connectedness has both binding and constraining dangers. There is a certain mistrust and vulnerability of closeness, and emotional interaction poses a threat to the self-image of the individual family member. On the other hand, separateness, sacrificing the warmth and emotional security of close family ties for autonomy and individual identity, threatens apprehension about the pain of separation. How a given family resolves these basic conflicts in ways that meet or frustrate the needs of the individual family members is that family's theme in the dimension of intimacy.

Family boundaries vary greatly.[4] Each family is seen as staking out its own "world" in which it lives. This may be narrow, restricted to the house, yard, or immediate neighborhood, as it is in some families. Or the family may be at home in many lands and climes with genuine interest in the entire world. The intensity of emotional experience that a family defines as appropriate may be constricted or permissive. Affection and hostility are expressed according to the internal boundaries set by a given family. A child is allowed to "talk back" or not, in line with the limits established by his parents. Such variations in family themes give each family its own unique characteristics which both express and set limits for each member of the family.

Three other types of family orientation, as described by Godfrey, are: (1) *past-oriented families*, (2) *present-oriented families*, or (3) *future-oriented families*.[5] In the family that is geared to the past, family standards are rigidly upheld, with the major sanctions being religion and the mores. The immediate family is recognized as part of the larger extended family, with each individual subordinated to the group as a whole. Family government is patriarchal. Children are trained by strict traditional methods. Women's spheres of activity are limited and subordinate to those of the men of the household. The father directs the economic affairs of the family in which economic interdependence is emphasized. Family solidarity is largely work-oriented, with farming seen as a family occupation. There are close ties with the church but few active connections with the school or other social and civic organizations.

---

[4] Richard Ardry, *Territorial Imperative* (New York: Atheneum, 1966).

[5] Eleanor Powell Godfrey, "A Construction of Family Types and Their Initial Empirical Validation," (Ph.D. study, Radcliffe College, 1951).

The family geared to the present views individual welfare as more important than group preservation. The immediate family is separated from the larger kinship group. Public approval is the major sanction, with methods of control derived from current practice and standards that are contemporary. Family government is equalitarian. Children are trained under the careful supervision of the mother according to currently popular methods. There is a well-defined division of labor between the sexes, but both men's and women's work are considered equally important. Husband and wife jointly control the money of the family and emphasize mature children's economic independence. Family solidarity is based largely on recreational ties. Farming as such is seen as a profitable business. There is little recreation with relatives, and individual family members are encouraged to be active in numerous organizations in the community.

The family geared to the future sees the needs of the individual and the group as equally important. The immediate family is most important, although past and future generations are considered. Standards are set by individual capacity, with methods derived freely from any source. The family is governed by group consensus. Child training is permissive and in terms of the nature of the individual child. The division of labor is functional, along personal lines of feasibility. Mutual economic responsibility is emphasized, with money allocated by the whole family. Family solidarity is based upon both work and play, and farming is seen as a way of life. There is a considerable amount of both family and organizational activity; relationships with relatives are along lines of personal friendship.

Although these three time-geared types of family orientation were found in corn belt families, they can be recognized too in the larger society. The past-oriented family is the traditional family found as typical of the family systems of old China, Japan, Germany, Poland, and Ireland, with vestiges still present in many communities throughout the United States. The present-oriented family appears similar to the new middle-class family in transition, broken away from old family ties and highly individualistic. The future-oriented family seems to be emerging in twentieth-century America as the family that is focused upon the development of its members as its primary goal.

FAMILY VALUES, SOCIAL CLASS, AND CHILD-REARING

A family brings up its children according to its values—consciously or unconsciously. Parents' values stem from the conditions of life their families have experienced. A family's values, then, are the link between the social structure and what happens in the family. For instance, families in the various social classes differ in the ways they rear their children. "Members of different social classes, by virtue of enjoying (or suffering) different conditions of life, come to see the world differently—to develop different conceptions of social reality, different aspirations and hopes and fears, different conceptions of the desirable."[6]

---

[6] Melvin L. Kohn, "Social Class and Parent-Child Relationships: An Interpretation," *American Journal of Sociology* 68, no. 4 (January 1963): 471.

Families differ by social class in ways that can be seen by comparing middle-class and lower-class family values in table 4–1. These differences hold generally for families in western middle and lower classes, although there has been some overlapping in both directions in recent years.

Middle-class occupations call for a high degree of self-direction, discipline, and personal competence. Middle-class parents' values stress the importance of individual freedom and responsibility, growth, change,

Table 4–1. *Middle-class and Lower-class Family Values*

Middle-class family values	Lower-class family values
1. Cleanliness (of clothes, body, hair, teeth, speech) is a virtue	1. Cleanliness is not important; often is difficult in crowded living
2. Religious affiliation and practices are important; conservative to liberal	2. Religious practices vary widely; if present are fundamentalist or Roman Catholic
3. Future plans rank high; savings, property, getting ahead are important	3. Present pleasures sought; little to look forward to in the future
4. Work and the joys of accomplishment are valued	4. Motivation lags; opportunities tend to be limited
5. Assuming responsibility and doing one's duty are expected	5. Work is a necessary evil; routine jobs offer few satisfactions
6. Sexual controls within family contexts are valued	6. Sex is open; "where one finds it"; less tenderness and permanence expected
7. Aggression is expressed symbolically in sports, verbal battles, etc.	7. Overt aggression is expected; symbolic hostility (ridicule, etc.) is punished
8. Good diction and verbal facility are very important	8. Dialect, vernacular, and street language are preferred to correct speech: "stuck up"
9. Moderation in drinking, smoking, drugs, and eating is important	9. Indulgence in drinking, drugs, smoking, and food is escape from harsh reality
10. Taking care of one's health and using professional services are expected	10. Ill health is lived with; home remedies are relied upon
11. Institutions (schools, laws, etc.) are supported and utilized	11. Loyalties are to kin; little backing or use of larger, formal institutions
12. Education, learning, reading, culture are highly valued in self and others	12. Schooling, learning, reading, etc., are not important in themselves

Source: Adapted freely from Boyd R. McCandless, *Children: Behavior and Development* (New York: Holt, Rinehart and Winston, 1967), pp. 588–593.

H. ARMSTRONG ROBERTS

Middle-class parents' values stress the importance of education.

and education. These values are reflected in their child-rearing practices that tend to rely on giving the child some freedom of choice, on reasoning with the child, and on encouraging his schooling, initiative, and self-control.

Working-class parents, limited by lower levels of education and jobs that call for conforming to regulations set down by authority figures, tend to bring up their children to conform. Discipline in the working-class family relies more heavily on

82

Table 4–2. *Characteristics Mothers Consider Most Desirable in a Ten-year-old, by Social Class*

Trait	Percentage of mothers choosing trait	
	Middle class	Lower class
Honesty	44	53
Happiness	46	36
Consideration	39	27
Dependability	24	21
Self-control	22	13
Obedience	20	33
Neatness and cleanliness	11	20

Source: Melvin L. Kohn, "Social Class and Parental Values," *American Journal of Sociology* 64 (1959): 337–352.

physical punishment of forbidden behavior, with less attempt to understand the intent behind the act than in middle-class families.[7]

Difference in emphasis in a context of a shared, single, dominant theme is evident in what mothers of the middle class and lower-class mothers consider most desirable characteristics of children, table 4–2.

A study of mothers and their preschool children found "that the middle-class mothers tended to use a more stimulating and emotionally warm mode of child-rearing, with emphasis upon the child's achieving autonomy through satisfactions from his own efforts rather than through maternal rewards and punishments. The working-class mothers, on the other hand, tended to play a more passive and less stimulating role with the child, with more emphasis upon control through rewards and punishments."[8]

Controlled observations of mothers' interactions with their children find significantly more contacting, directing, helping, lending cooperation, observing attentively, playing interactively, and teaching on the part of middle-class mothers, compared with lower-class mothers. Some 6,400 contacting responses were observed between middle-class mothers and their children, but fewer than 2,400 contacting responses were observed in the lower-class group. Middle-class mothers initiated six times as many directing responses and twice as many helping responses with their children as the lower-class mothers did with theirs.[9]

After reviewing many research reports on child-rearing patterns conducive to a child's success in school, Catherine Chil-

[7] Urie Bronfenbrenner, "Socialization and Social Class through Time and Space," in Eleanor E. Maccoby, Theodore M. Newcomb, and Eugene L. Hartley, eds., *Readings in Social Psychology* (New York: Henry Holt and Company, 1958), pp. 400–425; Kohn, "Social Class and Parent-Child Relationships: An Interpretation," pp. 471–480.

[8] Grace F. Brody, "Socioeconomic Differences in Stated Maternal Child-rearing Practices and in Observed Maternal Behavior," *Journal of Marriage and the Family* 30, no. 4 (November 1968): 660.

[9] Michael Zunich, "Study of Relationships between Child Rearing Attitudes and Maternal Behavior," *Journal of Experimental Education* 30 (1961): 231–241; see also M. Zunich, "Relationship between Maternal Behavior and Attitudes toward Children," *Journal of Genetic Psychology* 100 (1962): 155–165; and James Walters, Ruth Connor, and Michael Zunich, "Interaction of Mothers and Children from Lower-class Families," *Child Development* 35 (1964): 433–440.

man finds that such patterns tend to be those parental practices that take "an active, rational, self-confident, and optimistic approach to organized society—a society in which the individual can succeed, providing he acquires a wide range of skills and bends his efforts toward long-range goals. Parents value achievement and believe in its worth, both for themselves and for their children; these values and beliefs affect their practices with their children from infancy onward."[10]

Chart 4–1. *The Proportion of Children Enrolled in Preschools Is Lowest for Low-income Families*

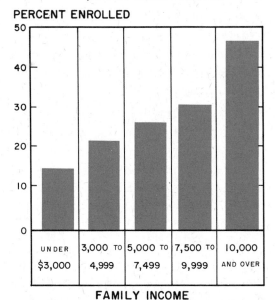

PERCENT ENROLLED

FAMILY INCOME				
UNDER $3,000	3,000 TO 4,999	5,000 TO 7,499	7,500 TO 9,999	10,000 AND OVER

Source: Elizabeth Herzog and Catharine Richards, eds., *The Nation's Youth,* Children's Bureau Publication, no. 460 (Washington, D.C., 1968), chart 25.

[10] Catherine S. Chilman, *Growing Up Poor,* Welfare Administration Publication, no. 13 (Washington, D.C., 1966), p. 42.

In contrast, child-rearing practices of the very poor tend to arise from an expectation of failure and a distrust of such middle-class institutions as the schools. Lower-class parents of both sexes tend to constrict the child's experience, rely on physical rather than verbal communication, use a more rigid approach, avoid abstractions in favor of concrete thinking, put less emphasis on education, training, and skill-development, have more tendencies toward magical thinking—than do middle-class parents. ". . . these values and attitudes provide poor preparation and support for many of the children of the very poor."[11]

The proportion of children enrolled in preschool programs is three times as large in the upper strata of social life than it is for children of low-income families (chart 4–1). Head Start programs may diminish the difference somewhat, but a large gap remains. The children most likely to have learning problems are those least likely to get the opportunities that preschool offers.[12]

Educationally handicapped in the critical early years, lower-class children are at a disadvantage all through their school years. A larger proportion of them get discouraged and drop out of school as soon as the law allows than is true of middle-class and upper-class children. Almost 65 percent of the high school dropouts are from families

[11] Ibid., p. 45.

[12] Elizabeth Herzog and Catharine Richards, eds., *The Nation's Youth,* Children's Bureau Publication, no. 460 (Washington, D.C., 1968), chart 25 and accompanying text.

FAMILY DEVELOPMENT

Chart 4–2. *High School Dropouts Are More Likely to Come from Low-income Families*

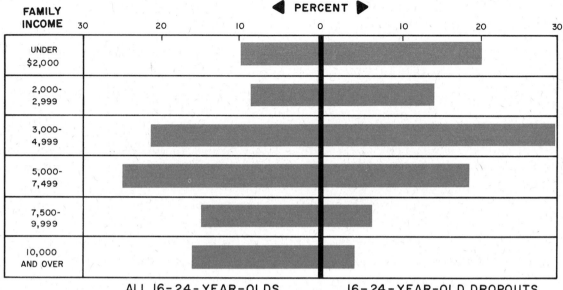

FAMILY INCOME

◀ **PERCENT** ▶

ALL 16–24–YEAR–OLDS   16–24–YEAR–OLD DROPOUTS

Source: Elizabeth Herzog and Catharine Richards, eds., *The Nation's Youth*, Children's Bureau Publication, no. 460 (Washington, D.C., 1968), chart 28.

with incomes under $5,000 a year; less than 40 percent of all sixteen- to twenty-four-year-olds are in these low-income families (chart 4–2). Among those who have the persistence to graduate from high school, a smaller proportion go on to college, as was seen in table 2–3, chapter 2. The basic problem is not lack of potential. An intensive survey by the Committee on Education and Labor of the House of Representatives found that four-fifths of the dropouts are capable of high school and perhaps of post–high school work.[13] The critical lack is not money—real as financial deprivation is.

The handicap stems from child-rearing practices that do not stimulate learning, encourage education, or give children confidence in their ability to succeed, all through the years.

Child-rearing practices in low-income families perpetuate "the culture of poverty" that persists among the disadvantaged. It is not that the very poor family, outside the mainstream of American society, is satisfied with its life, or that its values support it. Poor families, generally, aspire to the middle-class advantages thought of as "the American way of life." Like other parents, the poor would like their children to get a good education and to have nicer homes and better jobs than

[13] Herzog and Richards, eds., *The Nation's Youth*, text accompanying chart 28.

What they lack is not the fundamental family values, but the knowledge and competence for fulfilling them.[14]

TRENDS IN CHILD-REARING

The twentieth century has seen a basic shift in family values appropriate to the changing socioeconomic scene. Families at the beginning of the century typically lived on farms and valued hard work as essential for survival. Their children were raised to obey their parents, hold their tongues, and do a man's work around the place as soon as they were able. With the rapid advance of industrialization, urbanization, and affluence,[15] families became consumption-oriented and put a high valuation on personal freedom, development, and "having fun." As families shift their stance with the changing times, they pursue different values; as they develop new conceptions of themselves, their children, and their relationships, their child-rearing practices change accordingly. Child-rearing reflects family value orientations as seen in reviewing trends over the decades.

With the decline in the size of the work-ing class and the increase in the numbers of families in the "new middle class" has come a new emphasis on the kind of person one should be. The typical member of the "old middle class" (banker, tradesman, or small entrepreneur) grew up with a strong inner sense of direction that was implanted early by his elders. The new outer-directed[16] person depends upon others for guidance, in ways that are internalized early in more flexible, responsive, attentive, nurturing child-rearing.

Miller and Swanson's study of 582 mothers with one or more children under nineteen in the Detroit area[17] found the Riesman dichotomy in evidence in the two types of middle-class families: (1) entrepreneurial "older" middle-class families; and (2) bureaucratic "newer" middle-class families. They classified entrepreneurial families as those having (a) husband self-employed, (b) husband getting at least one-half of his income in profits, fees, or commissions, (c) husband working in a small-scale organization (only two levels of supervision), (d) husband or wife born on a farm, and (e) husband or wife born outside the United States. Bureaucratic families were classified as having none of these five characteristics; the husband works for someone else in an

---

[14] Chilman, *Growing Up Poor*, p. 25.

[15] Three-fourths of today's Americans feel they live better than Dad did, according to pollsters from Roper Research. Max Gunther, "How We Feel About Our Money," *Saturday Evening Post*, 240th year, no. 26 (December 1967), pp. 72–75.

[16] David Riesman with Nathan Glazer and Reuel Denney, *The Lonely Crowd: A Study of the Changing American Character* (New Haven: Yale University Press, 1950).

[17] Daniel R. Miller and Guy E. Swanson, *The Changing American Parent* (New York: John Wiley and Sons, 1958).

Table 4–3. *Entrepreneurial and Bureaucratic Child-rearing Methods*

Entrepreneurial	Bureaucratic
Stress self-control and internalization in control of impulses	Child is taught to fit in with others, to be a "nice guy," affable, unthreatening, adaptive, and to seek direction
Train child to change the situation	Child learns to go to parents for wisdom in social skills, even as adults
Stress activity and independence	
Encourage mastery	Person is trained to be cautious, precise, rational, secure, and unaggressive
Prefer sharp differences between sex roles	New levels of comfort and security with lessening psychic pressures are sought
More likely to:	New sense of participation in a responsible, moral community is emerging
Feed babies on schedule	
Begin toilet training early	Loyalty to the group is central
Use symbolic punishment	Child and adult are free to enjoy themselves and to express their feelings
Let babies cry	
Training is by suppression of impulsive drives	Individual should be warm, friendly, supportive of others
Egocentricity and hostility are more frequent	

States. Bureaucratic families were classified as having none of these five characteristics; the husband works for someone else in an organization of at least moderate complexity.

Entrepreneurial and bureaucratic families were found to use significantly different child-rearing methods, of which table 4–3 is a general summary.

With the increase in the size and complexity of large corporations has come an increase in the number of bureaucratically oriented families which encourage their children to be accommodative, to express their feelings freely, and to seek direction from the organizational programs in which they find themselves. The entrepreneurial family orientation at the present time is seen as a kind of anachronism, gaining less and less support from the values and institutions of the larger society. The bureaucratic family is an emergent type of family with child-rearing patterns compatible with contemporary values in American life.[18]

From Strict to Permissive Child-rearing

Analyzing more than a score of studies of child-rearing practices over the past twenty-five years, Bronfenbrenner reports[19] a clear trend away from strict, rigid methods of

---

[18] Ibid., p. 193.
[19] Bronfenbrenner, "Socialization and Social Class through Time and Space."

child care toward flexible, permissive ways with children. American mothers of both the lower and middle classes have become more flexible in caring for their infants. They are more likely now than previously to feed their babies on demand and to wean them later from both breast and bottle. They are more likely to be permissive in toilet training, beginning and completing bowel and bladder training at later ages. Those who are in touch with what the experts say in books, pamphlets, and in direct contact are changing more rapidly than those with little access to such sources.[20] A critical review of recent revisions of popular child-rearing manuals concludes, "The general emphasis on permissiveness in the early 1950's continues currently."[21]

Sibylle Escalona contrasts former with more recent thinking about young children thus:

> Ten years ago and less, authoritative public opinion subscribed to sentiments and rules which may be characterized as follows: Bodily and mental health is based upon an orderly, strictly scheduled existence from early childhood onwards. Prescribed formulae are superior to breast feeding, chiefly because the ingredients are known and nutrition becomes therefore, a controlled process. When babies or children cry without recognized legitimate cause it is best to let them cry it out. It is the responsibility of adults to teach children what is "right" and what is "wrong" in regard to meal times, sleeping hours, play interests and most other activities.

> It is now thought that it is up to us as adults to meet the needs of the younger child, rather than to expect early adaptation from him. To wit, self-demand schedules and all that goes with them. Among the needs of the young child we recognize the need for affection and for an intimate relationship with the mother as of very great importance, tending to evaluate it as more crucial than the need for good physical care. We prize self-expression, sincerity of feeling and spontaneous interest above good manners, self restraint or intellectual accomplishment.[22]

A review of sixty years of child training practices finds: "Three different schools of thought have prevailed with regard to how children should be raised. The 1890's and 1900's saw a highly sentimental approach to child rearing; 1910 through the 1930's witnessed a rigid, disciplinary approach; the 1940's have emphasized self regulation

[20] Elinor Waters and Vaughn J. Crandall, "Social Class and Observed Maternal Behavior from 1940 to 1960," *Child Development* 35 (1964): 1021–1032.

[21] Michael Gordon, "Infant Care Revisited," *Journal of Marriage and the Family* 30, no. 4 (November 1968): 578–583; see also Benjamin Spock, "How My Ideas Have Changed," *Redbook*, October 1963, pp. 51–54, 122–125.

[22] Sibylle Escalona, "A Commentary upon Some Recent Changes in Child-rearing Practices," *Child Development* 20, no. 3 (September 1949): 157–162.

and understanding the child. These sixty years have also seen a swing from emphasis on character development to emphasis on personality."[23]

The gap between the social classes in child-rearing appears to be narrowing.[24] Working-class fathers are found to be entering more into family activities with their wives and children, in intimate, nurturing ways.[25] High levels of employment and standards of living have made it possible for working-class families to aspire to many middle-class values. Moving more freely to take better jobs and to have nicer homes, they tend to pull away from more traditional kinship ties and find new satisfactions within the husband-wife-child family unit.[26]

---

[23] Celia B. Stendler, "Sixty Years of Child Training Practices," *Journal of Pediatrics* 36, no. 1 (January 1950): 122–134; quote from p. 134.

[24] Leone Kell and Joan Aldous, "Trends in Child Care over Three Generations," *Marriage and Family Living* 22, no. 2 (May 1960): 176–177.

[25] Urie Bronfenbrenner, "The Changing American Child: A Speculative Analysis," *Merrill-Palmer Quarterly* 7, no. 2 (April 1961): 73–84; and Wanda C. Bronson, Edith S. Katten, and Norman Livson, "Patterns of Authority and Affection in Two Generations," *Journal of Abnormal and Social Psychology* 58, no. 2 (March 1959): 143–152.

[26] Lee Rainwater and Gerald Handel, "Changing Family Roles in the Working Class," paper read to American Sociological Association, Los Angeles, 1963; see also interpretative comment by Reuben Hill and Joan Aldous, "Socialization for Marriage and Parenthood," chap. 22 in David A. Goslin, ed., *Handbook of Socialization Theory and Research* (Chicago: Rand McNally and Company, 1969), pp. 942–943.

From Traditional to Developmental Conceptions of Parents and Children

The first formulation of the traditional-developmental dichotomy of conceptions of family members came out of the author's original study of differential conceptions of parenthood.[27] The data were the verbatim responses of 433 mothers to the questions, "What are five things a good mother does?" (2,010 responses), and "What are five things a good child does?" (1,847 responses). Keeping the original wording used by the subjects, the responses were grouped into categories that distinguished traditional from developmental conceptions of both parents and children.

Traditional conceptions of motherhood were seen to be those having to do with what a mother expects herself to do *to* and *for* her home and children, i.e., keep house, make the child behave, etc. Traditional conceptions of childhood centered around the child's behaving in ways that please adults, i.e., obeys, respects property, runs errands willingly, etc. Traditional conceptions of both motherhood and childhood tend to be static, rigid, specific behavioral expectancies in line with former child-rearing orientations.

---

[27] Evelyn Millis Duvall, "Conceptions of Parenthood," *American Journal of Sociology* 52, no. 3 (November 1946): 193–203.

Table 4–4. *Child-rearing Changes from the 1880s to the 1960s*

1880s–Discipline was based upon authority, with instant, unquestioning obedience expected.

Training was directed toward "uprooting the evil in human nature" when widespread belief was that children are "conceived in sin and born in iniquity," and the clear duty of parents was to "whale the devil out of them."

Society for the Prevention of Cruelty to Children was organized "to resolutely and persistently attack cruel ways of treating children." Articles on prevention of cruelty to children mention: "whippings until bruised and sore," "shutting in dark closets until ill with fright," and "depriving of food until emaciated and feeble."

Frances Parker, G. Stanley Hall, William James, and Felix Adler started, respectively, the Cook County Normal School, studies on child development, psychology based upon experience at Harvard, and Society for the Study of Child Nature in New York.

1890s–Authority was still the basic point of view. Larkin Donton of the Boston Normal School expected "instantaneous obedience, with no sulkers, no laggards, no guerrillas, no independents, and the movement of all uniformly, quietly and instantly."

John Dewey founded Laboratory School, and Frances Parker founded an independent institute which was to become the School of Education, both at the University of Chicago.

The National Congress of Parents and Teachers was founded in 1897.

1900s–Discipline was a major issue. Sixteen out of eighteen schools reported corporal punishment in use, one in primary grades only, another "seldom," and others "good as a last resort," "cannot be dispensed with but might be reduced."

Guidance began to replace "training" in the literature. G. Stanley Hall published *Adolescence* (1904), the first work on the older child. William James's *Talks to Teachers* set the theme for the decade in stressing the importance of habits.

1910s–William Bagley, in *School Discipline* (1915), admonished never to punish in anger—to use switch on legs or ruler on palm of hands, but never to box the ears.

First edition of *Infant Care* published by the Children's Bureau, established in 1912, recommended, to stop thumb-sucking, pinning sleeve of baby's jacket down over "fingers of offending hand for several days and nights."

Freud, Montessori, John Dewey, and William H. Kilpatrick mentioned frequently in popular literature. The Progessive Education Association founded in 1918–1919 with emphasis on "freedom for children to develop."

1920s–John B. Watson's *Behaviorism* and *Psychological Care of Infant and Young Child*, which were widely followed, recommended kissing child on the forehead if at all, shaking hands with the child in the morning, never hugging, kissing, or letting child sit on your lap. The conditioned reflex, stimulus-response bonds, and laws of learning concepts current.

Child development institutes established in several universities, and the National Council on Parent Education founded, all with Laura Spelman Rockefeller Memorial grants.

Teachers College, Columbia University, announced a new course, "Training for Leadership in Education of Parents" in cooperation with the Child Study Association. "The child" and "child-centered" appear often in the literature.

1930s–Objectivity at its zenith, with great emphasis on the importance of routine, habit formation—i.e., "adhere without deviation to regular habits for sleeping, eating, and toileting beginning in early infancy." The parent was advised to be cool, detached, and unperturbed. High interest in specifics: sex education, allowances, and toilet training.

Table 4–4. *Child-rearing Changes from the 1880s to the 1960s*—Continued

National Council on Family Relations established 1938 as national clearinghouse for persons with professional interests in family living. Research in family life, child and adolescent development increased markedly. Corporal punishment rare in schools. Discussion of spanking as discipline continued among parents.

1940s—Family-centered approach to children seen in first National Conference on Family Life held at the White House in May 1948. Gesell and staff at Yale, Redl, Baruch, Hymes, and Spock advised accepting the child and his feelings without shame and gearing guidance to the readiness of the child. Spock's *The Common Sense Book of Baby and Child Care* became mothers' "bible," as permissive, "enjoy your youngster" attitude toward children became widely accepted.

1950s—Midcentury White House Conference on Children and Youth considered the role of the home, school, church, leisure-time agency, as well as vocational guidance, health, social services, and law enforcement in healthy personality development.

The developmental task concept, formulated earlier, widely used through this decade in the literature that discussed "the teachable moment," "developmental level," etc.

1960s—Golden Anniversary White House Conference on Children and Youth made recommendations for family life education at every age level, both in public schools and under private auspices. Research in family life and child-rearing steadily increased the quantity and quality of authoritative literature for professional and functional use.

Source: Adapted freely from Grace Langdon and Irving Stout, *The Discipline of Well-Adjusted Children* (New York: John Day Company, 1952), chap. 1; Children's Bureau, "Parents Welcome New Edition of Infant Care," *The Child*, January 1952, pp. 66–67, 76; and 1960 White House Conference on Children and Youth, *Recommendations: Composite Report of Forum Findings* (Washington, D.C.: U.S. Government Printing Office, 1960).

Developmental conceptions of motherhood emphasize a mother's encouraging her children to develop, enjoying and loving them, and viewing herself as a growing person, i.e., gives child freedom to grow, shares with the child, and gets enough recreation. Developmental conceptions of childhood center in his being a happy, healthy, growing person, i.e., is developing socially, enjoys growing up, etc. Developmental conceptions are recognized as dynamic, flexible, and growth-promoting. They emphasize encouraging development of the person rather than any specific form of discipline or type of behavior.

Parallel contrasts in traditionally and de-velopmentally oriented fathers were found in Elder's[28] exploration of fathers' conceptions of parenthood and childhood, following the Duvall methods. Traditional fathers disciplined their children for more reasons and with fewer methods. Developmental fathers were more interested in children's maturation, believed more in parent guidance literature and PTA meetings, and were more apt to help in child-rearing and to find parenthood enjoyable.

[28] Rachel Ann Elder, "Traditional and Developmental Conceptions of Fatherhood" (Master's thesis, Iowa State College, 1947); Rachel Ann Elder, "Traditional and Developmental Conceptions of Fatherhood," *Marriage and Family Living* 11, no. 3 (Summer 1949): 98–100, 106.

Using the traditional-developmental conceptions approach and methods developed earlier, a Florida State University team replicated the previous studies with university students and their parents, with remarkably similar results:

> Generally speaking, the traditional type of good father was defined in terms of providing for the family financially, disciplining and advising the children, and setting a good example . . . the traditional good mother as one who cares for the home and cooks, teaches religious values, and is a good example. The traditional good child is one who respects and obeys parents. . . .
>
> The developmental good father fosters the growth and development of the child and other family members, including himself in the home situation. The respondents viewed the developmental mother in much the same way as they saw the developmental father but added

the concept of having outside interests such as the PTA. The developmental child responses centered about growing in all areas of personality and social development.[29]

Traditional conceptions are significantly more frequent among working-class than middle-class parents, and among mothers of children over five years of age than among mothers of younger children. Developmental conceptions of both the good mother and the good child are significantly more frequent among middle-class than lower-class mothers, and among white than Negro mothers, at both lower- and middle-class levels.[30] Developmental fathers tend to be skilled, rather than semi-

---

[29] Ruth Connor, Theodore B. Johannis, Jr., and James Walters, "Intra-familial Conceptions of the Good Father, Good Mother, and Good Child," *Journal of Home Economics* 46, no. 3 (March 1954): 187–191.

[30] Duvall, "Conceptions of Parenthood."

Table 4–5. *Traditional and Developmental Conceptions*

Traditional conceptions	Developmental conceptions
A good child:	*A good child:*
Keeps clean and neat, is orderly, is clean, keeps himself neat, etc.	Is healthy and well, eats and sleeps well, grows a good body, has good health habits, etc.
Obeys and respects adults, minds his parents, does not talk back, respects teachers, etc.	Shares and cooperates with others, gets along with people, is developing socially, etc.
Pleases adults, has good character traits, is honest, truthful, polite, kind, fair, etc.	Is happy and contented, is a cheerful child, is emotionally well adjusted, etc.
Respects property, takes care of his things, is not destructive, hangs up his clothes, etc.	Loves and confides in his parents, responds with affection, has confidence, etc.
Is religious, goes to Sunday school, loves God, prays, follows Jesus, etc.	Is eager to learn, shows initiative, asks questions, expresses himself, accepts help, etc.

Table 4–5. *Traditional and Developmental Conceptions*—Continued

Traditional conceptions	Developmental conceptions
A good child:	*A good child:*
Works well, studies, goes to school, is dependable, takes responsibility, etc. Fits into the family program, has an interest in his home, does his share, helps out, etc.	Grows as a person, progresses in his ability to handle himself, enjoys growing up, etc.
A good mother:	*A good mother:*
Keeps house, washes, cooks, cleans, mends, sews, manages the household, etc. Takes care of the child physically, feeds, clothes, bathes him, guards child safety, etc. Trains the child to regularity, establishes regular habits, provides a schedule, etc. Disciplines, corrects child, demands obedience, rewards good behavior, is firm, etc. Makes the child good, instructs in morals, builds character, prays for, sees to religion, etc.	Trains for self-reliance, encourages independence, teaches how to adjust to life, etc. Sees to emotional well-being, keeps child happy and contented, helps child feel secure, etc. Helps child develop socially, provides toys and companions, supervises child's play, etc. Provides for child's mental growth, reads to child, provides stimulation, educates, etc. Guides with understanding, gears life to child's level, interprets, answers questions, etc. Relates lovingly to child, enjoys and shares with child, is interested in what child says, etc. Is a calm, cheerful, growing person oneself, has a sense of humor, smiles, keeps rested, etc.
A good father:	*A good father:*
Is a strong individual, always right, and the child is his ward "Knows" what the child "should" be, so does not seek to understand child as an individual Is interested only in activities which he determines are his responsibility for child's "good" Places emphasis on giving things to and doing things for the child Is interested in child's accepting and attaining goals set by the father Finds satisfaction in child's owing father a debt which can be repaid by child's obedience Feels parenthood is a duty which the church and/or society expect him to discharge	Is an individual, as is his child Seeks to understand the child and himself Places emphasis on the growth of the child and himself Is interested in child's determining and attaining child's own goals Finds satisfaction in child's becoming a mature individual Feels that parenthood is a privilege which he has chosen to assume

Source: Traditional and developmental conceptions of a good child and a good mother are categories of verbatim responses of 433 mothers reported in Evelyn Millis Duvall, "Conceptions of Parenthood," *American Journal of Sociology* 52, no. 3 (November 1946): 195–196. Traditional and developmental conceptions of a good father are derived from constructed father types emerging from Rachel Ann Elder, "Traditional and Developmental Conceptions of Fatherhood" (Master's thesis, Iowa State College, 1947), p. 21.

skilled or unskilled workers, who are more likely to be traditional in their conceptions of motherhood, fatherhood, and childhood.[31] These consistent tendencies are interpreted as follows:

In its transition from the traditional institution type of family to the person-centered unit of companionship that it is becoming, conceptions of the role of the parent and the child are shifting. These changes do not appear all at once and with equal force throughout the total society, but are evidenced first in little islands of the new that break off from the mass of tradition and become established in subgroups within the culture. These developmental islands are characterized by such concepts as respect for the person (both child and adult), satisfaction in personal interaction, pride in growth and development, and a permissive, growth-promoting type of guidance, as opposed to the more traditional attempts to "make" children conform to patterns of being neat and clean, obedient and respectful, polite and socially acceptable.

Traditional conceptions of parenthood remain in the lower-middle and upper-lower class levels, where recent migration, household drudgery, cramped living, and infrequency of opportunity to meet with other modes of adjustment keep both parents and children in line with traditional conceptions of role. The effort to achieve respectability so evident in the two lower class levels and among the minority racial group tends further to perpetuate conformity.

The tendency for mothers of younger children toward more developmental replies may be interpreted in a number of ways. The evidence points to the possibility that conformity is demanded of families with children old enough to have some life outside the family circle. As children become old enough to go to school and to range further afield in the community, the social pressures toward conformity are felt both by them and by their mothers.

Thus, we hypothesize a seesaw progress even within the more advanced groups. Some inexperienced mothers view their roles along new lines and break with the past in their efforts to make a more adequate adjustment to a changed social situation. As their children grow older and begin to represent them in the larger world, the earlier flexibility is modified by the demands of the more traditional mass.[32]

Reuben Hill's study of three generations of the same families shows clear trends toward more equalitarian patterns generation by generation, less conventional allocation of roles in the family, and more consensus on family values in the younger gen-

---

[31] Elder, "Traditional and Developmental Conceptions of Fatherhood" (both works of this title cited above).

[32] Duvall, "Conceptions of Parenthood," pp. 202–203.

erations. Through the years of this century, since the grandparents married in the early 1900s, the trends in the same family lines have been toward more education, better jobs, higher incomes, and increasingly more developmental ideologies about both parenthood and childhood. In the author's summary, "the grandparent generation is predominantly fatalistic, prudential, optimistic, present or past oriented and traditional in parental ideologies. The parent generation is predominantly fatalistic, prudential, optimistic, present oriented and shows mixed developmental-traditional in parental ideologies. The (married) child generation is least fatalistic of the three, prudential, moderately optimistic, most future oriented, and most developmental in parental ideologies."[33]

Increase in Developmentalism

Concern for wholesome development of the human personality has increased in recent years. Developmentalism does not imply unrestrained permissiveness, but rather the kind of setting that is conducive to optimal development, with the freedom, and the controls that are good to grow in, both as parents and as children. College students are found to be more developmental than are their parents, as table 4–6 shows.

Table 4–6. *Mean Developmental Scores of Conceptions of Good Father, Good Mother, and Good Child by Fathers, Mothers, and Adolescents*

Respondent	Good father	Good mother	Good child
Father	51.2	39.6	20.6
Mother	51.1	31.5	24.5
Adolescent	65.1	62.8	34.6

Source: Ruth Connor, Theodore B. Johannis, Jr., and James Walters, "Intra-familial Conceptions of the Good Father, Good Mother, and Good Child," *Journal of Home Economics* 46, no. 3 (March 1954): 190.

Grandmothers are significantly more authoritarian and less permissive than are the mothers of the same children.[34] A study of grandmother-mother pairs in the same urban community elaborates and extends earlier findings that developmentalism is found more among young than older mothers, and bears a positive relationship to the amount of their formal education.[35] Today's college girls are significantly more developmental than their mothers, who were in turn more likely to have permissive values than were the students' grandmothers, showing a trend over the past three generations toward increasing developmentalism.[36]

---

[33] Reuben Hill, *Family Development in Three Generations* (Cambridge, Mass.: Schenkman Publishing Company, 1970), summary of chap. 2.

[34] Ruth Staples and June Warden Smith, "Attitudes of Grandmothers and Mothers toward Child-rearing Practices," *Child Development* 25 (1954): 91–97.

[35] Duvall, "Conceptions of Parenthood," p. 202.

[36] Kell and Aldous, "Trends in Child Care over Three Generations," pp. 176–177; see also Hill, *Family Development in Three Generations*, chap. 2.

Continuing studies of three-generational families find the grandparent generation more traditional, fatalistic, and past-oriented, in contrast to the young couples, who are more adaptable. Young husbands and wives have more flexibility, are more companionable and communicative. Hill reports that young couples today appear better able to meet new and unusual problems because they have a sense of common direction, superior ability to communicate, and greater adaptability.[37]

Since developmentalism is associated with education and comfortable levels of living, it can be expected to increase. Improved standards of living and general education as well as specific family life education for more of the population may in time be expected to narrow the gap between the haves and have-nots and to make the developmental "traditional" in times to come. As the 1950 White House Conference on Children and Youth predicted, ". . . Within another generation the new ways of bringing up children may themselves become traditional. . . . If this happens, young parents' confidence should increase, since they will not feel so alone and so much in disagreement with the older generation."[38]

---

[37] Reuben Hill, "Transmission of Conceptions of Parenthood by Generations," Twin City Study, in progress.

[38] Helen Witmer and Ruth Kotinsky, *Personality in the Making* (New York: Harper and Brothers, 1952), p. 102.

EFFECTS OF CHILD-REARING PRACTICES ON PARENTS AND CHILDREN

A study of parents with preschool children living in a university community confirms the general observation that parents with a developmental ideology are more permissive with their children than are parents holding traditional conceptions of what constitutes a good child. Using parents' "pick-up policy" regarding children's clutter allowed in the living room and the number of types of children's activities permitted indoors, Blood[39] found that permissive parents, as compared with restrictive parents, reported (1) parents' lives more disrupted by children's behavior, (2) parents' activities more often disturbed by children's noisiness, (3) parents' privacy more difficult to achieve, (4) parents have greater difficulty controlling children's activities, (5) living room furnishings more often damaged by children, and (6) living rooms more frequently cluttered with children's things.

Developmentally oriented parents appear able to pay the price their permissiveness costs them as adults. They apparently can

---

[39] Robert O. Blood, Jr., "Consequences of Permissiveness for Parents of Young Children," *Marriage and Family Living* 15, no. 3 (August 1953): 209–212.

take the immediate consequences of their child-rearing practices because they put their children's developmental progress high in their value orientation, because they do not expect to have a model picture-book home while their children are small, because they "child-proof" the house by adapting to what reasonably can be expected of little children, because they realize that the sacrifice of some of their adult values (for neatness, quiet, etc.) is only for a while, and that as children grow older there will be less discrepancy between the interests and values of the two generations.

Restrictive fathers are found to be constricted, submissive, suggestible individuals with little self-assurance.[40] Permissive fathers, in contrast, tend to be self-reliant, ascendant, and functionally effective. These findings are in line with what is known about the authoritarian personality,[41] who tends to be the kind of person most comfortable with traditional child-rearing practices.

Fundamentally, developmental parents appear to be the kind of men and women who by personality, life history, and family orientation are inclined to accept the growing body of evidence (from child develop-

ment research, nursery school experience, and clinical findings) that supports their inner predispositions to encourage and enjoy the development of their children and themselves.

Effects of Child-rearing Practices on a Child's Personality

There are so many factors in child development that it may be impossible to say with assurance that one particular method will surely produce any predictable consequence in the growing child's personality. There are, however, findings in recent research that suggest significant relationships between parent-child interaction, child-rearing practices, and the emerging personality of the child. The following are representative.

Relating children's behavior in nursery school to the atmosphere within their homes, Baldwin found a number of related factors.[42] Family climates of warmth, activity, and democracy produce more curious, emotional, nonconforming, and competitive children in the nursery school than do cold, authoritarian, and low-activity families.

Longitudinal records of the complete childhood of 140 children studied at the

[40] Jack Block, "Personality Characteristics Associated with Fathers' Attitudes toward Childrearing," *Child Development* 26, no. 1 (1955): 41–48.

[41] T. W. Adorno, Else Frenkel-Brunswik, Daniel J. Levinson, R. Nevitt Sanford, in collaboration with Betty Aron, Maria Hertz Levinson, and William Morrow, *The Authoritarian Personality* (New York: Harper and Brothers, 1950).

[42] Alfred L. Baldwin, "Socialization and the Parent-Child Relationship," *Child Development* 19, no. 3 (September 1948): 127–136.

Table 4–7. *Child-rearing Patterns Related to Emotionally Healthy Personality Development*

Conducive (In families at any level)	Unfavorable (Characteristic of poor families)
1. Respect for child as individual whose behavior is caused by a multiple of factors. Acceptance of own role in events that occur.	1. Misbehavior regarded as such in terms of concrete pragmatic outcomes; reasons for behavior not considered. Projection of blame on others.
2. Commitment to slow development of child from infancy to maturity; stresses and pressures of each stage accepted by parent because of perceived worth of ultimate goal of raising "happy," successful son or daughter.	2. Lack of goal commitment and of belief in long-range success; a main object for parent and child is to "keep out of trouble"; orientation toward fatalism, impulse gratification, and sense of alienation.
3. Relative sense of competence in handling child's behavior.	3. Sense of impotence in handling children's behavior, as well as in other areas.
4. Discipline chiefly verbal, mild, reasonable, consistent, based on needs of child and family and of society; more emphasis on rewarding good behavior than on punishing bad behavior.	4. Discipline harsh, inconsistent, physical, makes use of ridicule; based on whether child's behavior does or does not annoy parent.
5. Open, free, verbal communication between parent and child; control largely verbal.	5. Limited verbal communication; control largely physical.
6. Democratic rather than autocratic or laissez-faire methods of rearing, with both parents in equalitarian but not necessarily interchangeable roles. Companionship between parents and children.	6. Authoritarian rearing methods; mother chief child-care agent; father, when in home, mainly a punitive figure. Little support and acceptance of child as an individual.
7. Parents view selves as generally competent adults and are generally satisfied with themselves and their situation.	7. Low parental self-esteem; sense of defeat.
8. Intimate, expressive, warm relationship between parent and child, allowing for gradually increasing independence. Sense of continuing responsibility.	8. Large families; more impulsive, narcissistic parent behavior. Orientation to "excitement." Abrupt, early yielding of independence.
9. Presence of father in home and lack of severe marital conflict.	9. Father out of home (under certain circumstances).
10. Free verbal communication about sex, acceptance of child's sex needs, channeling of sex drive through "healthy" psychological defenses, acceptance of slow growth toward impulse control and sex satisfaction in marriage; sex education by both father and mother.	10. Repressive, punitive attitude about sex, sex questioning, and experimentation. Sex viewed as exploitative relationship.

Table 4–7. *Child-rearing Patterns Related to Emotionally Healthy Personality Development—*
Continued

Conducive *(In families at any level)*	Unfavorable *(Characteristic of poor families)*
11. Acceptance of child's drive for aggression but channeling it into socially approved outlets.	11. Alternating encouragement and restriction of aggression, primarily related to consequences of aggression for parents.
12. Favorable attitude toward new experiences; flexibility.	12. Distrust of new experiences. Constricted life; rigidity.
13. Happiness of parental marriage.	13. High rates of marital conflict and family breakdown.

Source: Catherine S. Chilman, *Growing Up Poor*, Welfare Administration Publication, no. 13 (Washington, D.C., 1966), pp. 28–29.

Fels Research Institute provide extensive data for such relationships as are pertinent here. Among the conclusions of this investigation is that a child's need for achievement (which is related to accelerated rates of mental growth) develops in a family situation in which the mother uses democratic principles in disciplining the child, and, at least in the case of boys, tends to stress independent achievement at an early age.[43]

Getzels and Jackson found that parents of very bright adolescents seem to be more "vigilant" with respect to their children's behavior and academic progress, while families of highly creative children tend to permit and accept more divergence.[44]

Studies of 261 boys and girls between five and twenty-one years of age, selected as well adjusted by their teachers, found many types of discipline used in their homes, but a common core of factors by which parents accounted for their children's favorable adjustment. The parents said they enjoyed being parents; they believed in having fun together with their children; they appreciated their children and trusted them; and most important of all they rated "loving the children and letting them know it."[45]

[43] Lester W. Sontag, Charles T. Baker, and Virginia L. Nelson, *Mental Growth and Personality Development: A Longitudinal Study*, monograph of the Society for Research in Child Development, serial no. 68, vol. 23, no. 2 (1958), p. 139.

[44] Jacob W. Getzels and Philip W. Jackson, "Family Environment and Cognitive Style: A Study of the Sources of Highly Intelligent and of Highly Creative Adolescents," *American Sociological Review* 26, no. 3 (June 1961): 359.

[45] Grace Langdon and Irving Stout, *These Well-Adjusted Children* (New York: John Day Company, 1951).

Extensive studies at Harvard University find that children of warm mothers mature more rapidly socially, and that "the unhappy effects of punishment have run like a dismal thread through our findings." Mothers who punished their children's toilet accidents ended up with bed-wetting children. Mothers who punished aggressive behavior severely had more aggressive children than did mothers whose punishment for aggression was light. In the long run, punishment was found to be ineffectual as a technique for eliminating the kind of behavior toward which it was directed.[46]

Recent trends toward the pursuit of excellence and the thrust for achievement in both home and school, as well as evidence pointing up the dangers of too much permissiveness, may already be at work in a swing toward setting controls and limits to the freedom allowed a child. As Nye found, "a middle way giving major responsibility but not discontinuing supervision and guidance entirely appears to be associated with least delinquent behavior."[47]

Catherine Chilman's searching analysis of vast amounts of research on child-rearing in the United States finds significant factors characteristic of the various subcultures.

Table 4–7 lists in comparative columns those child-rearing practices that have been found conducive to mental health as contrasted with less fortunate patterns more characteristic of very poor families. The challenge is clear both in the mass of data Dr. Chilman explores and in her statement of the problem American families face in developing children capable of taking advantage of our complex society without breaking under the strain.

"Since children of very poor families are apt to contribute, in time, a disproportionate share of their numbers to the mentally ill, the delinquent, the broken family, and the socially rejected, as well as to the undereducated and the unemployed, it seems important to consider the development of the whole child, as he is reared in the so-called culture of poverty. If he is to escape effectively from the many-faceted frustrations that beset the very poor, he must escape as a whole person, not just as an efficient and employed cog in the economic complex."[48]

Out of her years of work with children at the Menninger Foundation, Topeka, Kansas, Dr. Lois Barclay Murphy lists the factors that build strong, well-knit personalities with a high degree of mental health:

1. A good start physiologically
2. Emotional nourishment
3. Adequacy of sensory stimuli

---

[46] Robert R. Sears, Eleanor E. Maccoby, and Harry Levin, *Patterns of Child Rearing* (Evanston, Ill.: Row, Peterson and Company, 1957), p. 484.

[47] F. Ivan Nye, *Family Relationships and Delinquent Behavior* (New York: John Wiley and Sons, 1958), p. 100.

[48] Chilman, *Growing Up Poor*, p. 2.

4. Opportunity for motor development and freedom from excessive pressure for performance
5. Stable relationships with mother during the period of establishing clear concepts of self and others
6. Stable, respected interests and possessions
7. Opportunity to exercise autonomy, initiative, and industry, and to achieve mastery over various areas of the environment
8. Feeling supported, accepted, a source of pride and satisfaction to parents
9. Opportunity to cope with gradual doses of frustration and difficulty
10. Participation in group life with some recognizably consistent pattern (freedom from demoralizing value conflicts).[49]

Democratic child-rearing is not anything that comes "naturally." It requires a firm set of family values and a willingness to pursue them diligently. It protects the rights of each member of the family, regardless of age or sex. It shares responsibilities with all family members according to their capacities. It fosters neither laissez-faire anarchy nor unrestricted license, but values rather self-disciplined, goal-directed individuals. It demands the courage and the capacity for verbal and non-verbal communication, openness and responsiveness with others, and the ability to handle abstractions as well as concrete things and thoughts. It thrives best within a relatively favorable climate where the struggle for survival is not ever-present. "It requires a sure sense of personal identity, a wealth of psychological defenses, and an optimistic, rather than a depressed life style."[50]

The values of democracy are not easily attained, but they are important to Americans. As Eleanore Luckey expresses it:

> To grow up to the full stature of thinking humanity—to reach what we believe is man's highest purpose—the fulfillment of his individual, God-created potential! This is what democracy is!
>
> The ultimate hope of humanity, as I see it, rests in man's own individual capacity to be concerned for others—to love others, if you will—in such a way that will cut across all lines of political difference, social class, race, sex, philosophy, religion. The home where there are mature, loving parents offers the optimal environment for the fostering of such persons. . . . Democracy means freedom with responsibility—it's going to take a nation of very grown-up people to make it go.[51]

---

[49] Lois Barclay Murphy, "Effects of Child-rearing Patterns on Mental Health," *Children* 3, no. 6 (November-December 1956): 218.

[50] Chilman, *Growing Up Poor*, p. 36.

[51] Eleanore Braun Luckey, "Family Goals in a Democratic Society," *Journal of Marriage and the Family* 26, no. 3 (August 1964): 278.

SUMMARY

Family values are conceptions of what is desirable that are shared by members of a family. A family's value orientations arise out of the issues of life it faces. A family may be child-oriented, home-oriented, or parent-oriented. Some families are past-oriented, others present-oriented, and still others are future-oriented. Family values are related to social class status, and they express themselves in child-rearing practices. There are significant differences in child-rearing patterns among middle-class, working-class, and very poor families that affect many dimensions of a child's life. Family values shift with the changing socio-economic scene in the larger society. In general, the trends have been from strict to permissive child-rearing, and from traditional to developmental conceptions of parents and of children, with evidence that developmentalism is increasing as more Americans adopt middle-class family values. A family's child-rearing practices affect both parents and children in a variety of ways. Developmentally-oriented parents pay a price for their child-rearing policies in loss of privacy and other parental values, but they are the kind of persons who can encourage and enjoy their children's development as well as their own. The way a child is reared influences his personality development in ways that can be detailed. Measured characteristics have been listed by those who have analyzed the many research studies available in their own and others' professional experience. Democratic child-rearing, highly valued by America's families, rests upon a number of mature attributes and capabilities of parents that call for development not only of children, but of adults as well.

SUGGESTED ACTIVITIES

1. Draft a proposal for needed educational services for parents of low-income groups in your area, based upon the research findings and interpretations reported in Dr. Catherine Chilman's *Growing Up Poor* (Washington, D.C.: Welfare Administration Publication, no. 13, May 1966). If possible, interview the administrative head of your community's welfare program for his or her appraisal of the workability of the various items of your proposal. Write up the interview as a concluding section of your paper.

2. Review Lorraine Hansberry's play *A Raisin in the Sun* in terms of the family themes that the Younger family seems to represent. Illustrate with quotes from the drama.

3. Conduct a study of the ideologies of the members of your class and their parents by providing each of them with cards on which to write (a) five things a good mother does, (b) five things a good father does, and (c) five things a good child does. Tabulate the statements as developmental or tradi-

tional according to the criteria in this chapter. Compare the developmental and traditional scores of males and females in the class, and of student and parent generations. Report your findings to the class with your interpretations of the data.

4. Plan a symposium of members of at least three generations—a student, a parent, a grandparent—on child-rearing practices as they remember them when they were young. Try to match the participants for social class and educational backgrounds as closely as possible.

5. Write a letter to yourself as a parent (actual or potential), reminding yourself of the policies and practices that you feel are best in child-rearing. Summarize briefly at the close the ways in which your recommendations for the rearing of your children differ from the ways in which you yourself were reared. In what ways are they similar?

6. Outline procedures for "child-proofing" the home of a young couple who want to be flexible with their young children and who are comfortable in the developmental point of view both for themselves and for their children. Itemize in detail the changes that should be made in every room of the home in order to meet the child's needs and still maintain comfort and pleasure for the parents.

7. Review Dr. Brim's study (see readings, below), and write a reaction paper of your own on the major points that are covered in this research.

8. Write a term paper reviewing Robert W. White, *Lives in Progress: A Study of the Natural Growth of Personality* (New York: Dryden Press, 1958), with particular stress on the family orientation and child-rearing practices that seem related to the development of Hartley Hale, Joseph Kidd, and Joyce Kingsley. Document your comments from both the White book and the references in this chapter of your text.

9. Prepare a table comparing current child-rearing patterns in the United States and in the Soviet Union, using material in Urie Bronfenbrenner, *Two Worlds of Childhood: U.S. and U.S.S.R.* (New York: Russell Sage Foundation, 1970). Summarize your tabular comparison and indicate what you feel is implied for America's stance toward our children, now and in the future.

READINGS

Adorno, T. W., Else Frenkel-Brunswik, Daniel J. Levinson, R. Nevitt Sanford, in collaboration with Betty Aron, Maria Hertz Levinson, and William Morrow. *The Authoritarian Personality*. New York: Harper and Brothers, 1950.

Baldwin, Alfred L. "Socialization and the Parent-Child Relationship." *Child Development* 19, no. 3 (September 1948): 127–136.

Bayley, Nancy, and Earl S. Schaefer. *Correlations of Maternal and Child Behaviors with the Development of Mental Abili-*

ties: Data from the Berkeley Growth Study. Monograph of the Society for Research in Child Development, serial no. 97, vol. 29, no. 6 (1964).

Brim, Orville G., Jr. *Education for Child Rearing.* New York: Russell Sage Foundation, 1959.

Brody, Grace F. "Socioeconomic Differences in Stated Maternal Child-Rearing Practices and in Observed Maternal Behavior." *Journal of Marriage and the Family* 30, no. 4 (November 1968): 656–660.

Bronfenbrenner, Urie. "Socialization and Social Class through Time and Space." In *Readings in Social Psychology,* edited by Eleanor E. Maccoby, Theodore M. Newcomb, and Eugene L. Hartley, pp. 400–425. New York: Henry Holt and Company, 1958.

Bronfenbrenner, Urie. "The Changing American Child: A Speculative Analysis." *Merrill-Palmer Quarterly* 7, no. 2 (April 1961): 73–84.

Bronfenbrenner, Urie. *Two Worlds of Childhood: U.S. and U.S.S.R.* New York: Russell Sage Foundation, 1970.

Bronson, Wanda C., Edith S. Katten, and Norman Livson. "Patterns of Authority and Affection in Two Generations." *Journal of Abnormal and Social Psychology* 58, no. 2 (March 1959): 143–152.

Duvall, Evelyn Millis. "Conceptions of Parenthood." *American Journal of Sociology* 52, no. 3 (November 1946): 193–203.

Farber, Bernard. *Family Organization and Crisis: Maintenance of Integration in Families with a Severely Mentally Retarded Child.* Monograph of the Society for Research in Child Development, serial no. 75, vol. 25, no. 1 (1960), pp. 39–63.

Gordon, Michael. "Infant Care Revisited." *Journal of Marriage and the Family* 30, no. 4 (November 1968): 578–583.

Havighurst, Robert J., and Allison Davis. "A Comparison of the Chicago and Harvard Studies of Social Class Differences in Child Rearing." *American Sociological Review* 20, no. 4 (August 1955): 438–442.

Hess, Robert D., and Gerald Handel. *Family Worlds: A Psychosocial Approach to Family Life.* Chicago: University of Chicago Press, 1959.

Johnsen, Kathryn P., and Gerald R. Leslie. "Methodological Notes in Research in Childrearing and Social Class." *Merrill-Palmer Quarterly* 2, no. 4 (October 1965): 345–358.

Kell, Leone, and Joan Aldous. "The Relation between Mothers' Child-Rearing Ideologies and Their Children's Perceptions of Maternal Control." *Child Development* 31, no. 1 (March 1960): 145–156.

Kohn, Melvin L. "Social Class and Parent-Child Relationships: An Interpretation." *American Journal of Sociology* 68, no. 4 (January 1963): 471–480.

Kohn, Melvin L., and Carmi Schooler. "Class, Occupation, and Orientation." *American Sociological Review* 34, no. 5 (October 1969): 659–678.

Langdon, Grace, and Irving Stout. *These Well-Adjusted Children*. New York: John Day Company, 1951.

Miller, Daniel R., and Guy E. Swanson. *The Changing American Parent*. New York: John Wiley and Sons, 1958.

Riesman, David, with Nathan Glazer and Reuel Denney. *The Lonely Crowd: A Study of the Changing American Character*. New Haven: Yale University Press, 1950.

Sears, Robert R., Eleanor E. Maccoby, and Harry Levin. *Patterns of Child Rearing*. Evanston, Ill.: Row, Peterson and Company, 1957.

Sewell, William, Paul Mussen, and Chester Harris. "Relationships among Child Training Practices." *American Sociological Review* 20, no. 2 (April 1955): 137–148.

Sontag, Lester W., Charles T. Baker, and Virginia L. Nelson. *Mental Growth and Personality Development: A Longitudinal Study*. Monograph of the Society for Research in Child Development, serial no. 68, vol. 23, no. 2 (1958).

Stendler, Celia B. "Sixty Years of Child Training Practices." *Journal of Pediatrics* 36, no. 1 (January 1950): 122–134.

Vincent, Clark E. "Trends in Infant Care Ideas." *Child Development* 22, no. 3 (September 1951): 199–209.

Waters, Elinor, and Vaughn J. Crandall. "Social Class and Observed Maternal Behavior from 1940 to 1960." *Child Development* 35 (1964): 1021–1032.

Wolfenstein, Martha. "Trends in Infant Care." *American Journal of Orthopsychiatry* 33 (1953): 120–130.

5 FAMILY LIFE CYCLE STAGES IN THE GENERATION SPIRAL

To every thing there is a season, and a time to every purpose under the heaven:

A time to be born, and a time to die; a time to plant, and a time to pluck up that which is planted . . .

A time to weep, and a time to laugh; a time to mourn, and a time to dance . . .

A time to get, and a time to lose; a time to keep, and a time to cast away. . . . Ecclesiastes 3:1–6

Knock on any family door, and what will you find within? No one can tell you exactly, for every family differs in many ways from any other. But generally, if you know three things about a family, you can predict somewhat reliably what you will find going on within it: (1) where a family is in time—in its life cycle, within an era of social change, and in a given season, day, and hour, (2) who lives in the family home, and (3) how the family rates in the community, as seen in its social status. If you know these three things, you can tell even before you meet the family what the important elements to look for are and what forces you may find in action there.

Family Tempos and Rhythms

Families have a developmental history marked by periods of dynamic action and spelled by intervals of relative calm. This is true even within a day, a week, a season. Typically, the family day begins with the bustle of arising, washing, dressing, collecting the day's equipment, and getting into the day's activity. This first spurt of energy is followed in many homes by the midday pause with nobody home but mom and the dog. By late afternoon there is the rush of homecoming with reports of the day, fixing equipment, cleaning up, and preparing the evening meal. In many families there is a period of eating together with family attention focused upon itself. Outside pressures then are suspended momentarily, and a high degree of family interaction is possible. Between the evening meal and bedtime, activities vary by the age and interests of the family members, the stage of the family life cycle, and its orientation. Young parents may go out for the evening, leaving a sitter to stay with the baby. The family may spend a quiet evening at home, with the peace broken by intervals of conflict over the choice of television programs, the use of the telephone, or the pressures of privacy and group demands. There may be guests in who are entertained by the whole family, by the adults only, or by the children. Retiring tends to be serially routinized, with the youngest going to bed first, and the others according to age and interest.

Weekly rhythms are fairly predictable in most families. Monday through Friday routines are built upon work and school schedules. Saturday and Sunday are the weekend intervals filled with shopping and food storage, cleaning and making ready for the coming week, in addition to individual and whole-family recreation (travel, trips, picnics, hobbies, movies, entertaining, and "just being lazy") and religious services for the various family members.

In most parts of the country there are seasonal variations characterized by spring, with its housecleaning, gardening, and storage of winter clothing and equipment; summer, with more out-of-doors living, sports, and vacation activities; autumn, with the busyness of organizational, educational, and vocational life, and getting the home ready for the fall and winter activities in the community. Late in the fall, there is the flurry of "getting ready for the holidays" in home, school, and community, with the bustle of seasonal entertaining and festivities in various settings. By midwinter, families settle down to indoor activities with routines established for getting things done before spring rolls around again.

LIFE-SPANS OF TODAY'S FAMILY MEMBERS

In much the same way that actuarial tables of an insurance company can predict life expectancy, so, in a measure, one can plot the generalized family expectancies through which family members pass. Anyone may personally depart from the statistical profile of family experience at any point in the schema. Such variations do not invalidate the predictions which hold true at a given time for the population as a whole.

Using norms of present-day American life as indicated in data from the United States Bureau of the Census and the National Center for Health Statistics, a woman's life may be outlined as follows.

She comes into her family of orientation at birth; she goes to kindergarten at five,[1] starts school at six, enters her teens at thirteen, and marries when she is about twenty. At this point she leaves her family of orientation and enters her family of procreation. Her first child is born about two years later, and her last child arrives when she is about thirty years of age. By the time she is twenty-seven, her first child goes to kindergarten, and a year later to school. He becomes a teenager when she is about thirty-five, and he marries when she is in her early forties. Her last child marries before she is fifty (earlier for daughters, later for sons). She shares her middle age in the empty nest with her husband until his death, which comes when she is in her mid-sixties. Then she has a decade, more or less, of widowhood until her own death.

Of course, no woman is a cold statistic, but a living person who will pass through several phases distinct from those that have gone before or those that come later in her life. These phases can be seen as a series of long and short pulsations that vary in length and intensity throughout life. She starts with the long period of girlhood that lasts the first dozen years of her life. Her career as a young woman is marked by her teen years that typically close with her marriage in her early twenties. Then come a series of intensely active periods: bearing and rearing infants and small children, having school-age children in the home, relating to teenagers in the family, and launching young adult children into lives of their own.[2] Now life slows down as she shares the empty nest with her husband for the long leisurely phase of sixteen years, more or less, until she is widowed by his death when she is in her sixties. The last stage of her own aging years continues for another decade or so.[3]

Female college graduates usually marry two to three years later than the average American woman. Girls with no high school education tend to marry before they are eighteen. Those who have completed their high school education usually marry by the time they are twenty.[4] Generally,

---

[2] The launching-center stage begins as the first child leaves home for marriage, college, work, or military service, and ends as the last child leaves home for a life of his or her own.

[3] One computation, using life tables for 1949–1951, shows that 65.3 percent of all brides eventually become widows in their early sixties and have an average period of widowhood of 18.7 years. Robert J. Myers, "Statistical Measures in the Marital Life Cycles of Men and Women," *International Population Conference, 1959* (Vienna: Christopher Reiser's Sons), pp. 229–233, quoted in Paul C. Glick and Robert Parke, Jr., "New Approaches in Studying the Life Cycle of the Family," *Demography* 2 (1965): 194–195.

[4] U.S. Bureau of the Census, *Population 1960: Age at First Marriage* (Washington, D.C.: U.S. Department of Commerce, Bureau of the Census, 1966), table 9, "Years of School Completed—Persons Ever Married 14 to 79 Years Old, by Age at First Marriage," p. 124.

---

[1] Nearly two-thirds (64.1 percent) of all five-year-olds in the United States are enrolled in kindergarten, according to the National Center for Educational Statistics, "Preprimary Enrollment of Children Under Six" (October 1968), table 3.

Table 5–1. *Profile of the Life of a Modern American Wife and Mother*

76		Death	75±
72			
68	Widow	Death of husband	66±
64			
60			
56			
52			
	Middle-aged and aging wife (empty nest)	Last child marries	50±
48			
44	Mother at launching stage	First child marries	45± 42±
40			
36	Mother of teenagers	First child teenager	35±
32			
	Mother of school-age children	Last baby born	30±
28		First child in school	28±
	Mother of preschool children		
24			
	Childbearing mother	First baby born	22±
20	Young wife	Marries	20±
16			
		Enters teens	13
12			
8			
		Goes to school	6±
4			
0		Born	0

Family of Procreation (ages 20±–50±)

Family of Orientation (ages 0–20±)

Source: Based upon current data from the U.S. Bureau of the Census and the National Center for Health Statistics, Washington, D.C.

women with four or more years of college enter marriage two to four years later. Because the college-educated woman marries later than her less-well-educated sister, she has her first baby at a later age and enters the next stages of the family life cycle somewhat later. However, the smaller number of children that college-educated women have offsets their later age at marriage to some extent. So, the life cycle profiles for the college woman and the typical American woman in the United States tend to parallel each other in the latter half of life, from the launching stage onward.

After a woman marries, there is an intensely active phase of childbearing and rearing that lasts about twenty-five years, to be followed by an equally long period that remains after the children are grown and gone. It is easy to see the woman's role in the child-rearing stage, but can you see her just as clearly twenty-five years later?

The typical American woman spends the first two decades of her life growing up and getting ready to have children, the next twenty-five to thirty years bearing and rearing children, and the last twenty-five to thirty years alone or with her husband after their children have grown and gone. More than half of her married life remains after her children have left home. Such a view of life through the years raises many questions about the kind of education a girl needs, not only for the immediate future, but also for the years ahead. What will a woman need to prepare herself for the long middle years after her parental role is over? What will be necessary for the period of widowhood that stretches on for half her later years? Does this have implications for life insurance plans? What does it say about mate selection that will not unduly prolong the period of widowhood? What is indicated in terms of interests and activities with carry-over possibilities for the later phases of life? One's roles as a woman are played out not only in the quick-moving years of young womanhood, but through the ever-changing tempos of the entire family life cycle.

Plotting the profile of the life of the man in the American family using medians and norms from the United States Bureau of the Census and the National Center for Health Statistics' data provides the following outline that differs slightly from that of the American woman. Like her, the male enters his family of orientation at

Table 5–2. *Profile of the Life of a Modern American Husband and Father*

Age	Stage	Event	Year	Family
76		Death of other spouse	75±	
72	Widower(?)			
68		Death of one spouse	68±	
64				
60				
56				
52	Middle-aged and aging husband (empty nest)	Last child marries	52±	Family of Procreation
48	Father at launching stage	First child marries	47± 45±	
44				
40	Father of teenagers	First child teenager	38±	
36				
32	Father of school-age children	Last baby born	32±	
	Father of preschool children	First child in school	31±	
28	Childbearing father	First baby born	25±	
24	Beginning family	Marries	22±	
20				
16		Enters teens	13	Family of Orientation
12				
8		Goes to school	6±	
4				
0		Born	0	

Source: Based upon current data from the U.S. Bureau of the Census and the National Center for Health Statistics, Washington, D.C.

birth, starts kindergarten at five, goes to school at six, and becomes a teenager at thirteen. He marries two years later than the woman, when he typically is twenty-two years of age, more or less. At this point he becomes part of his family of procreation. His first child is born a little more than two years after his marriage, when he is about twenty-five, more or less. His last child is born when he is in his early thirties, and he becomes a father of teenagers when he is about thirty-eight years of age. When he reaches his mid-forties, he becomes the father of the bride (or groom) when his first child marries. Soon after he reaches fifty his last child is married; by this time he probably is a grandfather. From now on he and his wife live in an empty nest, their parenting roles over. The chances are that he retires in his mid-sixties. Characteristically, then, he is the first spouse to die, but if he survives beyond the average, he may or may not be widowed through his final years. The chief differences between the length of the various phases of his life and those of his wife are the slightly longer period before marriage, by two years, more or less, and the shorter middle-aged and aging periods due to his shorter life-span.

Of course there is no such thing as the average man. Each man has the particular ages and stages in his life cycle which are peculiar to him. On the average, however, he can anticipate spending most of his adult life as a husband and father. He and his wife will spend the first two years or so as a couple before their first child arrives.

Then, after his last child has married and left home, he may expect another fourteen years (plus or minus) as a member of a couple again. His second decade of life will be spent in becoming a young man, his third in becoming a father. His forties will be characterized by children and teenagers and young adults being launched into lives of their own. His fifties and sixties, after the peak of child-rearing responsibilities are over, will be relatively quiet ones on the family scene, with just himself and his wife and their life as grandparents. The chances are that he will leave his wife a widow, with all the implications of life insurance, retirement plans, housing requirements, and the rest of the factors involved for them both in planning their later years.

PREDICTABLE STAGES IN THE DEVELOPMENT OF FAMILIES

There is a predictability about family development that helps us know what to expect of any family at a given stage, regardless of who or where it is. Much as an individual grows, develops, matures, and ages, undergoing the successive changes and readjustments from conception to senescence, no matter who he or she is, so families likewise have a life cycle that is seen in the universal sequence of family development.

The family life cycle, as a frame of reference, is a way of taking a long look at family life. It is based upon the recognition of the successive patterns within the continuity of family living over the years. It opens the way for study of the particular problems and potentials, rewards and hazards, vulnerabilities and strengths of each phase of family experience from beginning to end. It recognizes the peculiar rhythms and tempos that pulse through family living, now soft and sweet, now loud and tempestuous, now swift, now slow, in movements that every family everywhere knows in its harmonies and dissonances of living together through the years.

Families take form in the marriage and early establishment of the newly married couple. They develop rapidly as husband and wife assume, with the coming of their first child, additional roles as father and mother. As successive children are born, family members enlarge their roles to encompass the additional children as individuals and as members of the growing family group. Each addition to the family brings not only an increase in the number of family members, but a significant reorganization of family living, so that no two children are born into exactly the same family.

As children grow older, their parents are growing older also, changing in their needs and desires, their hopes and expectations, as well as their responses to the demands and pressures of growing children. Concurrently, the children are progressively changing in their relationship to their parents, to their brothers and sisters, and to other relatives.

Families mature as their children grow up, through childhood, into adolescence, and finally into lives and homes of their own. Families that once expanded to accommodate the requirements of growing children later must contract as they release these same children as young adults. The big, bustling years when family life runs at a hectic pace eventually give way to the long, slow-moving years of the empty nest, when the middle-aged and aging parents face the later half of their marriage together as a pair. With the prolongation of life, these later years present new opportunities and problems.

Each family grows through the years in its own particular way. Just as the individual person is born, grows and develops, matures, and ages, undergoing the successive changes and development from conception through senescence in his own way, so a family lives out its life cycle in its own unique fashion.

Stages in the Family Life Cycle

The family life cycle may be divided into few or many stages on the basis of several factors. It is possible to think of a two-stage family life cycle: (1) *the expanding family stage*, taking the family from its inception to the time its children are grown, and

(2) *the contracting family stage*, in which children are being launched by the family into lives of their own, and in which the family contracts through the later years with one or both of the original pair still at home. Such a two-stage cycle delineation is usually too gross for definitive study, but the factor of shifting plurality patterns in the family was one of the first used to see stages in the family life cycle.

As early as 1931, Sorokin and others[5] discussed a four-stage family life cycle based upon the changing family member constellation within the family: (1) married couples just starting their independent economic existence, (2) couples with one or more children, (3) couples with one or more adult self-supporting children, and (4) couples growing old.

E. L. Kirkpatrick and others[6] saw the stages of the family life cycle in terms of the place of the children in the educational system in a four-stage cycle: (1) preschool family, (2) grade school family, (3) high school family, and (4) all adult family.

In plotting the changing income and outgo financial patterns through the family life cycle, Howard Bigelow[7] elaborated on the school placement factor in a cycle he demarked into seven periods: (1) establishment, (2) childbearing and preschool period, (3) elementary school period, (4) high school period, (5) college, (6) period of recovery, and (7) period of retirement.

The most complex breakdown of the family life cycle into stages, to date,[8] elaborates the eight-stage cycle of this text into a twenty-four-stage cycle. Following not only the predictable development of a family as the oldest child grows, this proposal also keeps the youngest child in focus. Such a delineation calls for two preschool family stages, three school-age, four teenage, five young adult, and five launching stages. The first of these is the beginning family stage. The next twenty make provision in each family life cycle stage for a possible youngest child who theoretically plunges the family back into an earlier age group interest as younger children arrive. Dr. Rodgers explains, ". . . the solution follows Duvall quite closely. Birth, entry into school, departure from the family system, retirement, and dissolution of the system are easily identifiable. We can do this, however, for the additional position of last

---

[5] P. Sorokin, C. C. Zimmerman, and C. J. Galpin, *A Systematic Source Book in Rural Sociology* (Minneapolis: University of Minnesota Press, 1931), vol. 2, p. 31.

[6] E. L. Kirkpatrick et al., *The Life Cycle of the Farm Family in Relation to Its Standard of Living,* Agricultural Experiment Station Research Bulletin, no. 121 (Madison, Wis.: University of Wisconsin, 1934).

[7] Howard F. Bigelow, "Money and Marriage," chap. 17 in Howard Becker and Reuben Hill, eds., *Marriage and the Family* (Boston: D. C. Heath and Company, 1942), pp. 382–386.

[8] Roy H. Rodgers, "Proposed Modification of Duvall Family Life Cycle Stages," paper presented at the American Sociological Association meetings, New York City, August 31, 1960.

child, as well as first-born, which is a modification of the Duvall approach."[9]

The twenty-four categories in this schema are:

1. Beginning Families (defined as childless couples).
2. Families with Infants (all children less than 36 months old).
3a. Preschool Families with Infants (oldest child 3–6 years; youngest child birth–36 months).
3b. Preschool Families (all children 3–6 years).
4a. School-age Families with Infants (oldest child 6–13 years; youngest child birth–36 months).
4b. School-age Families with Preschoolers (oldest child 6–13 years; youngest child 3–6 years).
4c. School-age Families (all children 6–13 years).
5a. Teenage Families with Infants (oldest child 13–20 years; youngest child birth–36 months).
5b. Teenage Families with Preschoolers (oldest child 13–20 years; youngest child 3–6 years).
5c. Teenage Families with School-agers (oldest child 13–20 years; youngest child 6–13 years).
5d. Teenage Families (all children 13–20 years).

6a. Young Adult Families with Infants (oldest child over 20 years; youngest child birth–36 months).
6b. Young Adult Families with Preschoolers (oldest child over 20 years; youngest child 3–6 years).
6c. Young Adult Families with School-agers (oldest child over 20 years; youngest child 6–13 years).
6d. Young Adult Families with Teenagers (oldest child over 20 years; youngest child 13–20 years).
6e. Young Adult Families (all children over 20 years).
7a. Launching with Infants (first child launched; youngest child birth–36 months).
7b. Launching with Preschoolers (first child launched; youngest child 3–6 years).
7c. Launching with School-agers (first child launched; youngest child 6–13 years).
7d. Launching with Teenagers (first child launched; youngest child 13–20 years).
7e. Launching with Young Adults (first child launched; youngest child over 20 years).
8. Middle Years (all children launched to retirement).
9. Aging (retirement to death of one spouse).
10. Widowhood (death of first spouse to death of survivor).[10]

---

[9] Roy H. Rodgers, "Improvements in the Construction and Analysis of Family Life Cycle Categories" (Ph.D. dissertation, University of Minnesota, 1962), p. 62.

[10] Ibid., pp. 64–65.

Chart 5–1. *Percentage at Each Age of Married and Widowed Men and Women, by Stage of the Family Life Cycle (The divorced are not shown since the percentage never rises above 4.9.)*

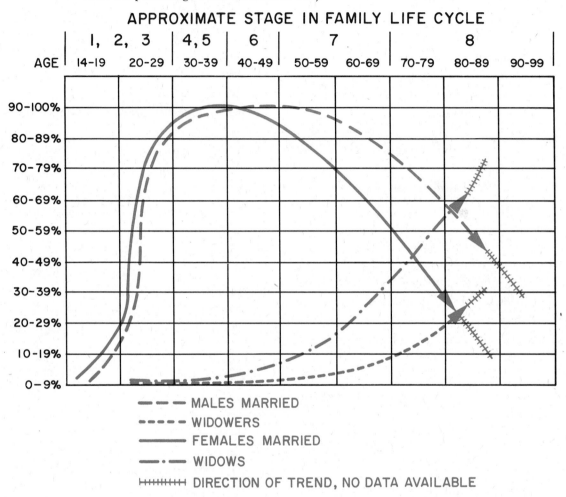

APPROXIMATE STAGE IN FAMILY LIFE CYCLE

	1, 2, 3		4, 5	6	7		8	
AGE	14-19	20-29	30-39	40-49	50-59	60-69	70-79	80-89	90-99

90-100%
80-89%
70-79%
60-69%
50-59%
40-49%
30-39%
20-29%
10-19%
0-9%

- – – – MALES MARRIED
- - - - - WIDOWERS
———— FEMALES MARRIED
—·—·— WIDOWS
++++++++ DIRECTION OF TREND, NO DATA AVAILABLE

Source: Ruth Shonle Cavan, *The American Family*, 4th ed. (New York: Thomas Y. Crowell Company, 1969), p. 232; with data from U.S. Bureau of the Census, *Statistical Abstract of the United States, 1967* (Washington, D.C.: U.S. Government Printing Office, 1967), p. 33.

This elaboration may prove helpful in research design, but it is unnecessarily detailed for our use here.

This book recognizes and depicts the family life cycle as consisting of eight stages:

Stage 1. Married Couples (without children)

Stage 2. Childbearing Families (oldest child birth–30 months)

Stage 3. Families with Preschool Children (oldest child 2½–6 years)

Stage 4. Families with Schoolchildren (oldest child 6–13 years)

Stage 5. Families with Teenagers (oldest child 13–20 years)

Stage 6. Families as Launching Centers (first child gone to last child's leaving home)

Stage 7. Middle-aged Parents (empty nest to retirement)

Stage 8. Aging Family Members (retirement to death of both spouses)

The age and school placement of the oldest child are used as criteria of family cycle stage placement from arrival of the first child in the family up to the launching center stage, when we shift focus to the situation facing those remaining in the original family. Families as launching centers (stage 6) is the stage that begins with the leaving home of the first child and concludes with the departure of the last child into marriage, military service, work, or whatever pulls him or her as a young adult into a life of his or her own.

This treatment is organized around a modification of the seven-stage family life cycle structured by the cochairmen for the National Conference on Family Life in 1948.[11] It represents a combination of the several factors used in determining family life cycle stages: (1) plurality patterns,

(2) age of the oldest child, (3) school placement of the oldest child, and (4) functions and statuses of families before children come and after they leave. This combination of factors seems to be workable for the study of the majority of American families, and to parallel such reliable data as are available to date both from the United States Bureau of the Census and from less extensive research studies.

Overlapping of Family Life Cycle Stages

In defining the stages in terms of the oldest child, the presence of other children in the family is not explicitly recognized. A clean-cut sequence of stages of the family life cycle such as that outlined above seems to occur only in the one-child family. In families with more than one child, there are several years of overlap at various of the stages. The average mother of two or more children is in the period of childbearing for a longer period than stage 2 indicates; she has preschool children over a longer span of time than is predicted for stage 3; she has school-age children longer than is considered in designating stage 4; she has teenagers in the home for a longer period than that covered by stage 5.

There is no simple solution to the conceptual problem of overlap of stages of the family life cycle in families of more than one child. Since our thesis is that families grow and develop as their children do, our

---

[11] Evelyn Millis Duvall and Reuben Hill, cochairmen, "Report of the Committee on the Dynamics of Family Interaction," prepared at the request of the National Conference on Family Life, Washington, D.C., February 1948, mimeographed.

answer to the question of overlapping of stages is that a family grows through a given stage with its oldest child, and in a sense "repeats" as subsequent children come along. We see a family being pushed out into new unknowns in its experience as its oldest child becomes a preschooler, goes to school, gets into the teens, and finally leaves for a life of his own. As younger children come along, they arrive in a family already somewhat familiar with these normal events and stages of children's growth through the induction given by the eldest. Thus, while a family may be seeing its firstborn into preschool, a younger sibling arrives in a preschool family rather than a childbearing family, because of the family's involvement with the older child also. Actually that family is not solely a childbearing family, because it is already grappling with the problems and pressures of its preschooler at the same time that it nurtures its newborn. And so it goes through the years that children are in the home. The oldest child is always taking his family with him out into the growing edges of family experience. Younger children necessarily arrive into a different family than that into which the firstborn came, if only in the degree of its experience with children of his age.

The problems of delineating family life cycle stages which will hold for all families are many because families themselves are so varied. Some couples marry early and others not until much later. Some couples have their first baby in the first year of their marriage, others not until years afterwards,

and still others never have children. Some babies arrive one after another in quick succession, while others are spaced by as much as a dozen years or more. Some children follow a regular progression through elementary school, high school, and college, while others cease being schoolchildren when they are scarcely in their teens. Even more difficult to take into account are the many forms of broken and rebuilt families—with all that is involved in divorce, remarriage, and the establishment of families in which "your children," "my children," and "our children" are all part of the same family. Military service but partially launches many young men from their parental families, for although they leave home, their independence is incomplete when they must return to finish their educational plans and finally get settled in lives of their own. No less indefinite is the status of the girl who may be a wife of an absent serviceman and yet still a daughter at home with her parents.

Whatever schema for defining family life cycle stages is used, it is merely a convenient division for study of something that in real life flows on from one phase to another without pause or break. The genius of the concept is the explicit awareness that each stage has its beginnings in the phases that are past and its fruition in development yet to come. Being cyclical by definition, the family life cycle and each of the stages within it has no beginning and no end. No matter where you start to study the family life cycle, there are always relevant roots in the near and distant past that must be considered. Wherever you are at the moment, you have grown out of the stage just before and are heading into the stage ahead.

Married Couples as "Families"

Three stages of the family life cycle, as we define it, deal with the husband and wife as a couple: stage 1 as a married couple before children come, and stages 7 and 8 as a married couple after their children have grown and gone. It can be argued that a couple without children is not a family, but more accurately a married couple.

But, seeing the whole family in focus through the years, the newly married couple appear as "the beginning family" which develops very quickly in the majority of cases into the childbearing family. The norm is for the young married couple to be a family-in-the-making not only in that their children eventually make a family of them, but they think of themselves as potential parents long before children actually arrive. In terms of the time factor alone, many couples spend as much or more of their early married stage as expectant parents as they do as bride and groom.

The middle-aged or aging couple who have already been through the childbearing, rearing, and launching stages of the family cycle are still a couple, true. But they are parents of grown children, too. They quite probably have grandchildren. They keep up the home base more often than not. They make a home for varying lengths of time for their married children and grandchildren; perhaps for their own aging parents and other older relatives. They continue to think of themselves as "family" and to function as family members long after their own children are grown and off in homes of their own. Therefore, we designate them as in the later stages of the family life cycle.

Length of Time in Each of the Stages

Remembering that few families are "typical" in the ways they move through the family life cycle, it is possible nevertheless to plot the time usually taken by American families to move through each of the eight stages of their life cycle. This is done by utilizing United States census data that provide profiles of families as well as of individuals by recognized milestones in their life histories.

Americans usually think of a family as one in which there is a father and mother and two or three young children. Advertisements beam on such a picture of family life. Church and school materials often portray this stage of the family life cycle as though it were the only one that mattered. Commercial word pictures commonly assume that the family with young children is *the* family. Holiday sentiments and everyday assumptions put this stage of the family life cycle so much in the foreground that none other seems to exist. Such a stereotype is understandable. Certainly the child-rearing and childbearing stages are highly important in family relationships, in the family's contact with school, church, and community, in the development of the personalities of the children, and for the family as a consumer, with its bulging appetites for more and ever more goods. Yet this stage in the family life cycle is but a small fraction of the whole. It consists of but a few years, an average of a dozen or so, out of the total of fifty to sixty years in the life of the average family.

In marriage and family life courses in schools and colleges, it is usual to spend the greater part of the time on the processes leading to marriage, the adjustments of the newly married pair, and their functions as expectant and actual parents. This, of course, is justifiable in that it reflects the readiness of the student, as well as the significance of the husband-wife relationship for the stability of the family. Yet at the same time such an emphasis misrepresents the time the married pair have together in the family they have established. Young adults, about to finish their education, establish themselves vocationally, and get married, can better make the decisions necessary for these immediate goals by keeping their probable entire family life cycle in mind.

If they are a man and woman of the average ages the United States Bureau of the Census reports as typical at first marriage, birth of children, marriage of last child, and death of spouse, then the family cycle they may envisage for themselves is largely ignored in courses that focus solely on the young married couple. As is seen in chart 5–2, one-half of the marriage typically is spent as a couple after the children have grown and gone.

The significance of the duration of the various stages, not only for education, but for budgeting, housing, health, recreation, home management, and a host of other family resources and services excites the imagination and will be dealt with in part in the subsequent chapters devoted to each of the stages of the family life cycle.

TWENTIETH-CENTURY CHANGES IN THE FAMILY LIFE CYCLE

Today, more children survive the early years; more mothers come through childbearing safely; and a larger percentage of men and women lives to round out the lifespan than did formerly. Marriage is at younger ages, and both husband and wife can anticipate considerably more years of marriage and family living now than was typical at the close of the last century.

Research into family development through three generations of present-day families finds changes in the timing of fam-

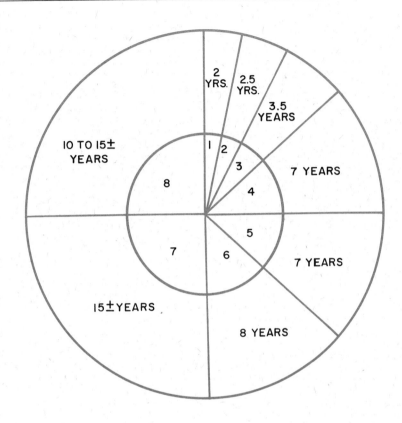

1. Married Couples (without children).	**5.** Families with Teenagers (Oldest child 13 – 20 years).
2. Childbearing Families (Oldest child, birth – 30 months).	**6.** Families as Launching Centers (First child gone to last child leaving home).
3. Families with Preschool Children (Oldest child 30 months – 6 years).	**7.** Middle-aged Parents (Empty nest to retirement).
4. Families with Schoolchildren (Oldest child 6 – 13 years).	**8.** Aging Family Members (Retirement to death of both spouses).

Source: Based upon data from the U.S. Bureau of the Census and from the National Center for Health Statistics, Washington, D.C.

Table 5–3. *Years Married at Critical Points in Family Life Cycle Stages in Three Generations*

Critical point in family life cycle	Number of years married		
	Grand-parents married 1907	Parents married 1931	Married children married 1953
First child born	1.67	1.69	1.66
Second child born	4.45	5.27	4.59
Third child born	6.58	9.8	6.83
Last child born	14.6	10.4	*
First child launched	22.4	20.7	*
Last child launched	33.8	25.0	*

Source: Reuben Hill, *Family Development in Three Generations* (Cambridge, Mass.: Schenkman Publishing Company, 1970), chap. 4, derived from chart 4.01.

* Married children's family life cycle not completed at the time of the study.

ily life cycle stages through this century, as shown in table 5–3.

The grandparent generation, marrying in the first decade of the twentieth century, married at a later age, bore children at closer intervals, and continued childbearing for a longer period, producing more children than recent generations. The parent generation married in the depression and delayed having children longer than did the grandparent or the married children generations. The grandparent generation spent more years having and rearing and releasing its children than have the two more recent generations. Trends in family life cycle changes over three generations are noted in twelve significant differences, summarized below.

Trends over Three Generations[12]

1. Marriage occurs at earlier ages now than in former generations.
2. Fewer children are now born into families than in earlier generations.
3. Voluntary child-spacing is more probable now than in earlier generations.
4. Children are spaced more closely than in parents' generation (during the depression).
5. Grown children are launched earlier now than in previous generations.
6. Launching stage is shorter than in earlier generations.
7. Periods of childbearing, child-rearing, and releasing grown children are shorter now.
8. There is an earlier empty nest for middle-aged couples now than formerly.
9. Middle-aged couples have a longer time together after their children are grown and gone.
10. There is a possibility of more years together after retirement now than formerly.
11. There is a likelihood of longer life for individuals now than in earlier generations.

[12] Adapted from Reuben Hill, *Family Development in Three Generations* (Cambridge, Mass.: Schenkman Publishing Company, 1970), chap. 4; and Glick and Parke, "New Approaches in Studying the Life Cycle of the Family," pp. 187–202.

12. Each family member has a larger number of older living relatives than formerly.

"Changes during the twentieth century in age at marriage, size of completed family, spacing of children, and life expectancy have had substantial effects on the life cycle of the average family. The youngest women for whom data are available compare as follows, on the average, with women who are forty to sixty years older: The youngest women marry one to two years younger and complete their childbearing two to three years younger; their age at the marriage of their last child is four to five years younger, and their length of married life is about nine years longer."[13]

The forecast for the American family life cycle of the future, in general, is: More persons in their late twenties and thirties will more likely marry than ever before. Teenage marriages, already declining, will continue to taper off, and then can be expected to level out. There will be a tendency for women's first marriages to be at somewhat later ages through the next decade or so. Husbands and wives will be closer together in age than formerly. More

[13] Glick and Parke, "New Approaches in Studying the Life Cycle of the Family," p. 196.

Chart 5-3. *Generational Overlap of Four Family Life Cycles*

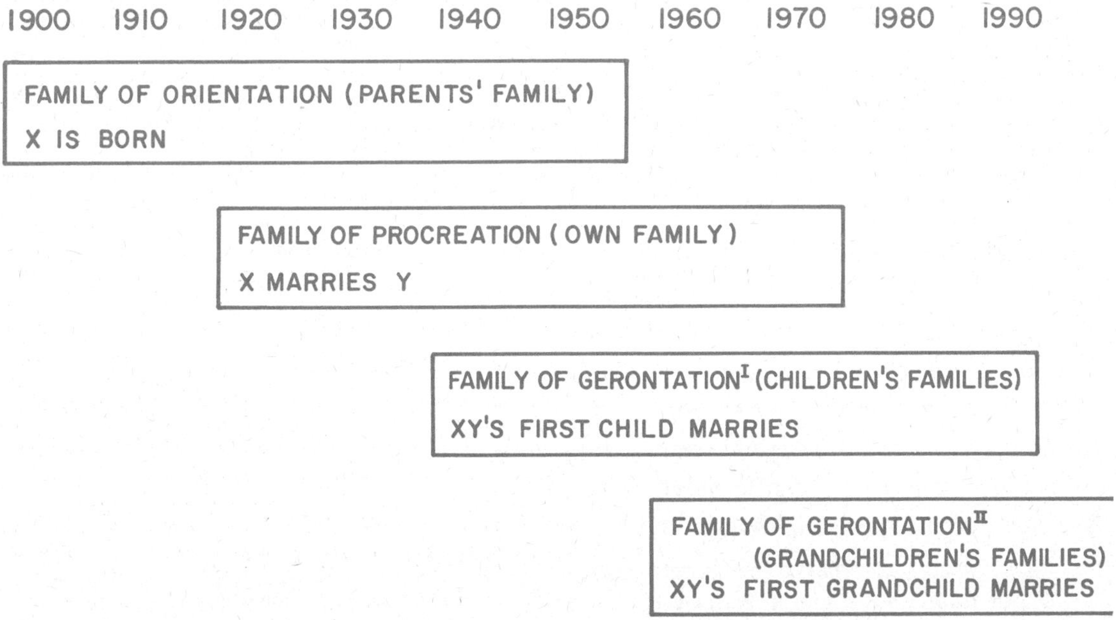

| 1900 | 1910 | 1920 | 1930 | 1940 | 1950 | 1960 | 1970 | 1980 | 1990 |

FAMILY OF ORIENTATION (PARENTS' FAMILY)
X IS BORN

FAMILY OF PROCREATION (OWN FAMILY)
X MARRIES Y

FAMILY OF GERONTATION[I] (CHILDREN'S FAMILIES)
XY'S FIRST CHILD MARRIES

FAMILY OF GERONTATION[II]
(GRANDCHILDREN'S FAMILIES)
XY'S FIRST GRANDCHILD MARRIES

Source: U.S. census data and projections for girls and women, whose generations are shorter than males' because females marry earlier, in general.

married couples will survive jointly to retirement and beyond. As economic conditions improve, further declines in divorce and separation may be expected. American families will remain about the same size. Within the next twenty years, five out of six aged persons not in institutions will maintain their own homes. Married couples will continue to keep house by themselves, as practically all of them do now. As further development of marriage and family projections are made, the forecasting of trends in marriage and family life can be expected to be made with even greater certainty.[14]

The Generation Spiral

Typically a family develops through a somewhat predictable sequence of stages that follow one another in reliable progression. Before one family unit has completed its cycle, its grown children have been launched to start out on theirs. Most twentieth-century American family members have the privilege of seeing a second, third, and perhaps even a fourth family life cycle spun off, as children marry and rear their children, who grow up, marry, and have children, who in turn marry and repeat the family life cycle pattern while older members of the family are still living.

Chart 5–3 is a schematic portrayal of family development from one generation to the next through the twentieth century. Using as a base line the length of time the original husband and wife have been married, their first child is seen coming at the usual interval. She marries at the median age for girls and raises her children, who begin to marry about twenty years later.

The original husband and wife can be expected to survive the marriage of all their children and participate in the induction of sons- and daughters-in-law into the family. Both of the original parents live to see their grandchildren born and raised and most of them married before their lives are terminated. The original woman lives to see the marriage of practically all her grandchildren, and not unusually has the experience of seeing her great-grandchildren well under way before she too passes on. Thus, at midcentury, the American family typically consists of four or more generations in its extended forms. Dr. Ruth Albrecht predicts that, with increased longevity, generations will be added to the family so that five- and six-generation families seem likely in the future. She suggests that if a girl with two parents, three grandparents, and two great-grandparents marries the boy with two parents and four grandparents, they will have possible interpersonal relationships with thirteen parent figures.[15]

---

[14] Drawn from Robert Parke, Jr., and Paul C. Glick, "Prospective Changes in Marriage and the Family," *Journal of Marriage and the Family* 29, no. 2 (May 1967): 256.

[15] Ruth Albrecht, "Intergeneration Parent Patterns," *Journal of Home Economics* 46, no. 1 (January 1954): 31.

This continuous spinning off of grown children's, grandchildren's, and future generations' family life cycles we view as *the generation spiral* (chart 5–4). As older family members disappear in death, their family life cycles fade away, but their emotional, intellectual, cultural, biological, material, and personal legacies continue on through the generation spiral of which they have been a part in their own family life cycle.

Reuben Hill's study of three-generation families confirms the fact of ongoing interaction in a continuing flow from one generation to the next. He finds generational sharing of activities, visiting, and help exchanges that are three generations in depth, with most frequent interaction between adjacent generations. The middle generation (parents of married children) is found to be the lineage bridge between the elder and the younger generations in the same family. Each generation turns to the kinship network for help in solving problems—the grandparent generation for help with illness and household management, the parent generation for emotional gratification, and the married children's generation for assistance with finances and child care.

> . . . three generation lineages develop networks of interdependence based upon a wide range of help exchanges and frequent kin contacts that approximate modified extended families in their symbiotic functioning. The viability of these networks is advanced by the heavy involvement of the middle generation as a lineage bridge initiating more activity

Chart 5–4. *The Generation Spiral— A Schematic Presentation*

Source: Adapted from the cover design of Takashi Koyama, *The Changing Social Position of Women in Japan* (Paris: UNESCO Publication, 1961).

and giving more help both up and down the generation ladder than it receives and by means of this kinkeeping activity moderating the strains occasioned by non-reciprocity in giving and receiving in the network.[16]

These three-generation families report more instances of help given and received between them as grandparents, parents, and married children than from any other source of assistance. Health and welfare agencies, religious organizations, and professional persons in the community supplied few of the family needs in times of trouble, compared to family members in

[16] Hill, *Family Development in Three Generations*, chap. 13.

Chart 5–5. *Sources of Help Received by Three Generations, over a Year's Time, by Percentages of Instances*

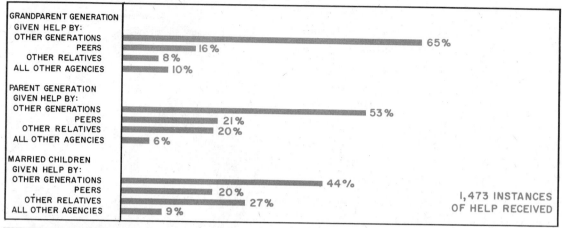

GRANDPARENT GENERATION GIVEN HELP BY:
- OTHER GENERATIONS — 65%
- PEERS — 16%
- OTHER RELATIVES — 8%
- ALL OTHER AGENCIES — 10%

PARENT GENERATION GIVEN HELP BY:
- OTHER GENERATIONS — 53%
- PEERS — 21%
- OTHER RELATIVES — 20%
- ALL OTHER AGENCIES — 6%

MARRIED CHILDREN GIVEN HELP BY:
- OTHER GENERATIONS — 44%
- PEERS — 20%
- OTHER RELATIVES — 27%
- ALL OTHER AGENCIES — 9%

1,473 INSTANCES OF HELP RECEIVED

Source: Reuben Hill, *Family Development in Three Generations* (Cambridge, Mass.: Schenkman Publishing Company, 1970), chap. 3, "Interdependence among the Generations."

Chart 5–6. *Help Given by Three Generations, over a Year's Time, by Percentages of Instances*

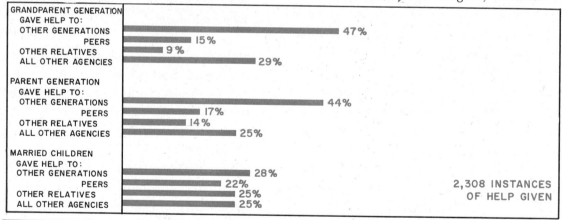

GRANDPARENT GENERATION GAVE HELP TO:
- OTHER GENERATIONS — 47%
- PEERS — 15%
- OTHER RELATIVES — 9%
- ALL OTHER AGENCIES — 29%

PARENT GENERATION GAVE HELP TO:
- OTHER GENERATIONS — 44%
- PEERS — 17%
- OTHER RELATIVES — 14%
- ALL OTHER AGENCIES — 25%

MARRIED CHILDREN GAVE HELP TO:
- OTHER GENERATIONS — 28%
- PEERS — 22%
- OTHER RELATIVES — 25%
- ALL OTHER AGENCIES — 25%

2,308 INSTANCES OF HELP GIVEN

Source: Reuben Hill, *Family Development in Three Generations* (Cambridge, Mass.: Schenkman Publishing Company, 1970), chap. 3, "Interdependence among the Generations."

older and younger generations, who most often stepped in with help. In one given year there was evidence of a vast network of interaction between the generations, of which 3,781 instances were exchanges of various kinds of help—in illness, financial binds, child care, household problems, and emotional stress. In this mutual interdependence, members of each generation report more received from than given to their relatives by significant percentages (charts 5–5 and 5–6).

FAMILY DEVELOPMENT

The many ways in which families rely upon one another within the generation spiral have been noted in earlier studies through the years.[17] The popular notion of the modern family as a vulnerable little nuclear unit consisting only of husband, wife, and their children, unsupported by other caring relatives, is not borne out by research. Empirical evidence points rather to a modified extended family within a rich network of generational interaction.[18]

Rapid Increase in Interpersonal Relationships as Families Grow

The size of the family increases by arithmetical progression—first two persons as husband and wife marry and settle down to establish a family, then the first baby comes along, followed by the second sibling, and so on as long as the family grows in size. The complexity of family relationships increases much more rapidly. According to the law of family interaction, with the addition of each person to a family or primary group, the number of persons increases in the simplest arithmetical progression in whole numbers, while the number of personal interrelationships within the group increases in the order of triangular numbers.[19]

To find the number of interpersonal relationships within a family, the following formula is used, in which x equals the number of interpersonal relationships, and y equals the number of persons:

$$x = \frac{y^2 - y}{2}$$

Applying this formula to a specific family, the following series emerges: number of persons in the family—2 3 4 5 6 7 8 9 and so forth; number of relationships in the family—1 3 6 10 15 21 28 36 and so forth.

Thus we see that a family consisting of a mother, father, and three children has a total of five individuals with a total of ten interpersonal relationships: father with mother, father with first child, father with second child, father with third child; mother with first child, mother with second child, mother with third child; first child with second child, first child with third child; second child with third child.

---

[17] Evelyn Millis Duvall, *In-Laws: Pro and Con* (New York: Association Press, 1954); Marvin B. Sussman and Lee Burchinal, "Kin Family Network: Unheralded Structure in Current Conceptualizations of Family Functioning," *Marriage and Family Living* 24, no. 3 (August 1962): 231–240.

[18] Eugene Litwak, "The Use of Extended Family Groups in the Achievement of Social Goals: Some Policy Implications," *Social Problems* 7 (Winter 1959–1960): 177–187; Marvin B. Sussman, "Relationships of Adult Children with Their Parents in the United States," chap. 4 in Ethel Shanas and Gordon F. Streib, eds., *Social Structure and the Family: Generational Relations* (Englewood Cliffs, N.J.: Prentice-Hall, 1965), pp. 62–92; and Hill, *Family Development in Three Generations,* chap. 3, "Interdependence Among the Generations."

[19] James H. S. Bossard, "The Law of Family Interaction," *American Journal of Sociology,* January 1945, p. 292.

Chart 5–7. *Possible Number of Interpersonal Relationships in a Three-child Family, by Stage in the Family Life Cycle*

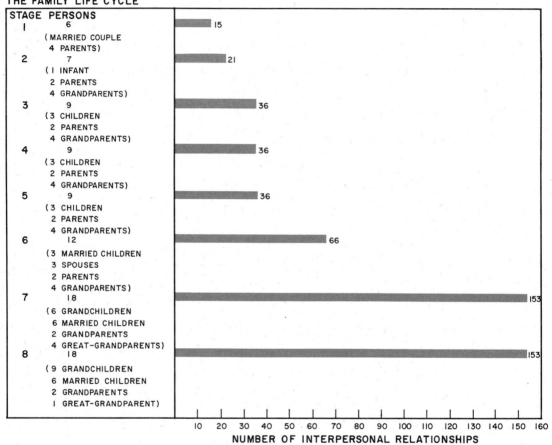

NUMBER OF FAMILY
MEMBERS AT EACH STAGE OF
THE FAMILY LIFE CYCLE

STAGE	PERSONS
1	6
	(MARRIED COUPLE
	4 PARENTS)
2	7
	(1 INFANT
	2 PARENTS
	4 GRANDPARENTS)
3	9
	(3 CHILDREN
	2 PARENTS
	4 GRANDPARENTS)
4	9
	(3 CHILDREN
	2 PARENTS
	4 GRANDPARENTS)
5	9
	(3 CHILDREN
	2 PARENTS
	4 GRANDPARENTS)
6	12
	(3 MARRIED CHILDREN
	3 SPOUSES
	2 PARENTS
	4 GRANDPARENTS)
7	18
	(6 GRANDCHILDREN
	6 MARRIED CHILDREN
	2 GRANDPARENTS
	4 GREAT–GRANDPARENTS)
8	18
	(9 GRANDCHILDREN
	6 MARRIED CHILDREN
	2 GRANDPARENTS
	1 GREAT–GRANDPARENT)

NUMBER OF INTERPERSONAL RELATIONSHIPS

Assuming all four grandparents are living, the family with three children consists of nine persons within the generation spiral (four grandparents, two parents, and three children), within which a total of thirty-six interpersonal relationships is possible. As the three children marry, their three spouses swell the number of family members to twelve, and their interrelationships to sixty-six, not counting any of the new in-laws. When each of the married children's families has its second child, there now is a probable number of interpersonal relationships totaling 153. As the great-grandparents die, they are replaced by new births in the youngest generation. The last remaining great-grandparent in the final stage of her life cycle quite possibly is part of an eighteen-person family, with more than 150 interpersonal relationships in its generation spiral. Chart 5–7 shows graphically how rapidly family relationships increase through the family life cycle, merely within the generation spiral, and not counting any of the relatives by marriage, nor the aunts, uncles, cousins, and other kin who are considered part of the family.

Family Life Cycle Analysis— Problems and Promise

There are a number of unsolved problems in family life cycle study. The first is that actual families do not follow statistical models derived from census data. Some family units do not fit any system of stages thus far designed—how many will not be known until there are more longitudinal family studies. The second is that any particular schema of stages has some advantages but fails to meet other specifications adequately. The two-stage family life cycle (expanding and contracting families) is too gross for detailed analysis. The twenty-four-stage cycle suggested by Rodgers is too complex to handle with ease. The eight-stage family life cycle has the disadvantage of explicitly focusing on the oldest child with vision of the younger children in the family blurred by implication and inference. However admittedly imperfect, family life cycle analysis along these lines is a productive way of studying the complexities of contemporary American families.

The family life cycle approach emphasizes the dynamics of family interaction as shifting and changing from one period to another in family experience. It is this dynamic quality that seems best to match the active life of real families. It is the long look longitudinally through the life history of a family that keeps in perspective each moment and each person in relationship to all others—past, present, and future. Furthermore, there is evidence that the family life cycle is superior to other variables in explaining and anticipating family behavior.[20] With further refinement, it may become a major tool in appraising and predicting many aspects of family living.

SUMMARY

Families are many and varied. They are similar in that they develop through the years in ways that are in part predictable. Every family develops through a family life cycle in which it becomes established in the marriage of the man and his wife, enters into childbearing and child-rearing with the coming of children, becomes an arena of interacting family members as the children grow up, and in time launches the

[20] John B. Lansing and Leslie Kish, "Family Life Cycle as an Independent Variable," *American Sociological Review* 22, no. 5 (October 1957): 512–519.

children into lives of their own. The middle-aged and aging couple live through their remaining years in an empty nest that is still a home base for their married children, their grandchildren, their other relatives, and so continues to be in fact part of the family cycle. The eight stages of the family life cycle differ in form and function, and in length of time spent in each one before the next stage comes. Each succeeding generation overlaps those that have gone before and those that come after, within the generation spiral. Interdependence of the generations in the family has been found in which each family member lives within a kin network rich in interpersonal relationships. As the family increases in size, the number of its possible relationships rapidly enlarges in ways that can be plotted mathematically. Family life cycle analysis is productive in studying the complexities of modern American families.

SUGGESTED ACTIVITIES

1. Compile a list of your relatives and, counting yourself as one of the family members, compute the number of possible interpersonal relationships you now have, according to the law of family interaction.

2. List the forms of family life in America today that are not explicitly accounted for in the family life cycle stages as outlined in this chapter. Include especially (a) couples without children, (b) families broken by death, divorce, or separation, (c) remarriage of husband, wife, or both, (d) families with stepchildren, (e) unmarried parents, (f) others. Describe one such family as you have listed and indicate its possible placement in the family life cycle. Give your reasons for assigning it to the stage to which you feel it belongs.

3. Plot your expected life line following the profile for American man or woman in charts 5–1 and 5–2, using data to date with projections into the future.

4. Prepare a biography of your family up through the present time by stages of its development as far back as you can recall or gather from what older members of the family have told you. Include the most important events your family has experienced during the past year, with some indication of how the various situations were handled. Finally, anticipate the problems and opportunities facing your family in the immediate future. Keep this paper for review at the end of the course.

5. List the names of ten men and women of various ages, known to you, and opposite each indicate the stage of the family life cycle in which he or she now is. Give data documenting each designation.

6. Write a paper on woman's education today, taking into account the competencies she will need during her career as a woman, a wife, a mother, and in the many other social roles she must face during her lifetime.

7. Discuss the implications of the family life cycle for courses in marriage and family in high schools, colleges, and in adult education.

8. Review in terms of family life cycle insights *The Fourposter*, by Jan de Hartog (a three-act play, Random House, 1951), and/or Thornton Wilder's one-act play *The Long Christmas Dinner*.

9. Prepare a paper on the implications of family life cycle orientation for modern-day professional work with families in various areas of life. Document from a variety of journals and other professional sources.

10. Develop a critique of the various methods of dividing the family life cycle into stages for the purposes of research, service, and teaching, indicating the strengths and weaknesses of each.

11. Discuss the prevalence of intergenerational assistance in terms of its implications for family continuity, personal independence, welfare programs, and other related aspects of the family in society.

12. Draft a pictorial schema of the generation spiral that represents the ways in which family life cycles spin off into one generation after another, as suggested in the schematic presentation in chart 5–6.

13. Arrange for a presentation and discussion of the play *Ring around the Family* (available from the Family Life Education Division, American Social Health Association, 1740 Broadway, New York, New York 10019, thirty minutes, 1970).

READINGS

Aldous, Joan. "The Consequences of Intergenerational Continuity." *Journal of Marriage and the Family* 27, no. 4 (November 1965): 462–468.

Aldous, Joan, and Reuben Hill. "Social Cohesion, Lineage Type, and Intergenerational Transmission." *Social Forces* 43, no. 4 (May 1965): 471–482.

Cavan, Ruth Shonle. *The American Family*. 4th ed. New York: Thomas Y. Crowell Company, 1969. Pt. 3, "The Cycle of Family Life," pp. 231–512.

Cavan, Ruth Shonle, ed. *Marriage and Family in the Modern World: A Book of Readings*. 3d ed. New York: Thomas Y. Crowell Company, 1969. Chap. 13, "Nuclear Family and Kinship Web," pp. 353–369.

Clark, Lincoln H., ed. *Consumer Behavior*, vol. 2, *The Life Cycle and Consumer Behavior*. New York: New York University Press, 1955.

Dublin, Louis I. *Factbook on Man from Birth to Death*. New York: Macmillan Company, 1965.

Glick, Paul C. *American Families*. New York: John Wiley and Sons, 1957.

Hardy, James M. *Focus on the Family.* New York: Association Press, 1966.

Hill, Reuben. *Family Development in Three Generations.* Cambridge, Mass.: Schenkman Publishing Company, 1970. Chap. 3, "Interdependence among the Generations."

Kenkel, William F. *The Family in Perspective.* New York: Appleton-Century-Crofts, 1960. Chap. 14, "Basic Concepts: The Family Life Cycle and Developmental Tasks."

Kirkpatrick, Clifford. *The Family as Process and Institution.* 2d ed. New York: Ronald Press Company, 1963. Pt. 3, "Life Cycle of Family Experience," pp. 175–535.

Lansing, John B., and Leslie Kish. "Family Life Cycle as an Independent Variable." *American Sociological Review* 22, no. 5 (October 1957): 512–519.

Lidz, Theodore. *The Person: His Development throughout the Life Cycle.* New York: Basic Books, 1968. Pt. 2, "The Life Cycle," pp. 93–506.

Milne, Lorus J., and Margery Milne. *The Ages of Life.* New York: Harcourt, Brace and World, 1968.

Parke, Robert, Jr., and Paul C. Glick. "Prospective Changes in Marriage and the Family." *Journal of Marriage and the Family* 29, no. 2 (May 1967): 249–256.

Rodgers, Roy H. *Improvements in the Construction and Analysis of Family Life Cycle Categories.* Kalamazoo, Mich.: Western Michigan University, 1962.

Shanas, Ethel, and Gordon F. Streib, eds. *Social Structure and the Family: Generational Relations.* Englewood Cliffs, N.J.: Prentice-Hall, 1965.

Toman, Walter. *Family Constellation.* New York: Springer Publishing Company, 1961.

Wattenberg, Ben J., and Richard M. Scammon. *This U.S.A.* Garden City, N.Y.: Doubleday and Company, 1965.

6 DEVELOPMENTAL TASKS OF FAMILIES AND THEIR MEMBERS

The proper study of mankind is man.   Alexander Pope

Growth is the only evidence of life.   John Henry, Cardinal Newman

Families develop through the family life cycle within the generation spiral in ways that are predictable. Within the family unit, individuals grow and develop throughout their lives according to universal patterns that can be traced in every family member. Human growth and development proceed according to known principles that hold for all persons. Each individual grows in his own way and at his own rate, within a developmental process followed by all. These patterns and principles of human development provide a foundation for understanding how families and their members undertake their developmental tasks.

development have been largely products of the twentieth century. Longitudinal studies of many groups of infants and children through adolescence and adulthood have yielded data on patterns of development that all individuals follow, as well as knowledge of individual differences at each stage of growth. Studies of childhood, of adolescence, and of young, middle-aged, and aging adults have accumulated profiles of human development throughout the lifespan. Observations of trained clinicians combine with statistical evidence to provide a remarkably consistent profile of human development from conception to the end of life.

THE NATURE OF HUMAN GROWTH AND DEVELOPMENT

Theory, research, and clinical contributions to knowledge of human growth and

Freud's Schema of Child Development

Freud mapped the course of child development out of his recognition of the effect of early experience upon an individual's later attitudes. He identified the first six stages of human development as: (1) *oral stage,* dominant during the first year, when the infant depends upon feeding for his physical survival and emotional well-being; (2) *anal stage,* during which the toddler is expected to conform to adult expectations that center in his bowel and bladder training; (3) *phallic stage,* when the preschooler becomes impressed with power in himself and with his body; (4) *oedipal stage,* during the early school years when the boy renounces his earlier tie to his mother and identifies with his father, while the girl becomes more feminine through her identification with her mother; (5) *latency stage,* which follows the resolution of the oedipal conflict, as a period characterized by reality orientation; and (6) *adolescence,* that begins with genital maturation and is completed with heterosexual maturity and the ability to give and to receive love.

Erikson's Eight Stages in the Life Cycle of Man[1]

Erik Erikson has identified eight stages of life as critical in human psychosocial development. He points to the struggle between the negatives and positives in each crisis that must be resolved if the next developmental stage is to be reached. He emphasizes that no victory is completely or forever won as an individual goes from stage to stage in his psychosocial development.[2]

1. *Infancy: trust versus mistrust.* The first "task" of the infant is to develop "the cornerstone of a healthy personality," a basic sense of trust—in himself and in his environment. This comes from a feeling of inner goodness derived from "the mutual regulation of his receptive capacities with the maternal techniques of provision"—a quality of care that transmits a sense of trustworthiness and meaning. The danger, most acute in the second half of the first year, is that discontinuities in care may increase a natural sense of loss, as the child gradually recognizes his separateness from his mother, to a basic sense of mistrust that may last through life.

2. *Early childhood: autonomy versus shame and doubt.* With muscular maturation the child experiments with holding on and letting go and begins to attach enormous value to his autonomous will. The danger here is the development of a deep sense of shame and doubt if he is deprived of the opportunity to learn to develop his will as he learns his "duty," and therefore learns to expect defeat in any battle of wills with those who are bigger and stronger.

---

[1] From "Youth and the Life Cycle," an interview with Erik H. Erikson by Kathryn Close, March-April 1960 issue of *Children,* interprofessional journal published by the Chidren's Bureau, Department of Health, Education, and Welfare.

[2] For detailed treatment see Erik H. Erikson, "Growth and Crises of the 'Healthy Personality,'" in *Problems of Infancy and Childhood,* supp. 2 of Milton J. E. Senn, ed., *Symposium on the Healthy Personality* (New York: Josiah Macy, Jr., Foundation, 1950); and Erik H. Erikson, *Childhood and Society* (New York: W. W. Norton and Company, 1950).

3. *Play age: initiative versus guilt.* In this stage the child's imagination is greatly expanded because of his increased ability to move around freely and to communicate. It is an age of intrusive activity, avid curiosity, and consuming fantasies which lead to feelings of guilt and anxiety. It is also the stage of the establishment of conscience. If this tendency to feel guilty is "overburdened by all-too-eager adults," the child may develop a deep-seated conviction that he is essentially bad, with a resultant stifling of initiative or a conversion of his moralism to vindictiveness.

4. *School age: industry versus inferiority.* The long period of sexual latency before puberty is the age when the child wants to learn how to do and make things with others. In learning to accept instruction and to win recognition by producing "things," he opens the way for the capacity of work enjoyment. The danger in this period is the development of a sense of inadequacy and inferiority in a child who does not receive recognition for his efforts.

5. *Adolescence: identity versus identity diffusion.* The physiological revolution that comes with puberty—rapid body growth and sexual maturity—forces the young person to question "all sameness and continuities relied on earlier" and to "refight many of the earlier battles." The developmental task is to integrate childhood identifications "with the basic biological drives, native endowment, and the opportunities offered in social roles." The danger is that identity diffusion, temporarily unavoidable in this period of physical and psychological up-heaval, may result in a permanent inability to "take hold," or, because of youth's tendency to total commitment, in the fixation in the young person of a negative identity, a devoted attempt to become what parents, class, or community do not want him to be.

6. *Young adulthood: intimacy versus isolation.* Only as a young person begins to feel more secure in his identity is he able to establish intimacy with himself (with his inner life) and with others, both in friendships and eventually in a love-based mutually satisfying sexual relationship with a member of the opposite sex. A person who cannot enter wholly into an intimate relationship because of the fear of losing his identity may develop a sense of isolation.

7. *Adulthood: generativity versus self-absorption.* Out of the intimacies of adulthood grows generativity—the mature person's interest in establishing and guiding the next generation. The lack of this results in self-absorption and frequently in a "pervading sense of stagnation and interpersonal impoverishment."

8. *Senescence: integrity versus disgust.* The person who has achieved a satisfying intimacy with other human beings and who has adapted to the triumphs and disappointments of his generative activities as parent and co-worker reaches the end of life with a certain ego integrity—an acceptance of his own responsibility for what his life is and was and of its place in the flow of history. Without this "accrued ego integration" there is despair, usually marked by a display of displeasure and disgust.

Piaget's Conception of Cognition-Development[3]

Piaget's work on the foundations of cognition during the first of life puts renewed emphasis on early human development and experience. He sees a definite order in which behavior and thought make their appearance out of a child's interaction with his environment. The infant is born with reflexes and built-in complexes of the senses, nerves, and muscles that the baby exercises and learns to use during his early sucking practice in the first month of life; that Piaget sees as "exercising ready-made sensormotor schemata." Sometime after the baby's first month, he varies and combines his nursing behavior as he looks while he sucks, or turns his head toward moving objects in what Piaget calls "primary circular reactions." Next come "secondary circular reactions," when the infant initiates and anticipates others' behavior and reaches out to them. This is close to what Erikson refers to as the basis of trust. Near the end of the first year the infant imitates, plays games, and becomes a social being who recognizes that what he does brings about some expected consequence, in what Piaget calls "coordination of secondary schemata." Between the first and second years of life, the toddler is curious, "into everything," craving more and more environmental stimulation in "tertiary circular reactions." Between eighteen and twenty-four months vocabulary spirals, and the infant changes into a child who operates more by symbols, remembers where things are and looks for them, and delights in problem-solving in the stage Piaget sees as "internalization of sensormotor schemata."

Between eighteen months and four years, during the child's "preconceptual phase," he accumulates images and forms "intuitions." By nine or ten a child is able to order objects serially by length, later by weight, and at eleven or twelve by volume, in "concrete operations." The third period, beginning at eleven or twelve, is a landmark in that the individual now can deal with propositions as well as concrete objects. This leads to the "formal operations" that provide the intellectual ability for the scientific method.

Bloom's Review of Longitudinal Studies

Benjamin S. Bloom has analyzed 1,000 longitudinal studies of individuals repeatedly measured and observed at different points in their development. He found the results of many studies in enough agreement to enable him to describe development quantitatively for thirty human characteristics.

---

[3] J. McV. Hunt, *Intelligence and Experience* (New York: Ronald Press Company, 1961), gives an especially lucid interpretation of Piaget's work; see also Jean Piaget and Bärbel Inhelder, *The Psychology of the Child* (New York: Basic Books, 1969).

Seven of these (listed in table 6–1) have reached 50 percent of their mature state by predictable ages: height by age two and one-half, general intelligence by four, aggressiveness in males by three, dependency in females by four, general school achievement by the third grade, and reading comprehension and vocabulary by age nine.[4]

Thurstone's work,[5] reviewed by Bloom, found 80 percent of adult performance in children and adolescents in a number of characteristics: perceptual speed by age twelve, space and reasoning factors by fourteen, number and memory factors by age sixteen, verbal comprehension by eighteen, and word fluency that reaches the 80 percent level by twenty. Longitudinal studies of college students[6] find ego development reaching 80 percent levels by age eighteen and flattening out in a plateau by twenty-five.

Critical Periods in Human Development

Critical periods in human development occur when specific organs or other aspects of an individual's growth undergo most rapid change. It is during a period of most rapid growth that a characteristic is most greatly affected by environmental factors. For instance, pregnant women who took thalidomide, or who contracted German measles during the first three months of pregnancy, bore infants whose defects (if observable) were in those parts of the body undergoing most rapid development at the time of the drug or viral attack.

Physical organs of the embryo emerge according to a precise schedule that is important for their full normal development, and for their articulation into the rest of the organism. In this sequence of development each organ has its time of origin. This time factor is as important as the place of origin. If the eye, for example, does not arise at the appointed time, "it will never be able to express itself fully, since the moment for the rapid outgrowth of some other part will have arrived, and this will tend to dominate the less active region and suppress the belated tendency for eye expression. . . ."

The organ which misses its time of ascendancy is not only doomed as an entity; it endangers at the same time the whole hierarchy of organs. "Not only does the arrest of a rapidly budding part, therefore, tend to suppress its development temporarily, but the premature loss of supremacy to some other organ renders it impossible for the suppressed part to come again into dominance so that it is permanently modified. . . ." The result of normal development

[4] Benjamin S. Bloom, *Stability and Change in Human Characteristics* (New York: John Wiley and Sons, 1964), chaps. 2–4, 7.

[5] L. I. Thurstone, *The Differential Growth of Mental Abilities* (Chapel Hill, N.C.: University of North Carolina Psychometric Laboratory, 1955).

[6] Nevitt Sanford, ed., *The American College* (New York: John Wiley and Sons, 1962).

Table 6–1. *Critical Periods in Human Development (Theory and Research)*

Age	Period	Freud	Erikson	Piaget	Bloom	Thurstone and others
23	Parenthood		Generativity			
22						
21	Marriage Adulthood		Intimacy			
20						Word fluency
19						
18						Verbal comprehension Ego development
17						
16						Number and memory factors
15	Adolescence		Identity	Formal operations		
14						Space and reasoning factors
13	Teenage					
12						Perceptual speed
11						
10						
9			Industry	Concrete operations	Reading comprehension	
8					Vocabulary General school achievement	Intelligence
7		Latency				
6	School-age					
5		Oedipal	Initiative	Preoperational: Intuitive		
4		Phallic	Imagination	Preconceptual	Dependency General intelligence	
3	Preschool	Anal		Sensorimotor Means—end behavior	Aggression in boys	
2			Autonomy	Internalization	Height	
1	Infancy	Oral	Trust	Circular reactions		
0	Birth			Reflexes		

Sources with approximate ages from Freud, Erikson, Piaget, Bloom, Thurstone, Sanford, works cited above.

is proper relationship of size and function among the body organs: the liver adjusted in size to the stomach and intestine, the heart and lungs properly balanced, and the capacity of the vascular system accurately proportioned to the body as a whole. Through developmental arrest one or more organs may become disproportionally small; this upsets functional harmony and produces a defective person.[7]

Theory and research into many facets of human development find critical periods at which a given characteristic or ability emerges. New development arises out of foundations already present. Growth is sequential, as each new aspect of development emerges from previously established structure or skills.

Research findings underline Freudian and Eriksonian observations of the critical importance of the earliest months of life as the infant learns to nurse and develops a sense of trust—in himself, his mother, and his world. Piaget points to the critical significance of the first weeks and months in the development of intelligence and the ability to learn. Hundreds of studies have traced the development of many human characteristics in ways that point up the significance of critical periods for the successful emergence of physical, intellectual, and personality factors. Some of these are indicated in table 6–1, at ages approximated by Freud, Erikson, Piaget, Bloom, Thurstone, and others.

Patterns and Principles of Development

Human growth, development, and decline involve a number of types of change, twelve of which are listed in table 6–2.

Each individual is unique in both inherited and environmentally learned aspects, but there is a universally recognizable pattern of development throughout the life-span. Human growth and development occur according to a number of principles, listed in table 6–3.

DEVELOPMENTAL TASKS OF INDIVIDUALS

Developmental tasks are defined as tasks that arise at or about a certain time in the life of an individual, successful achievement of which leads to his happiness and to his success with later tasks, while failure leads to unhappiness in the individual, disapproval by society, and difficulty with later tasks.[8] These growth responsibilities are

---

[7] Erikson, *Childhood and Society*, pp. 61–62; and C. H. Stockard, *The Physical Basis of Personality* (New York: W. W. Norton and Company, 1931).

[8] Robert J. Havighurst, *Human Development and Education* (New York: Longmans, Green and Company, 1953), p. 2.

Table 6–2. *Twelve Types of Change in Human Growth, Development, and Decline*

1. Changes in specificity (embryonic growth and development proceeds from simple cells to specific, functioning organ systems)

2. Changes in efficiency (digestive system is more efficient in childhood than in either infancy or aging)

3. Changes in kind (adult hair differs from baby down and also from thin, drying, aging hair)

4. Changes in color (skin and hair darkens through childhood; hair loses color, and skin darkens in later years)

5. Changes in number (teeth change from none visible at birth to fifty, more or less, in the preschooler; then school child gets permanent teeth, which may be lost over the years)

6. Changes in size (organs and stature become larger through the first twenty years; some shrinking of body size is to be expected in later years)

7. Changes in shape (profile of the body differs in infancy, childhood, adolescence, and adulthood in ways that are predictable)

8. Changes in texture (bones are soft in infancy; harden in childhood; and become brittle in aging)

9. Changes in flexibility (infant and child's body is elastic and flexible; adult muscles and joints stiffen through the years)

10. Changes in control (infant has little control; adult enjoys full control; aged lose some ability to control physical processes)

11. Changes in teachability (child learns many skills readily; adults with more difficulty)

12. Changes in physical satisfaction (infant, child, and adolescent enjoy physical activities; older adult finds less satisfaction in declining powers)

Model freely adapted and expanded from Boyd R. McCandless, *Children: Behavior and Development* (New York: Holt, Rinehart and Winston, 1967), p. 412.

jobs to be done by an individual as he develops. As his physical growth proceeds from one stage of development to the next, the individual must learn to use his new-found powers; i.e., the infant progressively learns to suck, to drink, to swallow soft foods, and eventually to chew and eat at the family table. Teething occurs automatically in time; learning to eat solid foods and to hold a spoon are developmental tasks of early childhood.

Developmental tasks arise at critical periods in an individual's growth, when others expect specific performance of him. A child is expected to learn to read when he goes to school; when he does, he and others (teachers, parents, and other kinfolk) are happy about his progress, and he goes on to more complex abilities in school and elsewhere. Should he find reading difficult to the point of failure, for any of a number of reasons, his school progress is slowed; he is unhappy about himself, and he faces others' disapproval.

Table 6–3. *Principles Inherent in Development*

1. Development results from both biological maturation and individual learning.

2. Development of human characteristics tends to be orderly, regular, and predictable.

3. Growth rates vary within the different stages of individual development.

4. Each individual grows at a pace appropriate for him, at his stage of development, in his environment.

5. Development tends to be sequential, with each added increment built upon earlier ones.

6. Development of specific characteristics is based upon previous progress in similar or associated forms.

7. Growth and development are most rapid during the early stages of life.

8. The first months and years are crucial foundations for later development.

9. Early verbal learning is essential for the development of later complex human skills.

10. Socially prescribed expectations order the major events of a lifetime in a given society.

11. Norms for given ages and stages function as social prods or brakes on behavior.

12. Development proceeds in a specific direction, from a known beginning to an expected end.

13. Anticipated end points in development serve as personal goals for individuals.

14. Personal goals are both individually and socially determined.

15. Attainment of personal goals brings a sense of fulfillment and success.

16. Developing individuals face certain responsibilities for maturing and achieving at every stage of life.

17. Individuals may be expected to be at work on developmental tasks appropriate to their stage of development.

18. Developmental tasks successfully accomplished lead to further developmental levels.

19. No one else can accomplish the developmental tasks an individual faces.

20. Few developmental tasks are completed in isolation; most depend upon social interaction.

21. Helping persons (parents, teachers, etc.) can be of great help to a child at work on one or more of his developmental tasks.

22. Modification of environment has least effect on characteristics at their periods of least development.

23. Rates of growth and development may be modified most at times of most rapid change.

24. Assistance in development is most effective at times of fastest growth and readiness.

For further documentation and detail see: Benjamin S. Bloom, *Stability and Change in Human Characteristics* (New York: John Wiley and Sons, 1964); Charlotte Buhler, "Social Roles and the Life Cycle," American Sociological Association address, Washington, D.C., 1962; Bernice L. Neugarten, "Continuities and Discontinuities of Psychological Issues into Adult Life," address presented at the American Psychological Association Annual Convention, San Francisco, August 31, 1968, mimeographed; Elizabeth Lee Vincent and Phyllis C. Martin, *Human Psychological Development* (New York: Ronald Press Company, 1961), pp. 19–25; earlier editions of Robert J. Havighurst, *Human Development and Education* (New York: Longmans, Green and Company, 1953); and Evelyn Millis Duvall, *Family Development*, 3d ed. (Philadelphia: J. B. Lippincott Company, 1967), p. 42.

Origins of Developmental Tasks

Developmental tasks have two primary origins: (1) physical maturation, and (2) cultural pressures and privileges. A secondary origin derived from the first two is found in the aspirations and values of the individual.

As the individual grows, he matures. Growth is much more than just added stature and bulk. It involves the elaboration and maturation of muscle, organ, bone, and neural systems of the organism that develop according to a predictable sequence within the individual. Certain developmental tasks come primarily from the maturation of one or more aspects of the organism. Examples are many. As the infant's leg and back muscles develop strength enough, and the neural connections mature to the place where the child has conscious control over their movement, he faces the developmental task of learning to walk. When the adolescent girl's body develops into one resembling that of a woman and she begins to menstruate, she must come to terms with her femaleness and develop a wholesome acceptance of herself as a woman. Later, when she becomes middle-aged, menopause is a reality that must be met with the new developmental task of accepting the termination of her reproductive life and facing the challenge of aging. And so it is with many other developmental tasks throughout the life of both men and women.

Cultural pressures are seen in the many rewards and penalties the individual receives (and anticipates) for his various behaviors. Society, in the form of peers, associates, parents, teachers, and all "the significant others" of his life, expects and often puts pressures upon the person to conform to the prescribed ways of behaving within that culture. These expectations and pressures emerge at the times believed appropriate in the culture for the individual to function in the roles and statuses assigned to him. Unfortunately they may be too soon or too late for an individual.

By the time a child reaches a certain age, he is expected to eat solid foods, at another age to be toilet trained, at another to walk, at another age to talk, at another to respect property rights, at another to mingle socially with members of the other sex, at another to marry and "settle down," and so on through his entire life-span. Regardless of what they are and when they come into effect, these expectancies exert pressures upon the individuals of the culture to behave in certain ways and so are an important origin of his developmental tasks. Examples in our society are: learning to read, learning to handle money responsibly, learning how to gain a place for oneself with one's age-mates, and establishing oneself as an acceptable member of a dating crowd as a teenager and among the young married set as a husband or wife.

Developmental tasks differ from culture to culture. Each cultural group has its own developmental definitions and expectations.

They also vary from region to region in our country, even from class to class in the same area, resulting in many persistent problems among children of different ethnic and cultural backgrounds.

Encouragement and support by family and friends are often essential in achieving developmental tasks that the individual alone might find too difficult. As cultural pressures play upon the maturing organism, the emergent personality is formed, with all of its idiosyncratic values and aspirations, which themselves then influence greatly the direction and form of future developmental tasks. Two examples of developmental tasks derived primarily from the personal aspirations and values of the individual are choosing a vocation and achieving a personal philosophy of life, both of which are always responsive to the life around the person.

Basically, a developmental task is a thrust from within the individual to develop in such a way as to narrow the discrepancy between his present behavior and what he might achieve. The push to change usually comes from inside the person but may be evoked by others' demands and expectations. It receives its direction from the cultural definition of what is expected of such an individual at his stage of development. A developmental task, while culturally defined, is neither a chore nor a duty, in the sense that it is externally imposed. It is rather a growth responsibility the individual assumes for his own development as he relates himself to his life situation.

MAGNUM—PHOTO BY CORNELL CAPA

The child who is loved and knows it has the inner security needed to keep working on his or her developmental tasks.

The individual's assumption of a given developmental task consists of at least four interrelated operations: (1) perceiving new possibilities for his behavior in what is expected of him or in what he sees others, more mature than he, accomplishing, (2) forming new conceptions of himself (identity formation), (3) coping effectively with conflicting demands upon him, and (4) wanting to achieve the next step in his development enough to work toward it (motivation). To illustrate: a small boy sees somewhat bigger boys riding their bicycles (operation 1—perception); he conceives of himself as a potential bicycle rider (operation 2—identity formation); he resolves the conflicts between his mother's protests that he might get hurt and his own fears of failure with the expectancies of his peers, and the demands of his father that he become "a big boy" (operation 3—coping with conflicting demands); and finally, he wants to learn to ride a bike enough to practice what it takes to become proficient in it (operation 4—motivation).

Most of the growth responsibilities the individual is faced with result from the combined impact of his biologic maturing, the environmental forces that play upon him, and his own personal drives, ambitions, and value orientation. Thus, being weaned results from his physiological maturation (teething, etc.), as well as from the cultural pressures in the form of maternal insistence that he take solid foods and his own desire to be a "big boy" and eat as the others in the family do. Teenage dating emerges partly from the biologic maturing of puberty, partly from the cultural pressures of friends and family to have a girl or boyfriend and go out to young people's activities in the community, and partly from the person's own aspiration to belong, to be accepted, to be a recognized member of the younger set in the neighborhood.

The Teachable Moment

When the time comes that the body is ripe for, culture is pressing for, and the individ-

ual is striving for some achievement, the teachable moment has arrived. It is at the convergence of the several origins of the developmental task that its accomplishment is most highly motivated; at that time the individual is most truly *ready for* the next step in his development. Before that the person is not mature enough for the desired outcome, and so efforts to push him through a premature accomplishment may be largely wasted. Readiness also implies that the person has lived fully at his present stage and so is not being hurried into the next stage.

An illustration is found in the early efforts to toilet train an infant. In the 1920s and 1930s, this training was often attempted while the baby was but a few weeks old. At that age, his sphincters were not ready for such control; his neural connections were not matured enough to make possible his cooperation; and his own aspirations were in quite another direction. It is not surprising to find that these precocious demands of the parent upon the child met with failure and often created persistent conflict. Knowledge of child development has modified these expectancies, and today good practice is to wait for signs that the baby is ready for toilet training before assisting him to achieve the task. This concept of readiness is well established in the field of human development.

The concept of the teachable moment goes a bit deeper in indicating specifically the three dimensions in which readiness emerges—in the physical organism, in the social pressures, and in the personal values of the individual. It has importance for anyone responsible for the growth, development, and guidance of others: teachers, supervisors, parents, indeed anyone who works with, or cares about, other people. For it gives a gauge of what we expect of given persons and at what time we may anticipate change. This ability to predict what persons at various stages of development are, or soon will be, ready for is of paramount importance to curriculum formulators and educators in general. If we assume that the general purpose of both family life and education is to assist the individual to grow up to his own best potential, we see that some knowledge of developmental tasks and especially of the teachable moments at which these tasks arise is highly relevant.

> *There is a tide in the affairs of men,*
> *Which, taken at the flood, leads on to*
> *   fortune;*
> *Omitted, all the voyage of their life*
> *Is bound in shallows and in miseries.*

> Shakespeare,
> *Julius Caesar,* IV, 3.

Developmental Tasks of the Individual through His Life

The developmental tasks an individual faces through the years of his life from birth to death are innumerable. It would be impossible to completely list all of the growth responsibilities to be achieved by any one person. Yet, there are certain general categories of tasks that make possible a cataloging of the more common developmental tasks within our culture. Such a formulation is found in table 6–4.

Such a listing of the individual's developmental tasks is not all-inclusive, nor is it universally applicable. Different cultures and subcultures make different demands upon their members. In most of the cultures of the world today, the general expectancies change from time to time, so that the developmental tasks of one generation differ somewhat from those of the preceding or of the succeeding one.

Whatever the society in which the individual grows up, he faces the developmental tasks peculiar to it at every stage of his life-span. The successful achievement of his developmental tasks brings the individual from a state of helpless dependence as an infant, through varying dimensions of independence as an adolescent, to a mature level of interdependence with his fellow-man that lasts through the greater part of adulthood.

Interacting Developmental Tasks of Family Members

This progression is not regular and all-of-a-piece. At any moment, children are striving to meet their growth needs, parents to reconcile conflicting demands, and each individual to find himself within the security and threats of his world.

Table 6–4. *Developmental Tasks in Ten Categories of Behavior of the Individual from Birth to Death*

	Infancy (birth to 1 or 2)	Early childhood (2–3 to 5–6–7)	Late childhood (5–6–7 to pubescence)
I Achieving an appropriate dependence-independence pattern	1. Establishing oneself as a very dependent being 2. Beginning the establishment of self-awareness	1. Adjusting to less private attention; becoming independent physically (while remaining strongly dependent emotionally)	1. Freeing oneself from primary identification with adults
II Achieving an appropriate giving-receiving pattern of affection	1. Developing a feeling for affection	1. Developing the ability to give affection 2. Learning to share affection	1. Learning to give as much love as one receives; forming friendships with peers
III Relating to changing social groups	1. Becoming aware of the alive as against the inanimate, and the familiar as against the unfamiliar 2. Developing rudimentary social interaction	1. Beginning to develop the ability to interact with age-mates 2. Adjusting in the family to expectations it has for the child as a member of the social unit	1. Clarifying the adult world as over against the child's world 2. Establishing peer groupness and learning to belong
IV Developing a conscience	1. Beginning to adjust to the expectations of others	1. Developing the ability to take directions and to be obedient in the presence of authority 2. Developing the ability to be obedient in the absence of authority where conscience substitutes for authority	1. Learning more rules and developing true morality
V Learning one's psycho-socio-biological sex role		1. Learning to identify with male adult and female adult roles	1. Beginning to identify with one's social contemporaries of the same sex
VI Accepting and adjusting to a changing body	1. Adjusting to adult feeding demands 2. Adjusting to adult cleanliness demands 3. Adjusting to adult attitudes toward genital manipulation	1. Adjusting to expectations resulting from one's improving muscular abilities 2. Developing sex modesty	
VII Managing a changing body and learning new motor patterns	1. Developing physiological equilibrium 2. Developing eye-hand coordination 3. Establishing satisfactory rhythms of rest and activity	1. Developing large muscle control 2. Learning to coordinate large muscles and small muscles	1. Refining and elaborating skill in the use of small muscles
VIII Learning to understand and control the physical world	1. Exploring the physical world	1. Meeting adult expectations for restrictive exploration and manipulation of an expanding environment	1. Learning more realistic ways of studying and controlling the physical world
IX Developing an appropriate symbol system and conceptual abilities	1. Developing preverbal communication 2. Developing verbal communication 3. Rudimentary concept formation	1. Improving one's use of the symbol system 2. Enormous elaboration of the concept pattern	1. Learning to use language actually to exchange ideas or to influence one's hearers 2. Beginning understanding of real causal relations 3. Making finer conceptual distinctions and thinking reflectively
X Relating oneself to the cosmos		1. Developing a genuine, though uncritical, notion about one's place in the cosmos	1. Developing a scientific approach

Early adolescence (pubescence to puberty)	Late adolescence (puberty to early maturity)	Maturity (early to late active adulthood)	Aging (beyond full powers of adulthood through senility)
1. Establishing one's independence from adults in all areas of behavior	1. Establishing oneself as an independent individual in an adult manner	1. Learning to be interdependent—now leaning, now succoring others, as need arises 2. Assisting one's children to become gradually independent and autonomous beings	1. Accepting graciously and comfortably the help needed from others as powers fail and dependence becomes necessary
1. Accepting oneself as a worthwhile person really worthy of love	1. Building a strong mutual affectional bond with a (possible) marriage partner	1. Building and maintaining a strong and mutually satisfying marriage relationship 2. Establishing wholesome affectional bonds with one's children and grandchildren 3. Meeting wisely the new needs for affection of one's own aging parents 4. Cultivating meaningfully warm friendships with members of one's own generation	1. Facing loss of one's spouse, and finding some satisfactory sources of affection previously received from mate 2. Learning new affectional roles with own children, now mature adults 3. Establishing ongoing, satisfying affectional patterns with grandchildren and other members of the extended family 4. Finding and preserving mutually satisfying friendships outside the family circle
1. Behaving according to a shifting peer code	1. Adopting an adult-patterned set of social values by learning a new peer code	1. Keeping in reasonable balance activities in the various social, service, political, and community groups and causes that make demands upon adults 2. Establishing and maintaining mutually satisfactory relationships with the in-law families of spouse and married children	1. Choosing and maintaining ongoing social activities and functions appropriate to health, energy, and interests
	1. Learning to verbalize contradictions in moral codes, as well as discrepancies between principle and practice, and resolving these problems in a responsible manner	1. Coming to terms with the violations of moral codes in the larger as well as in the more intimate social scene, and developing some constructive philosophy and method of operation. 2. Helping children to adjust to the expectations of others and to conform to the moral demands of the culture	1. Maintaining a sense of moral integrity in the face of disappointments and disillusionments in life's hopes and dreams
1. Strong identification with one's own sex mates 2. Learning one's role in heterosexual relationships	1. Exploring possibilities for a future mate and acquiring "desirability" 2. Choosing an occupation 3. Preparing to accept one's future role in manhood or womanhood as a responsible citizen of the larger community	1. Learning to be a competent husband or wife, and building a good marriage 2. Carrying a socially adequate role as citizen and worker in the community 3. Becoming a good parent and grandparent as children arrive and develop	1. Learning to live on a retirement income 2. Being a good companion to an aging spouse 3. Meeting bereavement of spouse adequately
1. Reorganizing one's thoughts and feelings about oneself in the face of significant bodily changes and their concomitants 2. Accepting the reality of one's appearance	1. Learning appropriate outlets for sexual drives	1. Making a good sex adjustment within marriage 2. Establishing healthful routines of eating, resting, working, playing within the pressures of the adult world	1. Making a good adjustment to failing powers as aging diminishes strengths and abilities
1. Controlling and using a "new" body		1. Learning the new motor skills involved in housekeeping, gardening, sports, and other activities expected of adults in the community	1. Adapting interests and activities to reserves of vitality and energy of the aging body
		1. Gaining intelligent understanding of new horizons of medicine and science sufficient for personal well-being and social competence	1. Mastering new awareness and methods of dealing with physical surroundings as an individual with occasional or permanent disabilities
1. Using language to express and to clarify more complex concepts 2. Moving from the concrete to the abstract and applying general principles to the particular	1. Achieving the level of reasoning of which one is capable	1. Mastering technical symbol systems involved in income tax, social security, complex financial dealings, and other contexts familiar to Western man	1. Keeping mentally alert and effective as long as is possible through the later years
	1. Formulating a workable belief and value system	1. Formulating and implementing a rational philosophy of life on the basis of adult experience 2. Cultivating a satisfactory religious climate in the home as the spiritual soil for development of family members	1. Preparing for eventual and inevitable cessation of life by building a set of beliefs that one can live and die with in peace

Source: An elaboration of Caroline Tryon and Jesse W. Lilienthal III, "Guideposts in Child Growth and Development," *NEA Journal*, March 1950, p. 189.

At times members of the family mutually support and sustain one another. During certain stages of the family life cycle, the developmental tasks of both children and parents call for the same general direction of energies, so that the family moves as a unit toward the meeting of the developmental requirements of each member. Such a time comes when the children are established in school and daily bring home to their parents the stimuli and broadened horizons that both mother and father are striving for as mature adults at the school-age stage of the family life cycle.

Just as "naturally," upon occasion, the goals, needs, striving, and developmental tasks of family members are in conflict. If we hold the entire family in focus, we see that many of the normal tangles of members during the family's life cycle are due to incompatibility of the diverse developmental strivings of family members at critical points of growth.

From time to time the developmental tasks of the husband may conflict with those of his wife. A simple illustration is found in the young husband's developmental task of developing competency with his do-it-yourself projects that clutter up the house at the time when his wife is trying to maintain a pleasant, attractive home amid the already heavy demands of infants and small children.

Developmental tasks of children conflict with those of their parents at several stages in the family life cycle. In adolescence the young person is struggling to emancipate himself or herself from the authority of the parents, whose own developmental tasks as parents call for sustained guidance and supervision of the not-yet-adult child. At such a time, storms brew and break within the family as normally as they do in the weather, when two or more energy systems moving in opposite directions collide.

Now unified, now atomized, each family lives out its own unique history in pulsing, throbbing rhythms and ever-changing tempos. Each family is an arena of interacting personalities, each trying to achieve his own developmental tasks within the pattern of family life that in turn is evolving in interaction with the larger society of which it is a part.

FAMILY DEVELOPMENTAL TASKS

As a social group, a family must come to terms with certain basic conditions, called *functional prerequisites*,[9] essential for its survival, continuity, and growth. The *basic tasks* of American families may be listed as:[10]

---

[9] Talcott Parsons, *Essays in Sociological Theory, Pure and Applied* (Glencoe, Ill.: Free Press, 1949), pp. viii, 6–7, 42–51.

[10] Adapted from course outlines in family development developed by Carlfred Broderick, Pennsylvania State University; Reuben Hill, University of Minnesota; and Roy Rodgers, Western Michigan University and University of Oregon.

1. Physical maintenance—providing shelter, food, clothing, health care, etc.

2. Allocation of resources—meeting family needs and costs, apportioning material goods, facilities, space, authority, respect, affection, etc.

3. Division of labor—deciding who does what, assigning responsibility for procuring income, managing the household, caring for family members, and other specific tasks

4. Socialization of family members—guiding the internalization of increasingly mature and acceptable patterns of controlling elimination, food intake, sexual drives, sleep, aggression, etc.

5. Reproduction, recruitment, and release of family members—bearing or adopting children and rearing them for release at maturity, incorporating new members by marriage, and establishing policies for inclusion of others: in-laws, relatives, step-parents, guests, family friends, etc.

6. Maintenance of order—providing means of communication, establishing types and intensity of interaction, patterns of affection, and sexual expression—by administering sanctions insuring conformity to group norms

7. Placement of members in the larger society—fitting into the community, relating to church, school, organizational life, political and economic systems, and protecting family members from undesirable outside influences

8. Maintenance of motivation and morale—rewarding members for achievements, satisfying individual needs for acceptance, encouragement, and affection, meeting personal and family crises, refining a philosophy of life and sense of family loyalty (through rituals, festivals, etc.)

These eight basic tasks confront the family as a group in all social classes and subcultures, through changing times and throughout the family life cycle. All eight basic tasks at any given stage in the family life cycle are the *family developmental tasks* of that period in its history as a family.

Most developmental tasks of most persons, as children and as adults, are worked out within the family through their lifetimes. The modern family assumes as one of its primary functions that of promoting the continuing development of each of its members throughout the entire life cycle. So families, as families, can be seen to have responsibilities, goals, and developmental tasks that are specifically related to the development of their members. All these developmental tasks of both family members and families as a whole shift as the family changes and are constantly being modified by the interplay of forces both within and without the family in every society, in every age.

A family developmental task arises at a given stage in the family life cycle as the family meets the needs of its members and satisfies the requirements for its continued growth and development as a family unit. Family developmental tasks parallel the developmental tasks of individuals and can be similarly defined: A family developmental task is a growth responsibility that arises at a certain stage in the life of a family, successful achievement of which leads to satisfaction and success with later tasks, while failure leads to unhappiness in the family, disapproval by society, and difficulty with later family developmental tasks.

Family developmental tasks are those growth responsibilities that must be accomplished by a family at a given stage of development in a way that will satisfy its (1) biological requirements, (2) cultural imperatives, and (3) personal aspirations and values, if the family is to continue to grow as a unit.

Much as individual developmental tasks change over the years, so family developmental tasks shift with each stage of the family life cycle. Family developmental tasks cluster around the meeting of the requisites for family continuation and growth at a particular period in the life of a family. Family developmental tasks, then, are basic family tasks particularized and specified for a given stage of development in the family life cycle.

As norms are clarified, it becomes possible to locate a given family at a particular stage in the family life cycle as on schedule, ahead of schedule, or behind schedule. Child development specialists speak intelligibly of a child being "precocious" or "retarded," as "early maturing" or "late blooming." So students of family life may become professionally expert in appraising family development by progress in the accomplishment of family development tasks at any given stage of the family life cycle.

The developmental tasks of any given family are many, complex, and difficult to enumerate in detail. Families differ from one another in many, many ways. However, just as it is possible to predict, in general, the developmental tasks of an individual at any given developmental level, so too, we can describe, in general, the family developmental tasks of American families throughout the family life cycle. Chapters 7 through 15 follow the developmental tasks of individual family members and of the family as a whole through an eight-stage family life cycle.

Stage-critical Family Developmental Tasks

Earlier in this chapter there was explicit recognition of critical periods in human development when an individual is undergoing most rapid change. In a like manner, it is possible to delineate stage-critical developmental tasks when a given family is assuming new responsibilities that arise out of the rapid changes it is undergoing at given stages in its life cycle. Some of these are suggested in table 6–5.

The marriage of the husband and wife in stage 1 joins the pair and links their parental bonds in the larger kin network. The engaged couple bridges the family life cycles of its families of orientation and its

Table 6–5. *Stage-critical Family Developmental Tasks through the Family Life Cycle*

Stage of the family life cycle	Positions in the family	Stage-critical family developmental tasks
1. Married couple	Wife Husband	Establishing a mutually satisfying marriage Adjusting to pregnancy and the promise of parenthood Fitting into the kin network
2. Childbearing	Wife-mother Husband-father Infant daughter or son or both	Having, adjusting to, and encouraging the development of infants Establishing a satisfying home for both parents and infant(s)
3. Preschool-age	Wife-mother Husband-father Daughter-sister Son-brother	Adapting to the critical needs and interests of preschool children in stimulating, growth-promoting ways Coping with energy depletion and lack of privacy as parents
4. School-age	Wife-mother Husband-father Daughter-sister Son-brother	Fitting into the community of school-age families in constructive ways Encouraging children's educational achievement
5. Teenage	Wife-mother Husband-father Daughter-sister Son-brother	Balancing freedom with responsibility as teenagers mature and emancipate themselves Establishing postparental interests and careers as growing parents
6. Launching center	Wife-mother-grandmother Husband-father-grandfather Daughter-sister-aunt Son-brother-uncle	Releasing young adults into work, military service, college, marriage, etc., with appropriate rituals and assistance Maintaining a supportive home base
7. Middle-aged parents	Wife-mother-grandmother Husband-father-grandfather	Rebuilding the marriage relationship Maintaining kin ties with older and younger generations
8. Aging family members	Widow/widower Wife-mother-grandmother Husband-father-grandfather	Coping with bereavement and living alone Closing the family home or adapting it to aging Adjusting to retirement

family of procreation into the generation spiral. The members of the newly married pair leave their parents' homes at the launching center stage, with its family developmental tasks, and enter their own marriage at its establishment phase, with all the changes and developmental tasks involved in building a marriage.

Family Aspirations and Goals

Ask a family what it is trying to do at any given time, and the answer may be in terms of its aspirations as a family. One family is building a new home; another is saving up for a vacation; a third is trying to pay its bills and get out of debt, while another is attempting to put its children through school, or to nurse an ill member back to health, or to release a young adult into marriage. Family aspirations are specific to the individual family in its social setting at a particular time. They tend to shift from time to time as one objective has been met (i.e., the home has been built, or the vacation is over), and others appear (i.e., the new home must be furnished, and the family in its new setting tries to get into the circles within the community to which it wants to become related). Family aspirations, then, are the short-term tension-reducing objectives that are defined by a family and its social set as important.

Beyond the specific, temporary, and individual aspirations of a given family are objectives that society as a whole has for families generally. National goals are in terms of family health, family safety, family stability, family standards of living, family levels of education and culture, and family competence in developing effective citizens for a free society. As the report of the President's Commission on National Goals specifies in part 1, "Goals at Home":

The status of the individual must remain our primary concern. All our institutions—political, social, and economic—must further enhance the dignity of the citizen, promote the maximum development of his capabilities, stimulate their responsible exercise, and widen the range and effectiveness of opportunities for individual choice.[11]

Family goals can be seen as lying between the short-term aspirations of a given family at a particular time and the long-term national goals for all families within the society. Family goals ideally facilitate the psychosocial development of family members step by step through life. Family goals are expressed in the contemporary processes that dominate a family's developmental tasks at any stage of the family life cycle. Thus, family goals at the establishment phase of family life center on adjusting to living as a married couple. When children come, family goals are in terms of providing for their care, nurture, and development. As children mature, family goals are focused upon loosening family ties and releasing young adults into homes of their own. Family goals profoundly influence family functioning and developmental tasks at every stage of the family life cycle.

Families, as families, are seen to have responsibilities, goals, and developmental tasks that are specifically related to the

---

[11] President's Commission on National Goals, *Goals for Americans* (New York: Prentice-Hall, Spectrum Books, 1960), p. 3.

development of their members. All these developmental tasks of both family members and families as a whole shift as the family grows and changes, and are constantly being modified by the interplay of forces both within and without the family in every society, in every age.

Successful Families

The success of a family can be appraised in several ways. Frequently used measures of family success are: (1) how well the family is meeting its short-term aspirations, (2) how well the family is attaining the goals that society has set for it, and (3) how well the family is achieving its developmental tasks.

1. It is not unusual today to find families defining their success in terms of the things they have acquired and the status they have achieved. Such family members may compare their present status with that of a previous period and feel that they have succeeded, as they have "bettered themselves" by moving up the social ladder to a higher status. They measure success by how well they are living up to their particular aspirations and ambitions.

2. The second way of appraising family success is in terms of the family's social contribution. Zimmerman and Cervantes[12]

define the successful family as one that (a) avoids disruption by divorce and desertion, (b) avoids interference by the police, and (c) puts its children through school. In their study of 60,000 American families, they define successful families as those that meet all three of these tests. Beyond such minimal criteria are other tangible evidences of a family's producing members who make positive contributions to the larger society, or serving as a constructive example of good family living in one of many ways.

3. Successful families in the framework of this text are defined as those that (a) encourage and assist their members in the achievement of their developmental tasks, and (b) effectively accomplish the appropriate family developmental tasks at every stage of the family life cycle to date in its history. When the basic family tasks are being accomplished effectively stage by stage through its career, a family is considered to be successful.

A family is successful, then, when its members—adult and child, male and female —are getting support, acceptance, and opportunities for working through the developmental tasks they each must achieve in order to move smoothly into the next stage of their development, and the family as a whole is meeting effectively the developmental tasks of its present stage in the family life cycle.

Much as individuals sometimes succeed and sometimes fail to accomplish one or more of their developmental tasks, so fami-

---

[12] Carle C. Zimmerman and Lucius F. Cervantes, *Successful American Families* (New York: Pageant Press, 1960), p. 7.

lies too at times function effectively and at other times find the going rough. Families find, as do individuals, that success leads to further success, while failure tends to increase the difficulty of the tasks that lie ahead. Difficulty in certain areas is greater at some stages of the family life cycle than at others, as is seen in the comparative overview in chapter 16.

The successful American family today is a flexible group of persons who mean enough to each other to have the courage to innovate and the willingness to explore new possibilities in the working through of its developmental tasks and those of its members. When family goals are defined in terms of raising mature persons capable of withstanding the stresses and strains of modern living and contributing creatively to society, the developmental task concept has special relevance.

SUMMARY

Families are the nurturing centers for human personality. Individuals, though unique, develop through a life cycle that resembles that of all other persons. In each of the eight stages in the life cycle of man there are developmental crises that must be fought through successfully if the next developmental stage is to be reached: (1) infancy: trust versus mistrust, (2) early childhood: autonomy versus shame and doubt, (3) play age: initiative versus guilt, (4) school age: industry versus inferiority, (5) adolescence: identity versus identity diffusion, (6) young adulthood: intimacy versus isolation, (7) adulthood: generativity versus self-absorption, and (8) senescence: integrity versus disgust.

Erikson's developmental stages parallel those of Sigmund Freud; they are comparable to Piaget's observations of the foundations of cognition; and they have been found applicable in more than a thousand research studies analyzed by Bloom. All point clearly to the importance of critical periods in human development as the times when most change is taking place. A dozen types of change in human growth, development, and decline and more than a score of principles inherent in development are identifiable.

Developmental tasks originate in the biologic maturing of the individual and the cultural pressures that are exerted upon him. As cultural pressures and opportunities play upon the maturing individual, his personality emerges with the personal aspirations and values that further influence and give direction to his developmental tasks. A developmental task is a thrust from within the individual to narrow the discrepancy between his present behavior and what he might achieve. Operationally, the individual's assumption of a given developmental task consists of (1) perception and new possibilities, (2) identity formation in the new direction, (3) coping with conflicting demands, and (4) motivation sufficient to assume the task. The developmental tasks of the individual have been outlined from birth to death in ten categories of human behavior. The developmental tasks of various members of the family interact so that sometimes they are in conflict and sometimes they mutually support each other.

Basic tasks of American families necessary for continued survival, continuity, and growth are: (1) physical maintenance, (2) allocation of resources, (3) division of labor, (4) socialization of family members, (5) reproduction, recruitment, and release of family members, (6) maintenance of order, (7) placement of members in the larger society, and (8) maintenance of motivation and morale. These eight basic tasks at any given stage in the family life cycle are the family developmental tasks of that period in its history as a family.

A family developmental task is a growth responsibility that arises at or about a certain stage in the family life cycle, successful achievement of which leads to satisfaction and success with later tasks, while failure leads to unhappiness in the family, disapproval by society, and difficulty with later family developmental tasks. Family developmental tasks are essential for continued growth through each stage of the family life cycle. Family developmental tasks shift as the family grows, and they are modified by the interplay of forces from within and without the family throughout the family life cycle. Stage-critical family developmental tasks arise at times when a family is undergoing most rapid change.

Family aspirations are short-term specific objectives defined by a given family as important. National standards and goals for families are those held by the society as a whole for its families. Family goals, lying between its short-term aspirations and long-term national goals, focus upon the developmental tasks that are critical at a given stage in the family life cycle.

Success in family life can be appraised by the way in which a family is satisfying its aspirations, by the social contribution of the family and its members, and by the extent to which it accomplishes its family developmental tasks and facilitates the accomplishment of the developmental tasks of its members.

SUGGESTED ACTIVITIES

1. Write a paper suggesting principles inherent in *family* development that theoretically might be extrapolated from the listing of twenty-four principles inherent in development in table 6–3. Document your hypotheses as adequately as you can from the readings at the chapter end and from any of the footnoted references that seem applicable. Be prepared to defend your thesis in a class discussion.

2. Compose a private letter to yourself outlining some the developmental tasks you are attempting to accomplish at this period of your life. Document each developmental task with data relative to its origins in terms of your maturation, as well as your cultural pressures and personal aspirations. Illustrate with anecdotal material and appraise roughly the degree of success or failure you are currently finding in each of your developmental tasks at the moment.

3. Compare the concept of "the principle of readiness" with that of "the teachable moment." In what ways do the two resemble one another? What are their differences?

4. Make a chart outline of *The Fourposter*, by Jan de Hartog (Random House, 1952), indicating developmental tasks of various members of the family and of the family as a whole by stages of the family life cycle depicted. Illustrate with quotations, and document when needed from primary sources.

5. Role play a situation illustrating the statement, "Each family may be seen as an arena of interacting personalities, each trying to meet his own basic needs within the pattern of family life." List the implications for family developmental tasks in the situation portrayed.

6. Support or refute the statement, "Parents, who themselves have urgent needs, make most of the adjustments in building complementary roles between themselves and their children." Would your conclusion be the same at the early stages of family development as for the later stages in the family life cycle? Explore and explain.

7. Defining the successful family as one that encourages its members to achieve their individual developmental tasks and accomplishes effectively its family developmental tasks at any given stage in the family life cycle, set up criteria by which family success might be appraised objectively at each stage of the family life cycle, for each of the eight basic tasks outlined in this chapter. State each criterion as simply and as specifically as possible so that it clearly measures the degree of success or failure being experienced for each family task through each stage of the family life cycle.

8. Prepare a graphic presentation of the relationship between the individual developmental tasks throughout the life of a person, as listed in table 6–4, and the stage-critical family developmental tasks through the family life cycle (table 6–5). Discuss the ways in which family and individual family members influence one another in their concurrent efforts to achieve their developmental tasks.

READINGS

Blood, Robert O., Jr., and Donald M. Wolfe. *Husbands and Wives: The Dynamics of Married Living.* Glencoe, Ill.: Free Press, 1960. Pp. 10, 76–77.

Bloom, Benjamin S. *Stability and Change in Human Characteristics.* New York: John Wiley and Sons, 1964.

Child Study Association of America. "Living and Growing with Our Children: Impact on Parents of Children's Growth Phases." *Child Study* 32, no. 3 (Summer 1955).

Duvall, Evelyn Millis. "Changing Roles in the Family Life Cycle." *Journal of Home Economics* 42, no. 6 (June 1950): 435–436.

Erikson, Erik H. *Childhood and Society.* New York: W. W. Norton and Company,

1950. Esp. chap. 7, "Eight Stages of Man."

Farber, Bernard, William C. Jenne, and Romolo Toigo. *Family Crisis and the Retarded Child*. Research Monograph Series A, no. 1, pp. 7–10. Washington, D.C.: Council for Exceptional Children, 1960.

Freud, Sigmund. *New Introductory Lectures on Psychoanalysis*. Edited by James Strachey. New York: W. W. Norton and Company, 1965.

Geismar, L. L., and Beverly Ayres. *Measuring Family Functioning*. St. Paul, Minn.: Family Centered Project, Greater St. Paul Community Chest and Councils, 1960. Chap. 2, "Conceptual Problems in Evaluating Family Functioning."

Havighurst, Robert J. *Human Development and Education*. New York: Longmans, Green and Company, 1953.

Hill, Reuben. *Family Development in Three Generations*. Cambridge, Mass.: Schenkman Publishing Company, 1970.

Hill, Reuben. "Interdisciplinary Workshop on Marriage and Family Research." *Marriage and Family Living* 13, no. 1 (February 1951): 13–28.

Hummel, Al J., and Clifford A. Smith. *The Task Method of Program Planning*. Omaha, Nebr.: Omaha Young Men's Christian Association Publications, 1959.

Hunt, J. McV. *Intelligence and Experience*. New York: Ronald Press Company, 1961.

Lidz, Theodore. *The Person: His Development throughout the Life Cycle*. New York: Basic Books, 1968.

Milne, Lorus J., and Margery Milne. *The Ages of Life*. New York: Harcourt, Brace and World, 1968.

Neugarten, Bernice L., ed. *Middle Age and Aging*. Chicago: University of Chicago Press, 1968.

Piaget, Jean. *The Origins of Intelligence in Children*. Translated by Margaret Cook. New York: International Universities Press, 1966.

Piaget, Jean, and Bärbel Inhelder. *The Psychology of the Child*. New York: Basic Books, 1969.

Pollak, Otto. "A Family Diagnosis Model." *Social Service Review* 34, no. 1 (March 1960): 19–28.

President's Commission on National Goals. *Goals for Americans*. New York: Prentice-Hall, Spectrum Books, 1960.

Smart, Mollie S., and Russell C. Smart. *Children: Development and Relationships*. New York: Macmillan Company, 1967.

Vincent, Elizabeth Lee, and Phyllis C. Martin. *Human Psychological Development*. New York: Ronald Press Company, 1961.

White, Burton L. "The Initial Coordination of Sensorimotor Schemas in Human Infants—Piaget's Ideas and the Role of Experience." Reprinted from *Studies in Cognitive Development*, edited by David Elkind and John H. Flavell, pp. 237–256. New York: Oxford University Press, 1969.

Zimmerman, Carle C., and Lucius F. Cervantes. *Successful American Families*. New York: Pageant Press, 1960.

PART 2 EXPANDING FAMILIES

7

MARRIED COUPLES— ESTABLISHMENT PHASE

To have and to hold from this day forward,
For better, for worse, for richer, for poorer,
In sickness, and in health, to love and to cherish,
Till death us do part. Book of Common Prayer

The establishment phase of the family life cycle begins with the couple at marriage and continues until they become aware of the fact that the wife is pregnant. Usually lasting about one year, this may be a period of a few months or many years. It may last for the duration of the marriage, as in the homes of childless couples. It may be a brief phase of only a few weeks.

Typically, there are two members in the family at the establishment phase: husband and wife. The man is about twenty-two and the woman about twenty, median ages for first marriage currently. As a two-person group they maintain one interpersonal relationship—that of husband and wife. They each confront individual developmental tasks as young adults, with developmental crises in terms of intimacy versus isolation. The major family goal at this stage is adjusting to living as a married pair.

Marriage marks a drastic role shift from the parent-child relationship in the family of orientation to the husband-wife relationship within the marriage. Marriage and family may be seen as two separate social systems with different purposes and tasks within a given household. The family system ministers primarily to the needs of the children, the marriage primarily to the needs of husband and wife.[1]

READINESS FOR MARRIAGE

Marriage usually is undertaken by young adults who have had some two decades of personal development and hopefully are ready to marry and establish families of their own. The young man and woman have completed their adolescence, and physically, emotionally, vocationally, financially, and personally are more or less ready for the responsibilities and privileges of

[1] Floyd M. Martinson, *Marriage and the American Ideal* (New York: Dodd, Mead and Company, 1960), p. 343.

being married. Getting married offers the young pair the opportunities of legally living together as man and wife and establishing a new family unit. Marriage satisfies the anticipation both persons have of what is appropriate for them as young adults.

There are norms and expectations throughout all of life that serve as prods or brakes on behavior.[2] People generally are aware of these social clocks that influence their behavior. They sense what it means to be early, late, or on time in such major transitions as getting married and starting a family. Marrying at seventeen is quite different psychologically and socially from marrying at thirty-seven or fifty-seven, and such later ages are not usually considered as "right" or "normal" as is marriage of two people in their twenties.

Early Marriage

The too-young individual is generally seen as lacking readiness for the many tasks that being married involves. Teenage marriages are recognized as more vulnerable to annulment, separation, and divorce than are those of young adults.[3] Premature marriage cuts off the full development of the young person's individual autonomy, often curtails his or her education, and limits the couple's vocational possibilities and financial security. Why, then, do so many teenagers turn to marriage?

Numerous research studies exploring the factors related to early marriage have found that young marriages are predominantly those of teenage girls to somewhat older males. Characteristics of girls who marry before they are out of high school are summarized in table 7–1.

Age is not the only determinant for success or failure in marriage. Some of the factors related to competence and satisfaction in marriage at any age are presented predictively in table 7–2.

Student marriages are hard to finance. One study of couples married while in high school found that financial assistance from parents' families included food, durable goods, and cash, and that such family help increased with the length of the young marriages.[4] Research on a Michigan population of married college students found financial problems present at all social class levels.[5] Student couples were both gainfully employed up to forty hours a week

[2] Bernice L. Neugarten, "Continuities and Discontinuities of Psychological Issues into Adult Life," address presented at the American Psychological Association Annual Convention, San Francisco, August 31, 1968, mimeographed.

[3] Lee G. Burchinal and Loren E. Chancellor, "Survival Rates among Religiously Homogamous and Interreligious Marriages," *Social Forces* 41 (May 1963): 353–362.

[4] Vladimir de Lissovoy, "High School Marriage in Pennsylvania," reported at the Annual Conference of the National Council on Family Relations, Washington, D.C., October 1969.

[5] J. Ross Eshleman and Chester L. Hunt, "Social Class Influences on Family Adjustment Patterns of Married College Students," *Journal of Marriage and the Family* 29, no. 3 (August 1967): 485–491.

Table 7–1. *Schoolgirls Who Marry (Data Keyed by Number to Supporting Research References)*

Factors related to early marriage	Girls who marry young tend to have:
Early heterosexual involvement	Started dating early (2, 3, 7, 9) Started going steady early (3, 7, 9) Gone steady more often (3) More often felt they were in love (3) Dated older fellow (3, 9) Become premaritally pregnant (1, 3, 7, 8, 9)
Personal inadequacies	Poor social adjustment (6, 9) Emotionally less stable (9) Lower intelligence test scores (5, 6) Poor school records (6)
Limited interest in education	Little interest in further education (9) Low level of aspiration (9) Parents with little interest in college education (9)
Unsatisfactory family situation	More disagreements with parents (7, 9) More brothers and sisters (5) Less stable, intact homes (6) Less attachment to father (7) Mothers who married in their teens (3)
Social disadvantage	Lower socioeconomic status (2, 3, 6) Rural or small-community background (1, 5) Little church contact (6)
High expectations of marriage	More close friends who married while in school (3) Expectations of being happier in marriage than before (8)

Keyed References:

1. Anderson, Wayne J., and Sander M. Latts, "High School Marriages and School Policies in Minnesota," *Journal of Marriage and the Family* 27, no. 2 (May 1965): 266–270.
2. Bayer, Alan E., "Early Dating and Early Marriage," *Journal of Marriage and the Family* 30, no. 4 (November 1968): 628–632.
3. Burchinal, Lee, "Adolescent Role Deprivation and High School Age Marriage," *Marriage and Family Living* 21, no. 4 (November 1959): 378–384.
4. Burchinal, Lee G., "How Successful Are High School Marriages?" *Iowa Farm Science* 13 (March 1959): 7–10.
5. De Lissovoy, Vladimir, and Mary Ellen Hitchcock, "High School Marriages in Pennsylvania," *Journal of Marriage and the Family* 27, no. 2 (May 1965): 263–265.

6. Havighurst, Robert J., Paul Hoover Bowman, Gordon P. Liddle, Charles V. Matthews, and James V. Pierce, *Growing Up in River City* (New York: John Wiley and Sons, 1962), chap. 9, "Marriage."
7. Inselberg, Rachel M., "Social and Psychological Factors Associated with High School Marriages," *Journal of Home Economics* 53, no. 9 (November 1961): 766–772.
8. Ivins, Wilson, "Student Marriages in New Mexico Secondary Schools," *Marriage and Family Living* 22, no. 1 (February 1960): 71–74.
9. Moss, J. Joel, and Ruby Gingles, "The Relationship of Personality to the Incidence of Early Marriage," *Marriage and Family Living* 21, no. 4 (November 1959): 373–377.

Table 7-2. Forecast of Marital Competence and Satisfaction

Factor	Poor chance	Good chance
Personality	Immature, few interests, poor personal and social adjustment, limited interpersonal skills	Mature, flexible, well adjusted, and generally competent in interpersonal relationships
Education	Dropouts	At least high school graduation and some further education for both
Dating history	Started to date early; went steady early; sexual involvement early	General social skills with members of both sexes developed in dating; gradual love development
Courtship	Hurried; less than six months' acquaintance; no engagement period	Several years' courtship relationship; at least six months' engagement
Reason for marriage	Impulse, "on a dare," premarital pregnancy, to escape boredom or failure, because everyone else is	Desire for home and family; to establish a deep, meaningful relationship with beloved
Pregnancy	Premarital conception	Pregnancy delayed until full year following marriage
Social status	Lower	Middle or better
Parental attitudes	Oppose the marriage, rejecting the mate, grudging assistance	Supportive; provide assistance with respect for young couple's autonomy; consult young pair upon occasion
Wedding	Elopement and civil ceremony	Conventional, hometown, church-sanctioned; family and friends present
Economic basis	Uncertain income, poor-paying jobs, little security of employment, help from relatives urgently needed	Realistic planning on known income, both with salable skills and willingness to work, reasonable expectations of present and immediate future, mature responsibility

Source: Freely adapted from Lee G. Burchinal, "Trends and Prospects for Young Marriages in the United States," *Journal of Marriage and the Family* 27, no. 2 (May 1965): 251, based upon research results from numerous sources and inferences to be further tested.

in addition to their home and school work in most cases. Furthermore, marrying while in college put an end to the wife's education.[6]

----

[6] Ibid., p. 490.

Nevertheless, when college students were asked if they would marry when they did if they were starting out all over again, 75 percent said they would not wait until after college to marry; 15 percent would wait;

and 10 percent were uncertain.[7] When asked if they would advise others to marry in college, 70 percent of the Michigan college students replied in the affirmative; 25 percent said they would not; and the other 5 percent were undecided.[8]

The closer one gets to being married, the greater the feeling of being ready for it, according to student replies on a self-administered marital preparedness instrument.[9] Dr. Rhona Rapoport of Harvard has developed a battery of ten items indicating an individual's readiness for taking over the new roles of husband or of wife, as seen in the degree to which the individual shows signs of:

1. being ready to be an exclusive sexual partner
2. being able to enter freely into an intimate sexual relation with one's partner
3. having tenderness and affection for the other
4. showing interest in the other's emotional life and development
5. sharing intimacies with the other
6. merging his own plans with those of the other

7. having a realistic appraisal of the personal characteristics of the prospective spouse
8. having a realistic conception of the economic problems entailed in being married
9. formulating a realistic picture of his own capacities to contribute to the needs of the new family unit
10. being ready to become a husband or a wife.[10]

Youth leaders, parents, and teachers who would be effective in preventing premature marriages of very young people find guidelines in implications of research in young marriage along the lines of helping the young people with whom they live and work to develop (1) feelings of worth, (2) sense of purpose, (3) feeling of being needed, (4) awareness of friends and family who care about them and want them to succeed, (5) interest in learning about oneself and others, (6) acceptance and respect for their family roots, (7) eagerness for family life education and preparation for marriage, (8) willingness to assume responsible codes of sexual conduct, (9) eagerness in continuing their education, (10) aspiration to prepare for a challenging vocation, (11) involvement in stimulating, growth-promoting projects in home, school, and community, (12) admiration for worthy adult models in their lives, and (13) respect for

[7] Harold T. Christensen and Robert E. Philbrick, "Family Size as a Factor in the Marital Adjustment of College Students," *American Sociological Review* 17, no. 3 (June 1952): 306–312.

[8] Eshleman and Hunt, "Social Class Influences on Family Adjustment Patterns of Married College Students," p. 490.

[9] Michael J. Sporakowski, "Marital Preparedness, Prediction and Adjustment," *Family Coordinator* 17, no. 3 (July 1968): 155–161.

[10] Rhona Rapoport, "Normal Crises, Family Structure, and Mental Health," *Family Process* 2, no. 1 (March 1963): 78.

counseling that deals wholesomely with self-defeating attitudes and hangups in the realm of sex and marriage.[11]

Premarital counseling is important not only for the help it gives in readying young people for marriage, but also as a positive experience with a resource to utilize as future marital problems arise. Many a troubled marriage limps along too long before getting help. A study conducted by a large metropolitan family service agency found that the average married couple did not come for counseling until six and a half years after their marital troubles began.[12] The roles of husband and wife are demanding, and their developmental tasks as a couple are challenging—too challenging to be left to chance, romance, pluck, or luck.

DEVELOPMENTAL TASKS OF THE ESTABLISHMENT PHASE

At the time of their marriage, the husband is attempting to achieve his developmental tasks as a young adult male, while his wife is concurrently working out her growth responsibilities as a young adult female. The young man must learn what it means to be a young adult with young adult responsibilities in his home and community. He must learn what is expected of him as a husband, and what it means to be a married man. Simultaneously, the young wife is learning what it means to be a wife, a young married woman both in her home and in the community. Sometimes the developmental tasks of husband and wife complement and mutually support each other. At other times the efforts of one conflict with those of the other. This is the nature of the dynamics of interaction in marriage and family living, as is suggested in table 7–3.

The distinction should be made between the conflict of developmental tasks of the husband and wife and conflict arising out of the couple's difficulties in accomplishing their tasks. The young wife may be ineffectual as a sex partner at first, experiencing some degree of sex conflict with her husband. But, in such a case, it is not the developmental tasks of the husband and wife that conflict. It is rather the husband's inexpertness or the wife's difficulties in working through the complementarity of sex roles that result in their conflict as sex partners. The husband may find it hard to become socially "domesticated," involving some marital conflict, but his task in this direction complements his wife's.

There are some complementary and some conflicting aspects in many of the

---

[11] Mary Jane Hungerford, "Preventing High School Marriages," *Family Life* 28, no. 9 (September 1968): 4.

[12] Clark W. Blackburn, "The Psychological Attitudes of Young Couples and the Harmony of the Couple," address presented at the International Family Conference of the International Union of Family Organizations, Rome, Italy, July 6, 1965, mimeographed, p. 23.

Table 7–3. *Complementary and Conflicting Developmental Tasks of Husbands and Wives*

Developmental tasks of the young husband	Developmental tasks of the young wife	Complementary and conflicting possibilities
Becoming established in an occupation	Making a home and managing the household	Complementary: Shared responsibility in homemaking
Getting specialized training	Getting settled in her home	Conflicting: Husband engrossed in work away from home, while wife tries to elicit his active cooperation in homemaking
Assuming responsibility for getting and holding a job	Establishing and maintaining household routines	
Working toward security and advancement in his work	Learning the many skills of homemaking and housework	
Assuming responsibility for the support of his family	Becoming a financial helpmate in establishing the home	Complementary: Both are economic partners through establishment phase
Earning the family income	Working until her husband is established	Conflicting: Her work threatens his status as breadwinner
Planning for the long pull of family support through the years	Seeing her work as secondary and possibly intermittent	
Fulfilling his military service requirements	Maintaining a home base with her husband in service	Conflicting: Husband is pulled away from home, while wife's efforts are in maintaining unity and integrity of home through their separation
Choosing the time for service	Deciding where and how to live while he is away	
Juggling educational, marital, occupational plans with the demands of military service	Keeping a sense of being married during her husband's absence	
Absenting himself from home for the duration of his service	Continuing educational, vocational, and family activities after her marriage	
Establishing mutually satisfying sex relationships	Becoming a satisfactory sex partner	Complementary: Each has the task of communicating intimately with the other
Awakening his wife sexually	Learning her sex role as wife	
Developing competency as a husband	Responding effectively and participating in their mutual fulfillment	
Becoming "domesticated" as a married man	Assuming hostess and companionship roles as a married woman	Complementary: Both husband and wife are learning to move in tandem in their social life as a couple
Sharing leisure time with his wife	Planning for recreational activities as a couple	
Developing mutual interests	Accepting and refusing social invitations	
Cultivating joint activities	Entertaining their friends, associates, and families	
Getting into the young married set		

developmental tasks of husband and wife. When the two people are drawn together in mutually supportive ways as they work on their individual developmental tasks, we see those tasks as complementary. When the working through of their tasks as husband and wife tend to pull the couple in opposite directions, the tasks are conflicting. The difference is in the lines of force, in the pull toward or away from the other. In conflicting developmental tasks the lines of force between the pair oppose and repel. In complementary tasks the lines of force pull the two together and operate toward unity, as we see in chart 7–1.

The two persons who come together in marriage have much to learn about each other, and about what it means to be married. It takes conscientious effort and a great deal of interpersonal perception to become aware of one another as distinct individuals with preferences, interests, values, and predispositions firmly rooted in each personality. Differences emerge to be recognized and evaluated. Some are simple idiosyncrasies that can be modified for the good of the union. Others are so important that ways must be found of coping with conflicts between the partners.

Being married involves a new way of life for both the new husband and his bride. Somehow they must develop together the patterns of daily living that express and satisfy them both. Every day brings decisions that must be made, problems to be solved, and plans to be laid for the development of the home they are establishing together. Some of these ongoing interde-

Chart 7–1. *Conflicting and Complementary Developmental Tasks*

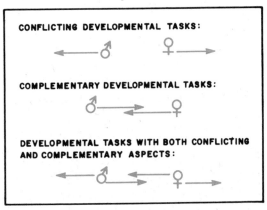

pendencies are filled with mutual satisfaction. Others are burdensome to one or both members of the pair. Each couple approaches their husband-wife-couple roles with varying degrees of readiness, flexibility and indecision. At first this all may be done in a spirit of playing at being married, until one day they begin to feel that they are really established in a going marriage.

Developmental Tasks of the Married Couple

The developmental tasks of the newly married couple arise in both the husband and wife first out of their physiological maturation, with its adult drives for ongoing sexual fulfillment. The second origin of the developmental tasks of the newly married couple is found in the cultural expectations and pressures for the married pair to settle down and behave as married couples are supposed to in the given community. Thirdly, the man and woman are moved by their own personal aspirations to establish their marriage according to the dreams that both of them have built through the years.

The multiple nature of the origins of the developmental tasks at this stage makes for some difficulties in itself. What the culture expects and what the young couple want do not always coincide. What the realities of the situation are and what the married pair dream of as right for them are rarely identical. The young woman who has built up extravagant ideas of what she must have at the time she marries may be disappointed when hers does not turn out to be a fashionable wedding or a modern home correct to the latest detail. The dreams of the husband and wife may mesh in many respects, but be miles apart in others. Being married first of all involves coming to terms with what is expected—by one's culture, by one's mate, by oneself, and as a couple.

The developmental tasks of the married couple are basic for the establishment of

COURTESY OF THE ADVERTISING COUNCIL, INC.

The bride and groom each have personal aspirations to establish their marriage according to the dreams that both of them have built through the years.

the family. Although they differ from family to family, from class to class, and from culture to culture, they may be listed in their more general aspects as follows:

1. establishing a home base in a place to call their own
2. establishing mutually satisfactory systems for getting and spending money
3. establishing mutually acceptable patterns of who does what and who is accountable to whom
4. establishing a continuity of mutually satisfying sex relationships
5. establishing systems of intellectual and emotional communication
6. establishing workable relationships with relatives
7. establishing ways of interacting with friends, associates, and community organizations
8. facing the possibility of children and planning for their coming
9. establishing a workable philosophy of life as a couple.

Each couple enters marriage with its own potentials and problems; each copes with the tasks of being married and making the transition from their previous roles and statuses with varying degrees of competence, creativity, and courage. Their success is dependent upon their skill in accomplishing their developmental tasks both as individuals and as a married couple.[13]

---

[13] Robert and Rhona Rapoport, "Work and Family in Contemporary Society," *American Sociological Review* 30, no. 3 (June 1965): 381–394.

Establishing a Home Base to Call Their Own

One of the first questions to be faced by a couple considering the possibilities of marriage is, "Where will we live?" If they are still in school or college, they may explore the resources for married students on or near the campus. If the boy is soon to leave for military service, they consider where the wife will live while he is away. Young married couples change their residence often, now more than ever. In one three-generation family study, 12 percent of the grandparent generation, 21 percent of the parent generation, and 24 percent of the married child generation had moved at least once during the first year of marriage. By the second year of marriage, mobility for all three generations was even higher: 42 percent of the grandparents, 48 percent of the parents, and 50 percent of the married child generation had moved from one home base to another.[14]

Couples with both schooling and military service out of the way find more stability in their home base as they choose the place where they can settle down and invest themselves and their resources in making a real home. At first this probably will be a rented place near their work and pos-

---

[14] Reuben Hill, *Family Development in Three Generations* (Cambridge, Mass.: Schenkman Publishing Company, 1970), chap. 5, "Planning Residential Location and Home Improvements."

sibly near friends and family. It may be a furnished room or two for the couple marrying "on a shoestring," or a commodious house or apartment for the more affluent. Newly married members of the upper class sometimes move into a new house completely furnished for them by one or both of their families, but this is rare. Most couples must together puzzle out their homemaking plans from the possibilities at hand and the promises ahead.

Establishing Mutually Satisfactory Systems for Getting and Spending Money

At the time of first marriage, the husband is usually young, inexperienced, and so relatively poorly paid. Yet the needs and wants and dreams of the young couple call for more money than will be available to them for some time. A successful family, in the eyes of today's man or woman, is one able to buy not only the necessities of life in terms of shelter, food, and clothing, but also such important "extras" as education, preventive medical care, leisure-time activities, and cultural opportunities. Much of the trouble in "making ends meet" among couples who marry before they have completed their education stems from their efforts to be self-supporting, even when this means sacrificing their schooling. Their parents have already invested heavily in

their education, and often would rather help out the young married couple for a while than have their son or daughter drop out of school upon marriage. This is not always an easy arrangement, and many couples avoid it if at all possible. Some young husbands carry a part-time job in addition to their full-time employment or school load. This makes strains in the establishment phase, when relaxed time together is so important for the building of the marriage.

The most frequent solution is found in the wife's ability and willingness to work during the establishment phase of the marriage. Two out of every three wives between sixteen and thirty-four years of age with no children in the home are gainfully employed. This is significantly higher than the proportion of wives working outside the home at any other stage in the family life cycle.[15]

Unforeseen problems often arise in this connection. Not all women have the salable skills that will net them enough to be worthwhile. Not all women have health and energy enough to handle both a job and a home, however simplified the latter may be. Not all men either know how or feel constrained to share the household responsibilities with their working wives.

The more optimistic side of the picture is found in the many men and women who

[15] See table 16–4, chap. 16; data from the Bureau of Labor Statistics, Washington, D.C.

are learning the new roles required for a real partnership in getting and spending the family income. As more and more married women enter the working force and bring home their paychecks, decisions about the spending of the family income tend to become cooperative, democratic, and based on joint planning of husband and wife.

One study of married students indicates that an overwhelming majority (86.8 percent) of the couples made their financial plans jointly. Some 84.1 percent of them budgeted their money, and nearly three-fourths of the couples who used financial plans (74.2 percent) kept records of their expenditures.[16] This is in sharp contrast to older patterns of handling money, where the woman often did not know how much income there was or how it was spent, but, like Vinnie Day,[17] cajoled what sums she could from her reluctant mate, who held the purse strings with a firm hand.

With both husband and wife increasingly responsible for getting and spending the

[16] Alice C. Thorpe, "How Married Students Manage," *Marriage and Family Living* 13, no. 3 (Summer 1951): 104–105, 130.

[17] Clarence Day, *Life with Father* (New York: Alfred A. Knopf, 1935).

EWING GALLOWAY

By reading labels and intelligently comparing values, young married couples stretch their money as far as it will go.

family income, there arises more consideration of the principles of wise purchasing. When both have planned for the purchase of some new item, they both are concerned with "getting the best buy." Courses, classes, units, and single lectures in consumer buying and subscriptions to such guides as *Consumer Reports* and *Consumers' Research Bulletins* have greatly increased in recent years. Today one sees an occasional young couple reading labels on packaged products and intelligently comparing the values of competing commodities. With a limited amount of money and a large number of needs, today's early married couple wants to know how to stretch the family dollars as far as they will go.

Establishing mutually satisfactory systems for getting and spending money as a developmental task involves at least four specific challenges: (1) coming to terms with the realities of one's own financial situation in the face of the appealing claims of modern advertising, high pressure salesmanship, and "keeping up with the Joneses" pressures, (2) finding mutually comfortable sources of income for the immediate and the distant future, (3) establishing ways of deciding how the money will be spent, for what and by whom, and (4) developing sound financial plans and buying methods. These challenges must be met in some way during the early days of the marriage. Successful methods express the values of the couple and are based upon the realities

of their situation. Upon the successful accomplishment of this developmental task rests the future financial health of the family.

Establishing Mutually Acceptable Patterns of Who Does What and Who is Accountable to Whom

Traditionally the roles of husband and wife were rigidly defined and underwent little variation by the individual couple. There was man's work and woman's work, and each knew which was which. The man was the head of the house, and his wife and children respected his authority and bowed to it. Today's newly married couples have no such definite outlines to follow in the division of responsibilities and the assignment of the roles within the union. They must work them out for themselves within the new patterns of freedom characteristic of the modern age.[18]

Nowadays more women find a place for themselves outside the home in remunerative work and volunteer service within the larger community. Concurrently men are becoming increasingly familiar with the household and its operation. Thus we find that among the married students already

[18] Debi D. Lovejoy, "College Student Conceptions of the Roles of the Husband and Wife in Family Decision-making," *Family Life Coordinator* 9, nos. 3–4 (March–June 1961): 43–46.

cited,[19] most of the husbands regularly help with the housework (77.2 percent). Husbands as well as wives are found taking the laundry to the nearby laundromat and casually enjoying menu-planning, as foods are bought for the week ahead. Men as well as women today engage in meal preparation with the help of packaged products, quick-frozen foods, modern kitchen equipment, and outdoor grills and barbeques. Merchandising that directly appeals to the male food handler (men's aprons, chef outfits, etc.) both represents and facilitates this trend.

Establishing a Continuity of Mutually Satisfying Sex Relationships

Part of the enigma of marriage stems from the fact that American codes have not yet reached agreement concerning the eternally troublesome questions of sex and love.[20] Being in love is presumed by most young people to be a sufficient answer in itself to any questioning of an adequate reason for a marriage. Elders, generally speaking, think that love is not enough to marry on, and they make a good case for their point of view. But to Joe and Jane in their teens or early twenties, the principal and impelling fact which stimulates them to marry, and to marry each other, is the unanswerable imperative that "it *is* love."

Sex is, at its best, one of life's great fulfillments, but this blessing is unequally distributed among married couples, and frustration is experienced by many in their search for fulfillment. Sexual maladjustments of one sort or another are confusing and irksome to many couples, especially during the first few years of marriage. Generally speaking, much of the trouble stems from the contradictions between the couple's expectations, on the one hand, and the inaccuracy of their knowledge regarding the subtleties of "the facts of life."[21] The problem is not, of course, wholly a matter of knowledge and intent. It is greatly complicated by the fact that husbands and wives both bring to marriage numerous and significant unconscious needs

[19] Thorpe, "How Married Students Manage," pp. 104–105.

[20] See Sylvanus M. Duvall, *Men, Women, and Morals* (New York: Association Press, 1952). For abundant statistical data see Alfred C. Kinsey, Wardell B. Pomeroy, and Clyde E. Martin, *Sexual Behavior in the Human Male* (Philadelphia: W. B. Saunders Company, 1948); and Alfred C. Kinsey, Wardell B. Pomeroy, Clyde E. Martin, and Paul H. Gebhard, *Sexual Behavior in the Human Female* (Philadelphia: W. B. Saunders Company, 1953).

[21] Inadequacies in knowledge in this area may be met in part by reading such books as Eustace Chesser, *Love Without Fear* (New York: Signet Books, 1949); Evelyn Millis Duvall and Reuben Hill, *When You Marry*, rev. ed. (New York: Association Press; Boston: D. C. Heath and Company, 1967); and Hannah and Abraham Stone, *A Marriage Manual*, rev. ed. (New York: Simon and Schuster, 1952).

and wants.[22] We perceive our true selves only dimly, as if through a dense mist into which we can occasionally peer, with distortions and mirages common. But the illusion persists that we really know ourselves, our needs, our desires, and also those of our mates.

Individual needs growing out of different hereditary makeup, different background of experience, and differing conceptions of the purpose of sex create barriers to mutual gratification. Accumulating frustrations bring forth angered epithets like "prude," "cold," "sensual," "beastly," "oversexed," and the like. It requires time,[23] more patience than some people have, more information than many can get, and skills of a specific nature to find mutual fulfillment. The almost innumerable avenues of sex satisfaction present further difficulties. Intimate personal acts which embellish the sexual experience for one mate may offend the fastidiousness of the other. Guilt, shame, indecision, and, many times, deep and abiding hostility become ingrained in the very fabric of sex in marriage. Hostilities may, over a long time, grow and fester into an impairment of the whole marital structure.

There are often painful discoveries such as lack of sexual response of the wife, the "insatiability" of the husband, jealousies with or without foundation in fact, or inabilities to forgive indiscretions in the past. These may have been confessed by the spouse in the attempt to relieve guilt feelings, only to find his or her marriage bond threatened by candor. There is evidence that previous sex experience is not necessarily conducive to good sex adjustment in marriage.[24]

In time, sexual difficulties, like other conflicts and disappointments, work out one way or another. The nature of this accomplishment is indeed varied. Failure is seen in resignation to one's fate, chronic frustration concealed (or ill-concealed), overt hostility to the mate, or generalized irritability. Progress is found in discovery of unexpected strength in self or mate, realization that success is worth working for and that the race for it can be fun, selective forgetting of earlier frustrated goals, and learning the knowledges, skills, and attitudes that make for mutual fulfillment.

The husband and wife who work out together a continuity of mutually satisfying sex relationships early in their marriage not only find a source of deep satisfaction for the present, but they also establish a firm foundation upon which other tasks

[22] John Levy and Ruth Munroe, *The Happy Family*, rev. ed. (New York: Alfred A. Knopf, 1962).

[23] Judson T. Landis, "Length of Time Required to Achieve Adjustment in Marriage," *American Sociological Review* 11, no. 6 (December 1946): 666–677.

[24] See David F. Shope and Carlfred B. Broderick, "Level of Sexual Experience and Predicted Adjustment in Marriage," *Journal of Marriage and the Family* 29, no. 3 (August 1967): 424–433; and also text and references in Evelyn Millis Duvall, *Why Wait Till Marriage?* (New York: Association Press, 1965).

FAMILY DEVELOPMENT

can be undertaken, and future happiness as a couple can be built.

Establishing Systems of Intellectual and Emotional Communication

One of the biggest jobs facing the recently married couple is that of communicating with each other. Two people may live in the same house and share the same bed and board, but unless they establish effective systems of communication between them, they might as well be miles apart. She may live through the days in tight-lipped silence; he may pout and mope through the evenings, with no awareness of what "is eating" either of them, unless and until they have developed the signs and signals, the words and gestures that keep the state of affairs open to them both.

Human beings do not live in emotional vacuums, but in a climate of feeling that changes quite as often as the weather. Each of us at times feels loving and at times feels hateful; at times is high and at other times low; is sometimes mad and sometimes sad. Mental hygiene findings have indicated without question that the healthful way to live is to recognize emotional states for what they are, as they arise, and to deal with them realistically. Pretending that all is well while one seethes inside is hypocrisy, and it is corrosive if it becomes habitual.

If two people are to live intimately together in marriage, they must learn to express their feelings in acceptable and healthful ways. They must develop ways of communicating for the mutual planning and furtherance of mutual services and for the necessity of sharing the meanings of a moment in true companionship—understanding and being understood in a system of satisfying mutual identification.

In a study of the development of the relationship of recently married couples, Bolton finds that some couples discover an immediate ability to communicate freely with one another. One young wife reports, "We communicated right away. We spoke the same language. There was a mutual understanding of feelings about things without having to go into detail." A young husband says, "I can tell by the kind of tenseness in her body whether she wants to be kissed or not. There's a lot of things like that by which I can tell her mood—whether she's quiet, the way she curls her lip, whether she looks up when I talk to her."

Couples reporting an awareness of spontaneous empathy describe it as some feeling of homogamy and of responsiveness. They seem to feel an immediate meshing of behavior without resorting to words. But the development of lasting communication appears to depend more upon the use of words or upon gestural cues translated into verbal intentions.

Most couples are found to develop a private vocabulary consisting of terms of endearment, special names, and unique symbolic meanings attached to jokes, rituals, or events shared in the relationship. Some couples work out special techniques for facilitating communication under tension. As a whole the form of communication remains relatively stable throughout the relationship. The evolution of the relation occurs more in the content than in the form of communication. Indeed, the conclusion is that "the mode of communication is one of the most stable and fundamental personality characteristics."[25]

Communication is an intricate complex of words, gestures, signs, and symbolic actions that have meanings to the communicating people. Some of these words and meanings are universal. Some are peculiar to the language and cultural group. More subtle systems are highly individual and must be built up within the new relationship. One of the joys of courtship, engagement, and the honeymoon is found in the development and the practice of intimate, personal gestures and symbols that have meaning only for the two persons. They identify "our song"; they walk by "our house" or through "our park"; and they repeat little ceremonies that convey more than words could the special significance each has for the other. Special gestures of affection become their own language of love that channels love feelings and adds immeasurably to the satisfaction they get in each other's company.

It may be relatively easy to get through to each other with love and affection. But learning how to handle the inevitable negative feelings that arise from time to time is a difficult assignment for many couples. No two people see eye to eye about all things. No two people feel the same way about everything they share in life together. So some conflict is to be expected in marriage, especially during the establishment phase, when the two people are learning to mesh their former ways of living into a unity of habits, aspirations, and values.

The romantic illusion prevalent in America calls for two people in love living "happily ever after" in a state of perpetual bliss that offers no room for the disagreements and differences that two normal people inevitably find cropping up between them. So, when the first quarrels occur, one or both of the pair mistakenly may feel that the marriage is failing, their love is not lasting, or they were not "made for each other" after all. The couple that is able to see conflict as a part of the close, intimate marriage relationship accepts its reality and assumes the responsibility for meeting constructively the differences that arise.

One of the critical tests of the adequacy of the communication established within a marriage is found in the way in which the two people meet a conflict situation. As long as they keep silent and pretend that they have no problems, little progress can be made in getting through to each other. When one person leaves the conflict situation in anger or in tears or in patient

[25] Charles D. Bolton, "The Development Process in Love Relationships" (Ph.D. dissertation, University of Chicago, 1959), pp. 242–243.

Table 7–4. *A Pattern for Problem-solving*

Steps	Key questions	Purpose
1. Face the problem	What is the matter? Why do I/we think it is a problem?	To get problem into words. To uncover the fear involved.
2. Look at the causes	What has been happening? What has made it a problem now?	To get the buildup of the problem. To get a clear statement of what is bringing it to a head.
3. Set some goals	What do I want to accomplish for myself? For the other person? What do we/I want the situation to be?	To be sure of desires for self. To be sure that decisions will benefit others as well as self. To set a definite change to work toward.
4. Get more knowledge and understanding	What knowledge from the biological, psychological, and social sciences is applicable? Have I found all the available material in technical and popular literature? What has been the experience of other people in similar situations?	To increase understanding. To gain insight.
5. Be the other person (Try to be each of the other persons or groups of persons involved in the problem)	Just how would I, as this other person, think about it? And as this other person, what does he or she feel?	To get the other person's point of view and emotional slant. To allow thinking and feelings of others be a framework for the next step.
6. Consider what to do	What could we/I do about it? Will that bring me to my goals? Will it fit the thoughts and feelings of the other person?	To get a list of possible actions. To be sure they lead to the goals. To be sure they will be acceptable to the other person.
7. Make a plan of action	Just how can this be done? Who will do each part? How will I do it? Who will help me?	To plan how to do it. To develop a one-two-three plan. To select the person to help at each point if needed.
8. Check the plan with the goals	Will this plan lead you to your goals? Does it provide for each goal?	To be sure the plan is really directed at the desired solution. To be sure it covers all the goals set.
9. Plan the follow-up	What shall I/we watch for to be sure the plan is working?	To encourage watchfulness in using the plan. To encourage abandonment if it seems to be failing.

Source: An adaption of "A Pattern for Counseling," by L. A. Lynde, extension specialist in parent education, January 30, 1947.

martyrdom, communication between the partners is poor. As the husband and wife make a real effort to share their true feelings and to accept without anxiety or fear the fact that their feelings and values do differ, they are able to learn to bridge their differences.

Table 7–4, "A Pattern for Problem-solving," evolved in family life education classes at Oklahoma State University as a guide for the development of skills in solving interpersonal problems.

Two people do not need to be identical to fit together well in action. Their differences and discrepancies may complement one another. They achieve a good fit when they harmonize their needs and values, whether these are alike or unlike.[26] Developing patterns of resolving conflicts and making decisions that protect one another's values are related to developing empathy, mutual supportiveness, understanding, and genuine communication as a married couple.[27] There is some evidence that married people are about as responsive to strangers as they are to their spouses, and that strangers tend to be nicer to them, which is seen as a built-in source of marital instability.[28] On the other hand, the same researchers at the National Institute of Mental Health found that when spouses are faced with apparent discrepancies in their responses, they tend to reinterpret their replies so that they seem to be in agreement, thus attempting to maintain couple unity at all costs.[29]

Unity as a couple is established by the network of bonds that weave the two into two-in-one. The bonds are open systems of communication through which each gets across to the other for the comfort, the love, the understanding, the sympathy, the loyalty, and the sense of purpose a man or woman needs to feel truly married. Without such communication a person may ache with loneliness even while beside the mate. With a well-established communication system, the husband and wife feel united even though they may be separated by many months and miles.

Establishing Workable Relationships with Relatives

The man and woman marrying for the first time undergo a basic role shift from their parental homes to their own home-in-the-making. Simultaneously they find themselves in three families: her family of orientation, his family of orientation, and the family they are founding together as their family of procreation. The success of the marriage depends in part upon how com-

---

[26] Rapoport, "Normal Crises, Family Structure, and Mental Health," pp. 68–80.

[27] Harold L. Raush, Wells Goodrich, and John D. Campbell, "Adaptation to the First Years of Marriage," *Psychiatry* 26, no. 4 (November 1963): 368–380.

[28] Robert G. Ryder, "Husband-Wife Dyads versus Married Strangers," *Family Process* 7, no. 2 (September 1968): 233–238.

[29] Robert G. Ryder and D. Wells Goodrich, "Married Couples' Responses to Disagreement," *Family Process* 5, no. 1 (March 1966): 30–42.

petently both husband and wife "forsake all others and cleave only to each other as long as they both shall live," to paraphrase the biblical injunction. For twenty years, more or less, the woman has been a daughter in her parents' home; now suddenly her husband must come first. For years, the young man has been a free agent, accountable only to his parents; now he is expected to be devoted exclusively to his wife. Difficulties in making these role shifts are seen in in-law problems through the early years of marriage.

Relationships with in-laws may be dreaded before marriage and avoided thereafter, in the stereotyped fear of intrusion that forms the basis of the universal mother-in-law joke and general mother-in-law avoidance.[30] Recent studies of newlyweds find that some couples have little contact with their parents, while others visit and telephone them often and still use their parents' closet space, automobile, checkbook, maid, and advice upon request. These family-oriented couples appear to value satisfactions with friends and the anticipation of parenthood more than their own intimate interaction. The couples who have cut themselves off from their parents tend to have a high degree of affective expression and investment in sexuality, and less interest in the prospect of child care, at least during the first four months of marriage.[31]

Studies of established marriages find that kinfolk are often counted on as friendly allies among young couples today quite as much as by their parents and grandparents. In fact, the youngest generation is least likely to say that each generation should go its own way (table 7–5).

---

[30] Evelyn Millis Duvall, *In-Laws: Pro and Con* (New York: Association Press, 1954).

[31] Wells Goodrich, Robert G. Ryder, and Harold L. Raush, "Patterns of Newlywed Marriage," *Journal of Marriage and the Family* 30, no. 3 (August 1968): 383–391.

Table 7–5. *Maintaining Intergenerational Relationships—Opinions by Generations*

Opinion		Grand-parents	Parents	Married children
A young couple and their parents-in-law should go their separate ways and see each other only occasionally	Agree	60%	42%	36%
	Disagree	29	46	42
	Undecided	11	12	22
Children who move up in the world tend to neglect their parents	Agree	22	20	9
	Disagree	64	69	74
	Undecided	14	11	17
A young couple has a real responsibility for keeping in touch with parents-in-law	Agree	65	65	74
	Disagree	13	21	14
	Undecided	22	14	12

Source: Reuben Hill, *Family Development in Three Generations* (Cambridge, Mass.: Schenkman Publishing Company, 1970): chap. 3, "Interdependence among the Generations."

A Cornell University study of recently married couples finds little evidence of young families being isolated from their parental families.[32] Some parents make such tangible contributions to the new household as cash, food, clothing, furnishings, equipment, furniture, and services such as baby-sitting, lodging, use of equipment, and household help.

Sussman and others find mutual help between the generations widespread among both middle- and working-class families. They find that couples receive financial aid from parents most often (1) during the early years of marriage, (2) when the parents approve the marriage, and (3) when the young people marry while still in school. Beyond the giving of tangible gifts to the young couple, there is a service network in families in which such assistance as help during illness, child care, visiting, escorting, shopping, and advice flow between parents and married children in both directions as voluntary mutual kin responsibilities through the years. Turning to relatives when trouble comes, rather than going first to community agencies set up for such service, is a common practice among the families studied.[33]

It is clear that few young married couples live to themselves alone, but rather within a total joint family of his relatives and hers. One of their tasks early in marriage is to establish those mutually satisfying relationships that it takes to thrive as members of the larger family. These interactions, most intense with parents of the pair, also branch out to siblings and other relatives.

Establishing Ways of Interacting with Friends, Associates, and Community Organizations

Being alone together is expected during the engagement and the honeymoon periods, but there comes a time when the married pair is ready for social activities. Friends, associates, and the larger community expect the couple to be active as a young married pair in the married set.

Getting into the young married set of the neighborhood is a developmental task that comes easily to the couple that settles down in the home community. It may pose problems for large numbers of young husbands and wives who move into a new area where they know no one and must find for themselves the companions and the social activities that interest both of them. The mixed marriage may require redefinitions of who is considered a pleasant companion and what is an acceptable social activity. Different experiences bring different defi-

[32] Alma Beth Clark and Jean Warren, *Economic Contributions Made to Newly Married Couples by Their Parents* (Ithaca, N.Y.: Cornell University, 1963), p. 5.

[33] Marvin B. Sussman and Lee Burchinal, "Kin Family Network: Unheralded Structure in Current Conceptualizations of Family Functioning," *Marriage and Family Living* 24, no. 3 (August 1962): 231–240.

nitions of how home is used. Jane, a minister's daughter, sees her home almost as a social center and expects neighbors and friends to drop in unannounced, while Jane's Joe sees their home as a refuge, with privacy and undisturbed quiet as prime values.

The demands upon the married couple made by the husband's job vary from the annual picnic of the plant, to which workers and their families are invited, to the exacting pressures made upon the corporation wife by the young executive's boss. The amount of business entertaining a young couple is expected to do depends upon his job, their social standing, and their social mobility. "Having the boss to dinner" has become a stereotyped problem situation in popular thinking that not incorrectly describes the anxiety and effort involved in becoming established as a socially acceptable married pair.

The extent to which the young husband and wife participate in community organizations depends on their previous involvements, on their social status, and on the length of time married. Lower-class families tend to be less active in community work than are members of the middle and upper classes. Young married couples are not as active in the community as are families established a number of years. The young husband and wife are highly mobile and busy getting themselves established, a task already achieved by longer-married couples. The children of the established family bring father and mother out to participate in neighborhood, school, church, and political projects that do not appeal as personally to the couple without children. The previous involvements of the young man or woman in union affairs, social activities, political campaigns, or church functions may continue to absorb the individual, especially if these interests are shared with the mate.

There may be some problems over the religious affiliations of the couple, especially if theirs is an interfaith marriage. Generally, there is more instability in mixed marriages than in those within the same faith. Three studies in various regions of the country (populations totaling 24,184) found significantly higher percentages of mixed marriages ending in divorce than do those in which the husband and wife share the same religious faith, as is summarized in table 7–6.

Sylvanus M. Duvall suggests several questions to be examined by two people attempting to establish a mixed marriage:

1. How intense is the loyalty of each to his own religious group?
2. How many complicating factors are there, such as relatives and influential friends?
3. What aspects of religion does each feel most strongly about?
4. Is there danger that religious differences will be used as a means by which one can dominate the other?
5. Are there other strong bonds to compensate for the religious differences?

6. What compromises are both willing to make to solve the problem?
7. What specific decisions can be made in regard to:
   a. Who, if either, will change his church relationship?
   b. If each retains his separate faith, where will they attend church, if at all?
   c. In what faith, if any, will the children be brought up?[34]

---

[34] Duvall and Hill, *When You Marry*, pp. 315–322; see also Raban Hathorn, William Genné, and Mordecai Brill, eds., *Marriage: An Interfaith Guide for All Couples* (New York: Association Press, 1970).

Table 7–6. *Percentage of Marriages of Mixed and Nonmixed Religious Faiths Ending in Divorce or Separation, as Revealed by Studies of Marriages in Michigan, Maryland, and Washington*

Religious categories	Landis Study* in Michigan (N = 4,108)	Bell Study† in Maryland (N = 13,528)	Weeks Study‡ in Washington (N = 6,548)
Both Catholic	4.4%	6.4%	3.8%
Both Jewish	5.2	4.6	—
Both Protestant	6.0	6.8	10.0
Mixed, Catholic-Protestant	14.1	15.2	17.4

Source: Data excerpted from Judson T. Landis, "Marriages of Mixed and Non-Mixed Religious Faith," *American Sociological Review* 14, no. 3 (June 1949): 403.
* Ibid., pp. 401–407.
† Howard M. Bell, *Youth Tell Their Story* (Washington, D.C.: American Council on Education, 1938), p. 21.
‡ H. Ashley Weeks, "Differential Divorce Rates by Occupation," *Social Forces* 21, no. 3 (March 1943): 336.

Even in marriages within the same faith there often are difficulties over the degree of interest in religious activities. A common conflict occurs when the wife wants to go to church regularly with her husband, while he prefers to sleep late on the one morning of the week when that is possible. The patterns a couple develops for resolving such differences and expressing their own wishes, desires, values, and beliefs take time to work out. These accomplishments are greatly aided by discussing the possible problems and their solutions in the premarital period, and then being willing to rethink and rework the tentative working agreements as needed during the establishment phase of the marriage.

Facing the Possibility of Children and Planning for Their Coming

The modern American couple marries with the anticipation of having children. Many have their first baby within the first year, some within the first nine months. Cross-cultural studies indicate that about one-fifth of all first births in the United States were conceived before marriage.[35] When marriage occurs after the first pregnancy

---

[35] Harold T. Christensen, "Studies in Child Spacing: I—Premarital Pregnancy as Measured by the Spacing of the First Birth from Marriage," *American Sociological Review* 18, no. 1 (February 1953): 53–59.

has already begun, the couple faces the developmental tasks of both the establishment and the expectant phases of stage 1 of the family life cycle concurrently.

The overwhelming majority of Americans believe in planned parenthood. On the basis of intensive interviews with a nationwide sample of white couples with wife under forty, researchers found attempts to avoid conception at some time virtually universal (94 percent) among couples with no fecundity impairment. Among fecund Catholic wives, 70 percent were past users and an additional 10 percent were acknowledged future users of both artificial and rhythm methods of family limitation.[36] However, many first babies are unplanned. One study of 424 married college students found that only slightly more than one-third had definitely planned their first child.[37]

Unplanned pregnancies may be a crisis for the couple, for either member of the pair, as well as for the child-to-be. Coming within the establishment phase of the newly founded family, a pregnancy may make it difficult for the wife to go with her husband as he completes his military service;

it may necessitate the wife's cutting short her educational plans; it may pull the young husband from long-range professional plans, and into some vocation where money is quicker and advancement sooner; it may mean the bringing in of one or both sets of parents for financial and personal help; or it may, if the couple is ready for a child, cement the marriage as nothing else can do.

Inability to conceive a child is another challenge to be faced. Infertility is encountered by something less than 15 percent of all married couples. During Bible days when a married woman did not become pregnant she was considered "barren." This term is no longer used by informed people for two reasons. First, because the condition is often caused by some inadequacy in the male, most frequently insufficiently motile sperm; and, second, because the inability to have a child is frequently a temporary condition that responds well to treatment. Infertility clinics in connection with hospitals in many communities, as well as private physicians in recent years, have increased the fecundity of many young married couples who want to become parents. Couples who have been married more than one year without conceiving a child are wise to go for examinations of both husband and wife and to accept treatment as indicated before becoming discouraged or jumping to the conclusion that theirs is a sterile union.

---

[36] Ronald Freedman, P. K. Whelpton, and Arthur Campbell, *Family Planning, Sterility, and Population Growth* (New York: McGraw-Hill Book Company, 1959), pp. 61, 104.

[37] Shirley Poffenberger, Thomas Poffenberger, and Judson T. Landis, "Intent toward Conception and the Pregnancy Experience," *American Sociological Review* 17, no. 5 (October 1952): 616–620.

Nine out of ten couples who are childless from choice have no interest in children.[38] The wife's participation in activities outside the home is directly related to her interest in and liking for children, as well as to the effectiveness of her family planning.[39] The more education a woman has, the less likely she is to want either no children at all or a very large family. The married college woman tends to prefer two or three children, according to a number of studies.[40]

Marital dissatisfaction tends to discourage the usual preference for children.[41] Well-adjusted married pairs tend to want children and to have the size family they prefer.[42]

More firstborn babies arrive during the first year of marriage than at any other time. By the end of the second year of marriage two-thirds of the white mothers (66.2 percent) and three-fourths of all nonwhite mothers (75.7 percent) in the population have had their first baby.[43]

Establishing a Workable Philosophy of Life as a Couple

Presumably the young adult has some kind of philosophy of life by the time he or she is old enough to marry. With marriage comes the weaving of one's convictions and values with those of the partner into a philosophical whole that gives unity to the marriage. Marriage provides for the young husband and wife many opportunites for testing previous orientations and situations that challenge former conclusions. Together the two people in marriage must choose those alternatives that best represent their present positions. Together over a period of time they develop a philosophy of life by which they can live.

Pressures during the early establishment phase of marriage push the young married couple into taking one stand or another on a good many issues. As a married pair they must decide what church they will attend, or if they will affiliate with any religious group. They face the current political situation with either indifference or dedicated loyalties. As soon as they are married they

[38] Lois Pratt and P. K. Whelpton, "Social and Psychological Factors Affecting Fertility," *Milbank Memorial Fund Quarterly* 33, no. 4 (October 1955): 1243.

[39] Ibid., vol. 34, no. 1 (January 1956): 1271.

[40] Ibid., and Robert O. Blood, Jr., and Donald M. Wolfe, *Husbands and Wives: The Dynamics of Married Living* (Glencoe, Ill.: Free Press, 1960), pp. 122–123.

[41] Ibid., p. 123.

[42] Robert B. Reed, "Sociological and Psychological Factors Affecting Fertility: The Interrelationship of Marital Adjustment, Fertility Control, and Size of Family," *Milbank Memorial Fund Quarterly* 25 (October 1947): 383.

[43] U.S. Bureau of the Census, "Marriage, Fertility, and Childspacing: August 1959," *Population Characteristics,* Current Population Reports, series P-20, no. 108 (July 12, 1961), p. 51.

meet the question of the filing of joint or individual income tax returns with temptations for "saving" as much as they can on their tax, on the one hand, or submitting a completely honest statement on the other. These are the decisions that reflect and refine a philosophy of life.

As a newly established unit of society they find themselves forced to take some kind of position—in their social groups, in the neighborhood, at work, as they read the daily paper, listen to the news reports over the radio, and fall into casual conversations—on the widely discussed issues of the day. In a hundred different weekly situations they are testing and establishing the philosophy by which they are to live—in the attitudes they take toward the new family from another ethnic background, recently moved into the neighborhood; in the way they feel and talk about an incident of aggression in the central square; in the position they take on the new zoning law that is being voted upon; in the way they behave when given too much change for a purchase; in the way they act toward the man who carries away their trash, or the deference they show the people above them in the community; in the degree of perfection they expect of themselves, of each other, and of others. In all these situations, and more, they are weaving the philosophy of life by which they as a couple are to live.

Establishing a philosophy of life for the average couple does not involve writing out a personal family creed. Few families come to that degree of explicit awareness of the philosophies by which they live. But whether it becomes explicit or not, the philosophy of life is there, worked out in everyday life together.

This does not imply that the couple must come to exactly the same stand on every issue of life. In some areas they may agree to disagree, each recognizing the other's right to feel as he or she must, believe what makes sense, and act according to his or her own convictions. But over and beyond the personal philosophy that moves each person to be himself is the philosophy of life as a couple that must be established explicitly or implicitly in early marriage.

CHALLENGES AND HAZARDS OF THE ESTABLISHMENT PHASE

The likelihood of divorce rises rapidly after the first few months of marriage, reaches a peak at the close of the first year, and steadily declines through the rest of the marriage.[44] Few couples realize how vul-

[44] National Center for Health Statistics, *Vital Statistics of the United States: Marriage and Divorce,* vol. 3 (Washington, D.C.: National Center for Health Statistics, 1965), table 2–5, pp. 2–8; see also Hugh Carter and Paul C. Glick, *Marriage and Divorce: A Social and Economic Study* (Cambridge, Mass.: Harvard University Press, 1970).

Chart 7–2. *Percentage of 409 Couples Reporting Various Periods of Time after Marriage to Achieve Adjustments*

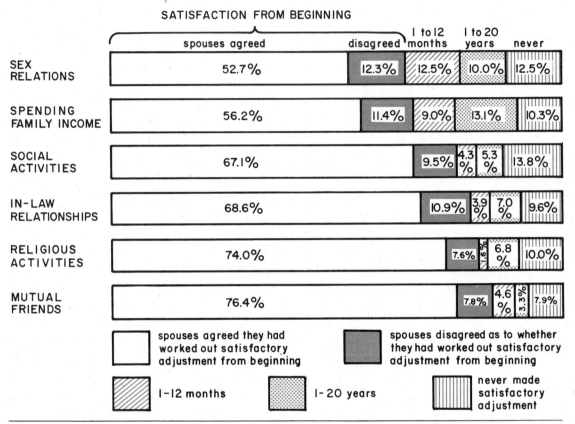

SATISFACTION FROM BEGINNING

	spouses agreed	disagreed	1 to 12 months	1 to 20 years	never
SEX RELATIONS	52.7%	12.3%	12.5%	10.0%	12.5%
SPENDING FAMILY INCOME	56.2%	11.4%	9.0%	13.1%	10.3%
SOCIAL ACTIVITIES	67.1%	9.5%	4.3% / 5.3%		13.8%
IN-LAW RELATIONSHIPS	68.6%	10.9%	3.9%	7.0%	9.6%
RELIGIOUS ACTIVITIES	74.0%	7.6%	1.6%	6.8%	10.0%
MUTUAL FRIENDS	76.4%	7.8%	4.6%	3.3%	7.9%

☐ spouses agreed they had worked out satisfactory adjustment from beginning

▩ spouses disagreed as to whether they had worked out satisfactory adjustment from beginning

▨ 1-12 months

▦ 1-20 years

▥ never made satisfactory adjustment

Source: Judson T. Landis, "Adjustments After Marriage," *Marriage and Family Living* 9, no. 2 (May 1947): 33.

nerable marriage is during the establishment phase. The tendency to think that marriage solves all problems is one real hazard facing the romantic couple who expect to find immediate and unending bliss as soon as they are married.

Some couples work out mutually satisfactory adjustments from the beginning. But a sizable percentage never do, and others work at their developmental tasks for several months to many years before they agree that all is well. Chart 7–2 summarizes the time couples happily married for twenty years or more reported it took them to make their marriage adjustments in six areas of their lives together.

Young people lacking the maturity to enjoy the responsibilities and privileges of marriage are ill-prepared for the many concurrent roles they must play as husband

and wife. When the marriage is combined with continuing education, military service, vocational establishment, high mobility, and/or dependence upon parents, it is filled with hazards for the young pair.

Financial strain is particularly great during the early years of marriage. Then a couple faces the high costs of getting and furnishing a place to call their own in line with advertising pressures and their efforts to impress their friends. At that time, when their costs may be greater than they ever will be again, the husband's income as a new worker is at a low point in his career. In order to start out in the style to which they would like to become accustomed, many a newly married couple goes into debt or buys more on the installment plan than they can afford.

The wife's working to help out during the establishment phase can itself create problems that must be solved. Unless the couple learns to live on the husband's income, they face additional adjustments when the wife drops out of work to have the first baby. Fitting homemaking tasks into the residue of time left after a full working day can be overtiring. Expecting a husband's help at home when he is swamped with his job, his further education, and his anxiety about military service may be more than he can measure up to.

Fallacious stereotypes about in-laws increase the difficulties the young couple has in accepting proffered help from one or both sets of parents, and can make for unnecessary strain between the young husband and wife and their relatives on both sides of the family.[45] Taboos, misconceptions, and fictions about love, sex, and marriage are disruptive, especially during the early years of marriage.[46] Yet they are rampant in the culture and continue to be reinforced through the mass media.

Resources for Establishing the Marriage

The honeymoon, as a period of privacy during which the couple may explore the intimate personal side of marriage, is an important resource for the newly married couple. Making good use of the honeymoon depends upon the attitudes the couple has as they embark upon it.[47] One study found 57 percent of the women saying they felt happy and expectant, and 28 percent confident and calm. But 21 percent also reported they were fatigued and exhausted; 16 percent felt apprehensive and fearful; and 20 percent were overstimulated and tense.[48] In time, resentments and dis-

---

[45] Duvall, *In-Laws: Pro and Con.*

[46] Ibid., and E. E. LeMasters, *Modern Courtship and Marriage* (New York: Macmillan Company, 1957), chap. 3, "Folklore about Marriage in Our Society," pp. 48–65.

[47] Lee G. Burchinal, Glenn R. Hawkes, and Bruce Gardner, "Personality Characteristics and Marital Satisfaction," *Social Forces* 35, no. 3 (March 1957): 218–222.

[48] Betty Hannah Hoffman, "Are Honeymoons Happy?" *Ladies' Home Journal,* June 1961, pp. 36–37, 104.

appointments drain off in socially accepted ways, while, through it all, the two are thrown together with the expectation of success by all who know them.

Some tasks of the honeymoon period are *intrapersonal*. Rhona and Robert Rapoport[49] list these as (1) developing competence to participate in an appropriate sexual relationship with one's marital partner, and (2) developing competence to live in close association with the marital partner. They find in their exploratory studies that young couples are often concerned about their sexual competence. Brides tend to be anxious about the possible pain of intercourse, whether their husbands will be patient and gentle with them, and whether they will be able to satisfy their husbands. Bridegrooms' fears center in their possible inability to be potent with their wives. Both members of the pair may be concerned about whether their autonomy will be threatened by the intimacy of marriage.

The honeymoon usually is the first experience of living intimately with a person of the other sex. It is then that feelings about sharing the same bed, about undressing in front of one another, about using the bathroom, and other such homely details of interaction come to the fore.

Other tasks of the honeymoon are *interpersonal:* (1) developing the basis for a mutually satisfactory sexual relationship, and (2) having a mutually satisfactory shared experience as a basis for developing a continuing husband-wife relationship. The husband and wife learn to cooperate and to sense their ability to work together. Getting married and establishing a marriage is a critical role transition for which many young people are often inadequately prepared.

Churches, YMCAs, YWCAs, and other youth- and family-serving agencies have established themselves in most communities as agencies interested in helping young men and women get a good start in marriage. Their services often include classes for engaged couples and young married couples, premarital and marital counseling services, special consultations in various aspects of marriage, and provision of films, books, pamphlets, and not infrequently some types of group discussion and therapy.

Schools and colleges in rapidly increasing numbers offer courses in family life education and related subjects designed to acquaint the student with the knowledge, skills, attitudes, and values that make for success in marriage.

Colleges and university centers in recent decades have greatly increased their research studies in marriage and family life. The implications of marriage research findings and clinical evidence are a substantial part of the many marriage texts now available for the young husband, wife, or couple interested in becoming informed in any of

[49] Rhona Rapoport and Robert N. Rapoport, "New Light on the Honeymoon," *Human Relations* 17, no. 1 (1964): 33–56.

the various areas involved in the establishment of their marriage.

SUMMARY

Married couples in the establishment phase of the family life cycle are building foundations upon which their life together is to be based. This calls for readiness to be married often lacking in very young marriages. Resources both within the young couple and to be tapped in the community may be helpful in preventing premature marriages. This period has many important developmental tasks as the couple attempts to satisfy their need for adult sexual fulfillment in marriage (biological origin), measure up to what is expected of them as a married couple (cultural origin), and merge their values as a couple (origins in personal aspirations).

The developmental tasks of this phase of the family life cycle may be summarized as (1) establishing a home base in a place they can call their own, (2) establishing mutually satisfying systems for getting and spending money, (3) establishing mutually acceptable patterns of who does what and who is accountable to whom, (4) establishing a continuity of mutually satisfying sex relationships, (5) establishing systems of intellectual and emotional communication, (6) establishing workable relationships with relatives, (7) establishing ways of interacting with friends, associates, and community organizations, (8) facing the possibility of children and planning for their coming, and (9) establishing a workable philosophy of life as a couple.

Each of the developmental tasks involved in establishing a marriage has hazards and challenges that must be met successfully if the couple is to develop and grow satisfactorily. Success in developmental tasks does not come all at once, but it must be achieved if the couple is to find happiness together. Upon the accomplishment of the developmental tasks of the establishment phase rests the future success of the developmental tasks still to come in the stages ahead for the couple in the family life cycle.

Resources available to help couples satisfactorily achieve the developmental tasks of the establishment phase are: the honeymoon period that protects the young couple in a circle of privacy in which the first intimate personal adjustments to married living may be made; encouragement and support from family, friends, and community in becoming a married couple and learning to live as a married pair; family life education in schools, churches, and community settings that prepares young people for marriage responsibilities ahead; premarital counseling; marriage and family research, with its implications for mate selection and preparation for marriage; marriage and family books that translate research and clinical evidence into discussions and recommendations that are functionally most relevant for the couple.

SUGGESTED ACTIVITIES

1. Review any five of the marriage texts listed in the readings, with special attention to the amount of space given the various tasks of the establishment phase of the beginning family. Count the number of pages in each text devoted to each of the developmental tasks (as described in this chapter) and make a chart by texts and tasks of the coverage of each. Discuss your findings.

2. Write a letter to your sister who is to be married soon, suggesting the resources she may want to avail herself of as her wedding date approaches, as well as after the ceremony. Tell her why you recommend the services you do.

3. Investigate the living units available in your community for a young married couple by answering a representative sampling of the advertisements in your local paper for rooms, apartments, and homes available for rent. How much rent will a young married couple have to pay for various types of housing in your area? In what condition are the available places?

4. Survey the married students in your area in terms of (a) working wives, (b) part-time employment of student-husbands, (c) other sources of income, and (d) use of budgets or other financial plans by the couple. Write up your findings in a report on "How Married Students Get and Spend Their Money."

5. Explore the factors discussed in the literature on sex adjustments in marriage for possible reasons why the task of achieving a mutually satisfying sex relationship is less often accomplished from the beginning than other aspects in building a marriage. Review your findings with an experienced physician, marriage counselor, or worker in a marriage counseling service in your community for futher interpretation of the nature of this developmental task. Summarize your material in a short report.

6. Find out what research studies have to say about which in-law is the most difficult, what husbands and wives report as objectionable behavior on the part of in-laws, and what makes for good in-law relationships. *In-Laws: Pro and Con* in your readings may be a helpful resource in this assignment.

7. View the kinescope "In-Laws" (No. 11 in the 1956 Marriage Series), produced by and available from the University of Michigan Television Center, Ann Arbor, Michigan, in which Robert O. Blood, Jr., and Evelyn Millis Duvall discuss in-law relationships in marriage. Discuss.

8. Consider the importance of emotional maturity in the accomplishment of the developmental tasks of early marriage in a series of psychodramas illustrating immature and relatively mature ways of meeting one or more of the usual early marriage challenges.

9. Practice problem-solving approaches to husband-wife differences in a series of "talk-

out" sessions, as developed by Dr. Hazel Ingersoll, Department of Family Relations and Child Development, Oklahoma State University. She divides the class into couples (man and woman preferably, or a pair of men or of women). Each pair takes roles of husband and wife, chooses a problem from such a list as is given below, and practices talking out differences. Stress is placed on considering feelings and attitudes of individuals as well as the facts of the case. Talk-out sessions go on simultaneously for a while, then volunteer pairs do spontaneous demonstration "talk-outs" before the entire group. Problem situations such as the following are suggested:

a. Who will manage the money—husband or wife?

b. Working wife versus wife as a full-time homemaker.

c. Simple small-town life versus living in a large city.

d. He thinks entertaining is a waste of money; she thinks it is important.

e. She wants a large church wedding, but he wants a simple family ceremony.

f. He wants to accept a job in a foreign country; she wants to stay home.

g. She insists on going to church and Sunday school; he likes to stay home and sleep late on Sunday.

h. He expects her to move into a large ranch house with his father; she objects.

READINGS

Bach, George R., and Peter Hyden. *The Intimate Enemy: How to Fight Fair in Love and Marriage.* New York: William Morrow and Company, 1968; New York: Avon Books, 1970.

Bartz, Karen Winch, and F. Ivan Nye. "Early Marriage: A Propositional Formulation." *Journal of Marriage and the Family* 32, no. 2 (May 1970): 258–268.

Blood, Robert O., Jr., and Donald M. Wolfe. *Husbands and Wives: The Dynamics of Married Living.* Glencoe, Ill.: Free Press, 1960.

Bowman, Henry. *Marriage for Moderns.* 6th ed. New York: McGraw-Hill Book Company, 1970.

Burgess, Ernest W., and Paul Wallin, with Gladys Denny Shultz. *Courtship, Engagement, and Marriage.* Philadelphia: J. B. Lippincott Company, 1954.

Chilman, Catherine S. "Dating, Courtship, and Engagement Behavior of Married, Compared to Single, Undergraduates, with an Analysis of Early-Marrying and Late-Marrying Students." *Family Life Coordinator* 15, no. 3 (July 1966): 112–118.

Christensen, Harold T. *Marriage Analysis.* Rev. ed. New York: Ronald Press Company, 1958.

Clark, Alma Beth, and Jean Warren. *Economic Contributions Made to Newly Married Couples by Their Parents.* Ithaca, N.Y.: Cornell University, 1963.

Duvall, Evelyn Millis. *In-Laws: Pro and Con.* New York: Association Press, 1954.

Duvall, Evelyn Millis, and Reuben Hill. *Being Married.* New York: Association Press; Boston: D. C. Heath and Company, 1960.

Eshleman, J. Ross. "Mental Health and Marital Integration in Young Marriages." *Journal of Marriage and the Family* 27, no. 2 (May 1965): 255–262.

Goodrich, Wells, Robert G. Ryder, and Harold L. Raush. "Patterns of Newlywed Marriage." *Journal of Marriage and the Family* 30, no. 3 (August 1968): 383–391.

Havighurst, Robert J. *Human Development and Education.* New York: Longmans, Green and Company, 1953. Chap. 16, "Developmental Tasks of Early Adulthood."

Hill, Reuben. *Family Development in Three Generations.* Cambridge, Mass.: Schenkman Publishing Company, 1970. Chap. 3, "Interdependence among the Generations."

International Union of Family Organizations. *Young Families in the Society.* Paris: IUFO General Secretariat, 1969.

Laing, Ronald D., H. Phillipson, and Russell A. Lee. *Interpersonal Perception.* New York: Springer Publishing Company, 1965.

Landis, Judson T., and Mary G. Landis. *Building a Successful Marriage.* 5th ed. Englewood Cliffs, N.J.: Prentice-Hall, 1968.

Levy, John, and Ruth Munroe. *The Happy Family.* Rev. ed. New York: Alfred A. Knopf, 1962.

Lidz, Theodore. *The Person: His Development throughout the Life Cycle.* New York: Basic Books, 1968. Chaps. 11–14.

Lovejoy, Debi D. "College Student Conceptions of the Roles of the Husband and Wife in Family Decision-Making." *Family Life Coordinator* 9, nos. 3–4 (March–June 1961): 43–46.

Margolius, Sidney. "Why Young Couples Spend More than They Earn." *Redbook,* February 1966, pp. 56–57, 104–107.

Martinson, Floyd M. *Marriage and the American Ideal.* New York: Dodd, Mead and Company, 1960. Pt. 3, "Marriage."

Masters, William H., and Virginia Johnson. *Human Sexual Inadequacy.* Boston: Little, Brown and Company, 1970.

Rainer, Jerome, and Julia Rainer. *Sexual Pleasure in Marriage.* New York: Julian Messner, 1959.

Rapoport, Rhona. "The Transition from Engagement to Marriage." *Acta Sociologica* 8, fasc. 1–2 (1964): 36–55.

Rapoport, Robert, and Rhona Rapoport. "Work and Family in Contemporary Society." *American Sociological Review* 30, no. 3 (June 1965): 381–394.

Raush, Harold L., Wells Goodrich, and John D. Campbell. "Adaptation to the First Years of Marriage." *Psychiatry* 26, no. 4 (November 1963): 368–380.

Ryder, Robert G. "Husband-Wife Dyads versus Married Strangers." *Family Process* 7, no. 2 (September 1968): 233–238.

Ryder, Robert G. "Married Couples' Responses to Disagreement." *Family Process* 5, no. 1 (March 1966): 30–42.

Shope, David F., and Carlfred B. Broderick. "Level of Sexual Experience and Predicted Adjustment in Marriage." *Journal of Marriage and the Family* 29, no. 3 (August 1967): 424–433.

Sporakowski, Michael J. "Marital Preparedness, Prediction and Adjustment." *Family Coordinator* 17, no. 3 (July 1968): 155–161.

Vincent, Elizabeth Lee, and Phyllis C. Martin. *Human Psychological Development*. New York: Ronald Press Company, 1961. Chap. 11, "Early Adulthood," and chap. 12, "Courtship, Marriage, and Family Life."

Womble, Dale L. *Foundations for Marriage and Family Relations*. New York: Macmillan Company, 1966.

8

PREGNANCY—
THE PROMISE
OF PARENTHOOD

*Age is not all decay, it is the ripening, the swelling of
fresh life within, that withers and bursts the husks.*

George Macdonald

The expectant phase of the beginning family starts with the awareness that the wife is pregnant and continues until the birth of the first child. This phase is no longer than nine months, and may be considerably shorter if the woman is already pregnant at marriage. Although short in length, the expectant family phase is long on tasks and responsibilities as the married pair concurrently develop their marriage relationship and their roles as parents-to-be.

There are two positions in the beginning family—that of husband and of wife, both maintaining a single basic relationship as a married couple. They are usually in their early twenties, facing the developmental tasks of early adulthood along with those of the family-in-the-making. The developmental crises of this phase are both those involved in intimacy patterns with the spouse and those inherent in bearing children, which Erikson calls "generativity" (chapter 6). The major family goal of this

phase is adjusting to pregnancy. How husband and wife feel about their new roles as parents-to-be varies greatly.

There is no one pattern of response when she misses her first menstrual period. Rather there are four possible reactions: (1) they both accept the fact that they have become an expectant family; (2) they both reject the baby months before he/she is due; (3) the husband accepts the pregnancy, while the wife does not; and (4) she is delighted, but he grouses about it. Pregnancy that is welcomed by some couples is an unbearable threat to others.

PARENTHOOD—
BY CHANCE OR CHOICE

More than 40 percent of the children born to the poor of this country are unwanted—a total of 450,000 a year. A recent survey of married women in the United States found more unwanted births among the poor (42 percent) than the near-poor (26 percent) or the more affluent (17 percent).[1] Many of these unwanted babies can be expected to become problems—to themselves and their families and for society as a whole. They are tomorrow's dropouts and delinquents, a new generation of the underprivileged from the moment of their birth.

Abortion

When a single girl finds herself unwillingly pregnant, she has five options: (1) marriage, (2) adoption, (3) keep her child, (4) abortion, and (5) suicide, as counselors with the Michigan Clergy for Problem Pregnancy Counseling recognize with their clients.[2]

When a married woman finds herself unwillingly pregnant, her alternatives are to bear or not to bear the unwelcome child. If she bears the baby reluctantly, she, her family, and the little newcomer face possibilities of problems that may go on for years. If a woman decides to relieve herself of the fetus, she can get a safe abortion if she has money enough. Widely circulated statistics of abortions performed legally in hospitals in New York City early in the sixties revealed more than nine out of ten women were patients in private rooms who could afford to pay well for their freedom from pregnancy. Less affluent women patronize abortion mills, doctors or nurses willing to operate outside the law, midwives, or neighbors, or they resort to self-administered treatments that are rarely effective in emptying the uterus, but can and do cause serious damage to health and life. In one typical year, women whose deaths were associated with abortions in New York City were 56 percent black, 23 percent Puerto Rican, and 21 percent white.[3]

Some legislators oppose liberalizing laws that make abortion a criminal offense. Most states have such restrictive legislation on their books; others are reviewing, revising, or repealing their abortion laws. Some church leaders oppose abortion for any reason, while others advocate the repeal of all abortion laws.[4]

---

[1] Charles F. Westoff, Emily C. Moore, and Norman B. Ryder, "The Structure of Attitudes toward Abortion," *Milbank Memorial Quarterly*, January 1969.

[2] "Clergy and Abortions," *Time*, November 28, 1969, p. 82.

[3] Harriet Pilpel, "The Right of Abortion," *Atlantic* 223, no. 6 (June 1969): 69–71.

[4] For instance, Pope Paul VI insists, "We must again declare that the direct interruption of the generative process already begun and above all, directly willed and procured abortion, even if for therapeutic reasons, are to be absolutely excluded as licit means of regulating birth" (*Humanae Vitae*, July 1968); on the other hand, Father Robert Drinan, dean of the Boston College Law School, and such Protestant bodies as the American Baptist Convention would like to see all abortion legislation repealed and the decision left to the woman and her doctor.

While lawyers and others debate the question in four out of five states of the union that "compel the unwilling to bear the unwanted," in Washington, D.C., United States District Court Judge Gerhard A. Gesell declared unconstitutional the law that makes it a crime for any doctor to perform an abortion except for the preservation of the mother's life or health. His interpretation of recent Supreme Court rulings leads him to believe that "a woman's liberty and right of privacy extends to family, marriage, and sex matters, and may well include the right to remove an unwanted child at least in the early stages of pregnancy."[5] Meanwhile, in a survey by *Modern Medicine* of 40,089 physicians, 87 percent of the doctors favored more liberal abortion laws. Married women themselves are overwhelmingly in favor of abortion if the mother's health is threatened.[6] Many authorities believe that every child has a right to be wanted by a family ready to provide the love and care he needs to develop his full human potential.

Family Planning

Preventing conception is the most widely used and recommended method of family planning in the United States. While search goes on for the perfect contraceptive (safe, effective, available, acceptable, inexpensive, and easy to use), millions of women regularly use one of the various oral contraceptives, intrauterine devices, or other methods of controlling their fertility. Voluntary sterilization, a safe procedure already legal in most states, is acceptable as more permanent prevention of conception for those for whom future childbearing would be unfortunate for any of a number of reasons.

Most married women in this country control their fertility. However, there are an estimated five million women living in poverty for whom family planning facilities are not available as yet. Therefore, the President's Committee on Population and Family Planning recommends "that the Federal Government rapidly expand family planning programs to make information and services available . . . on a voluntary basis to all American women who want but cannot afford them."[7]

Population Control

Population growth is seen as a critical worldwide problem. Dr. Philip Handler, president of the National Academy of Sciences, warns, "The greatest threat to the human race is man's own procreation. Hunger; pollution; crime; overlarge, dirty cities—even the seething unrest that leads

---

[5] "Constitutional Rights," *Time*, November 21, 1969, p. 65.

[6] Westoff, Moore, and Ryder, "The Structure of Attitudes toward Abortion."

[7] U.S. Department of Health, Education, and Welfare, *Population and Family Planning: The Transition from Concern to Action* (Washington, D.C.: U.S. Department of Health, Education, and Welfare, 1968), p. 16.

FAMILY DEVELOPMENT

Chart 8–1. *Population Increase of the United States, 1790–1970*

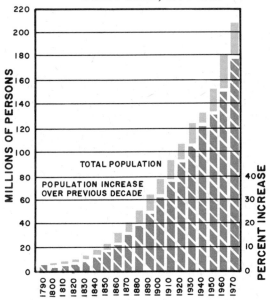

Source: U.S. Bureau of the Census, graphically presented by the Campaign to Check the Population Explosion.

Chart 8–2. *Increase of Women of Childbearing Ages, 20–29, for 1930–1980*

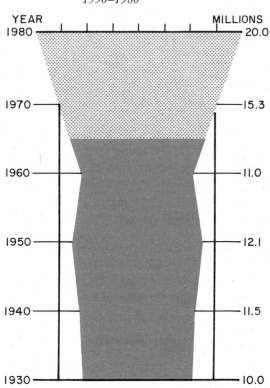

Source: Robert C. Cook and Goody Solomon, " 'Boom Babies' Come of Age: The American Family at the Crossroads," *Population Bulletin* 22, no. 3 (August 1966): 67. Used by permission of Population Reference Bureau, Washington, D.C.

to international conflict and war—all derive from the unbridled growth of human populations."[8] The spiraling growth of the population of the United States is clearly seen in chart 8–1 that shows the decade-by-decade population increase and the percentage increase each previous decade since the end of the eighteenth century. Chart 8–2 indicates the increase in the number of women of childbearing ages to be expected in the years ahead, which makes population control measures imperative if the United States is to avoid a dangerously

dense population. These females are already here, and, like their mothers, they will expect to marry and to have children in due time. Unless they are helped carefully to plan their families, overcrowding, poverty, pollution of air, water, and other natural resources, and further social problems will outrun the measures designed to solve them.

---

[8] "Overpopulation" (interview with Dr. Philip Handler), *This Week Magazine*, June 29, 1969, pp. 14–15.

Table 8–1. *Complementary and Conflicting Developmental Tasks during Pregnancy*

As the young couple go through the first pregnancy, there are times when their individual tasks complement each other in shared accomplishment as parents-to-be. Just as naturally, there are times when their individual developmental tasks conflict, and husband and wife are pulled in opposite directions. Illustrative instances are:

Developmental tasks of the expectant father	Developmental tasks of the expectant mother	Complementary and conflicting possibilities
Starting a family Planning the first child's arrival Learning what it means to become a father Giving his wife his support through her pregnancy and childbirth	Starting a family Planning the first child's arrival Learning what it means to be a mother Proceeding successfully through the pregnancy and childbirth experience	Complementary: both work together in the common task of becoming parents for the first time
Becoming a man in a man's world Finding himself among his fellow workers and male colleagues Taking jeers and taunts of other men good naturedly as his wife's condition becomes apparent Continuing some activities with "the boys" that do not include their wives necessarily	Becoming a woman in a woman's world Identifying with her women friends and neighbors in personal, special female ways Participating in baby showers and other "women only" affairs Borrowing and lending, sharing and being shared within the feminine fellowship of her relationship with "the girls"	Conflicting: the husband is pulled into male circles, and his wife is being absorbed in feminine interests and functions
Being responsible as the main support of the family Getting to work on time Carrying a full load as a breadwinner	Seeing her chief jobs as mother-to-be as well as wife Letting up on her outside interests as the pregnancy advances Becoming content to be wife and mother primarily	Complementary: common task of nest-building Conflicting: he is pulled outward, and she is pulled inward in her childbearing

Involuntary Childlessness

Only a rare married couple chooses to have no children at all. For the most part, childlessness is the result of some impairment of the reproductive system of husband or wife or both. Many of these conditions can be successfully treated, or they may right themselves in time.

More common are spontaneous miscarriages in which the uterus empties itself, usually in the first trimester of pregnancy. It is estimated that 400,000 to 600,000

American women involuntarily lose an embryo, in miscarriage, each year. Most women who lose one or more embryos early in pregnancy are able to have full-term babies later on. Some are helped by surgery, nutritional therapy, hormones, or psychotherapy to carry pregnancy through to term. A few become discouraged after numerous pregnancy failures and either go childless or adopt one or more children to bring up as their own. Adopted children place their families within the family life cycle in the same way that children born to the couple do, by age.

DEVELOPMENTAL TASKS OF THE EXPECTANT FAMILY

The developmental tasks of the expectant family arise in the biological reality of gestation, the cultural images of appropriate parenting roles, and the individual aspirations that both father-to-be and mother-to-be bring to their first experience in parenthood. The developmental tasks of this period in the family life cycle cannot be denied. They are peculiarly urgent and insistent. Whether the potential mother and father are ready or not, the pregnancy will come to term in the usual nine months. If the married couple is to make a comfortable adjustment to pregnancy, and to have their first baby with more of a sense of fulfillment than of distress, they must accomplish a number of developmental tasks that are particularly relevant to this stage in the family life cycle. These are, in brief summary:

1. arranging for the physical care of the expected baby
2. developing new patterns for getting and spending income
3. revaluating procedures for determining who does what and where authority rests
4. adapting patterns of sexual relationships to pregnancy
5. expanding communication systems for present and anticipated emotional needs
6. reorienting relationships with relatives
7. adapting relationships with friends, associates, and community activities to the realities of pregnancy
8. acquiring knowledge about and planning for the specifics of pregnancy, childbirth, and parenthood
9. maintaining morale and a workable philosophy of life.

Arranging for the Physical Care of the Expected Baby

No one has to teach birds their nesting rites and responsibilities. Their instincts guide them through the whole process. Not so with humans. They must learn their nesting tasks, step by step through the expectant phase.

Some husbands and wives take the coming of their first baby casually and do very little in providing a place for it before its arrival. The story is told of the young parents who simply dumped the contents of a dresser drawer in a box and plopped the new baby in the drawer, which served as a bed until the infant was big enough to sleep with its brothers. A maternity hospital reports that occasionally a baby arrives with no clothes to wear, no blankets, and no home to go to, but this is not the usual story, especially for the first baby. Later siblings may "make do" with provisions dating back to the arrival of their elder brothers and sisters, but some special provision is usually made for the first baby.

There are young couples who must make drastic shifts in their housing in order to make way for the expected first baby. Some modern apartment houses rule against children. A married couple whose first home has been in such a building must search out a more hospitable home base before their baby arrives. The husband and wife who have been floating from place to place in a series of rented rooms now want to settle down in something more permanent. The couple that has been living with one set of parents quite likely now desires to find a place of their own. There are couples who must find something less expensive than they have been enjoying in hous-

ing as soon as a baby is expected. Even more numerous are the young families-in-the-making who move to more desirable neighborhoods, sensing the importance of suitable neighbors, congenial companions, adequate play space, and good schools.

The husband and wife who stay on where they have been living make some rearrangements in their living space when a baby is expected. Room is cleared and provided for the baby's sleeping, eating, bathing, and playing. This may be a separate nursery complete with new baby furniture and sundry equipment, or it may be a corner that is equipped for baby care, away from the main household traffic. The differences in spatial arrangements are not important as long as husband and wife see eye to eye on them. Trouble comes when the definition of the demands of expectant parenthood differs greatly between the husband and wife.

A frequent problem arising in reorganizing the household for the first baby is that of the wife wanting more elaborate preparations and expensive rearrangements than the husband deems necessary. As the principal breadwinner, he is aware of the new responsibilities that will fall on him as father and so is reluctant to undertake any unnecessary expenditures. How the two resolve their dilemma is dependent in part upon how well they achieve the other developmental tasks they face as expectant parents.

Developing Earning and Spending Patterns

Fully 58 percent of all women expecting their first baby work during their pregnancy.[9] The coming of the first baby reduces the couple's income when the wife quits her job to devote herself primarily to motherhood while her children are young. Some married couples save the wife's first earnings against the time when they will need money for the costs of having children, buying and equipping their home, and establishing the financial security the mother of young children needs during the childbearing and child-rearing stages that lie ahead. Other newlyweds, who have been spending their joint income, are reduced to living on the husband's earnings alone at the time when costs increase with the arrival of the first baby.

The cost of having a baby was relatively low in the days when children were born in their parents' bed with only the family doctor, midwife, or neighbor in attendance. Today most babies are born in hospitals, where the costs are necessarily higher. Recent estimates of the costs of having a baby and raising it through its first year in the United States appear in table 8–2.

[9] National Center for Health Statistics, *Employment During Pregnancy* (Washington, D.C.: U.S. Department of Health, Education, and Welfare, 1968), p. 5.

Table 8–2. *Estimated Median Costs of Having a Baby, United States, 1969*

Usual items of expense	Estimated median cost
Medical expenses (doctor, hospital, post-maternity checkups, etc.)	$ 542
Pediatrician (newborn's care in hospital, inoculations, and first-year care)	128
Clothing (mail-order catalogue prices for infant wear the first year)	160
Furnishings (equipment, furniture, blankets, at national mail-order prices)	270
Infant food (government and industry estimates for nonnursing babies)	200
Diapers and laundering	200
Baby-sitters	40
Drug supplies and toiletries	35
Photographs	76
Total first-year costs	$1,651

Source: Kathleen D. Fury, "How Much Does a Baby Cost?" *Redbook*, July 1969, p. 49.

Costs range widely, by place of residence (large-city prices are usually higher than those in small communities), by income, and by individual values. Some couples prefer to borrow infant furnishings and supplies rather than to scrimp on baby-sitting services the first year. Others elect to have nearby relatives serve as sitters when needed and save their money for necessities. Clinic care for mother and infant costs less than private patients pay. Infant food costs are kept low if the mother nurses her baby and prepares some of his foods from stocks at hand. Home laundering costs are less than commercial diaper ser-

Table 8–3. *Estimated Cost of Raising a Child, 1969 (By Age of Child, Region, and Urbanization, in Family of Husband, Wife, and No More Than Five Children, with Food Expenditures at Level of Low-cost Food Plan), in Dollars*

Age of child (years)	Farm* North Central	South	North-east	Rural nonfarm North Central	South	North-east	West	Urban North Central	South	North-east	West
Under 1	$ 920	$ 1,040	$ 930	$ 970	$ 1,100	$ 1,100	$ 1,250	$ 1,130	$ 1,080	$ 930	$ 1,150
1	950	1,080	970	1,000	1,140	1,140	1,300	1,170	1,120	970	1,190
2	910	1,040	920	910	1,000	1,080	1,190	1,080	1,030	930	1,110
3	910	1,040	920	910	1,000	1,080	1,190	1,080	1,030	930	1,110
4	960	1,100	980	960	1,060	1,130	1,250	1,140	1,080	990	1,170
5	960	1,100	980	960	1,060	1,130	1,250	1,140	1,080	990	1,170
6	1,000	1,130	1,020	990	1,080	1,200	1,290	1,170	1,090	1,000	1,220
7	1,040	1,170	1,070	1,030	1,120	1,250	1,340	1,220	1,140	1,050	1,270
8	1,040	1,170	1,070	1,030	1,120	1,250	1,340	1,220	1,140	1,050	1,270
9	1,040	1,170	1,070	1,030	1,120	1,250	1,340	1,220	1,140	1,050	1,270
10	1,090	1,220	1,130	1,080	1,170	1,310	1,390	1,270	1,190	1,110	1,330
11	1,090	1,220	1,130	1,080	1,170	1,310	1,390	1,270	1,190	1,110	1,330
12	1,200	1,300	1,200	1,170	1,250	1,400	1,500	1,340	1,280	1,180	1,400
13	1,230	1,330	1,240	1,200	1,280	1,440	1,540	1,380	1,310	1,210	1,430
14	1,230	1,330	1,240	1,200	1,280	1,440	1,540	1,380	1,310	1,210	1,430
15	1,230	1,330	1,240	1,200	1,280	1,440	1,540	1,380	1,310	1,210	1,430
16	1,330	1,460	1,330	1,320	1,410	1,560	1,680	1,550	1,420	1,300	1,550
17	1,330	1,460	1,330	1,320	1,410	1,560	1,680	1,550	1,420	1,300	1,550
Total	$19,460	$21,690	$19,770	$19,360	$21,050	$23,070	$25,000	$22,690	$21,360	$19,520	$23,380

Source: Jean L. Pennock, "Cost of Raising a Child," *Family Economics Review,* March 1970, p. 16, table 3.
Note: Data rounded to nearest $10.
* Data for West not available.

vices, which are more convenient. Many a couple wants to splurge on its first baby and runs up the financial outlay beyond what is essential. This is an understandable celebration of becoming parents that may be worth the price to some young couples.

"It isn't the initial cost, it's the upkeep," that makes child-rearing expensive. The family's costs for raising its children rise with inflation, and in many items with a child's age, as is seen in table 8–3, consist-

ing of data from a 1969 United States Department of Agriculture study. The costs of raising a child vary by region of the country, as well as by urban-rural residence. Total costs through a child's seventeenth year range from $19,360 for a rural non-farm child in the North Central region to $25,000 for a rural nonfarm child in the West. Housing takes up to 30 percent of the total annual cost over a child's first seventeen years—the largest proportional expenditure per child. Food is a close second and may exceed housing, even at low-cost levels. Clothes cost another 10 to 12 percent of the family outlay per child, as do also expenses for recreation and personal care, with transportation even more costly. Medical care costs from 4 to 6 percent, and education about 1 percent per child, up to the time he is ready for college.[10]

Where is all the money coming from for initial costs of having the baby, its upkeep through the years, the many new needs as a family, the insurance, the savings, and all the rest at the very time that the wife stops work to give her time entirely to having and raising children? The answer varies from couple to couple, from social class to social class.

Depending upon its orientation, resources, and values, the young family may decide from among a variety of solutions to their financial problems. The young family may float a loan, or dip into savings, or look to their parents for help, or go into debt or into an orgy of installment buying. But whatever it does, the decision is there to be made.

Determining Who Does What and Where Authority Rests

Today's young mother-to-be assumes a multiplicity of roles. She carries on the responsibilities of her household; she works as long as her physician allows throughout the pregnancy; she is at home in classroom and laboratory as she tries to finish her education before maternity is upon her; she is found in her smart maternity garments as hostess or playmate along with her husband at neighborhood gatherings in the companionship roles so important today. Any one of these roles has been a full-time job for some women in the past—housewife, worker, mother-to-be, schoolgirl, hostess-companion. The modern young woman carries them all, with the help of her husband.

Now that men have a reasonably short working week (as compared with the sixty or more hours in the nineteenth-century work week), they have more time at home. Household tasks in the modern home, with its electrified equipment and packaged goods, are less arduous, more fun, and require less technical knowledge. Any man who wants to can whip up a tasty meal in today's kitchen. And many of them do. Now with wives out of the home carrying the variety of roles characteristic of modern woman, husbands are finding a new place for themselves in the family.

During the first trimester of pregnancy, when many expectant mothers feel nauseated upon awakening in the morning, a husband may get breakfast and bring his wife something to eat that will ease the discomfort of her arising before he leaves for work. During pregnancy, heavy cleaning may be forbidden the pregnant woman by

---

[10] Jean L. Pennock, "Cost of Raising a Child," *Family Economics Review,* March 1970, pp. 15–17; see also "Raising a Child Costs Plenty," *Family Financial Planning,* July 15, 1970, p. 1.

her doctor; her figure enlarges, making stooping over uncomfortable, so other tasks may be assigned to the husband. By the time the first baby is born, many couples have rearranged their previous definitions of who does what to make way for the new roles and realities of parenthood.

Outsiders become a new source of authority in many an expectant family's home. What the doctor has prescribed or proscribed is taken as law, more conscientiously now than it will be for further pregnancies, in many homes. The elder women of the family may come into the picture in many ways that are threatening to the authority of the young husband. One of the hazards of this phase of family living lies in the ego-shattering experience he goes through in being low man in the hierarchy of influence in his own home:

> It's foolish I know, but I'm jealous of my own obstetrician.
>
> I hate to admit that I don't know all there is to know, but frankly, I'm lost with all this gobbledegook the wife talks over with the Doc.

Many young couples make their first trip to the obstetrician or family doctor together. There they bring up as a couple the questions they want answered and together establish the relationship with the doctor that makes carrying out the prescribed regimen of pregnancy and birth a cooperative enterprise in which doctor, wife, and husband participate. Such a mutual assumption of responsibility pro-vides effective ways of achieving the developmental tasks involved for the couple and is to be recommended wherever possible.

Adapting Patterns of Sexual Relationships to Pregnancy

When a woman becomes pregnant, there are obvious changes in her body that remind both her and her husband that she is something much more than just a sexual being for the pleasures of marriage. One of the first of these changes is the filling out of her breasts early in pregnancy. In recent generations, a woman's breasts have become powerful sex symbols, almost to the point of fetishism. In premarital petting, as well as during the foreplay in marriage, love play involving the breasts is prominent in heterosexual lovemaking. But with the rounding out of the mammary glands in pregnancy comes the realization that these organs are soon to be shared with the little newcomer already on the way. For some husbands this means an abrupt change in types of sex play. As the pregnancy progresses, both husband and wife shift earlier patterns of sexual relationships to accommodate to the realities of the physical situation. These changes may or may not adversely affect the sexual relationship of the marriage (table 8–4).

Both husband and wife tend to report decreasing sexual desire as the pregnancy progresses, suggesting that both men and

Table 8–4. *Percentages of Husbands and Wives Reporting How First Pregnancy Affected Their Sexual Adjustment*

Reported effect	Percentage of husbands reporting	Percentage of wives reporting
No effect	58%	58%
Unfavorable	23	25
Favorable	19	17
	100%	100%

Source: Adapted from Judson T. Landis, Thomas Poffenberger, and Shirley Poffenberger, "The Effects of First Pregnancy upon the Sexual Adjustment of 212 Couples," *American Sociological Review* 15, no. 6 (December 1950): 770.

women are influenced by psychological as well as physiological factors during the expectant period, at least among married college students. There is a strong tendency for husbands to identify with their wives during the first pregnancy. Such a spirit is evident in the young father-to-be who says, "We are pregnant at our house."

Expanding Communication as Expectant Parents

With the knowledge that the wife is expecting their first baby, a married couple's conversation enlarges to include plans for their child and their new roles as parents-to-be. A recent Cornell University study of 852 couples compared the effect of pregnancy, the birth of the first child, and the arrival of the second child on the marriage of the parents. Dr. Feldman found that parent-hood has a pervasive influence on marriage from the pregnancy of the first child through the rest of the family life cycle. Couples expecting their first baby talked more about children than did those married for the same length of time without the wife's becoming pregnant. Expectant husbands and wives had less confidence in their ability to cope with a baby than did those who were not expecting a baby. In fact, the closer the event, the more tension there was about their performance and its consequences, especially on the part of the husbands. Husbands expecting their first babies felt more inadequate in anticipation of changing the baby, getting the child to sleep, and in caring for the baby when the wife was away than was estimated on the part of husbands who were not expectant fathers. Neither pregnant wives nor their husbands viewed pregnancy as being a delicate condition. They were less concerned about the pregnant wife's appearance, moods, and situation than were couples who had yet to experience pregnancy personally. In general, those without children saw pregnancy as more debilitating than it actually is.[11]

First pregnancy involves concentrating on the critical developmental tasks of parents-to-be in what Erik Erikson calls "generativity—concentration on establish-

[11] Harold Feldman, "Parent and Marriage: Myths and Realities," address presented at the Merrill-Palmer Institute Conference on the Family, November 21, 1969, mimeographed.

ing the next generation." This is important not only for the infant, but also for the continued development of the young parents and their marriage. Otherwise, the young adults are in danger of "regression to pseudo-intimacy."[12]

Pregnancy is an emotional experience for the husband and wife who have never been parents before. Although the danger of childbearing is dramatically less now than two or more generations ago, childbearing is still associated with illness—discomfort, pain, analgesics, stitches, doctors, nurses, days in the hospital, babies in sterile nurseries—in many an expectant parent's mind. To go through pregnancy and childbirth with resolute enthusiasm, if not radiant eagerness, a young woman must truly want her baby. She gets some of the courage she needs from her fantasies about the baby as a member of the family, about how she will nurse and care for the child, and about her husband as a devoted father. One young husband set a place for the baby as soon as the doctor confirmed his wife's pregnancy. She interpreted, "He's crazy just a little, but you see we've waited for this baby so long, I've dreamt of his sitting there at the table too."

Some men whose wives are expecting their first baby go through symptoms of pregnancy themselves.[13] Others say they

feel hemmed in, trapped, afraid of approaching their wives sexually, guilty for getting their wives pregnant, jealous of the little newcomer's place, depresssed and anxious about their own inadequacies. Pregnancy is no laughing matter for either the man or the woman of the house, even when it elicits their latent strengths and brings them deep satisfaction.

Pride over their proven fertility, satisfaction in the wife's prenatal progress, plans for their child's future, and the sense of fulfillment as parenthood approaches are but a few of the positive emotions expectant parents learn to express. Couples who learn to communicate the decisional and emotional realities of pregnancy and childbirth tend to be those who have already accomplished their earlier developmental tasks of accepting their feminine and masculine sex roles, and now are ready for the experience of parenthood.

Reorienting Relationships with Relatives

For every first baby born there is a new mother, a new father, and also new grandparents, aunts, uncles, cousins, and many other new constellations in the family circle. Family members who have been relatively successful in "keeping hands off" during the couple's honeymoon and establishment periods feel more closely involved with the new household as soon as a baby is expected.

---

[12] Erik Erikson, "Identify Versus Self-Diffusion," in Milton J. E. Senn, ed., *Symposium on the Healthy Personality* (New York: Josiah Macy, Jr., Foundation, 1950), pp. 134–143.

[13] Helene S. Arnstein, "When Father is Pregnant," *Ladies' Home Journal*, November 1968, pp. 182, 184.

FAMILY DEVELOPMENT

Relatives may vie with each other in showering gifts upon the new baby. These often reflect their own unfulfilled desires rather than the needs of the new family. Even more hazardous are the old wives' tales and well-meant advice that conflicts with that of the doctor.

There is a positive side to the picture. Nowadays, when nurses are hard to come by, and the new mother and tiny baby return from the hospital soon after the birth, a young couple is fortunate in having the willing hands of a mother or mother-in-law to help them through the lying-in period until the young mother can fully take over. A relevant study turned up many appreciative comments:

When our daughter was born, who but Mom-in-law would have come and stayed to cook, clean, care for a baby and mother, keep a household running smoothly, and yet have unbounded love and sheer joy in doing all this? (*Mrs. M., Indiana.*)

Last month we added a daughter to our family and we asked Tom's Mom to lend us a helping hand for a while. She immediately took a month's leave of absence from her work and home duties, to give us her time during the busiest of everyone's life—the Holiday Season. (*Mrs. T., Indiana.*)

When my child was born my own mother could not be with me and although my mother-in-law, who is in business for herself and finds it hard to get away, was at time needed at home,

she came to me and saw me through it all. (*Mrs. J., Illinois.*)

My husband and I have been married five and a half years. At first I resented my mother-in-law. Our first baby was born a year after we were married. She came five hundred miles to help care for me and the baby. (*Mrs. L., Kansas.*)[14]

Reorienting relationships with relatives of both sides of the family is an important developmental task during the expectant phase. Its success contributes a sense of accord and belonging to the parents-to-be and paves the way for many helpful, mutually supportive relationships in the years to come. Grandparents and other relatives can be liabilities or assets to the young family, depending in large part upon the accomplishment of this developmental task before the first child arrives.

Adapting Relationships with Friends, Associates, and Community Activities to the Realities of Pregnancy

As the pregnancy progresses, the recreational and social life of the couple has to be readapted to the realities of the situation. Some activities are sharply curtailed, and others stop altogether, while a regimen more suitable for the expectant mother is

14 Evelyn Millis Duvall, *In-Laws: Pro and Con* (New York: Association Press, 1954), pp. 94–95.

put into effect. Instead of gay nights out on the town, the couple may find more of their evenings given to a game of cards with old friends, or taking walks together, or reading aloud some of the current literature on bringing up baby.

Some couples find such adaptive procedures difficult. This wife did, who says, "He just does not dare go north fishing while I'm carrying this baby for him. If he does, I'll—I'll leave him and he knows I'm not fooling." Or this one, a young veteran, reflects, "You have to grow up fast when you get out of the Army and your wife is pregnant, and you aren't through school yet. I almost lost my wife in the process. She went back home to her mother and our son was two months old before I even saw him. We finally got together as a family again, but we almost didn't make it."

If the wife's insecurity in her pregnancy makes her jealous of her husband's night out with the boys, or his bowling league, or his educational and vocational projects, or any of his leisure-time pursuits that are not specifically related to the pregnancy, something will have to give. The husband may give in and defer to his wife through the period, or the wife may weather it on her own with either immature resentment or determination to grow up and be a woman through it all. Usually outside loyalties and involvements with friends and associates tend to drop off in importance as the pregnancy progresses. They possibly will never return to their former state, for with parenthood come even more confining days and nights.

New associations become a part of the expectant phase as the young mother-to-be is inducted into the women's clubs and organizations for which her new status makes her eligible. She may attend expectant mothers' classes or join a sewing circle where she will have congenial companionship while she makes maternity clothes and the wee garments for the layette. In general, she is now drawn more into feminine association than before, and if she has learned to enjoy being a woman, she will like the new woman's world that her baby and she enter together.

The hazard lies in the husband's being left out of it all as the pregnancy continues. His wife, who before shared everything with him, now shares her physical problems with the doctor, and her practical plans for the baby with friends whose personal experience parallels hers. Baby showers are given for *her* to which *he* is not invited. If he puts on his hat and coat and goes out for the evening, it is understandable. It takes a wise young husband and wife to work out a mutually acceptable social life that gives each of them freedom for the associations that are most personally meaningful, at the same time that they pursue enough joint activities to continue to enjoy life as a couple. A comfortable balance of their individual autonomy and integration as a couple forms a basis for their life together for the years ahead.

Acquiring Knowledge about and Planning for the Specifics of Pregnancy, Childbirth, and Parenthood

The old taboos about refusing to talk about sex and reproduction have broken down in recent decades. Today a husband and wife facing their first pregnancy want to know what is happening, and they both are learning to put their questions into words. This is harder for some than for others; more difficult for men than for women, perhaps, but it is being done.

One of the reasons why men find their wife's first pregnancy difficult is that in the areas of sex and reproduction a man hates to admit that he doesn't know all there is to be known. Up to now we have been rearing our sons that way. Parents tell sons less about reproduction than they tell daughters. The earthy and vulgar jokes

COURTESY OF CLARA ELIZABETH FUND FOR MATERNAL HEALTH

Expectant fathers' classes are available in many a modern community.

about sex and pregnancy of locker room and tavern are difficult to reconcile with the tenderness a man feels for his wife when she feels miserable in her pregnancy. Didn't he "get her that way?" Along with the pride he feels over his proven virility is more than a little guilt that he is causing her distress.

Recent advances in genetics, with the unraveling of the mystery of life programmed into the DNA and RNA molecules of the genes of living cells, make inheritance a personal mystery story that expectant fathers and mothers can read and discuss.[15] Men as well as women find such materials fascinating, especially as they follow the development of their own first child. In many a modern community, classes are available for parents-to-be interested in getting valid answers to their questions. Here are representative expectant fathers' queries:

Is a man's reproductive system as complicated as his wife's?

How is the baby fed before he is born?

Do smoking, drinking, and taking drugs harm the unborn child?

What are Rh babies, and how are they helped?

Do twins run in families?

Is it all right to have sex relations during pregnancy?

How soon will we know whether we have a boy or a girl?

How much does it cost to have a baby?[16]

Meanwhile, an expectant mother is getting answers to her questions from her doctor, the prenatal clinic, or the preparation-for-motherhood classes she attends. She wants to understand the normal process of bearing and giving birth to a child. She wants to know how she can best cooperate in what she eats, what she does, and how she feels about it.

Social class differences in the expectant phase are many. In general, members of the middle and upper classes seek out more earnestly, take more seriously, and follow more conscientiously the advice of physicians and other experts than do members of the lower class, for whom childbearing tends to be taken for granted as another part of life to be endured. Women of higher intelligence and higher social status tend to (1) be more careful in planning their first pregnancy and adjusting to it, (2) have better diet, (3) be more eager to

[15] See Amram Scheinfeld, *Your Heredity and Environment* (Philadelphia: J. B. Lippincott Company, 1965).

[16] Such queries as these are discussed in Aline B. Auerbach and Helene S. Arnstein, *Pregnancy and You* (New York: Child Study Association of America, 1962); N. J. Berrill, Jerome Kagan, Carlo Valenti, and John Lear, "The Child: What Science Is Learning about Human Personality and Growth," *Saturday Review*, December 7, 1968, pp. 71–88; Donald Harting, "What Expectant Mothers Need to Know: Interview on Results of Official Studies," *U.S. News and World Report*, February 14, 1966, pp. 54–58; and Jane S. Lin-Fu, "New Hope for Babies of Rh Negative Mothers," *Children* 16, no. 1 (January–February 1969): 23–27.

breast-feed the baby, and (4) use birth control more effectively than do mothers of the lower classes, according to a number of studies.

The middle- or upper-class woman may bombard her doctor with questions about his plans for her delivery, his preference for anesthetic, his opinion of "natural childbirth," rooming-in, and breast-feeding. She may need to be reassured about the possibilities of birth anomalies, or the incidence of trouble with incompatibility of Rh blood types in pregnancy, or any of the other difficulties with which she has had some personal or vicarious experience.

If anything happens and she loses this first baby, she needs more help than ever. Disappointed potential motherhood can be a terrifying thing, even if she is assured that she can have another baby someday. If the couple faces the possibility of remaining childless, they must come to terms with what they are going to do about it.

Most married couples unable to have children of their own turn to adoption as a way of fulfilling their dreams of children in the home. The majority of the more than 100,000 children adopted annually in the United States are placed with persons unrelated to them (table 8–5).

Communities provide a variety of services for adopting children. Medical, legal, and social services to the natural parents, especially the unmarried mother, the adoptive parents, and the child himself, as well as legislation specifying procedures for adopting children are included.

Table 8–5. *How America's Children Are Adopted, by Percentage of Placements*

Adopted by relatives		48%
Adopted by nonrelatives		52
Placed by social agencies	61%	
Placed independently	39	

Source: 1960 White House Conference on Children and Youth, *Children in a Changing World* (New York: Columbia University Press, 1960), chart 40, "Social Agencies Protect Children Who Are Being Adopted," p. 46.

Maintaining Morale and a Workable Philosophy of Life

Husband and wife expectant for the first time face the developmental task of rewarding each other for their achievements and satisfying critical needs for acceptance, encouragement, and affection during the pregnancy period. The expectant mother may wake up miserable through the first trimester and feel big and misshapen during the latter part of her pregnancy. Then she has especial need for her husband's reassurance of his devotion and of his eagerness for the baby. As the father-to-be feels pushed out and yet terribly responsible for her condition and for the support of the family in the making, he too requires understanding and emotional support.

At few other times in the whole life cycle do men and women become more self-conscious about such questions as: Who are we? What is our way of life? Is this the kind of life we want to bring our children

Chart 8–3. *Decrease in Maternal Mortality, 1930–1965 (Maternal Deaths per 10,000 Live Births)*

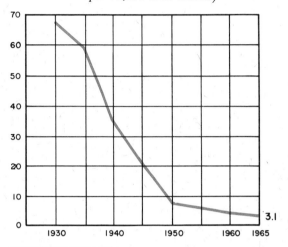

Source: Compiled from Metropolitan Life Insurance Company, *Statistical Bulletin*, June 1947, p. 5; July 1951, p. 2; and February 1954, pp. 8–9; and National Center for Health Statistics, Washington, D.C., recent data.

Chart 8–4. *Percentage of All Births in Hospitals in the United States, 1935–1967*

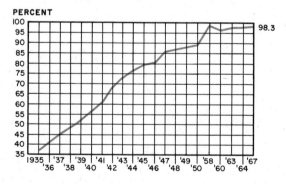

Source: Compiled from Metropolitan Life Insurance Company, *Statistical Bulletin*, December 1947, July 1951, and February 1954; U.S. Department of Health, Education, and Welfare, Public Health Service, *Natality Statistics Analysis, United States, 1963* (Washington, D.C.: Public Health Service, 1966), p. vi; and U.S. Department of Health, Education, and Welfare, Public Health Service, *Monthly Vital Statistics Report*, 1965, and December 4, 1968, p. 3.

up in? What kind of parents will we be? What can we do to make ourselves the persons our children can be proud of? In this sense the expectant phase is a critical period in the life of the couple, for it means that the life-style is now seen not only through the eyes of each of the pair as persons or from the point of view of the couple, but also from the viewpoint of the unborn generation, their children. This testing, evaluating, and maintaining of a workable philosophy of life runs through all other decisions and developmental tasks of the period. The beginning family successful in achieving this task is well on the way to family integration and a sense of identity upon which future periods and stages may be built.

HAZARDS AND DIFFICULTIES OF EXPECTANT FAMILIES

The danger of losing the wife in childbirth is dramatically less now than in earlier decades of this century, as is seen in chart 8–3. The greatly improved chance of a mother surviving childbirth is directly related to the increased percentage of births in hospitals, shown in chart 8–4. Now, when almost all babies are born in hospitals, they and their mothers are assured of good medical and nursing care, emergency help when needed, as well as postpartum attention.

FAMILY DEVELOPMENT

Despite the great improvement in maternal health, there still remain difficulties and problems of the expectant family that may be summarized briefly as follows:

1. Modern housing must be drastically adapted for the coming of the first baby. Many places do not allow children; others have inadequate facilities for babies, and so major rearrangements for coming of children must be made.

2. Double family income shrinks to one at a time when costs balloon. Wife drops out of work to have and raise her baby at a time when expenditures rise rapidly, putting strains on the family budget and necessitating careful financial and family planning.

3. Husband or wife is not ready to assume new role as parent-to-be. Immature husband cannot accept sharing wife or adapt to changes in schedule too well. Infantile wife is not ready to settle down and have a family.

4. There is an increase in emotional instability in early pregnancy. ". . . wives as a whole experience some heightened emotional tension in the early part of pregnancy as compared with their previous emotional stability."[17]

5. Married couples often are isolated from the supporting help of parental families.

Modern marriages are often established far from families of orientation, making it more difficult for members of the family to rally their resources and services to aid the new family at the birth of the baby.

6. Ignorance and superstition increase the difficulties of being expectant parents. Fallacies and current fictions about pregnancy, reproduction, and childbirth confuse the husband and wife and make their following healthful regimens more difficult.

7. There is fear of labor and childbirth experience. "Some anxiety is generally experienced," is the conclusion of one study of married college students in which 63.2 percent of the wives studied indicated they feared the labor and childbirth.[18]

8. The pregnancy is unplanned and the baby unwanted. Difficulties occur in working through the developmental tasks of the period and accepting the baby when it comes.

Resources and Services for Expectant Families

Preparation for parenthood begins in childhood. As boys and girls are brought up by parents who want children, who love them, and who let them know it, they get a good feeling about having children that strongly influences their own attitudes toward parenthood. As children have their questions

[17] Shirley Poffenberger, Thomas Poffenberger, and Judson T. Landis, "Intent toward Conception and the Pregnancy Experience," *American Sociological Review* 17, no. 5 (October 1952): 618.

[18] Ibid., p. 620.

answered by their parents, teachers, and leaders in an ongoing, integrated program of sex education, they are not as influenced by unfounded fears, superstitions, and ignorance and are better prepared for pregnancy, childbirth, and parenthood. Classes in preparation for marriage give both man and woman some idea of what to expect in marriage and family life as well as a chance to clarify their values and develop the positive attitudes that go a long way toward preparing for the realities of living together as a family.

Widely available prenatal care in clinics or with private physicians provides regular checkups throughout pregnancy. This is supplemented in many communities by classes for expectant parents, covering prenatal development, childbirth, and early infant care. Once an expectant mother is under professional guidance, she learns what to expect and how to keep herself and her baby in good health.

It is easier to accept the inconveniences that go with pregnancy as others in a class for expectant parents are having similar experiences or are raising questions like one's own. Many a man feels sheepish the first time he goes to a fathers' forum, but his tensions ease as he finds other men like himself trying to understand the physical adjustments and emotional disturbances that often accompany pregnancy.

Modern obstetrics, nursing, and hospital care now more frequently take into account the emotional and familial factors of having a baby that, in older, more rigid systems, unnecessarily increased the woman's panic in childbirth. Her physician now wins her confidence not only in his skill, but also in herself as a woman who understands what is happening. He instructs her on how to cooperate in a comfortable pregnancy and a good delivery. The nurse who sees her patient not just as another light to be answered, but as a flesh-and-blood person with feelings to be considered and new responsibilities to learn can be very helpful in giving the support that is needed during labor. She offers instruction that may be needed to get breast-feeding off to a good start and baby and mother comfortable in each other's company.

Films on the progress of pregnancy, prenatal development and care, the nature of labor, the birth of a baby, and postnatal care are used widely by many agencies. A number of museums have explicit exhibits of the growth of embryo and fetus in the uterus, childbirth, and early child development. The Dickinson-Belskie models of prenatal development and childbirth are extensively used, as are also a wide assortment of books and pamphlets on marriage, family relations, and the specific aspects of beginning families of greatest interest to parents-to-be.

Young couples themselves are ingenious in innovating ways of helping each other through expectant parenthood. One consumers' cooperative has a clearinghouse for the exchange of maternity garments and infant furnishings, by which these expensive items can be loaned from one expectant family to another with only the repair, cleaning, and replenishing costs involved for any one family. Other neighbors get together in their planning of social activities that fit the needs of young families. Potluck suppers, beach parties, community sings, and evenings around a campfire take the place of the dancing and night-clubbing that once occupied the same younger set in their courting and early marriage days. Now they are "settling down" to equally enjoyable activities that can carry through the expectant family phase into the child-bearing periods just ahead.

We need have no fear that young couples are floored by the developmental tasks and hazards of childbearing. More families are having babies today than ever before. Couples expecting their first baby are at the threshold of a great adventure. As they move from being a married couple to becoming a family "with baby makes three," they find new joys and satisfactions out of the successful accomplishment of the new tasks and responsibilities that are inherent in being in the expectant phase of family living.

The Dickinson-Belskie models of prenatal development and childbirth are effectively used in classes for expectant parents.

SUMMARY

The expectant phase of the beginning family stage covers the period of the first pregnancy. Many unwanted pregnancies cause both personal and social problems. Abortion laws are being reconsidered so that an unwilling woman need not bear an unwanted child. Preventing conception is the most widely used method of family planning in the United States, both as a family resource and to curb spiraling population growth. There are four possible responses to the knowledge that husband and wife have become an expectant family: (1) they both accept their new status; (2) both reject the pregnancy and the unborn child; (3) he is pleased, while she is unhappy about it; and (4) she is delighted, but he grouses about it.

Developmental tasks of the expectant family are (1) reorganizing housing arrangements to provide for the expected baby, (2) developing new patterns for getting and spending income, (3) evaluating procedures for determining who does what and where authority rests, (4) adapting patterns of sexual relationships to pregnancy, (5) expanding communication systems for present and anticipated emotional constellations, (6) reorienting relationships with relatives, (7) adapting relationships with friends, associates, and community activities to the realities of pregnancy, (8) acquiring knowledge about and planning for the specifics of pregnancy, childbirth, and parenthood, and (9) testing and maintaining a workable philosophy of life.

In our present-day society the expectant family faces a number of difficulties in the successful accomplishment of its various developmental tasks. Promising new services and greatly improved established resources increase the chances of the survival of mother and baby in childbirth and the neonatal period and of the effective achievement of the family developmental tasks during the expectant phase.

SUGGESTED ACTIVITIES

1. Compute the costs of having a baby in your neighborhood on the basis of prevailing rates for the doctor's services, hospital costs, basic layette, infant furnishings, etc.

2. Interview a practicing obstetrician in your community on the common complaints of pregnant women and of women in labor and childbirth, with special emphasis on the kinds of supportive therapy he finds most generally helpful. Relate his experience to what you now know about the developmental tasks of women in first pregnancy and childbirth.

3. Write a paper on "How Well Are We Preparing Youth for Parenthood?" using as references one or more of the following research reports:

   a. Duvall, Evelyn Millis, "What Kind of Parents Will Today's Teen-Agers

Be?" *National Parent-Teacher* 54, no. 1 (September 1959): 4–6, 36.

b. English, O. Spurgeon, Max Katz, Albert E. Scheflen, Elliot R. Danzig, and Jeanne B. Speiser, "Preparedness of High School and College Seniors for Parenthood," *A.M.A. Archives of Neurology and Psychiatry* 81, no. 4 (April 1959): 85, 469–496.

c. Remmers, H. H., "Future Parents' Views on Child Management," *Report of Poll No. 53, The Purdue Opinion Panel* (Lafayette, Ind.: Purdue University, 1959).

d. Walters, James, and Clara Fisher, "Changes in the Attitudes of Young Women toward Child Guidance over a Two-Year Period," *Journal of Educational Research* 52, no. 3 (November 1958): 115–118.

4. Review the series of *Pierre the Pelican* bulletins sent to expectant mothers by the Louisiana Association for Mental Health, 1528 Jackson Avenue, New Orleans, Louisiana 70130, on the explicit and implicit hazards and challenges of each trimester of pregnancy.

5. Go through Dickinson and Belskie's *Birth Atlas* (available through the Maternity Center Association, 48 East Ninety-second Street, New York, New York 10028) of photographs of the growth of the fetus and the birth of a baby with an expectant couple with whom you have offered to share the pictures in exchange for the privi-lege of recording verbatim their questions, page by page. Discuss these questions in terms of what is revealed in the interest in and knowledge about pregnancy, fetal growth, and birth by married men and women typical of the couple you studied.

6. Visit the library of your county medical association or local maternity hospital and list the films, pamphlets, and books available for expectant parents. According to their records, how many individuals availed themselves of these services during the current year? From what social class levels did these expectant parents come? Write an interpretive comment on your findings.

7. Prepare a debate on, "Resolved, that all abortion laws be repealed," documenting both arguments for and against with carefully chosen, valid data.

8. View currently available family planning films, and write a review on one or more of them, indicating something of the content, the audience for which the film(s) were intended, and your appraisal of the effectiveness with which their message came through. Consult your local Planned Parenthood Association for film listings from which to make your selection.

READINGS

Auerbach, Aline B., and Helene S. Arnstein. *Pregnancy and You.* New York: Child Study Association of America, 1962.

Bernstein, Rose. "Unmarried Parents and Their Families." *Child Welfare* 45, no. 4 (April 1966): 185–193.

Berrill, N. J. *The Person in the Womb.* New York: Dodd, Mead and Company, 1968.

Cook, Robert C., and Goody Solomon. "'Boom Babies' Come of Age: The American Family at the Crossroads." *Population Bulletin* 22, no. 3 (August 1966).

Duvall, Evelyn Millis. *In-Laws: Pro and Con.* New York: Association Press, 1954. Chaps. 6, 16.

Duvall, Evelyn Millis, and Reuben Hill. *Being Married.* New York: Association Press; Boston: D. C. Heath and Company, 1960. Chaps. 18–19.

Frank, Richard, and Christopher Tietze. *Successful Family Planning Made Easy and Inexpensive.* Chicago: Community and Family Study Center, University of Chicago.

Gebhard, Paul, Wardell Pomeroy, Clyde Martin, and Cornelia Christenson. *Pregnancy, Birth, and Abortion.* New York: Harper and Brothers, 1958.

Genné, William. *Husbands and Pregnancy: The Handbook for Expectant Fathers.* New York: Association Press, 1956.

Guttmacher, Alan F., Winfield Best, and Frederick S. Jaffe. *Birth Control and Love.* New York: Macmillan Company, 1969.

Herzog, Elizabeth. "The Chronic Revolution: Births Out of Wedlock." *Clinical Pediatrics* 5, no. 2 (February 1966): 130–135.

Huxley, Aldous. "The Politics of Population." *Center Magazine* 2, no. 2 (March 1969): 13–19.

International Conference on Abortion. *The Terrible Choice: The Abortion Dilemma.* New York: Bantam Books, 1968.

Lewis, Abigail. *An Interesting Condition: The Diary of a Pregnant Woman.* Garden City, N.Y.: Doubleday and Company, 1950.

Lidz, Theodore. *The Person: His Development throughout the Life Cycle.* New York: Basic Books, 1968. Chap. 15.

Louisiana Association for Mental Health. *Pierre the Pelican: Prenatal Series.* New Orleans: Louisiana Association for Mental Health.

Martin, Phyllis, and Elizabeth L. Vincent. *Human Biological Development.* New York: Ronald Press Company, 1960.

Maternity Center Association. *A Baby Is Born: The Picture Story of Everyman's Beginning.* New York: Maternity Center Association.

Neubardt, Selig. *A Concept of Contraception.* New York: Trident Press, 1967.

Porter, Sylvia. "What It Costs *Now* to Have a Baby." *Ladies' Home Journal* 87, no. 7 (July 1970): 32–33.

President's Committee on Population and Family Planning. *Population and Family*

Planning. Washington, D.C.: U.S. Department of Health, Education, and Welfare, 1968.

Rainwater, Lee, ed. "Family Planning in Cross-National Perspective." *Journal of Social Issues* 23, no. 4 (October 1967): entire issue.

Rainwater, Lee, and Karol K. Weinstein. *And the Poor Get Children: Sex, Contraception, and Family Planning in the Working Class.* Chicago: Quadrangle Books, 1960.

Raymond, Louise. *Adoption and After.* New York: Harper and Brothers, 1955.

Scheinfeld, Amram. *Your Heredity and Environment.* Philadelphia: J. B. Lippincott Company, 1965.

Smart, Mollie S., and Russell C. Smart. *Children: Development and Relationships.* New York: Macmillan Company, 1967. Chaps. 2–3.

Stolka, Susan M., and Larry D. Barnett. "Education and Religion as Factors in Women's Attitudes Motivating Childbearing." *Journal of Marriage and the Family* 31, no. 4 (November 1969): 740–750.

Vincent, Clark. "Unwed Mothers and the Adoption Market: Psychological and Familial Factors." *Marriage and Family Living* 22, no. 2 (May 1960): 112–118.

Wrage, Karl. *Man and Woman: The Basics of Sex and Marriage.* Philadelphia: Fortress Press, 1969. Pp. 159–222.

9 CHILDBEARING FAMILIES

You are the bows from which your children
as living arrows are sent forth. Kahlil Gibran

The childbearing stage of the family life cycle begins with the birth of the first baby and continues until the firstborn is in preschool. During this period the husband and wife have their first experience as parents. They enter the stage as a married couple and leave it as established parents with one or more children. This stage of family life proceeds at a rapid pace through a series of overlapping phases. These involve the changing nature of the parents' roles and tasks of settling down as parents, the child's developmental progress, and family developmental tasks that appear, are satisfied or left incomplete, and are replaced by other urgencies that demand the attention of the young family.

Settling Down as a Family

The first phase of the childbearing family is one of rejoicing. The man has come through the crisis of the birth of his first child with a sense of relief and satisfaction. He throws out his chest as he passes cigars and announces the coming of his firstborn. The woman emerges from the first fatigue of childbirth with a sense of accomplishment, a sensation of being in on the process of creation itself. She puts a ribbon in her hair and relaxes in the luxury of bed care and postpartum attention, replete with telephone calls from well-wishers, congratulations from her friends, and the beaming pride of her parents and her husband's family. There is a new tenderness from her mate. There are flowers, gifts for the baby, and a general spirit of celebration.

By the end of the first week mother and baby have made their first efforts to learn to live together. The mother has already taken the step that leads her into, or away from, active nursing of her baby. The baby has made his first adjustment to nursing and is either succeeding well or having trouble at his mother's breast. The new father's visits to the hospital are full of detailed accounts of what the baby is doing, how the nurses love him, how much handsomer, or brighter, or bigger, or quieter he is than the others in the nursery, and speculations as to which relative he resembles most closely.

With the homecoming of mother and baby from the hospital comes the end of the first flush of elation and the realization that parenthood is a strenuous responsibility. Now the care of the newborn is no longer in the capable hands of the nursing staff, but becomes a round-the-clock task of the young family. Baby's feeding schedule has to be worked out in ways that satisfy him and make sense in terms of the household. His bath time at first is marked by the nervous fumbles of the new mother, whose experiences in handling a tiny baby are limited.

Keeping the baby clean and dry seems to be an ever-present challenge at first, and the diaper pail fills up at an alarming rate, or so it seems to the young mother who assumes as one of her responsibilities the daily laundry connected with infant care. Discouragement is so common at this time that it is generally known popularly as "postpartum blues." Even in her weakened condition, she might manage all this if only she could get a good night's sleep. But many a newborn takes time to adjust to day and night schedules at home, and his howls between 2:00 and 4:00 A.M. not only rob his parents of sleep, but also increase their insecurity about their competence in caring for him.

The coming of the first child is a crisis, in that it calls for reorganization of the family. Roles must be reassigned; new needs must be met in new ways; and family values have to be reoriented. The parents may want babies, but be dismayed to discover what they are like. Studies of hundreds of couples over the years concur that parenthood is a critical experience, and that marital satisfaction drops sharply with the coming of the first baby.[1] One interpretation is that their first child forces the young parents to take the last major step into the adult world, as they encounter the developmental tasks of being responsible for another human being. Thus it is parenthood even more than marriage that demands maturity in both husband and wife.

There may be a nurse for the baby in the upper-class family. In middle- and lower-class homes some female relative, generally one of the baby's grandmothers, comes in for a while and does the housework and the baby's laundry, gets the meals, and tries to keep things together until the mother regains her strength and has made some progress in caring for her baby.

Lacking such a willing relative, the young husband may bear the brunt of the new burden, hurrying home from work to pitch in and help his wife with all she

[1] E. E. LeMasters, "Parenthood as Crisis," *Marriage and Family Living* 19, no. 4 (November 1957): 352–355; Everett D. Dyer, "Parenthood as Crisis: A Restudy," *Marriage and Family Living* 25, no. 2 (May 1963): 196–201; Harold Feldman and Michael Rogoff, "Correlates of Changes in Marital Satisfaction with the Birth of the First Child," research report read at the American Psychological Association meetings, San Francisco, September 3, 1968; and Harold Feldman, "Parent and Marriage: Myths and Realities," address presented at the Merrill-Palmer Institute Conference on the Family, November 21, 1969, mimeographed.

Table 9–1. *Physical Development—Newborn to Two Years*

Developmental dimension	Newborn	Infant (0–2 years)
Height	Eighteen to twenty-two inches	Twenty-six to thirty-five inches
Weight	Six to eight pounds	Birth weight triples in first year; by two years about thirty pounds
Proportions	Head large (one-quarter of total height); chest large; abdomen small; legs short	Face grows rapidly; trunk, legs, and arms lengthen
Bones	Cartilage present in ankles, wrists, soft spots in skull	Soft spots in skull closed at one year; leg and arm bones elongated
Muscles	Heart and smooth muscles developed; skeletal muscles uncoordinated; sphincters weak	Coordination improving; sphincters strengthening; back, leg, and arm muscles developing rapidly
Sense organs	Sees, distinguishing light from dark; tastes; smells; and feels with little discrimination	One week, hears; three months, coordinates eyes; all senses developing; equilibrium weak
Posture	Prone (on stomach) or supine (on back)	Three months, raises head and shoulders from prone position; four months, sits erect when held by hands; eight months, sits alone; nine months, creeps, crawls, stands by chair; twelve months, stands alone, soon walks
Manual skills	Random movements of hands; lashing when angry and with crying	Four to five months, scoops up block with hand; eight months, picks up blocks in both hands; nine months, thumb and finger opposed in pincer grasp of tiny objects; two years, prefers one hand to the other
Hair	Varies widely: none too much; often not typical of later hair; is generally lost	Typical color and texture established by second year
Teeth	None usually	Second year, sixteen temporary teeth in order: four to fifteen months, eight incisors; twelve to eighteen months, four molars; eighteen to twenty-four months, four canines
Digestion	Stomach empties every three to four hours; liquids only	First solids two to six months; three meals a day in first year; eats family foods by second year
Urination	Kidneys functioning; no bladder control; voiding about twenty times daily	Bladder grows slowly; voiding every two hours; may be dry by two years (varies widely)

Table 9–1. *Physical Development—Newborn to Two Years—Continued*

Developmental dimension	Newborn	Infant (0-2 years)
Respiration	Some wheezing; low susceptibility to infection; rapid breathing: thirty-four to forty-five inhalations a minute	Regular breathing established; steadies to twenty-five to thirty-five inhalations a minute; increased susceptibility to infection
Vocalization	Cries, hiccups, sneezes	Range rapidly increases to grunts, gurgles, babbling, imitating sounds, single words, phrases, short sentences
Heartbeat	One hundred and thirty per minute at rest	Decreases to one hundred and twenty-five to ninety per minute by two years
Blood pressure	Low: about forty millimeters	About eighty millimeters

For further detail, see Mollie S. Smart and Russell C. Smart, *Children: Development and Relationships* (New York: Macmillan Company, 1967), chaps. 3–4; Elizabeth Lee Vincent and Phyllis C. Martin, *Human Psychological Development* (New York: Ronald Press Company, 1961), pp. 127–140.

couldn't accomplish around the edges of baby care through the day. The strain of double duty for them both on a day and night basis may take its toll in frayed nerves and a kind of chronic fatigue that is characteristic of the period in many a young family.

After a while, the baby becomes stabilized around a predictable schedule and sleeps through the night most of the time. The mother's strength returns, and she becomes more skilled in caring for the baby as a normal part of her day's work. Now bath time is fun for both. The daily outing becomes a lark, and shopping an outing. The outsiders who have helped out during the baby's first days at home have left, and father, mother, and baby settle down as a family. Thus begins the long pull of parenthood, with its alternating phases of pride, pressure, and enjoyment.

INFANT DEVELOPMENT

Babies normally grow rapidly during the first months of their lives—faster than they ever will again. In fact, development slows down from the moment of conception, so that each period of growth is faster than any that will succeed it. If an individual continued to treble his weight every six to twelve months, as he does his first year, he would become a multi-ton monster in time.

Human development is sequential with each new step in growth laid upon the foundation of what has gone before. Infant development provides the base for what a person is to become. It is, therefore, the most important period of development in all its facets—physical, intellectual, emotional, social.

Physical development advances most rapidly anteriorly during prenatal life and infancy, as seen in the large head and small abdomen and legs in the neonate. Within a week after birth the baby is capable of seeing, hearing, tasting, smelling, feeling, and responding to stimuli around him. These sensory capacities provide the channels for his intellectual development.

Intellectual development occurs progressively as an infant learns. During his first month he uses the abilities he was born with as he waves his arms and legs, cries, sucks, burps, and hiccoughs. The more he does these things, the better he does them, and the more sure of himself he becomes. Between his first and fifth months, the baby combines his skills as he looks or clutches while he sucks, sucks anything he can grasp, turns his head to watch moving objects, and begins to need active stimulation. Between the fifth and ninth months, the baby learns to initiate behavior, to look for lost objects, and to anticipate attention as a familiar person approaches. By the end of his first year, the infant normally works hard to get something he wants; he imitates others, plays games, and enjoys socializing; he probably has mastered pulling himself upright, and possibly has begun to walk. Through the latter half of his second year, the baby is into everything, exploring his world, and the more stimulation he gets, the better he likes it. The closer he gets to age two, the better he is at problem-solving, talking, remembering where things are, and finding them, and he operates more by symbols as he moves out of infancy and into early childhood.[2]

Stimulation encourages an infant's intellectual development, according to a number of tutoring projects for infants and their mothers in underprivileged areas. Tutoring consists of trips to stores, the fire station, zoo, and library; the use of story books, records, puzzles, blocks, drawing materials, crafts; and conversation with the infant as well as encouraging support for the mother in her efforts to enrich her baby's life. Workers suggest that the ultimate intellectual level of a child could be established at the age of twenty-one months, much earlier than had previously been thought possible.[3]

The ways in which parents relate to their babies significantly affect their development. Studies show that parents behave differently with their infant sons and daughters, thus reinforcing sex-appropriate

---

[2] See Piaget's formulation of cognitive development in chap. 6; and Boyd R. McCandless, *Children: Behavior and Development* (New York: Holt, Rinehart and Winston, 1967), pp. 48–54.

[3] Catherine S. Chilman, *Growing Up Poor*, Welfare Administration Publication, no. 13 (Washington, D.C., 1966), pp. 81–87; Ira J. Gordon, "Stimulation via Parent Education," *Children* 16, no. 2 (March–April 1969): 57–59; John Leo, "I.Q.s of Underprivileged Infants Raised Dramatically by Tutors," *New York Times*, December 26, 1968; and Earl S. Schaefer, "A Home Tutoring Program," *Children* 16, no. 2 (March–April 1969): 59–61.

behavior in the first year of life.[4] The relationships a woman reports having had with her own mother influence the ways she in turn relates to her infant.[5] Infants shape their mothers' behavior in noticeable ways, as seen in direct observation of mother-infant pairs.[6]

Learning disorders, disturbed behavior, and difficulty in dealing with problems may result from early deprivation and frustration. The evidence is that it is impossible to "spoil" a baby. Parents are wise to meet babies' needs with a minimum of frustration. When an infant is left to cry out his discomfort and distress, he learns that no one comes to answer his cries, so he either turns inward and away from others or toward them with anger.

---

[4] Susan Goldberg and Michael Lewis, "Play Behavior in the Year-Old Infant: Early Sex Differences," *Child Development* 40, no. 1 (March 1969): 21–31; Howard A. Moss, "Sex, Age, and State as Determinants of Mother-Infant Interaction," *Merrill-Palmer Quarterly* 13, no. 1 (1967): 19–36.

[5] Howard A. Moss, Robert C. Ryder, and Kenneth S. Robson, "The Relationships between Pre-Parental Variables Assessed at the Newlywed Stage and Later Maternal Behavior," paper presented at the 1967 meetings of the Society for Research in Child Development.

[6] Howard A. Moss, "Methodological Issues in Studying Mother-Infant Interaction," *American Journal of Orthopsychiatry* 35, no. 3 (April 1965): 482–486; and Richard Q. Bell, "Stimulus Control of Parent or Caretaker Behavior by Offspring," mimeographed paper from National Institute of Mental Health, pp. 30–31.

Recommendations for Infant Care

Research and clinical evidence indicate that early child care fostering good physical, mental, emotional, social, and cognitive development has seven basic elements:[7]

1. Providing adequate nutrition—proteins, vitamins, minerals, and other necessary nutrients.

2. Dealing with a baby in distress—colic, diarrhea, infection, etc.

3. Stimulating in accordance with an infant's needs, tolerance level, and capacity for enjoyment.

4. Communicating with the baby—tactile and conversational contacts especially important.

5. Giving opportunities for the exercise of emerging sensory-motor functions—feeling, touching, banging, throwing, and combining things; relating supportively with other children and adults.

6. Encouraging the infant's efforts to develop new skills, to cope with problems, and to amuse, comfort, feed, and progressively care for himself.

7. Continuing warm relationships—mother, father, siblings, and other relatives and friends.

---

[7] Freely adapted from Lois Barclay Murphy, "Children under Three . . . Finding Ways to Stimulate Development," *Children* 16, no. 2 (March–April 1969): 48–49.

DEVELOPMENTAL TASKS OF INFANCY AND EARLY CHILDHOOD

This first period of life takes the infant from birth, when he emerges as a helpless bundle of potentials, to the place where he is somewhat independent of others. At the end of this period, the child has acquired a measure of autonomy, is taking solid foods, has achieved independent locomotion, and has mastered the first steps in a complex system of communication. Each of these accomplishments represents many hours of practice in real efforts on the part of the child to achieve the developmental tasks involved. These developmental tasks can be summarized as follows:

1. Achieving physiological equilibrium following birth:

Learning to sleep at appropriate times.
Maintaining a healthful balance of rest and activity.

2. Learning to take food satisfactorily:

Developing ability to nurse—to suck, swallow, and adjust to nipple comfortably.
Learning to take solid foods, to enjoy new textures, tastes, and temperatures, to use cup, spoon, and dishes competently in ways appropriate to his age.

3. Learning the know-how and the where-when of elimination:

Finding satisfaction in early eliminative processes.
Wanting to adapt to expectations of time and place of functioning as developmental readiness and parental pressures indicate.
Participating cooperatively and effectively as ready in the training program.

4. Learning to manage one's body effectively:

Developing coordination (eye-hand, hand-mouth, reach, grasp, handle, manipulate, put and take).
Acquiring skills in locomotion through kicking, creeping, walking, and running.
Gaining assurance and competence in handling oneself in a variety of situations.

5. Learning to adjust to other people:

Responding discriminatingly to others' expectations.
Recognizing parental authority and controls.
Learning the do's and the don'ts of his world.
Reacting positively to both familiar and strange persons within his orbit.

6. Learning to love and be loved:

Responding affectionally to others through cuddling, smiling, loving.

Meeting emotional needs through widening spheres and varieties of contact.

Beginning to give self spontaneously and trustfully to others.

Exploring rights and privileges of being a person.

Finding personal fulfillment with and without others.

---

7. Developing systems of communication:

Learning patterns of recognition and response.

Establishing nonverbal, preverbal, and verbal communicative systems.

Acquiring basic concepts ("yes," "no," "up," "down," "come," "go," "hot," etc.).

Mastering basic language fundamentals in interaction with others.

---

8. Learning to express and control feelings:

Managing feelings of fear and anxiety in healthful ways.

Developing a sense of trust and confidence in one's world.

Handling feelings of frustration, disappointment, and anger effectively in accordance with his development.

Moderating demanding attitudes as time goes on.

---

9. Laying foundations for self-awareness:

Seeing oneself as a separate entity.

Thus A Child Learns

Thus a child learns: by wiggling skills through his fingers and toes into himself, by soaking up habits and attitudes of those around him, by pushing and pulling his own world.

Thus a child learns: more through trial than error, more through pleasure than pain, more through experience than suggestion, more through suggestion than direction.

Thus a child learns: through affection, through love, through patience, through understanding, through belonging, through doing, through being.

Day by day the child comes to know a little bit of what you know, to think a little bit of what you think, to understand your understanding. That which you dream and believe and are, in truth, becomes the child.

As you perceive clearly or dully, as you think fuzzily or sharply, as you believe foolishly or wisely, as you dream drably or goldenly, as you are unworthy or sincere—thus a child learns.

Frederick J. Moffitt
Associate Commissioner for
Elementary, Secondary, and Adult Education
New York State Education Department

DEVELOPMENTAL TASKS OF THE MOTHER OF THE INFANT AND YOUNG CHILD

The first baby arrives in most families when the husband and wife are still working to establish their relationship as a married couple. Therefore, there is an

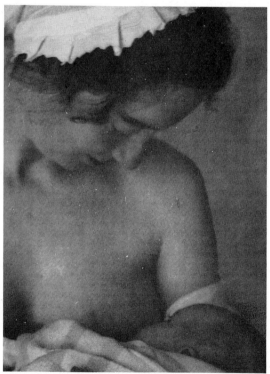

COURTESY OF NELL DORR: FROM "MOTHER AND CHILD"

As a mother nurses her baby, she expresses her love by cuddling and holding him close—communication that even the littlest infant can understand.

inevitable overlapping of the developmental tasks of the young wife with those of the young mother during the baby's infancy. The young woman carries concurrently the unfinished business of being a competent and happy wife with that of becoming an effective and fulfilled mother. She masters many new skills during the infancy of her firstborn. One of the first questions she must answer is how her baby will be fed. Western cultures do not encourage a mother to nurse her baby. Feelings of false modesty, uncertainty about lactation, modern dress styles, community involvement beyond the home, busy medical and nursing personnel, and husband's reluctance may deter a young mother. If she decides that it will not be possible or convenient for her to breast-feed her baby, she must learn to prepare, sterilize, refrigerate, and warm a formula for bottle-feedings. She may prefer to breast-feed for the baby's sake (fewer infections; less diarrhea, colic, and diaper rash; higher levels of arousal and alertness; and the emotional benefits of frequent fondling and being held in his mother's arms) or for the maternal advantages (speedier contraction of the uterus from hormonal stimulation of lactation, lower incidence of breast cancer, convenience of sterile, warm, ever-ready milk, and the satisfactions of suckling).[8]

---

[8] Richard Q. Bell, "Level of Arousal in Breast-fed and Bottle-fed Human Newborns," *Psychosomatic Medicine* 28, no. 2 (March–April 1966): 177–180; also "Maternity: Back to the Breast," *Time,* July 19, 1968, pp. 53–54.

At the close of the childbearing stage, the young mother hopefully has learned to know and to love her baby, and to have confidence in herself as a wife, a mother, and a person. These attitudes and values come as she achieves the developmental tasks of this stage of her development, which, in summary form, include:

1. Reconciling conflicting conceptions of roles:

Clarifying her role as a wife-mother-person.

Reconciling differences in conceptions of roles held by herself, her husband, and the various relatives, friends, and significant others.

Developing a sound workable conception of what she expects of her child.

Coming to comfortable understanding of her husband's role as a young father.

2. Accepting and adjusting to the strains and pressures of young motherhood:

Gearing activity to lessened physical vigor in the periods of involution and lactation.

Cooperating in the processes involved in effective infant feeding.

Balancing the demands of the child, the expectations of the husband, and her commitments as a person with the limits of her abilities.

3. Learning how to care for her infant with competence and assurance:

Assuming responsibility for the care of the child.

Mastering the skills of feeding, bathing, protecting, and maintaining a healthy, happy baby.

Learning how to anticipate and to recognize the needs of the baby.

Becoming increasingly able to enjoy caring for the young child.

4. Establishing and maintaining healthful routines for the young family:

Learning how to choose, prepare, and serve nutritious foods for both adult and infant needs.

Reorganizing family routines to meet the changing needs of the growing child within the family context.

Assuring a sufficiency of rest, relaxation, and sleep for the baby, the young husband, and herself.

Readjusting time schedules to make way for the necessities and for some purely pleasurable activities within the young family.

5. Providing full opportunities for the child's development:

Enriching the physical situation within the limits of family resources.

Providing plentiful variety of experiences in exploring, manipulating, and learning for the infant and small child.

Protecting the furnishings and equipment in ways that keep to a minimum the physical restraint of the growing child (child-proofing the home).

Learning to enjoy and to wholeheartedly encourage the child's development and progress.

Accepting the child as himself without undue pressure, disappointment, or comparison.

6. Sharing the responsibilities of parenthood with her husband:

Recognizing the importance of the father-child relationship from the beginning.

Encouraging the participation of the young father in the care of the baby and small child in appropriate ways.

Bringing the young father into the planning, decision-making, evaluating processes that make him feel that his wishes and values are being respected and appreciated.

Establishing the habits of thinking of the child as "ours" rather than "mine."

7. Maintaining a satisfying relationship with her husband:

Protecting her husband's values as a person through the demanding pressures of young parenthood.

Reestablishing ways of being a couple with the unique values of husband-wife companionship throughout the infancy of the first child.

Maintaining the joys of being a wife in the sexual, recreational, emotional, intellectual, and spiritual aspects of married living.

8. Making satisfactory adjustments to the practical realities of life:

Assisting her husband in the financial and housing planning for the family.

Adapting happily to the limitations of space and resources of the family.

Innovating ways of enriching the family experience by new use of available facilities and resources.

Supplementing the family income when it seems wise or necessary in ways that safeguard the well-being of all members of the family.

9. Keeping alive some sense of personal autonomy through young motherhood:

Retaining some satisfying contacts with personal interests and stimuli.

Continuing some aspect of personal development that is especially meaningful within the realities of the present family situation.

Utilizing the unique experiences of young motherhood for the fulfillment inherent within it.

Following her child's growth experiences out into new horizons of personal insight and growth.

10. Exploring and developing the satisfying sense of being a family:

Initiating family recreation in which the whole family may participate with pleasure—picnics, trips to zoo and beach, music, automobile trips, etc.

Participating with other young families in community functions.

Joining with other young wives and mothers in cooperative endeavors.

Providing for whole-family participation in church, neighborhood, and community activities suitable to this stage in family development.

Maintaining mutually supportive contacts with parental families.

This is quite an assignment for the young wife and mother. No wonder so many young women feel so overwhelmed during this phase of their lives. In the big, old-fashioned family (in which the young couple lived near, or sometimes with, their parental families), there was a sharing of functions and responsibilities of childbearing and rearing with the support of other members of the extended family that lessened the burden on the young mother. In the simple folk society, infants and young children are cooperatively cared for by any conveniently located adult.

Young families today are usually removed from former day-to-day supportive relationships of the extended family. The inexperienced mother is alone with her baby for most of the waking day, and shares with her mate the child's care around the clock and calendar. In addition to caring for the baby and providing opportunities for his development, the young mother does the shopping, prepares food for the family, washes the dishes, cleans the house, washes, irons, and puts away the clothes, assumes responsibility for the family's social life, tries to be a good wife for her husband, and picks up the ever-present litter that goes with infancy.

A recent Cornell University study of 1,296 mothers found those with infants under one year of age spending 50 percent more time doing housework than mothers whose youngest child is a teenager (9.3 versus 6 hours a day).[9] Fatigue is a problem for mothers of infant-toddlers, significantly more than for mothers of older children.[10]

The developmental tasks of the young mother are demanding. She succeeds in them as she gains confidence and acquires competence in her multiple roles. A family-affirming society might provide a variety of services and resources for childbearing families. At the present time, most young mothers do what they can with the help of their husbands.

[9] Kathryn E. Walker, "Time Spent in Household Work by Homemakers," *Family Economics Review*, September 1969, pp. 5–6.

[10] Elizabeth Wiegand and Irma H. Gross, *Fatigue of Homemakers with Young Children*, Agricultural Experiment Station Technical Bulletin, no. 265 (East Lansing, Mich., 1958).

DEVELOPMENTAL TASKS OF THE FATHER OF THE INFANT AND YOUNG CHILD

The young father is not as directly responsible for his baby as is his wife, and yet he faces certain inevitable developmental tasks arising directly out of his new status as father. The very fact that it is his wife rather than himself who is most intimately related to the child's birth, nursing, and early care gives rise to some unique developmental tasks. Of course, it is humanly possible, as it is among other species, for the father to escape entirely the experiences of living intimately with his own young offspring. There are men, especially among the lower classes, who take little or no responsibility for the bearing and rearing of the child. In earlier times, a man left the care of the young child to the women of the household almost entirely. A father began his active role when his youngster could handle himself well enough to go along on hunting, fishing, or short treks near home. Until then, or at least until the child was "housebroken," father's life was relatively undisturbed by baby.

Nowadays, a man improvises along with his wife as both of them attempt to live with the disturbing little newcomer in ways that will be mutually pleasant and satisfying. Now as always, a man is expected to be the primary breadwinner and set up his little family in the style to which he wants them to become accustomed. But here too, there are puzzling variations from the older norms. All in all, the young husband-father has quite a surprising number of developmental tasks during the childbearing stage of the family life cycle, as we see in a summary of them:

1. Reconciling conflicting conceptions of role:

Settling upon a satisfactory role for himself as father out of the many conflicting possibilities in conceptions in himself, his wife, both families, friends, and others of influence.

Coming to terms with what he expects of his wife, now mother of his child, out of the conflicting expectations in each of them and in their significant other responsibilities.

Reconciling conflicting conceptions of childhood to a point of assurance in what to expect in his own child.

2. Making way for the new pressures made upon him as a young father:

Accepting a reasonable share of responsibility for the care of the child, compatible with the realities of the situation at home and on his job.

Being willing to accept without undue stress or complaint his wife's increased emotional and physical need of him during the time when she is not yet functioning at peak effectiveness.

Assuming his share of responsibilities in representing the new family in the community in appropriate ways.

---

3. Learning the basic essentials of baby and child care:

Acquiring enough of the knowledges and skills of early child care to be able to function effectively in the baby's personal life.

Practicing the fundamentals required in caring for a tiny baby and small child both alone and with the mother present.

Learning enough about early child development to know what to expect and understand what is relatively normal at a given stage of development.

Becoming increasingly able to enjoy intimate personal interaction with the baby.

---

4. Conforming to the new regimens designed as most healthful for the young family:

Adapting his eating habits to facilitate the new food intake patterns of mother, baby, and young family as a whole.

Working out ways of getting enough sleep and rest around the edges of the young child's needs and disturbances.

Designing new approaches in recreation that will fit in with the needs and limitations now operating in the family.

Being willing to experiment with any promising possibilities that seem worth trying, rather than insisting that "life go on as usual."

---

5. Encouraging the child's full development:

Investing in the equipment and resources that will be most helpful and useful.

Cooperating in child-proofing the home for the period of young childhood.

Planning with his wife for the enriching experiences that will provide opportunities for the child's well-rounded development.

Encouraging the child as it is, or may become, rather than as a "chip off the old block" or a vessel for unfulfilled personal ambitions and dreams.

---

6. Maintaining a mutually satisfying companionship with his wife:

Wooing her back into tender sweetheart and intense lover roles as she recovers from childbirth and the arduousness of the first mothering responsibilities.

Seeing to it that the husband-wife relationship is neither chronically nor critically submerged beneath new parenting responsibilities.

Taking the initiative, when necessary, in renewing satisfying activities as a couple that may have been suspended during the pregnancy, childbirth, and lying-in periods.

7. Assuming the major responsibility for earning the family income:

Carrying breadwinner responsibilities willingly.

Augmenting the family income in ways that are appropriate as may become necessary.

Being willing to accept assistance, as it may be required, from either set of parents, from the wife's supplemental earnings, from savings, from loans or other mortgages on the future, at this time of relatively high needs and low income.

Assisting in financial planning that will keep expenditures within available resources.

8. Maintaining a satisfying sense of self as a man:

Continuing personal interests and pursuits compatible with childbearing responsibilities and limitations.

Finding new levels of fulfillment in the new experiences of fatherhood.

Growing as a person in the maturing experiences of sharing fully with his developing baby and with the full bloom of womanhood in his wife.

Mastering the infantile, jealousy-provoking impulses that might alienate him from his little family at the very times when they need each other most.

9. Representing the family within the wider community:

Serving as chief representative of his family in the workaday world.

Recognizing that he is the one to whom his wife looks for adult stimulus, interest, and activities while she is confined with baby care.

Bringing home the ideas, the people, the projects that will keep the young family in touch with the larger community during childbearing days.

Carrying on the community participation compatible with the pressures at home and on the job.

10. Becoming a family man in the fullest sense of the term:

Finding satisfactions in whole-family activities.

Cooperating with his wife and baby in the new pursuits that appeal to them.

Initiating experiences for the whole family that will broaden horizons and enrich their life together as a family unit.

Enjoying the new dimensions of life with other relatives now rekindled with the new roles as aunts, uncles, cousins, and grandparents of the new baby.

Needless to say, all this is more than the average man bargained for when he fell in love and got married. As Frederick Lewis Allen used to say, "Everything is easier to get into than out of." And parenthood is surely a good example. It is so easy for most people to conceive, and so hard to deliver; so easy to dream of settling down and having a family, and so hard to meet the realities of family life when they flood in upon one.

Few men have been adequately prepared for what to expect when children come. They only rarely go through schools where boys as well as girls receive an educational program in preparation for marriage and family life. They come up in homes where little has been expected of them in direct child care. Until a man's first child appears, he usually has had very little first-hand experience with a baby. He doesn't know what to expect. He finds that his fingers are all thumbs in his first attempts to change or bathe or dress a baby.

Most difficult of all may be the intimate sharing of his wife with the intrusive little rival that now claims so much of her attention. The husband has had his wife all to himself during their courting and honeymoon days and has learned to take her for granted as his partner and companion during the establishment phase of marriage. He now must see her time, energy, and love directed to the demanding baby in ways that may fill him with intense feelings of being left out and neglected. It is a mature husband indeed who can early feel enough centrally involved in the new relationships

to get the deep sense of belonging necessary for his security as a husband and father. One of the usual hazards to be expected in this stage of the family life cycle is for the mother to devote herself disproportionally to the new baby, and for the young father to retreat emotionally to a doghouse of his own making. Until he can share his wife maturely and participate with her in the experiences of parenthood, he may feel like little more than a fifth wheel around the place.

How well the young husband juggles the conflicting loyalties and expectations and manages the multiplicity of roles opening up to him depends in large measure on how ready he is for fatherhood and how successful he is in accomplishing the developmental tasks inherent in the childbearing stage of family life. As he succeeds in achieving his own developmental tasks, he will be able to participate effectively in working through the family developmental tasks necessary for the survival, continuation, and growth of the family as a unit.

DEVELOPMENTAL TASKS OF THE CHILDBEARING FAMILY

With the coming of the first baby, the couple now becomes a family of three persons: mother, father, and baby. The interrelationships within the family have jumped from one (husband-wife) to three (husband-wife, father-child, and mother-child). Husband and wife are typically in their mid-twenties as this stage begins, and thirty, more or less, as it ends, two and one-half years after the baby's birth.

The developmental tasks of the family in the childbearing stage are basically concerned with establishing the young family as a stable unit, reconciling conflicting developmental tasks of the various members, and mutually supporting the developmental needs of mother, father, and baby in ways that strengthen each one and the family as a whole.

With the coming of the first baby, there appears for the first time a new mother, in the sense that this woman has never been a mother before, a new father who must learn what it means to function as a father, and a new family that must find its own way of being a family. While the baby is learning what it means to become a human being by growing, developing, and achieving his developmental tasks, his mother is learning how to be a mother; his father is practicing what it means to be a father, and the new family is settling itself into family patterns for the first time in its history. This involves the simultaneous working out of the developmental tasks of the baby, the mother, the father, and the family as a whole. The basic developmental tasks of the childbearing family are discussed briefly in the sections that follow.

Adapting Housing Arrangements for the Life of the Little Child

In millions of families around the world, no special provisions are made for the infant and little child. He or she is carried about by the mother or an older sibling, either in arms or in some kind of shawl or sling or even wrapped tightly on a board. The baby sleeps with the parents until he is old enough to fend for himself with the other children of the household. There are many homes in the United States where a child never knows a bed of his own, where everything is "share and share alike" within the home from the baby's first appearance until he is grown and leaves for a home of his own.

As the standard of living improves among American families, giving the baby a special place of his own and readapting the family housing for the comfort and convenience of the little child has become the norm. Families with infants and small children are more likely to move than families at other stages of the life cycle.[11] Interviews with members of three-generation families find most couples staying put the first year of their marriage, and then

[11] U.S. Bureau of the Census, "Mobility of the Population of the United States: March 1967 to March 1968," *Population Characteristics*, Current Population Reports, series P-20, no. 188 (August 14, 1969), p. 11; see also chart 16–1, chap. 16.

Table 9–2. *Child-proofing the Home during the Childbearing Stage (Outlined Suggestions for Keeping Little Children from Getting Hurt or Destroying Property)*

Item	Danger	Child-proofing suggestions
Furniture	Tipping over on child	Select big-bottomed, heavy, plain pieces (especially lamps and tables)
	Painful bumps	Rounded corners better than sharp
	Drawers dumped	Safety catch on all drawers (catch pegs at back hold them)
	Breaking treasured items	Pack away breakables or put in inaccessible places; use wall or hanging lamps instead of table and floor lamps wherever possible
	Soiling upholstery	Choose expendable items, or slipcover with washable fabrics, or upholster in durable, easily cleaned, figured patterns that can take it (feet, sticky fingers, moist surfaces, etc.)
Floors and floor coverings	Chilling in drafts and cold surfaces	Weatherstrip under outside doors in cold weather; supplement heating at floor level; cover with rugs
	Slipping and falling	Avoid hazardous waxing; discard throw rugs; keep traffic lanes as clear as possible
	Soiling rugs	Choose colors that do not show dirt, in patterns rather than plain; select washable or reversible rugs; plan to discard after childbearing stage is over
	Marring floors	Cover with relatively indestructible surface; plan to refinish after heavy-duty phases of family living pass
Walls	Marking and scratching	Choose washable papers or paints, or spray with washable plastic; convert a sizable section into blackboard (paint or large strips of paper), where child may mark; supply child with washable crayons; plan to redecorate when children are older
Tabletops	Scarring and staining	Cover with formica, linoleum, terrazzo, marble, or other surface not harmed by wetting, soiling, and pounding; use secondhand items at first
Toys	Littered	Provide low shelves and accessible storage places
	Harmful paints and surfaces	Select things child can suck and chew without harm
	Sharp edges and corners	Choose toys that will not hurt child in bangs and bumps
	Swallowing	Nothing smaller than a plum for baby
	Breaking	Give child sturdy things he cannot easily break (frustrating him, and you)

Table 9–2. *Child-proofing the Home during the Childbearing Stage*—Continued

Item	Danger	Child-proofing suggestions
Bathroom fixtures	Falling baby	Provide convenient bathing, changing, and toileting facilities for care of baby and little child
	Clinging child	Encourage child's independence as he becomes ready by low steps by washbowl, low hooks for his towel, washcloth, and cup
	Training problems	Supply equipment he can manage himself when he is ready to care for his needs
	Running water	Allow for child's joy in water play by providing time and place for it with some supervision
Locked cupboards	Breaking treasures	Hang key high for door of good dish cabinet, etc.
	Swallowing poisons	Lock up paints, varnish, cleaning compounds, ammonia, lye, medicines, insecticides
	Inflicting wounds	Keep tools, guns, knives, and all other such objects locked away
Stairs and windows	Falling	Put gates at top and bottom of all stairways; give time to child as he learns to go up and down stairs; bar or tightly screen windows
Electric outlets	Shocking child	Cap low outlets; protect cords and keep to reasonable lengths; fence off with heavy furniture so child cannot introduce his finger, tongue, or object into outlet
Entranceways	Cluttering	Provide shelves for rubbers, mittens, and other small objects; make room for baby buggy, sled, stroller, etc.
	Soiling	Supply washable mats at outside doors to keep dirt from being tracked in; keep rubbers, boots, and wheeled objects near door
	Falling	Keep doorway gated or door closed or screen locked when baby begins to get around
Kitchen	Burning	Provide play space near but not at the stove; keep handles of pans turned in rather than out
	Lighting gas	Make burner knobs one of the "no-nos" that baby may not touch
	Lighting matches	Keep matches on high shelves; establish firm "no-no" policy on them
	Tripping workers	Fence off child's play area from main traffic lanes in kitchen, or provide high-chair play during meal preparation
	Cutting	Hang knives high on wall

Table 9–2. *Child-proofing the Home during the Childbearing Stage*—Continued

Item	Danger	Child-proofing suggestions
General	Hurting baby	Minor cuts, bruises, bangs, burns, etc., are taken in stride; major ones are turned over immediately to medical attention (keep doctor's number and other resources on telephone pad)
	Damaging the house	Keep perspective of child being more important than things; use temporary, expendable things while children are small; plan to redo the place as youngsters near the teen years (they'll push for that anyway)

moving to more appropriate housing with the arrival of their first baby.[12]

Developmental parents accept the fact that a little child is born with ten hungry fingers that must "get into things." They know that the rough and tumble of the baby's early exploration, soiling, and fumbling must be allowed for in the home they share with him. Rather than cooping him up indefinitely or forbidding him access to their living quarters, they so arrange the household that he may enjoy it with them with a minimum of restraint. To avoid the continual *"no!"* and to protect their belongings as well as their child, they child-proof the home.

Meeting the Costs of Family Living at the Childbearing Stage

A baby born into a typical American family is fortunate. He will enjoy a higher stan-dard of living than a child born in any other culture. His family will have a higher income year by year than would be average in any other country.

Even in a country of high income, and at a time of prosperity characteristic of this period in the American economy, millions of families have incomes below that considered adequate at current prices, and many children grow up in low-income families with the deprivations of housing, nutrition, education, and other disadvan-

Table 9–3. *Percentage of Families by Family Income, in the United States, 1965*

Family income before taxes	Percentage of families
Under $3,000	17%
$3,000 to $4,999	16
$5,000 to $6,999	19
$7,000 to $9,999	24
$10,000 to $14,999	17
$15,000 and over	8
Median: $6,900	100%*

Source: U.S. Department of Agriculture, *Family Economics Review*, September 1966, p. 20.
* Due to rounding of figures, the column does not total 100 percent.

[12] Reuben Hill, *Family Development in Three Generations* (Cambridge, Mass.: Schenkman Publishing Company, 1970), chaps. 5, 9.

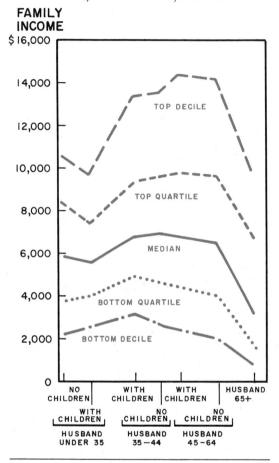

Chart 9–1. *Dispersion of Family Income, for Husband-wife Families*

FAMILY
INCOME

TOP DECILE

TOP QUARTILE

MEDIAN

BOTTOM QUARTILE

BOTTOM DECILE

NO CHILDREN | WITH CHILDREN | WITH CHILDREN | HUSBAND 65+

WITH CHILDREN | NO CHILDREN | NO CHILDREN

HUSBAND UNDER 35 | HUSBAND 35–44 | HUSBAND 45–64

Source: Reprinted by permission from Paul C. Glick and Robert Parke, Jr., "New Approaches in Studying the Life Cycle of the Family," *Demography* 2 (1965): 201.

educated middle-class couple is the fact that the first baby comes while they are still struggling to establish themselves financially. The young husband at the childbearing stages of the family life cycle is typically at the bottom of the vocational ladder with less income than he will have at any other time in his life as a worker. The typical pattern is for the man to start modestly and from then on to enjoy steady increases in income up to his forties in lower-paid jobs, and to his fifties in higher-paid positions, followed by gradual reductions as he nears, reaches, and passes his retirement (chart 9–1).

The costs of the family at the childbearing stage tend to balloon because it is then that the past, present, and future needs of the family are simultaneously part of the family budget. The first baby comes on the heels of the establishment stage of the family, when payments for furniture, equipment, house, car, and other high-cost items are still being made. The first child represents current costs in terms of doctor and hospital bills, baby furnishings, layette, special foods and medicines, baby-sitter fees, and at least some new clothing for the mother after nine months of pregnancy. With the coming of the first child the future is sharply focused by realization of the importance of insurance. Such protection means safeguarding the mother and children during the childbearing and rearing stages, saving for the rainy days when sickness, accident, or other crises drain the family purse or put the breadwinner out of

tages of lower-class status discussed in chapter 2. The median money income of families in the United States has been steadily increasing. Since prices also continue to rise, families' purchasing power increases slower than their income.

Even more pertinent for the college-

FAMILY DEVELOPMENT

work, as well as financing education, cultural advantages, and a comfortable future for the family members.

This meeting of past, present, and future financial needs in the childbearing family stage spirals costs when family income is relatively low and when the wife is likely to be no longer gainfully employed. Therefore, the pinch is on, and making ends meet is a real challenge to the young family. Families each with its own problems and possibilities meet this developmental task in many ways.

The young father may get an additional part-time job in an effort to make ends meet. This will supply more income, but at the cost of his time with his family, and possibly in fatigue, irritability, and strain. The young mother may go back to full-time employment soon after the baby is born. This will maintain the family income at the previous level, but it sacrifices the mother's full-time care of the child, their early hour-by-hour companionship, with its satisfactions both for the baby and for the mother. Actually, if the mother has to replace herself in the home with a paid household helper, her work may not net the family much. If her mother, or his, is available for the early child care and housework, the employment of the young mother may make financial sense, as it does in many lower-class homes.

Some young mothers have the kinds of salable skills that continue to supplement the family income even with a small child in the home. The young woman who can type, tutor, sew, or do baking or cooking, or other moneymaking projects can often continue to earn some money even during the active childbearing and rearing stages. Some young women can do such things easily and well. Others find extra activities beyond those of caring for the children and the household an added strain that cannot be comfortably handled.

The couple may borrow money for some high-cost purchases—mortgaging their future by that much but having the equipment when they need it most. Installment buying may be of this sort, with payments over a period of years for such things as the car, the refrigerator, the washing machine, and the other items that mean much when children are small. The danger is in loading up on installment purchases beyond the ability to pay comfortably over the months and years to come. Borrowing is feasible only if the family can see enough income in the foreseeable future to take care of the payment of the loan, with its accumulated interest charges, within a reasonable length of time. Borrowing in a period of financial strain may be unwise, for it adds interest charges to the already too heavy expenditures.

Savings laid away earlier may be used for such items as the automobile, the first baby, or the furniture. The grandparents may pitch in with gifts that assure the young family of what they need as they need it. Some families can do these things well. Where there are tendencies to jealousy or rivalry between the two in-law families, or emotional immaturity and dependency on the part of one or both of the young parents, expensive gifts from grandparents may be hazardous.

"Making do" is one way of balancing the budget during this stage in the family life cycle. Many young families recognize that the household can be kept simple and inexpensive while the children are coming and growing, with furnishings that are expendable and with little importance put on appearance. Later, when the children are old enough to appreciate nice things and to share in their care, the old, inexpensive, beat-up things may be replaced.

Which course the young family follows in accomplishing this developmental task of meeting the costs of the family at the childbearing stage depends upon how they are approaching and meeting a number of their other developmental tasks of the period, especially those having to do with the allocation of responsibility, developing systems of communication, adapting relationships with relatives and friends, and working through a philosophy of life.

Reworking Patterns of Mutual Responsibility and Accountability

The first child brings new responsibilities in terms of round-the-clock care, including the intricacies of feeding, bathing, soothing, and diagnosing distress signals. Daily laundry of baby clothing is a new responsibility. Making formula for the bottle-fed baby is a daily job. Cleaning up the household swollen by the new activities incident to child care is an ever-present chore. At the same time the former responsibilities of earning the family income, shopping, cooking, dishwashing, housecleaning, mopping, bed-making, and all the rest continue as before.

There are some responsibilities that will be automatically allocated to one or the other of the parents: the father assumes the role of primary breadwinner, the mother of nursing the baby. Everything else that must be done in the young family may become the responsibility of either partner on either a short-term or a long-term basis. The usual pattern in the American family is for the wife to assume responsibility for child care, housework, laundry, and food preparation for both the baby and the adults, with the assistance of the husband in those chores in which he is particularly interested or capable. For instance, now that the young mother is confined with the care of the baby, the husband may assume more responsibility for marketing and other errands that he can take care of on his way home from work.

As both parents increasingly share the responsibilities for the family's welfare, certain chores may be relegated to the husband and others to the wife on the basis of individual strength. An example is found in the number of young husbands who take over some of the heavy cleaning and carrying jobs until the young mother has regained her strength and has the time and energy for all the housework again. It works the other way too. In some beginning families the shopping is done by both members of the pair in weekly marketing excursions. With the coming of the first baby, the wife now enjoys getting out of the house and taking the baby for a daily airing, and so now shops more often while she is out with the baby.

The wife, who is home most of the time with the baby, relates to the husband at his return home what has transpired through the day and how she and the child have fared. She brings up for his approval purchases made or contemplated and decisions that must be made one way or the other in the immediate and distant future. The husband in turn tells his wife of progress and problems on the job and goes over with her alternatives that may be theirs for improving their financial or vocational position.

As the baby grows, he becomes accountable to his parents for the behavior that is expected. This has its beginnings long before the thirty-month age when the child is well launched into a set of expectancies of what to do and when and how. What constitutes good behavior and what is "being bad" varies enormously by families, by cultural groups, and by developmental-traditional orientation. But in every home the child soon learns that he must assume certain responsibilities for himself and his conduct, and that he is accountable to his parents for what he is and does. These responsibilities increase as the child grows; are least when he is a tiny infant; and grow as he develops more and more toward the "age of responsibility."

Reestablishing Mutually Satisfying Sexual Relationships

It is usual for the sex life of the couple to decrease during the pregnancy, childbirth, and neonatal periods. By six weeks after the birth of the baby, the woman's pelvis is back to normal; the postnatal discharge has ceased; involution is complete; and normally she is physically able to enjoy an active sex life again. The reestablishment of their sex relations is not a simple physiological problem; it has many intricate psychological aspects for both the wife and her mate. Research finds that having a baby is hard on a marriage, with more sex problems in which the wife is more concerned, and the husband more dissatisfied.[13]

Many a young mother experiencing for the first time the challenges of motherhood becomes absorbed in its responsibilities and satisfactions so much that the husband is pushed into the background,

13 Feldman, "Parent and Marriage: Myths and Realities."

unless he or she takes the initiative in keeping their mate-love central in the family. It may be the man of the house who reestablishes some of the wooing and courtship processes that will get them both occasionally out of the house with its constant reminders of the baby. The renewal of sweetheart roles will often rekindle the banked fires of desire in both of them. It may be the wife who takes the initiative in reestablishing full marital relationships as soon as she is ready. One of the first steps the wife takes in this direction is that of making herself attractive for her man again.

Throughout the pregnancy she may have felt the loss of her sexual attractiveness, as her body became swollen with child and the maternal functions gained ascendancy. Now that the baby has safely arrived and is well on the way to healthy infancy, the young mother is free to take an interest in becoming attractive to her husband again. She may get some stylish new clothes to fit her now-slim silhouette. She may get a new hairdo and pay new attention to her figure and skin care. Quite likely she will watch her diet to keep her weight in line during lactation at the same time that she assures her baby of sufficient milk.

Medically and emotionally there may be some specific problems. It is usual in most hospitals to perform an episiotomy, cutting the perineum enough to let the baby through without the danger of tearing maternal tissue. Normally the perineum heals in a few days, but the itching of the healing tissues continues a while. For some time afterwards, the memory of the pain in the sensitive area may make the reestablishment of sexual relations difficult. A young mother may complain that "the doctor sewed me up too tight," when the main trouble is the tightening of the tissues as she involuntarily tenses during stimulation of the area. Patient thoughtfulness on the husband's part and active cooperation of the wife are usually all that is necessary for those who previously have known a good sex adjustment.

For couples whose early sex life has been frustratingly inadequate, the nursing period may be used as a protective device by the young mother. In some societies, and in some families here and now, the mother has been known to prolong the nursing of the infant as a way of protecting herself from the sexual advances of her husband. In still others, the young mother may complain of fatigue, ill health, or pain as a way of avoiding the reestablishment of active sex life as long as possible.

Happy families soon find their way through the emotional and physical problems involved. The best of them find that the infant's call for attention may interrupt the most tender embrace from time to time. It is at such times that the couple's communication systems and philosophy of life stand them in good stead as they meet the baby's need and return to each other in good humor without the overtones of frustrated, disgruntled impulses spoiling their relationship one with another.

Refining Communication for Childbearing and Rearing

Something new is added to family inter-communication when a baby comes into the household. The newborn makes his needs known through a series of signals and distress calls that have to be "received" by his parents with appropriate responses if he or they are to be comfortable. As he is able to communicate his wishes and feelings, and as his parents become increasingly skillful in understanding his communicative efforts, both baby and parents get a feeling of satisfaction in their interrelationship. When this developmental task is difficult, the baby and the parents find each other unsatisfying, even to the point of mutual frustration.

CAMERA PRESS—PIX

As the mother and father cuddle and fondle the baby, the baby learns to respond.

As the mother and father cuddle and fondle the baby, expressing their love for him in close person-to-person contacts, the baby learns to respond. He smiles when his mother or father comes near. He gurgles when they pick him up. He pats them when they care for him. He soon learns to hug, nestle, kiss, snuggle, and to express in the ways of his particular family the love he feels in response to those who love him.

Long before the child is two years old, he has learned the basic response patterns appropriate for his little world. He has learned a degree of trust and confidence in his parents. He has learned how to express his annoyance and impatience with those around him. He has laid down the foundation of his emotional being in the loves and hates, fears and anxieties, joys and satisfactions that he has experienced and expressed during his early life with his family. His basic security as a personality rests upon the faith that he early develops in his world through his trust in his parents and his feeling that he is able to communicate, to be understood, and to have his needs met as they arise. By the time the family leaves the childbearing stage of the family cycle, the baby has learned the fundamentals of language and is talking in ways that may be understood not only by his parents, but also by others outside the family. He uses a growing number of concepts accurately and is fast becoming a fully communicating member of his family.

Husband and wife must reestablish effective communication as they become parents. They have new feelings to share in the prides, joys, anxieties, annoyances, and insecurities of early parenthood. The danger is that their marriage may be eclipsed by their new family roles. Feldman finds that parents of infants talk less with each other, especially about personal things, than they did before their babies came.[14] They tend to have fewer gay times, to laugh less, to have fewer stimulating exchanges of ideas, and to feel resentful more often. In general, the coming of the first baby has a sobering effect on the parents and a depressing effect on the marriage. Recent team research finds that with the coming of the first child, there is a shift from "we" to "I" in conversations of husband and of wife.[15] The advent of children is found by others to cause husband and wife to do less together, and to grow apart from each other.[16]

Sharing one's mate with the newcomer involves still other communication systems in which there is mutual recognition of the multiple involvements of both the man

[14] Harold Feldman, "The Development of the Husband-Wife Relationship," a study supported in part by the National Institute of Mental Health, unpublished data received through personal correspondence, March 24, 1961, with permission.

[15] Harold L. Raush, Karol A. Marshall, and Jo-Anna M. Featherman, "Relations at Three Early Stages of Marriage as Reflected by the Use of Personal Pronouns," mimeographed paper from the National Institute of Mental Health, pp. 11, 20.

[16] Robert O. Blood, Jr., and Donald M. Wolfe, *Husbands and Wives: The Dynamics of Married Living* (Glencoe, Ill.: Free Press, 1960), pp. 156, 174.

and the woman as mates, as parents, and as persons. The young father now must recognize his wife as also "mother" with the coming of their first baby. She must become accustomed to seeing her husband as also "father" as soon as children come. Sometimes these terms are actually employed and continue throughout the life of the family. In other families, these designations are used only occasionally in jest, but they serve their purpose of assisting the partners to accept, express, and internalize the new roles as parents that both of the partners face.

The young family is successful in accomplishing the several-faceted developmental task of refining communication systems to accommodate the new constellation of emotional interactions when it emerges from the childbearing stage with a well-knit sense of being a family. When difficulties in achieving the task are unresolved, the family may emerge from the stage with problems of poor integration that carry over to complicate further stages in its development.

Reestablishing Working Relationships with Relatives

With the coming of the first baby, grandmother comes into her own in many a home. She is welcomed as the one who holds things together during the baby's first days at home while the mother is fully absorbed in the baby's care and in regaining her strength. As the young mother is increasingly able to take over the full responsibility for her household with the assistance of the baby's father, the grandmother's role recedes in importance. About that time, other relatives begin to come by to see the new baby, call on the new mother, and bring gifts, advice, and warnings that have to be absorbed and dealt with one way or another.

In-law jealousies and juggling for power not infrequently emerge with the coming of the first baby. One parental family gives more, does more, demands more, or expects more of the little new family than does the other. If one or both of the parents are immature or on the defensive, the imbalance of grandparental interest may fan the flames of envy, jealousy, and insecurity to a white heat of passionate resistance.

In the mixed marriage, the interest of the grandparents in seeing that the new baby is baptized in the church of their faith rather than that of the other mate may become a battle royal, involving both grandparental families in armed camps in which "anything is fair in love and war." This may take the form of anything from covert hints and maneuvers to open aggression and abuse, as we saw in the many cases of in-law relationships both pro and con analyzed earlier.[17] Even if the home is of one faith, there may be, with the coming

17 Evelyn Millis Duvall, *In-Laws: Pro and Con* (New York: Association Press, 1954), chaps. 5, 8.

of the first baby, interference in religious practices, financial plans, household routines, social activities, and so on until the young family finds its own autonomy as a family unit.

The childbearing family is now a unit in the larger family circle, with all the problems and promises appertaining thereto. As the young family establishes itself as a comfortably interdependent unit within the larger whole, giving and receiving in ways that are mutually satisfying, it is ready for the years of interlocking family interrelationships that lie ahead. No man can live to himself alone. Few families, even today in our age of individualism, are entirely independent. Most of us profit by serving and being served by our own flesh and blood, the brothers and sisters, parents, uncles, aunts, and cousins that make up our larger families.

Fitting into Community Life as a Young Family

Families tend to keep to themselves during the nesting time. Young families are apt to be highly mobile during the period when the young husband is transferred from place to place as he gets established vocationally. Community contacts in any one location tend to be temporary at best. Old friends and family are left behind. Old interests and group ties may be weakened. After a man and his wife have become parents, they have little in common with their childless friends. They are not as available for gadding about as they were before the baby came. When the cost of a baby-sitter must be considered with every social affair the couple is invited to, they think twice before accepting the invitation.

Baby-sitters not only charge for their services, but they run up other costs as well. The inexperienced high school girl may give the young parents a feeling of severe insecurity that rises to fever pitch when some adolescent indiscretion is discovered. The older available woman may lack the physical stamina, the point of view, or the mental poise for dealing with the active little child. There has been such a shift in ideologies about the care of children since the older woman was herself a young mother that it may be extremely difficult to trust to her the type of child care procedures that seem important now (chapters 3 and 4). Even if the ideal baby-sitter is found and groomed for her tasks, there still remain the scheduling problems inherent in trying to fit together the needs of the young family with the available time of the sitter. In the "good old days," parents were freed for life as a couple in neighborhood and community affairs by the resident adults, who accepted as one of their roles in the larger family the staying with children that was expected from time to time. Nowadays it is much harder for the little new family, more removed from the extended family, to keep active in community life while their children are small.

Young parents today have developed some ingenious ways of working through this developmental task. In some neighborhoods, parents take turns minding each other's children, thus freeing each other for more social life. There are examples of parents' sitter-pools, by which parents sign up as available for the care of their neighbors' children in exchange for like service in return. The sitters are experienced young parents themselves. Other reported satisfactions are in serving in each other's families, enjoying the resources of each other's homes, and realizing through practical experience that one's own child is no worse than his age-mates in similar homes. A disadvantage is that, while the one parent is doing duty in sitting for another family, the other parent is home alone with his or her own children. Since this is usually at the quiet hours of the family day, when the children are asleep and the adults are free for their life as a couple, there may be something of a problem.

Among lower-class families there generally is more of the old-world custom of taking the baby along in shawl or bundle to any of the community or church affairs that continue to interest the mother of the family. But since such families rarely participate actively in the wide variety of community activities, family participation as such does not increase during the childbearing stage.

Upper-class families frequently have a nurse whose responsibility it is to care for the baby from the time it comes home from the hospital until he or she is old enough to be sent away to school. The nurse frees the mother and father from the day-by-day and night-by-night care of the little child, and so they are more apt to continues their previous activities in work and play, clubs and charities, benefits and concerts, less disturbed by their parenting responsibilities (except in times of emergency, such as the child's serious illness) than is the middle-class parent.

Planning for Further Children in the Family

It is possible to conceive again as soon as marital relations are resumed after the birth of the first child. Some women, believing that lactation postpones pregnancy, continue to nurse the first baby as long as possible in an effort to delay the coming of a second child. Others refuse to resume sexual contact with their husbands until they are ready to accept the responsibility of the possibility of another pregnancy. More effective today is the medical assistance given the couple that allows them marital access at the same time that they are relieved of further parenting responsibilities until they are ready for their next child. The belief is that a child should be wanted before it is born, and that this is more readily assured if the parents are helped to plan their families.

Chart 9–2. *The United States Infant*
Mortality Rate Is Dropping

NUMBER OF DEATHS UNDER ONE YEAR
PER 1,000 LIVE BIRTHS (LOG SCALE)

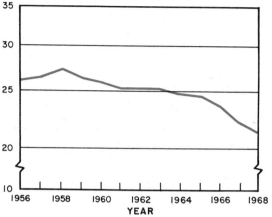

Source: Elizabeth Herzog and Catharine Richards, eds., *The Nation's Youth*, Children's Bureau Publication, no. 460 (Washington, D.C., 1968), chart 36; updated from U.S. Department of Health, Education, and Welfare, National Center for Health Statistics, "Births, Marriages, Divorces, and Deaths for 1968," *Monthly Vital Statistics Report* 17, no. 12 (March 12, 1969).

The procedure is a simple one. When the woman goes for her checkup six weeks following the birth of her child, her physician advises her on the practice that will best meet her situation. The method is important, but even more important for the well-being of the family is the philosophy underlying whatever is done.

The question of future children comes soon if something happens to the firstborn. It may be hopelessly atypical in some way. Mongoloidism, hydrocephalus, and spina bifida are three such conditions apparent at birth. Or the baby may die, as more than seventy thousand do each year (75,300 in 1968 in the United States), even as in-

fant mortality rates decline each succeeding year (chart 9–2). Some infants die suddenly for no apparent reason, making it important that parents be reassured that: (1) sudden death syndrome (SDS) is neither predictable nor preventable; (2) its victims do not suffocate or suffer; (3) it is not hereditary or infectious; (4) the disease is old as biblical times; (5) it occurs all over the world; and (6) SDS kills one in every five hundred infants born in the United States.[18]

After the first shock and disbelief at losing their firstborn, a couple may postpone their next baby out of fear of a second disappointment, or they may make plans for their next child as soon as possible, in an attempt to take their loss philosophically. These are not easy decisions, but they must be accomplished as stage-critical developmental tasks of the childbearing family.

Reworking a Suitable Philosophy of Life as a Family

There is a fivefold crisis in family living at the childbearing stage that is essentially philosophical in nature:

1. Seeing through the drudgeries to the fundamental satisfactions of parenthood.

[18] Margaret R. Pomeroy, "Sudden Death Syndrome," *American Journal of Nursing*, September 1969.

2. Valuing persons above things.
3. Resolving the conflicts inherent in the contradictory developmental tasks of parents and young children, and of fathers and mothers.
4. Establishing healthy independence as a married couple.
5. Accepting help in a spirit of appreciation and growth.

Faced with the daily round of diapers, dishes, and distractions, a young mother may feel weighed down with drudgeries to the point where she loses her sense of perspective. The young father, burdened with his new responsibilities and pressures to make ends meet, may become chronically harassed and under strain. The young couple who sense through their daily duties the deep-down satisfactions involved in having their own child to care for find ways to shrug off needless worries and to adopt a lighthearted approach to their family life and with each other. They find joy in little everyday happenings. They delight in their youngster's development, as well as in his emerging skills and cute doings and sayings. They discover the spiritual meanings of their own family living as they free themselves for the fulfillments of parenthood.

Things are in the saddle in many a family at the childbearing stage. The parents have invested a great deal of themselves and their resources into equipping a home they can be proud of. Along comes Junior with none of the adult values of neatness and cleanliness in his makeup, but rather bent on active exploration of as much of his world as he can get into his mouth, or pound to a pulp, or sit on, or wet and mess. The family soon has its back to the wall in the struggle of values as to which comes first—persons or things, parents or children. Ideally, each learns from the others in time. The baby learns that there are certain things that must not be touched, and certain values that are too precious to parents to ignore. While the parents are socializing their lusty little human, the infant, in turn, is changing a new mother and father into a set of experienced parents able to relax and take the daily issues.

It is at this stage that a family works through the dynamics of its primary and secondary orbits. The basic conflict is between the mother-child and the wife-husband relationship. Struggling through conflicting pressures to the full realization of the importance of keeping the husband-wife relationship primary often involves some tears, not a few tense moments, and a young mother torn by conflicting loyalties within herself. Resolving such a basic conflict rests first of all upon the philosophy of family life that sees the husband-wife relationship as central for the stability and well-being of the entire family.

Accepting help in the form of assistance and gifts from relatives, professional guidance of physicians, marriage counselors, child-guidance experts, or whatever is needed is dependent in large measure upon the philosophy of the family. If the young family is developing the philosophy of humility in open recognition of the interdependence of all humans, then they as family members can accept help with appreciation. Maturing families, as well as persons, grow from serving and being served by those in whom they have confidence. Especially now, the young father and mother can learn a great deal from parent-education experiences, as well as family counseling opportunities in which they talk over their problems, evaluate their progress, and plan for their future as a family.

If each new day in the life of the childbearing family started out without reference to those that had preceded, life might be hectic indeed. Each new situation would be faced without the benefit of precedents and established procedures. Each person would be confronted with a multitude of possibilities that could be frighteningly confusing. Each new developmental task of individual or family would be borne by the persons involved with its full weight. Fortunately the tasks of family life are not that heavy upon anyone, partly because of the early establishment of family rituals that help routinize into familiar patterns many of the aspects of living together around the clock and calendar. Rituals that are commonly part of the childbearing stage of the family life cycle are outlined below.

Rituals of awakening in the morning.

Little child comes into parents' bed.
Ritualized games and language play.

Breakfast rituals.

Eating from special dishes.
Names for foods and functions given by the baby used within the family.

Naps for baby and mother ritualized.

Special blankets and toys.
Ceremonies and routines.

Shopping on daily outings.

Baby takes special possessions.
Child allowed certain privileges.

Father's homecoming.

Child watches for father from window.
Father brings home gifts and surprises for baby.
Mother and child welcome returning father in own special ways.

Bedtime bath for child.

Special toys and procedures.
Father may participate in particular functions.

Bedtime routines and ceremonies.

Stories, songs, prayers at child's bedtime.
"Drink a water" demands for further attention.
Special light or customs to give child assurance.

Special holidays.

Birthday celebrations ritualized.
Visits to see relatives.
Vacations and trips with baby.
Photographing baby in special holiday settings.
Sitter routines when parents celebrate as a couple.

Rituals add a great deal to the life of the childbearing family. They provide the workable routines that ease the parents' days and nights. They give the little child a sense of reliable, secure expectations of what comes next, and they provide the simple, sweet sources of satisfaction that come to mean most in family living.

SUMMARY

Changing feelings and tempos are to be expected as father, mother, and baby settle down as a family. Infant development (physically, mentally, emotionally, and socially) is gradual, progressive, and to some extent predictable. Early enrichment of a baby's life is important for his optimum development and growth, as he strives to achieve his developmental tasks. The mother of the young child has developmental tasks she must accomplish as a mother, as a wife, as a person. The father at the childbearing stage has a series of complicated developmental tasks as a father, husband, and man that he must work through as a person. The developmental tasks of the childbearing family as a whole are several: adapting housing arrangements for the life of the little child (child-proofing the home during the childbearing stage), meeting the costs of family living at the childbearing stage, reworking patterns of responsibility and accountability, reestablishing mutually satisfying sexual relationships, refining intellectual and emotional communication systems for childbearing and rearing, reestablishing working relationships with relatives, fitting into community life as a young family, planning for further children in the family, and reworking a suitable philosophy of life as a family. Rituals of family living at the childbearing stage ease the parent's job, give security to the youngster, and bring satisfactions to the family.

SUGGESTED ACTIVITIES

1. Consulting authoritative child development sources for norms of development from birth through thirty months, make a master chart of the step-by-step progress

the normal infant makes from the period of restless dependency to relatively poised independence as a little child able to communicate, get around, and master many aspects of himself and his world.

2. Review one or both of the films, *Helping the Child Accept the Do's* and *Helping the Child Accept the Don'ts* (Encyclopaedia Britannica Films, Inc., black and white, ten minutes each), with especial emphasis on the ways in which a child learns what is expected of him in a variety of situations.

3. Take pad and pencil to a nearby park, tot-lot, or other place where young mothers congregate with their babies. Record everything that is done and said by both a selected mother and her child for a five-minute interval. Write a paper incorporating your verbatim record and interpreting the behaviors included in terms of the developmental tasks of both mother and baby that might be inferred at this stage and in this situation.

4. Interview four mothers whose first babies are two years old or younger on the question, "What part of the daily routine with your baby do you find hardest to work out comfortably?" Capture in your recording of the interviews not only the areas in which the mothers report difficulties but also their attitudes and feelings about themselves, their babies, and their adequacy as mothers in childbearing families. Comment critically on your findings in terms of the hazards young mothers find

in achieving their developmental tasks during the childbearing stage.

5. Review the first eighty-five pages of *Fathers Are Parents, Too,* by O. Spurgeon English and Constance J. Foster (New York: G. P. Putnam's Sons, 1951) for implicit and explicit factors relating to the developmental tasks of the young father during the childbearing stage.

6. Write a letter to your sister who has told you of her concern over her first child's thumb-sucking, telling her what is considered good practice in dealing with thumb-sucking today, the developmental basis for the recommendations, and readings that may be still further helpful to her.

7. Outline a course of study to be used for a "Grandmothers' Refresher Course in Child Care" that would help a present-day grandmother bring up to date her concepts, ideas, and understandings of child development and guidance through the first three years of a baby's life. Contrast throughout present-day practices with those prevalent twenty to thirty years ago (when she brought up her children) using such references as were generally current then as manuals of baby care, in books, magazines, and government bulletins and pamphlets.

8. Prepare a paper on the major causes of infant death, documenting with material from medical journals and official data. Indicate which conditions appear to be preventable, and recommend procedures

for further lowering the infant mortality rate.

9. Contrast expected family rituals at the childbearing stage for families at the lower-, middle-, and upper-class levels, documenting your materials with quotations from James H. S. Bossard and Eleanor S. Boll, *Ritual in Family Living* (Philadelphia: University of Pennsylvania Press, 1950), chapter 6, as well as excerpts from selected fiction and biography representative of the three class levels.

10. Chart the complementary and conflicting developmental tasks of the mother, the father, and the baby of the childbearing family, using the materials detailed in this chapter in the style developed in chapters 7 and 8. Discuss the relative mutuality of this stage as compared with the previous two stages of the family life cycle.

READINGS

Auerbach, Aline B. *How to Give Your Child a Good Start*. Rev. ed. New York: Child Study Association of America, 1961.

Bayley, Nancy. "Comparisons of Mental and Motor Test Scores for Ages 1-15 Months by Sex, Birth Order, Race, Geographical Location, and Education of Parents." *Child Development* 36 (1965): 379–411.

Bayley, Nancy, and Earl S. Schaefer. *Correlations of Maternal and Child Behaviors with the Development of Mental Abilities: Data from the Berkeley Growth Study*. Monograph of the Society for Research in Child Development, serial no. 97, vol. 29, no. 6 (1964).

Bloom, Benjamin S. *Stability and Change in Human Characteristics*. New York: John Wiley and Sons, 1964.

Caldwell, Bettye M. "The Effects of Infant Care." In *Review of Child Development Research*, vol. 1, edited by Martin L. Hoffman and Lois Wladis Hoffman, pp. 9–87. New York: Russell Sage Foundation, 1964.

"Children under Three: Some Approaches for Stimulating Optimal Development." *Children* 16, no. 2 (March-April 1969): entire issue.

Chilman, Catherine S. *Growing Up Poor*. Welfare Administration Publication, no. 13. Washington, D.C., 1966.

Clay, Vidal S. "The Effect of Culture on Mother-Child Tactile Communication." *Family Coordinator* 17, no. 3 (July 1968): 204–210.

English, O. Spurgeon, and Constance J. Foster. *Fathers Are Parents, Too*. New York: G. P. Putnam's Sons, 1951.

Escalona, Sibylle. *The Roots of Individuality: Normal Patterns of Development in Infancy*. Chicago: Aldine Publishing Company, 1969.

Escalona, Sibylle, and Grace M. Heider. *Prediction and Outcome*. New York: Basic Books, 1959.

Faegre, Marion L., John E. Anderson, and Dale B. Harris. *Child Care and Training*. 8th ed. Minneapolis: University of Minnesota Press, 1958.

Feldman, Harold. "Parent and Marriage: Myths and Realities." Address presented at the Merrill-Palmer Institute Conference on the Family, November 21, 1969. Mimeographed.

Flavell, John H. *The Developmental Psychology of Jean Piaget*. Princeton, N.J.: Van Nostrand, 1963.

Goldberg, Susan, and Michael Lewis. "Play Behavior in the Year-Old Infant: Early Sex Differences." *Child Development* 40, no. 1 (March 1969): 21–31.

Hess, Robert, and V. Shipman. "Early Experience and the Socialization of Cognitive Modes in Children." *Child Development* 36 (1965): 869–886.

Jacoby, Arthur P. "Transition to Parenthood: A Reassessment." *Journal of Marriage and the Family* 31, no. 4 (November 1969): 720–727.

Kagan, Jerome, and M. Lewis. "Studies of Attention in the Human Infant." *Merrill-Palmer Quarterly* 11 (1965): 95–127.

Lidz, Theodore. *The Person: His Development throughout the Life Cycle*. New York: Basic Books, 1968. Chaps. 4 and 5, "The Neonate and the New Mother" and "Infancy," pp. 93–158.

Louisiana Association for Mental Health. *Pierre the Pelican: Post-Natal Series*. New Orleans: Louisiana Association for Mental Health.

McCandless, Boyd R. *Children: Behavior and Development*. New York: Holt, Rinehart and Winston, 1967.

Maccoby, Eleanor, ed. *The Development of Sex Differences*. Stanford, Calif.: Stanford University Press. 1966.

Martin, William E., and Celia Burns Stendler. *Child Behavior and Development*. Rev. and enl. ed. of *Child Development*. New York: Harcourt, Brace and Company, 1959.

Moss, Howard A. "Sex, Age, and State as Determinants of Mother-Infant Interaction." *Merrill-Palmer Quarterly* 13, no. 1 (1967): 19–36.

Mussen, Paul H. *The Psychological Development of the Child*. Englewood Cliffs, N.J.: Prentice-Hall, 1963.

National Institute of Child Health and Human Development. *Perspectives on Human Deprivation: Biological, Psychological, and Sociological*. Washington, D.C.: U.S. Department of Health, Education, and Welfare, 1968.

Piaget, Jean. *The Origins of Intelligence in Children*. Translated by Margaret Cook. New York: International Universities Press, 1966.

Pohlman, Edward W. *The Psychology of Birth Planning*. Cambridge, Mass.: Schenkman Publishing Company, 1969.

Pope, Hallowell. "Negro-White Differences in Decisions Regarding Illegitimate Children." *Journal of Marriage and the Family* 31, no. 4 (November 1969): 756–764.

Scheinfeld, Amram. *Your Heredity and Environment*. Philadelphia: J. B. Lippincott Company, 1965.

Smart, Mollie S., and Russell C. Smart. *Children: Development and Relationships*. New York: Macmillan Company, 1967. Pt. 1, "Infancy," pp. 31–169.

10 FAMILIES WITH PRESCHOOL CHILDREN

The child is father of the man. Wordsworth

While the first child is between two-and-one-half and five years of age, the preschool family typically has a second and possibly a third child, making a total of three to five persons, with the possibility of from three to ten interpersonal relationships. The possible positions in the family are husband-father, wife-mother, son-brother, and daughter-sister, each with its own developmental tasks. While the adults struggle with their child-rearing and personal tasks, the preschool child faces the crisis of initiative (expanding imagination) versus guilt (developing conscience), while younger siblings retrace, each in his or her own way, the developmental stages the eldest has completed.

From the preoccupation of babyhood, the preschool child is emerging as a social being who can share with others and participate as a member of his family. His pace of physical growth is slowing down, and many of his body activities are becoming routine. Progress in his emotional and intellectual development is increasingly apparent in his growing ability to express himself in speech and in his greatly increased acquaintance with his environment.

Development of the preschool child varies greatly by individual and is dependent upon opportunities to learn and grow; it follows in broad summary the outline in table 10-1.

INDIVIDUAL DIFFERENCES

Each child is unique, grows at his own pace, and is unlike any other human being in all respects. Such normative listings as that found in table 10-1 are indicative only of where *most* children of a given age are in the development of various characteristics. Much of a child's development is not included in such gross categories as height, weight, vocabulary, and mental, emotional, or social life. Within any of these broad groupings of characteristics are tremendous differences in literally thousands of qualities and wide variations in patterns of growth and status of development among children of any age. Some children mature rapidly, others slowly, but most within the

Table 10–1. *Development of the Preschool Child*

Characteristic	Two and one-half to four years of age	Four to six years of age
Height	Thirty-three to forty-four inches (range)	Thirty-eight to forty-eight inches (range)
Weight	Twenty-three to forty-eight pounds (range)	Thirty to fifty-six pounds (range)
Bones	All seven ankle bones begun; bridge of nose forming; fusions occurring in skull; spinal curvature beginning	
Muscles	Steady growth and development; coordination increasing; sphincters maturing and becoming controllable	
Sense organs	Equilibrium improving	Farsighted by six years
Locomotion	Walks up and down stairs; runs well; jumps; tiptoes; hops with both feet; rides tricycle	Skips; gallops; hops on one foot; alternates feet in descending stairs; walks straight line
Manual skills	Small muscle skills developing in drawing, building, etc.	
Eye-hand coordination	Uses spoon; pours; puts shoes on; copies circle; draws straight line; catches ball; builds with blocks	Dresses self; cuts with scissors; copies square; designs and letters; throws and catches ball
Teeth	Four molars appear; twenty temporary teeth by three years	Loss of baby teeth begins
Digestion	General diet	Appetite slackens; less interest in food
Urination	Sense of bladder fullness developing	Complete control by six years usually
Respiration	Twenty to thirty inhalations per minute	Increased susceptibility to infection
Vocabulary	896 words by three years; 1,540 words by four years; simple sentences; "what" and "where" questions predominate	2,072 words by five years; 2,562 words by six years; more complex sentences of six to eight words; "how," "when," and "why" questioning
Thinking	Increasingly flexible through preschool years; concepts first through concrete experience become abstract with experience in grouping objects, dealing with time, space, numbers, and processes; varies widely with intelligence and interaction with others	
Character	Increasing knowledge of rules; growing ability to judge right from wrong, to control himself, to internalize standards, and to make explicit demands upon himself	
Dominant emotions	Anger, temper tantrums, and negativism	Fears peak; fighting especially among boys; sympathy, empathy in simple forms evident
Social life	Parallel play; imaginary playmates; dramatizations	Social adjustment under way; varies by playmates available

For further detail see Mollie S. Smart and Russell C. Smart, *Children: Development and Relationships* (New York: Macmillan Company, 1967), chaps. 6–9; Elizabeth Lee Vincent and Phyllis C. Martin, *Human Psychological Development* (New York: Ronald Press Company, 1961), pp. 127–140; Character Research Project, *The Growth and Development of Christian Personality*, 4th ed. (Schenectady, N.Y.: Union College, n.d.).

ranges indicated in general patterns of child development derived from study of many children over the years. No individual child is a statistic, but a living, growing human being best understood for himself, in relation, when helpful, to other children of about his age and stage of development.

Physically, children range from broad and stocky to tall and thin, from large- to small-boned, from robust to weak, from obese to underweight, according to the norms. These differences can be plotted on the Wetzel grids in ways that help doctors understand how a given child is progressing in his own growth track.

Mentally, children range from slow to quick within the "normal" IQ of 90 to 110, more or less. Below this are various levels of retardation, and above are the bright children some of whom test out as geniuses. Musical ability, rhythm, creativity, imagination, language sense, and other special talents or handicaps manifest themselves in some children quite early, and in others more slowly or not at all.

Emotionally some children are fearful, anxious, or easily upset, while others seem to fear little or nothing. Some children are loving cuddlers, while others are less affectionate "by nature," it seems. Some children anger easily, lose their tempers, and fight their way through situations, while others just as "naturally" cope more rationally with their problems. Some children tend to be outgoing and friendly, while some are shy and retiring, and still others can react either way depending upon how they feel about the situation and the people involved.

Individual differences arise from a complex of sources. Children are born different from others in the ways they are programmed to be and become in the genetic factors they have inherited through the DNA and RNA molecules found in the cells of their bodies (coloring, body type, handedness, for instance). Some differences among children are congenital, arising in the developing embryo or fetus before birth (thalidomide or Rh problems, congenital syphilis or rubella, for instance). Inherited and congenital factors are more difficult to change than are the host of acquired characteristics that arise after birth. These come from the way a child is nurtured and how he responds to the signals he receives from others (or from within himself). There is a tremendous difference between the TLC (tender, loving care) a child receives from two parents who love and rear him in a happy home and the neglect a child knows at the hands of an unloved and unloving mother or the "battered baby" syndrome seen in young children who have been beaten by one or both of their parents. Wide variations are found between privileged and underprivileged children not only in their nutrition and general health, but also in their interest in learning, their response to others, and their basic stance toward life.

The indications are that child development is all of a piece, that children who are mentally alert and emotionally healthy tend also to be physically well developed.[1] Psychological states affect biological processes and vice versa in children as well as in adults, according to clinical evidence from psychosomatic medicine. Even within this broad generalization there are many exceptions, depending upon the repertoire of response an individual has for his many life situations. Much is dependent upon the ways in which children accomplish their developmental tasks step by step through their growing years. In no other period of his life does a person have quite such a dramatic complex of roles and developmental tasks as confront the preschool child, who now for the first time begins to see himself and to be seen by others as no longer a baby, but a person in his own right.

---

[1] E. M. Abernethy, *Relationships between Physical and Mental Growth*, monograph of the Society for Research in Child Development, vol. 1, no. 7 (1936); Mary Cover Jones and P. H. Mussen, "Self-Conceptions, Motivations, and Interpersonal Attitudes of Early- and Late-Maturing Girls," *Child Development* 29 (1958): 492–501; W. A. Ketcham, "Relationship of Physical and Mental Traits in Intellectually Gifted and Mentally Retarded Boys," *Merrill-Palmer Quarterly* 6 (1960): 171–177; Paul H. Mussen and Mary Cover Jones, "The Behavior-Inferred Motivations of Late- and Early-Maturing Boys," *Child Development* 29 (1958): 61–67; and J. M. Tanner, "The Regulation of Human Growth," *Child Development* 34 (1963): 817–847.

DEVELOPMENTAL TASKS OF PRESCHOOL CHILDREN

1. Settling into healthy daily routines of rest and activity:

Going to bed and getting his needed rest without a struggle.
Taking his nap or rest, and learning to relax when he is weary.
Enjoying active play in a variety of situations and places.
Becoming increasingly flexible and able to accept changes.

2. Mastering good eating habits:

Becoming adequate in the use of the customary utensils for eating.
Accepting new flavors and textures in foods with interest.
Enjoying his food with lessening incidents of spilling, messing, and toying.
Learning the social as well as the sensual pleasures of eating.

3. Mastering the basics of toilet training:

Growing in his ability to indicate his needs for elimination.
Cooperating comfortably in the toilet training program.

Finding satisfaction in behaving appropriately as to time, place, and ways of toileting expected of boys/girls of his age.

Becoming flexible in his ability to use the variety of resources, places, and personnel available to him.

4. Developing the physical skills appropriate to his stage of motor development:

Learning to climb, balance, run, skip, push, pull, throw, and catch in whole-body use of large muscle systems.

Developing manual skills for buttoning, zipping, cutting, drawing, coloring, modeling, and manipulating small objects deftly.

Becoming increasingly independent in his ability to handle himself effectively in a variety of physical situations.

5. Becoming a participating member of his family:

Assuming responsibilities within the family happily and effectively.

Learning to give and receive affection and gifts freely within the family.

Identifying with parent of the same sex.

Developing ability to share his parents with another child and with others generally.

Recognizing his family's ways as compared with those of his friends and neighbors.

6. Beginning to master his impulses and to conform to others' expectations:

Outgrowing the impulsive, urgent outbursts of infancy.

Learning to share, take turns, hold his own, and enjoy the companionship of other children, and at times play happily alone.

Developing the sympathetic, cooperative ways with others that ensure his inclusion in groups.

Learning appropriate behavior for situations in which he is (times and places for noise, quiet, messing, nudity, etc.).

7. Developing healthy emotional expressions for a wide variety of experiences:

Learning to play out his feelings, frustrations, needs, and experiences.

Learning to postpone and to wait for satisfactions.

Expressing momentary hostility and making up readily afterwards.

Refining generalized joy or pain into discriminating expressions of pleasure, eagerness, tenderness, affection, sympathy, fear, anxiety, remorse, sorrow, etc.

8. Learning to communicate effectively with an increasing number of others:

Developing the vocabulary and ability to talk about a rapidly growing number of things, feelings, experiences, impressions, and curiosities.

Learning to listen, take in, follow directions, increase his attention span, and respond intellectually to situations and to others.

Acquiring the social skills needed to get over feelings of shyness, self-consciousness, and awkwardness, and to participate with other people comfortably.

9. Developing the ability to handle potentially dangerous situations:

Learning to respect the dangers in fire, traffic, high places, bathing areas, poisons, animals, and the many other potential hazards.

Learning to handle himself effectively without undue fear in situations calling for caution and safety precautions (crossing streets, greeting strange dogs, responding to a stranger's offer of a ride, etc.).

Becoming willing to accept help in situations that are beyond him without undue dependence or too impulsive independence.

10. Learning to be an autonomous person with initiative and a conscience of his own:

Becoming increasingly responsible for making decisions in ways appropriate to his readiness.

Taking initiative for projecting himself into situations with innovations, experiments, trials, and original achievements.

Internalizing the expectancies and demands of his family and culture groups in his developing conscience.

Becoming reasonably self-sufficient in situations in accordance with his own makeup and stage of development.

11. Laying foundations for understanding the meanings of life:

Beginning to understand the origins of life, how the two sexes differ, and who he or she is as a member of his or her sex.

Trying to understand the nature of the physical world, what things are, how they work and why, and what they mean to him.

Accepting the religious faith of his parents and learning about the nature of God and the spiritual nature of life.

The preschool boy or girl must achieve enough independence to be comfortable without his parents in a variety of situations. He or she must become reasonably self-sufficient both in the home and in outside settings, in keeping with his particular stage of development. The child who has preliminary practice in crossing streets, managing his outside garments, going to the toilet alone, washing his own hands, using his handkerchief, and in handling everyday routines, accidents, and minor crises will be ready to enter school feeling self-confident enough to be ready for its challenges. If his parents have introduced stories, songs, pictures, conversations, ex-

Table 10–2. *Child's Readiness for Kindergarten: A Check Test*

	Always	Usually	Sometimes	Rarely
1. The child knows his name, address, and father's name.				
2. He is free from those physical defects which can be corrected.				
3. He knows the way to school and can find his way home again.				
4. He has been taught how to cross streets.				
5. He recognizes policemen, is not afraid of them, and will follow their directions.				
6. He can go to the toilet, manage his clothing by himself, and conform to expected modesty patterns.				
7. He can hang up his coat, put on his outdoor clothing, and recognize his own belongings.				
8. He is content to stay with adults other than those he knows well.				
9. He has had opportunities to play with children his own age and gets along well with them.				
10. He is familiar with some of the places in the neighborhood which are of interest to children his age (post office, grocery store, firehouse, a building under construction, etc.).				
11. He can entertain himself with constructive tasks for short periods of time.				
12. He is interested in books and will spend some time looking at them quietly.				
13. He attacks a new job willingly and welcomes new situations without fear.				
14. He is in the habit of sharing certain household tasks with other members of the family.				
15. He is patient about waiting his turn and respecting property rights of others.				
16. He can keep his temper, his tears, and his other emotional outbursts under reasonably good control.				
17. He is curious about many things and, with a little help from an adult, can follow up his interests.				

Source: Adapted freely from Fay Moeller, "Understanding Our Children," mimeographed (Storrs, Conn.: University of Connecticut Extension Service, 1954).

cursions, and creative play materials into his life, he will be able to enter school as a contributor as well as a recipient. When the preschool child has successfully accomplished the developmental tasks of this stage, he is ready to go to school. The check test on readiness for kindergarten details some of the specific learnings derived from the preschooler's developmental tasks.

Preschool Experiences

Many of a child's developmental tasks are facilitated with the social interaction, physical environment, and competent direction of a good preschool. Experience in nursery school, kindergarten, Project Head Start, day care center, or any of the other recently developed programs designed to encourage the young child's development has been shown to have measurable value. One project involving inner-city, low-income families' children tested before and after two years' nursery schooling found an average IQ gain of 14.7 points on the Stanford Binet scale.[2]

Major objectives of nursery schools for culturally deprived children are seen as: (1) stimulating children to perceive aspects of the world around them and to fix these aspects by their use of language; (2) developing more extended and accurate speech;

(3) developing a sense of mastery over aspects of the immediate environment and an enthusiasm for learning; (4) developing the ability to make new discoveries, to think, and to reason; (5) developing purposive learning activity and the ability to attend and to concentrate on an activity for longer periods of time.[3]

The majority of Americans favor federally funded day care centers for young children so that "mothers living in poor areas can work, and so that children can get early educational training," according to a recent Gallup poll, table 10–3.

Table 10–3. *Most Americans Favor Federally Funded Day Care Centers*

Respondents	*Percentage*		
	Favor	*Oppose*	*No opinion*
Women	68%	27%	5%
Men	59	34	7
Negroes	83	11	6
Whites	63	32	5
21–29 years	77	21	2
30–49 years	63	32	5
50 and over	60	32	8
Community Size:			
500,000 and over	70	23	7
50,000–500,000	67	29	4
2,500–50,000	58	38	4
Under 2,500	58	35	7
National Totals	64%	30%	6%

Source: Gallup poll, July 1969.

[2] Ivor Kraft, Jean Fuschillo, and Elizabeth Herzog, *Prelude to School: An Evaluation of an Inner-City Preschool Program*, Children's Bureau Research Reports, no. 3 (Washington, D.C., 1968).

[3] Benjamin S. Bloom, "Early Learning in the Home," first B. J. Paley lecture, University of California at Los Angeles, July 18, 1965, mimeographed, pp. 23–24.

Preschool offers a little child an opportunity to play with other children and to explore a variety of materials, settings, and situations.

Preschools for children of affluent parents have proven their worth over many decades. Before many public schools had kindergartens, parents who realized the importance of early child development enrolled their little children in private preschool programs. Some of these were cooperatives in which parents participated as well as their children, with the added advantages of parent education and whole-family involvement.[4] What is new about the preschool movement today is the wider public recognition of the importance of early childhood education and the more

[4] Katharine Whiteside Taylor, *Parents and Children Learn Together* (original title: *Parents Cooperative Nursery Schools*), 2d ed. (New York: Teachers College, Columbia University, 1967).

general acceptance of social responsibility for enriching the lives of disadvantaged children. Nonwhite three- and four-year-olds enrolled in school increased twofold when Project Head Start went into effect. The percentage of nonwhite children of preschool age increased from 10 percent in 1964 to 19 percent in 1968, while enrollment of three- and four-year-old white children increased from 9 percent to 15 percent.[5]

DEVELOPMENTAL TASKS OF PARENTS OF PRESCHOOL CHILDREN

Parents help the young child achieve his many developmental tasks by accepting his increasing range of skills and physical activity and by finding satisfactory roles in which physical help is gradually diminishing and other kinds of help gradually increasing. They must assume responsibility for supervising the child and yet avoid unnecessary worry and fear, whether in connection with a child's physical competence or growing social interests.

One of the perpetually surprising features of family life is the fact that it never

---

[5] U.S. Bureau of the Census, "School Enrollment: October 1968 and 1967," *Population Characteristics,* Current Population Reports, series P-20, no. 190 (1969), p. 1.

stays put. No sooner has a fence been built to keep a two-year-old out of the street than he is a three-year-old, capable of understanding why he must keep to the sidewalk. The period of teaching the youngster to keep dry is succeeded by one of helping him to get used to sharing his parents with a new baby. Just as a child has reached a stage when his mental growth has made him an increasingly interesting companion, he is away at nursery school or kindergarten, and his parents begin to be outsiders, unaware of what is happening to him during many of his waking hours.

Providing a Wholesome Home Environment

As their child enters a wider set of relationships and presses for independence, parents need to maintain a sense of balance that recognizes helpfully that the child is still young, still dependent, and still in need of guidance and help in many areas.

Using television constructively is an especial challenge to American parents. Preschool children are fascinated with television programs, both those designed for children and for adults. A Nielson study finds many evening shows having a larger number of two- to five-year-olds watching than any daytime show. The effects are particularly unfortunate for low-income children, who are found to watch television up to five to seven hours each weekday.

The National Commission on the Causes and Prevention of Violence concludes that television has been so filled with violence that it is teaching American children moral and social values "inconsistent with a civilized society."[6]

Television is potent in shaping children's attitudes toward and expectations of themselves and others long before they can read and write. Used constructively, television can enlarge a child's world and bring him face to face with persons, places, ideas, and ideals. Recommendations for parents' guidance of children's television viewing include:

1. Become aware of what children are watching, rather than consistently using the TV set as a baby-sitter
2. Turn off undesirable programs and interpret why to your child—"Our family does not like such behavior."
3. Prepare a television guide for young children, using pictures of the clock, channel numbers, and television characters for children not old enough to read
4. Help little children see TV commercials as ways people try to sell things to be chosen or not by those who do the buying

5. Tell local television stations and the networks your choices, your objections, and your preferences
6. Request that the recommendations of the violence commission be implemented:
   a. an overall reduction in programs that require or contain violence
   b. elimination of violence from children's cartoon programs
   c. adoption of the British practice of scheduling crime, Western, and adventure stories containing significant violence only after children's bedtime
   d. permanent federal financing for the Public Broadcast Corporation to enable it to offer high-quality alternatives to violent programs for children
   e. intensified research by the networks into the impact of television violence.[7]

A little child especially needs the comfort of being loved, appreciated, and enjoyed for himself. Both parents may need to check upon possible tendencies toward trying to make the child over, tweaking and pulling at him in little criticisms rather than giving encouraging and appreciative little pats. They must recognize that it is

[6] "TV Violence 'Appalling,'" *U.S. News and World Report*, October 6, 1969, pp. 55–56; Eliot A. Daley, "Is TV Brutalizing Your Child?" *Look*, December 2, 1969, pp. 99–100; and "Excerpts from Summary of Violence Commission's Report," *New York Times*, December 13, 1969, p. 22.

[7] Richard L. Tobin, "When Violence Begets Violence," *Saturday Review*, October 11, 1969, pp. 69–70; see relevant research cited in Urie Bronfenbrenner, "The Split-Level American Family," *Saturday Review*, October 7, 1967, pp. 60–66.

their job to help the child develop the capacities he has rather than to try to build up their self-esteem by pushing him beyond what he can do. Being aware of dangers in visiting "the curse of the norm" on any child and enjoying the unique individuality of each child are paired developmental tasks of prime importance.

Creating Together an Atmosphere of Love

Studies show that wives and husbands at the preschool family stage have less emotionally-charged interaction with each other than they had earlier in their marriages.[8] They have fewer arguments, feel resentful or misunderstood less often, and they tend less often to refuse to talk because they are angry with each other now than they have since they married. At the same time, the marriage has fewer positive supports at the preschool stage than it formerly did. Husband and wife have fewer gay times away from home and less often laugh together, work together on a stimulating project, or calmly discuss something with each other than formerly. By now the parents seem to

have settled into the business of child-rearing with fewer negative feelings and less fun as a married pair than they had earlier.

At this stage the parents may need to strengthen their creative partnership and express their affection in ways that will keep their relationship from falling to a humdrum level. Expression of affection for each other may seem like an odd "task" to set up, but lack of such expression ranks high among the grievances husbands and wives list when trying to analyze their sources of unhappiness.[9] Apparently it is easy to fall into the habit of assuming that the other partner will take for granted the love each really wants and needs.

Accepting Their Weaknesses Gracefully

Somehow parents have to learn to take their unavoidable failures, mistakes, and blunders without piling up feelings of guilt, blame, and recrimination. One way of doing this is to try to be sympathetic toward, instead of full of blame for, each other's faults in connection with dealing with the children. In a day when so much

[8] Harold Feldman, "The Development of the Husband-Wife Relationship," a study supported in part by the National Institute of Mental Health, unpublished data received through personal correspondence, March 24, 1961, with permission.

[9] Lewis M. Terman, assisted by Paul Buttenwieser, Leonard W. Ferguson, Winifred Bent Johnson, and Donald P. Wilson, *Psychological Factors in Marital Happiness* (New York: McGraw-Hill Book Company, 1938), chap. 5, "The Interpretation of Domestic Grievances."

emphasis is placed on parent-child relations, while so little is known about how to keep from foisting one's own frustrations and insecurities on one's children, parents need each other's help in striking a balance between worry and nonchalance, between self-recrimination and indifference. We all make mistakes, but if our basic attitudes are wholesome, loving, and friendly, the mistakes are going to be more than offset by good feelings.

Continuing to Develop as Individuals and as a Married Couple

This is a time when a man and woman must learn to nourish mutual tastes, interests, and friendships as an aid to making the satisfactions of marriage permanent and enduring and to providing for each other the satisfactions that strengthen their belief in themselves and give them status. The many demands and pressures upon each parent may tend to leave little time for them to enjoy each other and the hobbies or pursuits that may have been initially responsible for drawing them together. The mother may be so concerned with the demands of child care and homemaking that she gives little thought to her need for continuing to develop as a person. The father may be so taken up with his work that he no longer takes time for just enjoying life with his wife.

FAMILY DEVELOPMENTAL TASKS AT THE PRESCHOOL STAGE

While the preschool child is achieving his developmental tasks, and the adults are attempting to accomplish theirs as parents and as husband and wife, the family as a whole is concurrently facing the family developmental tasks of the preschool stage:

1. Supplying adequate space, facilities, and equipment for the expanding family

2. Meeting predictable and unexpected costs of family life with small children

3. Sharing responsibilities within the expanding family

4. Maintaining mutually satisfying sexual relationships and planning for future children

5. Creating and maintaining effective communication within the family

6. Cultivating relationships within the extended family

7. Tapping resources and serving needs outside the family

8. Facing dilemmas and reworking philosophies of life.

Supplying Adequate Space, Facilities, and Equipment for the Expanding Family

Housing now should promote the growth of the preschooler, afford a good start for his younger sibling, and allow some privacy and comfort for the parents. Nothing can be a greater challenge to good family growth than inadequate room to work out the problems of group and individual maturation. Fathers with preschool children spend significantly more time out of the

MERRILL-PALMER INSTITUTE—
PHOTO BY DONNA J. HARRIS

This is the stage when climbing, pulling, and hauling equipment give the preschooler the large-muscle exercise and skill-development opportunities he needs.

home than men whose children have grown. Among the reasons for fathers' absenting themselves from their young families is their need for privacy and a chance to concentrate on their own projects.[10]

Inefficient houses and inadequate household equipment complicate the mother's already onerous task of dividing her time between the needs of her children and the demands of the household. Facilities adequate for the differential sleep and rest requirements of the several members of the family are a real asset. Parents now especially need privacy for their more intimate moments together without the ever-present interest of the inquiring preschooler, "Watcha doing?" The child-proofing of the house mentioned earlier carries over into this stage with all its safeguards, especially now, when protecting the new baby without unduly restraining the preschool child becomes an additional factor of importance.

This is the stage when climbing, pulling, and hauling equipment give the preschooler the large-muscle exercise and skill-development opportunities he needs, at the same time that it takes him out from under foot, assuring both his parents and his new sibling of some relief from his boisterous activity. When the entire neighborhood seems compressed and hemmed in through social barriers, the problem of full expression of the individual and the family is com-

[10] Ruth H. Smith, Donna Beth Downer, and Mildred T. Lynch, "The Man in the House," *Family Coordinator* 18, no. 2 (April 1969): 107–111.

pounded. Play facilities, recreational areas, parks, and their availability to all are important in providing an outlet for family tensions.

Meeting Predictable and Unexpected Costs of Family Life with Small Children

If the family income is fairly steady, it is possible to budget carefully for the normal expenditures of the growing family: so much for food, clothing, sitter fees, recreation, utilities, rent or house payments, and the rest. When the income fluctuates, as it does with periods of unemployment or sickness or accident, major adjustments may need to be made.

The preschool stage is notorious for its unpredictabilities. The family may be getting along fine, with income matching outgo, when suddenly something happens that throws the whole financial picture out of focus. In early childhood there is a multiplicity of minor illnesses, any one of which can upset the family budget temporarily. Now when the older child ranges further afield in the neighborhood, to nursery school, kindergarten, play lot, park, and beach, he comes in contact with many more children than he met as long as he was content in house and yard. These increased contacts multiply exposure to infections that make childhood diseases

common for the preschooler and quite often for the baby sister or brother as well.

Accidents, falls, burns, and cuts are even more distressing because of the factor of suddenness that is added to the distress of actual incapacity. Children's accidents are frequently of great importance in the amount of guilt they arouse in the parents. When a long continued illness or an abrupt accident results in a deforming handicap or a crippling condition, it may necessitate critical shifts in the economic aspects as well as the emotional relationships of the family. Intelligent medical and social management are often necessary to keep the illness at the physical level from producing emotional maladjustment in its wake.

The high costs of medical care, continuing insurance drains, installment buying, debts, and mortgages complicate even well-planned family economics and are disastrous to those less carefully organized. Recent years have seen some advance in general recognition of such financial hazards facing young families with the development of such cushioning resources as group hospitalization and medical service plans, well-baby clinics, cooperative nurseries, child guidance clinics, mental hygiene services, family service facilities, parent education agencies, adult and child recreational programs, and special facilities for the care and education of all types of exceptional children. That such helpful resources are not yet generally available, or even known, to the rank and file of fam-

Chart 10–1. *Working Wives and Mothers, by Age of Children*

LABOR FORCE RATES^{1/} (PERCENT)

——— With Children 6 to 17
•••••• With No Children Under 18
—•—• All Wives
— —— With Children Under 6

Source: Elizabeth Waldman and Yvonne Olson, "Marital and Family Status of Workers," *Monthly Labor Review,* April 1968, p. 18.
1 Labor force as a percentage of population.

ilies who need them is all too true in most communities.

Nationally, grants-in-aid to the several states, funneled through the Children's Bureau, are available for maternal and child health, crippled children, child welfare services, etc., as is also the mental hygiene program under the United States Public Health Service.

The preschool family characteristically gets along on the single income of the husband. Even during years when the percentage of working wives in the total population increased, three out of four mothers with children under six years of age were not working (chart 10–1). Now when little children must be cared for, it is the exceptional mother who leaves home to earn money, even at a time when family needs are great. This is the period when the family tightens its belt and tries to make ends meet on the husband's income alone.

Sharing Responsibilities within the Expanding Family

Daily round-the-clock child care, involving "chasing the children," who play in yard and neighborhood, to properly supervise their play and protect them from danger, as well as attending to the needs of the infant and doing the housework (marketing, cooking, baking, cleaning, dishwashing, sewing, washing, ironing), is generally assigned the young wife and mother in our society. In former days these many responsibilities were divided among other grown and growing members of the family. In the old-fashioned farm family, there was always a pair of willing hands to mind the baby or do an errand or set the table. Margaret Mead reminds us that most primitive peoples recognize that it takes more than one adult to care for small, helpless children and recommends that American families innovate ways of sharing small-child care more broadly today.

We have established a strange and lonely way of life, as grandmothers, aunts, grown daughters, and domestic help have progressively been banished from the home. We must devise new ways for real neighborhood sharing of the care of children, more cooperative nursery schools, more sharing of minor crises, so that the neighborhood takes over what the family used to do. And we need more generosity on the part of parents toward the grandparents, the childless aunts and uncles, all of whom could share a lot of the care of children if the parents were willing to really share their children. The present-day mother is alone in the house with her small children too much, and she has her hands too full.[11]

Until real help from the outside can be recruited, it may fall to the husband to share with his wife the tasks of child-rear-

[11] Fifth Journal Forum, "The Plight of the Young Mother, *Ladies' Home Journal*, February 1956, p. 62.

ing and housekeeping through the preschool stage of the family life cycle. The young father returns home from work to find his wife busy with her end-of-the-day chores, the children irritably clinging to her while she tries to get the evening meal. He steps in and volunteers to take the children off her hands or to do some of the chores that she has not been able to finish through the hectic pace of the day. He may be tired, but he comes in fresh from the outside without the mutual annoyance and frustration that is so often a part of the young mother's hour-by-hour life with active young children. He can whisk them off for a frolic or give them their baths or take over their feeding with a light touch just because he has been out of the home all day.

An exploratory study of the percentage of time married men spend in various ac-

Table 10–4. *What Husbands Do in the Home, by Percentage of Time Spent and Stage of the Family Life Cycle*

Activities in/out of the home	Preschool		School-age		Empty nest		Postretirement	
In the house:								
Household tasks	12.6		3.9		4.6		9.0	
Food operations		2.9		2.7		2.2		4.6
House care		2.1		1.4		2.2		3.9
Laundry		.3		.5		.2		.5
Care of children		7.3	—		—		—	
Business	.1		.2		8.1		.3	
Conversation	3.6		4.9		4.7		5.0	
Personal care	4.5		3.2		9.3		8.5	
Eating	5.2		3.9		6.2		5.3	
Leisure	9.9		14.8		18.3		29.6	
Out of the house	64.5		66.1		48.8		42.1	

Source: Ruth H. Smith, Donna Beth Downer, and Mildred T. Lynch, "The Man in the House," *Family Coordinator* 18, no. 2 (April 1969): 109.

Families with Preschool Children

tivies finds fathers of preschool children more involved in household responsibilities than are husbands at any other stage of the family life cycle. Fathers of young children spend more time in child care than in all other household tasks combined (table 10–4).

Father's presence in a child's life is important for his or her full development. A little girl gets a sense of being a desirable, capable feminine person both through identifying with her mother and by attracting the interest of her father—the first important man in her life. Association with a strong, limit-setting, affectionate father is critical in the establishment of a boy's masculinity in the first five years of life.[12]

The more strenuous tasks of floor-mopping, window-cleaning, washing, or trash-dumping may be saved for the man of the house by the woman whose strength is barely adequate for the many other demands upon it. Some young families have established such heavy allocations of responsibilities to the young husband and father that he may be severely exploited by a wife who reserves more and more of the day's work for him to do when his day's work is presumably finished. The young husband is apt to be sorely pressed for time and energy at this stage of his life. This is the time when the man of the house is trying to get ahead on his job. He possibly is taking an evening course or two with an eye to advancement. He may be doing what overtime he can get to help make ends meet. Even if he is willing to help out at home, there is a limit to what any one person can do comfortably and well.

The preschool child is old enough to assume some real responsibilities. He gradually takes over more and more of his own care in toileting, washing his face and hands, dressing and undressing, and picking up his toys, with help or supervision as needed. As he enters the preschool period, he or she has begun to take a real interest in what is going on in the household and wants to participate. The little girl of two and a half or three begs to help make beds, to sweep the floor, and to wash dishes when her mother is occupied with these tasks. The child identifies with the parent of the same sex and likes nothing better than acting out the sex role. Parents are wise not to discourage these efforts on the part of the small child "to help." They share with the child the jobs he or she can join in, not so much in the interest of the child's labor, but especially because helping makes the youngster a real participant in his family. The child learns thus to internalize his or her sex role.

Many a young family sails smoothly through the preschool family stage in these days. Modern equipment in kitchen and laundry eases the load that the young mother must carry. Miracle fabrics are

---

[12] Henry B. Biller, "Masculine Development: An Integrative Review," *Merrill-Palmer Quarterly* 13, no. 4 (October 1967): 253–294; Alexander Mitscherlich, *Society without the Father* (New York: Harcourt, Brace and World, 1969); and Paul Popenoe, "Fathers In and Out of the Home," *Family Life* 28, no. 2 (February 1968): 1–2.

easy to keep clean and need practically no ironing. Prepared baby foods and frozen products that can be readied for use in a few moments are a godsend. The modern young mother's ability to plan her work, putting the essential tasks on the agenda and letting the relatively unimportant things slide, removes much of the strain from daily routines. Spacing the arrival of the children so that each is assured the care it needs without unduly taxing the mother's strength does much to keep the young family on an even keel during the preschool stage, when life can so easily become pretty hectic.

Success in achieving this developmental task is not just a matter of how much or how little there is to be done, but rather of how decisions are made, how roles are assigned, and how the several family members feel about their responsibilities. If each family member feels pride and pleasure in doing his tasks, if each is accountable to the others for common concerns, if each feels needed and appreciated, the family is finding happiness and integration as a working unit.

Maintaining Mutually Satisfying Sexual Relationships and Planning for Future Children

By the time the first child is a preschooler, his parents have been through the full process of conception, pregnancy, childbirth,

and establishment as a full-fledged family at least once. Learning theory would suggest that the experienced couple should be able to take further pregnancies and children more in stride now than when their first baby came, but there is evidence that the second child has even more negative effect on a couple's marital happiness and satisfaction than did their firstborn.

Dr. Harold Feldman's study comparing couples without children, those expecting their first baby, and those with one child with husbands and wives beyond the child-rearing stage of the family life cycle finds that the second child has an even greater negative effect on marital happiness and satisfaction than did the first. Evidence that parental roles are hard on the marriage are several: "lowered satisfaction in marriage, perceived negative personality change in both partners, less satisfaction with the home, more instrumental conversation, more child-centered concern and more warmth toward the child, and a curvilinear effect for sexual satisfaction although ending lower."[13]

Couples with but one child expected that their situation would get better as the child got older. They looked forward to their children's interfering less with their marriage, to having the house look better, to being less tired, nervous, blue, tied

[13] Harold Feldman, "Parent and Marriage: Myths and Realities," address presented at the Merrill-Palmer Institute Conference on the Family, November 21, 1969, mimeographed, pp. 18–19.

down, and to having more and better sexual relations as their children became more mature.[14]

Child spacing studies find that the intervals between births in a family tend to increase.[15] These longer intervals can be seen as "breathing spaces" in which a family reestablishes itself and mobilizes its resources after the birth of one child before attempting the next.

Finding the time, privacy, and energy for tender, close relationships as a married couple may be difficult when children are young. Sharing bed or room with a child old enough to be aware of what is going on robs a husband and wife of much-needed privacy. Days and nights of nursing a sick youngster rob even the most loving husband and wife of their ardor for each other. Just getting through the day's work may bring the couple to bed too tired for anything but sleep. Knowing from experience the power of their fertility tends to make the woman wary of her husband's approaches unless she has confidence in the family planning procedures. What once was entered into with joyous abandon now may become a marital duty unless the couple provides for their sex life together amid the welter of other demands.

Creating and Maintaining Effective Communication within the Family

The Tower of Babel had nothing on family life at the preschool stage. The baby babbles and gurgles and sputters and fusses and "practices" his vowels. The preschool child's language development is more rapid than it ever will be again. Research finds that typically he learns to use hundreds of new words each year, and that his use of complete sentences is established by the time he is three.[16] Speech and learning are so closely associated that in a real sense a little child learns as he talks, and he talks as he learns in increasingly effective ways.

With the coming of the new baby, the emotional constellations of the family shift, as the firstborn accepts his displacement as well as he can, and as the parents find a place in their home for the little newcomer at the same time that they safeguard the security of the older child. There may be a tendency for parents to be emotionally warmer with the second baby than they were with their first.[17] This

---

[14] Ibid., p. 17.

[15] Gerald Leslie, Harold Christensen, and Glenn Pearman, "Studies in Child Spacing: The Time-Interval Separating All Children in Completed Families of Purdue University Graduates," *Social Forces* 34, no. 1 (October 1955): 77–82.

[16] D. McCarthy, "Language Development in Children," in L. Carmichael, ed., *Manual of Child Psychology* (New York: John Wiley and Sons, 1954), pp. 492–630.

[17] J. K. Lasko, "Parent Behavior toward First and Second Children," *Genetic Psychology Monograph* 49, no. 1 (February 1954): 99–137.

probably is not so much that they love the second baby more, but rather that they have become more familiar with their roles, and so are able to relax and enjoy the new baby more fully than they could in their first experience as parents.

Understandable as the parents' feelings and emotional expressions are, it may be hard for the firstborn to accept their open display of affection for the little new rival. Therefore, the mother and father may need to create new modes of emotional communication with the older child that will give him the assurance that he is loved and needed and wanted for himself. Wise parents provide some special time with their firstborn when the new baby does not intrude. It sometimes helps to let the firstborn know that just because he is older, he occupies a special place in their lives that no younger sibling can ever fill. Some increase in responsibility for the firstborn may be reassuring to him if it is not overdone. The older child sometimes has to let his parents know of his need for being babied too, in regressive acts: wetting himself when he has long since learned to be dry, wanting to take his milk from a bottle when he has already established more mature eating and drinking habits, wanting to be cuddled and fussed over as the baby is, even trying to put himself in the baby's place—literally in the buggy or the crib. These are signals a sensitive parent can read that indicate the older child's need for more close, demonstrable affection and

attention than he has been getting. Ridiculing, belittling, ignoring, or denying a child's effort to communicate his emotional needs cripple the communication systems and bottle up explosive feelings with unfortunate results to the youngster, the younger sibling, and the family as a whole.

The child who is prepared for the coming of his new baby sister or brother can take with less distress the jealousy and rivalry so usually generated by his displacement by the new rival. Before the baby comes, the older child needs from his parents an understanding of what is happening and an assurance that this is to be *his* baby as well as theirs, and that they will love him after the baby comes, as they have before. In this a mother or father can get helpful books to read to the preschool youngster, as well as find sound guides on the early sex education of their children, of which the following are examples:

Andry, Andrew C., and Steven Schepp, *How Babies Are Made* (New York: Time-Life Books, 1968).

Bell, Evelyn S., and Elizabeth Farogh, *The New Baby* (Philadelphia: J. B. Lippincott Company, 1938).

Cockefair, Edgar, and Ada Milam Cockefair, *The Story of You* (Madison, Wis.: Milam Publications, 1955).

Ets, Marie Hall, *The Story of a Baby* (New York: Viking Press, 1948).

Gruenberg, Sidonie M., *The Wonderful Story of How You Were Born* (Garden City, N.Y.: Hanover House, 1952).

Kaufman, Dorothy Brennan, *Where Do Babies Come From?* (Detroit: Harlo Press, 1965).

Levine, Milton I., and Jean H. Seligmann, *A Baby Is Born* (New York: Golden Press, 1966).

Peller, Lili, and Sophia Mumford, *Our New Baby* (New York: Vanguard Press, 1943).

Shane, Harold, and Ruth Shane, *The New Baby* (New York: Simon and Schuster, 1948).

Little children are so ever-present and so demanding of the time and attention of their parents that husband and wife may need to inaugurate new times and ways for getting through to each other. The little children may be fed by one or both parents and then put to rest while the parents have an occasional quiet meal together, or the preschooler can be given some special time of his own by either the father or the mother just before the family meal, so that he can relate the excitements of his day and get some of his more pressing questions out of the way before the family as a whole assembles for mealtime. One young family developed a "green light" system by which the "traffic" of conversation could flow in both directions across the table, each in its turn, thus assuring the parents of some access to each other between the gusts of chatter from their preschool youngsters.

This developmental task is being achieved in the family as each member of the family increasingly feels free to express his ideas, his feelings, and his values with assurance of their acceptance by the others in the family. The expanding stage of the family life cycle is so explosive and so full of new experiences, feelings, decisions, and needs to evaluate that communication systems become extremely important at the very time that they are most difficult to keep open and in good working order. But few things are more important to happy family life.

Cultivating Relationships within the Extended Family

At few stages in the family life cycle can relatives be as important as during the preschool period. Grandparents can do much to ease the pressures upon the parents while children are young. A loving relative who is on hand while the new baby is coming, and through the illnesses and accidents that occasionally hit the young family, cushions these crises in many a home.[18] An aunt and uncle may get valuable experience at the same time that they relieve the young parents in child care. They may take over for a long evening or over a weekend or

---

[18] Reuben Hill, *Family Development in Three Generations* (Cambridge, Mass.: Schenkman Publishing Company, 1970), found kinship exchanges of help accounting for 70 percent of 3,781 mutual services in one year's time. Married children, with their pressures of rearing youngsters, were the most needful and received the most help from their relatives (chapter 3).

FAMILY DEVELOPMENT

even for a week or two while father and mother slip off to regain their perspective as a couple on a brief vacation, on a business trip, or for a quick visit to old friends.

Problems come up, of course, when the substitute parents do not agree with the child guidance procedures or philosophy that the parents are trying to practice. A grandmother can "spoil" her young charges in ways that take weeks to rehabilitate if she is not aware of the parents' goals for their children. Or a too-rigid program of discipline suddenly imposed by some well-meaning aunt or uncle may boomerang in any number of ways. These things are being openly discussed in many families today in ways that allow the parents to brief explicitly any child-serving relative on what is the usual practice, and why; what the child is and is not customarily allowed to do, and why; and what routines are followed most conscientiously, and which can be let slide when the situation warrants.

Children are remarkably resilient creatures and can take a great deal of inconsistency from the various adults that attend them, as long as they feel basically secure. Although there are some procedures and policies that are considered better than others according to sound child-development principles (chapter 4), few children can be severely damaged by occasional lapses or changes of pace. Extremists who insist that grandparents are bad for children fail to see how much a child can learn from being differently handled by different persons, or how much a youngster benefits from the sense of ongoing family relations he gets as he clamors for tales of when his mother or father was young. One nine-year-old puts both values neatly when he says solemnly, "I like to go to Grandma's house, because she scolds so soft, and she tells me all about the olden days when Daddy was a little boy just like me."

Tapping Resources and Serving Needs outside the Family

One hazard of the family with little children is its preoccupation with itself. The young father is seen putting in a full day on his job, rushing to night school or union meeting to better his chances for advancement, and helping out at home in the many roles he feels are his in the family. The young mother is tied down with little children so much day after day that she may long for adult companionship, stimulation, and contact.

The little child will lead the family out into wider horizons if he is allowed to range further afield. He goes to nursery school and then to kindergarten, bringing home with him new problems and experiences and later taking his parents out to parents' meetings, neighborhood projects, and community affairs. The preschooler is big enough now to go to Sunday school, and often starts his family in church activities that carry through the years. Periodic trips to the pediatrician or family doctor for preventive shots and checkups, as well as treatment for the various illnesses that befall him, bring both him and his parents into relationship with the health facilities of the community. His enjoyment of the park, the zoo, the playground, the fire department, and the bakery frequently gets his whole family out for jaunts into activities and facilities never before explored.

The young mother finds meanings in life as a person outside the family at intervals around her homemaking and child care responsibilities. It may be in some parents' group, community service project, church circle, political campaign, course of study in the evening, or Saturday afternoon employment that she finds her identity as a woman and brings home, after a few hours of wider horizons, the perspective and point of view that enrich the family as a whole. Here it is that the stereotyped reactions of the "Woman's place is in the home" or "Little children need a mother's care," if interpreted too rigidly, can be suffocating not only to the young woman but to her family as well. A major complaint of college-educated mothers of young children is that they long for intervals of adult association, mature stimulation, and challenging activities with persons their own age. This is one of the prime motivators back of the young mother's desire for a job. Openly recognized by the family, many opportunities besides gainful employment may appear as satisfying, unless the financial needs of the family require it.

The young father, driven through his twenties and thirties by efforts to get himself established vocationally and to keep his little family afloat financially, may push himself so hard that he has little time for continuing his interests as a person or for enjoying his family on their new horizons. This is especially true in some middle-class families, where mobility drives keep a man lashed by hopes for advancement and chained to his job and its demands. Upper-class fathers find it easier to keep up their club memberships (for business and professional reasons, it's true), and to maintain regular programs of recreation, with other men as well as in the young married couple set. Lower-class families make the poorest articulations with the wider community in the health, recreational, educational, vocational, and social aspects of life, as studies previously quoted (chapter 2) so emphatically indicate.

Coping with Special Problems

Many children are growing up in one-parent homes, or with neither their own mother nor father to care for them. Some six million children live with their mother only, and another three milion live with neither parent.[19] Other children live with

[19] U.S. Bureau of the Census, "Household and Family Characteristics: March 1966," *Population Characteristics*, Current Population Reports, series P-20, no. 164 (April 12, 1967), table D, p. 3; table 1, p. 9.

stepfathers after their mothers have been widowed or divorced and remarried. Many of these rebuilt families provide the love and security preschool children need, but, in almost all, some problems have to be met which add their stress to those already present in young children.

Longitudinal studies find that virtually all children must cope with crises as they grow up. These efforts of theirs include problem behavior such as aggression, that peaks at about age five for most young-sters.[20] Preschool children's aggressive behavior has been effectively reduced by affiliation-arousing stories such as that about a lonely dog looking for someone to play with.[21]

Children with developmental problems pose special difficulties for their families. Brain-damaged children are found to have tendencies toward excitability, overreaction, impulsiveness, lack of control, and defective motivation.[22] Farber finds that

the more helpless a severely retarded child is, the more adverse is his effect on the rest of the family.[23] One mother of a handicapped child reports confidentially, "The slow and steady erosion of relationships within a family is the more destructive because of the attitudes of neighbors, and the general public, so often condemnatory and critical of both parents and child."

Facing Dilemmas and Reworking Philosophies of Life

By the time the oldest child is four or five and the next baby already on the scene, the family is face to face with a number of dilemmas that challenge its way of life. Kirkpatrick mentions several that are particularly relevant at this stage of the family life cycle: (1) freedom versus order and efficiency, (2) free expression of personal potentialities versus stable goal expectations, (3) personal self-expression versus child-rearing, (4) work achievement versus love-reproduction functions, (5) flexible training versus rigid child-rearing, (6) high aspiration levels for children versus realistic expectations, (7) family loyalty versus community loyalty, and (8) extensive casual association versus restrictive inten-

[20] B. R. McCandless, Carolyn Balsbaugh, and Hannah L. Bennett, "Preschool Age Socialization and Maternal Control Techniques," abstract in *American Psychologist* 13 (1958), following p. 320; and Lois Barclay Murphy, "Preventive Implications of Development in the Preschool Years," in G. Caplan, ed., *Prevention of Mental Disorders in Children* (New York: Basic Books, 1961), pp. 218–248.

[21] J. E. Gordon and E. Smith, "Children's Aggression, Parental Attitudes, and the Effects of an Affiliation-Arousing Story," *Journal of Personal and Social Psychology* 1 (1965): 654–659.

[22] Mary F. Waldrop, Frank A. Pedersen, and Richard Q. Bell, "Minor Physical Anomalies and Behavior in Preschool Children," *Child Development* 39, no. 2 (June 1968): 391–400.

[23] Bernard Farber, *Effects of a Severely Mentally Retarded Child on Family Integration*, monograph of the Society for Research in Child Development, vol. 24, no. 2 (1959): 1–112.

One dilemma that challenges the preschool family is that of freedom (to clutter, to mess, to spill, and to play with a minimum of restraint) versus order and efficiency.

sive association.[24] Each horn of each dilemma has its values and its price. Freedom is greatly to be desired, but its price is conflict and confusion in the family. On the other hand, order and efficiency are values, but at the cost of personal frustration and submission to authority. And so it goes. Every family must work out, in ways that make sense to its members and

to itself as a unit, those answers to the eternal questions of life that suit them in their situations.

A simple "nonintellectual" family may deny its absorption in philosophical matters, yet every day is full of decisions and choices that depend upon how the family conceives of itself and what is operational definitions of life are. These conceptions of their common life are constantly undergoing change: (1) with the addition of each new member; (2) with the stimuli of

---

[24] Clifford Kirkpatrick, *The Family as Process and Institution*, 2d ed. (New York: Ronald Press Company, 1963), chap. 4, "Family Types and Dilemmas."

FAMILY DEVELOPMENT

other ways of life in the community and among their associates; (3) with the new ideas and insights any of the family members get (in association with others, in reading, in educational, social, religious, and other contexts); (4) with the old and new tastes of joys and satisfactions that ought to be safeguarded; and (5) under the various stresses, strains, and challenges that back them to the wall and force them to take another look at life as they are living it.

SUMMARY

Families with preschool children are those whose first children are between two-and-one-half and five years of age. There quite possibly is a second child, and sometimes a third, born into the family before the stage is completed, who will be preoccupied with the developmental tasks of infancy, while the preschool child is working on his developmental tasks, and the parents are attempting to accomplish those they face as parents, as married partners, and as persons. Family developmental tasks of this stage may be seen as (1) supplying adequate space, facilities, and equipment for the expanding family, (2) meeting predictable and unexpected costs of family life with small children, (3) sharing responsibilities within the expanding family, (4) maintaining mutually satisfying sexual relationships and planning for future children, (5) creating and maintaining effective communication within the family, (6) cultivating

relationships within the extended family, (7) tapping resources and serving needs outside the family, and (8) facing dilemmas and reworking philosophies of life.

SUGGESTED ACTIVITIES

1. Prepare a paper on the kibbutz of Israel based upon authoritative sources such as Bruno Bettelheim, *The Children of the Dream* (New York: Macmillan Company, 1969), and two critical reviews of this book: Urie Bronfenbrenner, "The Dream of the Kibbutz," *Saturday Review,* September 20, 1969, pages 72–73, 83–85; and also Albert I. Rabin, "Of Dreams and Reality: Kibbutz Children," *Children* 16, no. 4 (July-August 1969): 160–162. Compare the advantages and disadvantages of collectives for children with American family child-rearing in the preschool years.

2. Outline a feasible program in preparation of the firstborn child for the coming of a new baby into the family, using references suggested in this chapter and/or other sound materials. Discuss the relevance of each step in the program for the achievement of the goals for the child and for the family.

3. Role-play several of the family situations presented in either Jackson's *Life among the Savages* or McConnell's *Trampled Terraces* (full references in readings for this chapter), portraying the child's as well as the parents' roles in each situation presented. Discuss the nature of the conflict between the developmental tasks of little children and the developmental tasks of parents of little children in each connection. Indicate in what ways these are normal conflicts of developmental tasks between the generations or how they may be atypical of this stage. Document your opinions as far as you can from materials in your readings and in the chapter.

4. Copy on the blackboard one of Hank Ketcham's cartoons of Dennis the Menace showing a predicament in which the developmental tasks of the child are in opposition to those of his parents. Discuss.

5. Review the film *Preface to a Life* (twenty-nine minutes, sound, produced by Sun Dial Films, Inc., for National Institute of Mental Health, United States Public Health Service, 1950), looking especially into how a preschool child feels about the coming of the new baby into his family. What did the parents do that helped? What made the problem more difficult for the firstborn? What else might have been tried?

6. Invite a preschool teacher to tell you what she finds most usual in the behavior of her children. Discuss what the children seem to be after in these situations in terms of what you know about their developmental tasks.

7. Elaborate any one of Kirkpatrick's dilemmas of family life that particularly applies to the preschool stage, citing illustrations and giving sources for both aspects of the dilemma you have chosen (see readings).

8. Write a paper on the development of trust and of autonomy in early childhood, using as basic references Erik Erikson, *Childhood and Society* (New York: W. W. Norton and Company, 1950), and Robert J. Havighurst, *Human Development and Education*, part 1 (see readings).

9. Discuss what is meant by the concept of a child's identifying with the parent of the same sex. Give illustrations and sources, and indicate the relationship between this tendency and the accomplishment of the developmental tasks of early childhood.

10. Write a paper on the role of the father in the preschool family, touching on the amount of responsibility he may assume in homemaking and child care, and what effect he has upon the development of the child. Document with research reports in the professional literature and with interviews gathered from fathers and mothers of preschool children in a nearby nursery school or kindergarten.

READINGS

Bettelheim, Bruno. *The Children of the Dream.* New York: Macmillan Company, 1969.

Biller, Henry B., and Stephan D. Weiss. "The Father-Daughter Relationship and the Personality Development of the

Female." *Journal of Genetic Psychology* 116 (1970): 79–93.

Boston Children's Hospital Medical Center. *Accident Handbook: A New Approach to Children's Safety.* New York: Dell Purse Book, 1966.

Breckenridge, Marian E., and E. Lee Vincent. *Child Development.* 5th ed. Philadelphia: W. B. Saunders Company, 1965.

Children's Bureau. *Your Child from 3 to 4.* Children's Bureau Publication, no. 446. Washington, D.C., 1967.

Child Study Association of America. *Behavior: The Unspoken Language of Children.* New York: Child Study Association of America, 1967.

Duvall, Evelyn Millis. *Family Living.* Rev. ed. New York: Macmillan Company. Chaps. 15–17.

English, O. Spurgeon, and Constance J. Foster. *Fathers Are Parents, Too.* New York: G. P. Putnam's Sons, 1951.

Faegre, Marion L., John E. Anderson, and Dale B. Harris. *Child Care and Training.* 8th ed. Minneapolis: University of Minnesota Press, 1958.

Ginott, Haim G. *Between Parent and Child.* New York: Macmillan Company, 1968.

Havighurst, Robert J. *Human Development and Education.* New York: Longmans, Green and Company, 1953. Chaps. 2–3.

Hendrickson, Norejane Johnston. *Teaching Preschool Children from Low Income Families.* Columbus, Ohio: 1787 Neil Avenue, 1965.

Hoffman, Martin L., and Lois Wladis Hoffman, eds. *Review of Child Development Research.* New York: Russell Sage Foundation, 1964.

Hurlock, Elizabeth B. *Developmental Psycology.* 3d ed. New York: McGraw-Hill Book Company, 1968. Chaps. 5, 10–11.

Jackson, Shirley. *Life among the Savages.* New York: Farrar, Strauss, and Young, 1953.

Jones, Eve. *Natural Child Rearing.* New York: Free Press, 1959.

Ketcham, Hank. *Dennis the Menace* and *More Dennis the Menace.* New York: Henry Holt and Company, 1953.

Kirkpatrick, Clifford. *The Family as Process and Institution.* 2d ed. New York: Ronald Press Company, 1963. Chap. 4, "Family Types and Dilemmas."

Kraft, Ivor, Jean Fuschillo, and Elizabeth Herzog. *Prelude to School: An Evaluation of an Inner-City Preschool Program.* Children's Bureau Research Reports, no. 3. Washington, D.C., 1968.

Langdon, Grace, and Irving Stout. *These Well-Adjusted Children.* New York: John Day Company, 1951.

McCandless, B. R., Carolyn Balsbaugh, and Hannah L. Bennett. "Preschool Age Socialization and Maternal Control Techniques." Abstract in *American Psychologist* 13 (1958), following p. 320.

McConnell, Raymond. *Trampled Terraces.* Lincoln, Nebr.: University of Nebraska Press, 1950.

Martin, William E., and Celia Burns Stendler. *Child Behavior and Development.* Rev. and enl. ed. of *Child Development.* New York: Harcourt, Brace and Company, 1959.

Murphy, Lois Barclay, and collaborators. *The Widening World of Childhood.* New York: Basic Books, 1962.

Parsons, Talcott, and Robert F. Bales. *Family, Socialization and Interaction Process.* Glencoe, Ill.: Free Press, 1955. Chap. 2, "Family Structure and the Socialization of the Child."

Read, Katherine H. *The Nusery School: A Human Relationships Laboratory.* Philadelphia: W. B. Saunders Company, 1966.

Ridenour, Nina, and Isabel Johnson. *Some Special Problems of Children Aged Two to Five Years.* Rev. ed. New York: Child Study Association of America, 1969.

Ross Laboratories. *Developing Self-Esteem.* Columbus, Ohio: Ross Laboratories, 1959.

Ross Laboratories. *When Your Child Is Contrary.* Columbus, Ohio: Ross Laboratories, 1967.

Ross Laboratories. *Your Child and Discipline.* Columbus, Ohio: Ross Laboratories, 1959.

Ross Laboratories. *Your Child's Appetite.* Columbus, Ohio: Ross Laboratories, 1960.

Ross Laboratories. *Your Child's Fears.* Columbus, Ohio: Ross Laboratories, 1960.

Ross Laboratories. *Your Child's Quarrels.* Columbus, Ohio: Ross Laboratories, 1957.

Smart, Mollie S., and Russell C. Smart. *Children: Development and Relationships.* New York: Macmillan Company, 1967.

Smith, Leona J. *Guiding the Character Development of the Preschool Child.* New York: Association Press, 1968.

Stone, L. Joseph, and Joseph Church. *Childhood and Adolescence.* New York: Random House, 1957. Chaps. 6–7.

Taylor, Katharine Whiteside. *Parents and Children Learn Together* (original title: *Parents Cooperative Nursery Schools*). 2d ed. New York: Teachers College, Columbia University, 1967.

Vincent, Elizabeth Lee, and Phyllis C. Martin. *Human Psychological Development.* New York: Ronald Press Company, 1961.

Yarrow, M. R., J. D. Campbell, and R. V. Burton. *Childrearing: An Inquiry into Research.* San Francisco: Jossey-Bass, 1968.

11 FAMILIES WITH SCHOOLCHILDREN

*Children begin by loving their parents; as
they grow older they judge them;
sometimes they forgive them.* Oscar Wilde
The Picture of Dorian Gray

The stage of the family life cycle characterized by school-age children starts when the first child goes to school, at five to six years of age, and continues until he or she becomes a teenager at thirteen. Before the end of this period, it is likely that the family has seen the birth of younger siblings and that the family has reached its maximum size in number of members and of interrelationships. Typically the American family at this stage consists of four to six persons, who maintain from six to fifteen interpersonal relationships. The possible range in age is from infancy (youngest child) through forty, plus or minus (father), while the eldest child is a school-ager. The parents' crisis continues to be that of self-absorption versus finding fulfillment in rearing the next generation. The school-age child's developmental crisis is risking a sense of inferiority as he develops the capacity of work enjoyment (industry). The family developmental tasks revolve around the major goal of reorganization to make way for the expanding world of school-agers.

These are busy, full years of family living, with children running in and out of the house, with many projects under way, the adults busy keeping the household in good running order and following their youngsters out into wider contacts in the larger community. Concurrently, the school-ager, his younger siblings, his parents, and his entire family work at their developmental tasks, sometimes in harmony, sometimes in discord, but always with the urgency that accompanies growth.

DEVELOPMENT OF SCHOOL-AGE CHILDREN

Elementary schoolchildren differ considerably within a wide range of normal physical, mental, and social development. They enter school as little children and emerge seven years later at various stages of puberty. Growth in height is steady until between nine and twelve, when early-developing youngsters, especially girls, grow taller through the pubertal growth spurt. Weight increases gradually, and more mature distribution of fat occurs in most children. Appetite varies from poor to ravenous, and digestion is generally good. Bladder control is established with only infrequent lapses. Bone replaces cartilage in the skeleton, and permanent teeth come in as baby teeth are lost. Muscular strength and skills increase, bringing a sense of mastery to many a child. The school years are a vigorous, healthy period for most children.

Intellectually, schoolchildren are involved in what Piaget has called "concrete operations." Children develop concepts (mental tools making sense of a multitude of particulars) through ordering and classifying objects and ideas. This includes collecting and arranging things, learning to read, playing with words and their meanings, and enjoying riddles, jokes, and jingles. They begin to see order in the universe through their study of mathematics and science, to know where places are through geography, and to understand the sequence of events through history. Everything they learn later in school is largely determined by what has been learned by the end of the third grade, and by the time they reach the eighth grade, they will have completed 75 percent of their development of general learning.[1]

Parents are the significant people in the schoolchild's life, but other boys and girls become increasingly important throughout the school years.[2] In recent years schoolchildren show little tendency to avoid members of the other sex. They have friends of both sexes, and most of them report having a sweetheart while still in elementary school.[3] Sex role differentiation is well under way as children of both sexes gain understanding as to what activities are appropriate for boys (playing with guns, trucks, bat and ball, etc.), for girls (playing with doll carriages and housekeeping toys, etc.), and for either sex (playing at the beach, in the country, in playground or park, etc.).[4]

When eight- to eleven-year-old boys are asked, "What is expected of boys?" they reply that grown-ups expect them to be noisy, to get dirty, to mess up the house, to be naughty, to be outside more than girls, not to be crybabies or softies, and to get into more trouble than girls. Further-

---

[1] Benjamin S. Bloom, *Stability and Change in Human Characteristics* (New York: John Wiley and Sons, 1964), p. 110.

[2] Dale B. Harris and S. C. Tseng, "Children's Attitudes toward Peers and Parents as Revealed by Sentence Completions," *Child Development* 28 (1957): 401–411.

[3] Gertrude M. Lewis, *Educating Children in Grades Four, Five, and Six* (Washington, D.C.: U.S. Office of Education, 1960); and Carlfred B. Broderick and Stanley E. Fowler, "New Patterns of Relationships between the Sexes among Preadolescents," *Marriage and Family Living* 23, no. 1 (February 1961): 27–30.

[4] Ruth E. Hartley and F. P. Hardesty, "Children's Perceptions of Sex Roles in Childhood," *Journal of Genetic Psychology* 105 (1964): 48.

more, they feel that as boys they cannot do many of the things girls do, but that girls may do many of the things boys do.[5] Growing up either as a boy or a girl involves the successful completion of many age-specific developmental tasks during the school years.

DEVELOPMENTAL TASKS OF SCHOOL-AGE CHILDREN

The developmental tasks of schoolchildren are both those of continuing previous learnings and opening up whole new areas of life.

1. Learning the basic skills required of schoolchildren:

Mastering the fundamentals of reading, writing, calculating, and the scientific, rational approach to solving problems.
Extending understandings of cause-and-effect relationships.
Developing concepts essential for everyday living.
Continued development in ability to reason and to do reflective thinking.

2. Mastering the physical skills appropriate to his development:

Learning the games, the sports, and the various roles in activities pursued by children of his age and sex in his community (ride a bike, swim, skate, play ball, row a boat, climb a tree, etc.).
Developing abilities needed in personal and family living (bathe and dress himself, care for his clothing, make his bed, cook and serve food, clean up after activities, maintain and repair simple household equipment, etc.).

3. Developing meaningful understandings of the use of money:

Finding socially acceptable ways of getting money for what he wants to buy.
Learning how to buy wisely the things he most wants with what he has, and to stay within his available resources.
Finding the meanings of saving for postponed satisfactions.
Reconciling differences between his wants and his resources, and those of others both poorer and richer than he.
Getting basic orientation into the nature of money in everyday life in the family and in the larger community.

4. Becoming an active, cooperative member of his family:

Gaining skills in participating in family discussions and decision-making.

[5] Ruth E. Hartley, "Sex-Role Pressures and the Socialization of the Male Child," *Psychological Reports* 5 (1959): 457–468.

Assuming responsibilities within the household with satisfactions in accomplishment and belonging.

Becoming more mature in giving and receiving affection and gifts between himself and his parents, his siblings, and his relatives within the extended family.

Learning to enjoy the full resources and facilities available within the family, and to take initiative in enriching them as he becomes able.

5. Extending his abilities to relate effectively to others, both peers and adults:

Making progress in his ability to adjust to others.

Learning to stand up for his rights.

Improving his abilities both to lead and to follow others.

Mastering expectancies in simple conventions, rules, customs, courtesies, and standards of his family and groups.

Learning genuinely cooperative roles with others in many situations.

Making and keeping close friends.

6. Continuing the learnings involved in handling his feelings and impulses:

Growing in his ability to work through simple frustrations.

Exploring socially acceptable ways of releasing negative emotions effectively.

Becoming more mature in channeling feelings into the ways and time and places appropriate within his culture.

Gaining skill in sharing his feelings with those who can help (parents, teachers, close friends, scout leaders, etc.).

7. Coming to terms with his or her own sex role, both now and as it will become:

Learning what is expected as appropriate behavior for boys, for girls, for men, for women, for married people, for parents, and for grandparents.

Clarifying knowledge about the nature of sex and reproduction.

Adjusting to a changing body in the pubertal growth spurt as teen years approach (accepting the new size and form, function and potentials of pubertal growth).

Thinking wholesomely ahead to what it will be like to be grown up as a man or woman.

8. Continuing to find himself as a worthy person:

Identifying with his own age and sex in appropriate ways.

Discovering many ways of becoming acceptable as a person; gaining status.

Growing in self-confidence, self-respect, self-control, and self-realization.

Extending the process of establishing his own individuality.

9. Relating himself to loyalties beyond the moment and outside himself:

Finding new meanings in religion, in the universe, in the nature of things.

Discovering satisfactions in music, art, drama, nature, and the literature of his culture, appropriate to his age.

Devoting himself to group goals (scouts, boys' and girls' clubs, etc.).

Laying foundations for patriotism, for pride in men's achievements through history, and for a sense of belongingness to the human race.

Gaining experience in essential morality in action at home and with others.

Learning and accepting the eternal realities of birth, death, and infinity.

How well a given boy or girl accomplishes any of these many complex developmental tasks before he or she enters the teens depends on many things. It depends first of all on how good a start that particular child had in development through the early years of childhood. The little child who succeeded in achieving most of the developmental tasks of infancy, early childhood, and the preschool years continues on in these achievements as his or her horizons expand through the school years. Success depends upon how many opportunities there are for development in the home, in the school, and in community life. It depends in large measure on how skilled parents and teachers are in anticipating, recognizing, and providing growth opportunities for the child's developmental tasks as they come along. But children differ widely, as do parents. And, while children are struggling through their growth stages, the parents too are hard at work on their developmental tasks.

DEVELOPMENTAL TASKS OF PARENTS OF SCHOOL-AGE CHILDREN

Parents know full well that they are needed through the bustling years of the school-age period. But by this time, household routines have become established, and the children are growing at a less rapid rate than they did as infants or preschoolers. Parents now can get their children in focus and understand them better because they are not changing so fast, and because parent-child intercommunication is better. School-age children generally are satisfied with their relationships with their parents, and are involved to a considerable degree in family activities, according to one study of 730 fifth-graders.[6] No other stage appears to offer so much in family solidarity.

Being Sensitive to and Providing for Children's Growth Needs

A recurring challenge to modern parents is to provide opportunities for the child to do things for himself which are within his abilities. It is helpful to the accomplishment of the child's developmental tasks if

[6] Glenn R. Hawkes, Lee G. Burchinal, and Bruce Gardner, "Preadolescents' Views of Some of Their Relations with Their Parents," *Child Development* 28, no. 4 (December 1957): 393–399.

A recurring challenge to modern parents is providing opportunities for children to do things within their abilities.

he can share in family decisions, responsibilities, and opportunities. Family discussion and joint planning offer openings for school-agers to join with their parents and their brothers and sisters in establishing family policies and getting firsthand experience in democratic interaction and orderly ways of doing things.

Overly cautious parents may curtail their schoolchild's activities because they fear he will be hurt. Actually, the accidental death rate for school-age children is lower than at any other time in the life cycle. The National Safety Council estimates acciden-

tal deaths per 100,000 population of each age group as: 18.4 for five- to fourteen-year-olds, 44.0 for under five-year-olds, 56.1 for fifteen- to twenty-four-year-olds, 42.1 for twenty-five- to forty-four-year-olds, 52.2 for forty-five- to sixty-four-year-olds, and 157.4 for those over sixty-five years of age.[7] Thus in the chance of meeting accidental death, the school-ager statistically is more than twice as safe as his parents, nearly three times as safe as his grandparents, and more than eight times as safe as his retired great-grandparents. Schoolchildren who tend to have accidents more than others are found to have emotional problems, and to have parents who are anxious, insecure, and nonassertive.[8]

Parents are under pressure from neighbors and other members of their social class to have their children measure up to the demands and expectancies of the culture. This tends to shape even the most developmental family into more traditional lines as soon as the children reach school age, as we saw in chapter 4. "What will the neighbors think?" or "What will the teacher say?" are powerful pressures to conform in the school-age family. When traditional striving for good manners collides with

[7] National Safety Council, *Accident Facts* (Chicago: National Safety Council, 1960), p. 14.

[8] Irwin Marcus, Wilma Wilson, Irvin Kraft, Delmar Swander, Fred Southerland, and Edith Schulhofer, *An Interdisciplinary Approach to Accident Patterns in Children,* monograph of the Society for Research in Child Development, serial no. 76, vol. 25, no. 2 (1960): 53–54.

developmental conceptions of parent-child rapport, the traditional patterns win out in most homes studied. Two examples:

Billy, age ten, hurries home to snatch his lunch and get back for an important school football game. As he gobbles, he tells his mother excitedly all about the team. As he pauses for breath, his mother breaks in severely, "Billy, take your elbows off the table. How many times must I tell you? And, stop eating so fast!"

Immediately Billy wilts. He obediently removes his elbows and hurries through the remainder of the meal in silence. . . .

Mother has a point. Billy will have to learn good manners. But what is more important at the moment—good manners or good feelings shared between mother and son? How ready will Billy be next time to share his excitements with his mother?

Mary dashes home from school. She breaks in on her mother's club meeting with all the ladies sitting around. Mary is twelve, happy, friendly, and outgoing. She is unselfconscious. She says cheerily, "Hello, Mrs. Brown," as she stumbles over Mrs. Smith's feet.

Mother rises to the situation. She must teach Mary some manners right now. She must save her own face by scolding Mary. So she speaks, sweetly but pointedly, "Mary, my dear! Do look where you are going!" Then she turns to her guests, saying, "Mary is just at the awkward age, so you'll have to excuse her."

Is Mary's face red? Does she approach the next roomful of guests with more or less ease as a result of this experience? Has her feeling of friendliness increased or decreased? Is she closer to or farther from her mother now?

Enjoying Life through Children's Eyes

Parents who can relax and enjoy their children find life unfolding all around them as they see it through children's eyes. Long-forgotten joys and pleasures are renewed as they are shared with children who delight in them. New vistas and fresh perspectives from different vantage points open up with a child companion. What might have been an ordinary business trip turns out to be an adventure when a ten-year-old goes along:

I was at the meetings in Omaha for three days; took Janice along, and we had a great time. As you would guess, I did many things I would not have done had I gone alone: climbing on foot to the top floor of the hotel and looking out over the city from the fire escape; climbing to the very top seat in Omaha's immense auditorium; walking all the way across the Missouri River bridge to Council Bluffs and standing midway on the bridge with one foot on the Iowa side

MAGNUM—PHOTO BY CHARLES HARBUTT

Parents who can relax and enjoy their children find life unfolding all around them.

of the line and the other foot on the Nebraska side; going to the top of the Woodman of the World Building. . . .

There was much other fun too: being proud of how sweet she looked; enjoying her ways of packing and unpacking; watching her select items at Bishops Cafeteria and her enjoyment of her favorites; appreciating the fact that she surprised me the second afternoon and

did the wash for us in the bathroom sink . . . observing the things she enjoyed most. . . . People without children miss half the fun in the world![9]

Enjoying one's children means accepting them as persons in their own right. Parental acceptance includes: unconditional love for one's children, seeing them as persons with the right to express their real feelings, valuing the unique personality of each of their children, and recognizing children's need to pull away from their parents as they become increasingly autonomous individuals.[10]

Interviews with several hundred children ranging in age from six to fourteen on what they considered the perfect parent to be like turned up such characteristics as: enjoys being home and available to children, awake and ready to play rather than too often sleepy, generous, open-minded, patient, slow to anger and quick to forgive.[11]

Dr. Eleanore Luckey throws further light on parental enjoyment of children with her comparative study over the years of forty satisfactorily married couples and forty unsatisfactorily married pairs. She and her colleagues find that children are the pri-

---

[9] David Fulcomer, personal communication; see also Benjamin Spock, "The Wonderful World of Little Children," *Ladies' Home Journal*, June 1960, pp. 47–58.

[10] Blaine M. Porter, "Measurement of Parental Acceptance of Children," *Journal of Home Economics* 46, no. 3 (March 1954): 176–182.

[11] Sam Bloom, "The Perfect Parent," *McCall's*, August 1969, pp. 51, 95–98.

mary, if not the only, satisfaction of unhappily married couples, while companionship is of much greater significance for the couple's happiness in satisfactory marriages.[12]

What Is a Boy?[13]

By Alan Beck

Between the innocence of babyhood and the dignity of manhood we find a delightful creature called a boy. Boys come in assorted sizes, weights, and colors, but all boys have the same creed: To enjoy every second of every minute of every hour of every day and to protest with noise (their only weapon) when their last minute is finished and the adult males pack them off to bed at night.

Boys are found everywhere—on top of, underneath, inside of, climbing on, swinging from, running around, or jumping to. Mothers love them, little girls hate them, older sisters and brothers tolerate them, adults ignore them, and Heaven protects them. A boy is Truth with dirt on its face, Beauty with a cut on its finger, Wisdom with bubble gum in its hair, and the Hope of the future with a frog in its pocket.

When you are busy, a boy is an inconsiderate, bothersome, intruding jangle of noise. When you want him to make a good impression, his brain turns to jelly or else he becomes a savage, sadistic, jungle creature bent on destroying the world and himself with it.

A boy is a composite—he has the appetite of a horse, the digestion of a sword swallower, the energy of a pocket-size atomic bomb, the curiosity of a cat, the lungs of a dictator, the imagination of a Paul Bunyan, the shyness of a violet, the audacity of a steel trap, the enthusiasm of a firecracker, and when he makes something he has five thumbs on each hand.

He likes ice cream, knives, saws, Christmas, comic books, the boy across the street, woods, water (in its natural habitat), large animals, Dad, trains, Saturday mornings, and fire engines. He is not much for Sunday School, company, schools, books without pictures, music lessons, neckties, barbers, girls, overcoats, adults, or bedtime.

Nobody else is so early to rise, or so late to supper. Nobody else gets so much fun out of trees, dogs, and breezes. Nobody else can cram into one pocket a rusty knife, a half-eaten apple, 3 feet of string, an empty Bull Durham sack, 2 gum drops, 6 cents, a sling shot, a chunk of unknown substance, and a genuine supersonic code ring with a secret compartment.

A boy is a magical creature—you can lock him out of your work shop, but you can't lock him out of your heart. You can get him out of your study, but you can't get

12 Eleanore Braun Luckey and Joyce Koym Bain, "Children: A Factor in Marital Satisfaction," *Journal of Marriage and the Family* 32, no. 1 (February 1970): 43–44.

him out of your mind. Might as well give up—he is your captor, your jailer, your boss, and your master—a freckled-face, pint-sized, cat-chasing, bundle of noise. But when you come home at night with only the shattered pieces of your hopes and dreams, he can mend them like new with the two magic words—"Hi Dad!"

What Is a Girl?[14]

By Alan Beck

Little girls are the nicest things that happen to people. They are born with a little bit of angelshine about them and though it wears thin sometimes, there is always enough left to lasso your heart—even when they are sitting in the mud, or crying temperamental tears, or parading up the street in mother's best clothes.

A little girl can be sweeter (and badder) oftener than anyone else in the world. She can jitter around, and stomp, and make funny noises that frazzle your nerves, yet just when you open your mouth, she stands there demure with that special look in her eyes. A girl is Innocence playing in the mud, Beauty standing on its head, and Motherhood dragging a doll by the foot.

Girls are available in five colors—black, white, red, yellow, or brown, yet Mother Nature always manages to select your favorite color when you place your order. They disprove the law of supply and demand—there are millions of little girls, but each is as precious as rubies.

God borrows from many creatures to make a little girl. He uses the song of a bird, the squeal of a pig, the stubbornness of a mule, the antics of a monkey, the spryness of a grasshopper, the curiosity of a cat, the speed of a gazelle, the slyness of a fox, the softness of a kitten, and to top it all off He adds the mysterious mind of a woman.

A little girl likes new shoes, party dresses, small animals, first grade, noise makers, the girl next door, dolls, make-believe, dancing lessons, ice cream, kitchens, coloring books, make-up, cans of water, going visiting, tea parties, and one boy. She doesn't care so much for visitors, boys in general, large dogs, hand-me-downs, straight chairs, vegetables, snow suits, or staying in the front yard. She is loudest when you are thinking, the prettiest when she has provoked you, the busiest at bedtime, the quietest when you want to show her off, and the most flirtatious when she absolutely must not get the best of you again.

Who else can cause you more grief, joy, irritation, satisfaction, embarrassment, and genuine delight than this combination of Eve, Salome, and Florence Nightingale? She can muss up your home, your hair, and your dignity—spend your money, your time, and your temper—then just when your patience is ready to crack, her sunshine peeks through and you've lost again.

---

[14] Copyright New England Mutual Life Insurance Company, Boston, Mass., quoted with permission.

FAMILY DEVELOPMENT

Yes, she is a nerve-racking nuisance, just a noisy bundle of mischief. But when your dreams tumble down and the world is a mess—when it seems you are pretty much of a fool after all—she can make you a king when she climbs on your knee and whispers, "I love you best of all!"

Letting the Child Go and Grow

Encouraging a child's growth involves letting him go. As the school years progress, there are longer and longer absences from home. He is away from home through the school hours, which often include the lunch period as well as morning and afternoon sessions. If he or she is getting normally involved in sports and clubs and friendship groups, the after-school hours increasingly are given to these interests, with the youngster coming home tired and bedraggled just in time for the evening meal. There are frequent requests to spend the evening at someone else's home and occasions when spending the night with a close buddy is terribly important. Soon there are weekend trips with scouts or other youth groups, and then come the longer periods during summer vacation when children of school age are off to camp or visiting relatives for weeks at a time. All this is good for the child's development of independence, widening social experience, and general personality growth.

As children become increasingly involved with friends their own age, their orientation increasingly is toward their peers. Parents can encourage these associations, for research shows that children who are well-adjusted family members tend to retain family identifications, norms, and values even as they associate with others.[15] Mothers with emotionally satisfying friendships may find it easier to let their children go. Unfortunately, however, those old enough to have school-age children tend to have fewer close friends than do both younger and older housewives.[16]

School-agers often quote other adults as authority figures. A secure parent can take a child's, "But the teacher says so," as an indication that the youngster is stretching away from home in intellectual as well as physical respects, with new models, new attitudes, and new viewpoints to explore beyond the immediate family. Parents who can empathize with their children's interests and loosen the apron strings at this point have less difficulty untying them in another few years, when the youngsters become teenagers.

Parents who cultivate interests beyond their children probably have less difficulty letting them go than do those who devote their lives to their children. Ongoing research at Cornell finds husbands and wives

15 Charles E. Bowerman and John W. Kinch, "Changes in Family and Peer Orientation of Children between the Fourth and Tenth Grades," *Social Forces* 37, no. 3 (March 1959): 206–211.

16 James H. Williams, "Close Friendship Relations of Housewives Residing in an Urban Community," *Social Forces* 36, no. 4 (May 1958): 358–362.

with school-age children working together on projects more often than do those at either the preschool or the teenage stage of the family life cycle.[17] This is the time when building a boat, equipping a summer camp, and fixing up the house preoccupy father and mother. Now, too, entertaining others in the home and going as a family to company picnics and social affairs with the husband's work associates are at an all-time high.[18] Such activities shared with the children suggest an overall parental stance of involvement in whole-family pursuits that may develop into continuing interests for the married pair as a couple.

FAMILY DEVELOPMENTAL TASKS AT THE SCHOOL-AGE STAGE

Married seven years or more, by the time their eldest is in school, the husband and wife have been parents for at least six years and have settled into familiar ways with each other and with their children. The developmental routes traversed by the oldest child are gone over again by the younger children each in his turn, each in his own way. Family developmental tasks at this stage include:

1. Providing for children's activity and parents' privacy
2. Keeping financially solvent
3. Cooperating to get things done
4. Continuing to satisfy each other as married partners
5. Effectively utilizing family communication systems
6. Feeling close to relatives in the larger family
7. Tying in with life outside the family
8. Testing and retesting family philosophies of life.

Providing for Children's Activity and Parents' Privacy

Now that families live mostly in cities, towns, and suburbs, homes are smaller and space is more limited, both indoors and out, than it once was. Thanks to better nutrition and preventive medical care, today's children are bigger, stronger, and more vigorous, age for age, than was true a generation or two ago. No comparable change has occurred in the desire of parents for privacy and a little peace and quiet in their lives. Today's developmental family's house during the preschool and school-age periods is cluttered, toy-strewn, and noisy.

[17] Harold Feldman, "The Development of the Husband-Wife Relationship," a study supported in part by the National Institute of Mental Health, unpublished data received through personal correspondence, March 24, 1961, with permission.

[18] Robert O. Blood, Jr., and Donald M. Wolfe, *Husbands and Wives: The Dynamics of Married Living* (Glencoe, Ill.: Free Press, 1960), pp. 158–159.

Providing outlets for the needed exploration and activity of vigorous growing children within the limits of cramped housing, small yards, remote playgrounds, traffic-filled streets, and cranky neighbors is not an easy task. Lower-class neighbors in some places settle the problem by letting the children roam the streets, play in the alleys, and run the risks of life and limb. Social clubs and settlements set up programs that help in some of these congested areas, but the needs are still unfulfilled. Upper-class families usually have more space and, except for those urban cliff dwellers who live in crowded metropolitan apartment houses, have areas the children can call their own to play in, either on the home grounds or at their private schools. Many middle-class families feel the pinch in living so closely with their children in common living quarters; space requirements must be worked out in elaborate rituals and routines.

This is the time when many families move out of congested areas and into the suburbs, where children can have space for play, enjoy congenial companions, and attend good schools and community activities. The price that these families pay for such a move is real, both in monetary and psychic terms.[19] The family reorganizes itself around a mother-head. Father comes home too tired and is there too infrequently to play the role he could if he lived nearer his work.

The irony is that just when a man is most needed around the house for all the repairs and refurbishing that are part of home-ownership, the man is not as readily available as he was when they lived in the city, where services around the place were provided without tapping the man of the house. The pressure is eased somewhat by the five-day week, which gives father to his family Saturdays and Sundays—unless the golf bug bites him first, that is!

Keeping Financially Solvent

The triple threat of keeping up payments, keeping up with the Joneses, and keeping out of debt is a real strain now. Costs will zoom even higher before there is any relief. But now, when the firstborn is in school and younger children are coming along, comes the bulging budget characteristic of expanding families. In low- and moderate-income families, where food, clothing, and medical costs are always a big part of the household expenses, these items take a big bite out of what money there is. Fixed costs such as car expenses, rent or house payments and maintenance, utilities, insurance, bus and lunch money, as well as all the expected items like dues, school collections, allowances, and recreation add to the financial burden. No wonder many a family man may look a little frayed at times.

[19] See Richard Gordon, Katherine Gordon, and Max Gunther, *The Split-Level Trap* (New York: Bernard Geis Associates, 1960); and John Keats, *The Crack in the Picture Window* (Boston: Houghton Mifflin Company, 1957).

Moonlighting, in which the man of the house takes a second job to make ends meet, is not uncommon now. Before the end of the school-age period, Junior may have a paper route and be earning some of his own money, and Mother may have found a full- or a part-time job that fits the demands of her growing brood. The highest labor force rate for women of all ages in one recent year was among wives with children in school.[20] Grandparents help out by giving the grandchildren clothing, taking the family on vacation trips, purchasing big items of equipment, sitter services, and nursing care through childhood sicknesses and childbirth of the little newcomer.[21] Income tax exemptions for the children and unemployed wife are a help, but are by no means adequate to cover the costs of child-rearing at this stage of family living.[22] Many a middle-class father gets what overtime he can or pieces out his earnings with a part-time job during his "leisure" hours.

[20] Elizabeth Waldman, "Marital and Family Status of Workers," *Monthly Labor Review*, April 1968, p. 19.

[21] Marvin B. Sussman, "The Help Pattern in the Middle Class Family," *American Sociological Review* 18, no. 1 (February 1953): 22–28; and Evelyn Millis Duvall, *In-Laws: Pro and Con* (New York: Association Press, 1954), pp. 89–99.

[22] Reuben Hill estimates that income tax exemptions meet about one-twentieth of the cost of rearing his children in any given year; each child's exemption is worth from a fifty to seventy-five-dollar cut in tax per child per year, while it costs on the average one thousand dollars a year per child to rear him or her to age eighteen (Louis Dublin and Alfred Lotka, *The Money Value of a Man* [New York: Ronald Press Company, 1946], chap. 4, pp. 44–58).

The lower-class family frequently solves the problem by the mother's employment, leaving the children under the casual supervision of whoever happens to be home. The upper-class family's financial problems are less, for by definition the upper-class home is more affluent. But even so, the strain of keeping up appearances, sending the youngsters to the proper private schools, maintaining memberships in exclusive clubs, and participating in the right charities adds up faster than the money rolls in, in many a supposedly well-to-do family. Here the problems are compounded by pride. What lower-status families can do without losing face become last resorts to the families "on the hill."

Cooperating to Get Things Done

Each family has its own ways of getting things done. Mother does everything. Father pitches in as he can. Older children care for the younger ones. Grandmother may be close enough to help out. A maid works by the day or month. In one way or another food has to be purchased, prepared, and served. Clothes have to be washed, ironed, mended, and put away. Dishes have to be washed, the house cleaned, beds made, and belongings put where they belong. The too-young, the too-sick, and dependent members of the family must be cared for, and extended family relationships must be kept in good repair. Someone must answer the doorbell, the phone, the questions of the youngsters, and the demands of salesmen. Someone has to plan the meals, supervise the spending, and attend to the special and the everyday routines, in even the sketchiest family situation.

Casual impressions of homemaking in this push-button age are that now the housekeeping day has been so shortened, thanks to the marvels of science, that there is really very little to do around the house. Actually quite the opposite is the case. A recent study of fifty-two midwestern homemakers with two to four school-age children indicated that these women spent more time in laundering now than was spent by a similar group of homemakers twenty-five years ago, automatic washers to the contrary notwithstanding![23] Interpretations are two: (1) our miracle fibers take special care, and no longer can the family wash all go through together, and (2) our standards are higher; we have more clothing, and we expect to be cleaner now than people did a generation ago.

Increased standards of living put a heavier load of responsibility on the home than used to be expected. It is no longer enough to put food on the table. It must be a carefully balanced meal, supplying just the right number of calories for the individual family members; attractive in color; tasty as to the right combination of textures, flavors, and personal preferences; full of vitamins, body-building proteins, minerals, and even trace minerals. It isn't enough to keep a child neat, clean, and obedient; today we must be concerned for his growth as a personality (chapter 4). It isn't enough to keep a man's shirt buttons on; now a wife must be concerned and interested with all that goes into mending a wounded ego and keeping her husband a growing, happy person. It isn't enough to keep house for the family; now a woman is expected to do her share of community housekeeping in working for a school bond issue, getting out to parent-teacher meetings, and helping run the block meeting, or whatever is the pressing issue of the day. It is the plethora of new tasks and expectations that takes the time and energy of families at this stage in the life cycle.

Cooperation is the answer, not only for getting things done, but for helping everyone grow in the process. What becomes "a chore" if one person gets stuck with it all the time becomes "a project" when the whole family pitches in and works together to get a job done. Cooperative efforts in meal-preparation, serving, and cleaning up make for pleasant companionship as well as shared responsibilities. Daily routines, weekly cleaning, and seasonal gardening, housecleaning, leaf-raking, and holiday preparations are planned by the family; tasks are allocated on the basis of interest, ability, and preference and are accomplished with family members working side by side.

---

[23] Dorothy G. Van Bortel, "Conception of Woman's Role in the Home in Two Social Classes," reported at the Seventh Annual Symposium, University of Chicago, Committee on Human Development, February 25, 1956.

In a nationwide study of boys in the fourth through the eighth grades in public, private, and parochial schools, the Survey Research Center asked the boys, "What things that you do at home or in school or with your friends, make you feel important and useful?" The largest percentage of the eleven- to thirteen-year-olds (40 percent) mentioned some adult role around the house. The next most frequent mention was that of achievement and use of skills (28 percent). Other high-ranking items were "recognition by parents and adults" (12 percent) and "giving help" (18 percent).[24] These findings are in line with the general tendency of children to find satisfaction in working constructively with adults as members of a team.

Continuing to Satisfy Each Other as Married Partners

If the woman has received good postnatal care and has established a satisfactory sex response in the marriage, she now is at the peak of her sexual powers. Her main problem now is in getting over enough of her busyness to relax and give herself wholeheartedly to her husband. The man old enough to have school-age children is beyond the peak of his sexual capacities, but still a virile man with needs not only for sexual intercourse, but also for the renewal of faith in himself as a man that a truly loving wife can give him so well.

The couple successful in accomplishing this developmental task is usually one who keep their love for each other central in their family life. Yet the evidence is that wives are decreasingly satisfied with their husbands' love through the family life cycle.[25] Mothers of preschool children are more satisfied with their husbands' affection than any other group of wives. But, by the time the school-age stage of the family life cycle arrives, fewer wives are satisfied with the affection they receive from their mates—a decline that continues through the rest of the marriage.

Marital satisfaction is found to be at a low ebb during the school-age stage of the family life cycle in two widely separate studies published simultaneously. One investigation of marital interaction through the years of marriage finds the lowest levels of satisfaction of 147 husbands and wives in finances, task performance, companionship, sex, and relationships with children while there were schoolchildren in the home.[26]

At the same time, a Cornell University study of marital satisfaction over the family

---

[24] Survey Research Center, *A Study of Boys Becoming Adolescents* (Ann Arbor: University of Michigan, 1960), p. 215.

[25] Blood and Wolfe, *Husbands and Wives*, p. 232.

[26] Wesley R. Burr, "Satisfaction with Various Aspects of Marriage over the Life Cycle: A Random Middle Class Sample," *Journal of Marriage and the Family* 32, no. 1 (February 1970): 29–37.

life cycle finds fewer husbands and wives of the 1,598 studied reporting satisfaction in their marriage "all the time" during the school-age stage than at any other time in their lives together. Furthermore, significantly more wives report negative feelings such as feeling resentful, misunderstood, or not needed while dependent children were in the home than at any other time in their marriages.[27]

Effectively Utilizing Family Communication Systems

It may be that decline in mates' satisfaction with each other results from the eclipse of the husband-wife relationship by the responsibilities of parenthood. The school-age family is a network of communication ties, with possible interpersonal relationships numbering fifteen in the four-child family. The children now are full of experiences to relate, questions to ask, and sheer exuberance to express. Each is uniquely at work on his developmental tasks within his position in the family. Boy or girl, first-born or younger child, each struggles to establish his identity as a person in the family, who is and must be different from his siblings.[28] Unless they are twins, their ages differ so widely that their interests as children of school age, preschool stage, and infancy are worlds apart. Yet they compete for the resources of the family (the use of the television set is a good example),[29] for status and affection, and for the special recognition that all children need in intimate association.

The school-age youngster comes home from his rigorous day in classroom and playground full of the pent-up emotions that could not be fully expressed in front of teachers and classmates. He brings his frustrations, disappointments, and unexpressed hostilities home, where he very likely takes them out on the first available family member. This is not to be condemned. One of the chief functions of family life is to serve as an emotional reconditioning center for its members. But this does not make for peace and quiet. On the contrary, feelings explode all over the place; the children get into squabbles seemingly without provocation. Junior topples over the baby's blocks; baby scrawls in Mary's book; she teases Junior; and they are at it again.

One group of mothers exploring children's squabbles in their own homes dis-

---

[27] Boyd C. Rollins and Harold Feldman, "Marital Satisfaction over the Family Life Cycle," *Journal of Marriage and the Family* 32, no. 1 (February 1970): 20–28; find detailed data from this research in tables 16–6 and 16–7, chap. 16.

[28] Helen L. Koch, *The Relation of Certain Formal Attributes of Siblings to Attitudes Held toward Each Other and toward Their Parents*, monograph of the Society for Research in Child Development, serial no. 78, vol. 25, no. 4 (1960).

[29] Robert O. Blood, Jr., "Social Class and Family Control of Television Viewing," *Merrill-Palmer Quarterly* 7, no. 3 (July 1961): 205–222.

covered that most of the quarreling took place in the late afternoon between the time the schoolchildren returned home and the evening meal was served. Hypothesizing that a juice break might build up blood sugar levels and reduce tension, these mothers found that after-school snacks alone did not decrease the number and length of the episodes of tension. However, the squabbles decreased significantly in the homes where the mother awaited her schoolchildren's return home with an interest in their feelings and reports of the day.[30]

These results of a very simple experiment parallel those of the famous studies of factory workers in which it was the *attention* paid the people that increased their work output and job satisfaction.[31] They give a challenge to family members who must weather the emotional storms that generate outside to blow their full fury within the home. Not only the children, but father and mother too, bring home their tensions and unresolved conflicts from office, factory, or PTA meetings. The family that is satisfactorily providing effective means by which tension can be drained off before they become either chronic or critical is one that keeps communication free and full.

One mother who is aware of the importance of these functions has the makings of a picnic supper in her pantry for the occasional afternoon when her husband comes home looking as though he has had "one of those days." As soon as she takes a good look at her husband's face, she suggests a picnic for the whole family, or a quiet tête-à-tête for just the two of them, with the children having their picnic supper on the back porch or yard. This is a way of not only helping her husband through a difficult time, but is also effective in maintaining the kind of sensitive communication needed in the hurly-burly of family life.

It works the other way too. An emphatic husband returning home to find his wife at the end of her rope, with the youngsters irritable and the house a mess, may take her out for dinner, with a quickly imported sitter for the children more than paying for her charge in the release the husband and wife get when they need it most.

The most valuable aspect of marriage from the wife's point of view is companionship in doing things with her husband. This outranks all other aspects, including love, understanding, standard of living, and the chance to have children, in the eyes of most wives.[32] The Detroit Area Study further finds that the more education a wife has, the more likely she is to be satisfied with her husband's companionship. College-educated wives, usually married to college-educated husbands, are more satisfied with their marital companionship than are wives on any other educational or income level.[33]

---

[30] Unpublished study by the author.
[31] F. U. Roethlisberger and W. J. Dickson, *Management and the Worker* (Cambridge, Mass.: Harvard University Press, 1940).

---

[32] Blood and Wolfe, *Husbands and Wives*, p. 150.
[33] Ibid., pp. 170–171.

When communication systems are open within a family, love can flow through, removing the waste products of everyday living and renewing the spirit of every member, for love is a two-way flow, going and returning between each person and the next, taking away one's hates and angers and bringing back the warmth of belonging and the joy of living in a family. Like a river that purifies itself as long as it keeps running freely, so the stream of human emotions within a family renews and refreshes the human spirit so long as communication systems run free.

Feeling Close to Relatives in the Larger Family

Relatives come into their own during the school-age stage of family living. When a boy is old enough to handle himself with some independence, his uncles and cousins may take him along on a fishing trip, to ball games, and all the rest of the activities that delight the young man of the family. A school-age boy or girl is old enough to visit relatives for a week or more, even a whole summer vacation without becoming homesick or being too dependent upon a hospitable household. Going to grandparents' home for special holidays is a thrill now, when the children are old enough to appreciate such treats, and to take care of their own needs and interests in new settings with only casual supervision.

With family routines fairly well established and the children knowing the ropes of everyday family living, it is possible for them to take over for a few days at a time with a visiting relative keeping a general eye on things, while the parents leave for a brief holiday or business trip. "Sitting" now becomes a mutual process in which the youngsters share their interests and achievements with the aunt, uncle, or grandparent in charge, at the same time that they tap this rich source of family lore and gain a sense of the continuity of family living from those who knew their parents when they were small.

Even more important than what the relatives *do* for the school-age boy or girl is what they *are*. In even the most homogeneous family, there are so many differences in personality strengths and weaknesses, behavior patterns, and value systems represented in the members of the extended family group that these variations are of great interest to all. The family is worried about one of its black sheep, who has stepped out of line again, and hashes over his past history, the details of the current escapade, and their opinions as to why he has turned out so badly. The family is proud of some honor bestowed upon one of its relatives and proudly exhibits mementos of the glorious moment, the picture of the person with prestige, and regales even the most casual visitor with the wonderful qualities that have helped this special one turn out so well. One relative is ill, another is mentally unstable, a third is out of work, still another is leaving for an extended voyage, and so on and on through the multitude of permutations and combinations of experiences and predispositions represented in the members of any family.

All this is grist for the chlidren's mill. As they get close to these differing relatives and hear them discussed in the family, they see value systems in action. They find themselves lining up on one side or the other in accordance with their own personality needs and tasks of the moment. The twelve-year-old girl may ardently defend some impulsive cousin who has run away to be married in defiance of her family, not because the girl actually believes that such actions are wise, but because this represents for her the emancipation she is mobilizing for and has not yet accomplished personally. The ten-year-old boy may idolize a young uncle who flexes his muscles and talks big about the manly art of self-defense, not because he is going to turn out to be a prizefighter, but because growing up to be a strong man is the boy's goal for himself.

Feeling close to the relatives of the family is accomplished through the years in the letter-writing, visiting, holiday observances, vacation-sharing, gift-giving, services rendered and received, and all the other ways in which the members of the family maintain contact with each other. The process is furthered by the family loyalties that bind the family together, regardless of what any member may or may not do. The task is delayed or incomplete in the little family

in which such high standards of perfection are maintained that it ostracizes any relative who steps out of line. Sniping at in-laws is one way of venting hostilities against the mate, or mutual dislike of any relative on either side of the family may be a common bond between a couple. Complete harmony in the larger family is rarely realized, but, to the extent to which it is achieved, it contributes much to the ongoing life of the family.

Tying in with Life outside the Family

The school-ager takes the family with him out into the larger community. Pressure is on the parents to become active in the parent-teacher association, to visit the school for special parents' functions, to participate in parents' study groups, and to become an active part of community life as soon as their children are enrolled in school.

Father now gets tied into father-son affairs with his boy through church and youth programs, as well as in the informal going and coming within the neighborhood. As soon as the youngster becomes a little leaguer, he becomes a part of the male set in town, with other men and boys recognizing him and his father and the rest of the family in ways that are new and exciting.

Mother is asked to bake a cake for a scout bake sale or to help serve at a Camp Fire Girls' mothers' tea. She may take on the job of den mother, or teach a Sunday school class, or help her youngsters canvass for Red Cross funds as soon as her own children are drawn into community projects and group life.

Life in the larger community becomes of more personal interest when children are intimately involved. Raising interest in a new school building or getting pledges for the Community Fund or a special neighborhood project now makes sense in a personal way, when the family's own children are directly benefited. Candidates for political office may have been only remote pictures in the newspaper before; now they are seen for the issues for which they stand, for the kind of family life they represent, and for what they promise to do for the welfare of the community. Corruption may once have seemed like something that is always with us, but when children get out into the streets, ridding the city of its harmful elements becomes urgent family business. The teacher shortage, once a general social problem, now becomes an imminent family concern. And so it goes. As the child grows up and goes forth into the world, he takes his family with him into larger and larger circles of interest and influence. Widening participation in community life helps mature the family as well as the individual, and this is one of the developmental tasks that must be tackled and worked through together.

FAMILY FACTORS IN SCHOOL ACHIEVEMENT

Americans believe in education. More than sixty-one million men, women, and children are involved full time as teachers, administrators, or students in the nation's schools. Another 132,000 adults serve as trustees of local schools, on state boards of education, or for institutions of higher learning.[34] Practically all (96.5 percent) of the nation's five- to thirteen-year-olds are in school in the 1970s, and more than nine out of ten of them will stay in school through their seventeenth year.[35] This represents an immense investment of time and resources in education, generally recognized as important both for the country as a whole and for the full development and participation of each individual in today's complex society.

Educational achievement depends not only on the competence of the school staff, but also on the families from which the pupils come. Wide differences in children's school achievement are found to be signifi-

---

[34] "The Magnitude of the American Educational Establishment (1969–1970)," *Saturday Review*, October 18, 1969, p. 83, from estimates of the U.S. Office of Education and the National Education Association.

[35] U.S. Bureau of the Census, "Revised Projections of School and College Enrollment in the United States to 1985," *Population Estimates*, Current Population Reports, series P-25, no. 365 (May 5, 1967), table 2, series B-2, pp. 5–8, and table A, p. 9.

cantly related to the home's influence on both a child's language development and his general ability to learn. School achievement depends on such family factors as: (1) *achievement press* (parents' aspirations for the child and their interest in, knowledge of, and standards of reward for the child's educational achievement); (2) *language models* (the quality of the parents' language and the standards they expect of the child's speech); (3) *academic guidance* (the availability and quality of academic guidance and help provided in the home); (4) activity in the home (stimulation provided in the home to explore various aspects of the larger environment); (5) intellectuality (intellectual interests and activities in the home); and (6) work habits (household routines and emphasis on regularity in the use of time and space).[36] Moreover, there is evidence that achievement strivings during the first four years of school are predictive of future achievement in adolescence and adulthood.[37]

Nationwide responses of mothers of first-graders indicate that parents of high-achieving compared to low-achieving children read more aloud to their children, talk longer with their children about school and other things of interest to the youngsters, permit less use of television, play more mentally stimulating games in the family, and see college as essential for their sons and daughters.[38]

Dr. Catherine S. Chilman summarizes the findings of more than a score of studies on child-rearing patterns characteristic of children who are educationally achieving compared with practices and patterns more often found in very poor families (table 11–1).

Testing and Retesting Family Philosophies of Life

As soon as the yard child gets out into the street and begins to go to school, he comes face-to-face with ways of life that are different from those of his family. Some of these variations on the theme of life look good to him, and he brings them home in questions about and demands for a new order of things. The family then must test its way of life in terms of child-introduced community pressures. Something has got to give. Either the family gives way to the child's pleas that "all the other kids are doing it," or the youngster faces up to the finality of "this is the way we do it in *our* family." Either outcome is the result of

---

[36] Bloom, *Stability and Change in Human Characteristics*, p. 124.

[37] Howard A. Moss and Jerome Kagan, "Stability of Achievement and Recognition Seeking Behaviors from Early Childhood through Adulthood," mimeographed (Yellow Springs, Ohio: Fels Institute), p. 21.

[38] "How to Help Your Child Do Well in School," *U.S. News and World Report*, October 6, 1969, pp. 49–50, reporting a survey by Gallup International for the Institute for Development of Educational Activities, an affiliate of the Charles F. Kettering Foundation.

Table 11–1. *Family Factors Conducive to and Limiting of Children's School Achievement*

Conductive	Limiting (more typical of low-income families)
1. Infant and child given freedom within consistent limits to explore and experiment.	Limited freedom for exploration (partly imposed by crowded and dangerous aspects of environment).
2. Wide range of parent-guided experiences, offering visual, auditory, kinesthetic, and tactile stimulation from early infancy.	Constricted lives led by parents; fear and distrust of the unknown.
3. Goal-commitment and belief in long-range success potential.	Fatalistic, apathetic attitudes.
4. Gradual training for and value placed upon independence.	Tendency for abrupt transition to independence: parents tend to "lose control" of children at an early age.
5. Parents serve as model of educational-occupational success and continuing development; high achievement needs in parents.	Tendency to educational-occupational failure; reliance on personal versus skill attributes of vocational success.
6. Reliance on objective evidence.	Magical, rigid thinking.
7. Much verbal communication with a flexible, conceptual style and emphasis on both speaking and listening.	Little verbal communication, especially of an interactive, conceptual, flexible kind.
8. High value placed on academic success.	Academic achievement not highly valued.
9. Democratic child-rearing attitudes.	Authoritarian child-rearing attitudes.
10. Collaborative attitudes toward the school system.	Fear and distrust of the school system.
11. Value placed on abstractions.	Pragmatic, concrete values.

Source: Catherine S. Chilman, *Growing Up Poor*, Welfare Administration Publication, no. 13 (Washington, D.C., 1966), p. 43.

some testing and review of the merits and penalties of a certain stand or value.

By the time the boy or girl reaches the third or fourth grade in school, these culture conflicts may be in the form of episodes of open rebellion. The preadolescent finds adults generally trying. Both boys and girls are skeptical of the other sex and band together in tight little groups of children of the same age and sex. Boys now reject such adult-imposed "sissy stuff" as cleanliness, obedience, and politeness, and often become antagonistic, rebellious, uncooperative, restless, and very noisy. Dr. Luton D. Ackerson, studying 5,000 nondelinquent boys and girls at the Illinois Institute for Juvenile Research, found that behavior problems are more frequent among the nine- to thirteen-year-olds than among any other age group—more fighting, rudeness, and disobedience among preadolescent children than among either the younger or the older age groups.[39] These problems are so characteristic of the third- to sixth-grader that Fritz Redl defines preadolescence as "that phase when the nicest children begin to behave in the most awful way."[40]

Another study of third- to sixth-grade boys finds that those children whose parents were both coercive and autonomy-granting were successfully assertive academically as well as in social influence and friendship.[41] Such data suggest strongly that school-agers need firm controls from their parents, as well as a chance to prove

---

[39] Quoted in *Junior Guidance Newsletter* (Chicago: Science Research Associates), December 1952.
[40] Ibid., p. 1.

[41] Lois Wladis Hoffman, Sidney Rosen, and Ronald Lippitt, "Parental Coerciveness, Child Autonomy, and Child's Role at School," *Sociometry* 23, no. 1 (March 1960): 15–22.

Religious practices on a whole-family basis may help a youngster feel secure.

FAMILY DEVELOPMENT

themselves autonomously. Other significant adults—teachers, scout leaders, relatives, and friends of the family—further reinforce family values for a child.[42]

When mother and father have successfully undertaken their developmental tasks of developing a workable philosophy of life in the earlier stages of their marriage and in their individual personality development, they can accept the querying and the challenging of the school-age boy or girl without being personally threatened or feeling personally attacked or repudiated.[43] It is when one or the other of the parents feels basically insecure about the area under question that confusion reigns and the family fails to make progress in refining and developing its way of life to meet the test of real life situations. Actively interpreting why some things are wrong and others right, why some actions are good and others bad are aspects of this developmental task that families face all through the school-age stage. Such teaching is not easy, especially in this day and age when family values are changing, but nothing is more important to a family's basic integrity, or to a youngster's sense of what he and his family stand for in a world where

individuals have to stand for something, lest they fall for anything.[44]

Challenges and Resources of Families with Schoolchildren

Families with school-age children present at least seven challenges today: (1) economic pressures (four out of five families at this stage are in debt),[45] (2) limited space in home and neighborhood, (3) ethnic and racial tensions in changing communities, (4) inadequate school facilities for a rapidly growing population, (5) poor articulation of home and school, (6) neglected and rejected children growing up in inadequate homes, and (7) unsolved and undetected child behavior problems, uncertainties, and anxieties of parents.

Rearing children is a continuing challenge for parents. Each stage of child development has problems to be faced. Each child differs from all others, not only because he was born unique genetically, but also because he responds differently to others, to parental controls, and to life itself. Longitudinal studies indicate that earlier problems such as destructiveness,

[42] Carle C. Zimmerman and Lucius F. Cervantes, *Successful American Families* (New York: Pageant Press, 1960).

[43] O. Spurgeon English and Constance J. Foster, *Fathers Are Parents, Too* (New York: G. P. Putnam's Sons, 1951), chap. 6, "The Latency Period."

[44] Daniel R. Miller and Guy E. Swanson, *The Changing American Parent* (New York: John Wiley and Sons, 1958), and other sources quoted in chapter 4.

[45] John B. Lansing and Leslie Kish, "Family Life Cycle as an Independent Variable," *American Sociological Review* 22, no. 5 (October 1957): 514.

temper tantrums, and overactivity decline rapidly through the school years.[46] But firstborn children, more than their younger siblings, evidence problems of excessive demands for attention, restlessness in sleep, and physical timidity between ages six and twelve. Firstborn girls especially have problems indicating tension and withdrawal at the age of six and again at eleven. Firstborn boys now have more withdrawing and internalizing patterns than do second-born boys, who tend to be more overt and aggressive.

Quarreling, jealousies, rivalry, and other conflictive relationships between siblings reflect both struggles for parental attention and the different stance firstborn, second-born, and later children have as persons. Research finds that ordinal position influences personality development, as each child arriving in the family establishes his own role patterns and relationships with the others.[47] This explains in part the

often-heard observation that discipline that works with one child is ineffective with another, so that each youngster is a challenge to the child-rearing skills of his parents.

Childhood illnesses can be expected from time to time in school-age children, involving special care and family accommodations for the incapacitated. Even more challenging are the various handicaps that show up especially as children go to school. Numerically, eye conditions needing specialists' care lead all other children's handicaps, followed by emotional disturbances, speech problems, mental retardation, hearing impediments, and orthopedic conditions (chart 11–1).

Resources helpful to families with schoolchildren, in brief, suggestive summary, are:

1. Financial plans to spread the costs of rearing children

2. Increase and improvement of housing suitable for families with children, and of neighborhood facilities for active play

3. Widespread intergroup education and interpretation of the meanings and methods of living in a democratic melting-pot culture

4. Rapid expansion of school facilities, teacher recruitment, and education with enlightened public support

5. Parent-teacher cooperation in improving conditions for children and

[46] Jean W. Macfarlane, Lucile Allen, and Marjorie P. Honzik, *A Developmental Study of the Behavior Problems of Normal Children between Twenty-one Months and Fourteen Years* (Berkeley: University of California Press, 1954), pp. 146–186.

[47] James H. S. Bossard and Eleanor S. Boll, *The Large Family System* (Philadelphia: University of Pennsylvania Press, 1956); Walter Toman, *Family Constellation* (New York: Springer Publishing Company, 1961); Koch, *The Relation of Certain Formal Attributes of Siblings to Attitudes Held toward Each Other and toward Their Parents;* and the popular summary of recent research in Vance Packard, "First, Last, or Middle Child—The Surprising Differences," *Reader's Digest,* December 1969, pp. 25–32.

Chart 11–1. *Many Millions of Children Have Handicaps*

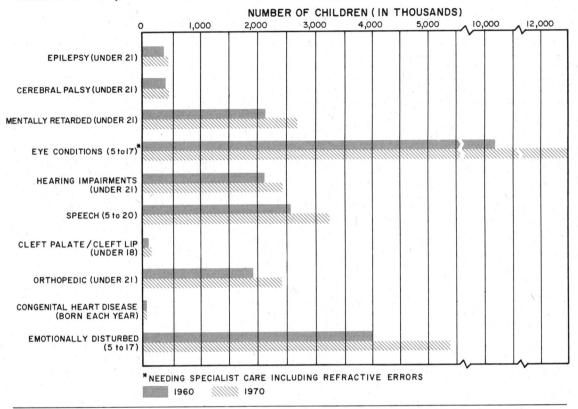

NUMBER OF CHILDREN (IN THOUSANDS)

Source: Elizabeth Herzog and Catharine Richards, eds., *The Nation's Youth,* Children's Bureau Publication, no. 460 (Washington, D.C., 1968), chart 38.

encouraging home-school teamwork through effective PTA programs, etc.

6. Widely accessible child-guidance services, effective mental health education, and adequate programs in parent education and family counseling

7. Community programs to strengthen families and to provide supplemental services for children whose homes have failed them.

SUMMARY

The school-age stage of family life represents the crowded years that begin with the firstborn going off to school and flow into the teen years as he becomes a teenager. Younger children have already arrived and are hard at work on their developmental tasks, while the school-ager works out his at the growing edges of the family, where all is new both to it and to him. He faces a multitude of growth responsibilities as he make a place for himself at school, with his peer group, and with adults, and becomes a participating member of his family and of the larger community. His parents meanwhile are occupied with their tasks as parents, as a married couple, and as individuals. Family developmental tasks of this stage may be summarized briefly: (1) providing for parents' needs for privacy, quiet, and order during the children's vigorous years; (2) keeping financially afloat while the family nears the flood stage of its needs; (3) cooperating to get things done; (4) continuing to satisfy each other as married partners; (5) elaborating communication systems within the expanding family; (6) feeling close to relatives in the larger family; (7) tying in with life outside the family; and (8) testing and retesting family philosophies of life.

The school-age family has its challenges in dovetailing the many developmental tasks of all members of the family in harmonious, satisfying ways. It has its rewards in the sense of accomplishment that comes from both individual and group achievements, as well as in the family solidarity that is peculiarly meaningful at this stage.

SUGGESTED ACTIVITIES

1. Prepare an address for the parents of a local elementary school along the lines of "How to Help Your Child in School," based upon material in the section on "Family Factors in School Achievement" in this chapter, and its research sources. Keep your approach positive and nonthreatening so that the parents may be encouraged in constructive practices rather than apply undue pressure on their children.

2. Conduct an informal survey of family practices in your community on the extent and ways schoolchildren's use of television is supervised or restricted. Compare with interviews with local schoolteachers on their observations of the effect of unlimited television viewing on children in their classes. Summarize your findings on the range of family practices and attitudes toward children's TV watching by representative parents and teachers, using verbatim quotes to illustrate the various positions taken.

3. Plan a budget for a school-age family with three children for (a) a low-income family, (b) a medium-income family, and (c) a high-income family. Base your figures on current prices and standards of living in your community. Discuss the ways in which the three budgets differ, and why.

4. Review the School-Age Study Course in the *PTA Magazine* for the current year, relating the materials covered to the developmental tasks of the school-age family.

5. Write a paper on the pros and cons of moving to the suburbs as children reach

school age. Interview at least one middle-class family which has chosen to remain in the city and a family of similar social status which has recently moved to a suburb for anecdotal material on the rewards and regrets of suburban versus urban living.

6. Develop a critique of the philosophies of child development at Yale University under Dr. Arnold Gesell and under Dr. Milton Senn, by comparing the references under the two names in your readings.

7. Prepare a list of recommendations for parents of school-age children who want to keep their marriage relationship from being overshadowed by their responsibilities as parents. Document with statistical and clinical evidence, and gear to both preventive and remedial proposals.

8. Role-play three ways of handling children's quarrels within the family where there are two or more children of school age or younger. Discuss your feelings and behaviors, and relate to relevant materials in this chapter and its references.

9. Review Carleton Washburne's *The World's Good* (New York: John Day Company, 1954) for ways in which parents and teachers can help push out a child's horizons toward world-mindedness and interest in other peoples around the globe.

10. Carefully review the research on the effects of working mothers on their children, their marriages, and their personality development (see references in chapters 3 and 11), and debate the proposition, "Resolved, that mothers with schoolchildren should be full-time homemakers."

11. Evaluate recent proposals for revamping modern education such as appear regularly in professional journals and books, including George B. Leonard, *Education and Ecstasy* (New York: Delacorte Press, 1969), and Eda J. LeShan, *The Conspiracy against Childhood* (New York: Atheneum Publishers, 1967), in terms of what you know about the development of school-age children.

READINGS

Barclay, Dorothy. *Understanding the City Child*. New York: Franklin Watts, 1959.

Brim, Orville G., Jr. *Education for Child Rearing*. New York: Russell Sage Foundation, 1959.

Burr, Wesley R. "Satisfaction with Various Aspects of Marriage over the Life Cycle: A Random Middle Class Sample." *Journal of Marriage and the Family* 32, no. 1 (February 1970): 29–37.

Chilman, Catherine S. *Your Child from 6 to 12*. Children's Bureau Publication, no. 324. Washington, D.C., 1966.

Duvall, Evelyn Millis, and Reuben Hill. *Being Married*. New York: Association Press; Boston: D. C. Heath and Company, 1960. Chap. 20, "Bringing Up Your Children."

English, O. Spurgeon, and Constance J.

Foster. *Fathers Are Parents, Too.* New York: G. P. Putnam's Sons, 1951. Chap. 6, "The Latency Period."

Frank, Mary, and Lawrence K. Frank. *How to Help Your Child in School.* New York: Viking Press, 1950.

Gardner, Riley W., and Alice Moriarty. *Personality Development at Preadolescence: Explorations of Structure Formation.* Seattle, Wash.: University of Washington, 1968.

Gesell, Arnold, and Frances Ilg. *The Child from Five to Ten.* New York: Harper and Brothers, 1946.

Havighurst, Robert J. *Human Development and Education.* New York: Longmans, Green and Company, 1953. Pt. 2, "Middle Childhood."

Hawkes, Glenn R., and Damaris Pease. *Behavior and Development from 5 to 12.* New York: Harper and Brothers, 1962.

Hess, Robert D., and Judith V. Torney. *The Development of Political Attitudes in Children.* Chicago: Aldine Publishing Company, 1967.

Hoffman, Lois Wladis. "Effects of Maternal Employment on the Child." *Child Development* 32, no. 1 (March 1961): 187–197.

Iscoe, Ira, and Harold Stevenson, eds. *Personality Development in Children.* Austin, Tex.: University of Texas Press, 1960.

Koch, Helen L. *The Relation of Certain Formal Attributes of Siblings to Attitudes Held toward Each Other and toward Their Parents.* Monograph of the Society for Research in Child Development, serial no. 78, vol. 25, no. 4 (1960).

Lane, Howard A., and Mary Beauchamp. *Understanding Human Development.* New York: Prentice-Hall, 1959.

Lewis, Gertrude M. *Educating Children in Grades Four, Five, and Six.* Washington, D.C.: U.S. Office of Education, 1960.

Lidz, Theodore. *The Person: His Development throughout the Life Cycle.* New York: Basic Books, 1968. Chap. 9, "The Juvenile."

Luckey, Eleanore Braun, and Joyce Koym Bain. "Children: A Factor in Marital Satisfaction." *Journal of Marriage and the Family* 32, no. 1 (February 1970): 43–44.

Macfarlane, Jean W., Lucile Allen, and Marjorie P. Honzik. *A Developmental Study of the Behavior Problems of Normal Children between Twenty-one Months and Fourteen Years.* Berkeley: University of California Press, 1954.

Martin, William E., and Celia Burns Stendler. *Child Development: The Process of Growing Up in Society.* New York: Harcourt, Brace and Company, 1953.

Miller, Daniel R., and Guy E. Swanson. *The Changing American Parent.* New York: John Wiley and Sons, 1958.

Mussen, Paul H. *The Psychological Development of the Child.* Englewood Cliffs, N.J.: Prentice-Hall, 1963.

National Institute of Child Health and Human Development. *Perspectives on Human Deprivation: Biological, Psycho-*

logical, and Sociological. Washington, D.C: U.S. Department of Health, Education, and Welfare, 1968.

National Manpower Council. *Work in the Lives of Married Women.* New York: Columbia University Press, 1958.

Prescott, Daniel A. *The Child in the Educative Process.* New York: McGraw-Hill Book Company, 1957.

Rollins, Boyd C., and Harold Feldman. "Marital Satisfaction over the Family Life Cycle." *Journal of Marriage and the Family* 32, no. 1 (February 1970): 20–28.

Senn, Milton J. E. "The Epoch Approach to Child Development." *Woman's Home Companion,* November 1955, pp. 40–42, 60–62.

Smart, Mollie S., and Russell C. Smart. *Children: Development and Relationships.* New York: Macmillan Company, 1967.

Stolz, Lois H. Meek. "Effects of Maternal Employment on Children: Evidence from Research." *Child Development* 31, no. 4 (December 1960): 749–782.

Stone, L. Joseph, and Joseph Church. *Childhood and Adolescence.* New York: Random House, 1957. Chaps. 8–9.

Strang, Ruth. *Helping Your Gifted Child.* New York: E. P. Dutton and Company, 1960.

Terman, Lewis M., and Melita H. Oden. *The Gifted Child Grows Up.* Stanford, Calif.: Stanford University Press, 1947.

Vincent, Elizabeth Lee, and Phyllis C. Martin. *Human Psychological Development.* New York: Ronald Press Company, 1961.

Weil, Mildred W. "An Analysis of the Factors Influencing Married Women's Actual or Planned Work Participation." *American Sociological Review* 26, no. 1 (February 1961): 91–96.

12 FAMILIES WITH TEENAGERS

*Old and young, even of the same breed, find themselves
at different phases in the vital cycle, and cannot agree
in mood, opinion, impulse or affection. Contact means
restraint on both sides, and a hearty unison can seldom be
established except amongst comrades of the same age.*

George Santayana

A family enters the teenage stage of the family life cycle when the oldest child becomes thirteen, and leaves it when the first child departs for marriage, for work, or for military service, as a young adult. Typically six or seven years in the teenage stage, the family may spend but three or four years, as in the case of the very early marriage or the school dropout who goes to work at sixteen. The stage lasts longer when the first child to be launched delays his leaving home until later.

The father at the teenage stage is usually close to or in his forties, with his wife on the average of two years younger, entering the stage in her mid-thirties and leaving it typically in her mid-forties. By this time she is in her menopause, and possibly has a "change of life baby" as the late-arriving infant is sometimes called. The other children by this time are most likely school-agers.

A family with four sons and daughters is made up of six persons, holding a maximum of four positions: husband-father, wife-mother, son-brother, and daughter-sister. Each has developmental tasks as parent, teenager, school-ager, or younger child. Father and mother cope with guiding the next generation with the possible risk of interpersonal impoverishment. The adolescent struggles toward a sense of identity against the danger of identity diffusion, inability to "take hold," or fixation on a negative identity. Concurrently, the school-ager is busy learning to make things and proving his ability to produce; the pre-school child adventures in curiosity and initiative against the tendency to feel guilty and vindictive; the possible late-born infant is getting a sense of trust in his world so critical at his stage of development. The overall family goal at the teenage stage is that of loosening family ties to allow greater responsibility and freedom in readiness for releasing young adults-in-the-making.

TEENAGERS TODAY

The proportion of teenagers in the population through the 1970s is smaller than it was during the 1960s, even though they are more numerous. In 1969, 11.25 percent of the population were teenagers (22.5 million of the total of over two hundred million Americans). By 1980 the population of the United States will be around 230 million, of which some 24 million (10.4 percent) will be in their teens.[1]

Americans' negative attitudes toward teenagers may be diminishing. Wide recognition that the vast majority of teenage boys and girls are responsible, law-abiding young people has tended to lessen former stereotyping of anyone between twelve and twenty as a potential troublemaker or an out-and-out delinquent.[2] Evidence that some adolescents are more vulnerable to delinquency than others is generally accepted. Research projects concur that most teenagers who violate the laws are disadvantaged, lower-class youngsters. Youth apprehended from the other social classes are more apt to be emotionally disturbed, as is clear from Dr. Miller's estimations of delinquency distribution, table 12–1.

Leaders now are aware of the plight of all minorities, including youth, whose path to fulfillment is rigorous. Research estimates that 30 percent of the teenage boys,

Table 12–1. *Distribution of "Delinquent" Individuals*

Social class status	Demonstrable emotional disturbance	Little or no serious emotional disturbance	Percentage of all delinquents
Lower class	15%	70%	85%
Non-lower class	10	5	15
Total	25%	75%	100%

Degree of Emotional Disturbance

Source: William C. Kvaraceus and Walter B. Miller, with the collaboration of Milton L. Barron, Edward M. Daniels, Preston A. McLendon, and Benjamin A. Thompson, *Delinquent Behavior* (Washington, D.C.: National Education Association, 1959), vol. 1, p. 54.

and 20 percent of the girls find the pathway to adulthood blocked and have great difficulty reaching responsible adulthood.[3] These are the youngsters who drop out of school at fifteen or sixteen with a history of failure, frustration, and maladjustment in school, home, and community.

Until 1900, 80 percent of the boys and 90 percent of the girls typically left school by age fifteen. The median age for leaving school at the turn of the century for the boy was fourteen, when he went to work on a farm or as an apprentice in a trade or business. Most girls finished grade school and then went to work in their own or other people's families until they married and established their own homes. This classic pattern, typical of the centuries that

---

[1] "Teen Era Phasing Out in Population Forecast," *Family Financial Planning* (New York: Women's Division, Institute of Life Insurance, 1969).

[2] William C. Kvaraceus and Walter B. Miller, with the collaboration of Milton L. Barron, Edward M. Daniels, Preston A. McLendon, and Benjamin A. Thompson, *Delinquent Behavior* (Washington, D.C.: National Education Association, 1959), vol. 1, pp. 24–31.

[3] Robert J. Havighurst, "Adolescence and the Postponement of Adulthood," *School Review*, Spring 1960, pp. 52–62.

Chart 12–1. *Median Income of Families by Years of School Completed and Race of Head*

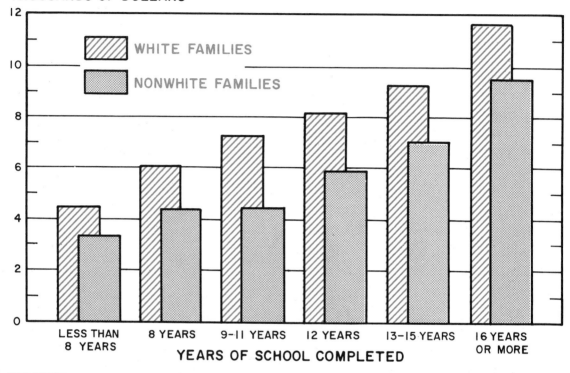

Source: U.S. Bureau of the Census, "Household and Family Characteristics: April 1953," *Population Characteristics,* Current Population Reports, series P-20, no. 53 (April 11, 1954); and U.S. Bureau of the Census, *Statistical Abstract of the United States, 1968* (Washington, D.C.: U.S. Government Printing Office, 1968), fig. 17, p. 327.

preceded our own, no longer fits in today's world, and so more often brings frustration and maladjustment to the teenager who follows it.

Dropouts in today's complex society are more likely to be unemployed than those who finish high school. Approximately 13 percent of elementary and high school dropouts were unemployed in one recent year, as compared with 6 percent of all high school graduates.[4]

High school enrollment has increased 10 percent, and college attendance by 46

[4] *Monthly Labor Review,* June 1969, pp. 36–43; and Virginia Britton, "U.S. Families—Recent Census Findings," *Family Economics Review,* December 1969, p. 6.

FAMILY DEVELOPMENT

percent since 1964,[5] indicating not only increased numbers in these age groups, but also greater awareness of the value of education on the part of today's young people and their families. There is a straight-line relationship between the amount of education and income in both white and nonwhite families, chart 12–1.

Money is not the primary objective of contemporary youth. Many more of them are influenced by the challenge and stimulation of a future career, the opportunity to make a meaningful contribution, and the ability to express themselves, than by the money that can be earned in a given line of work.[6]

Most teenagers today enjoy going to school. The Purdue Opinion Panel of representative high school students polled between 1953 and 1967 found three out of four teenagers saying that they like school (table 12–2). The small percentage of students expressing negative sentiments has been constant over the years. Teenagers' positive feelings about school have shifted from the unqualified, "I like it very much,"

Table 12–2. *How American High School Students Feel about School*

Student responses	1953	1958	1965	1967
I like it very much.	32%	27%	21%	16%
I like it most of the time.	43	46	51	57
I don't like it very much.	23	24	24	25
I dislike it.	2	3	2	2

Source: Thomas R. Leidy and Allan R. Starry, "Contemporary Youth Culture," *NEA Journal* 56 (October 1967): 8, from Purdue Opinion Panel polls between 1953 and 1967.

of 1953, to the more moderate, "I like it most of the time," of 1967, suggesting that teenagers today tend to be more perceptive, more critical, and more outspoken than young people their age were even a dozen or more years ago.

Achievement drive in a teenager appears to be closely related to his family relationships. Those with low drives for achievement tend to come from families where there is (1) a close mother-son relationship marked by dependence, (2) low standards of the "not caring" sort, and/or (3) too high and too early expectations beyond the child's readiness and ability.[7] Another study of adolescents' vocational aspirations found that high aspirers more frequently report (1) feelings of parental rejection, (2) demonstration of favoritism to a child in the family, (3) less attachment to parents,

[5] U.S. Bureau of the Census, "Fall School Enrollment Approximately 58.8 Million," *Population Characteristics*, Current Population Reports, series P-20, no. 179 (March 4, 1969); and U.S. Bureau of the Census, "Characteristics of Students and Their Colleges: October 1966," *Population Characteristics*, Current Population Reports, series P-20, no. 183 (May 22, 1969).

[6] Fortune-Yankelovich Survey, "American Youth: Its Outlook Is Changing the World," *Fortune*, January 1969, pp. 70–71; 179–181.

[7] David C. McClelland, "Cultural Variation and Achievement Motivation," paper delivered at the Twelfth Annual Symposium of the Committee on Human Development, University of Chicago, April 15, 1961.

(4) less childhood happiness, and (5) other indications of unsatisfactory interpersonal relationships in the family from which escape may be seen as lying up the occupational ladder.[8]

Distinguishing between two types of intellectual ability as high in IQ tests and high in creativity, a University of Chicago team found that the high-IQ adolescent appears to prefer safety, while the adolescent with high creativity chooses the anxieties and delights of growth. Parents of high-IQ students tend to recall more financial difficulties in their childhood, and so may have felt more insecurity than did the parents of students with high creativity, who tend to take risks, permit divergence, and to emphasize their children's openness to experience, values, interests, and enthusiasms.[9]

The dominant values of the period of history in which a youth grows up affect his vocational dreams. In the early 1960s 3,892 high school boys reported what they wanted to be in the following rank order: nationally famous athlete (37.3 percent), jet pilot (31.6 percent), atomic scientist (25.6

percent), and missionary (5.7 percent). In the same investigation girls looked toward occupations in this rank order: model (32 percent), nurse (29.2 percent), schoolteacher (20.6 percent), and actress or artist (18.4 percent).[10] Consistent with the current mood of the country, more teenagers of both sexes can be expected to go into both behavioral and natural sciences than did earlier generations.

Teenagers' interests and concerns with problems vary with the times. Replicating a 1935 study of 1,641 junior and senior high school students with a 1957 comparable investigation of 1,165 teenagers, Harris found significant increases within the twenty-two-year period in interests of both sexes in love and marriage, home and family relationships, and getting along with others. In 1957, both boys and girls significantly ranked problems of interpersonal relationships with parents, love, and marriage higher than did children in the thirties.[11]

Wide-ranging teenage concerns were apparent in the poll in which 6,181 youth participated following the Midcentury White House Conference on Children and Youth, wherein the problems ranked as

[8] Russell R. Dynes, Alfred C. Clarke, and Simon Dinitz, "Levels of Occupational Aspiration: Some Aspects of Family Experience as a Variable," *American Sociological Review* 21, no. 2 (April 1956): 212–215; see chap. 13 for further details.

[9] Jacob W. Getzels and Philip W. Jackson, "Family Environment and Cognitive Style: A Study of the Sources of Highly Intelligent and of Highly Creative Adolescents," *American Sociological Review* 26, no. 3 (June 1961): 351–359.

[10] James S. Coleman, *Social Climates in High Schools* (Washington, D.C.: U.S. Office of Education, 1961), p. 11.

[11] Dale B. Harris, "Sex Differences in the Life Problems and Interests of Adolescents, 1935 and 1957," *Child Development* 30, no. 4 (December 1959): 453–459.

"very important" by one-third to one-half of the young people were:[12]

Percentage
of Youth
Reporting As "Very Important" Problem

56%	Unhappy relationship between mother and father
56%	Draft and threat of war
49%	Developing healthy attitude toward sex
48%	Being misunderstood by parents
47%	Finding the right job
46%	Use of narcotics
45%	Finding the right girl or boy
42%	Responsible driving of automobile
37%	Use of alcohol
35%	Religious uncertainties
34%	Lack of respect for property rights of others
34%	Racial discrimination
33%	Religious discrimination
32%	Lack of close friends of my own age
32%	Lack of good home suitable for friends

The 1969 statewide survey of the problems of five thousand students in Connecticut schools found that the dominant concerns of seventh through eleventh graders continued to be in the areas of peer relationships, mental health (including self-understanding), and sex education.[13]

[12] National Midcentury Committee for Children and Youth, "Unhappy Homes and Draft Lead Youth Problems," *Progress Bulletin*, January 1953, pp. 1, 7.

[13] Ruth Byler, Gertrude Lewis, and Ruth Totman, *Teach Us What We Want to Know* (published for the Connecticut State Board of Education by the Mental Health Materials Center, New York, 1969).

These are the obviously urgent needs of today's teenagers that many of the nation's schools are attempting to meet in carefully designed curricula in family living and sex education.[14] Such efforts have special meaning for members of both generations in the family during adolescence, when teenagers' relationships with their parents are shifting.

Adolescents and Their Parents

Adolescence is a period of strain in most families as teenagers attempt to establish their identity and emancipate themselves from their parents. This is a time when parents feel that their children undervalue them, and when adolescents believe that adults generally depreciate teenagers. Widely separate studies find, however, that adolescents have a higher opinion of adults than do their parents, that both generations have favorable opinions of teenagers, and

[14] Family Health Education Project, *Junior and Senior High School Preparation of the Individual for Life* (a Title III E.S.E.A. project through Hinsdale District no. 181, Downers Grove, Ill., September 1969); S. R. Laycock, *Family Living and Sex Education: A Guide for Parents and Youth Leaders* (published for Canadian Health Education Specialists Society by Baxter Publishing, Toronto, Canada, 1967); Esther D. Schulz and Sally Williams, *Family Life and Sex Education: Curriculum and Instruction* (New York: Harcourt, Brace and World, 1968); and Hershel D. Thornburg, *Sex Education in the Public Schools* (Phoenix, Ariz.: Arizona Education Association, 1969).

that adolescents rate parent-adolescent relationships more favorably than do their mothers or fathers.[15]

Conforming teenagers who less often break rules and regulations tend more than others to have favorable images of their families, to rate their parents' discipline as fair and their family relationships as democratic and affectionate.[16] There is also evidence that lower-class families value conformity and respectability more than do middle-class parents, whose children tend

more to be encouraged to develop as persons in their own right.[17]

Gradually through adolescence, teenagers shift their orientation from family to friends, as table 12–3 indicates. In this transition, teenagers tend to be parent-oriented in important decisions regarding companions and ideas of right and wrong, and to follow their peers in matters of taste in dress, movies, television, and music.[18] On questions of educational plans and

---

[15] Robert D. Hess and Irene Goldblatt, "The Status of Adolescents in American Society: A Problem in Social Identity," *Child Development* 28, no. 4 (December 1957): 459–468; and Patricia Henderson Maxwell, Ruth Connor, and James Walters, "Family Member Perceptions of Parent Role Performance," *Merrill-Palmer Quarterly* 7, no. 1 (1961): 31–37.

[16] W. L. Slocum and Carol L. Stone, "A Method for Measuring Family Images Held by Teen-Agers," *Marriage and Family Living* 21, no. 3 (August 1959), 245–250.

[17] Elias Tuma and Norman Livson, "Family Socioeconomic Status and Adolescent Attitudes toward Authority," *Child Development* 31, no. 2 (June 1961): 387–399; Evelyn Millis Duvall, "Conceptions of Parenthood," *American Journal of Sociology* 52, no. 3 (November 1946): 193–203; and Melvin Kohn, "Social Class and Parental Authority," *American Sociological Review* 24, no. 3 (June 1959): 352–366; and other references in chap. 2.

[18] Nick Stinnett and James Walters, "Parent-Peer Orientation of Adolescents from Low-Income Families," *Journal of Home Economics* 59, no. 1 (January 1967): 37–40; and C. V. Brittain, "Adolescent Choices and Parent-Peer Cross-Pressures," *American Sociological Review* 28 (1963): 385–391.

Table 12–3. *Percentage of Students by Grade and by Orientation*

Orientation toward	Grade in school						
	4th	5th	6th	7th	8th	9th	10th
Family	87.1%	80.5%	80.2%	66.7%	41.7%	44.7%	31.6%
Neutral	6.9	12.2	11.2	9.3	18.3	22.4	20.2
Peers	5.9	7.3	8.6	24.1	40.0	32.9	48.1
Number	101	82	116	108	115	85	79

Source: Charles E. Bowerman and John W. Kinch, "Changes in Family and Peer Orientation of Children between the Fourth and Tenth Grades," *Social Forces* 37, no. 3 (March 1959): 206–211.

future life goals, parents have a stronger influence than do peers. Furthermore, in critical areas, teenagers' interactions with one another tend to support their parents.[19]

Gradually through the teen years young people find themselves as members of their own generation, as they explore the resources within and beyond their families for all they require to accomplish the developmental tasks that lead into effective adulthood.

DEVELOPMENTAL TASKS OF TEENAGERS[20]

1. Accepting one's changing body and learning to use it effectively:

Coming to terms with new size, shape, function, and potential of one's maturing body.

Reconciling differences between one's own physique and that of age-mates of the same and other sex as variations which are normal and to be expected.

Understanding what pubertal changes mean and wholesomely anticipating maturity as a man or as a woman.

Caring for one's body in heathful ways that assure its optimum development.

Learning to handle oneself skillfully in the variety of recreational, social, and family situations that require learned physical skills.

2. Achieving a satisfying and socially accepted masculine or feminine role:

Learning what it means to be a boy or girl in one's culture.

Anticipating realistically what will be involved in becoming a man or a woman.

Finding oneself within the leeway of sex-role expectations and practice allowed by one's family and community.

3. Finding oneself as a member of one's own generation in more mature relations with one's age-mates:

Becoming acceptable as a member of one or more groups of peers.

Making and keeping friends of both sexes.

Getting dates and becoming comfortable in dating situations.

Getting experience in loving and being loved by one or more members of the opposite sex.

Learning how to get along with a wide variety of age-mates in school, neighborhood, and community settings.

Developing skills in inviting and refusing, solving problems and resolving conflicts, making decisions, and evaluating experiences with one's peers.

[19] Denise B. Kandel and Gerald S. Lesser, "Parental and Peer Influence on Educational Plans of Adolescents," *American Sociological Review* 34, no. 2 (April 1969): 213–223.

[20] Freely adapted from the schema used by Robert J. Havighurst, *Human Development and Education* (New York: Longmans, Green and Company, 1953), chaps. 9–11.

4. Achieving emotional independence of parents and other adults:

Becoming free of childish dependencies upon one's parents.

Developing more mature affection for parents as persons.

Learning how to be an autonomous person who is capable of making decisions and running one's own life.

Growing through the dependence of childhood and the impulsive independence of adolescence to mature interdependence with others (parents, teachers, and all authority figures, especially).

Learning to be an adult among adults.

5. Selecting and preparing for an occupation and economic independence:

Seeking counsel and getting specific knowledges about possible fields of work within the limits of real possibilities.

Choosing an occupation in line with interests, abilities, and opportunities.

Preparing oneself through schooling, specialized training, and personal responsibility to get and hold a position.

Getting tryout or appenticeship experiences wherever possible in the lines of future vocational interests.

6. Preparing for marriage and family life:

Enjoying the responsibilities as well as the privileges of family membership.

Developing a responsible attitude toward getting married and having a family.

Acquiring knowledge about mate selection, marriage, homemaking, and child-rearing.

Learning to distinguish between infatuation and more lasting forms of love.

Developing a mutually satisfying personal relationship with a potential mate through processes of dating, going steady, effective courtship, and becoming involved with a loved one.

Making decisions about the timing of engagement, marriage, completion of one's education, fulfillment of military service requirements, and the multiple demands upon young people of marriageable age.

Becoming ready to settle down into a home of one's own.

7. Developing intellectual skills and social sensitivities necessary for civic competence:

Developing concepts of law, government, economics, politics, geography, human nature, and social organization which fit the modern world.

Gaining awareness of human needs and becoming motivated to help others attain their goals.

Acquiring problem-solving methods for dealing effectively with modern problems.

Gaining abilities to communicate competently as a citizen in a democracy.

Becoming involved in causes and projects outside oneself and becoming a socially responsible person.

8. Developing a workable philosophy of life that makes sense in today's world:

Achieving a mature set of values and the ethical controls that characterize a good individual in one's culture.

Desiring and achieving socially responsible behavior.

Selecting worthy ideals and standards to live by and identify with.

Practicing and working through the meanings of religious experience that motivate and inspire.

Finding oneself in the universe and among one's fellowmen in meaningful ways.

Each youth sustains within his breast
A vague and infinite unrest.
He goes about in still alarm,
With shrouded future at his arm,
With longings that can find no tongue.
I see him thus, for I am young.

By an Oklahoma High School Boy

Adolescents' developmental tasks were originally derived from intensive longitudinal studies. More recently, young teenagers have been able to identify their developmental tasks, as Dales' use of scalogram analysis illustrates.[21] Planning youth programs in terms of the developmental tasks of various age groupings in ways that make possible the measurement of progress now seems possible.[22] Criteria for success or failure and for early, expected, and late accomplishment of each of the developmental tasks of adolescence would give even a finer cutting edge to this useful tool.

Traditional tendencies in thinking, feeling, and behaving often hinder and delay a young person's development. Attitudes of shame, guilt, and embarrassment hurt, while wholesomeness helps a youth's full acceptance of himself and of other persons. Finding oneself vocationally is delayed by tendencies to live in a world of dreams and fantasy; it is helped by the willingness to cope with reality and the courage to explore real possibilities. Preparing for marriage and family life is blocked by outmoded restrictions and limitations in education and greatly helped by forward-looking programs for equipping young men and women to become competent husbands and wives, fathers and mothers. Becoming a competent citizen is often sidetracked by outmoded biases and stereotyped ideas ("you can't buck the system"); it moves toward its goal with worthy adults to emulate in determining a sound, acceptable set of values. Finding oneself as a person means coming to terms with oneself, as one was, as one is, and as one might become. Acceptance, encouragement, and guidance are pivotal requisites for teenagers in ac-

---

[21] Ruth J. Dales, "A Method for Measuring Developmental Tasks: Scales for Selected Tasks at the Beginning of Adolescence," *Child Development* 26, no. 2 (June 1955): 111–122.

[22] Al J. Hummel and Clifford A. Smith, *The Task Method of Program Planning* (Omaha, Nebr.: Omaha Young Men's Christian Association Publications, 1959); and James M. Hardy, *Focus on the Family* (New York: Association Press, 1966).

complishing these manifold tasks of growing toward mature adulthood.

DEVELOPMENTAL TASKS OF ADULTS IN THE FAMILY WITH TEENAGERS

Traditional tendencies in thinking, feeling, and behaving often are hazards for both parents, as we see in the charts that follow.[23]

As each of the adult members realistically accepts himself as he is—his physique, with its weaknesses and strengths, its defects and superiorities, his sex and the sex role he plays, his age and stage of maturity, all without inner conflict and undue sensitiv-

[23] Freely adapted from Leland H. Stott, chairman, Robert G. Foster, Robert J. Havighurst, and Fritz Redl, "Section V, The Family with Teenagers," for the Committee on the Dynamics of Family Interaction, preliminary report, Evelyn Millis Duvall and Reuben Hill, cochairmen, National Conference on Family Life, Washington, D.C., February 1948, mimeographed.

The Man of the Family as Father

Developmental Tasks, Goals, and Responsibilities	Traditional Tendencies in Thinking, Feeling, and Behaving
Providing "good" patterns for the roles of the growing adult man, loving husband, and accepting father.	Inability to regard adolescent "cockiness" and impudence as growth manifestations but interpret them as attacks upon parental dignity.
Learning to understand each child as an individual, believe in and trust him, respect his personality and delight in seeing him grow into adolescence and adulthood, and thus maintaining the confidential, affectionate, and companionable relationship earlier established. Providing time to spend with adolescent on a companionable basis, and to get the youth's point of view.	Tendency to more or less unconsciously look upon adolescent child as his rival for the attention of others and in importance and prestige.

Developmental Tasks, Goals, and Responsibilities	Traditional Tendencies in Thinking, Feeling, and Behaving
Understanding that growth is not identical with "improvement," that what the adolescent *needs* is often *not* what he seems to "deserve." Also that what the youngster *needs* has no relationship to the kind of treatment the father received when young.	Fear of loss of control, hence the tendency to be more autocratic toward the adolescent. Tendency to deal with child in terms of his own adolescent experiences —either try to repeat or to avoid what happened to himself. (Repeat the strict handling he received from his own parents, or avoid all firmness, not in terms of the child's needs but because of what happened to him.)
Getting insight into, and a realistic evaluation of, his own emotional reactions, not to stifle or hide them, but to avoid consciously or unconsciously overreacting to them in dealing with the child.	Tendency to fear his own emotions (fear of "spoiling" child through the expression of affection) and so become unduly cold and overstrict.
Arriving at a common understanding and cooperating with mother on matters of guidance and control of children.	Assumption of an authoritarian attitude, following perhaps the pattern of his own parental home, and attempting arbitrarily to order the lives and activities of his older children without consultation with mother or the young people. Taking no particular interest in, and assuming no part of the responsibility for, the guidance and control of children.

The Woman of the Family as Mother

Developmental Tasks, Goals, and Responsibilities	Traditional Tendencies in Thinking, Feeling, and Behaving
Providing "good" patterns for the roles of the *growing* adult woman, wife, and mother. Being alert to matters of her personal and social behavior, dress, and appearance that the adolescent may or may not be proud of.	Tendency not to think of her own attitudes, behavior, and appearance as being important for adolescent children.
Trying to understand each child as an individual, believing in and trusting him, respecting his personality, and delighting in seeing him grow into adolescence and adulthood, and thus maintaining a confidential, affectionate, and companionable relationship with the adolescent as well as with the younger children. Understanding also that what the child needs in the way of guidance has no relationship to the kind of treatment she herself received when young.	Tendency to be anxious upon seeing the child grow up. Tendency to deal with the adolescent in terms of her own adolescent experiences —either repeat or try to avoid what happened to herself (repeat strict handling of own parents or avoid firmness, not in terms of child's needs, but because of what happened to her). Tendency more or less unconsciously to feel that the adolescent daughter is her rival—is replacing her in the attention of the father—is outdoing her in attractiveness.
Understanding that growth is not identical with "improvement," that what the adolescent *needs* is often not what he seems to "deserve."	Tendency to be overconcerned with "improvement" in the child's behavior in relation to certain stereotypes of socially acceptable conduct.

The Woman of the Family as Mother (Continued)

Developmental Tasks, Goals, and Responsibilities	Traditional Tendencies in Thinking, Feeling, and Behaving
Getting insight into, and a realistic evaluation of, her own emotional reactions, not to stifle or hide them, but to avoid consciously or unconsciously overreacting to them in dealing with the adolescent.	Tendency to fear her own emotions (fear that her strong affection for child is "spoiling") and to try to compensate by becoming unduly cold and overstrict; or fear of her rejecting and aggressive wishes may result in a compensatory suppression of all control and firmness with an "overdose of overprotection."

The Man of the Family as Homemaker and Provider

Developmental Tasks, Goals, and Responsibilities	Traditional Tendencies in Thinking, Feeling, and Behaving
Taking a renewed interest in the activities of the home and cooperating with and supporting wife in adapting the household routines to the changing and varied demands of the family members at this stage.	Tendency to resist changes and to be irritated at variations from routines he has become accustomed to.
Relieving his wife of some of the actual work and assuming a share of the responsibility of the family and household management—encouraging and facilitating participation of children in the daily work.	Tendency to hold to the point of view that housework is woman's work and beneath the dignity of men. Tendency to follow the pattern of home participation set in his own parental home and to take for granted that that pattern is normal and desirable.

Developmental Tasks, Goals, and Responsibilities	Traditional Tendencies in Thinking, Feeling, and Behaving
Taking on more responsibility in the management of interpersonal relationships and problems, particularly in relation to adolescent children.	Feeling that the handling of the children is their mother's job and responsibility.
Regarding his responsibility for providing for the material requirements and the general economic security of his family as taking precedence over his own desires to speculate or to quit.	Irresponsibility in the matter of providing financially for the family—tendency to take chances and go into financial ventures that jeopardize the economic security of family, or to run away in one escape or another.
Acquainting the rest of the family with the realities of the family's financial situation and thus enlisting their intelligent sharing of responsibility.	Feeling that the money he makes is his own—that money matters are a man's business.
Enlisting the participation of the family in making decisions regarding important expenditures or financial ventures and regarding the equitable sharing and apportioning of the family funds.	Feeling that he, as head of the family, should continue to maintain complete control of the family finances.
Accepting and encouraging the wife's sharing of the economic burden of earning the family living if she is so talented and so minded.	Feeling that to provide the income to support the family is the task of man alone.

The Woman of the Family as Homemaker and Family Manager

Developmental Tasks, Goals, and Responsibilities | Traditional Tendencies in Thinking, Feeling, and Behaving

Checking on her health needs and habits and taking steps to ensure strength and energy for the job of making a home for a family with adolescents.

Tendency to neglect her own health at a time of life when it is especially important.

Reviewing her work habits and routines with the purpose of adapting them to the real needs and demands of all members of the family, including herself.

Tendency to overstress the housekeeping aspects—orderliness, cleanliness, things always in their places. Tendency either to follow slavishly or to repudiate the homemaking patterns of her parental home.

Reviewing homemaking schedules and routines with the view of obtaining optimum family participation and satisfaction.

Tendency to perfectionism—husband or children not able to participate in homemaking activities because they cannot do them to suit her.

Managing the family budget efficiently—buying economically and with an understanding of the nutritional requirements and other material needs of the family. Devising means of keeping family, including the father, informed as to costs, available goods, and relative values, and enlisting their intelligent cooperation in the use of the family's resources.

Tendency to be extravagant or unwise in buying.

Failing to cooperate fully with the "provider" or to enlist his sympathy and his understanding of the problems of managing efficiently the household budget. *Struggling* with the children rather than helping them to understand the problems of "making ends meet."

Acquiring the attitudes, knowledge, and skills necessary to create a "home atmosphere" which is comfortable, wholesome, easy, friendly, happy, and *to take joy and professional pride in that accomplishment.*

Tendency to feel that the status of the homemaker is low in comparison with business or professional work. Assuming an attitude of one betrayed—an attitude of self-pity. Failing to see the challenge or the possibilities for satisfaction and development in homemaking.

The Man of the Family as Husband

Developmental Tasks, Goals, and Responsibilities	Traditional Tendencies in Thinking, Feeling, and Behaving
Maintaining or reinforcing habits of personal care and grooming.	Tendency to "let down" with the approach of middle age, to be careless in care of clothes and in personal care and grooming.
Strengthening his attitudes of acceptance with respect to his wife—to be able more than ever to recognize the necessity for, and her right to be different—to be as she is, and to be able really to accept her thus.	Tendency to hold to a preconceived notion as to personality, talents, and behavior of a wife. Tendency to follow or to repudiate compulsively the husband-wife relationships of his own parents.
Maintaining or reestablishing habits of outward courtesy and attentiveness toward wife and a genuine concern for her comfort and welfare.	Tendency to take wife for granted, to forget to be courteous or to show appreciation of her or concern for her welfare and comfort.
Understanding the needs and tendencies of his wife at this particular stage and be increasingly alert to ways of facilitating her personal growth and satisfactions.	Tendency to assume a self-centered, individualistic attitude in his relationships with wife, to be concerned with his own satisfactions and exploitative in marital relations.
Cultivating a closer confidential and sharing relationship with his wife; to share with her his experiences—his triumphs and worries, etc. Being really interested in her activities, domestic and social. Regarding her as a partner and sharer in all aspects of their life together.	Tendency to regard men's and women's spheres of action as separate, to feel that he must maintain his authority, that a "woman's place is in the home," that she "has no business working outside the home," "has no sense about money," or that "it's her job to take care of the kids."
Cooperating in the development of new joint interests, activities, hobbies, etc.	Tendency to want to "take it easy"—to follow old established habits in the use of leisure, resisting something new.

The Woman of the Family as Wife

Developmental Tasks, Goals, and Responsibilities	Traditional Tendencies in Thinking, Feeling, and Behaving
Maintaining and enhancing her personal attractiveness and charm.	Tendency to "let down" with the passage of years—to forget the importance of being personally attractive, particularly to her husband.
Showing tender concern about husband's health and welfare. Being sympathetic with his need for quiet, for understanding, and for occasional "ego inflation."	Tendency to take husband for granted; to be nagging and critical when he needs sympathy and understanding; to be thoughtless and inconsiderate toward him.
Understanding her husband's needs for affection and response and being able to respond to them adequately.	Inability to respond maritally with warmth and affection; being self-centered; responding or not responding according to her present whim.
Being able to accept her husband's differences and peculiarities with sympathy and with interest.	Tendency to continue to try to make her husband over after her own preconceived notions, which may represent a compulsive adherence to, or a repudiation of, the husband-wife relationship of her own parents.
Maintaining or acquiring a genuine interest in husband's business or profession and thus being able to function as an understanding and sympathetic listener, confidante, and sharer in his triumphs and worries.	Boredom in relation to husband's work; tendency to be disparaging of his job; lack of appreciation of its importance; nagging with respect to the prestige value or income from the job.
Encouraging the development of additional joint activities and interests with husband.	Lack of inclination to participate in the type of activities in which husband is interested.

The Man of the Family as a Person

Developmental Tasks, Goals, and Responsibilities	Traditional Tendencies in Thinking, Feeling, and Behaving
Adjusting to the realities of constantly growing older—accepting realistically his present age and stage of development with its limitations as well as its potentialities for satisfactory functioning and enjoyment.	Tendency to continue to base feelings of personal prestige on the exploits and accomplishments of youth, maintaining image of self established in youth. Tendency to feel that life is "passing him by." Feeling that the supreme pleasures and satisfactions of life are limited to youth and young manhood.
Keeping up to date on current thinking, social attitudes, and changing folkways and mores.	Tendency to continue to think in terms of the norms and social standards of his youth, failing to move along with the times.
Broadening interests and knowledge, and thus growing in terms of civic and social responsibility.	Tendency to become so engrossed in making a living or achieving business or professional success as to have no time or energy for growth in other areas. Tendency to attitude that "politics is rotten business," and that government is the business of incompetent, irresponsible, and corrupt individuals.
Bolstering feelings of adequacy and self-confidence and personal worth by constantly developing new personal skills, hobbies, etc.	Tendency to foster basic feelings of inadequacy through lack of growth in skills and personal proficiency (sometimes compensated for in rigid, unyielding, domineering behavior toward wife, children, and associates).
Continuing to work toward his personal ideals and goals of achievement, always in terms of the realities of his own resources and limitations.	Tendency to seek to attain *through his child* the ideals and goals of achievement which he failed to achieve in his own life.

Developmental Tasks, Goals, and Responsibilities	Traditional Tendencies in Thinking, Feeling, and Behaving
Adjusting to the realities of constantly growing older—to approaching middle age. Accepting realistically and with equanimity her present age and stage of development with its limitations and its potentialities for satisfactory functioning and enjoyment.	Tendency to feel that she is "missing out," that life is passing her by. ⅄ Becoming anxious, irritable, complaining, or discouraged.⅄ Trying to "have her fling" while she can, or to recapture the appearance and the pleasures of youth. ⅄
Keeping up to date on current thinking, social attitudes, and changing folkways and mores.	Tendency to fall behind the times because of her preoccupation with home duties; tendency to neglect or sacrifice and submerge self for family.
Developing new interests and broadening scope of activities outside the home, and thus maintaining or reestablishing herself as an independently growing, yet interacting member of the family group.	Tendency to limit activities and interests more and more exclusively to home and family, and thus to have no time or energy for growth in other areas. Tendency to feel that civic and political problems are not the concern of women.
Bolstering feelings of personal adequacy and worth by developing new skills, hobbies, interests, and commitments.	Tendency to compensate for feelings of inadequacy by controlling or domineering over others by means of various devices or to "outdo" others in appearance, clothes, or show of wealth, etc. ⅄
Continuing to get satisfaction from her own efforts toward the achievement of personal ideals and goals.	Tendency to live and to experience the realization of her own dreams and ideals through, and in the life and the triumphs of, her daughter.

ity—he sets the pattern for a similar sort of self-acceptance on the part of the children. The adolescent girl then has the pattern for accepting with satisfaction her role as a girl and woman; and the boy, even though he may be small in stature or a bit behind schedule in his physical development, has before him a healthy pattern to follow and an understanding attitude in his parents to help him to live happily with himself and his family. Inseparable from the attitude of self-acceptance in the family is the tendency for each family member to accept the others with a basic respect that is founded on mutual understanding.

FAMILY DEVELOPMENTAL TASKS AT THE TEENAGE STAGE

While mother and father, teenager and younger siblings are working through their developmental tasks within the traditional tendencies and social pressures that oftentimes thwart and hinder them, the family as a whole is busy at the essential family developmental tasks of the teenage stage:

1. Providing facilities for widely different needs
2. Working out money matters in the family with teenagers
3. Sharing responsibilities of family living
4. Putting the marriage relationship in focus
5. Bridging the communication gap
6. Keeping in touch with relatives
7. Widening horizons of teenagers and their parents
8. Reworking and maintaining a philosophy of life.

Providing Facilities for Widely Different Needs

At no time in the family life cycle do family members feel as intensely about the house and its facilities as they do during the teenage family stage. Now the teenager's need for acceptance in larger social circles makes him (or oftener her) push for nicer, better, bigger, more modern furnishings and equipment. The house that some years ago was child-proofed and stripped of all breakable elegance now must bloom in the styles of the period, as teenagers see the house as a reflection of themselves and their family. One of the first signs of adolescence noted by mothers is a critical attitude of the youngster about the physical features of the home. Studies of the health and development of normal children find that with the onset of adolescence youngsters tend to compare their homes unfavorably with others in the community; they find it hard to accept the fact that they cannot use the telephone for hours on end, and they feel they should have top priority in the use of the bathroom.[24]

[24] Ruth M. Butler, "Mothers' Attitudes toward the Social Development of Their Adolescents," *Social Casework*, May-June 1956, reprint p. 3.

The dating adolescent girl wants an attractive setting in which she can entertain her boy and girl friends. She needs some privacy in these facilities at least part of the time, away from the ever-watchful eyes and ears of younger siblings, parents, and other family members. The rest of the family needs to be somewhat protected from the noisy activities of teenagers, with their radios turned up full blast, the record player blaring out the same popular tune over and over again, the giggles, the chatter, the shrieks, and the endless telephone conversations that mean so much to teenagers and yet so often fray the nerves of adults. Now, when so much emphasis is put upon popularity and social life, most families want to encourage their teenagers in their social growth, and so do what they can to provide the facilities for it.

Individual differences among the children of a family call for a variety of facilities during the teen years. Some boys enjoy the superior social-emotional adjustment of early maturation; others, less far along in their physical, emotional, and social development, tend to be less poised and conforming and more active and adventuresome as teenagers.[25] The big, well-developed teenager tends, therefore, to be involved in sports, social activities, and community projects, while the late-maturing boy throws himself into music, applied science, a series of hobbies, or a variety of other interests for which physical size and social competence are not requisites.

The teenage boy starts dating a little later, and he dates less frequently than the girl of the same age.[26] He does less of his dating and entertaining at home than does the girl, and so tends to demand less in refurbishing and "style." The pressures he puts on the home as a teenager are more apt to be in space for his hobbies and for his gang of buddies. As the fellows gather in the basement to fix a model plane, or in the yard to "soup up" the jalopy, or over the shortwave set in his room, there is bound to be some invasion of the house and its supplies for food and drink and rags and string and all the other necessities that go into the completion of a project—and a man!

Teenagers tend to crowd their parents in the use of household equipment as they begin to adopt adult ways. One study finds that in the shared equipment and space for leisure activities of teenagers and other members of the family, there are too many activities of diversified nature carried on in the same room.[27] Listing them as (1) quiet or private—reading, study, etc., (2) social—entertaining guests, music, records, television, etc., and (3) active—dancing, painting, carpentry, etc., the investigators recom-

25 Mary Cover Jones, "Psychological Correlates of Somatic Development," *Child Development* 36, no. 4 (December 1965): 899–911.

26 Samuel H. Lowrie, "Factors Involved in the Frequency of Dating," *Marriage and Family Living* 18, no. 1 (February 1956): 46–51.

27 Jerre L. Withrow and Virginia Y. Trotter, "Space for Leisure Activities of Teen-Agers," *Journal of Home Economics* 53, no. 5 (May 1961): 359–362.

mend creating three distinct activity areas: private, social, and active, used interchangeably depending upon the demands of the various family members.

While the teenager is crowding the house with his or her dating, recreational, and work interests, younger siblings are growing up, and their interests and needs must be taken into account. Younger brothers and sisters often resent teenage interests and activities and the break in customary patterns of former years of play together. At the same time, father and mother continue to be persons with rights and needs for a little peace and quiet in their lives. The home that fulfills this multidimensional demand for adequate facilities during the teenage stage has some tall stepping to do, with adaptations and elaborations that more than likely cost money—plenty of it, as we see in the next section.

Working Out Money Matters in the Family with Teenagers

The teenage family feels pressures for physical expansion and renewal of its facilities. Junior campaigns for a new car; sister for a party dress. The refrigerator is no longer large enough to meet the demand for snacks and meals of the many appetites represented in the family. It would be nice to have another bathroom, or a second television set, or a deep freeze, or a rumpus room, or a den where mother and father could find some place to call their own when the teenagers are entertaining, or some new furnishings to replace "this old stuff" that is suddenly so hideous in adolescent eyes. Meanwhile, father sees costs of college, social life, and weddings ballooning up ahead of him.

Adolescents are very much concerned with the problems of money. A great many junior and senior high school young people have difficulty keeping up with school expenses and feel embarrassed because of lack of funds.[28] Dates cost money—clothes and grooming for the girl, and, for the boy, actual financial outlay for entertainment and food on the date. There is a wide range in the costs of a date, all the way from less than a dollar for something simple to a great deal of money for elaborate special affairs. One study of freshman and sophomore college students reports that they spent two to three dollars for routine dates, five to six dollars for special dates, and twenty to thirty-five dollars for big affairs like homecoming, in a range of dating costs running from less than one dollar to three hundred dollars.[29] Current dating costs quite probably are even higher.

---

[28] Martin Bloom, "The Money Problems of Adolescents in the Secondary Schools of Springfield, Massachusetts" (Doctor of Education thesis, New York University, 1955).

[29] Ruth Connor and Edith Flinn Hall, "The Dating Behavior of College Freshmen and Sophomores," *Journal of Home Economics* 44, no. 4 (April 1952): 278–281.

This is the time when a teenager gets a part-time job that will not interfere too greatly with his school work and yet will bring him some regular money of his own. When employment is good, a teenage boy can find work in a neighborhood shop or store, golf links, or garage. The adolescent girl is in demand as baby-sitter, household helper, and in many places as saleswoman or clerk in a local store or office. These may be valuable experiences if they do not cut short the young person's educational program and if the income from self-employment may be jointly recognized in the family as of special interest to the adolescent.

Families differ greatly in money practices. Some appropriate the children's earnings as part of the family income, as once was traditional. Others consider the child's earnings as his to do with as he or she pleases. Still others keep a supervisory eye on teenagers' earnings, and while they respect the young person's wishes, try to counsel for wisdom in planning for future needs. There are still some traditional homes in which either the father or the mother holds the purse strings, and the young people have no voice in the family finances. In growing numbers are the more democratically oriented families in which family income and expenditures are discussed and money planning is done jointly, with all members of the family participating. In these homes, young people gain experience in handling money and in dealing with financial problems, at the same time feeling that their wishes and rights are being considered in the family as they grow up.

Wives tend to be earning money at this stage of the family life cycle. Some 50 percent of teenagers' mothers are gainfully employed.[30] Before they return to work, they are wise to consider how much take-home pay can be expected from the stated salary. Sylvia Porter, syndicated financial counselor, offers this minimal estimate of what it costs a wife returning to work at a salary of ninety dollars a week:[31]

Federal and state income taxes .... $	15.00
Group health and life insurance	1.85
Social security and other deductions	4.26
Transportation to and from work	2.50
Lunches	6.25
Baby-sitters	7.00
Extra clothes and personal care	3.50
Other extra expenses	4.25
Total expenses and deductions .... $	44.61
Net weekly income	45.39
Total net annual income $2,360.28	

Harder to calculate are other possible benefits (or psychic costs) of a wife's working—satisfactions or frustrations of the job, enrichment or strains in the husband-wife relationship, and improvement or threats to the mother-teenager relationship. There is some evidence that the adjustment

[30] U.S. Department of Labor, Bureau of Labor Statistics, *Marital and Family Characteristics of Workers*, Special Labor Force Report, no. 94 (March 1967), table J, p. A-15; see also table 16–4, on the effect of husbands' income on percentage of wives working.

[31] Sylvia Porter, "Spending Your Money," *Ladies' Home Journal*, January 1968, p. 24.

between adolescents and their parents is better when the mother is employed part-time than when she is a full-time home-maker.[32] One interpretation is that as children become adolescent, emancipating themselves is easier if their mother is not entirely dependent upon her children for her sense of being needed. If she has a part-time job, she not only helps out financially, but very likely she widens her horizons and extends her roles as wife, mother, and self-sufficient person.

Teenagers whose mothers are employed tend more than others to feel that the outside work does not threaten the marital relationship. Furthermore, both boys and girls usually accept their mothers' employment, especially in those homes where the father participates in household tasks.[33] Family situations differ widely, and many wives find it impossible or impractical to work outside the home. With the removal of traditional taboos about women working, a family has a choice about the matter today. That so many families in the teen-age stage find economic and emotional pressures eased when the mother has some gainful employment is a trend worthy of note.

Sharing Responsibilities of Family Living

By the time a girl becomes a teenager, she sometimes enjoys preparing a family meal or buying new curtains for her room out of her own money. The boy who does a better job than his father at making household or automobile repairs gets satisfaction from these new responsibilities in the home.[34] Teenagers are still accountable to their parents, but they progressively assume more and more responsibility for their behavior and for the family's well-being as they mature. The traditional family, with its father-head, is on the wane in twentieth-century America, and democratic patterns are more frequent in families with teenagers.[35]

Studies show that most household tasks are jointly undertaken by the various members of the family, with no one member assuming complete responsibility. Too frequently, however, teenagers are found

[32] Ivan Nye, "Adolescent-Parent Adjustment: Age, Sex, Sibling Number, Broken Homes, and Employed Mothers as Variables," *Marriage and Family Living* 14, no. 4 (November 1952): 331; also research in progress under Margaret S. Jessen of the Woodland Public Schools, Woodland, California, on "Factors in Parents' Understanding of Adolescent Attitudes," reports that working mothers tend to show more understanding than mothers at home.

[33] Karl King, Jennie McIntyre, and Leland Axelson, "Adolescents' Views of Maternal Employment as a Threat to the Marital Relationship," *Journal of Marriage and the Family* 30, no. 4 (November 1968): 633–637.

[34] Ruth M. Butler, "Is Disrespect Inevitable?" *PTA Magazine* 57, no. 7 (March 1963): 24–26.

[35] Vivian Briggs and Lois R. Schulz, "Parental Response to Concepts of Parent-Adolescent Relationships," *Child Development* 26, no. 4 (December 1955): 279–284.

doing the simpler, less interesting jobs, such as setting and clearing the table (by the girls), and removing the trash by the teenage boy—the major chore that he claims as his own in most families. The parents take on the more important activities—the mother preparing the meals, and the father fixing broken things—which might give teenagers and their younger brothers and sisters pride in achievement.[36]

Mother and father clearly hold the balance of power in deciding who will participate in the various activities involving family members. Although most decisions are jointly made by two or more family members, significantly more parents than teenagers have a voice in the social activities that affect them. For example, four out of five fathers (83.8 percent) decide who uses the family car, a decision that about half of the mothers (51.9 percent), less than one out of four teenage sons (23.8 percent), and 13.4 percent of the teenage daughters have a voice in making. Twice as many parents as teenagers decide who will go on outings or summer vacations, and half again as many mothers as teenage daughters decide who will use the living room.[37]

It is the father who earns the money (97.9 percent), pays the bills (97.9 percent), and shops for the family car (91.3 percent). Mother has the major voice in selecting the household equipment, furniture, and clothing for the family. Less than half of all teenagers polled participate in any of the family economic activities.[38]

Putting the Marriage Relationship in Focus

By the time father and mother have been married fifteen or more years, they may have become so preoccupied with their parenthood responsibilities that their marriage no longer holds a central place in their lives. The man of the house tends to be absorbed in his work roles and associations. His wife, carrying through the years major responsibility for the home and children, may feel "bogged down," work-worn, and devoid of the glamour that her teenagers' magazines portray so fetchingly. Putting the marriage back in focus may be a major family developmental task at this stage.

Studies of husband-wife relationships through the family life cycle find a steady decline in the wife's satisfaction with her husband's love as the children grow older.[39]

---

[36] Theodore B. Johannis, Jr., "Participation by Fathers, Mothers, and Teenage Sons and Daughters in Selected Household Tasks," *Coordinator* 6, no. 4 (June 1958): 61–62; and Evelyn Millis Duvall, *Today's Teen-Agers* (New York: Association Press, 1966), chap. 16, pp. 191–200.

[37] Theodore B. Johannis, Jr., and James M. Rollins, "Teenager Perception of Family Decision Making about Social Activity," *Family Life Coordinator* 8, no. 3 (March 1960): 59–60.

[38] Theodore B. Johannis, Jr., "Participation by Fathers, Mothers, and Teenage Sons and Daughters in Selected Family Economic Activity," *Coordinator* 6, no. 1 (September 1957): 15–16.

[39] See chart 16–4 and supporting research in chap. 16.

At the teenage stage of the family life cycle, the middle-aged husband shows little of the ardor that his teenagers demonstrate in their lovemaking. The wife feels taken for granted, always on tap to serve family needs, with few of the fulfillments that are supposed to go with marriage.

Wives about the same age as their mates are more satisfied with marital love than wives older or younger by four or more years.[40] The middle-aged woman, old enough to have teenage children, may be especially vulnerable. The college-educated find greater fulfillment in their marriages than do those with less education, possibly because their schooling meant deferred gratification in adolescence and the development of a richer repertoire of emotional and sexual expression.

As the family reaches the teenage stage, its children are more active socially than they were at younger ages. Boyfriends call for the adolescent daughter, whose excitement in getting ready for her dates has a certain contagion that carries over to her parents, who relive in her some of their courtship experiences. Now husband and wife drive their teenagers to parties and various social events, where they, with other adults, are expected to stay as chaperones. This may explain in part why married couples with teenagers more often have a gay time away from home than they did when their oldest child was still a schoolager.[41]

Now that the oldest child is old enough to be left in charge of the home for short intervals, husband and wife are freer to get away for an occasional evening, or to have a weekend trip together from time to time as the husband's schedule allows. Letting the adolescents perk things up in the family as they want to is often fun for the parents as well as the youngsters. As mother gets a smart new outfit, she gets the feelings that go with it and once more attracts her husband's interest in her as a woman. When father gets into the tweed jacket his son insists is right for him, he assumes the gay blade air that seems appropriate; he throws back his shoulders, pulls in his tummy, and woos his own wife as only he can charm her. Keeping a marriage vigorously alive consists of much more than so-called marriage hygiene: it rests upon the eagerness of the husband and wife to attract and be attractive to the other—with the life and the lilt that are to be found in a radiantly alive marriage.

Bridging the Communication Gap

The major problem in communication at this stage of the family life cycle is being

---

[40] Robert O. Blood, Jr., and Donald M. Wolfe, *Husbands and Wives: The Dynamics of Married Living* (Glencoe, Ill.: Free Press, 1960), p. 227.

[41] Harold Feldman, "Development of the Husband-Wife Relationship: A Research Report," mimeographed (Ithaca, N.Y.: Cornell University, 1965), p. 41.

available to each other both as husbands and wives and as parents and children. Parents with teenagers and parents with children at the preschool stage experience a collapse in the exchange of ideas more than at any other periods in the life of the marriage. The man and wife appear to be so involved in keeping the family intact and in order that their own contact with each other intellectually and emotionally is damaged. The adolescents are so absorbed with their problems and so noisy in their interaction with each other and with the younger children in the family that the parents may have little opportunity for interchange of their own thoughts and feelings.

They now keep their ideas to themselves; they have fewer arguments than they had earlier in their marriage, even though both husband and wife feel misunderstood quite as often as they did when their eldest was of school age.[42]

It is generally agreed that one function of communication in marriage is that of sharing with one's partner the pleasant and the unpleasant events which have happened during the day while each has been at work at his or her own tasks. Yet few of the wives in the Detroit Area Study spontaneously mentioned interaction with their husbands after a bad day. During the honeymoon stage of the marriage 70 percent of the brides appear to have kept their problems to themselves. This percentage of wives increases as the marriage continues, until at the teenage stage 98 percent of the wives report neither positive nor negative interaction with their husbands at the end of a bad day.[43] It is safe to assume that the reason is not that mothers of adolescents have no bad days, but rather that their communication with their husbands has declined to the point where they no longer burden their mates with their problems.

Although a few teenagers are found to report all their difficulties to their mothers and fathers, most of them have trouble confiding in their parents.[44] Sex and petting are the two subjects ranked by both boys and girls as most difficult to discuss with their parents. Four out of five boys had trouble talking about sex with their fathers, and 84 percent with their mothers. Nine out of ten girls had trouble discussing sex with their fathers, and 64 percent with their mothers; 12 percent of the girls were totally blocked from talking about sex with their mothers, 24 percent with their fathers, and 10 percent had no communication whatever with their parents in these areas. In the light of the developmental tasks of adolescence, it may well be that parents' silence in such matters of critical concern accounts for some of the mutual alienation

---

[42] Ibid.

[43] Blood and Wolfe, *Husbands and Wives*, p. 188.

[44] Marvin C. Dubbé, "What Do Your Adolescents Tell You?" mimeographed (Portland, Ore.: E. C. Brown Trust, n.d.); and Marvin C. Dubbé, "What Young People Can't Talk over with Their Parents," *National Parent-Teacher* 52, no. 2 (October 1957): 18–20.

and suspicion that exist between teenagers and their parents.

Little children can be openly dependent. Teenagers frequently are irritated by evidences of their continuing need for their parents. Watch a central school letting out in the afternoon. As the children come to find parents waiting to take them to a picnic or music lesson, the younger child usually welcomes his mother with enthusiastic warmth. Not so the junior or senior high school student, who more typically resents his parents' presence near the school building and has been known to greet his mother with the critical query, "What are you doing here?"

Parents who have been considered perfect by little children come in for criticism and faultfinding as these same children reach adolescence. The schoolboy brags about his father's prowess and boasts of his mother's beauty. The same young fellow as a teenager groans over his father's old-fashioned behavior and begs his mother not

H. ARMSTRONG ROBERTS

Effective communication between the generations is a decided advantage.

FAMILY DEVELOPMENT

to appear at a parent-teacher meeting in "that old thing." Adolescent criticism of parents is evidence of the young person's struggle to free himself from his close emotional attachment to his parents and to mature in his relationship with them.

The teenager who achieves emancipation from his parents emerges as a young adult capable of mature affection for his mother and father as persons. He becomes an autonomous person, capable of reciprocal interdependence with his parents, and of mature feelings of genuine affection and appreciation for them. But in the meantime, through adolescence, relationships between the generations are frequently strained.

There is some normal slackening off of telling parents everything as children get into their teens. Then it is normal for intimate confidences to be shared first with close friends within the peer group, and only secondarily with parents and other significant adults. Adults who recognize how normal it is for young people to identify now with their own generation, as they must if they are to emerge as full-fledged adults, restrain themselves from the prying pressures that only serve to alienate them further from their teenagers.

Wise parents guide their adolescents with a loose rein, letting them have their heads, knowing that they will not stray too far from the fold if they are not driven from it. Being available for companionable chats now and then is better than letting loose a barrage of questions as soon as the teenager

sets foot inside the door. Adolescents need parents and go to them willingly in families where communication systems are kept in good working order.

Some families experience more alienation between generations than do others. Ethnic groups in which the parents hold to the old ways, while the young people reach out to the new, find it hard to bridge the growing chasms between the generations. In general, middle-class and upper-class families maintain more democratic patterns of interaction and have fewer problems with their adolescent youth than do lower-class families.[45]

Youth is more explorative, daring, and up to the minute than are parents. Young people enjoy that contrast. They want to be out ahead. But it is also exceedingly important to the adolescent for dad and mom not to get *too* far behind. They take pride in their parents' progressive point of view and in their social and civic activities and interest. They are concerned about the way their parents look and behave in public. For parents to possess some social grace and an interest in cultural activities and events apparently gives the young per-

---

[45] Leonard G. Benson, "Family Social Status and Parental Authority Evaluations among Adolescents," *Southwest Social Science Quarterly* 36, no. 1 (June 1955): 46–54; Ivan Nye, "Adolescent-Parent Adjustment—Socio-Economic Level as a Variable," *American Sociological Review* 16, no. 3 (June 1951): 341–349; and Henry S. Maas, "Some Social Class Differences in the Family Systems and Group Relations of Pre- and Early Adolescents," *Child Development* 22, no. 2 (June 1951): 145–152.

son the needed sense of pride in them that facilitates their communication.

Keeping in Touch with Relatives

The teenage stage of the family life cycle is the testing time for the immediate relatives. If they pass youth's rigorous standards of acceptability, they can contribute much to and gain much from association with the young relatives. If they remain rigidly rooted in "old-fashioned" ways and ideas, young people eschew them heartily and will avoid them except under duress. An understanding grandparent can bridge the gap not only between the first and third generations but also between grandchild and parent. A sympathetic uncle, aunt, or cousin has a real role to play as a home away from home—a parent once removed, a guide without the heavy hand of authority, or the wise counselor who is not too close to the teenage boy or girl. The narrow-minded "old maid," male or female, married or unmarried, is rarely a welcome guest in the teenage family, for he or she brings too much implied criticism and personifies too clearly the frustrations that burden youth.

Broad-gauged or narrow, generous or stingy, wise or foolish, relatives have to be taken in their stride in most families. You dare not offend Aunt Amy no matter what you think of her. You cannot go and live with your sophisticated cousin however much you would love it. You need not imitate drifting Uncle Mike regardless of how much you envy his freedom. You go to family gatherings and size them all up, maintaining the courtesies that are expected and learning a great deal about your roots and your forebears as you see these kinfolk in action.

When graduation day arrives, and your relatives sit there beaming up at you, you can afford to be proud of your family and glad to be a part of them. You want to be worthy of them and to measure up to their expectations of you. You recognize yourself as a member of the larger family group and feel sorry for the boy or girl in your class who has no family to call his own.

Younger cousins and other relatives may idolize the teenager and play significant parts in his or her development. Relatives have a real place in the family, less perhaps in the teenage family than before or after, but a place, nevertheless, that is real and a part of family living that is important.

Widening Horizons of Teenagers and Their Parents

The teenage family ranges farther afield than it ever has before. The children are now old enough to enjoy a whole-family vacation to more distant points of interest than before was feasible. Trips to historic shrines and cultural areas now take on real meaning for the family. Individually, horizons expand too. The teenager goes off with his friends for a weekend or a summer. Father is away on business trips from time to time. Mother is sent as a delegate to the state or national convention of her favorite organization. The family is beginning to scatter in a preview of the individualization characteristic of the empty nest stage just ahead.

Teenagers normally reach out for associations with people outside the family. The adolescent must identify with the younger generation. Social growth is dependent upon friendships with members of both sexes and on the activities that go with dating, courtship, and becoming involved emotionally with one or more members of the other sex. During the entire second decade of life, members of the peer group are especially important to the young person. It is in the face-to-face contacts with friends of one's own age that decisions are made, skills are developed, and values are weighed in everyday interaction. Guidance, confidences, and counsel from beloved older friends (teacher, minister, youth leaders, etc.) may be more important to the teenager than one suspects. Such close ties outside the family may threaten the parent who is not prepared to release the teenage child. Accepting the teenager's intimate friends and the confidences that young people normally share, parents can take adolescence in their stride. Otherwise this task of growing out to others may be frightening for the parents who stand by and resist or retreat.

A frequent example is found in the teenager's early love experiences. For him or her the crushes and infatuations of early adolescence are important and especially precious. If one or both of the parents ridicule these early involvements as "puppy love" or ignore them as "kid stuff," they alienate their own youngster and only rarely weaken the outside ties. When the family can make this special friend welcome at home, treat him or her and the relationship with respect, and take it for what it is and nothing more, both the family and the adolescent are free to grow through the experience to new levels of maturity.

Group life is a magnet for the adolescent. Many a teenager wants to belong to more organizations and get into more activities than can comfortably be carried. He or she wants to belong to the band or the glee club, to the drama group or the ball team, to social clubs and hobby groups. Life is opening up, and everything must be tried and tested. Political organizations and social action groups quite distant from the family's orientation may be explored, as much to see what they are like as to stretch away from the family's affiliations into those peculiarly one's own.

Parents who can take these adventures of their youngsters as a normal part of growing up, without feeling unnecessarily afraid or personally threatened, can argue the merits of this cause or that with their budding citizen without going off the deep end in repression or repudiation. Families who can go along with their young people in the various explorations into new ways of looking at things can grow up with the flexibility that the modern age requires.

HAZARDS AND CHALLENGES OF TEENAGERS' FAMILIES

It is not easy to rear children in the modern scene, especially as they become teenagers. Loud voices of television, movies, and other mass media proclaim values of sex, sadism, violence, immaturity, materialism, and hedonism with regularity. Widely publicized increases in venereal infection, premarital pregnancy, drinking, drug usage, and hippie cults among youth suggest to many an anxious parent that their teenagers are espousing alien values at variance with those of the family. Parental values are more along the lines of consideration and moderation rather than violence, sexual restraint and monogamy rather than promiscuous eroticism, maturity and planning for future goals rather than irresponsible pleasure-seeking.[46]

Teenagers face hazards today from their downgrading in the public mind and the general anxiety that "kids are wild."[47] Teenagers' families face real problems in combatting delinquent tendencies, irresponsible conduct, truancy, questionable companions, confusions about love, sex, and marriage, and blocked pathways to adulthood as adolescents go through the teen years.

Anxious, threatened, insecure parents and those with outmoded traditional attitudes fail to give their adolescents the firm, understanding guidance they need, and too often alienate their children. As teenagers attempt to establish their identity and to emancipate themselves from their dependence upon their parents, they present urgent challenges to their families and to themselves. Both overdependency and overrebelliousness increase the difficulties in both generations in loosening the apron strings and allowing the maturing young person to find himself.

Family Dilemmas at the Teenage Stage

Modern families ride the horns of at least six dilemmas through the teen years:[48] (1) firm family control versus freedom for

---

[46] E. E. LeMasters, *Parents in Modern America* (Homewood, Ill.: Dorsey Press, 1969), chap. 10, "Parents, Mass Media, and the Youth Peer Group," pp. 176–191.

[47] Frank R. Donovan, *Wild Kids* (Harrisburg, Pa.: Stackpole Books, 1967).

[48] Evelyn Millis Duvall, "Family Dilemmas with Teen-Agers," *Family Life Coordinator* 14, no. 2 (April 1965): 35–38.

the teenager; (2) responsibility vested in parents versus shared with teenagers; (3) emphasis on social activities versus academic success; (4) mobility versus stability for the family and for the teenager; (5) open communication with outspoken criticism versus respect with peace and quiet; and (6) dedicated lives versus uncommitted stance toward life. Each dilemma involves the challenge of choices to be made and values to be held. Families grow strong as they work through their dilemmas with today's teenagers. Young people mature as they explore alternatives open to them and their families in the modern world.

A family cannot be buffeted about by every social wind that blows and feel steady and strong within itself. Conversely, a family that does not bend with the pressures of the times will break under their stress. With no convictions and values, the family is a tumbleweed, without roots or stability. With a philosophy of life that is too rigid and narrow, a family risks alienation of its teenagers and grown children and its own integrity as a unit.

The stresses of adolescence that so often shake families to their roots often grow out of conflicting value systems of the old and the new generation. Parents were brought up in one way of life, where definite standards of right and wrong prevailed. Circumstances have changed; teenage young people see life situations differently. The developmental tasks for the family involve holding fast to those verities that have continuing meaning, while venturing forth into wider, broader orientations that new levels of development and experience require. Successful in this concurrent maintenance and testing of values and truths by which life is lived, families weather the storms that beset them without losing their integrity as units or as individual members.

POSITIVE VALUES IN TEENAGE FAMILY LIFE

Family life, with its potentials for promoting human growth, becomes complicated and often threatened by the struggle and clash of diverse strivings, emotional difficulties, misconceptions, and rationalized behavior of individual family members. It is, nevertheless, the area of life from which come some of the deepest satisfactions in human experience. Fulfillment comes from adequate functioning. Those forms of functioning involved in human interaction can be the most satisfying of all.

Adults and youth in the family group are constantly striving toward their goals as persons and as family members. Many of the growth tasks and needs in terms of which the teenager strives to function are consistent and harmonious with the desires and felt responsibilities of the parents. But usually some yielding and a lot of "accepting" may be necessary on the part of youth as well as by the parents. It is in the very process thus of arriving at an integration of purposes (dynamic interaction) that both grow and experience deep satisfaction.

The adolescent, for example, needs to function more and more as a free agent in his own right. He is striving toward an independent adult status. The parent normally delights in the young person's attainments in the direction of adultlike functioning, and from them derives the satisfaction of the fulfillment of his own purposes and responsibilities. In adolescent strivings toward independence, however, there are likely to be some fumblings, errors in judgment, and behavior that looks like arrogance, impudence, and lack of respect for his elders. Parents are inclined to feel these concomitants of growth as threats to their status—assaults upon their dignity as parents. But parents can, through experience and some effort, come to take them for what they are, and become yielding and understanding.

The young person, on the other hand, senses any resistance the parent may feel to his strivings and awkward attempts at independence. He is inclined to resent that resistance. But if he also senses in his parent's behavior a genuine interest in his problems and some evidence of an understanding acceptance of him, he is able to yield a bit, eventually to accept the advice and counsel of his parent. Each grows through understanding the other. They both grow in their ability to accept others as they are. The relationship between them then grows closer, more affectionate and companionable.

In our culture the smallness of the family group limits the personal sources from which the child can draw for security and a sense of belonging. The kind of persons his parents happen to be, therefore, is for him an exceedingly important matter. If they are secure and growing individuals, happy in their relationships with each other, they are the greatest source of inner security a youngster can have. They not only provide a home atmosphere in which he can feel secure, but they also set the pattern of attitudes and interpersonal relationships which is conducive to human adjustment and growth.

When mutual respect for each other's point of view and a real concern for each other's well-being and peace of mind is the prevailing pattern of interaction, the child is inclined to follow that pattern. As he increasingly does so, the adult's confidence in him grows. He is allowed to assume more and more responsibility for his own activities and conduct. In such matters, for example, as being in at night he will not need to be *told* when he must be home. He clears his plans with his parents and gradually takes on the full responsibility himself. Because of his regard for his parents and his desire not to cause them worry or inconvenience, and especially because he knows they trust him, he meets family standards on his own responsibility. He thus achieves self-control and personal integration.

Parents need the love, confidence, and respect of their teenage children. They need it for the sense of success and accomplishment it gives them, for they have invested a great deal of themselves in the rearing of those sons and daughters. But they gain and maintain that love and respect only as they meet dependably, day by day, the developmental needs of their children. During adolescence those needs are as vital as at any other period of the child's development, and the understanding parent is just as necessary in the adequate meeting of those needs. Adolescents need parents, and they know it, most of the time.

SUMMARY

Teenagers today face special problems that confuse both them and the adults who live with them. While they struggle with their developmental tasks, and their parents work at theirs amidst the handicaps of traditional approaches, their families face their developmental tasks: (1) providing facilities for widely different needs, (2) working out money matters in the family with teenagers, (3) sharing responsibilities of family living, (4) putting the marriage relationship in focus, (5) bridging the communication gap, (6) keeping in touch with relatives, (7) widening horizons of teenagers and their parents, and (8) coping with the hazards, challenges, and dilemmas of teenagers' families in ways that preserve the positive values of families through the teen years.

SUGGESTED ACTIVITIES

1. Arrange for a showing of *Last Summer*, the 1969 film written and directed by Eleanor and Frank Perry, that describes what happens to four young adolescents in their final fling. In discussing the problems portrayed, Mrs. Perry says, "Conscience dies in the group"; Frank Perry comments, "Adolescents today are experimenting with some very dangerous things." Discuss these two points and others you collectively want to make. Write a review of the film from the point of view of problems teenagers face today.

2. Prepare a master chart of the several roles teenagers, their fathers, mothers, and families play in home and community (teenagers as sons or daughters, brothers or sisters, cousins, grandchildren, students, members of club, team, band, or class, workers, volunteers, etc.; fathers as husbands, workers, homemakers, and persons; mothers as wives, homemakers, workers, volunteers, and persons) indicating the possible conflicts to be expected between family members at the teenage stage, and the contradictions in the roles of the various members of the family at this stage of development.

3. Write a case history of some teenager whom you know well, listing the developmental tasks he or she is working on, with anecdotal material illustrating the relative success or failure with which each task is being achieved. Document.

4. Conduct an informal discussion among teenagers whose mothers work outside the home on either a part-time or full-time basis. Focus the discussion on how the adolescents feel about having their mothers work. Encourage full expression of both positive and negative attitudes. Keep notes sufficient to write up the group interview, with verbatim illustrations on how adolescents feel about their mothers' work.

5. Critically compare the various approaches recommended for bridging the generation gap found in the literature in such sources as:

Millard J. Bienvenu, Sr., *Parent–Teenager Communication,* Public Affairs Pamphlet, no. 438 (New York: Public Affairs Committee, 1969).

Evelyn Millis Duvall, *Today's Teen-Agers* (New York: Association Press, 1966), chaps. 16–18.

Bernice M. Moore, "Interaction among Generations," *Journal of Home Economics* 59, no. 8 (October 1967): 621–628.

Eva Schindler-Rainman, "Communicating with Today's Teenagers: An Exercise between Generations," *Children* 16, no. 6 (November-December 1969): 218–223.

6. Make a study of the therapeutic approaches being suggested by various professionals reporting in their respective journals on facets of their teenage practice. Start with such references as: Dale C. Garell, "A Hotline Telephone Service for Young People in Crisis," *Children* 16, no. 5 (October 1969): 177–180; Morris A. Wessel and Robert G. LaCamera, "The Pediatrician and the Adolescent," *Clinical Pediatrics* 6, no. 4 (April 1967): 227–233. Add recent reports on work with young drug-users, unwed teenage mothers, various types of juvenile delinquents, and other teenagers with problems.

7. Arrange a simple production of *High Pressure Area*, a short skit available from the National Association for Mental Health, 1790 Broadway, New York, New York 10019, depicting a provocative situation between an adolescent girl and her family. Discuss your reactions to the skit by identifying one by one with each of the principal characters: analyzing how the person felt and why, what he or she did and why, how he or she might have responded differently, and how these different responses might have altered the others' reactions and the course of the story.

8. Write a letter to your superintendent of schools, to your state department of education at your state capital, to the National Association of Secondary School Principals, 1201 Sixteenth Street, N.W., Washington, D.C. 20036, and to the United States

Department of Health, Education, and Welfare, Office of Education, Washington, D.C. In each case, inquire about what is being done in educating teenagers for friendship, love, marriage, and family living in the schools known to them. Collect and analyze your findings in the light of what you believe the need to be for education of a young person for mature living with the significant others of his life now and in the foreseeable future.

9. Discuss the following situation from case excerpts developed by Dr. Hazel Ingersoll, Department of Family Relations and Child Development, Oklahoma State University:

> Judy's mother loves to see Judy have a good time. She would, by her own admission, "work her fingers to the bone" for Judy. She wants Judy to have the most clothes and the most dates! She is overcome with joy when she is selected May Queen. She even suggests that she has a stage career all lined up for Judy. "And I'll go with her to see that she gets along all right. She will need me, then, more than now. And maybe she will meet and marry some rich nice young man." Meantime Judy's mother neglects her own appearance and has no life of her own apart from her child. She was widowed young after an early marriage and a frugal upbringing. What do you think are the mother's developmental tasks? How do they affect Judy? What suggestions do you have for Judy's mother? for Judy?

READINGS

Bachelor, Evelyn, Robert J. Ehrlich, Carolyn Harris, and Robert White, eds. *Teen Conflicts: Readings in Family Life and Sex Education.* Berkeley, Calif.: Diablo Press, 1968.

Bienvenu, Millard J., Sr. *Parent–Teen-ager Communication.* Public Affairs Pamphlet, no. 438. New York: Public Affairs Committee, 1969.

Broderick, Carlfred B. "Socio-Sexual Development in a Suburban Community." *Journal of Sex Research* 2, no. 1 (April 1966): 1–24.

Coleman, James S. *The Adolescent Society.* New York: Free Press, 1961.

Coopersmith, Stanley. *The Antecedents of Self-Esteem.* San Francisco: W. H. Freeman and Company, 1967.

Douvan, Elizabeth, and Joseph Adelson. *The Adolescent Experience.* New York: John Wiley and Sons, 1966.

Duvall, Evelyn Millis. *Today's Teen-Agers.* New York: Association Press, 1966.

Feuer, Lewis S. *The Conflict of Generations: The Character and Significance of Student Movements.* New York: Basic Books, 1969.

Ginott, Haim. *Between Parent and Teen-ager.* New York: Macmillan Company, 1969.

Group for the Advancement of Psychiatry. *Normal Adolescence.* New York: Group for the Advancement of Psychiatry, 1968.

Havighurst, Robert J., Paul Hoover Bowman, Gordon P. Liddle, Charles V. Matthews, and James V. Pierce. *Growing Up in River City*. New York: John Wiley and Sons, 1962.

Herzog, Elizabeth, and Catharine Richards, eds. *The Nation's Youth*. Children's Bureau Publication, no. 460. Washington, D.C., 1968.

LeMasters, E. E. *Parents in Modern America*. Homewood, Ill.: Dorsey Press, 1969.

Mead, Margaret. *Culture and Commitment: A Study of the Generation Gap*. New York: Doubleday, Natural History Press, 1969.

Mohr, George, and Marian Despres. *The Stormy Decade: Adolescence*. New York: Random House, 1958.

Offer, Daniel. *The Psychological World of the Teen-Ager: A Study of Normal Adolescent Boys*. New York: Basic Books, 1969.

Peck, Robert F., and Robert J. Havighurst. *The Psychology of Character Development*. New York: John Wiley and Sons, 1960.

Sklansky, Morris A., Sylvia W. Silverman, and Helen G. Rabichow. *The High School Adolescent: Understanding and Treating His Emotional Problems*. New York: Association Press, 1969.

Stone, L. Joseph, and Joseph Church. *Childhood and Adolescence*. Rev. ed. New York: Random House, 1968.

Time–Louis Harris Poll. "Changing Morality: The Two Americas." *Time*, June 6, 1969, pp. 26–27.

Wittenberg, Rudolph. *Adolescence and Discipline*. New York: Association Press, 1959.

Youth in Turmoil. New York: Time-Life Books, 1969.

PART 3 CONTRACTING FAMILIES

13 FAMILIES LAUNCHING YOUNG ADULTS

This time, like all times, is a very good one if we but know what to do with it. Emerson

There comes a time when the young of the family are ready to be launched from the home base. In twentieth-century American families this stage usually begins late in the teen years. It is sharply marked by the young person's departure from home to marry, to take a full-time job, to begin military service, to attend college—each of which removes the person from the parental home, never again to return as a child.

This stage begins with the first child leaving home as a young adult; it ends with the empty nest, as the last child leaves home for a life of his or her own. This stage may be an extremely short one, as is the case in the family with one child, a daughter who marries the year she graduates from high school. The stage may extend over a considerable period of time, as happens in an occasional family in which an unmarried son or daughter stays dependent in the home through the years. In mid-century United States the stage typically lasts six to seven years (chapter 5).

The processes of launching start during the earlier life cycle stages of the family, as the child or young person prepares for the decisions that will shape his future. His or her vocational future is planned or is left to chance long before the young person is out of school. Educational plans are formed, or they go by default early in the high school years. Timing for his military service depends in part upon his educational decisions. His or her marriage readiness is determined by previous successes or failures in making heterosexual adjustments. The process of cutting apron strings characterizes the teen years and sets the stage for the son's or daughter's emergence as an emancipated young adult. No matter how abrupt this may seem to be, the departure of the young person from his home is a process that has been going on through the years.

From maximum size at the beginning of the stage, the nuclear family shrinks during the launching period to the original married pair. From the multiplicity of interpersonal relationships with all the children at home, characteristic of the beginning of the stage, the family leaves this stage in its development with but one: the husband-wife relationship. Before the stage is completed, the husband-father may also be a grandfather, and the wife-mother a grandmother, as the first-married son or daughter has children. Thus later-launched siblings now hold positions of son-brother-uncle and daughter-sister-aunt. Similarly, with the marriage of the first child, the mother becomes a mother-in-law, the father a father-in-law, and their children brothers- and sisters-in-law of the newly recruited members of the family by marriage.

The launching stage is marked by the simultaneous release of the family's children and the recruitment of all new members (and their families) by marriage. Personal positional developmental tasks continue for the parents: as mother, homemaker, wife, person, and probably mother-in-law and grandmother; as father, provider, husband, person, and possibly father-in-law and grandfather. All of the children have their developmental tasks as young adults and younger children in the family of orientation, and, as they marry, as husbands and wives in the establishment phase of their family of procreation. Family developmental tasks are critical as the family shifts from a household with children to a husband-wife pair. The major family goal is the reorganization of the family into a continuing unity while releasing matured and maturing young people into lives of their own.

Factors Affecting Young Adults' Life Plans

Some young people plan farther ahead than do others. In general, as social class rises, the interest in life planning and the ability to predictably plan one's life increases. A study of 2,700 public, private, and trade high school students and 349 Yale undergraduates explored the question, "How far ahead have you planned your life?" The percentage of high school students planning five or more years ahead doubled from the lowest to the highest social class (from approximately 20 to 40 percent). The researchers conclude that "length of life planning had a reliable positive correlation with both the occupational and educational status of the young respondents' fathers."[1]

A further factor related to the young adult's plans for his life is the mobility of his family. Upward mobile parents tend either to carry their children along with them or to encourage their young people to climb; young people from nonmobile families tend to remain static in the great majority of cases (85 percent in one study).[2]

[1] Orville G. Brim and Raymond Forer, "A Note on the Relation of Values and Social Structure to Life Planning," *Sociometry* 19, no. 1 (March 1956): 54–60.

[2] Carson McGuire, "Conforming, Mobile, and Divergent Families," *Marriage and Family Living* 14, no. 2 (May 1952): 113.

Significantly more boys than girls tend to make extended life plans,[3] probably because a girl knows her future will be greatly influenced by her marriage and the plans of her husband. In both sexes there is more upward mobility drive among those whose family and interpersonal relations have been difficult than among those whose early interpersonal relations have been satisfying.[4] One relevant study shows that high levels of aspiration of 350 university students are related to (1) feelings of not being wanted by parents, (2) favoritism shown by parents, and (3) little attachment to parents (table 13-1).

[3] Brim and Forer, "A Note on the Relation of Values and Social Structure to Life Planning," p. 58.

[4] Evelyn Ellis, "Social Psychological Correlates of Upward Social Mobility among Unmarried Career Women," *American Sociological Review* 17, no. 5 (October 1952): 558–563; and Karen Horney, *The Neurotic Personality of Our Time* (New York: W. W. Norton and Company, 1938), pp. 162–187.

These findings support current psychoanalytic assumptions and general social theory that unsatisfactory interpersonal relationships in the family of orientation are significantly related to high aspirational levels. The hypothesis is that some young people, whose family life has been unhappy, struggle to better themselves as soon as they can cut loose from family ties. In some cases the high levels of aspiration are fantasies not related too closely to what is realizable. In others actual social mobility results from realistic efforts to improve.

The final factor influencing the young person's vision of who he may become is the factor of identification with some older person who serves as a model for the emerging young adult. The girl identifies with her teacher and wants to be just like her when she grows up. The boy greatly admires his coach or his leader at the YMCA and goes off like his hero for specialized training, possibly at the same col-

Table 13–1. *Interpersonal Relationships in the Family and Aspirational Level of 350 University Students*

Feelings of not being wanted by parents	Levels of aspiration		Favoritism shown by parents	Levels of aspiration		Degree of attachment to parents	Levels of aspiration	
	High	Low		High	Low		High	Low
Father .....(N = 117)....(N = 223)			Father ......(N = 95)....(N = 188)			Father .....(N = 110)....(N = 222)		
Some ....41.9........ 24.7			Yes ....45.3........ 30.9			Much ....33.6........ 50.9		
None ....58.1........ 75.3			No ....54.7........ 69.1			Little ....66.4........ 49.1		
Mother .....(N = 122)....(N = 223)			Mother ......(N = 95)....(N = 188)			Mother .....(N = 123)....(N = 223)		
Some ....34.4........ 20.2			Yes ....41.1........ 25.0			Much ....52.8........ 66.8		
None ....65.6........ 79.8			No ....58.9........ 75.0			Little ....47.2........ 33.2		

Source: Russell R. Dynes, Alfred C. Clarke, and Simon Dinitz, "Levels of Occupational Aspiration: Some Aspects of Family Experience as a Variable," *American Sociological Review* 21, no. 2 (April 1956): tables 1, 2, and 3, pp. 212–215.

lege and professional school. In such cases, the young adult patterns himself after the much admired adult and so makes the decisions and follows the course that brings him closer to his ideal.

To summarize, factors influencing the young adult's life planning and specific decisions upon leaving his family of orientation tend to operate in the following directions:

1. The higher the social class of the parents, the farther ahead the young person plans his life.

2. Young people from upward mobile families tend to continue climbing.

3. Young men tend to plan further ahead than do young women.

4. Young people from unhappy homes tend to have higher levels of aspiration than do young adults from satisfactory family backgrounds.

5. Young people who identify closely with an admired adult tend to pattern themselves after that older person in their own life plans.

DEVELOPMENTAL TASKS OF YOUNG ADULTS

The developmental tasks of young adults in the United States are intertwined with the decisions that must be made concurrently along several related lines. Throughout his life as a child and teenager, the individual lived within the expectancies of his age and grade. Now, upon his emergence from the norms of the age-grade system, he steps out into a life of his own, with his success or failure largely dependent upon the choices he makes as an individual. This very freedom is confusing, as Robert Havighurst vividly points out:

> Early adulthood seems . . . to be a period of storm and stress in America, and especially in the middle-class part of American society. The basic reason for this, when expressed in sociological terms, is that this is a relatively unorganized period in life which marks a transition from an age-graded to a social status-graded society. During childhood and adolescence one climbs the age ladder, getting new privileges and taking on new responsibilities with each step up the ladder. The ten-year-old has such and such privileges and such and such responsibilities, which enable him to look down on the eight-year-old, but also cause him to look up to the twelve-year-old. He climbs the age ladder, rung by rung, year by year, knowing that each step up gives him more prestige, along with new tasks and pleasures.
>
> This simple age-grading stops in our culture somewhere around sixteen to twenty. It is like reaching the end of the ladder and stepping off onto a new, strange cloud-land with giants and witches to be circumvented and the goose that lays the golden eggs to be

captured if only one can discover the know-how.

In the adult society prestige and power depend not so much on age as on skill and strength and wisdom, and family connections. Achieving the goals of life is not nearly so much a matter of waiting until one grows up to them as it was in the earlier years. There must be a strategy, based on an understanding of the new terrain, which can only be got by scouting around and getting the lay of the land for a few years. This is what young people do, and it often takes several years to learn how to get about efficiently and to go where one wants to go in the adult society in America.[5]

Choosing a Vocation

In some cultures a young man is expected to follow in his father's footsteps and carry on the family business. In the United States this pattern tends to hold largely in the upper-class families, where wealth and holdings necessitate grooming the sons of the family to carry on the family traditions. Young people today face many more vocational possibilities than were formerly available. In 1870 there were but 338 vocations, in contrast to tens of thousands by the late twentieth century in elec-

tronics, atomic energy, radar, television, plastics, medical, chemical, biological, and behavioral science.

Historically, a young woman groomed herself for marriage; all other interests were secondary. Today, a girl may be marriage-minded, but she is more active in civic affairs, and she looks forward to continuing some vocational interests both as an unmarried woman and as a wife and mother. Marriage still holds first place in the future plans of the great majority of American girls, but many of them think also in terms of developing vocational skills that will serve them through the years. As more fields open up for women, girls as well as boys face inevitable vocational choices.

Personal factors limit a young adult's fields of interest and influence the direction his lifework will take. Within a given direction, there is much to learn about specific vocations and about one's individual aptitudes, interests, preferences, and preparation. Part-time jobs, summer employment, and apprenticelike opportunities are helpful to many young people. Vocational guidance is available in many schools. Testing and counseling programs are designed to help young people find themselves in an occupational field suited to their abilities.

Parents who encourage their sons and daughters to explore various possibilities and to get the training needed for the chosen field greatly assist youth in accomplishing this developmental task. Attempt-

[5] Robert J. Havighurst, *Human Development and Education* (New York: Longmans, Green and Company, 1953), pp. 258–259.

ing to force a young person into a field in which he or she is not personally interested or suited often results in parental disappointment and failure of the young adult.

Getting an Education

The choice of a vocation determines in large measure the amount and the kind of education a young person must pursue. Conversely, the education a young person has influences his vocational opportunities. A boy who drops out of school to make "quick money" with which to buy a car and date his girl thereby limits his future possibilities for vocational choice and advancement as well as his earning capacity for the rest of his life. The mobile young person from a lower-class home may push on through school as the first in his family to graduate from high school and go on to college. In doing so, he broadens his vocational and economic future enormously.

The more education a boy has, the greater his lifetime earnings. In one recent year, the median American man who had graduated from college had lifetime earnings totaling well over one-half million dollars ($541,911), and the elementary school graduate less than half that amount ($246,525). The high school graduate in the meantime earned the intermediate sum of $340,520 (chart 13–1). College enrollments had increased to more than five million students by late 1969 and were estimated to reach ten and one-half million

Chart 13–1. *Estimated Lifetime Income, by Educational Achievement (Men 25 Years Old and Over, for the United States)*

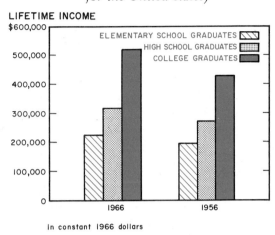

LIFETIME INCOME

In constant 1966 dollars

Source: U.S. Bureau of the Census, "Annual Mean Income, Lifetime Income, and Educational Attainment of Men in the United States, for Selected Years, 1956 to 1966," *Consumer Income,* Current Population Reports, series P-60, no. 56 (August 14, 1968), fig. 1, cover, and table F, p. 9.

by 1975, after which the number is expected to remain steady for several years.[6]

Getting an education is especially important today when there are relatively few nonskilled jobs, in comparison with the large number of highly skilled occupations requiring specialized training. A good general educational background is important not only for earning a living, but especially for living a life. The educated person who knows his way around in the physical and biological sciences, the humanities, and the social sciences is at home

[6] Associated Press release, December 11, 1969.

in much more of the world than the relatively illiterate. Every citizen today should have enough orientation to know how to tackle a problem and how to think through a point.

The question of how much education a girl should have has often been discussed. The general consensus today is that education is important for a woman, as a worker, as a wife and mother, as a citizen, and as a person. The girl with an education has something to offer that assures her of a better job at more money than is generally available to the less-well-educated woman. The statement, "when you educate a woman, you educate a family," recognizes that the woman's cultural background becomes the foundation of her family. Whatever she has learned of music, the arts, literature, medicine, history, philosophy, and religion can become part of the children's day-to-day education in the home. As a citizen and as a person, education is quite as important for a woman as it is for a man. This is recognized by members of both generations today.

Going to college, formerly a privilege of the well-to-do, has become a responsibility of modern youth. As recently as 1940, only one-third of the nation's high school graduates went to college; by the 1970s the majority of them did.[7] The reasons for this rapid increase were: the nation's rising affluence that made college a possibility for millions of young Americans whose forefathers had never aspired to higher education; coercive economic, social, and military pressures upon youth; the need for highly trained manpower in a complex industrial age; a general holding pattern before plunging millions of young people into competition with established adults; and conformity to the pace of conventional escalators to success. The results were not only the best-educated generation the nation ever had, but also violent protests by masses of involuntary students who felt they were on campus because they had to be, and might as well fight for some say in running it.[8]

An Urban Research Corporation study between January and June, 1969, found 215,000 students active in 292 major protests on 232 campuses having a total enrollment of one-third of the college student population of the United States. Demands of nonwhite students for more black faculty and students, black studies, and better facilities touched off 49 percent of the protests. Ranking second were demands for more student power (44 percent), and third were war-related concerns (22 percent) such as military recruiting, ROTC, military research, and stopping the war in Vietnam. The study concludes, "the striking finding about white student protests

---

[7] "Class of '69: The Violent Years," *Newsweek,* June 23, 1969, pp. 68–73.

[8] President Kingman Brewster, Jr., of Yale, in an address at Michigan State University, reported in "I'm Here Because I Have to Be . . . ," *Christian Science Monitor,* January 14, 1970, p. 9.

is that they were not dominated by the New Left."[9]

Psychological tests and intensive interviews with Harvard students find the alienated characterized by distrust, isolation, pessimism, hostility, and negativism. Alienated students appear to have dissatisfied, frustrated parents—mothers whose talents have not been fulfilled in marriage, who depreciate their husbands (whose idealism has been crushed by reality) and turn to their sons instead.[10] Historical review of student movements through the centuries in the Old World and the New concludes that conflict of generations has always been a driving force in history.[11] Educator Dr. Harold Taylor sees the student revolt as a constructive contribution of the younger generation to what might have continued as complacent university administration and teaching.[12] There is general recognition that this best-educated generation has not only the idealism of youth, but also the critical abilities and the power to act and to raise questions Americans should have asked long ago.

---

[9] John Herbers, "Analysis of Student Protests Finds Most Nonviolent with New Left a Minor Factor," *New York Times*, January 14, 1970, p. C-13.

[10] Kenneth Keniston, *Young Radicals: Notes on Committed Youth* (New York: Harcourt, Brace and World, 1968).

[11] Lewis S. Feuer, *The Conflict of Generations: The Character and Significance of Student Movements* (New York: Basic Books, 1969).

[12] Harold Taylor, *Students without Teachers: The Crisis in the University* (New York: McGraw-Hill Book Company, 1969).

Serving the Country

Young adults today tend to be socially sensitive and service-oriented. In a national survey of college and noncollege youth between the ages of seventeen and twenty-three, 93 percent said that service to others was important to them; 96 percent responded that doing work that is more than just a job was personally important; 86 percent would welcome more emphasis on personal responsibility; 79 percent felt that changing society was important; and 99 percent that love was important to them. At the same time only one out of eight young adults would welcome vigorous protests of minority groups, and 94 percent believed that society needs some legally based authority in order to prevent chaos. Very small minorities would do away with the military, the universities, trade unions, political parties, big business, and the mass media, but better than two-thirds of all young adults polled would like to see substantial changes made in all of these aspects of "the establishment." More noncollege youth than students felt obligated to serve the country regardless of their personal views about the justness of a war, and a total of 66 percent felt that resisting the draft was basically wrong.[13]

---

[13] CBS News, *Generations Apart* (Survey conducted for CBS News by Daniel Yankelovich, Inc.) (New York: Columbia Broadcasting System, 1969), pp. 5–6, 9–10, 22.

Military service is a responsibility that thrusts itself upon a young man at the time when he is leaving home to establish a life of his own. It is then that he is trying to achieve the universal developmental tasks of fitting himself for a vocation, completing his education, becoming socially acceptable, choosing and winning a wife, getting married, and settling into a home of his own. Many questions come tumbling in upon both the young man and his girl as he reaches draft age. There is no single answer to questions of how best to juggle the timing of education, career preparation and establishment, marriage, military service, and full citizenship.

Each young man, each young woman, each young couple today must work out the solution that makes the most sense in their particular situation. That so many young adults accomplish this task so well is a credit to the generation of young adults today. At the same time, it is understandable that many fellows and girls are anxious, baffled, and bewildered by the multitude of major decisions that must be made during this period. The impulsive, the impetuous, the hysterical fringe of the young adult population who rush into some premature "solution" (only to find themselves in one of the traps for the unwary) are the problematic minority.

There are many community, church, school, and family aids to young men and women facing the likelihood of military service. Today, more than ever before, young people need opportunities to think through, under qualified leadership, the many paths that stretch ahead for them, of which military service is but one. Boys need some preparation for what to expect in service, what the alternatives are, and how to choose the time that will be best for each of the demands and responsibilities they face as young adult males. Girls in their teens and early twenties are ready for discussion of what it means to be a woman, whom to marry and when, and what their role is in the many months and miles of separation from lover or husband that military service imposes. Together the sexes face the developmental tasks of dating, courtship, marriage, and family establishment in the midst of a military economy as they enter the launching years. The decisions about military service are made with vocational, educational, social, marital, familial, and personal values all crowding in for multifocused attention.

Becoming Marriageable

Today's young people have full responsibility for finding a place for themselves among their peers, making friends, getting dates, and becoming the kind of marriageable young men or women who can win and hold a mate. This is not an easy task. Many young women who are of good marriage potential miss out because of shyness, social ineptness, and inability to get along comfortably with eligible young men. Some of our most able young men lose themselves so completely in their vocational interests that they miss out on normal social contacts with members of the other sex. A man may be a good engineer or an outstanding physician, but if he has not learned to get along pleasantly with women and to find deep satisfaction in warm friendships with one or more especially compatible women, he may be easy prey for some unscrupulous female when the time comes for him to marry. There are many instances of a young man of outstanding ability hurriedly plunging into marriage with some relatively inferior woman largely because he has not developed the social, emotional, domestic sides of his personality.

Leonard S. is a case in point. He is a brilliant scientist, but in social affairs he feels lost. He is embarrassed at meeting new people. He is shy and uncomfortable with women generally. His conversational abilities are limited to the field of his specialty and superficial comments about the weather. He is now nearly twenty-seven, has never gone seriously with a girl, doesn't know how to dance, and has no contacts with mixed groups of young adults his own age. Several weeks ago, a girl behind the salad counter at the corner cafeteria began to flirt with him. At first he blushed and stammered some nonsensical reply. She told him she thought he was "real sweet," and on her day off brought her dinner out to eat with him. Things moved fast from then on, and they are to be married next Saturday. Leonard's family is shocked at his marrying a lower-class girl who never went beyond sixth grade. Leonard has questions himself about what he is getting into. The girl's family is happy about the financial security she will acquire by the marriage, but openly ridicules Leonard as a "brain." But, at the moment, Leonard is powerless to stop the affair.

Surely there are many factors contributing to such a situation as Leonard faces. The obvious ones are social inexperience and lack of competency with others in personal and social relationships. Failures in accomplishing these developmental tasks become problems for many teenagers and young adults. Such continuing failures seriously block or distort the processes that lead to marriage.

Among college students there is general agreement on the traits preferred in members of the other sex both as dating and as marriage partners. Both men and women students rate as "crucially important" in a date such qualities as (1) well groomed and well mannered, (2) sense of humor, (3) considerate, (4) emotional maturity, (5) ambitious and industrious, (6) health and vitality, and (7) sensible about money. Preferred traits for marriage partners include these seven qualities, plus the trait of affection (by more than 80 percent of both men and women). Much more than in dating partners, students value in marriage partners such characteristics as similar background, normal heredity, good earner or cook, intellectual and religious nature.[14] An eleven-university survey shows roughly similar percentages of men and women students listing such qualities of their ideal mate as highly important.[15]

No area is more confusing than that of sex expression before marriage. Both sexes have increasingly greater freedom, but premarital chastity continues to be the desirable alternative for many college students, with about a third feeling that premarital sex relations could never be justified, a fifth saying that virginity is a highly important factor in mate selection, and nearly two-fifths "not sure" they would break their engagement if this rule were broken.[16] More men than women are permissive in their sex attitudes and behavior. But, as love enters the relationship, men are only half as likely to engage in premarital intercourse (and women more than twice as apt to go all the way) with their loved ones as with friends and acquaintances.[17]

Reviewing changing sex standards, Reiss finds the majority of college men today adhering fairly closely to the double standard, modified by a feeling that abstinence is really the best policy. Most college women tolerate the double standard but feel that abstinence for both sexes before marriage is preferable, and that petting with affection is sometimes acceptable.[18]

Kirkendall's research into six levels of attachment (from prostitute and pickup to fiancée) between premarital sex partners suggests that such criteria as increasing trust, integrity, and self-respect within the interpersonal relationship be used as a basis for making moral judgments.[19]

Sex is not a simple biological response, but reflects the personalities of the partners and expresses the type of persons they are more dramatically than any other type of behavior. Sex is not and cannot be a strictly private affair, of concern only to the partners, for it is at the core of family life and is of central social concern. One of the most difficult tasks for a young man or woman is determining what is best in the expression of love and sex at a time when society no longer draws a clear line between right and wrong. A valid sex code that protects social, family, and personal values must be built.[20]

[14] Lester E. Hewitt, "Student Perceptions of Traits Desired in Themselves as Dating and Marriage Partners," *Marriage and Family Living* 20, no. 4 (November 1958): 344–349.

[15] Rose K. Goldsen, Morris Rosenberg, Robin M. Williams, Jr., and Edward A. Suchman, *What College Students Think* (Princeton, N.J.: D. Van Nostrand Company, 1960), p. 90.

[16] Ibid., p. 94.

[17] Winston W. Ehrmann, *Premarital Dating Behavior* (New York: Henry Holt and Company, 1959), p. 179.

[18] Ira L. Reiss, *Premarital Sexual Standards in America* (Glencoe, Ill.: Free Press, 1960), pp. 250–252.

[19] Lester A. Kirkendall, *Premarital Intercourse and Interpersonal Relationships* (New York: Julian Press, 1961).

[20] Sylvanus M. Duvall, *Men, Women, and Morals* (New York: Association Press, 1952); and "Sex Fictions and Facts," *Look* 24, no. 8 (April 12, 1960): 47 ff.; see also Evelyn Millis Duvall, *Why Wait Till Marriage?* (New York: Association Press, 1965).

Student preferences for responsible interpersonal relationships between dating partners as marriage becomes a possibility are apparent in the differences in characteristics chosen for serious dates as contrasted with those for casual campus dates (table 13–2).

The researcher observes from these data: "The over-all impression given . . . is one of increasing rapprochement between the sexes as they begin to get serious with one another. Moreover, this rapprochement centers about themes of emotional maturity, intelligence, and affectionateness which appear conducive to marital adjustment."[21]

Success in dating and in becoming marriageable seems to be dependent upon a number of factors. There is evidence that such success is closely related to personal and family background. One study finds that:

The seniors not dating presented a more negative, less wholesome picture in family relationships, feeling of self-regard, and social relations than did the other seniors. . . .

. . . A relatively large number of young people had worried during childhood about their physical characteristics, development and appearance. These students had had and were still having difficulty in their relations with others because of shyness and sensitivity. . . .

21 Robert O. Blood, Jr., "Uniformities and Diversities in Campus Dating Preferences," *Marriage and Family Living* 18, no. 1 (February 1956): 44. Note also John W. Hudson and Lura F. Henze, "Campus Values in Mate Selection: A Replication," *Journal of Marriage and the Family* 31, no. 4 (November 1969): 772–775.

Table 13–2. *Significant Differences between Percentage of Students Preferring Specified Characteristics in Casual and Serious Dating Partners for All Students, for Men Students, and for Women Students*

Items	Casual dates	Serious dates
A. *Discriminations Made by Both Sexes*		
1. Is emotionally mature	84.2	100.0
2. Is dependable	87.8	99.3
3. Is a well-rounded person	84.6	98.5
4. Is affectionate	69.6	97.6
5. Is a good listener	88.3	97.4
6. Gets along with friends of own sex	80.6	96.4
7. Is ambitious and energetic	65.3	84.7
8. Has my family's approval	24.5	72.1
9. Knows how to dance well	52.6	31.9
B. *Discriminations Made by Men Students*		
10. Has good sense, is intelligent	88.4	100.0
11. Is an intelligent conversationalist	85.3	100.0
12. Is honest, straightforward	80.0	96.8
13. Is willing to join a group	82.1	93.7
14. Has polished manners	66.3	81.1
15. Doesn't have a reputation for petting	38.9	74.7
16. Doesn't have a reputation for necking	34.7	67.4
17. Dates popular students only	9.5	3.2
C. *Discriminations Made by Women Students*		
18. Is willing to neck on occasion	34.3	67.7
19. Is willing to pet on occasion	8.2	32.1
20. Is good-looking, attractive	61.2	45.5
21. Goes to popular places	38.8	22.6

Percentage of respondents choosing item personal preferences

Source: Robert O. Blood, Jr., "Uniformities and Diversities in Campus Dating Preferences," *Marriage and Family Living* 18, no. 1 (February 1956): 43.

The most significant finding with respect to their *social relationships* was the relatively large number of young people who, by their senior year in high school, were having few social contacts, especially with the other sex.[22]

In some high schools, the path to popularity is through athletics for boys and activities for girls. In schools where more young men are headed for the professions, intelligence and good scholarship may be (to a lesser extent than athletics) a road to social acceptance.[23]

Opportunities for gaining social experience, as well as for dating, appear to be related to the social class of the young person's family (chapter 2). In general, a larger percentage of young people in the higher social class date, and they date more frequently and with more persons than do boys and girls from the lower socioeconomic groups.[24]

Success in dating and in gaining social experience tends to be cumulative. The more dating is done, the smoother it becomes. Studies of the frequency of dating among both high school and college students indicate that from the ages of sixteen to twenty-one years, the frequency of dating increases with age; furthermore, the earlier university students had begun to date in their teens, the more frequently they dated in college.[25]

Frequency of dating is significantly related to one's dating status. Those who are playing the field have fewer dates than do those who are going steady or are engaged. Among college students the findings of one study are: "Among the men those going steady in each age classification date around twice as frequently as those playing the field. Among the women . . . those going steady or engaged date much more frequently than those playing the field. These differences are statistically highly significant for each sex and for all age levels, except eighteen among the women."[26]

Going steady is usually defined as dating exclusively one person with whom there are generally recognized expectations, loyalties, and some mutual identification.[27] It has arisen in recent years, with the coming of large, heterogeneous high school populations and complex urban communities, for what seem to be several inter-

[22] Opal Powell Wolford, "How Early Background Affects Dating Behavior," *Journal of Home Economics* 40, no. 9 (November 1948): 505–506.

[23] James S. Coleman, *The Adolescent Society* (New York: Free Press, 1961).

[24] August B. Hollingshead, *Elmtown's Youth* (New York: John Wiley and Sons, 1949), pp. 229–230.

[25] Samuel H. Lowrie, "Factors Involved in the Frequency of Dating," *Marriage and Family Living* 18, no. 1 (February 1956): 49–51.

[26] Ibid., pp. 48–49.

[27] Robert D. Herman, "The 'Going Steady' Complex: A Re-examination," *Marriage and Family Living* 17, no. 1 (February 1955): 36–37.

Table 13–3. *Mean Number of Dates per Week by Sex, Age, and Dating Status of University Students Dating for Previous Month*

	Men					Women				
	Playing field		Going steady			Playing field		Going steady		
Age	Mean	No. of students	Mean	No. of students	Critical ratio*	Mean	No. of students	Mean	No. of students	Critical ratio*
18	1.2	110	2.5	39	4.6	2.0	119	2.5	68	1.9
19	1.5	165	2.8	90	8.3	2.2	129	2.9	100	3.5
20	1.7	112	3.5	77	8.3	2.2	105	3.6	69	6.0
21	1.8	91	3.2	55	5.5	1.9	62	3.6	66	6.8
Total	1.5	478	3.0	261	—	2.1	415	3.1	303	—

Source: Samuel H. Lowrie, "Factors Involved in the Frequency of Dating," *Marriage and Family Living* 18, no. 1 (February 1956): 49.

* A critical ratio of 3.5 or over is considered statistically significant, that is, the relationship between the two variables is such that it cannot be attributed to chance.

related reasons, in the words of young people themselves:

1. "If you go steady, you are more sure of a date when you want one." (*Date insurance*.)[28] Among high school students a frequent observation is, "If you go at all, you have to go steady."

2. "You aren't anybody in our school if you don't go steady." (*Group acceptance*.) High school students report that going steady is important for status reasons, and that "going steady was the thing to do in my high school."[29]

3. "Be seen twice with the same person, and you are going steady—the crowd sees to that." (*Social pressure*.) If John dates Mary a couple of times over the weekend, by Monday they are going steady, whether they have decided to or not, for by then their friends line up behind them as a pair and expect them to go steady from then on.[30] Such social pressure is found in many high school, community, and campus situations.

4. "Going steady is a lot easier and safer than dating unknowns." (*Personal security*.) A girl knows what her steady boyfriend will expect of her on a date; she is secure with him as she cannot be with a strange boy, whom she may or may not be able to manage. A boy is secure knowing his steady girl expects him, and he finds it easier and cheaper to go steady than to play

[28] Ruth Connor and Edith Flinn Hall, "The Dating Behavior of College Freshmen and Sophomores," *Journal of Home Economics* 44, no. 4 (April 1952): 280.

[29] Herman, "The 'Going Steady' Complex: A Reexamination," p. 39.

[30] Evelyn Millis Duvall, *The Art of Dating*, rev. ed. (New York: Association Press, 1967), p. 218.

the field. There is probably less exploitation in going steady than in random dating, as Herman observes.[31]

5. "We would rather go steady than to date anyone else available." (*Mutual preference.*) The two persons prefer each other to any other possibilities on the scene. They may be fond of each other, and so prefer associating with one another than with other, more casual dating partners.[32]

6. "When you go steady, you learn to adjust to one person, and to become more mature in your understanding of each other." (*Mature association.*) In this sense, going steady is good preparation for marriage based upon companionship and mutual understanding.[33]

Adults and many young people themselves see some of the problems related to going steady. In general, these tend to be: (1) going steady limits social contacts; (2) going steady interferes with work responsibilities and takes up too much time; (3) going steady often brings more emotional and sexual involvement than the two people are ready for; and (4) it is hard to get out of going steady after both names have been coupled together for a long time. Young people tend to agree that it is not wise to go steady too soon before the two people have had some general experience with members of the other sex. They recognize generally that going steady is not wise if the two people are to be separated for a considerable period of time. Then their social life will be severely curtailed if they try "to be true to each other," and yet they are not close enough to participate socially as a couple. College men and women are particularly aware of the importance of breaking off going steady when the two people have outgrown each other. The solution of the dilemma of becoming seriously involved with a steady who will not be a suitable mate is difficult to work through comfortably, posing a serious problem in present-day patterns in going steady.

The most favorable situations for those who want to become more marriageable are found in the families, in the schools and colleges, in the community programs that foster wholesome contact between the sexes in a wide variety of interests and activities. The responsibility is upon the young man or woman to develop the social skills and to introduce oneself into the situations where mingling with congenial persons is increasingly comfortable and competent. For those young adults who have reached marriage age without accomplishing this developmental task, there are at least two types of supportive services that might be helpful. The first is the introduction service that offers help, for a small charge, to those desiring friend-

---

[31] Herman "The 'Going Steady' Complex: A Reexamination," p. 40.

[32] Evelyn Millis Duvall, *Love and the Facts of Life* (New York: Association Press, 1963), p. 283.

[33] Ibid., pp. 285–286.

ship or marriage.[34] The second is the group counseling or educational program designed to help socially inept young men and women develop the specific skills, social graces, and personal adequacies needed to become more marriageable. The time may come when such programs of remedial socialization are widespread, just as programs in remedial reading, remedial speech, and the like are now generally available.

In summarizing this section, we recognize the relevancy of the concept of the "teachable moment" (chapter 6) in the process of becoming marriageable. If the person as a young teenager learns to dance and to date and to associate with his peer group acceptably, while the others are working on these same tasks, he gets group support in his efforts. When he is awkward, the others are too, so the learning process is tolerable. But if, for some reason, he or she has been delayed in this particular task, it will be more difficult later on when it must be done in relative solitude, carrying the added burden of feelings of personal inadequacy and social isolation. Social success in the past facilitates success in present efforts. The process of becoming marriageable is one that typically goes on through the entire second decade and some of the third decade of life for many, many persons.

[34] Ernest W. Burgess and Harvey J. Locke, *The Family: From Institution to Companionship* (New York: American Book Company, 1953), pp. 354–362.

Learning to Appraise and Express Love

Learning to love is a lifetime achievement. It begins in infancy, flowers in the teens and twenties, bears fruit in the rich, full years of childbearing and rearing, and colors and warms the rest of life. At no stage of life is it more difficult to assay and to express responsibly than in the teen and young adult years, when it is confused and intertwined with maturing sex drives.

In a culture that allows freedom of access between the sexes from an early age and establishes marriage on the basis of being in love, it is not surprising to find young people repeatedly asking three questions about love and its expression: (1) What is love? (2) How can you tell when you are really in love (enough to build a marriage on)? and (3) How far is it wise to go in physical expression of love and sex interests before marriage? Each of these questions is complex. There are no completely satisfying or well-substantiated answers to any of these questions. Yet, when so many young men and women want to base their behavior upon some understanding of what is involved, it behooves us to rally resources that are available for their use.

What is love? Love is the most powerful force known to man. It is indeed "the greatest thing in the world." It is also the most mysterious and the hardest to describe. In the outline below we see some outstanding attempts at definition or description made by men and women of various orientations through the years:

Apostle Paul

Love is patient and kind; love is not jealous or boastful; it is not arrogant or rude. Love does not insist on its own way; it is not irritable or resentful; it does not rejoice at wrong, but rejoices in the right. Love bears all things, believes all things, hopes all things, endures all things.[35]

Theologian Paul Johnson

Love is a growing interest in, appreciation of, and responsibility for another person.[36]

Poetess
Elizabeth Barrett Browning

How do I love thee? Let me count the ways.
I love thee to the depth and breadth and height
My soul can reach, when feeling out of sight
For the ends of Being and ideal Grace.
I love thee to the level of every day's
Most quiet need, by sun and candlelight.
I love thee freely, as men strive for Right;
I love thee purely, as they turn from praise.
I love thee with the passion put to use
In my old griefs, and with my childhood's faith.
I love thee with a love I seemed to lose
With my lost saints,—I love thee with the breath,
Smiles, tears, of all my life!—and, if God choose,
I shall but love thee better after death.[37]

---

[35] I Corinthians, 13:4–7.

[36] Quoted in Harold Mackey, "How Do I Love Thee?" *Family Coordinator* 18, no. 2 (April 1969): 122.

[37] "How Do I Love Thee?" from the *Standard Book of British and American Verse* (Garden City, N.Y.: Garden City Publishing Company, 1932), pp. 431–432.

FAMILY DEVELOPMENT

Anthropologist Ashley Montagu	To love and to be loved is as necessary to the organism as the breathing of air. Insofar as the organism fails in loving, it fails in living, for to live and love is, for a human being, the equivalent of healthy living. To live as if to live and love were one is not simply an ideal to be achieved, but a potentiality to be realized, a destiny to be fulfilled.[38]
Human relations professor F. Alexander Magoun	Love is the passionate and abiding desire on the part of two or more people to produce together the conditions under which each can be and spontaneously express his real self; to produce together the intellectual soil and an emotional climate in which each can flourish, far superior to what either could achieve alone. . . . Love is concerned with the realities of life; not with ideas about romantic idealism which cannot be embodied in life. Love sees faults as well as virtues. Love knows and unhesitatingly accepts the fact that no one is perfect. . . . Love is self-discovery and self-fulfillment through healthy growth with and for the other person.[39]
Biologist and philosopher Julian Huxley	As a biologist, but also as a human being, I want to affirm the unique importance of love in life—an affirmation badly needed in a tormented age like ours, where violence and disillusion have joined forces with undigested technological advance to produce an atmosphere of cynicism and crude materialism. . . . Personal love is indispensable both for the continuation of the species, and for the full development of the individual. Love is part of personal education; through love, the self learns to grow. . . . Love is a positive emotion, an enlargement of life; it leads on toward greater fulfillment and counteracts human hate and destructive impulses.[40]

---

[38] Ashley Montagu, ed., *The Meaning of Love* (New York: Julian Press, 1953), p. 19.

[39] F. Alexander Magoun, *Love and Marriage* (New York: Harper and Brothers, 1948), pp. 4, 16–17.

[40] Julian Huxley, "All about Love," *Look* 19, no. 14 (July 12, 1955): 29.

Human development educator Daniel A. Prescott	Love involves more or less empathy with the loved one. . . . One who loves is deeply concerned for the welfare, happiness, and development of the loved one. . . . One who loves finds pleasure in making his resources available to the loved one . . . the loving person seeks a maximum of participation in the activities that contribute to the welfare, happiness, and development of the loved one. . . . Love is most readily and usually achieved within the family circle but can be extended to include many other individuals. . . . The good effects of love are not limited to the loved one but promote the happiness and further development of the loving one as well. . . . Love is not rooted primarily in sexual dynamics or hormonal drives, although it may well have large erotic components.[41]
Psychologist and philosopher Harry A. Overstreet	The love of a person implies, not the possession of that person, but the affirmation of that person. It means granting him, gladly, the full right to his unique humanhood. One does not truly love a person and yet seek to enslave him—by law or by bonds of dependence and possessiveness. Whenever we experience a genuine love, we are moved by this transforming experience toward a capacity for good will.[42]
Psychiatrist Smiley Blanton	. . . It is in the joyful union of a man with a woman that the jangled forces of life fall at last into harmony. Here, in the eternal longing of one to join with the other, we may discern an infinite wisdom distilled from billions of years of patient evolution. Here lies the primordial pattern of all our striving and all our bliss. It is the secret spring that animates our deepest desires and shapes our loftiest dreams. It generates the restless tension, the driv-

---

[41] Daniel A. Prescott, "Role of Love in Human Development," *Journal of Home Economics* 44, no. 3 (March 1952): 174–175.

[42] Harry A. Overstreet, *The Mature Mind* (New York: W. W. Norton and Company, 1949), p. 103.

ing energy, that ever moves us to aspire and to achieve. From its profound yearning comes all creation, whether of the body or spirit. Man and woman, united in loving endeavor, truly encompass the sum and substance of human life.[43]

Clinical psychologist Rollo May

Loveliness shall be loved not because of infantile needs, or because it stands for breast, or because it is aim-inhibited sex, or because it aids adjustment, or because it will make us happy—but simply because it is lovely. Loveliness exercises a pull upon us; we are drawn to life by love.[44]

By the time a young person reaches the late teens and twenties, he or she is experienced in loving. One of the most important things he or she has learned within the family through the years of childhood and adolescence is to love.

Love does not simply spring forth some moonlight night without warning. We do not *fall* in love. We *learn* to love through a lifetime of experience in loving. By the time boy meets girl, a great deal has happened to both of them to make them ready for their interest in each other. In fact, by that time they both are old hands at loving, in many ways. Each has grown up through the phases of emotional maturity to the place where he and she are capable of loving and being loved. In a real sense we *grow* into love, both individually and as couples.[45]

If, through the years of growing up within the family, the young adult has learned how to love and be loved, he or she is ready for the urgent developmental tasks of appraising love feelings in terms of readiness for marriage. If there has been deprivation or distortion of love through the years of growing up, it may be exceedingly difficult to achieve and gauge the level of mature love that is needed as a foundation for a successful marriage.

The young person often needs a functional answer to the urgent question, "Is this *it*?" If the marriage is to be based

[43] Smiley Blanton, "Love or Perish," *Woman's Home Companion*, January 1956, p. 70, copyright, 1956, Crowell-Collier Publishing Company.

[44] Rollo May, *Love and Will* (New York: W. W. Norton and Company, 1969).

[45] Evelyn Millis Duvall, *Facts of Life and Love for Teenagers*, rev. ed. (New York: Association Press, 1956), p. 257.

Table 13–4. *Differences between Infatuation and Love*

Infatuation	Love
1. Is the term applied to past attachments, oftentimes	1. Is the term used to refer to a current attachment, usually
2. Focuses frequently on quite unsuitable persons	2. Object of affection is likely to be a suitable person
3. Parents often disapprove	3. Parents tend to approve
4. Feelings of guilt, insecurity, and frustration are frequent	4. Is associated with feelings of self-confidence, trust, and security
5. Tends to be self-centered and restricted	5. Kindlier feelings toward other people generally are associated
6. Narrowly focuses on but a few highly visible or fantasied traits	6. Broadly involves the whole personality
7. Most frequent among young adolescents and immature persons	7. Grows through the years with emotional maturity
8. Simultaneous attachments to two or more at the same time are possible	8. Loyalty centers in mutual commitment and involvement
9. Can reoccur soon after a previous affair is over	9. May slowly develop again after a previous lover has gone
10. Boredom is frequent when sexual excitement dies down	10. An ongoing sense of being alive when together precludes boredom
11. Partners depend upon external amusement for fun	11. Joy is in many common interests and in each other
12. Little change in the relationship over time	12. Relationship changes and grows with ongoing association
13. Shallow sensations come and go	13. Deepening feelings provide steady warmth as more of life is shared
14. Problems and barriers are usually disregarded	14. Problems are tackled and worked out as they arise
15. Romantic illusions have little regard for reality	15. Faces reality with faith in growth and improvement
16. Tends to last but a short time	16. Tends to last over a long period of time
17. Little mutual exploration of personality values and aspirations	17. Shares hopes and dreams, feelings and meanings
18. May be stereotyped "romance for romance's sake"	18. Tends to be highly individual, unique, and person-centered
19. Can exploit the other as a person	19. Has a protective, nurturing, caring concern
20. A poor basis for marriage	20. Enough to build a marriage on, perhaps—if other things are right

Source: Evelyn Millis Duvall and Reuben Hill, *When You Marry*, rev. ed. (New York: Association Press; Boston: D. C. Heath and Company, 1967), pp. 40–41, quoted with permission.

upon love, it becomes imperative to know whether the feeling one has toward a particular person is "the real thing," especially when love comes and goes, as apparently is quite usual. One study of 896 love affairs of college men and women found that 644 of them (71.8 percent) had been broken off.[46]

Opportunities for discussion, individual and group counseling, education for marriage, premarital conferences, and confidential relationships with trusted adults in the family, the community, the church, and in schools and colleges prove helpful to many young adults who are at the point of making personal decisions on the basis of the mutuality and potential permanence of their love feelings.

Whether a love affair goes on into marriage or breaks off after a few dates, there still remains the question of the degree of expression of affection between the two lovers. How much intimacy is appropriate to various situations and relationships? How far is it wise to go before marriage? These are two questions especially pertinent today. It is generally agreed that two lovers need to express their affection for each other, not only for their emotional well-being and development, but as good preparation for marriage. There is general recognition, too, that there is a progression of intimacy through the process of dating, going steady, being engaged, and getting married. Holding hands, kissing goodnight, and the lighter forms of contact are typical early in the relationship. As the involvement increases, there is commensurate development of intimacy patterns through what young people themselves generally recognize as "necking," "light petting," and "going all the way." At what point an unmarried couple stops depends upon a number of factors.[47]

According to one research study of two university populations, "there is a striking tendency for females to be less tolerant than males with respect to petting to climax, premarital sex intercourse, intercourse with prostitutes, and extramarital sex intercourse."[48] The influence of social class is seen in a study within another state university student group: "The marked tendency of males to descend the social ladder for dating companions seems to be motivated primarily by a desire to find willing sexual partners."[49]

---

[46] Clifford Kirkpatrick and Theodore Caplow, "Emotional Trends in the Courtship Experience of College Students as Expressed by Graphs with Some Observations on Methodological Implications," *American Sociological Review* 10, no. 5 (October 1945): 619–629.

[47] For detailed treatment see Jessie Bernard, *The Sex Game* (Englewood Cliffs, N.J.: Prentice-Hall, 1968); Vance Packard, *The Sexual Wilderness* (New York: David McKay Company, 1968); Ira L. Reiss, *The Social Context of Premarital Permissiveness* (New York: Holt, Rinehart and Winston, 1967); and Duvall, *Why Wait Till Marriage?*

[48] Clifford Kirkpatrick, Sheldon Stryker, and Philip Buell, "Attitudes towards Male Sex Behavior," *American Sociological Review* 17, no. 5 (October 1952): 586.

[49] Winston W. Ehrmann, "Influence of Comparative Social Class of Companion upon Premarital Heterosexual Behavior," *Marriage and Family Living* 17, no. 1 (February 1955): 52.

Similar findings are reported from other studies, indicating that girls from the lower classes are more willing and available sexual partners than those from higher educational and social levels.[50] Boys, too, show striking differences in premarital sex experience by social class as indicated by level of education achieved. Studying the percentage of total sex outlet in intercourse with companions among sixteen- to twenty-year-old boys, Kinsey found the highest percentage of sex intercourse among the least well-educated: 50.62 percent among males with less than eighth-grade education, 39.49 percent among males with high school education, and 9.13 percent among males with some education beyond high school.[51] No major change in the incidence of premarital coitus was reported two decades after Kinsey, although attitudes in the interim had changed in the direction of putting more responsibility on the individual for his conduct.[52]

Premarital pregnancies have been found more frequent: (1) during the depression years when marriage was more difficult, (2) among people who married young, (3) among couples who were married in a civil or secular ceremony, and (4) for those who were classified occupationally as laborers.[53]

The moral, as well as the emotional and psychological aspects of premarital sex behavior have been widely discussed.[54] A sociological exploration of the factors that distinguished happily married from divorced couples found, "A significantly larger percent of divorced than happily married men reported premarital intercourse."[55] Another student of the question suggests that the romantic ideal and permissiveness in sexual practice before marriage may be incompatible, when he says, "When a couple chooses to 'go all the way,' it should be prepared for the possibility that the romantic bubble may collapse in the process."[56] He cites loss of the sense of mystery, and of the image of per-

---

[50] Hollingshead, *Elmtown's Youth*, pp. 232, 240; and Alfred C. Kinsey, Wardell B. Pomeroy, Clyde E. Martin, and Paul H. Gebhard, *Sexual Behavior in the Human Female* (Philadelphia: W. B. Saunders Company, 1953), p. 78.

[51] Alfred C. Kinsey, Wardell B. Pomeroy, and Clyde E. Martin, *Sexual Behavior in the Human Male* (Philadelphia: W. B. Saunders Company, 1948), p. 378.

[52] See, for instance, Ira E. Robinson, Karl King, Charles J. Dudley, and Francis J. Clune, "Change in Sexual Behavior and Attitudes of College Students," *Family Coordinator* 17, no. 2 (April 1968): 119–123.

[53] Harold T. Christensen, "Studies in Child Spacing: I—Premarital Pregnancy as Measured by the Spacing of the First Birth from Marriage," *American Sociological Review* 18, no. 1 (February 1953): 52.

[54] Duvall, *Men, Women, and Morals,* chap. 9, "The Morality of Fornication," and bibliography, pp. 319–330.

[55] Harvey J. Locke, *Predicting Adjustment in Marriage: A Comparison of a Divorced and a Happily Married Group* (New York: Henry Holt and Company, 1951), p. 133.

[56] Robert O. Blood, Jr., "Romance and Premarital Intercourse—Incompatibles?" *Marriage and Family Living* 14, no. 2 (May 1952): 108.

fection, as well as the waning of interest in the other when the two have "gone the limit," as factors that may start one or both members of the pair to wondering if they were really meant for each other after all, with the possible outcome of a broken love affair and a search for a new partner.

The individual young man or woman faces the question of premarital sexual behavior not so much in terms of the findings of studies as in terms of conceptions of self. The young person who sees himself or herself as a person with a future, who has long-term professional and personal goals has a basis for conforming to responsible codes of premarital chastity, while the individual whose past has been bleak, whose future seems to offer little, and who tends to see himself as a creature of impulse feels there is nothing much worth waiting for. Success in the developmental tasks of building an adequate self-concept and meaningful philosophy of life through the years of childhood and adolescence in the family contributes to success in this task of learning to express responsibly the love and sex feelings of young adulthood.

Choosing a Marriage Partner

Three factors are found to play a part in choosing a life partner: propinquity, homogamy, and complementarity. Persons of both sexes tend to marry those who live and work near them. Residential propinquity is significantly related to mate selection in both urban and rural populations, in various regions and among the several racial groups. Studies of marriages in Philadelphia, Pennsylvania, and in New Haven, Connecticut, in the thirties both found more than half of the couples living within twenty blocks of each other at the time of their marriage.[57] In a later study in New Haven, one of the original researchers discovered an even higher percentage (an increase of 18.4 percent) of marriages among persons residing within an area of twenty blocks.[58] Studies in rural counties in Michigan and Minnesota turned up 58 percent and from 58 to 70 percent of the couples living in the same county respectively.[59]

A recent study of both Negro and white marriages in Nashville, Tennessee, finds that residential propinquity operates significantly more frequently among the colored than among the white populations (79.6 percent of the Negroes, as compared with 46.6 percent of the white couples liv-

[57] James H. S. Bossard, "Residential Propinquity as a Factor in Marriage Selection," *American Journal of Sociology* 38 (1932–1933): 219–224; and Maurice R. Davie and Ruby Jo Reeves, "Propinquity of Residence before Marriage," *American Journal of Sociology* 44 (1938–1939): 510–517.

[58] Ruby Jo Reeves Kennedy, "Premarital Residential Propinquity and Ethnic Endogamy," *American Journal of Sociology* 48 (1942–1943): 580–584.

[59] Howard Y. McClusky and Alvin Zander, "Residential Propinquity and Marriage in Branch County Michigan," *Social Forces* 19 (1940): 79–81; and Donald Mitchell, "Residential Propinquity and Marriage in Carver and Scott Counties, Minnesota," *Social Forces* 20 (1941): 256–259.

ing within a twenty-block radius).[60] Several factors possibly related to the high propinquity tendencies are suggested: (1) segregation, (2) neighborhood organization, and (3) neighborhood self-sufficiency (schools, churches, shopping centers, etc.).[61]

Homogamy, the tendency of marriage partners to have similar characteristics, has been shown in scores of studies of many characteristics, in thousands of couples, by hundreds of social scientists through recent decades.[62] Homogamy is especially evident in tendencies to marry within the same group, as Hollingshead has pointed out in his study of all marriages in New Haven during 1948:

The data presented demonstrate that American culture, as it is reflected in the behavior of newly married couples in New Haven, places very definite restrictions on whom an individual may or may not marry. The racial mores were found to be the most explicit on this point. They divided the community into two pools of marriage mates and an individual fished for a mate only in his own racial pool. Religion divided the white race into three smaller pools. Persons in the Jewish pool in 97.1 percent of the cases married within their own group; the percentage was 93.8 for Catholics and 74.4 for Protestants. . . . The ethnic origin of a person's family placed further restrictions on his marital choice. In addition, class position and education stratified the three religious pools into areas where an individual was most likely to find a mate. . . . In a highly significant number of cases the person who marries is very similar culturally to one's self.[63]

Neither propinquity nor homogamy tells us how mates are chosen within a pool of eligibles. To explore the theory of complementary needs as a factor in the dynamics of individual choice, Winch and others have conducted a series of studies that indicates that individuals tend to marry those persons who are purposefully *unlike* in significant personality characteristics.[64] The senior author concludes: "The bulk of the evidence, therefore, supports the hypothesis

---

[60] Alan C. Kerckhoff, "Notes and Comments on the Meaning of Residential Propinquity as a Factor in Mate Selection," *Social Forces* 34, no. 3 (March 1956): 207–213.

[61] Ibid., p. 212.

[62] A carefully selected bibliography of studies on homogamy is found in the footnotes of August B. Hollingshead, "Cultural Factors in the Selection of Marriage Mates," *American Sociological Review* 15, no. 5 (October 1950): 619–627.

[63] Ibid., p. 627.

[64] Robert F. Winch, Thomas Ktsanes, and Virginia Ktsanes, "The Theory of Complementary Needs in Mate Selection: An Analytic and Descriptive Study," *American Sociological Review* 19, no. 3 (June 1954); and Robert F. Winch, "The Theory of Complementary Needs in Mate-Selection: A Test of One Kind of Complementariness," *American Sociological Review* 20, no. 1 (February 1955): 52–56.

that mates tend to select each other on the basis of complementary needs."[65]

The element of personal choice is strongly influenced by powerful unconscious needs that apparently strive to be met through a mate whose personality complements rather than replicates one's own. In such interplay of mutually complementary need patterns may be the answer to the question of "What can he see in *her*?" That marriage partners may tend to choose those whose life-style and personality patterns mutually strengthen and encourage their development as persons is a theory that may yield still further insight in further research.

Granted that persons generally tend to marry those individuals who live and work nearby, and to choose mates from within their own social, religious, and racial groups, an increasingly large number of mixed marriages are taking place today. How successful marriage is that crosses religious, racial, nationality, or socioeconomic group lines depends upon a number of interrelated factors: (1) the motivation for the selection of the marriage partner, (2) responsibility of the sweethearts and mates for bridging the gulfs between them and their families, (3) ability of the two people to live with their differences. Since there are usually more problems in building a marriage that spans two different cultures, the two people face a greater task, and more is expected of them both in maturity and in responsibility than might be necessary in a homogamous union.

Choosing a suitable partner for marriage can be and often is a confusing task. Families help by standing by with assurance, encouragement, and opportunities for free exploration and development of available possibilities. Premarital counseling and education have proven of invaluable aid to many young men and women who want to be sure before they plunge into anything as serious as marriage.

Getting Engaged

Getting engaged may seem like a pleasant "task" to set up for young adults, but it is a many-faceted responsibility that is not easy for many a couple. Some of the more frequent questions young people ask about the engagement period are:

How soon should a couple get engaged? How long should an engagement be? Is it necessary for the man to ask the girl's father for her hand in marriage? Why does an engagement ring mean so much to a girl? How much freedom should be allowed the engaged couple? Does engagement mean "no stepping out?" Is it necessary to reveal your past

---

[65] Robert F. Winch, "The Theory of Complementary Needs in Mate Selection: Final Results on the Test of the General Hypothesis," *American Sociological Review* 20, no. 5 (October 1955): 555.

Table 13–5. *Relation between Engagement Success and Marital Success for Men and Women (Percentage Distribution for 666 Couples)*

Engagement success scores	Men			Women		
	Marriage success score			*Marriage success score*		
	Low	*Intermediate*	*High*	*Low*	*Intermediate*	*High*
High (180 and over)	0.0	16.0	84.0	0.0	9.1	90.9
Median (150–159)	6.7	38.7	54.7	6.7	32.2	61.1
Low (100–109)	40.0	40.0	20.0	28.6	57.1	14.3

Source: Ernest W. Burgess and Paul Wallin, *Engagement and Marriage* (Chicago: J. B. Lippincott Company, 1953), excerpts from table 81, p. 547.

to your fiancé(e)? Is it natural to have doubts about your engagement? About yourself? What are justifiable reasons for breaking an engagement? How can an unsatisfactory engagement be terminated without being painful? What is the engagement period for? What should be discussed during the engagement period? Is it wise for two people to visit each other's families before they marry? How can you know when you are really ready for marriage?[66]

No two persons will ever answer such questions in the same way. The answers to most engagement questions depend upon the two people, the nature of their relationship, the motivating forces within them both, their dreams, disappointments, and readiness. The way they conduct their engagement is predictive of their marriage success, as we see from how closely the engagement success scores parallel the marriage success scores for both men and women in the longitudinal study of 666 couples through engagement into marriage by Burgess and Wallin, reported in table 13–5.

Engagement rituals contribute to the success of the engagement period. Many an engaged pair shares the rituals of their respective families as a way of giving a sense of belonging to both families, and also as a way of selecting those common rituals that both may enjoy and want to continue in their own family-to-be. Having Sunday dinner with his or her family, participating in family celebrations, going on family picnics, and attending church and community functions with one or the other family are illustrations of the way rituals in the engagement weave the couple into the larger family life.

---

[66] Discussed in Duvall, *Love and the Facts of Life*, chap. 18, "What Does It Mean to Be Engaged?" pp. 298–315; and in Evelyn Millis Duvall and Reuben Hill, *When You Marry*, rev. ed. (New York: Association Press; Boston: D. C. Heath and Company, 1967), chap. 5, "Getting Engaged," pp. 87–111.

FAMILY DEVELOPMENT

Some engagement rituals are oriented toward the future in anticipating and preparing for their marriage and family life. Ritualized house-hunting, Saturday afternoon window-shopping, contributing to the piggy bank for special funds, calling on recently married friends, having a series of premarital conferences, and attending courses for engaged couples, all are practices that tend to emerge in engagement as future-oriented rituals.

By the time the couple is ready for marriage, they will have accomplished three important purposes of the engagement period: (1) to place themselves as a pair in their own eyes, and in the eyes of both families and their mutual friends, (2) to work through intimate systems of communication that allow for exchange of confidences and an increasing degree of empathy and the ability to predict each other's responses, (3) to plan specifically for the marriage that lies ahead, in terms of both the practical decisions of where and on what, as well as the value consensus of how the common life will be lived.

Being Married

Being married is a multiple developmental task for both partners. If the marriage is to get off to a good start in its establishment phase (chapter 7), several urgent questions must be faced: (1) Are our parents with us or against us in our marriage? (2) Where will we live, and on what? (3) Are we both really ready to settle down in marriage? (4) How well prepared for marriage are we? (5) What kind of ceremony will we have?

A marriage that starts off with the blessing of both sets of parents has much smoother going than if one or both families oppose the match. Modern young people growing up in an era of extreme individualism may operate under the illusion that they are not marrying into each other's families, and that what their parents think about their marriage is none of their business. Actually, the opinions of both families are very important and influence the marriage either positively or negatively in many crucial ways. The most immediate evidence of parental support is expressed in tangible financial assistance early in the marriage.[67]

Typically, the young married couple set up housekeeping in an apartment, postponing home-ownership until they are on their feet financially and have begun to have their children. Nationwide increases in apartment living and declines in new single-family houses occurring during the

---

[67] Marvin B. Sussman and Lee Burchinal, "Kin Family Network: Unheralded Structure in Current Conceptualizations of Family Functioning," *Marriage and Family Living* 24, no. 3 (August 1962): 231–240; Reuben Hill, *Family Development in Three Generations* (Cambridge, Mass.: Schenkman Publishing Company, 1970); and other evidence cited in chapter 7.

Chart 13–2. *More Apartments, Fewer One-family Homes*

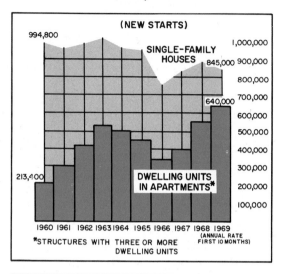

(NEW STARTS)

994,800

SINGLE-FAMILY HOUSES 845,000

1,000,000
900,000
800,000
700,000
600,000
500,000
400,000
300,000
200,000
100,000

640,000

213,400

DWELLING UNITS IN APARTMENTS*

1960 1961 1962 1963 1964 1965 1966 1967 1968 1969

(ANNUAL RATE FIRST 10 MONTHS)

*STRUCTURES WITH THREE OR MORE DWELLING UNITS

Source: "The Rush to Apartments," *U.S. News and World Report,* December 8, 1969, p. 47, with data from the U.S. Bureau of the Census.

1960s (chart 13–2) are expected to continue along with high building costs and standards of living.

Men with low incomes tend to avoid marriage, as is seen in Bureau of the Census data in which 35 to 40 percent of the men with incomes under $3,000 a year were single, as compared with less than 10 percent of the same age group (twenty-five to thirty-four years of age) with incomes over $6,000 a year (chart 13–3).

The too-young couple may be getting themselves caught in the tender trap of love and marriage, as a woman professor of education warns:

Funny . . . how ideas about love and marriage change with something so unromantic as the national economy. In the depression years of the 1930's the average young woman was willing or at least reconciled to waiting before mating. Now she knows that her parents can and probably will help. And she knows she can get a job that will enable her husband to manage. It may well be an uninteresting (if fairly well-paid) job with no chance for advancement, but she can thereby Help Her Husband with His Education—or make it possible for *him* to take, if necessary, a thirty-six-dollar-a-week job with a whale of a future. Perhaps she has always wanted to work her way up in a New York publishing house—or with the Department of State in Washington. She drops her plans like a hot cake to follow her husband to the spot on the globe where he can do what he wants to do—and she can't. It doesn't occur to her until later that she has walked wide-eyed into a trap.

She does not stop to think that, while the early sacrifices of the ardent young bride can be made with happy generosity, they will lead to later resentment when she discovers that she is an uninteresting person, unqualified for either self-respect or respect of others in a world that has moved ahead without her, where her own growth has been slowed and stunted. The husband will forget, in time, that it was she who helped him win success and grow beyond her very reach,

FAMILY DEVELOPMENT

Chart 13–3. *Percentage of Single Men Twenty-Five to Thirty-Four Years of Age, by Income and Education*

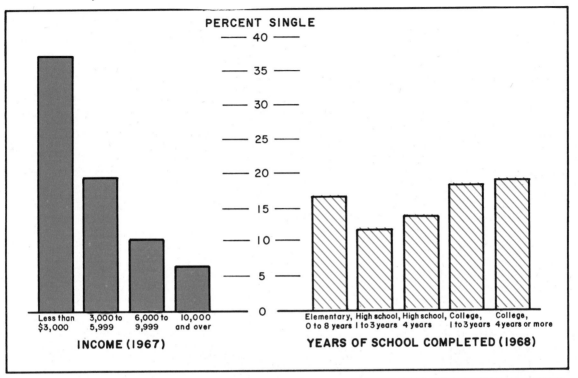

Source: U.S. Bureau of the Census, "Marital Status and Family Status: March 1968," *Population Characteristics,* Current Population Reports, series P-20, no. 187 (August 11, 1969), p. 2.

that it was she who took upon herself the limiting routines and denied her own personal goals.

An early marriage . . . can trap the husband as well as the wife. He is not allowed the time and leisure for intellectual growth. His perceptions and judgments are sharpened only in his own professional directions. Weighed down by his desperate pressures in earning power, he has too many responsibilities too early—financing his wife, the two, three or four babies, the mortgage. He does not have the leisure to write, experiment, explore, create. He too is cramped and harassed.[68]

Readiness for marriage is measured most easily by chronological age. Data on age

[68] Kate Hevner Mueller, "The Marriage Trap," *Mademoiselle,* Spring 1955, taken from release from *Mademoiselle,* pp. 1–2.

at marriage by success in marriage indicate that teenage marriages are the riskiest of all. However, the number of birthdays an individual has had is not as good an indication of his or her readiness for marriage as is emotional age, or maturity as a person. Discriminating questions like these are pertinent: Am I really ready to stop playing around and settle down with one person in marriage? Am I grown up enough to be responsible for my own behavior without blaming someone else or "running home to mother" when I get in a jam? Am I emotionally weaned from my parents? Are my motives for marriage to this person at this time sound and mature? Are we both prepared for what lies ahead for us?

Such questions as these, and many others, are usually freely discussed in functional courses in marriage and family living. Marriage and family courses have ranked high in American colleges over recent decades and were offered by 82 percent of the colleges surveyed in one recent year.[69] Studies have shown that college students are generally appreciative of such course work, their attitudes ranging from "favorable" to

[69] Davida P. Gates, "Sociology in Small Liberal Arts Colleges," *American Sociologist* 4, no. 4 (November 1969): 325.

Formal and informal education for marriage clears up many of the confusions young adults have about when and how and whom to marry.

"strongly favorable."[70] Of the married graduates who had taken the course in "Marriage and the Family" at Florida State University between 1930 and 1946, 34.8 percent responded to a poll by saying they believed the college course had helped them "a great deal," 52.8 percent "helped somewhat," and 12.4 percent "made no difference."[71] An evaluation of the effectiveness of the course at Syracuse University summarizes findings in part as follows:

. . . Students enrolled in a functional course in Family Relationships do make significant gains in their understanding; they do gain insights which they, themselves, consider to be of personal value; they do apply these understandings and insights in their efforts to solve personal problems they are currently experiencing on campus . . . individuals who formerly have had the course and who are now married are applying learnings and insights derived from the course. These people feel the application of learnings derived from the course has contributed much to the quality of their marriages.[72]

Review of more than eighty reports of a variety of methods used in evaluating marriage courses such as: (1) collecting student and alumni reactions to completed courses, (2) pre- and posttesting student knowledge, attitudes, and competence at the beginning and the end of courses, and (3) administering standardized tests to marriage course students and matched control groups before and after a course found marriage courses to be effective by all measures used to evaluate them to date.[73]

Courses in preparation for marriage are offered by many public and private schools, YMCAs, YWCAs, and other youth-serving agencies in many communities. Churches of all major faiths increasingly assume responsibility for preparing their teenage and young adult constituents for marriage and family life.[74] The Pre-Cana and Cana Conferences under Roman Catholic auspices, the excellent materials (course outlines, books, pamphlets, filmstrips, recordings, leader's guides, etc.) published by many Protestant denominations for their work in Christian Family Life programs, as well as the outstanding work done in many Jewish groups are all resources that may be tapped.

Weddings range from simple ceremonies in church or home with only members of the family present to elaborate high-society

[70] Lawrence S. Bee, "Student Attitudes toward a Course in Courtship and Marriage: Educational Implications," *Marriage and Family Living* 13, no. 4 (Fall 1951): 157–160.

[71] George H. Finck, "A Comparative Analysis of the Marriages and Families of Participants and Non-Participants in Marriage Education," *Marriage and Family Living* 18, no. 1 (February 1956): 63.

[72] Virginia Musick Moses, "A Study of Learnings Derived from a Functional College Course in Marriage and Family Relationships by Students as Undergraduates and as Married Alumni" (Dissertation, Syracuse University, 1955).

[73] Evelyn Millis Duvall, "How Effective Are Marriage Courses?" *Journal of Marriage and the Family* 27, no. 2 (May 1965): 176–184.

[74] Clark W. Blackburn, "The Church's Unique Opportunity in Family Development—A Communitywide View," *Lutheran Social Welfare Quarterly* 6, no. 2 (June 1966): 49–60.

affairs running into five or six figures. Americans spend more than seven billion dollars annually on weddings and their accompanying activities, averaging some $1,666 that the father of the bride spends for the expenses of the wedding day.[75]

Whatever the type of ceremony, the most important factors are the *persons*, rather than the things. A wedding that is planned to meet the needs of the situation in accordance with the wishes of the families and the values of the couple is a many-faceted responsibility involving a number of specific decisions.[76] These tasks are usually jointly assumed by the couple and their parents, with the bride and her parents taking the major responsibility for the social aspects of the affair.

DEVELOPMENTAL TASKS OF FAMILIES LAUNCHING YOUNG ADULTS

The popular stereotype has the family playing a passive role as its young adults leave home for lives of their own. Like Horatio Alger, the youth is seen striding from the door darkened by the figure of his weeping mother to go into the world and make his fortune. In reality, most families today, as they always have, play active roles over a considerable period of time in getting their young people successfully launched into the world.[77]

While the first child is at work getting established as an autonomous young adult, there probably are one or more younger children still in the family, each with his or her own developmental tasks to accomplish. So, the family's tasks are not only in assisting the young adult to become successfully autonomous, but also in maintaining a home base in which the other members of the family can thrive.

Family developmental tasks at the launching-center stage are:

1. Rearranging physical facilities and resources
2. Meeting the expenses of a launching-center family
3. Reallocating responsibilities among grown and growing children
4. Coming to terms with themselves as husband and wife
5. Maintaining open systems of communication within the family and between the family and others

[75] Bill Davidson, "Nothing's too Good for My Daughter," *Saturday Evening Post*, 239th year, August 13, 1966, pp. 28–35, citing U.S. Department of Commerce data.

[76] Evelyn Millis Duvall and Reuben Hill, *Being Married* (New York: Association Press; Boston: D. C. Heath and Company, 1960), chap. 9, "Your Wedding Plans," pp. 171–191.

[77] Marvin B. Sussman and Lee Burchinal, "Parental Aid: Prospects and Implications for Family Theory," mimeographed, September 1961.

6. Widening the family circle through release of young adult children and recruitment of new members by marriage

7. Reconciling conflicting loyalties and philosophies of life.

Rearranging Physical Facilities and Resources

These are the accordion years of family life. The young adult's room lies empty through the college year, or while he is away for service, only to suddenly become swollen over a holiday or through a leave, with the young person and his or her friends swooping in for a few days and nights. The family goes along on an even keel for some weeks and then must mobilize itself and all of its resources for a wedding, or a graduation, or both, that keeps the household humming and house bulging at the seams.

The physical plant is sorely taxed at this stage. The family car that dad uses to get to work, and that is needed for the weekly shopping, is in constant demand by the young man or woman of the family with engagements far and wide looming large in importance during the launching stage. Teenage siblings clamor for their share of the use of the car, the telephone, the television set, and the living room, until, as one harassed father described it, "This is the stage of life when a man is dispossessed in his own home." A mother comments somewhat ruefully that she doesn't mind the noise and the expense of young people in the home, but she will be glad to regain the use of her own living room when the courting couples have finally found homes of their own. Few families complain when facilities are sorely taxed at this stage of family living, but the fact remains that for many, the flexible rearrangement of available resources to meet the variety of functions within families at the launching-center stage is a task indeed.

Meeting the Expenses of a Launching-center Family

With some exceptions, families at this stage are at the peak load of family expenses. These are the years when the young adult needs financial help to carry him or her through college or other educational plans, to get specialized training and experience, to get established in the "starvation period" of any of the professions, to pay union initiation fees and dues as workers, to finance the wedding and the new home-in-the-making. Such costs are over and above the already established expenditures budgeted for the family. Many young people today help earn what they can, as young adults always have, but few are in a position to contribute heavily to the family budget at the very time that they are establishing themselves independently.

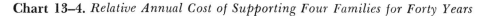

Chart 13–4. *Relative Annual Cost of Supporting Four Families for Forty Years*

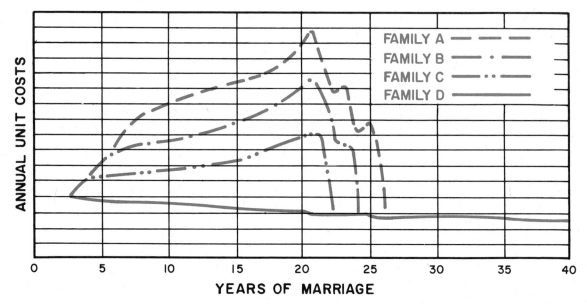

Family A consists of a husband and wife who bring up three children, a boy born at the end of the second year, a girl born at the end of the fourth year, and a boy born at the end of the sixth year of their married life.

Family B consists of a husband and wife who bring up two children, a boy born at the end of the second year and a girl born at the end of the fourth year of their married life.

Family C consists of a husband and wife who bring up one child, a boy born at the end of the second year of their married life.

Family D has no children.

It is assumed in each case that the husband and wife were married when he was twenty-five and she was twenty-three, and that each family supports each of its children for nineteen years, providing them with a high school education. On the nineteenth birthday, each child leaves home and becomes self-supporting.

Source: Howard F. Bigelow, *Family Finance* (Chicago: J. B. Lippincott Company, 1953), p. 333.

Family expenditures are highest when the oldest child is about nineteen in families of one, two, or three children. Costs mount until this period and rapidly decline as the children are launched. Only the family with no children escapes this peak load that comes typically twenty to twenty-five years after the parents' marriage (chart 13–4).

These are the years when a man is glad he is near the peak of his earnings; but even so, some supplementation may be necessary to carry the additional expenditures that go with launching-center functions.

The husband may do overtime as a laboring man or get a summer job as a teacher or a part-time job around the edges of his regular position. His wife now is possibly in the labor force. The young adult and other children in the family possibly have jobs of some kind on a part-time basis while in school and full-time after education is completed. These sources of income may not be sufficient to meet such special costs as are involved in an expensive wedding or college tuition and fees. The family may float a loan or borrow on life insurance or increase the mortgage on the house or tighten its belt wherever it can to meet the current emergencies. Providing for a family at the launching-center stage is a task, as few will deny.

Reallocating Responsibilities among Grown and Growing Children in the Family

Young adults and older teenagers thrive with real responsibilities of their own. Now is the time when father and mother can sit back and let the children run their own affairs in many a situation. These are the years when the "smothering mom" is a liability, and a dad who is too prone to "snoopervise" is a threat to the autonomy of the young adult. The happy family at the launching-center stage is one in which tasks and responsibilities are allocated among the members of the family on the basis of interest, ability, and availability.

The successful accomplishment of this task depends upon the flexibility of roles of the two parents as well as the growing abilities of the young adult(s) and younger siblings to assume and carry through effectively the tasks of the household. As young adults begin to take on more real responsibility for their own and for the family's welfare, the parents play the complementary roles of letting go and standing by with encouragement, reassurance, and appreciation.

Coming to Terms with Themselves as Husband and Wife

Being a parent is not easy at any stage in the child's growth. In many ways being a parent of older youth today is the hardest of all, for parents often vicariously live through all the terrors and threats of emancipation that beset their youth, at the same time that they as people are living through the "crisis of the middle years."

Being middle-aged today is a far more powerful business than it used to be in the day of Whistler's mother. Then, a woman in her forties was physically and psychologically ready to retire to her knitting. Today's middle-aged woman, thanks to better nutrition, medical services, lightened burdens at home, and shifting feminine roles, still has a "head of steam up," both physiologically and emotionally. She is apt to be vigorous, often feeling better than she has in her whole life. Even menopause, the dread of women in earlier eras, now can be taken in stride (chapter 14). The woman with nearly grown children has found her strengths and her weaknesses. She has tasted the sweetness of affection and learned to enjoy creative companionship with her husband and children. Husband and wife, now more often than they have in years, work together on projects and have stimulating exchanges of ideas.[78]

Now, suddenly, before she has quite prepared herself for it, her children are no longer children; they are taking their confidences and their loves outside. Her husband is engrossed in the peak of his business or career. Her house is in order. And she—where does she go from here? What loves can take the place of those so suddenly torn away? What tasks will absorb the energies and the skills that cry for channeling? If she clings to her children, she is a "mom." If her interests in her husband's career become too absorbing, she is a "meddler." If she spends her time in a dizzy round of matinees, bridge parties, and beauty parlors, she is a "parasite." If she devotes herself to a quest for her soul through devious cults and sundry religions, she is suspect. Her salable skills are at least two decades old where she left them to get married. As a modern, liberated woman, her sexual demands upon her husband may leave her frustrated and further threaten

him with a sense of personal inadequacy.[79] It may be partly for these reasons that, according to the Marriage Council of Philadelphia, by the age of forty, 50 percent of the husbands and 26 percent of the wives have had at least one extramarital affair, and some 63 percent of women married more than a decade claim they are less happy than they were when they first married.[80]

There is evidence to indicate that men face a crisis in the middle years, for the basic problem is the same for men and women alike. Briefly it is this. Throughout their lusty twenties and pushy thirties most American men, driving to "get ahead," fasten their eyes on distant goals and dream hopefully of success, but few reach the top. Those who do often struggle to maintain and improve their position in the competitive scheme of things where others are always jockeying for more favorable positions. The glamour dies in the struggle, and "success" for too many American men in their forties and fifties is but ashes in the mouth.

The multitude of hardworking fathers who never reach the top must face the realities of their limitations and accept their lot for what it is, mediocre and bitter though it may be. "I am just a minor guy in a minor rut, living life in a minor key," says one man.

---

[78] Harold Feldman, "The Development of the Husband-Wife Relationship," a study supported in part by the National Institute of Mental Health, unpublished data received through personal correspondence, March 24, 1961, with permission.

[79] Catherine S. Chilman, "Families in Development at Mid-Stage of the Family Life Cycle," *Family Coordinator* 17, no. 4 (October 1968): 297–312.

[80] *Marriage Council Newsletter*, September 1969, p. 1.

Men are further troubled by signs of diminished masculinity, so ever dear to American males. The slowing up characteristic of the middle-aged father, seen in contrast with the youthful vigor of his growing sons and daughters, is personally threatening to many men. Lessened potency and sexual excitation is too frequently attributed to monogamous monotony. The "dangerous period" for men comes when a man must prove his virility to himself, even with more youthful partners if need be. With the burden of guilt that this carries, is it any wonder that he is too easily upset by his son's girl troubles or his daughter's involvements? The timing of launching, both for parents and for young adults, today is unfortunate. Two types of crises piled one on top of the other mean trouble in many homes.

The question of "how well have we done by our children?" is pertinent. In the dark hours of the night, parents toss with the haunting fear that somehow, some way, they might have done a better job with those children who are now beyond their parental ministrations. Parents recognize that the family at the launching stage is being evaluated on its success through its products, the children. Yet the problems of their achieving full adulthood maritally, vocationally, and intellectually are so many and the solutions so few!

Someday we will know more about these things. We will be prepared for the head-on collisions of children and their parents bent on urgent, not-to-be-denied tasks. Today we stumble along doing amazingly well considering all the threats with which we live in the launching-center stage.

Maintaining Communication within the Family

Both happily and unhappily married men and women see communication as contributing to happiness in marriage above all other qualities. Secondly they value being in love with one another, and in third place they rank their emotional need for each other as important for marital happiness. In contrast, they put low in importance for their happiness such things as possessions and good food.[81]

Being able to get through to each other in the family is especially important during the launching stage. This is the time when the young adult is emerging from his family and is working through some of the most important and the most complex tasks of his life. The young person who can freely bring his questions and his alternative solutions to his parents as sounding boards can get invaluable help through their perspective.

At the same time, his parents face the possibility of critical young adults challenging their way of life. As Russell Baker wryly observes, "Now they are trapped

81 Judson T. Landis, "Functional and Dysfunctional Aspects of Stress in Happy and Unhappy Marriages," research reported at the annual meeting of the National Council on Family Relations, Washington, D.C., October 22–25, 1969.

between grandfather's wheezing and the homiletic tedium of two or three young fogies denouncing the shallowness of their goals."[82]

Only an understanding, nonjudgmental family can hope to keep the confidence of its young adults, busy with the gaining of true autonomy. Families who "make a scene" or create an issue over some youthful blunder lose, at least for the moment, contact with the young person at the very time when the generations may need each other most. This is especially true in the relationships the young adult is establishing outside the family. If the parents are unduly critical of visiting boyfriends, a girl often has to make a choice between complying with her parents' wishes or being true to her "heart" and loyal to her friend(s). This is a lot to ask of a young person. Yet, the evidence is that parental disapproval of boys dated has increased appreciably in the last three generations.

In a study made of young college-trained married women, their mothers, and their maternal grandmothers, a pattern emerges of increasing frequency of disapproval of boys dated, with the youngest generation reporting more disapproval than either the mothers or the grandmothers had known in their time (table 13–6).

The reasons for such a significant increase of parental disapproval of the boys

Table 13–6. *Parental Approval of Boys Dated in the Early Courtships of Respondents from Three Married Female Generations*

| | Generations | | |
Parental approval	First (grand-mothers)	Second (mothers)	Third (young wives)
Did not approve	62	91	109
Did approve	104	89	69
Uncertain	25	20	22
Unknown	9	0	0
Total	200	200	200

Source: Marvin R. Koller, "Some Changes in Courtship Behavior in Three Generations of Ohio Women," *American Sociological Review* 16, no. 3 (June 1951): 367.

a girl dates are a matter of conjecture. One may result from rapid social change, in which each generation departs farther from its predecessor than the former had from its parents. A second may be that the increase in social contacts in the larger community brings girls into contact with more boys and young men of whom parents disapprove than was possible in more limited situations characteristic of an earlier day. Still a third possible explanation is that parents had more control over courting couples and dating choices in former times and were therefore more likely to approve the dating partners than today, when friends are selected by the young person with little assistance from the family.

Families at the launching-center stage walk the tightrope between the pressures from outside the family and the forces of cohesion that integrate the family as a unit. This developmental task is one of the most

---

[82] Russell Baker, "Observer: Youth as a Tiresome Old Windbag," *New York Times*, October 17, 1967, p. 46.

FAMILY DEVELOPMENT

difficult to achieve satisfactorily. It is competently accomplished if a solid foundation of good parent-child relationships has been established, and if now at the "proving time" the young adults feel that whatever happens, their family is back of them, with faith in their ability to work things through and willingness to look at any situation with loving concern.

Widening the Family Circle

With the first marriage of one of the children of the family comes the first experience of sudden expansion of the extended family to include both the new family unit being established and also, with more or less interaction, the family of the son- or daughter-in-law. The family in its earlier expanding stages took upon itself one child at a time (except in multiple births), and that as a tiny infant. The widening of the family circle at the launching-center stage is dramatically different in two major respects: (1) the addition is multiple, consisting of the entire family of in-laws, and (2) the additional persons are at varying levels of maturity with a preponderance of adults.

The situation is complicated by the fact that while the young adult of the one family is intimately known within his or her own family, he or she, for awhile, remains an outsider to the young mate's family of orientation. If there is too close a bond between one young adult and his or her

parents, it is difficult to establish the new unit with equilibrium, as we see in the following analysis:

Every married couple belongs to three families. They belong first of all to themselves. They are the *we* of the new family they are founding together. But, at the same time, they belong also to *his* family and to *hers*. If they are to establish a strong family unit of their own, they must inevitably realign their loyalties to the place where *our* family comes before either *yours* or *mine*.

This is the elemental triangle of married living. Unless the cohesive force in the new family unit is stronger than that which ties either of the couple to the parental home, the founding family is threatened, as we see in the figures [chart 13–5].

In figure 1–A, *you* have in-law trouble because *my* family is too close. It may

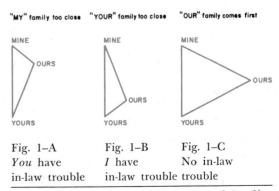

Chart 13–5. *The Elemental Triangle of Married Living*

"MY" family too close	"YOUR" family too close	"OUR" family comes first
Fig. 1–A	Fig. 1–B	Fig. 1–C
You have in-law trouble	*I* have in-law trouble	No in-law trouble

Source: Evelyn Millis Duvall, *In-Laws: Pro·and Con* (New York: Association Press, 1954), p. 279.

be because I am still immature and not ready to emancipate myself from my parental home. It may be that one or more members of my family are possessive and find it difficult to let me go. It may be that circumstances within my family require from me more loyalty and attention than I can comfortably give at the time that I am involved in building my own home and marriage. Whatever the reason, if the forces pulling me/us toward loyalties to *my* home are too strong, the development of *our* common sense of identity is delayed or weakened.

In figure 1–B, *your* family is too close, and so *I* have in-law trouble. Because *you* are bound so tightly to *your* family, I am pulled away from mine, and *we* make little progress in establishing *ours*.

In figure 1–C, *our* family unit comes first in our joint loyalties. We are threatened neither by the ties that bind us to *your* family, nor by the bonds that unite us to *mine*. We are able to make progress as a new family because the force of our common identification pulls us out and away together into a home of our own. Now we can share in the common heritage of both your family and mine because we are not threatened by the pull from either. Only thus are *we* free to enjoy being members of the entire extended family, without the stress of in-law strains.[83]

---

[83] Evelyn Millis Duvall, *In-Laws: Pro and Con* (New York: Association Press, 1954), pp. 278–279.

Reconciling Conflicting Loyalties and Philosophies of Life

In establishing his autonomy as a young adult, the son or daughter of the family has to question at least some of the premises by which life in his family has been lived. These are the days when many a young person tries out conflicting ways of life in an effort to test his background and catch a glimpse of his potential future. When a young adult is being launched from his home base into a life of his own, it is the one time within his life-span when he will be free to pull loose from old allegiances without basic threats and instabilities.

The young man or woman critically reviews his life within his family of orientation and makes comments from time to time that may severely challenge his parents and their ways with him. Ruth Ann startled her parents one night with her observation that she would never make last year's clothes do, and look as shabby as her mother in order to let any child of hers go to college. The fact that the family's sacrifice had been for *her* college education was not irrelevant! Junior soberly reflects one night when his father is working late at the office that life is too short to spend cooped up on any job; he promises himself that when he gets out into life of his own, he will never knuckle under to any position the way he has seen his father do through the years. Young Sam, son of a prominent

Republican leader, is active in a leftist organization in college. Mary, brought up in a pious home, refuses to continue in church as soon as she gets a job in the mill. Such illustrative cases are frequently cited, but there is evidence from a number of substantial studies of the remarkable congruence of values and attitudes between the young adult and parental generations.[84] Although differences emerge within the young adult generation itself, less than one-fourth of the most liberal students feel that the differences between their own values and those of their parents are very great. The majority of eighteen- to twenty-four-year-old men and women in and out of college clearly identify more with their families than with their own generation, according to their own reports (table 13–7).

Some young people get into trouble as they push out into strange new ways. Queenie, in Noel Coward's *This Happy Breed*, runs off with a married man, is deserted, tries to make a go of running a tea shop in southern France, and finally is brought back home to a reconciliation by a loyal lover who grew up next door. Not all youthful mistakes are as critical. Not all turn out so well in the end. But in some way or other most young people blunder as they try their wings and attempt to fly off into life on their own. Parents who are patient while these efforts are being made

[84] Several such university studies are reviewed in "No Silence Please," *Center Magazine* 2, no. 2 (March 1969): 83–86.

Table 13–7. *Young Adults' Values and Identification with Their Families and Peers*

	No college	Practical college*	Fore-runner college†
Differences between parents and your values:			
Very great	15%	11%	24%
Moderate	41	49	51
Slight	44	40	25
Identification and sense of solidarity with:			
Family	82%	78%	65%
Own generation	60	65	68

Source: *Fortune*-Yankelovich Survey, "What They Believe," *Fortune* 79, no. 1 (January 1969): 70–71, 179–181.
* Students in practical colleges have definite career plans (business, engineering, etc.).
† Students in forerunner colleges have intangible career plans (arts and humanities largely).

are of far more help than those who stand by clucking their fears as the fledgling leaves the nest. Families who stand by with assurance and encouragement, giving help as needed, especially in any of life's firsts (first formal party, first job, first trip away from home, and the rest), give their young people the stable home base that is needed for a successful launching.

While the young adults are gaining strength to live independently and showing by their words and actions that their lives are not going to be in all respects copies of their parents, the younger children in the family may be torn by the obvious conflicts between their parents and their older siblings. It is normal for younger children in the family to value highly the attitudes and judgments of their older brothers and sisters. During World War II, when large numbers of young men left for military service, there was a sudden upsurge of juvenile delinquency among the next younger teenage boys. Two explanations were given—one that they felt unneeded, in the sense that their older brothers were needed, and, secondly, that their models of behavior in showing what a young man is and does were no longer at home to keep them in line. Very possibly there were other factors operating too, but the influence of older young people on the lives of their younger brothers and sisters is not to be denied.

Families that keep a secure home base for the younger members of the family during the launching-center stage are those that attempt to accept comfortably the way of life the young adult has chosen. They do not feel too threatened by it. They help the younger siblings see that there are many good ways to live a life, and that when his time comes, he too will find his way for himself.

In a democratic society, in a democratic home, such a course is not hard to follow. Difficulties come in the autocratic, rigid ways in which little latitude is allowed, and where all must follow the one path already established by the dictator of the family.

SUMMARY

Families enter the launching-center stage as the first child leaves home as a young adult. The stage ends as the last child departs, leaving the parents in their empty nest. The stage may be short or long; typically it lasts from six to seven years. Developmental tasks of young adults in the United States include the following: choosing a vocation, getting an education, satisfying military service requirements, becoming marriageable, learning to appraise and to express love feelings appropriately, choosing a marriage partner, getting engaged, and being married. The developmental tasks of families as launching centers include: meeting costs as launching-center families, reallocating responsibilities among grown and growing children in the family, coming to terms with themselves and with each other as husband and wife amid the threats of the launching period, maintaining open systems of communication within the family and between the family and others, widening the family circle to include the new relatives by marriage within the extended family, and reconciling conflicting loyalties and philosophies of life.

This is a period full of teachable moments for the young adult and for all those who live with and love him. New possibilities, new problems, and new ways bring new tasks for the young person to accomplish. He is helped to achieve his developmental tasks as a young adult by family members who have confidence in him and who encourage him to become an autonomous person. He may find especially meaningful the courses, counseling, and guidance offered in many communities to assist the young adult in one or more of his growth responsibilities.

Parents at this stage are breaking the patterns and habits of two decades as they let their children go. Never again will the relationship between themselves and their offspring be quite the same. Fathers and mothers who successfully launch their children into the world are usually those whose emotional lives do not depend upon the continuing dependence of their children. This is the time when their ways of life are being challenged by their own flesh and blood. It is either a threat or a challenge, depending upon their basic security in a democratic acceptance of difference.

SUGGESTED ACTIVITIES

1. Report on details of current requirements for military service in the United States, with a focus on the options open to young men. Collect material on the nonmilitary ways young people of both sexes are serving their country today. Document with official rulings as well as other sources for both military and civil service.

2. Investigate the range of wedding costs in your community by getting prices of such items as gowns for brides and bridesmaids, flowers, cake and other refreshments (both on a catered and a noncatered basis), musicians' services, use of the church or wedding chapel, and other expenses of the wedding day. Interview one or more men whose daughters have recently married and report their feelings about the money outlay involved.

3. Review Jan de Hartog, *The Fourposter* (New York: Random House, 1952), act 3, scene 1, pages 89–104. Then chart the indicated developmental tasks of both Agnes and Michael as they meet the crisis of the marriage of their daughter, listing the revealing phrases (quotes) in the left-hand column and the developmental task implied in the right-hand column of your paper. Interpret and summarize.

4. Compare the launching of a conforming son, as revealed in the character of young Apley in John P. Marquand's *The Late George Apley* (Boston: Little, Brown and Company, 1937), with the mobile climber depicted in the character of Sammy in Budd Schulberg's *What Makes Sammy Run?* (New York: Bantam Books, 1945). Indicate in what significant ways the two patterns differ, and how the various developmental tasks of young adulthood are accomplished by the young men.

5. Poll the class on the question, "Is it wise to get as much education as is possible before going into service or getting married?" Tabulate replies and document with verbatim statements of the various positions taken. Discuss in terms of what you know about the multiple developmental tasks young adults face today.

6. Write an autobiography outlining specifically the factors in your life history that played some direct or indirect part in your choice of a vocation. Consider such factors

as the social class placement of your family, your mobility drives, your sex, your identification with some significant adult, vocational guidance and tests you have had, and other factors that are relevant.

7. Visit a class in personality development in your local YMCA, YWCA, church, or other community group, and observe what is being done to help young adults become more marriageable in your area. Write a report of your findings.

8. Write a paper on how much parents should try to influence the choice of a life mate. Give illustrations of parents who have tried to exert too much influence and those who have seemed not to care enough about the choice of their child's life partner. Show possible consequences of each extreme.

9. Chart the pros and cons of parental subsidy in the marriage of their young adult children. Summarize with a documented paper showing why you have placed the items mentioned where you did.

10. Debate the proposition that there are more intrafamily conflicts at the launching-center stage of the family life cycle than at any other period.

11. Discuss one or more of the following situations adapted from case excerpts developed as class discussion stimuli by Dr. Hazel Ingersoll, Department of Family Relations and Child Development, Oklahoma State University:

a. Jack and Martha came from different home backgrounds and from different parts of the country. Martha's parents had hoped she would marry a western boy. Jack wants Martha's parents to accept him and his New England ways; Martha wants to please his parents as well. During the engagement period they plan to spend their vacations in each other's home. How will they go about really getting to know and understand the early childhood experiences of each other? How can they use this interest in each other's background to further their relationships with their prospective in-laws? How can they come to understand and appreciate the differences in their upbringing? In what ways will these explorations facilitate their marriage adjustment?

b. Judy and her widowed mother have always been very close. Now Judy's mother thinks John is taking Judy away from her. Her whole life has been wrapped up in Judy. She is encouraging Judy to delay marriage and to go on with her career. She says, "We've worked and sacrificed so much for your education. Now you are giving up everything to marry this stranger!" John feels he is unwanted, so he has avoided Judy's mother as much as possible. Judy's mother cries and becomes ill when Judy talks about marriage, and because Judy can't bear to hurt her mother, she is considering asking her to live with John and her. John objects. What is the real problem here?

What might Judy do? John? Judy's mother? Judy and John as a couple? What developmental tasks does each individual face in this situation?

c. Al's parents had his life all planned. He was to devote his life to medicine, as his grandfather had done. After completion of medical training they envisaged him married to one of his own set and settled nearby. But Al, aware that he must soon enter military service, married Louise, a classmate, a girl his parents had never met. Louise had planned to finish school (one year more) and then work, but she became pregnant. Al, wanting her to have good care, asked his parents to take her in until his return. Louise objects because she feels the parents-in-law will treat her like a child and try to run her life. What developmental tasks are inherent in this situation for Louise, for Al, and for his parents? What difficulties may arise in the young couple's efforts to launch themselves as a separate family unit? What possible outcomes are there to the problem situation? Which course will best assure the various members and the two family units of achieving their developmental tasks?

d. Mary Ann's father "dotes" on her and thinks no man could ever be good enough for his daughter. Mary Ann, an only child, is very devoted to her father, so much so that she has chosen a man who is very much like him. Bill, her fiancé, resents the affection and attention Mary Ann gives her father, and the father wastes no words in his criticism of Bill. The father is accustomed to taking Mary Ann with him to games, etc. Now Mary Ann wants to go with Bill, or wants her dad to include Bill in their activities, but the tension between the men makes her uncomfortable. What is the source of Mary Ann's difficulty? What developmental task(s) is she struggling with? What can be done by each of the three persons to better the relationship?

e. Beverly is a city girl who is engaged to Tom, a student in the college of agriculture, who is going back to the ranch in partnership with his father. Beverly does not know anything about being the wife of a rancher. How best can she learn her new roles on the ranch? What may be involved in her relationship with her prospective mother-in-law, who is an experienced rancher's wife? What hazards and challenges, what resources and advantages do both of the young people face in the accomplishment of their developmental tasks in the months ahead?

12. Arrange a showing of *George and Betty: Career versus Marriage* (16mm, sound, color, ten minutes, available from Newenhouse-Novo, 1825 Willow Road, Northfield, Illinois 60093), during which the young women identify with Betty and the men with George in the film. As the movie draws to a close, ask volunteers to role-play how George and Betty work through their dilemma as a couple and as individuals. Discuss.

READINGS

Brenton, Myron. *The American Male.* New York: Coward-McCann, 1966.

CBS News. *Generations Apart* (Survey conducted for CBS News by Daniel Yankelovich, Inc.). New York: Columbia Broadcasting System, 1969.

Chilman, Catherine S. "Families in Development at Mid-Stage of the Family Life Cycle." *Family Coordinator* 17, no. 4 (October 1968): 297–312.

Duvall, Evelyn Millis. "How Effective Are Marriage Courses?" *Journal of Marriage and the Family* 27, no. 2 (May 1965): 176–184.

Duvall, Evelyn Millis, and Reuben Hill. *Being Married.* New York: Association Press; Boston: D. C. Heath and Company, 1960.

Erikson, Erik, ed. *The Challenge of Youth.* Garden City, N.Y.: Doubleday and Company, Anchor Books Edition, 1965.

Feuer, Lewis S. *The Conflict of Generations: The Character and Significance of Student Movements.* New York: Basic Books, 1969.

Fortune-Yankelovich Survey. "What They Believe." *Fortune* 79, no. 1 (January 1969).

Goldsen, Rose K., Morris Rosenberg, Robin M. Williams, Jr., and Edward A. Suchman. *What College Students Think.* Princeton, N.J.: D. Van Nostrand Company, 1960.

Havighurst, Robert J., Paul Hoover Bowman, Gordon P. Liddle, Charles V. Matthews, and James V. Pierce. *Growing Up in River City.* New York: John Wiley and Sons, 1962. Chaps. 8–10.

Hill, Reuben, and Joan Aldous. "Socialization for Marriage and Parenthood." Chap. 22 in *Handbook of Socialization Theory and Research*, edited by David A. Goslin, pp. 885–950. Chicago: Rand McNally and Company, 1969.

Keniston, Kenneth. *Young Radicals: Notes on Committed Youth.* New York: Harcourt, Brace and World, 1968.

Kirkendall, Lester A. *Premarital Intercourse and Interpersonal Relationships.* New York: Julian Press, 1961.

Kirkpatrick, Clifford. *The Family as Process and Institution.* 2d ed. New York: Ronald Press Company, 1963. Chaps. 12–17.

Klemer, Richard H. *A Man for Every Woman.* New York: Macmillan Company, 1959.

Landis, Judson T., and Mary G. Landis. *Building a Successful Marriage.* 5th ed. Englewood Cliffs, N.J.: Prentice-Hall, 1968.

Lidz, Theodore. *The Person: His Development throughout the Life Cycle.* New York: Basic Books, 1968. Chaps. 11–13.

May, Rollo. *Love and Will.* New York: W. W. Norton and Company, 1969.

Mead, Margaret. *Culture and Commitment: A Study of the Generation Gap.* New York: Doubleday, Natural History Press, 1969.

Reiss, Ira L. *The Social Context of Premarital Permissiveness.* New York: Holt, Rinehart and Winston, 1967.

Sutherland, Robert L., Wayne H. Holtzman, Earl A. Koile, and Bert Kruger Smith, eds. *Personality Factors on the College Campus.* Austin, Tex.: Hogg Foundation for Mental Health, University of Texas, 1962.

Udry, J. Richard. *The Social Context of Marriage.* Philadelphia: J. B. Lippincott Company, 1966.

14 MIDDLE-AGED PARENTS— THE GENERATION BETWEEN

Sing a song of seasons!
Something bright in all!
Flowers in the summer,
Fires in the fall. Robert Louis Stevenson

The family life cycle stage of the middle years starts with the departure of the last child from the home and continues to the retirement of the husband or the death of one of the spouses. This may be a period of only a few months or years, as in the case of a late launching of a son or daughter or an early retirement of the man of the house. The stage may abruptly stop with the premature death of either husband or wife. It may be delayed indefinitely by a dependent child who stays on at home.

Typically in the latter half of the twentieth century, the period of the middle years lasts longer than any stage in the family life cycle that a couple has had since their marriage. Up to the turn of the century, the likelihood was that a woman was widowed before her last child left home; or the mother may have died before seeing the first of her children married. Now the married couple have an average of sixteen to eighteen years together between the departure of their last child and the death of the first spouse (charts 5–1 and 5–2 and table 14–1).

The period of the middle years is new to this century for several reasons. Fewer children, spaced early in the marriage, give the parents an early release from childbearing and rearing. Medical advances postpone the time when death of the husband or the wife breaks the marital bond. More adults live out their life-span in good health now than previously could be expected. So, nowadays, most married pairs can expect a "breathing spell" between the busy years of child-rearing and the aging years when retirement, decreased physical vitality, reduced social life, and finally the death of first one and then the other of the pair must be anticipated.

THE MIDDLE YEARS OF LIFE

The husband and wife are usually close to fifty when they enter the postparental middle years, and somewhere near their mid-sixties when the man's retirement takes

Table 14–1. *Ages of Husband and Wife at Critical Stages in the Family Life Cycle in the United States, 1890, 1940, 1950, 1960, 1980*

Stage of the family life cycle	1890	1940	1950	1960 (averages)	1980 (projections)
Median age of wife at:					
First marriage	22.0	21.5	20.1	20.1	19-21
Birth of last child	31.9	27.1	26.1	25.9	26-28
Marriage of last child	55.3	50.0	47.6	47.1	47-49
Death of husband	53.3	60.9	61.4	63.5	65-67
Median age of husband at:					
First marriage	26.1	24.3	22.8	22.3	21-23
Birth of last child	36.0	29.9	28.8	28.0	28-30
Marriage of last child	59.4	52.8	50.3	49.1	50-52
Death of wife	57.4	63.6	64.1	65.5	68-70

Source: Paul C. Glick, "The Life Cycle of the Family," *Marriage and Family Living* 17, no. 1 (February 1955), pp. 3–9; Paul C. Glick, *American Families* (New York: John Wiley and Sons, 1957); Paul C. Glick and Robert Parke, Jr., "New Approaches in Studying the Life Cycle of the Family," *Demography* 2 (1965): 187–202; and averages for 1960 and projections for 1980 derived from Bureau of the Census data with methods similar to those used for earlier years; see also Robert Parke, Jr., and Paul C. Glick, "Prospective Changes in Marriage and the Family," *Journal of Marriage and the Family* 29, no. 2 (May 1967): 249–256.

them into the final stage of the family life cycle. Throughout the middle years the married couple alone constitute the nuclear family, maintaining their husband-wife interaction as the central interpersonal relationship. Now each occupies several positions with multiple roles in the family: husband, father, father-in-law, and grandfather, and wife, mother, mother-in-law, and grandmother, as well as son and daughter of aging parents. Husband and wife in the middle years are indeed the generation between, with both younger and older members of the family looking to them for strength and support from time to time. The crisis of this period is essentially that of accepting responsibility for life as mature adults, without which there is despair, disappointment, and a feeling of being abandoned in the later years of life.

The departure of the grown children from the home to establish their independence is a turning point for the family. In American life, mothers and fathers are expected to observe a hands-off policy toward their married children. The daily stream of thought, activities, tenderness, and love that once flowed from parents to children now must be diverted into other channels in order to allow the young married couple the opportunity to establish their own new family life.

Physical Reminders of Being Middle-aged

Middle-aged adults in a society that values youthfulness are often reminded that they are no longer young. Such physical realities as thinning and graying hair, wrinkling skin, and a tendency to put on weight, especially in the "potbelly" area, make both men and women aware of the onset of middle age. This is the time of life when friends and colleagues of one's own age drop dead of heart failure, or discover they must cope with cancer, high blood pressure, diabetes, hypothyroidism, or any of the other conditions that begin to manifest themselves in the middle years.

A wife may be more concerned for her husband's health now than she is of her own. She tends to develop a number of strategies for maintaining her husband's health and vigor in protective ways termed "body-monitoring" by university research teams.[1] Wife-initiated health programs for the husband often include planning vacation periods for his rest and relaxation; encouraging his getting regular exercise through physical fitness programs, sports, etc.; provision of high-vitamin, high-protein, low-cholesterol, and low-calorie diets; encouragement of regular physical checkups and adherence to whatever regimen the husband's physician prescribes for special problems; and sparing him as much as possible the everyday strains of the household.

Middle-aged women tend to be more concerned with their appearance than with their health as such. This is the time of life when many a woman tries to slim down to be able to wear youthful fashions, tints her hair to cover the gray, and turns to cosmetic creams, hand lotions, and "moisturizers" to preserve "the skin men love to touch."

Both middle-aged men and women become aware of a decline in physical strength, a decrease in stamina, a tendency to tire more easily, propensities to indigestion, insomnia, and "nervous headaches," as well as anxiety about their diminishing attractiveness in a culture where attractiveness is equated with being "young-looking."[2] Beside their handsome young adult sons and daughters they come out second best, and they know it.

Disengagement and Disenchantment Possibilities

The young feel young, the old feel old, but the trouble with being middle-aged is that there is no middle ground, only alternations between youth and senility. You play a hard game of tennis because you feel so good, and spend the rest of the week nursing sore muscles like an old man.[3]

[1] Robert C. Peck, "Psychological Developments in the Second Half of Life," chap. 9 in Bernice L. Neugarten, ed., *Middle Age and Aging* (Chicago: University of Chicago Press, 1968), pp. 88–92.

[2] Ibid., p. 88.

[3] Sydney J. Harris, "The Paradoxes of Middle Age," *Strictly Personal*, syndicated feature, June 16, 1964.

Such are some of the biological bases for the middle-aged's withdrawing from activities once enjoyed.

With the middle years there may be a drop in marital satisfaction and adjustment. Longitudinal studies of marriage find more loneliness and greater personal needs suggesting increased dependency, but with less intimacy as husband and wife, described as disenchantment.[4] A prominent divorce lawyer attributes man's "dangerous years" in the forties and fifties to the sense of being trapped and cheated that many a middle-aged married man feels. He has a sense that his life is slipping away from him, and he begins to wonder if all his struggles have been worth their cost. He begins to believe that his neighbors' grass is greener, and it is then that he may cast a wistful glance at another woman as a way of proving to himself that he can, or of bolstering up his flagging feeling of adequacy.[5]

The middle-aged wife, threatened by the loss of her life work as her last child leaves home, may turn to drinking for the courage she lacks in the monotony of her life. Clinical studies of alcoholism of women at the empty nest stage of the family life cycle find the basic reason to be an absence of a personal sense of identity: "None of the women in this group seemed clearly defined as a person in her own right. None seemed to have ever thought of themselves except in relation to their husbands or children. The question, 'Who am I?' is difficult at age 15; it is excruciating at age 50."[6]

Ever since MacIver dubbed this "the stage of the empty nest,"[7] it often has been discussed in terms of abandonment, when the middle-aged parents, after devoting their lives to their children, now are deserted, and thereafter find life bleak and barren. Evidence from the Kansas City Studies of Adult Life indicates that there is a dip in overall adjustment among fifty- to fifty-five-year-old adults that resembles what is popularly known as "middle-age depression." Not systematically associated with the sexual climacteric, or otherwise simply explained, there is a temporary period of poor adjustment in the lives of many otherwise normal men and women in their fifties.[8]

Rather than society withdrawing from the middle-aged and aging person, it has been suggested that the individual goes through a process of disengagement be-

[4] Peter C. Pineo, "Disenchantment in the Later Years of Marriage," *Marriage and Family Living* 23, no. 1 (February 1961): 3–11.

[5] Samuel C. Kling, "Why Middle-Aged Men Revolt," *Family Weekly*, October 26, 1969, pp. 6–7.

[6] Joan Curlee, "Alcoholism and the Empty Nest," *Bulletin of the Menninger Clinic* 33, no. 3 (May 1969): 170–171.

[7] R. M. MacIver, *Society: A Textbook of Sociology* (New York: Rinehart, 1937), pp. 199 ff.

[8] Robert F. Peck, *What Is Normal?* (Austin, Tex.: Hogg Foundation for Mental Health, 1961), p. 4; and Robert F. Peck, "Measuring the Mental Health of Normal Adults," *Genetic Psychology Monographs* 60 (1959): 197–255.

tween himself and society. Data from a panel of healthy adults between the ages of fifty and seventy within the Kansas City longitudinal studies point toward a perception of constriction even before life space actually decreases, following retirement. A person is seen as going through a process of mutual withdrawal in which disengagement begins in the sixth decade with a shift in self-perception, accompanied by a constriction in the variety of interactions, to be followed by a reduction in the amount of time spent in the company of others, eventually resulting in a self-centered and idiosyncratic style of behavior among the aged.[9]

Reactions to the middle years of life after

[9] Elaine Cumming, Lois R. Dean, David Newell, and Isabel McCaffrey, "Disengagement—A Tentative Theory of Aging," *Sociometry* 23, no. 1 (March 1960): 23–35.

H. ARMSTRONG ROBERTS

These are the years when a couple can tour the countryside, take a trip to faraway places, and enjoy their freedom for a weekend or a season.

the children have been launched vary. A Washington State University study appears to corroborate the disengagement theory when it finds that some mothers whose last child has left home participate less in community activities and are significantly more lonely at the empty nest stage than they were before.[10] At the same time Axelson finds no significant difference in the degree of satisfaction in seven basic areas of life as mothers and fathers move into the postparental period. Their financial worries and concern for the children now decrease significantly, while satisfaction with their marital adjustment and the activities they share with each other increases as their children marry and leave home.

Some middle-aged husbands and wives go in for a variety of self-enriching pursuits that range all the way from refurbishing the home or renewing their formal and informal educational pursuits to taking extended trips together to faraway places.

The empty nest is not as empty for some as it is for others. It can fill up with grandchildren, as one grandfather in his early fifties observes, "What's all this about the empty nest? The old nest here is bursting at the seams with five wonderful grandchildren and two sons-in-law extra—all besides the two daughters who used to roost with us!"

---

[10] Leland J. Axelson, "Personal Adjustment in the Postparental Period," *Marriage and Family Living* 22, no. 1 (February 1960): 66–68.

Complementary Roles of Husband and Wife in the Middle Years

One student of the roles played by middle-aged husbands and wives finds a direct relationship between the complementarity of their roles during the postparental years and their satisfaction with the period. Three-fourths of the husbands and wives interviewed evaluated the postparental phase of the family life cycle as better than or as good as the preceding stages, and only three individuals reported the postparental stage as worse than earlier periods of the marriage.[11]

Complementary roles have been defined as "interlocking systems in which each unit shapes and directs the other units in the system. This effect is reciprocal; changes in one role cannot be made without corresponding changes in other roles which are involved in it. For example, changes in the role of wife will be accompanied by changes in the role of husband; changes in the role of employer will involve changes in the role of employee. Changes in the role of mother will involve changes in the role of the father and in the role of the child."[12] Following this definition, Deutscher de-

---

[11] Irwin Deutscher, *Married Life in the Middle Years* (Kansas City, Mo.: Community Studies, 1959), p. 44.

[12] Eugene L. Hartley and Ruth E. Hartley, *Fundamentals of Social Psychology* (New York: Alfred A. Knopf, 1952), pp. 495–496.

scribes six different patterns of complementarity in the Kansas City middle-class panel of middle-aged adults that he interviewed:

1. *Reciprocal bolstering*, through appreciation, consideration and standing by with encouragement through crisis.

2. *Mutual activities*, in increased recreational pursuits that both enjoy together.

3. *Relaxing together*, as "joint idlers in a restful paradise of peace and quiet."

4. *Joint participation in husband's occupation*, in which the wife becomes absorbed in helping her husband in his work.

5. *Constructive projects*, in which both members of the couple join forces to fix things up, in one project after another.

6. *Separate interests*, as husband remains absorbed in his work and the wife goes on with what interests she has or can find.[13]

The self and other role images of both men and women appear to change as they grow older, in two distinctly different patterns. Men, oriented primarily outside the family in their young adulthood, show a gradual decline in affective expressiveness and a withdrawal from emotional investments as they age. In contrast, as women move through the middle years, they become more self-confident, emotionally more expressive, more expansive, and in some ways even dominant over their husbands.

The young woman is a bland figure, lacking in autonomy and symbolizing tenderness, intimacy, and sexuality. The more mature woman is the key figure in the family, struggling with problems of retaining and controlling the young, channeling her own needs for self-assertion, with great depths of feeling symbolized by impulsive, egocentric qualities. Women stress the aggressive qualities of the older woman, while men see her either as benignly maternal or as domineering.[14]

DEVELOPMENTAL TASKS OF MIDDLE-AGED COUPLES

Basically, the developmental tasks of the middle years may be seen as a complex of social roles. A social role is defined as a pattern of learned behavior appropriate to a given social status. A social role is devel-

[13] Irwin Deutscher, "Husband-Wife Relations in Middle-Age: An Analysis of Sequential Roles among the Urban Middle Classes" (unpublished manuscript, Department of Sociology, University of Missouri, July 1954), pp. 122–130.

[14] Bernice L. Neugarten and David L. Gutmann, "Age-Sex Roles and Personality in Middle Age: A Thematic Apperception Study," *Psychological Monographs* 72, no. 17 (1958): 32–33.

FAMILY DEVELOPMENT

Table 14–2. *Performance Scores of Kansas City Adults on the Developmental Tasks of Middle Age*

Area	Men (age 40–70) Social class*				Women (age 40–70) Social class*			
	I	II	III	IV	I	II	III	IV
Parent	6.00	5.50	5.21	3.90	6.44	5.48	5.88	4.84
Spouse	6.00	5.57	4.87	4.13	6.17	5.94	5.46	3.62
Child of aging parent	5.89	6.06	5.89	5.00	5.75	5.90	5.94	5.75
Homemaker	5.64	5.70	5.55	4.38	5.93	4.86	5.40	3.68
Worker	7.31	5.67	5.36	3.54	6.25	5.97	4.50	3.61
Leisure participant	5.97	5.64	4.21	3.50	6.32	5.05	4.33	2.66
Church member	4.19	3.39	3.19	3.06	4.70	3.57	4.23	4.18
Club and association member	5.55	3.03	2.47	1.89	5.13	2.34	1.91	0.84
Citizen	5.21	4.11	3.64	3.44	4.57	4.01	3.06	3.91
Friend	5.27	4.38	4.02	3.75	6.32	4.59	3.85	2.52

Source: Robert J. Havighurst and Betty Orr, *Adult Education and Adult Needs: A Report* (Chicago: Center for the Study of Liberal Education for Adults, 1956), p. 32.

* I—upper-middle; II—lower-middle; III—upper-lower; IV—lower-lower (as defined by Warner and other writers on social class in America).

oped by an individual as his response to what is expected of him by others, modified by his own perceptions, values, and aspirations.

A man or woman in modern society is expected to fill such social roles as (1) parent, (2) spouse, (3) child of aging parent, (4) homemaker (male or female), (5) worker, (6) user of leisure time, (7) church member, (8) club or association member, (9) citizen, and (10) friend. The quality of a person's life is judged generally by the way he or she fills these roles. When performance approaches the ideal expectations of American society generally, it is rated "high"; when performance is average (4 to 5 on a 0–9 scale), it is rated "medium"; while failure is rated "low." Actual scores on performance in each of ten social roles for men

and women in four social classes in the Kansas City study gives the multicelled picture seen in table 14–2.

Several observations are of interest in comparing the performance scores on the developmental tasks of middle age by social class, sex, and social role. In general we note that:

1. The higher the social class, the higher the performance score on developmental tasks for both men and women in all social roles.

2. Women tend to get higher scores than do men in such roles as parent and church member, but men do better than women as club and association members and as citizens, generally for all social class levels.

3. Scores range from .84 (lower-class women as club and association members) to 7.31 (upper middle-class men as workers), with more than half (47 out of 80) getting "medium" scores between 4 and 6, 24 out of 80 scoring less than 4 ("low"), and 9 of the 80 scoring over 6, or "high medium."

It is possible to appraise an individual's success in his social roles as one measure of his achievement of his developmental tasks as a mature adult. Failure to accomplish the developmental tasks of any stage in life leads to unhappiness and difficulty with later tasks, while success leads to satisfaction at the time and greater ease with future tasks. The middle-aged adults who are lonely and depressed may well be having more difficulty achieving their developmental tasks than are those whose satisfaction with life continues after the children have departed. One aspect of the Kansas City Studies of Adult Life finds social class differences in the ways men and women take the middle years of life. The upper lower-class man or woman views the years between forty and sixty as decline in which he or she is "slowing down," "a has-been." The upper middle-class man sees the middle years as the period of his greatest productivity and major rewards, the "prime of life." The upper-status woman feels the loss of her children from the home, but also a sense of mellowness and serenity when "you enjoy life—you're comfortable with yourself and the world—you're no longer *adjusting* as you were before."[15]

Intensive research over the past decade has been fruitful in describing the patterns followed by men and women in various walks of life as they enter, pass through, and leave the period of the middle years. The relative success or failure of men and women in the middle years of life is best appraised, as at younger stages in the life cycle, by their achievement of the developmental tasks as middle-aged adults, outlined as:

1. Setting adolescent children free and helping them to become happy and responsible adults.
*1a. As aunt or uncle, serving as model and, on occasion, as parent-substitute for nephews and nieces.
2. Discovering new satisfactions in relations with one's spouse.
*2a. Working out an intimate relationship with brothers and sisters.
3. Working out an affectionate but independent relationship with aging parents.
4. Creating a beautiful and comfortable home.
5. Reaching a peak in one's work career.

---

[15] Bernice L. Neugarten and Warren A. Peterson, "A Study of the American Age-Grade System," *Proceedings of the Fourth Congress of the International Association of Gerontology*, Merano, Italy, July 14–19, 1957, vol. 3, Sociological Division, pp. 497–502.

* Roles which unmarried people may perform more fully than the average person, as a partial substitute for the roles of parent and spouse.

6. Achieving mature social and civic responsibility.
7. Accepting and adjusting to physiological changes of middle age.
8. Making an art of friendship.
9. Making a satisfying and creative use of leisure time.
10. Becoming or maintaining oneself as an active club or organization member.
11. Becoming or maintaining oneself as an active church member.[16]

The developmental tasks of middle adulthood have a biological basis in the gradual aging of the physical body, a cultural basis in social pressures and expectations, and a personal origin in the individual life-style and self-concept that the mature adult has developed. Personal aspirations are by nature idiosyncratic and highly individual, and therefore difficult to gauge. Social expectations, on the other hand, tend to be general within a given culture and so can be listed and scored.

DEVELOPMENTAL TASKS OF THE MIDDLE-AGED WIFE AND MOTHER

1. Helping grown and growing children to become happy and responsible adults:

[16] Robert J. Havighurst and Betty Orr, *Adult Education and Adult Needs: A Report* (Chicago: Center for the Study of Liberal Education for Adults, 1956), p. 9.

Setting young adult children free as autonomous persons.

Freeing herself from her emotional dependence upon her children.

Relinquishing her central position in the affection of her grown and growing children and sharing them freely with their husbands, wives, and friends.

Standing by with assistance as needed, without hovering and smothering.

Withdrawing from active motherhood roles and diffusing nurturance drives into wider areas of mothering (through community service and interest in children and young people generally).

Accepting her young adult sons and daughters and their husbands, wives, and children as dear friends whose independence is respected and promoted.

Enjoying her grandchildren without intruding and meddling.

2. Discovering and developing new satisfactions as a wife with her husband:

Giving her husband the encouragement, reassurance, support, and appreciation he needs as a middle-aged man.

Enjoying her part in joint activities as a couple again.

Exploring new hobbies, vacation possibilities, friendship groups, and community projects they both may enjoy as a pair.

Becoming a desirable and desiring companion.

Plumbing the possibilities of deep and

abiding intimacy, in mutual understanding, empathy, and the sense of unity as a couple.

3. Working out an affectionate and independent relationship with aging parents:

Helping her own and her husband's parents find wholesome, happy ways of living out their sunset years.

Assisting both sets of aging parents to find satisfactory supports for their failing powers as needed.

Giving the expressions of interest, affection, and care that aging parents need from their grown children.

Serving as a buffer as need be between the demands of aging parents and the needs of the young adults.

Weathering the inevitable illnesses, accidents, and eventual death of aging parents in wholesome, supportive ways.

4. Creating a pleasant, comfortable home for her husband and herself:

Refurbishing the home for couple-living after the children have grown.

Reworking household facilities and routines for ease and comfort of upkeep.

Investing time, energy, and resources in making home a place of enjoyment and comfort according to the interests and values of husband and wife.

Getting satisfactions from achieving proficiency in one or more of her chosen roles.

Sharing the family home at intervals with grown children, grandchildren, and friends with satisfaction in hospitality.

Giving, receiving, and exchanging hospitality with grown children with mutual interdependence and freedom.

5. Finding satisfactions in her work if she is an employed woman:

Becoming more relaxed about the quantity of her work.

Making progress in line with her powers, wisdom, and proficiencies as a woman on the job.

Getting real satisfactions from being of service, being creative, being recognized as competent, and being a pleasant colleague and a growing person.

Balancing the values of her work with those of her homemaking and other roles to avoid strain and grossly unequal devotion to any one.

6. Achieving mature social and civic responsibility:

Becoming alert and intelligently informed about civic affairs and her role in them.

Taking an active part in one or more organizations at work on civic and political problems in the neighborhood, community, nation, or world.

Giving time, energy, and resources to causes beyond herself and her home.

Working cooperatively with others in the mutual responsibilities of citizenship.

Committing herself to the democratic ideal in any of its many manifestations.

7. Accepting and adjusting to the physical changes of middle age in healthful ways:

Taking menopause in her stride with whatever medical and psychological supports may be needed.

Accepting changes in skin, hair color, body tone, energy output, and physical rhythms without distress.

Eating a well-balanced diet high in proteins, fresh fruits, and vegetables.

Keeping her weight within normal limits.

Getting a healthful balance of sleep and exercise.

Going periodically for medical and dental checkups and following prescribed routines.

Dressing comfortably and attractively to please both herself and others.

Relishing the bloom and pace of maturity as a woman.

8. Making an art of friendship:

Cherishing old friends for themselves and the mutual experiences and values that have been built together through the years.

Choosing new friends from among the many interesting new contacts with "our kind of people" as well as novel, refreshing personalities.

Enjoying active social life with friends of both sexes and a variety of ages.

Giving and receiving freely in social interaction with her friends.

Accepting at least a few friends into close sharing of real feelings with intimacy and mutual security.

Becoming an increasingly friendly person who values her friends and her friendships highly.

9. Using her leisure time creatively and with satisfaction:

Choosing the interests and activities that she finds most rewarding without yielding too much to social pressures and "styles."

Learning to do some things well enough to become known for them among her family, friends, and associates.

Losing herself sufficiently in one or more areas of interest so that she gets creative satisfaction from her leisure hours.

Balancing her program of leisure activities with active and passive, collective and solitary, service-motivated and self-indulgent pursuits.

Keeping alive and interested in the world around her and her part in it.

10. Becoming or maintaining herself as an active club or association member:

Choosing her affiliations with discrimination.

Assuming real responsibilities in those she considers important.

Refusing conflicting, contradictory, or too burdensome invitations with poise.

Getting a sense of pleasure and satisfaction from her affiliations.

Enjoying a sense of belonging with kindred minds and spirits.

Working through her own ways of dealing with intraclub tensions, power systems, and personality problems within the membership comfortably and effectively.

---

11. Becoming or maintaining herself as an active church member, as may be socially expected and personally meaningful:

Finding a soul-satisfying place for herself in a religious affiliation in which she has an abiding faith.

Holding one or more responsible positions within the church.

Gaining personal satisfaction from worship and the rituals, ceremonies, and celebrations of her church.

Contributing her services and her resources to the upkeep of her church.

Serving in ways that help her contribute her best talents to the causes and purposes in which she believes.

Discovering new depths and meanings in the brotherhood of man and the fatherhood of God that go beyond the fellowship of her particular church.

Any woman who accomplishes all this is quite a woman! No one is expected to score high on every task, now or at any other time of life. Certain social roles, such as church membership, are expected in some communities but are not important in others. Some tasks will proceed smoothly and well. Others will labor or go by default. In those areas where she builds upon past successes, the middle-aged woman will be likely to find happiness and relative success in the tasks of the middle years. In the tasks in which she has had past difficulties, failures, or little experience, her accomplishments in the middle years may reflect her inexperience or incompetence.

Some of the developmental tasks of the middle years are particularly difficult for the middle-aged woman, partly because she does not relish them. It is an unusual woman who really enjoys relinquishing her active role as mother, to see her children, whom she has loved and cared for for twenty years, pack their suitcases and leave home. A woman's children represent for her, more than they do for her husband, not only an emotional investment of her adulthood until now, but also the main reason for her existence. Throughout her life as wife and mother, her children have been her job. Now, when they leave, she feels that they take with them her very reason for being. Unless she has prepared herself through the years for a life beyond her children, helping them become independent adults is apt to be a highly unpleasant and difficult job for her.

Difficult, too, may be the reestablishment of a close companionship with her husband now that the children have grown. If she has been a "devoted mother," she may have put the children first and her husband in second place in her thoughts and actions through the years. Now it may come as a shock to realize that she hardly knows this man of hers in terms of his deepest hurts and disillusionments, his dreams and aspirations, or even how he really feels about her. She may feel that they have grown apart through the years of child-rearing while he had to keep his nose to the grindstone to make ends meet, and she was so busy with the thousand and one details of homemaking. She may find life dull and drab in the same old routines with him day after day, and long for a fling before it is too late. Her efforts to get close to her mate now may make her feel self-conscious and embarrassed, but, if she has maintained a real fellowship with her husband as their children were growing up, she does not have as big a task now reestablishing a meaningful companionship. By now husband and wife have learned what to expect of each other. They have already established ways of coping with their problems and of meeting one another's needs that can bring to their later years a comfortable security as well as the possibilities of recurrent discovery and delight.

Menopause must be taken in stride both physically and psychologically as a developmental task of the middle years. Studies find middle-aged women expressing both ambivalence and anxiety about menopause beyond their personal experience with it. The majority view menopause as a disagreeable, disturbing, depressing experi-

H. ARMSTRONG ROBERTS

Reestablishment of a close relationship with her husband is especially important now that the children have grown and gone.

ence that is both unpredictable and mysterious. When these same women check attitudes toward menopause, the majority indicate that menopause has no effect on a woman's physical and emotional health or her sex relations. Half of the middle-aged women studied fear that menopause affects their appearance negatively, and 35 percent say that what they dislike most about menopause is that it is a sign of their getting older.[17]

17 Bernice L. Neugarten, "A New Look at Menopause," *Psychology Today*, December 1967, p. 44.

Now, more than ever, a woman wants to feel that she is attractive. The appearance of gray hair, wrinkles in her skin, flabbiness in upper arm or abdomen may be frightening reminders that she is no longer the appealing young thing she once was. She may lie about her age and prop up her sagging tissue; she may dye her hair or wear a wig. Or, she may cultivate the charm of mature femininity that will see her through for several decades.

Some developmental tasks of the middle-aged wife and mother are highly motivated and relatively pleasantly undertaken. Now, as at other times in the life cycle, there are certain teachable moments that are full of eagerness to learn and grow and achieve. The woman may get a special pleasure in helping her husband rearrange their lives to "live it up" a little now, when their responsibilities are not as great as they have been and their income is still near its peak. It may be fun to expand their recreational budget to take a trip or build a summer place or join a club they haven't been able to afford before. Redoing their home as a place they are proud to call their own may become a joyful task, highly motivated and richly rewarding in ways for all to see.

Becoming a satisfied and satisfying grandmother may be another easy, happy developmental task. In wanting to become worthy of these exciting new roles with these wonderful little people who are indeed her "own flesh and blood," she may take a refresher course in child care and learn more now than she ever knew about children and child development, her nature as a person, and of life itself.

Difficult or easy, late or soon, every wife and mother faces her new developmental tasks in her own way with the coming of her middle years. She is successful if she finds happiness and satisfaction in this stage of living. As she meets life's challenges now, she prepares herself for the aging years that lie ahead. She is all of a piece, building on what has gone before and laying the foundation now for what still lies ahead. This can be a time of fulfillment in which, for the first time in a woman's life, she is free to live on her own terms. For the first twenty years she did what her parents wanted her to do. For the next twenty-five years she did what her children wanted her to do. Now she and her husband are free to do what they want to do—if they can achieve the developmental tasks of this stage.

DEVELOPMENTAL TASKS OF THE MIDDLE-AGED HUSBAND AND FATHER

1. Setting young adult children free and helping them become happy, responsible adults:

Getting along with grown children as friendly equals in most areas of life.

Encouraging grown children to make their own choices of clothes, college, military service, friends, marriage partner, job, etc.

Supporting grown children where necessary, unobtrusively and without any strings attached.

Being an adviser as requested and an impartial "listener" for young people who are trying to work out their problems.

Expecting grown children to want and need autonomy, privacy, and freedom.

Giving and receiving affection and attention from grown children and their families.

Becoming a pleasant, beloved grandfather who finds joy in his grandchildren.

---

2. Discovering and developing new satisfactions with his wife:

Giving his wife the reassurance, the recognition (both in private and in public), the appreciation, and the affection she needs as a middle-aged woman.

Enjoying being with his wife and participating with her in a variety of shared activities.

Feeling close to his wife with mutual understanding and empathy.

Sharing his work, his thoughts, his feelings, and his hopes and disappointments with his wife and encouraging her to tell him of hers.

Developing mutually satisfying ways of attracting and holding her interest in him as a man, a male, and as a husband.

3. Working out an affectionate and independent relationship with aging parents:

Being friendly without too much dominance or dependence in relations with his own and his wife's parents.

Taking responsibility for failing parents as needed in ways that help them maintain their self-respect.

Keeping in touch with the needs, interests, and plans of his parents.

Working through, with the others involved, the best possible living arrangements when parents no longer are able to live by themselves.

Interpreting aging parents and young adult family members to each other as needed.

Giving personal support as illnesses, accidents, and eventual death of one or both parents bring their crises.

---

4. Creating a pleasant, comfortable home:

Taking a real interest in the physical upkeep of the home.

Assuming responsibility for the care of the heavier chores around the house, basement, and yard.

Helping plan for and taking a real interest in decorating the home and keeping it nice.

Enjoying full partnership in planning for the home, its remodeling, redecorating, and ongoing routines.

Taking pride in his and in his wife's accomplishments in making the home a good place to live in as a couple.

Finding pleasure in having grown children home at intervals for celebrations, vacations, and in times of need.

Assuming his share of responsibility for entertaining friends, associates, and members of the extended family.

---

5. Working productively and efficiently in his job:

Liking his work and doing well in it.

Being able to lead and to follow, to give and to take orders comfortably on the job.

Coming to terms with the degree of success that is his without regret or recriminations.

Getting satisfactions on his job from friendships with associates, feeling of being needed and of service, self-respect and prestige, and feeling of creative productivity.

Taking his work at a more leisurely pace as time goes on, letting established routines and wisdom on the job take the place of earlier overzealous drive.

Letting younger men take over without threat of lost status, and planning for his eventual retirement constructively.

---

6. Achieving mature social and civic responsibility:

Keeping informed and enjoying discussing civic affairs and national and international problems.

Understanding where he fits into the pressure groups and politics of the society.

Taking active part in some one or more movements for community improvement, civic reform, or national and world conditions.

Encouraging his wife and family to be good citizens.

Standing for democratic practices and the good of the whole in issues where vested interests may be at stake.

---

7. Accepting and adjusting to the physical changes of middle age in healthful ways:

Getting regular medical and dental checkups and keeping physically fit.

Using the glasses, hearing aid, or other helps prescribed for him as needed.

Eating what is good for him, in healthful quantities, avoiding excesses in rich, caloric foods, and keeping tobacco use and alcohol consumption within reasonable limits.

Getting some physical exercise appropriate to his age, strength, and endurance.

Dressing comfortably and attractively with attention to good grooming and the self-respect of cleanliness, neatness, and appropriateness.

Wearing his mature years with poise, without undue concern over such inevitables as balding, graying hair, and lessening vitality.

---

8. Making an art of friendship:

Choosing friends of various ages with mutual interests and ongoing satisfactions.

Enjoying old and new friends of both sexes

in a variety of settings, rituals, and functions.

Reciprocating hospitality and finding satisfactions in roles of both host and guest.

Being gracious to his wife's friends and associates, for themselves as well as for his wife's sake.

Sharing feelings intimately with close friends in whose fellowship he feels basically secure.

Considering himself a warm, friendly person with others generally.

---

9. Making satisfying and creative use of leisure time:

Welcoming the increased leisure of the middle years as a chance to do all the things he has never had time for before.

Choosing some activities that have personal meaning for him as well as doing some things for fellowship primarily.

Mastering some arts and skills sufficiently to gain recognition and a heightened sense of self-respect and pride from his workmanship.

Losing himself in some of his pursuits so that he is never at a loss for things to do.

Sharing an increasing number of his leisure-time activities with his wife.

Keeping alert and alive to the world around him.

10. Becoming or maintaining himself as an active club or association member:

Dropping the unrewarding affiliations that may have interested him early in his career but that may be burdensome or boring now.

Attending meetings and assuming responsibility in the associations he considers important.

Finding satisfactions in using his talents and abilities in group activities.

Enjoying fellowship with like-minded people.

Becoming a mature "elder statesman" in diplomatic roles within the relationships of his clubs.

---

11. Becoming or maintaining himself as an active church member, as may be socially expected or personally rewarding:

Coming to terms with what religion and his church mean to him.

Holding responsible positions in his church.

Finding personal satisfactions through the various rituals, activities, and programs of the church.

Enjoying the opportunities for service available through the church and its related activities.

Being increasingly willing to lose himself in causes that are bigger than he is and in movements that go beyond the present.

The husband and father in the middle years finds some of his developmental tasks easier than the parallel tasks his wife is facing. It probably is easier for him than it is for her to encourage the autonomy of their children, largely because the children have been her main responsibility, her number-one job through the years of their growing up. It usually is easier for a middle-aged man to find ongoing satisfactions in his work than it is for his wife, whose employment has probably been secondary to her homemaking responsibilities through the years.

In some areas of life the man in the middle years of the family life cycle may find difficulties greater than those his wife is facing. He may refuse to recognize his decline in vitality and brag that he can work and play as vigorously as he did twenty years ago. He may have been so preoccupied with his work through the years of getting established that he has built little foundation for more relaxed living with his wife and family. He may be dismayed in the face of so much leisure now available and postpone much-needed vacations or hurry back from those he takes, largely because he has never learned to play. Some men even feel guilty if they "play," since recreation used to be considered wasteful of time rather than re-creative.

After years of tight financing and trying to make ends meet within the pressures of his growing family, he may find that he has built habits of scrimping and "making do" that now are inappropriate. It may be a struggle for him to cooperate with his wife in making their home pleasant and comfortable. He may seem to be "tight" with their money now, when they might be enjoying it in ways that are rightfully theirs. He is likely to be uncertain about how much should be saved for the future and how much could be spent for today's pleasure.

Even grandfatherhood can be a challenging task. During the years when his own children were growing up, he may have been so involved outside the home that he never seemed to have the time for close companionship with them that now is possible with his grandchildren. He may not know what to do with little children, and so miss out on some of the joys and satisfactions that otherwise would be his. He can find peculiar pleasure in his grandchildren and contribute richly to them and to the entire family from the wisdom and richness of his years.

A man is sometimes a better father to his grandchildren than he was able to be to his own children. He is getting older now and the years have passed so swiftly that he is suddenly aware of all that he has missed. He wants to make up for lost time and one way to do it is to enjoy his grandchildren and savor their youth, though he had little inclination for this sort of thing when his own children were small. . . .

• • •

. . . Grandfather, who has read many men and women in his lifetime, often catches the tremble in the lip or the hangdog look of shame that a busy parent misses beneath the overt defiance. Being a wise man he has relinquished the intense competition of his earlier days, the ceaseless striving to keep up with the

Joneses, get ahead of a business rival, or acquire a new-model car every year. He has learned to be content with his lot whatever it may be. He is relaxed enough to have fun with his grandchildren and that is the master recipe for being good friends with children.

A thoughtful, well-seasoned, leisured man in a home where there are young children can be of great service in their well-rounded development. Grandfather has time to mend a broken toy or coax a stubborn one to work. He can read or tell stories. He is not too busy to admire the shape of a pebble a young one discovers on the beach and wonder with him about it—why it is different from all the others, from what far shores the ocean waves washed it, where it got its opalescent gleam.

• • •

Children need grandparents who have come to terms with life and accept it philosophically as parents seldom have yet learned or had time to· do. When those who are at the beginning of the journey hold hands with those who have travelled a long way and know all the turns in the road, each gains the strength needed by both. They are like the pair who were seen wandering together in the summer over the winding paths of a Maine island in Casco Bay.

"My grandfather takes me everywhere," the small boy told a summer visitor happily.

"He doesn't know it," the white-haired man smiled, "but he's the one who takes *me*. I'm blind, you see."[18]

A man may flee from the new expectations and possibilities of middle age. He may bury himself blindly in his accustomed work and refuse to anticipate his impending retirement. He may neglect his wife, his grown children, his grandchildren, and his friends. He can deny his own failing strength and refuse to accept his feelings of regret, frustration, disappointment, and panic. He may fail in any or all of the developmental tasks of this stage of life and be miserable in the process, nursing his neurotic symptoms and his grudges until he chucks it all in an early grave soon after retirement. Such failures to meet the challenge of the middle years do happen, but they are not necessary.

What has been called "the crisis of the middle years" seems in the light of recent research to be more like a phase in the process of disenchantment that continues throughout life. Studying men's and women's attitude changes from courtship through engagement into marriage, Hobart found men more quickly disillusioned than women after marriage, especially in the more romanticized areas of life. Postmarital disillusionment is especially characteristic in such areas as personal freedom, marital roles, having children, in-law relationships,

---

[18] O. Spurgeon English and Constance J. Foster, *Fathers Are Parents, Too* (New York: G. P. Putnam's Sons, 1951), pp. 260–261, 268–269, 271.

values on neatness, savings and money, and attitudes toward divorce.[19]

Study of Burgess and Wallin's one thousand couples investigated from engagement into marriage now continues after they have been married up to twenty years. Between the early and the middle years of marriage two evidences of disenchantment are noted: (1) a general drop in marital satisfaction and adjustment, and (2) a loss of intimacy—less frequent kissing, reciprocal settlement of disagreements, and more loneliness. The marital adjustment score declines more than any other from the early to the middle years of marriage.[20]

There is further evidence that many men and women fail to find happiness in the middle years. A study of the marital happiness and unhappiness of married persons (as rated by their brothers and sisters) reveals the forties and fifties as a difficult period for married women and the fifties as particularly hard for men.[21] The women's problems revolve around their joblessness as mothers when their children no longer need their services, the decreasing adequacy of their middle-aged husbands as sexual partners, and the problems of the menopause. For men, the unhappiness of the middle years tends to center in their occupational problems.

. . . Two groups of men are identified by our informants. One consists of men who have attained some degree of prominence and success in their chosen field, only to find that their wives have not kept pace with them in their upward climb. Such men often make a determined effort to remain loyal to their mates. Some of them are reported as succeeding; others fail and are aware of it; and still others appear to their siblings as failing in spite of outward evidences of success.

A second group of men, identified by their siblings, are in their fifties and have failed, absolutely or relatively, in their occupational efforts. Such failures lead them to rationalizations: they never had a chance to succeed, they say. Their wives were no help to them. If it were not for the handicaps which their wives imposed, they would have succeeded, as did other men. Such wives become scapegoats for the failure of their husbands. The husbands find comfort in the development of feelings of self-pity and animosity toward their wives.[22]

The findings of a study of 8,300 American business leaders and their wives seem to show that business success depends not so much on whom a man marries or on

[19] Charles W. Hobart, "Disillusionment in Marriage and Romanticism," *Marriage and Family Living* 20, no. 2 (May 1958): 156–162.

[20] Pineo, "Disenchantment in the Later Years of Marriage," pp. 3–11.

[21] James H. S. Bossard and Eleanor S. Boll, "Marital Unhappiness in the Life Cycle," *Marriage and Family Living* 17, no. 1 (February 1955): 10–14.

[22] Bossard and Boll, "Marital Unhappiness in the Life Cycle," p. 14.

what his wife does as on his talents, energies, and his singleness of purpose.[23] If these findings apply to vocational success generally, then it must be that a great many men unfairly blame their wives for their failures, to the impairment of the marriage relationship. If, at the same time, middle-aged women complain about the inadequacies of their husbands as sexual mates, as Bossard and Boll find many of them do, then the probabilities are that the marriage itself is threatened in the middle years.

Happiness in the middle years is an indication of success in one's developmental tasks and of good adjustment to the process of growing older. For example, a study of parents of university students finds that social participation is associated with life satisfaction among both men and women.[24] Life satisfaction rating scales[25] designed to measure relative success in the middle and later years use five criteria: (1) zest versus apathy (enthusiasm of response and degree of ego-involvement), (2) resolution and fortitude (personal responsibility for one's life), (3) congruence between desired and achieved goals (feeling of success in accomplishments one feels are important), (4) self-concept (physical, psychological, and social attributes), and (5) mood tone (spontaneous positively toned affective terms for people and things). Each of these criteria, rated on a five-point scale from high to low, yields an index of life satisfaction that distinguishes between individuals and between groups. The nonmarried (single, separated, divorced, and widowed men and women) have significantly lower life satisfaction scores than do married persons, suggesting that disenchantment is less within than outside of marriage.

A husband and father who is willing to keep on growing can, during his middle years, reap the harvest of good living that he has sown in earlier years. He can relax and enjoy the fruits of his labors, in the sense of "you can't take it with you," or in the spirit of this being "the last of life for which the first was made." He can rediscover the richness of marriage, the satisfactions of fellowship with grown children, the warmth of friendship, the excitement of adventure and novel experience, the rewards of productivity. But not one of these automatically "comes due" at this time without effort on his part. They all are satisfactions that accrue from success in achieving the developmental tasks of this stage of life. When he does a good job in them, he finds the happiness that goes with their successful accomplishment. As long as there is life, there can be growth, and the middle years are no exception.

[23] W. Lloyd Warner and James C. Abegglen, *Business Leaders in America* (New York: Harper and Brothers, 1956).

[24] Arnold M. Rose, "Factors Associated with the Life Satisfaction of Middle-Class, Middle-Aged Persons," *Marriage and Family Living* 17, no. 1 (February 1955): 15–19.

[25] Bernice L. Neugarten, Robert J. Havighurst, and Sheldon S. Tobin, "The Measurement of Life Satisfaction," *Journal of Gerontology* 16, no. 2 (April 1961): 134–143.

FAMILY DEVELOPMENTAL TASKS IN THE MIDDLE YEARS

The middle years in the family are a challenge to more than the individual husband and wife as middle-aged adults. This stage has its full complement of family developmental tasks that are necessary for family survival, continuity, and growth. These family developmental tasks can be briefly outlined as follows:

1. Maintaining a pleasant and comfortable home.
2. Assuring security for the later years.
3. Carrying household responsibilities.
4. Drawing closer together as a couple.
5. Maintaining contact with grown children's families.
6. Keeping in touch with brothers' and sisters' families and with aging parents.
7. Participating in community life beyond the family.
8. Reaffirming the values of life that have real meaning.

Maintaining a Pleasant and Comfortable Home

Most couples own their own homes by the time the last child is launched. Indeed, home ownership is more likely now than at any other stage in the family life cycle: 37.3 percent of the young married, 52.5 percent of young couples with youngest child under six, 66.7 percent of young marrieds with youngest child six or older, 69.9 percent of older married with children, and 71.4 percent of those whose children have been launched.[26] The chances are nine out of ten that the middle-aged couple stay on in the family home after their children have grown and gone.[27]

Reasons for remaining in the family home are several. The most powerful is probably the sense that this *is* home to husband and wife. Here their habits are built into the place. Here are their friends, neighbors, and the familiar ways of life that perhaps mean much to both of the couple. The husband still is on the job, and he is accustomed to going and coming from this place. The children come home for special celebrations now and then and seem to enjoy having a place to call their own within the home base. If the family has been a happy one, there are few unpleasant memories to escape and many reasons for

---

[26] John B. Lansing and Leslie Kish, "Family Life Cycle as an Independent Variable," *American Sociological Review* 22, no. 5 (October 1957): 512–519.

[27] Paul C. Glick, "The Life Cycle of the Family," *Marriage and Family Living* 17, no. 1 (February 1955): table 2, p. 7. (The 10.3 percent of husbands moving in the middle years compares with 55.8 percent of husbands under 25 years of age, 32.9 percent of husbands 25–34 years of age, and 18.2 percent of husbands 35–44 years old who change their place of residence.)

building themselves into the home for the enjoyment of the middle years as a couple.

Remodeling the home after the children leave is a pleasant project for the middle-aged couple. Now that the place is theirs alone, it can be refurbished around their particular interests rather than in terms of what the children need. One of the upstairs bedrooms may become a cozy den or hobby center. The back porch may be closed in for intimate dining. They may decide to make a bedroom and bath on the first floor, which saves steps while they are alone, and which comes in handy when sickness strikes or when aged relatives have to be given a home. The second floor may be rented out or closed off except for times when the grown children are home with their families. There is time and money now to remodel the kitchen for good management and efficient operation as well as for its functions as living center of the home with telephone at hand, a comfortable chair or two, and a pleasant place to eat. They may redecorate with an eye to entertaining freely, or to using home as a pleasant, comfortable haven from the world and its people. Whatever is done, it can express the needs, values, and interests of the husband and wife in their middle years and in the foreseeable future, when their own failing powers will call for convenient, safe housing facilities.

Safety is particularly a factor to consider in remodeling the home for the middle and later years. A handrail on the cellar stairs or a handgrip at the bathtub may prevent

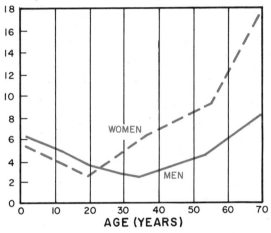

Chart 14–1. *Home Accidents Disabling for One Week or More by Ages in Years for Men and Women by Annual Frequency per 1,000 Persons*

Source: Adapted from Frederick Gutheim, *Houses for Family Living* (New York: The Woman's Foundation), p. 39.

a nasty fall. Conveniently located electric outlets are important. Good lights at work centers are more essential now than ever. A quick glance at the incidence of home accidents by age groups shows a sharp increase for both men and women after fifty in accidents that disable for one week or more (chart 14–1). Sensible middle-aged people plan for the gradual failing of their powers by making home as safe, convenient, and comfortable as they can while they are rethinking their homemaking functions for the later decades of life together as a couple.

After twenty or twenty-five years of marriage a man and his wife should have learned what is important to them in a home. If they enjoy their yard with its garden, it should be part of their plans for the future, but if it has been primarily for the children and of little or no interest to either of the married pair, then this may be the time to move into an apartment or a less burdensome house. If they do move, they will need to look not only for present comfort and convenience, but also for the years ahead. Their task is in arranging for a home that expresses their interests so that it becomes for both of them a satisfying place in which to live.

Assuring Security for the Later Years

In the middle years, the husband's income is still at or close to its peak, while costs have dropped sharply as the children have left home. Fewer couples have debts now than at any time since they were married.[28] The scrimping days of trying to make ends meet are over for most couples. The house is furnished; the car and the last baby are paid for; and the couple can relax and enjoy their earnings in the breathing spell that is theirs now before retirement and the costs of the later years are upon them. Two facets of this task call for special atten-

tion: (1) learning to spend money for personal gratification after years of self-sacrifice and thinking first of the children and their needs, and (2) planning for a secure old age.

Planning financially for the later years is highly motivated during middle age. Few parents want to be beholden to their grown children for support during their own old age. They realize that neither Social Security nor Old Age Assistance will keep them on anything more than a subsistence level. They may not have accumulated enough

Chart 14–2. *Family Income and Income per Family Member, for Husband-wife Families (United States, 1960)*

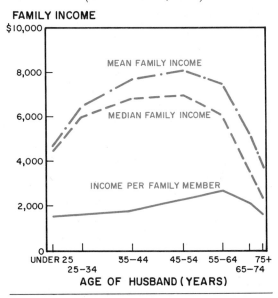

Source: Paul C. Glick and Robert Parke, Jr., "New Approaches in Studying the Life Cycle of the Family," *Demography* 2 (1965): 199.

---

[28] Lansing and Kish, "Family Life Cycle as an Independent Variable," p. 514.

during the peak years of child-rearing to make them feel as adequately prepared for the uncertainties of their later years as they would like. Realistically, most families can anticipate a sharp drop in income with the man's retirement (chart 14–2). And so they continue the pattern of putting their money away for a rainy day that has been established through their earlier years in the family. National analyses of saving by age groups indicate that middle-aged families tend to be the biggest savers and to place more emphasis on building up a reserve than any other age group.[29]

Planning for old age should include recognition of the fact that the average age at which men die is lower than the average age at which women die. In the older age groups, there are many more widows than widowers. In fact, after age seventy there are more widows than women living with husbands. Men need to provide not only for their own support in old age, but for the support of their widows. This is more than a matter of stocks and bonds and life insurance. It means helping prepare the wife to fend for herself if and when she is left alone.

Few happily married women want to think of widowhood as a personal possibility. Yet, when one or more of their husband's friends or associates drop off in the prime of life, they begin to realize the importance of preparing for what may become inevitable for them too one day. Several steps in preparing for widowhood are indicated: (1) Find one or more close confidants besides the husband. A good woman friend will do. An understanding lawyer-friend, a sensitive pastor, or an old friend of the family may be tapped to serve as counsel and confidential ear when widowhood comes. (2) Make sure that both husband and wife know the full state of their financial affairs. The older pattern of the husband carrying the full responsibility for the money matters in the marriage meant that many mature women were as babes in the woods when their husbands died. They were easy prey for charlatans and sundry "widows' rackets." Today's couples more often share responsibility for financial planning through the years and so leave the widow better prepared to carry on when she is left in charge. (3) Encourage one or more absorbing interests in life that keep pulling toward the future. A crocheted afghan is a start, but it is not enough for most women. Active work in the community gives her something to grow on and into. A job outside the home may do it. Whatever it is, a woman in the middle years must have something to live *for* as well as to live *on*. If it can be both, she is doubly protected.

The chances of the wife's working are greater in the middle years than at any other time in the family life cycle (chart

[29] Dorothy A. Brady and Marsha Froeder, "Influence of Age on Saving and Spending Patterns," *Monthly Labor Review* 78, no. 11 (November 1955): 1240–1244.

Chart 14–3. *Percentage of Husband-wife Families with Wife in Labor Force (United States, 1960)*

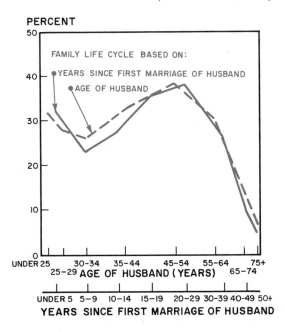

PERCENT

FAMILY LIFE CYCLE BASED ON:
- YEARS SINCE FIRST MARRIAGE OF HUSBAND
- AGE OF HUSBAND

AGE OF HUSBAND (YEARS)

UNDER 25 / 25–29 / 30–34 / 35–44 / 45–54 / 55–64 / 65–74 / 75+

YEARS SINCE FIRST MARRIAGE OF HUSBAND

UNDER 5 / 5–9 / 10–14 / 15–19 / 20–29 / 30–39 / 40–49 / 50+

Source: Paul C. Glick and Robert Parke, Jr., "New Approaches in Studying the Life Cycle of the Family," *Demography* 2 (1965): 197.

14–3). The middle-aged wife's income may be welcome for future security planning as well as for luxuries and pleasures. A combined income now may make it possible for the couple to buy a nice home, or fix up the old one, or take a long-dreamed-of trip abroad, spend a winter holiday in a southern clime, or budget more lavishly for their clothes and personal grooming than was possible before now. Some husbands are secure enough as males not to be threatened by their wives' earning power, enjoying the economic partnership involved in team earning, shared planning, and joint spending.

Learning to "live it up" may be more difficult a task in the middle years than is planning for the future. When two people have been future-oriented throughout their whole life together as a pair, it is not easy to suddenly shift into spending for present pleasures. Getting away for an occasional holiday while the children were growing up has prepared some couples for their freedom in the middle years. Spending something for immediate fun and pleasure through the years, even when the going has been rough, gives some basis for relaxing and just enjoying life now. Even finding pleasure in freedom and in enjoying life has to be learned, as many a lonely middle-aged or older person discovers. This is the nature of developmental tasks, built on the past, pointed toward the future at every stage of the life cycle.

Carrying Household Responsibilities Together

Typically, the middle-aged couple has no one but themselves to worry about in the daily routines of living. The grown children are in homes of their own; aging parents are being cared for independently; and the husband and wife are alone in the home, free to plan their daily routines as they will, without others' schedules to burden them.

Occasionally a married son or daughter will return home for a few weeks or months through a stint in military service, or for special training, or during an illness. Then the old place is crowded as two families try to live as one, getting into each other's way and having to work out new ways of doing old chores.

There may be times when the only way to care adequately for aging parents is to bring the dependent one into the home. Then husband and wife divide the care of the aging or invalid one as best they can, so that no one gets completely tied down unnecessarily. If the old person is bedridden, the burden may be heavy indeed, perhaps for a long period of time. If the elderly one is able to care for herself (or for himself, as is less likely), she may take over some of the household routine and free the middle-aged wife for a life of her own outside the home in gainful employment, volunteer or community work.

When husband and wife are home alone, their household responsibilities may be kept at the level that they personally most enjoy. They may keep house quite casually, deciding at the last minute to go out for dinner, or invite neighbors over for potluck, or take a piece of beef out of the freezer and broil a steak in the backyard. By the time a woman has reached her middle years, her skills in homemaking are at their peak, and she can care for her home with a minimum of effort and a maximum of enjoyment. By this time, too, her husband has learned how to share the work load and the companionship in getting things done in ways that satisfy them both.

Homemaking now can be fun, "just like playing house," as one fiftyish woman describes it.

Drawing Closer Together as a Couple

The most important task of the middle years is that of finding each other as husband and wife again. Not since their honeymoon days have the two been thrown as closely together, with no children or responsibilities of child-rearing to divert them from each other. From a distance it looks as though this is a state of affairs that both the man and the woman he chose to be his own would welcome. Yet, for many a couple it is a real task to be worked on and achieved to the point where life together has meaning and purpose and richness once more.

Widely separated studies find marital happiness, adjustment, and satisfaction declining throughout the marriage.[30] That

[30] Pineo, "Disenchantment in the Later Years of Marriage," pp. 3–4; Gerald Gurin, Joseph Veroff, and Sheila Feld, *Americans View Their Mental Health: A Nationwide Interview Study* (New York: Basic Books, 1960), p. 103; Harold Feldman, "The Development of the Husband-Wife Relationship," a study supported in part by the National Institute of Mental Health," unpublished data received through personal correspondence, March 24, 1961, with permission; and Robert O. Blood, Jr., and Donald M. Wolfe, *Husbands and Wives: The Dynamics of Married Living* (Glencoe, Ill.: Free Press, 1960), p. 265.

some couples succeed in finding happiness with each other through the middle years of their marriage is evident in the preponderance of postparental couples who find this stage better than the earlier years of their lives together.[31] The suggestion is that many men and women find childbearing and rearing a heavy responsibility, and once free to live on their own terms, they relax and find new satisfaction in their marriage. Working wives are found to be in better health and to feel better about the middle years than do nonworking middle-aged women.[32]

Drs. Masters and Johnson report that women who have had happy, well-adjusted, stimulating marriages go through the middle years with little or no interruption in the frequency of, interest in, or enjoyment of sexual activity with their husbands, who normally continue active marital relations well into their seventies and eighties.[33]

The Kinsey studies indicate that the mean frequencies of intercourse among married men continue to decline at a constant rate from the youngest to the oldest ages, with men at sixty having an average frequency of about once a week.[34] Middle-aged married women have as high or higher incidence of orgasm in their forties and fifties as they experience in their early twenties. Active incidences of married women reaching orgasm during ages twenty-one to twenty-five years is 88 percent; during ages forty-one to forty-five it is 93 percent; and during ages fifty-one to fifty-five it is 89 percent.[35] Clinical evidence seems to indicate that by middle age many women have overcome the repressions that limited their sex lives early in marriage, and with the passing of menopause, with its removal of the fear of pregnancy, enjoy sex experience more in their middle years than ever before in the marriage.[36]

With mature appreciation of sex, and of each other, a middle-aged couple may become capable of a more prolonged mutual orgasm that is far more deeply satisfying to both partners than anything they were able to achieve in their earlier years together. Meeting each other's needs emotionally as well as sexually draws the mates together as a couple. At this time the middle-aged man

[31] Irwin Deutscher, "The Quality of Postparental Life," chap. 29 in Bernice L. Neugarten, ed., *Middle Age and Aging* (Chicago: University of Chicago Press, 1968), p. 264.

[32] Bernice L. Neugarten and David Garron, "Attitudes of Middle-Aged Persons toward Growing Older," *Geriatrics* 14 (January 1959): 21–24.

[33] William H. Masters and Virginia E. Johnson, "Human Sexual Response: The Aging Female and the Aging Male," chap. 30 in Bernice L. Neugarten, ed., *Middle Age and Aging* (Chicago: University of Chicago Press, 1968), pp. 271, 275.

[34] Alfred C. Kinsey, Wardell B. Pomeroy, and Clyde E. Martin, *Sexual Behavior in the Human Male* (Philadelphia: W. B. Saunders Company, 1948), p. 253.

[35] Alfred C. Kinsey, Wardell B. Pomeroy, Clyde E. Martin, and Paul H. Gebhard, *Sexual Behavior in the Human Female* (Philadelphia: W. B. Saunders Company, 1953), p. 549, table 154.

[36] LeMon Clark, "Sex Life of the Middle-Aged," *Marriage and Family Living* 11, no. 2 (Spring 1949): 58–60.

and woman each need the reassurance, the appreciation, and the encouragement to be what they each are that comes from feeling fully accepted and truly close to each other in marriage. Failure in this task brings the aching loneliness so frequent in later years. Success in intimate interaction brings immediate contentment and paves the way for smooth going through the rest of life together.

Maintaining Contact with Extended Family Members

Becoming accepting and acceptable in-laws, welcomed and welcoming grandparents, in mutually satisfying intergenerational relationships is a highly rewarding developmental task to accomplish during the years immediately following the marriage of the grown children of the family. Fail in this task, and the family is fragmented, with loneliness and heartache accruing to members of all three generations (parents, grown children, and their children). Succeed, as many families do, and the middle-aged pair keeps a warm sense of being a family; the grown childen feel secure in their roots, with the traditions and values of ongoing family continuity.[37]

An exploratory study of several thousand in-law relationships attempted to discover what causes difficulties and what is conducive to harmony between in-laws. More than 75 percent of the factors making for in-law harmony had to do with mutual acceptance and mutual respect.[38] Problems arise when a middle-aged parent has difficulty letting a grown child go, or accepting the grown son's or daughter's choice of a mate. Mothers more than fathers have and become in-law problems, probably because their child-rearing responsibilities have been primary in their life interests through the years. The boy's parents more than the girl's are apt to find acceptance of the marriage and the marriage partner difficult, possibly because the girl's parents have had more of a hand in the mate choice, as Komarovsky suggests.[39] Acceptance of the mates chosen by grown children seems to be easier for developmentally oriented parents than for those who have clung possessively to their children all along.[40]

The chances are that the mother-in-law who can wholeheartedly and enthusiastically welcome her children-in-law has been a good mother in the developmental sense all along, while the selfish, pos-

---

[37] Marvin B. Sussman, "Kin Relations and Social Roles in Middle Age," mimeographed, 1959, p. 18.

[38] Evelyn Millis Duvall, *In-Laws: Pro and Con* (New York: Association Press, 1954), p. 336.

[39] Mirra Komarovsky, "Functional Analysis of Sex Roles," *American Sociological Review* 15, no. 4 (August 1950): 516.

[40] Marvin B. Sussman, "Family Continuity: Selective Factors Which Affect Relationships between Families at Generational Levels," *Marriage and Family Living* 16, no. 2 (May 1954): 112–120.

sessive mother finds it hard to be a good mother-in-law.

• • •

You (mother-in-law) have been "in training" for the full acceptance of your children-in-law for many years. As you accepted your children's friends and pals and playmates through the years of their childhood, you learned how to love others just because they were those your children loved. Adolescent crushes and love affairs you could take in your stride as further practice in letting children go and in accepting those they found lovable. So now, when the children marry, you can accept their mates, because you have learned to let your love for them swell to include their loved ones.[41]

Folklore has it that when grown children marry they become completely independent, neither asking for nor receiving assistance from their parents. Actually, there is a great deal of mutual support and help between the generations when grown children marry. Sussman's study of intergenerational help in middle-class families concludes that there are well-established patterns of giving and receiving between middle-aged parents and their children's families that are related to the continuity and success of intergenerational family relationships.

Parents . . . wished to help their newly married children to become established on their own class level or even a higher one, and, in turn, wanted affectional response from them. They believed children to be more appreciative of their financial and service help after marriage. This was because they now faced the problems of establishing a new household and family. Many children realize, perhaps for the first time, the efforts their own parents had exerted in providing for them. However, most parents have no intention of subsidizing their children's families permanently, and many learned that help given in moderation was more prudent than unrestrained giving. When given in moderate amounts, it did not create conflict with the new family head. Parents also indicated that by mutual aid with married children in nursing care, house repairing, vacation planning, and similar activities, they enriched one another's lives, took pride in their achievements, and felt that each had some part in the other's success.[42]

Becoming a satisfying grandparent involves a great many roles new to the middle-aged man or woman. Standing by and seeing their grown children bring up their children in ways that differ from former methods of child-rearing is not an easy task. Yet because styles in child training are changing, there usually are some areas in which today's young parents repudiate

---

[41] Duvall, *In-Laws: Pro and Con,* pp. 347–348.

[42] Marvin B. Sussman, "The Help Pattern in the Middle Class Family," *American Sociological Review* 18, no. 1 (February 1953): 27–28.

older ways in the rearing of their children. It is likely that middle-aged grandparents will be stricter and less permissive and developmental than their own grown children are. Or, on the other hand, some grandparents tend to be more indulgent with their grandchildren than they ever were with their own children. This often is resented by the young parents, not only because it undermines their authority and "spoils the children," but also because they remember how much more severely these same parents were with them as children. Helping without interfering, loving without smothering, being available without being intrusive: these are complex tasks for grandparents generally.

Grandparents can be a blessing when they are available to help out in a family crisis: a critical or chronic illness, an accident, the birth of a new baby, a period of military service or other necessary separation of the young husband and wife, temporary unemployment, or other situation that mobilizes all family resources for meeting the new problem. In occasional baby-sitting and inviting grandchildren to visit them, grandparents can do a great deal to relieve young parents of the confining burdens of child care. Furthermore, they as grandparents can greatly enrich the lives of their grandchildren with the perspective, the memories of the former days when the parents were themselves children, the continuity of the family, and the mellow wisdom of maturity.

Much has been said about the relief from their children that grandparents provide for parents. Little usually is said of the need children may have for some relief from their parents. It is quite possible that grandparents serve a real purpose in providing for children a different touch, another approach, a new setting and emotional climate that is not possible in the day-in-day-out contact with parents alone.[43]

Margaret Mead sees today's grandparents as experts in change, who have much to offer children in a sense of wonder at man's achievements during their lifetime. They, who have seen the first airplane, talking movies, television, computers, and satellites, can share with their grandchildren faith in a future in which almost anything can happen.[44]

More parents between forty-five and fifty-four report satisfying relationships with their children than any other age group.[45] To enjoy the fellowship of growing children, to be accepted by them as pleasant companions, to hear their confidences, and to share the mysteries of life with them are deep-down satisfactions. To feel the satisfaction of a job well done as grown children establish themselves in their families and carry on some of the

---

[43] Duvall, *In-Laws: Pro and Con*, p. 147.

[44] Margaret Mead, "What Is Modern Grandparent's Role?" *Redbook*, June 1966, pp. 28, 30.

[45] Gurin, Veroff, and Feld, *Americans View Their Mental Health*, pp. 136–137.

Table 14–3. *Intergenerational Visiting by Men and Women*

Frequency of visits	Parents—Grandparents		Married children—Parents		Married children—Grandparents	
	Male	*Female*	*Male*	*Female*	*Male*	*Female*
Daily or weekly	36%	54%	74%	69%	32%	41%
Monthly	52	39	23	25	16	15
Quarterly	9	6	—	6	36	33
Yearly	3	—	3	—	16	10
Total	100%	100%*	100%	100%	100%	100%*

Source: Reuben Hill, *Family Development in Three Generations* (Cambridge, Mass.: Schenkman Publishing Company, 1970), chap. 3, table 3.01.

* Due to rounding of figures, the columns may not total 100 percent.

family traditions and values are rewards indeed. Grandparents who early learn to master the arts of intergenerational relationships build not only for the moment but also for the years that lie ahead as their grandchildren grow up and become adolescents, are launched, and go on into their homes. Today's middle-aged men and women can anticipate many more years of the family life cycle and often live to see child-rearing go around a second, third, or even fourth time.

Personal contact with younger and older family members is maintained through frequent visits by large percentages of both men and women in all age groups in a recent three-generation family study in the greater Minneapolis area (table 14–3).

With the coming of the middle years in the family there is time, money, and interest in cementing relationships in the family generally. During the peak years when children were growing, life was too busy to go visiting very much, or even to write the letters, send the gifts, and keep in touch with brothers' and sisters' growing families. In the middle years, when one's own children are grown and gone, there often is a desire to become reacquainted with nephews and nieces and to come closer to the other relatives in the larger family circle.

There are certain hazards to be avoided in relationships with brothers' and sisters' families. In an exploratory study of in-law relationships, the one more difficult than any other, except for the mother-in-law, was that of sister-in-law. The findings indicate that some sisters-in-law are possessive, meddling, and intrusive in much the same way that mothers-in-law offend. In addition, there seems to be a considerable amount of sibling rivalry (competitiveness, jealousy, envy, comparing, bickering, and belittling) continuing on into adulthood. Sisters-in-law are especially susceptible to this problem in the larger family interrelationships.[46]

[46] Duvall, *In-Laws: Pro and Con*, chap. 11, pp. 221–243.

FAMILY DEVELOPMENT

Problems with brothers' and sisters' families sometimes arise out of efforts to plan for the care of aging parents. When one's parents need financial support, or when one or both of them need a home in their later years, the problem may precipitate a crisis among the grown children in terms of whose responsibility it is and which one should do what to help carry the load. Old grudges may be dredged up and old resentments aired until feelings run so high that the whole family is unpleasantly involved. Bitterness in the family is of little comfort through the middle and later years. Better by far is the effort to work things through harmoniously with the others in the larger family.

Aging parents who are financially quite independent and whose health does not yet require special care still need the attention and loving interest of their grown children. There are strong social pressures for "being nice to" one's aging parents, with everything from neighborhood gossip to newspaper headlines pouring criticism down upon the heads of the men and women who woefully neglect their parents in their later years. Respect for elders is not as strong in the Western world as it is in the East, but even so, some filial devotion is expected in terms of occasional visits, letters, telephone calls, and gifts on special days. Many of the little rituals help aging parents to feel that they are loved and appreciated.

For many mature men and women, giving affection and attention to aging parents is an easy task. For others, whose earlier relationships with their parents have been uncongenial or full of conflict, there may be real problems.[47] It is likely that keeping close to aging relatives is more difficult for the upward mobile man or woman than it is for the married couple whose ways of life are still quite similar to those of their parents. Being ashamed of the old-fashioned, old-world ways of parents of an ethnic group is a frequent hazard to the comfortable accomplishment of this task.

Cavan anticipates a decline of tension between middle-aged adults and aging parents as urbanization and acculturation increase. As older family members are fully accepted, they, their adult children, and the grandchildren benefit.[48]

Participating in Community Life

There are times for staying in and times for getting out of oneself. During the child-bearing stage of the family life cycle, little families keep much to themselves. But when children have grown and gone, and the middle-aged husband and wife are alone with fully half of their adult lives together stretching ahead of them, it is a

[47] See Robert M. Dinkel, "Parent-Child Conflict in Minnesota Families," *American Sociological Review*, August 1943, pp. 412–419; and also sections of chap. 14 on these problems.

[48] Ruth Shonle Cavan, "Family Tensions between the Old and the Middle-Aged," *Marriage and Family Living* 18, no. 4 (November 1956): 323–327.

time for getting out and building a broad base for life together. One middle-aged woman who keeps active in many projects outside her home says that she feels that these are the years when she is storing up sweetness for the rest of life. Much as the honeybee fills up the many cells of the honeycomb for the winter months that lie ahead, so a middle-aged human stores up memories of activities enjoyed, projects completed, and friendships made as safeguards against loneliness in the later years when activities, of necessity, must be curtailed.

Participation in life beyond the confines of the home is of many types and forms through the middle years. The man has his work, and many satisfied, active women have theirs too. Dr. Rose's study of life satisfaction among middle-aged, middle-class men and women turns up a larger proportion of satisfied than dissatisfied women among those gainfully employed outside the home.[49] Recreational interests too are related to life satisfaction in the middle years, as the study finds:

> Desire for having more amusement is associated with life satisfaction among both women and men. A significantly larger proportion of the relatively dissatisfied wives and husbands (44 and 39 percent, respectively) than of the satisfied ones (22 and 13 percent, respectively) would like to go out more often in the evenings for entertainment than they do now. The same relationship holds when this diversion is specified to take place with the spouse (52 and 64 percent of the relatively dissatisfied women and men, as compared with 33 and 40 percent of the very satisfied).[50]

Sussman's investigation of what middle-aged parents do when their grown children leave found that most couples increase their mutual undertakings both within and outside the home. Such joint interaction patterns as listening to the radio, viewing television, playing games, conversing, entertaining friends, doing housework and home repairs, dining out, attending clubs, movies, and concerts, taking long vacation trips, and acquiring a summer place all increased with the leave-taking of the children. These new activities were associated with increased leisure and affluence that come as children no longer have to be reared.[51] That many parents find pleasure in their newfound freedom to do what they like is reflected in an excerpt from an interview with Mrs. Baxter, who said: "Now we are living for the first time! We are in a much better position to do things now that they

[49] Rose, "Factors Associated with the Life Satisfaction of Middle-Class, Middle-Aged Persons," pp. 15–19.

[50] Ibid., p. 18.

[51] Marvin B. Sussman, "Activity Patterns of Postparental Couples and Their Relationship to Family Continuity," *Marriage and Family Living* 17, no. 4 (November 1955): 338–341.

(children) are not our responsibility. We redecorated our house last year, and Mr. Baxter changed his position the first of the year. I don't feel it would have been possible if the children were still living at home."[52]

More than ever before the couple in the middle years of the family life cycle can contribute to community life and general welfare. These are the years when a woman is free to take an active part in some community project in which she has become concerned. While her children were small, she did well to get to the parent-teacher meetings in their school. Now she may attend state and national meetings; she may hold a responsible office; she may go to the state capital to plead for a worthy piece of legislation. At the same time the middle-aged man is taking on more responsible positions in his club, organization, or union.

The middle-aged of the working class tend to spend most of their leisure around home or "with the boys" (lower-lower class), while the successfully active in the community are middle-class men and women, according to findings of the Kansas City Study of Adult Life.[53] Intensive interviews with upper-middle-class college-educated women ranging in age from forty-seven to sixty-five found most of them satisfactorily

COURTESY OF AMERICAN MUSIC CONFERENCE

A middle-aged couple can enjoy much more social life and joint participation outside the home than has been possible before.

adapting to middle age. They were in excellent health; their marital relationships were improving; some were working; others were active in volunteer and church work; in fact, great involvement with people was the primary role change of the middle years for them.[54]

Many women see the middle years as a period of greater freedom for self-expres-

---

[52] Ibid., p. 340.

[53] Robert J. Havighurst and Kenneth Feigenbaum, "Leisure and Life-Style," *American Journal of Sociology* 64, no. 4 (January 1959): 396–404.

[54] Ida Fisher Davidoff and May Elish Markewich, "The Postparental Phase in the Life-Cycle of Fifty College-Educated Women" (Doctor of Education project report, Teachers College, Columbia University, 1961).

sion. They now have the chance to expand their activities or to develop previously latent or dormant interests and talents. Their lives in the middle years are characterized by marked changes in activity and by major shifts in their self-image.[55] Social participation is found to be associated with life satisfaction among both men and women in studies of the middle-aged parents of University of Minnesota students. Working mothers were the more satisfied with their lot, especially if they found job status and satisfaction in their work. It was the middle-aged women who had married young before they had learned the skills needed to change their central roles in middle life who were the most dissatisfied with their lives.[56]

Success in participation within the community in the middle years is dependent on the foundations laid for it in the earlier years of marriage. As the family has projects and purposes beyond its own immediate interests through the years, it has laid the track upon which may run the trains of accomplishment in the middle and later years. Some new activities are possible for the middle-aged couple, but the likelihood is that the man and woman in their middle years will continue on with extensions of their previous interests and activities.

---

[55] Bernice L. Neugarten, "Adult Personality: A Developmental View," *Human Development* 9 (1966): 61–73.

[56] Rose, "Factors Associated with the Life Satisfaction of Middle-Class, Middle-Aged Persons," pp. 15–19.

SUMMARY

The couple's philosophy of life is being reaffirmed in everything they do toward the accomplishment of all the other developmental tasks of the middle years. They express their value systems as they create and maintain a pleasant and comfortable home, as they enjoy their financial peace of mind and plan for old age security, as they carry out their household responsibilities together, as they draw closer together as a couple, as they work out warm mutually satisfying relationships with the families of their grown children, as they keep in touch with their brothers' and sisters' families, as well as with their aging parents, as they participate within the larger community and find themselves as persons, as a couple, as family members, as workers, as citizens, and in all the other roles that society expects of them and that their personal aspirations define for them.

Few there are who have to talk long and loud about what life means to them or what values they are living for. Most men and women speak most eloquently about what matters to them in the stand they take in current issues, in the way they are willing to be counted in a controversy, in what they do about what they believe to be right and just and good and true. By the time a husband and wife reach their middle years together, they have worked through the lifestyle that makes sense to them as a couple, so that it brings them a sense of peace and satisfaction (success), or so that it rankles as a conflict point between them (failure).

It's never too late to learn. Even in the reaffirmation of life's values, a couple can still make progress toward developing unity and integrity in the leisure of their middle years. Nothing can bring greater satisfaction than finding that life all adds up, and that together the two know who they are and where they are headed in the business of living.

In summary of the middle years, we may say that the family typically consists of husband and wife; the children are grown, married and in homes of their own. Although the parents miss the companionship and youthful gaiety of their children, they also feel a sense of relief that the responsibility of child-rearing is ended; a sense of achievement that their children are safely launched in the adult world; and a sense of relaxation in the peace of the quiet household.[57]

SUGGESTED ACTIVITIES

1. Grounding your generalizations in research such as that cited in this chapter, and in other professional sources, show the relationship between success in achieving the developmental tasks of the middle years, educational and social status levels, and other earlier life experiences of husband and wife before and after they married.

2. Reconcile to your satisfaction the seemingly contradictory evidence on the decline or increase in marital happiness in the middle years, documenting your conclusions with evidence from both statistical and clinical or interview sources.

3. Chart the complementary nature of the developmental tasks of the middle-aged man and his wife, by indicating how the tasks of the two tend to draw them together and to operate in the same direction through the middle years. Star and discuss the exceptions that seem to be conflicting rather than mutually supportive.

4. Conduct a panel of women whose children have recently married on "How It Feels to Become a Mother-in-Law." Encourage the women to speak freely of the problems, confusions, and satisfactions they are finding in these new roles. Ask them what they have had to learn about taking in a new son- or daughter-in-law as a member of the family. Plumb the problems they have faced in reorganizing their relationships with their own children as they marry. Summarize their experiences briefly for both the pros and cons of mother-in-lawhood.

---

[57] Ruth Shonle Cavan, Ernest W. Burgess, and Robert J. Havighurst, "Section VII, The Family in the Later Years," for the Committee on the Dynamics of Family Interaction, preliminary report, Evelyn Millis Duvall and Reuben Hill, cochairmen, National Conference on Family Life, Washington, D.C., February 1948, mimeographed.

5. Make a call upon some family in the middle years that is known to you and, through direct questioning and informal observation, discover what developmental tasks the middle-aged couple is working on most actively at the moment, what problems they seem to be facing, and what satisfactions and successes are apparent.

6. List all the helps you can think of that growing and grown children could give their own parents that would be of some assistance in their achievement of the developmental tasks of the middle years. Include intangibles as well as specific practical suggestions.

7. Write a letter to yourself outlining what you recommend as an ideal program for the middle years of your own life. How will it differ from the middle age of your own parents? Of other middle-aged people known to you? Why? What will you have to do to pave the way for these ideal circumstances in life in the middle years?

8. Debate the proposition that middle-aged parents should help their grown children's families financially. Use all the data you can find that give statistical support to your arguments, at the same time that you give adequate weight to the social, emotional, and psychological aspects of parental subsidy and young adult dependence. Use actual case excerpts to document points on both sides of the question where possible.

9. Discuss one or more of the following situations adapted from case excerpts developed as class discussion stimuli by Dr. Hazel Ingersoll, Department of Family Relations and Child Development, Oklahoma State University:

a. Mrs. Flint is in her forties and is still a vigorous woman. Her only child has gone away to school, and now she finds herself without an interest in life. She writes to Joan daily and urges her to come home every weekend. She complains about young people today being so "heartless." Dr. Flint, a physician, is a very busy man. He married Mrs. Flint when she was a nurse in the hospital where he interned. He dislikes seeing his wife so disinterested in life and wonders what he can suggest that will help her. What developmental tasks confront Mrs. Flint? What can she do? How can Dr. Flint be of real help? What should Joan do?

b. Mr. Douglas is a fine man and a respectable citizen. He has been hardworking and honest all his life. When he was first married, he had great dreams of success in his career, but the children came along pretty rapidly, and Betsy, his wife, was often ill. He found himself, instead of following his desire to be a great musician, a music teacher in a small-town high school. At middle age he realized that success had passed him by. He looked about him to see the compensations—a small home, a busy wife, and four growing children. "Well one never knows which way fate will lead! Maybe

I'm luckier than I think, but I can't help regretting what might have been." How can his family members help this father overcome his sense of failure?

c. Mr. Allison has always been a sportsman and, in his own words, "as healthy as a baby." When he goes camping with "the boys," he attempts to show them how young he still is by performing strenuous athletic feats. At parties he sometimes embarrasses his daughter by his attention to her girl friends. He prefers dancing with them to dancing with his own age group. Mrs. Allison laughs and says, "Oh, Daddy is just an overgrown boy, you know. We have to humor him." What developmental tasks does he need to accomplish? Any suggestions for making aging more attractive?

d. Alice's mother and dad have been "jogging along" in marriage for twenty-five years. They take each other pretty much for granted. Daddy jokes about his increased girth and his bald head. Mom says, "Well, I'm no spring chicken either." Alice is a bit irked with her parents for "letting themselves go." As she puts it, "they appear to enjoy middle age! I wish they would try to stay young like other parents!" Discuss the attitudes of both parents and of Alice, evaluating the predominant attitudes and suggesting what developmental tasks they satisfy. How may Alice's attitude toward her parents be affecting their tasks of middle age? What does one do when young adults are ashamed of parents who do not look young and fashionable?

READINGS

Axelson, Leland J. "Personal Adjustment in the Postparental Period." *Marriage and Family Living* 22, no. 1 (February 1960): 66–68.

Blanton, Smiley, and Arthur Gordon. *Now or Never: The Promise of the Middle Years.* Englewood Cliffs, N.J.: Prentice-Hall, 1959.

Blood, Robert O., Jr., and Donald M. Wolfe. *Husbands and Wives: The Dynamics of Married Living.* Glencoe, Ill.: Free Press, 1960.

Bossard, James H. S., and Eleanor S. Boll. "Marital Unhappiness in the Life Cycle." *Marriage and Family Living* 17, no. 1 (February 1955): 10–14.

Cavan, Ruth Shonle. "Family Tensions between the Old and the Middle-Aged." *Marriage and Family Living* 18, no. 4 (November 1956): 323–327.

Chilman, Catherine S. "Families in Development at Mid-Stage of the Family Life Cycle." *Family Coordinator* 17, no. 4 (October 1968): 297–312.

Cumming, Elaine, and William E. Henry. *Growing Old.* New York: Basic Books, 1961.

Davis, Maxine. *Get the Most out of Your Best Years.* New York: Dial Press, 1960.

Deutscher, Irwin. *Married Life in the Middle Years*. Kansas City, Mo.: Community Studies, 1959.

Duvall, Evelyn Millis. *In-Laws: Pro and Con*. New York: Association Press, 1954.

English, O. Spurgeon, and Constance J. Foster. *Fathers Are Parents, Too*. New York: G. P. Putnam's Sons, 1951. Chap. 16.

Feldman, Harold. *Development of the Husband-Wife Relationship: A Research Report*. Ithaca, N.Y.: Cornell University, 1965.

Glick, Paul C., and Robert Parke, Jr. "New Approaches in Studying the Life Cycle of the Family." *Demography* 2 (1965): 187–202.

Gruenberg, Sidonie M., and Hilda Sidney Krech. *The Many Lives of Modern Woman*. New York: Doubleday and Company, 1952.

Gurin, Gerald, Joseph Veroff, and Sheila Feld. *Americans View Their Mental Health: A Nationwide Interview Study*. New York: Basic Books, 1960.

Havighurst, Robert J. *Human Development and Education*. New York: Longmans, Green and Company, 1953. Chap. 17.

Havighurst, Robert J. "The Social Competence of Middle-Aged People." *Genetic Psychology Monographs* 56 (1957): 297–375.

Havighurst, Robert J., and Betty Orr. *Adult Education and Adult Needs: A Report*. Chicago: Center for the Study of Liberal Education for Adults, 1956.

Hill, Reuben. *Family Development in Three Generations*. Cambridge, Mass.: Schenkman Publishing Company, 1970.

Hurlock, Elizabeth B. *Developmental Psychology*. 2d ed. New York: McGraw-Hill Book Company, 1959. Chaps. 12–13.

Jewish Vacation Association. *Women in the Middle Years*. New York: Jewish Vacation Association, 1960.

Lidz, Theodore. *The Person: His Development throughout the Life Cycle*. New York: Basic Books, 1968. Chap. 16, "The Middle Years," pp. 457–475.

Neugarten, Bernice L., ed. *Middle Age and Aging*. Chicago: University of Chicago Press, 1968.

Neugarten, Bernice L., and associates. *Personality in Middle and Late Life*. New York: Atherton Press, 1964.

Neugarten, Bernice L., and David L. Gutmann. "Age-Sex Roles and Personality in Middle Age: A Thematic Apperception Study." *Psychological Monographs* 72, no. 17 (1958).

Perlman, Helen Harris. *Persona: Social Role and Personality*. Chicago: University of Chicago Press, 1968.

Peterson, James A. *Married Love in the Middle Years*. New York: Association Press, 1968.

Pineo, Peter C. "Disenchantment in the Later Years of Marriage," *Marriage and Family Living* 23, no. 1 (February 1961): 3–11.

Rose, Arnold M. "Factors Associated with the Life Satisfaction of Middle-Class, Middle-Aged Persons." *Marriage and Family Living* 17, no. 1 (February 1955): 15–19.

Shanas, Ethel, and Gordon F. Streib, eds. *Social Structure and the Family: Generational Relations.* Englewood Cliffs, N.J.: Prentice-Hall, 1965.

Sussman, Marvin B. "Activity Patterns of Post-parental Couples and Their Relationship to Family Continuity." *Marriage and Family Living* 17, no. 4 (November 1955): 338–341.

Sussman, Marvin B. "Family Continuity: Selective Factors Which Affect Relationships between Families at Generational Levels." *Marriage and Family Living* 16, no. 2 (May 1954): 112–120.

Sussman, Marvin B., and Lee Burchinal. "Parental Aid to Married Children: Implications for Family Functioning." *Marriage and Family Living* 24, no. 4 (November 1962): 320–332.

15 AGING FAMILY MEMBERS

Grow old along with me!
The best is yet to be,
The last of life for which the first was made. . . .

Robert Browning

The final stage of the family life cycle begins with the man's retirement, goes through the loss of the first spouse, and ends with the death of the second. Because women live longer than men and usually are younger than their husbands, they more often are widowed than are men.

The aging family stage begins with two positions, husband and wife, and ends with one, the surviving spouse. Beginning with one interpersonal relationship, the nuclear family ends with none. The aging couple continues to be "family" to their grown children, grandchildren, and great-grandchildren, facing individual developmental tasks as aging man and woman, mates, parents, and grandparents, and family developmental tasks of the final stage of the family life cycle. The challenge of senescence is ego integrity, without which despair may mark the final years. The goal of this period is successful aging through continued activity and comfortable disengagement.

THE AGING IN AMERICA

The number of persons over sixty-five years of age in America's population has in-

creased steadily through the twentieth century (table 15–1). By the early 1970s there were about twenty million persons sixty-five years of age or older in the United States, with millions more about to retire in the decade to come. Four out of five men and women over sixty-five are no longer working, and so have less income than they have had for many years. Half of the over-sixty-five population never went

Table 15–1. *Over-sixty-five Population of the United States, 1900–1990*

Year	Population over 65
1900	3,100,000
1910	3,985,000
1920	4,929,000
1930	6,706,000
1940	9,031,000
1950	12,287,000
1960	16,658,000
1970	19,585,000
1980	23,063,000
1990	27,005,000

Source: U.S. Bureau of the Census, "Projections of the Population of the United States, by Age, Sex, and Color to 1990, with Extensions of Population by Age and Sex to 2015," *Population Estimates,* Current Population Reports, series P-25, no. 381 (December 18, 1967), series B, and earlier data from the Bureau of the Census, released by the Population Reference Bureau, Information Service, June 4, 1969.

to high school, and about three million are illiterate. Most older people are women, many of whom are already widowed. Most older men are husbands; 40 percent of the retired men in the population have wives who are not yet sixty-five years old.[1]

Some older men and women become petulant, demanding, and difficult to please. Life becomes a burden for them and for those who care for them. They resent the "insults of aging" as they gradually lose their physical attractiveness and powers, their jobs and status, their loved ones, and their former sources of satisfaction and fulfillment.[2]

Other aging men and women find the "golden years" of life the most fruitful of all, as they gather the harvest of a lifetime and keep on vigorously growing to the very last. Oliver Wendell Holmes observed in his later years that being seventy years young is far better than being forty years old. Helen Keller, deaf-blind since early childhood, at seventy-seven was traveling all over the world, writing and lecturing in humanitarian service, when she said, "Joy in adventure, travel and love of service to my fellow men were stronger than physical handicaps."[3]

Out of a group of typical older people studied, half of those between the ages of sixty-five and sixty-nine answered the question "How old do you feel?" by replying "middle-aged" or even "young." Not until the group past eighty years was polled did everyone say that they felt "old" or "aged."[4]

Why do some people age so gracefully and continue to find life good in the later years, while others get old before their time and fail to find their latter decades as "the best is yet to be?" The simplest answer is that old age is not a disease; it is a time of life. And, just as other stages of life, it has its challenges and rewards, its tasks and responsibilities.

Three patterns of aging in the United States are seen by David Riesman:[5] (1) the autonomous—persons like Toscanini, whose essential aliveness of spirit kept the body alive too; (2) the adjusted—typified by the American executive or professional man who is not supposed to allow himself to age, but must keep himself "well preserved"; and (3) the anomic—the fate of some men forced to retire, or suddenly widowed, who die shortly thereafter in a metaphorical suttee; "such people live like cards, propped up by other cards."[6]

All older people must learn the new roles appropriate to their stage of life, in which some do well and others fail.

---

[1] U.S. Department of Health, Education, and Welfare, as reported in "Runaway Problem of Retirement: More and More Old People," *U.S. News and World Report*, August 5, 1968, p. 77.

[2] See Robert J. Havighurst and Ruth Albrecht, *Older People* (New York: Longmans, Green and Company, 1953), chap. 2.

[3] Helen Keller, "My Luminous Universe," *Guideposts*, June 1956, p. 2.

[4] Havighurst and Albrecht, *Older People*, p. 9.

[5] David Riesman, "Some Clinical and Cultural Aspects of Aging," *American Journal of Sociology* 59, no. 4 (January 1954): 379–383.

[6] Ibid., p. 383.

The movement through adulthood and old age involves changes in role activity. As one's children grow up and move away, as one's aging parents grow old and feeble, as physical energy and attractiveness decrease, as death takes away husbands, wives, and friends, as retirement takes away work, as the fires of ambition die down—as those things happen, people must learn to get new satisfactions in place of old ones out of new activities in place of old ones. They must withdraw emotional capital from one role and invest it in another one.[7]

Aging men and women find that some of their former roles are now greatly reduced, while other roles are intensified as the years roll by. Less time may be given in the later decades to active working for money, and more to enjoying the fruits of former labors. Less emphasis is now on the responsibility for young children, and more on the companionship of grandchildren and perhaps great-grandchildren. Fewer strenuous physical activities and more time for reflective thought and emotional interaction are possible now. Less time in being tied down to one place and more freedom to travel, to pull up stakes and settle in a new location, and to go where one will, and when, and with whom, in a new freedom of choice are open to many a man and woman. The possibilities are many; the chances for

growth and development continue on for the human personality as long as there is a will to assume responsibility for them.

DEVELOPMENTAL TASKS OF THE AGING HUSBAND

The man of the house faces two crucial developmental tasks through the later years: (a) finding life meaningful after he retires, and (b) adjusting to decreasing physical health and strength. All other developmental tasks tend to stem from this primary pair, as is seen in reviewing the outlined tasks of the aging husband below.

1. Finding life meaningful after retirement:

Continuing on some central interests and purposes.
Gaining status and recognition from some ongoing activities.
Feeling needed and creative for what he is and does.

2. Adjusting to his income level as a retired worker:

Tapping resources built up in his peak years of earning power.
Supplementing income with remunerative activities.

---

[7] Robert J. Havighurst, "Flexibility and the Social Roles of the Retired," *American Journal of Sociology* 59, no. 4 (January 1954): 311.

Adjusting living standards to the realities of current income.

3. Making satisfactory living arrangements with his wife:

Deciding where and how they will live out their later years.
Fitting physical arrangements to health and economic situation.
Carrying out household routines without undue burden.

4. Keeping well and taking care of himself physically:

Getting regular health examinations and care.
Eating an adequate diet of well-chosen foods.
Keeping neat, clean, and pleasantly groomed.

5. Maintaining social contacts and responsibilities:

Enjoying old friends and making new ones.
Carrying some responsibilities for life outside himself.
Maintaining adequate roles as a citizen.

6. Finding emotional satisfactions in intimate contact with his loved ones:

Reestablishing close, warm relationships with his wife.

Keeping in touch with his children and grandchildren.
Feeling he belongs to his kinfolk in warm, meaningful ways.

7. Facing the possibility of death in constructive ways:

Working out a meaningful philosophy of life and death.
Preparing for the inevitability of a last illness and death of his wife and himself.
Adjusting to widowerhood if his wife dies before he does.

DEVELOPMENTAL TASKS OF THE AGING WIFE

The married woman faces certain developmental tasks in common with her aging husband and others that are more peculiarly hers as wife. She has already adjusted to being stripped of her main lifework in her middle years as she released her grown children. She personally is affected by her husband's retirement, and she vicariously carries her husband's struggles to work out his retirement problems, but the task remains primarily his. She, too, faces the challenges of adjusting to decreasing physical attractiveness, strength, and health. She, too, must continue to find life meaningful, and to feel that she belongs to others in satisfying ways. She faces the task of meeting the loss of her spouse more often than does her husband, because statistically wives tend to outlive their husbands by several years. Some of the developmental tasks of the aging married woman are:

1. Helping her husband find life meaningful after retirement:

Encouraging him in the pursuit of new interests and the continuation of the central purposes to which he has formerly devoted himself.

Assisting him to find recognition for his accomplishments.

Making him feel important as a person, for what he is as well as what he does.

2. Adjusting to the retirement level of income:

Adjusting living standards to the realities of their economic situation.

Supplementing her husband's income as is appropriate.

3. Making a pleasant, comfortable home in whatever circumstances they choose:

Adjusting happily to the situation in which they are to live out their years.

Keeping home safe and pleasant for their lives as older people.

4. Taking care of herself physically:

Adjusting comfortably to aging processes[8] without undue rebellion or regret at her lost youth.

Maintaining good health practices in diet, exercise, prescribed routines, and regular health checkups and care.

Keeping fit and attractive through good grooming and healthy pride in her appearance.

5. Keeping socially alive and active:

Cherishing old friendships and finding joy in new friends and acquaintances.

Carrying some responsibilities for clubs and group life.

Keeping posted and active in civic life.

6. Growing emotionally through satisfying contact with her family:

Growing close to her husband in new intimacy patterns appropriate to the later years.

---

[8] That aging means a slowing down of the processes of life is illustrated by the rate of blood flow through the human body. At twenty it takes blood twenty seconds to reach the heart; at forty it takes twice as long; and at sixty, three times as long, because the heart, although beating just as fast, does less and less work per beat through the years. N. J. Berrill, "The Time of Our Lives," *Saturday Evening Post*, August 12, 1961, p. 42.

Maintaining close, meaningful contacts with her children and grandchildren.
Feeling needed in some significant ways, for what she is and does.

7. Living through the death of her husband wholesomely:

Meeting bereavement courageously.
Going on alone in life after being a member of a wedded pair for most of her adult years.
Working out meaningful ways of living as a widow.

8. Facing death as inevitable and as a part of life:

Finding comfort in religion or a philosophy of life and death.
Accepting and adjusting to the realities of life and death constructively.

DEVELOPMENTAL TASKS OF AGING FAMILIES

The developmental tasks of both the aging husband and wife are intertwined with the aging family's developmental tasks, which can be simply summarized as:

1. Finding a satisfying home for the later years
2. Adjusting to retirement income

3. Establishing comfortable household routines
4. Nurturing each other as husband and wife
5. Facing bereavement and widowhood
6. Caring for elderly relatives
7. Maintaining contact with children and grandchildren
8. Keeping an interest in people outside the family
9. Finding meanings in life.

Finding a Satisfying Home for the Later Years

Research studies indicate that aging families want a number of things in their homes for their remaining years: (1) quiet, (2) privacy, (3) independence of action, (4) nearness to relatives and friends, (5) residence among their own kind of people, (6) inexpensiveness, and (7) closeness to transportation lines and community activities to be found in libraries, shops, churches, etc.[9]

Most often the aging man and his wife continue on as long as they can at the place they have been calling home. There things are familiar; they are known among the neighbors and are close to family and friends. Aging families in the middle-income brackets can remain on as usual, while the poorer third of older people are

[9] Havighurst and Albrecht, *Older People*, p. 162.

forced into shabby quarters that are cheap. The upper third of older people tend to get better housing as they grow older.[10]

Migration to warmer climates is a well-known phenomenon in the United States, but the flow of older persons into the South, Southeast, and Southwest represents but a small percentage of men and women over sixty-five from any one community.[11]

Questions older couples are advised to consider in choosing a retirement site are:

1. Do we "feel good" in this place?
2. Have we tested the locale in earlier visits and vacations?
3. Do we have congenial friends (or the promise of them) there?
4. Are climate and geography right for us now and in the predictable future?
5. Are there opportunities, facilities, and companions for continuing our interests, avocations, and possible vocational extensions?
6. What cultural, intellectual, and social groups and activities will be stimulating and satisfying there?
7. Are good medical and hospital services readily available?
8. Is the place accessible, so that we can get around when we no longer drive our own car?
9. Do the churches and religious programs there promise us continued spiritual growth?
10. Can we comfortably carry the cost of living in this community, now and in the foreseeable future?
11. Could we be reasonably happy and contented there if we were limited in strength and motility?
12. Is it a locale for the expression of activities and habits to which we are already accustomed, or merely those we think we might like?
13. What assurance have we that these conditions and new friends will wear well, and that we can live with them for the rest of our lives? Even after one of us has gone?
14. How accessible will we be to members of our famiy? Too close? Too far away?[12]

The percentage of older parents living with their children is small. In one year, roughly 28 percent of the aged in the United States were living with their children.[13] Older persons sharing living arrangements with their adult children feel more satisfied and more permanently set-

---

[10] Ibid., pp. 162–163; and Charles R. Manley, Jr., "The Migration of Older People," *American Journal of Sociology* 59, no. 4 (January 1954): 324–331. Both studies indicate the greater migration among the higher income levels of older persons.

[11] Only 2 percent during the six-year period of the Prairie City study reported in Havighurst and Albrecht, *Older People*, p. 165.

[12] Adapted freely from A. Donald Bell, "Preparing for Fulfillment in Retirement," *Family Life Education* 15 (Summer 1969): 3–4.

[13] Ethel Shanas, "The Living Arrangements of Older People in the United States," paper prepared for the Fifth Congress, International Association of Gerontology, August 1960.

tled than any other group.[14] Cavan suggests that separation of the generations may not be the best solution for the aging, their middle-aged children, their grandchildren, or the stability of the family.[15]

Nevertheless, the long-term trend appears to be toward a declining percentage of aged persons living with their grown children. Summarizing recent research on filial relations with aging parents, Schorr says:

Living together is frequently a situation in which *both* parties benefit, though a set of scales would tip one way or the other. And whatever the material balance, the receiver often renders service or repays with fondness, an important coin in itself. Conflict between such drives as advancement of one's own family and ties to the older generation is not necessarily intergenerational conflict; parents are as much wedded to their children's advancement as are the children. Though to the onlooker, on occasion, adult children may be living disproportionally well compared with their parents, it may be that the parents would not have it otherwise and take pleasure in their children's success.[16]

Living with married children can be a hardship to members of all three generations. One study highlights some of the bases for the general belief that "no roof is big enough for two families," especially when one is the aging mother-in-law:

The three-generation household was recognized by most of the informants as a hazardous type of family living in which the combined virtues of diplomat, statesman, and saint are needed. The elders have had considerable authority in the past and they do not find it easy to relinquish power to their own children. The husband and wife have just begun to live their lives independently and somewhat resent the intrusion of a threat to this newly found authority. The youngest generation, in turn, are baffled by the splitting of authority among their elders and their own desires to be "grown up."[17]

As in so many other decisions in family life, there is no one best answer to the question of aging parents making their home with their married children. What works well for one family would not be suitable for another. What would be appropriate at one period in the life of the family would not fit at another. "The task before us is to learn when this may be sound and when it may be disastrous, and the techniques

---

[14] Carol L. Stone, "Living Arrangements and Social Adjustment of the Aged," *Coordinator* 6, no. 1 (September 1957): 13.

[15] Ruth Shonle Cavan, "The Old and the Middle-Aged," unpublished paper, pp. 6–7.

[16] Alvin L. Schorr, *Filial Responsibility in the Modern American Family* (Washington, D.C.: U.S. Government Printing Office, 1960), p. 17.

[17] Marvin R. Koller, "Studies in Three-Generation Households," *Marriage and Family Living* 16, no. 3 (August 1954): 206.

that work in living together, so that we may equip our families to make sound choices."[18]

Hundreds of cases of husbands and wives who have found ways of making a home for their aging parents that worked out happily for all concerned volunteer their recommendations for harmonious three-generational living along the following lines.

When You Live with Your In-laws

1. Develop together a clear understanding of financial, household, and other responsibilities so that each one may know just what is expected of him or her.

2. Be reasonable in your expectations of one another. No one is perfect. Everyone makes mistakes from time to time. Perfectionists are hard to live with in any family.

3. Make some provision for protecting the personal property of each member of the family. It may be little more than a closet or a bureau of his or her own, but everyone welcomes some place for his things that will be respected as his alone.

4. Respect each person's need for privacy. It is not only the great who need their "islands of solitude," as Adlai Stevenson suggested. The elderly, the adolescent, and all the rest of us from time to time desire undisturbed privacy. We have the right to open our own mail, answer our own phone calls, and make our own friends with some sense of privacy.

5. Encourage each member of the household to develop his own talents and to pursue his own interests in his own way. This means you, too.

6. Jointly plan for whole-family activities so that each may have a share in deciding what is to be done and what part he or she will play in the affair.

7. As disagreements arise, and they will from time to time, take the time to hear the other(s) out. Listen well enough to get what the situation means to those who differ from you. Respond to their feelings as well as to the "sense" of the situation.

8. Unify the larger family unit, sharing the household by celebrations and rituals that bring the family closer together in its own most meaningful ways.

9. Take a positive attitude toward your joint living arrangement by being appreciative of the benefits derived from sharing the household, rather than merely bemoaning the sacrifices involved.

10. Gain some perspective by realizing that through the ages, families have lived more often together than in the little separate family units more popular today.[19]

Wherever home is, there are certain desirables in good housing that make home pleasant at any time, but are particularly

---

[18] Schorr, *Filial Responsibility in the Modern American Family*, p. 18.

[19] Evelyn Millis Duvall, *In-Laws: Pro and Con* (New York: Association Press, 1954), pp. 323–324.

important for the later years. Henry Churchill, architect, includes features such as these:

One-floor layout. This is desirable for any age—for the creeper, the housewife, the sick, and cardiac.

If not a one-floor home, the stairs should be easy and the handrails solid; the stairs should be well lighted. . . .

Floors should be warm and resilient. . . .

The possibility of reasonable privacy. . . .

Convenient arrangement of space, such as easy access to the bathroom, kitchen, entrances, and minimum laundry facility. That is to say, good planning.

Sunlight, of course.

Good lighting; no dark halls, closets, or corners; plenty of switches.

Safe cooking equipment. . . .

Nonslip bathtubs, strong grab bars. . . .

No drafts—sensible and easy-opening windows, perhaps louvred subsill ventilation.

Reduction of transmitted noise wherever possible. . . .

Outside sitting space, sunny and sheltered from the wind. . . .

Well-planned and accessible closet and storage space.

Doors wide enough for wheelchairs. . . .[20]

Within the framework of good housing, there are specific practices suggested as sensible for aging persons' homes by the National Safety Council: putting a light near the bed, tacking down or removing throw rugs, lighting the bathroom upon entering, wearing glasses when opening the medicine cabinet, taking it easy on hot days, wearing a hat when working in the sun, carrying loads that are not too heavy, and holding the handrail in going downstairs. Since accidents increase greatly through the latter decades of life (chart 14–1), such precautions are important preventives for aging family members who want to remain active and independent as long as they can.

There comes a time in the life of some older men and women when it may no longer be possible to stay on at home. The very old, the critically or chronically ill, the

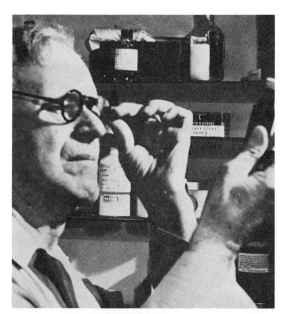

COURTESY OF THE NATIONAL SAFETY COUNCIL

Lighting the bathroom upon entering and wearing glasses when opening the medicine cabinet are recommended safety practices for older persons.

---

[20] Julietta K. Arthur, *How to Help Older People* (Philadelphia: J. B. Lippincott Company, 1954), pp. 118–119.

Table 15–2. *Percentage of Persons over Sixty-five Years of Age in Prairie City in Four Categories of Physical Well-being or Disability*

Physical state	Percentage of men and women reporting
No obvious disability (Able to be out and around the city)	79
Up and about but ill (Limited activity because of obvious defect or illness)	13
Homebound (Not confined to bed, but cannot leave their homes)	6
Bedridden (Permanently bedfast and ill a long time)	2
Total	100

Source: Robert J. Havighurst and Ruth Albrecht, *Older People* (New York: Longmans, Green and Company, 1953), p. 65.

Table 15–3. *Labor Force Participation Rates of Men over Sixty-five, 1900–1975*

Year	Percentage of men over 65 employed
1900	63.2
1920	57.1
1930	55.5
1940	43.3
1950	45.0
1955	42.9
1960	41.2
1965	39.6
1970	38.0
1975	36.5

Source: Philip M. Hauser, "Changes in Labor-Force Participation of the Older Worker," *American Journal of Sociology* 59, no. 4 (January 1954): 315; data drawn from U.S. Bureau of the Census, "Projected Growth of the Labor Force in the United States under Conditions of High Employment: 1950 to 1975," *Labor Force*, Current Population Reports, series P–50, no. 42 (December 10, 1952), and from John Durand, *The Labor Force in the United States, 1890–1960* (New York: Social Science Research Council, 1948), pp. 208 ff.

infirm, and the socially isolated older person frequently needs care that cannot be given within his or her home. These are the people who need some kind of institutional or foster home care, for which adequate provisions must yet be made in many communities.[21] Fortunately, the percentage of older persons who are completely disabled is relatively small, as we see from the health survey in Prairie City, summarized in table 15–2.

In this representative sample of older people, eight out of ten are fairly well and vigorous, and not more than two out of ten are so ill or feeble as to need nursing care. One specialist in problems of the aging points out that the extension into the home of hospital, home management, housekeeping services, social casework, food, and visiting nurse services is enabling many infirm and ill to remain at home where they seem best satisfied.[22]

Whatever the situation, whatever the decisions that have to be made, the developmental tasks of the aging man and his wife must be accomplished as a team.

[21] Specific, practical helps are found in detail in Arthur, *How to Help Older People*, chaps. 8–14, and in their related appendices.

[22] Clark Tibbitts, "Retirement Problems in American Society," *American Journal of Sociology* 59, no. 4 (January 1954): 301–308.

Together they make their home where it suits them best, for as long as it meets their needs. As they accomplish this task successfully, they are content in their surroundings and happy in their physical setting. As they fail to work out the fundamental responsibilities of finding a satisfactory and satisfying home for their later years, they face the unhappiness that so often accompanies failure in any of the developmental tasks at any stage of the life cycle.

Adjusting to Retirement Income

In the United States, it is generally assumed that a man retires at or about age sixty-five. This is true particularly of men employed in industry and in some professions, such as teaching, where policies for retirement are fixed. In general, fewer men are employed now after age sixty-five than was true in earlier decades, as we see in table 15–3.

COURTESY OF THE LIBRARY OF CONGRESS

There is nothing mandatory about retirement for many men who continue to work on through their later years.

Chart 15–1. *Family Income in the United States by Education and Age of Head*

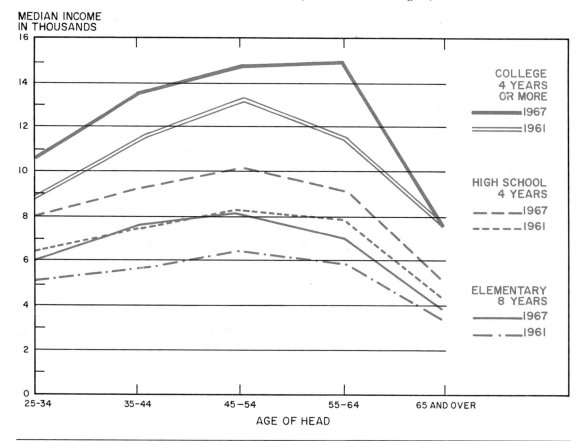

MEDIAN INCOME
IN THOUSANDS

COLLEGE
4 YEARS
OR MORE
—— 1967
=== 1961

HIGH SCHOOL
4 YEARS
— — — 1967
- - - - 1961

ELEMENTARY
8 YEARS
—— 1967
— · — 1961

AGE OF HEAD

Source: U.S. Bureau of the Census, "Income in 1967 of Families in the United States," *Consumer Income,* Current Population Reports, series P-60, no. 59 (April 18, 1969).

There is nothing mandatory about retirement for many men. A good many self-employed men continue to work on through their later years for a variety of satisfactions: (1) a basis for self-respect and a sense of worth, (2) a source of prestige and recognition by others, (3) an avenue of social participation, (4) a source of intrinsic enjoyment and of creative satisfaction and self-expression, (5) a way of being of service to others, and (6) a continuation of pleasant routines and habits.[23] The doctor, the lawyer, the writer, the farmer, the artist, the carpenter, and the businessman who is not retired under company policy often continues to work long after retirement age,

[23] Havighurst and Albrecht, *Older People,* p. 109.

FAMILY DEVELOPMENT

Table 15–4. *Adequacy of Family Income in Three Generations*

	Grand-parents	Parents	Married children
Do without many needed things	28.0%	4.7%	1.2%
Have the things we need but none of the extras	23.5	5.9	4.8
Have the things we need and a few of the extras	30.5	61.0	76.0
Have the things we need and any extras we want	3.5	14.2	16.8
Have the things we need and any extras we want, and still have money left over to invest	14.5	14.2	1.2
Total	100.0%	100.0%	100.0%
Number of families	85	85	83

Source: Reuben Hill, "Decision Making and the Family Life Cycle," in Ethel Shanas and Gordon F. Streib, eds., *Social Structure and the Family: Generational Relations* (Englewood Cliffs, N.J.: Prentice-Hall, 1965), p. 123.

thus postponing the problems of retirement for himself and his family.

Sharp curtailment of family income is one of the immediate retirement adjustments. For instance, between 1961 and 1967, when incomes were rising for men of all educational levels, there was a sharp decline in family incomes as family heads neared retirement (chart 15–1).

The financial pinch felt by aging family members is significantly greater than that of middle-aged parents or their married children, as is seen in the responses of the members of the three generations studied by Reuben Hill, table 15–4.

Many men stop working because of poor health and may find medical costs a severe problem. Hospital care ranges from an average of fifty-five dollars a day to as much as one hundred dollars in leading medical centers.[24] Medicare legislation in 1965 took a giant step forward in medical care for older Americans.

Medicare is a federally sponsored hospital and medical insurance program for persons sixty-five or older which provides basic protection against the costs of inpatient hospital care, posthospital extended care, posthospital home health care, supplemental protection against costs of physicians' services, medical services and supplies, home health care services, outpatient hospital services and therapy, and other services. Medicare pays most, but not all, hospital and medical costs for people who are insured. It is available to persons over sixty-five upon application through the local Social Security office.[25]

Medicaid, an assistance program jointly financed by federal, state, and local taxes,

[24] Stanley Rosenthal, "Medical Costs Are Getting Out of Hand," *Forbes*, March 15, 1968, pp. 101–124.

[25] U.S. Department of Health, Education, and Welfare, Medical Services Administration, Social and Rehabilitation Service, *Medicaid, Medicare: Which Is Which?* (Washington, D.C., 1969).

pays medical bills for eligible needy and low-income persons: the aged, the blind, the disabled, members of families with dependent children, and some other children. Medicaid differs from state to state, since each state designs its own Medicaid program within federal guidelines. Medicaid pays for at least these services: inpatient hospital care, outpatient hospital services, laboratory and X-ray services, skilled nursing home service, physicians' services, and also in many states such services as dental care, prescribed drugs, home health care, eyeglasses, clinic services, and other diagnostic screening and preventive and rehabilitation service. Medicaid can pay for what Medicare does not pay for people who are eligible for both programs. Persons

may apply for Medicaid at their local welfare office.[26]

By 1967, 98.1 percent of persons sixty-five years old and over were covered by hospital insurance, as compared with 54.0 percent of the same age group with hospital insurance coverage in 1963 (chart 15–2).

Postponing retirement as long as possible makes sense for many an able older worker and his family. Each year of employment after sixty-five increases the amount of retirement benefits. Working men and women are better off than the retired of the same age and occupational level, both economically and psychologically. Several studies indicate that while older workers

[26] Ibid.

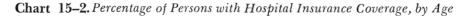

Chart 15–2. *Percentage of Persons with Hospital Insurance Coverage, by Age*

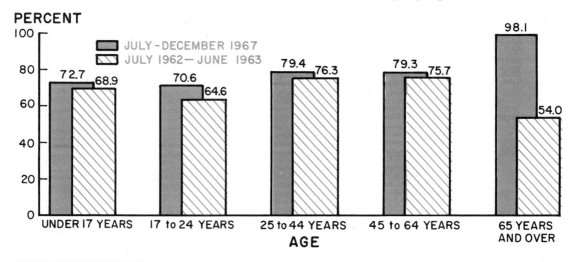

Source: U.S. Department of Health, Education, and Welfare, Public Health Service, *Monthly Vital Statistics Reports* 18, no. 3 (June 23, 1969): 1.

tend to slow up somewhat, their steadiness on the job, their efficiency, and their regular attendance are quite as good as among workers at younger age levels.[27] The thinking of students on the problem leans toward a general recommendation of more flexible retirement ages, with more opportunities for creative activity for the man or woman who wants to continue active production than are now available.

Retirement means not only sharply reduced family income, but losses of a psychological and social nature as well. Work means an emotional investment for many middle-class persons, who generally assume that the more experience one has, the more valuable one is on the job. Such basic feelings of security are derived from one's job that one study indicates that retirement for many people "is like walking over a cliff, not only depriving the person of emotional security of work and work colleagues, but also because it is a complete undermining of the seniority system on which they have counted."[28]

Age for age, retired persons think of themselves as older than do men and women who are still actively at work. Data from the series of studies in social gerontology conducted by the Department of Sociology and Anthropology at Cornell University disclose significantly larger percentages of retired as compared with employed persons at all age levels under seventy, and at seventy and over, who think of themselves as "old." As one of the retirants in these studies says, "When did I start to feel old? Why when I stopped working. I was always real proud that I'd come to Chicago and got a job and supported myself. Then when I couldn't work anymore, why I wasn't good for anything."[29]

Adjusting to retirement is a complex task, involving, as it does, not only getting along on a sharply reduced income for many aging families, but also finding life meaningful after active participation as a worker has stopped. Personal and social supports are being encouraged to ease the economic burden of the aging. Age at retirement, now relatively rigid for many millions, could be much more personally adapted to the abilities and interests of the individual to the benefit of all concerned. Until more flexible practices in retirement are general, millions of aging families must tighten their belts, rely on relatives, accept private or public assistance, or do what they can to make ends meet during the later years of life.

[27] Sidney L. Pressey, "Employment Potentialities in Age, and Means for Their Possible Increase," in New York State Joint Legislative Committee on Problems of the Aging, *Growing with the Years,* Legislative Document, no. 32 (Albany, N.Y., 1954), pp. 92–94.

[28] Martin B. Loeb, "The Social Factors in the Study of Aging" (unpublished research paper, September 1955), pt. 2, pp. 5–6.

[29] Zena Smith Blau, "Changes in Status and Age Identification," *American Sociological Review* 21, no. 2 (April 1956): 200.

Establishing Comfortable Household Routines

One of the most baffling tasks facing the aging couple involves getting used to having both husband and wife home together all day. Always before, except for brief periods of illness or layoffs, the husband has been away at work through the working day, leaving the home and its care in the hands of the wife. Now that both of the pair are at home all day, every day, the man may "rattle around like a pebble in a pail," as one older man puts it, with nothing to do except get in his wife's way and feel that he is a nuisance around the place.

The problem is quite different for the wife. She, in a sense, "retired" some years ago when the last child was launched and by now has made her adjustment to life. In another sense she never really "retires" as long as there are meals to prepare, beds to make, and household routines to see to. In her later years, she will taper off in the amount of heavy physical work she undertakes. She may get some additional equipment to carry some of the load that now is too burdensome for her failing strength. She may hire some of the heavy work done on a regular or a seasonal basis, but fundamentally her job continues as housekeeper and homemaker.

Interviews with retired men and their wives find the women continuing such traditional responsibilities as laundry, ironing, dusting, and making beds, but with retirement such tasks as moving and fixing furniture, repairing a faucet, removing and burning trash, and paying household bills shift from the wife to the husband.[30]

Retired men are also found to spend much less time out of the house than those at earlier stages of the family life cycle, and they are more than twice as active in household tasks as they have been anytime since their children were young (table 10–4).

In many a family today, patterns of working jointly as homemakers have been established through the years, so that now, in the postretirement period, the two continue on in the double harness to which they have become accustomed. Responsibilities are assumed on the basis of interest, ability, and strength, with the husband routinely assuming some chores, the wife others, and both tackling together the jobs that they enjoy doing as a team. As illness strikes, or one of the partners is out of the home for a time, the other then can take over, because he or she is already familiar with the processes involved. Decisions are jointly made; authority is assumed by the couple as a unit; and each is accountable to the other, and to the realities of the situation, in the family that has already laid a foundation for joint homemaking responsibilities through the various stages of the family.

---

[30] John A. Ballweg, "Resolution of Conjugal Role Adjustment after Retirement," *Journal of Marriage and the Family* 29, no. 2 (May 1967): 277–281.

Nurturing Each Other as Older Husband and Wife

With the processes of aging comes a variety of human needs that husband and wife mutually can meet for each other and for themselves as a couple. Physical vitality declines. Eyes, ears, and perhaps teeth need mechanical assistance in the form of glasses, hearing aids, and dentures. In time they find they do not get around as much or as far or as easily as they did. All these things are normal and to be expected in the later years. Even more disconcerting is the accident or the illness that incapacitates one or the other and throws the burden of the household and the personal nursing on the able member of the pair.

Illnesses and accidents of old age are more costly,[31] critical, and chronic than at earlier ages through the life cycle. Since women tend to live longer than men, on the average, it is usually the woman who nurses her husband through the illnesses that beset him in the later years. At first she may consider his condition as temporary. In time comes the realization that the husband cannot recover and that the disease causes death, and only after a long period of disability. The wife's acceptance of the chronic nature of her husband's illness is made easier by the fact that many of the illnesses of the aging begin with mild disabilities and progress very slowly toward complete helplessness; so she adjusts slowly, taking each change as it comes. One by one she takes over responsibilities new to her. She may have to make decisions in which she has had little practice or previous experience, such as taking charge of the finances of the household. She may have to give physical care and at times even protect her husband from the results of his mental wanderings. Care of a chronically ill husband is one of the most difficult tasks that the older wife meets.

The husband faced with the illness of his wife may have an even greater task, in that much of what is now expected of him is unfamiliar to him as the man of the house. His wife, who has always provided for his needs, now helplessly awaits him to serve her. He must know how to cook an edible meal, care for a disabled patient, keep the house reasonably neat and clean, and function in what traditionally is the woman's sphere of the home.

Traditionally-oriented men who have never learned to be at home in the house are apt to be uncomfortably awkward when the burden of homemaking falls upon them. Men who define their roles as males more flexibly, who have always been at home within the intimate, everyday routines of family living, find these tasks much easier and far more comfortable.

---

[31] Odin Anderson, Patricia Collette, and Jacob Feldman, *Family Expenditure Patterns for Personal Health Services* (New York: Health Information Foundation, 1960), p. 11.

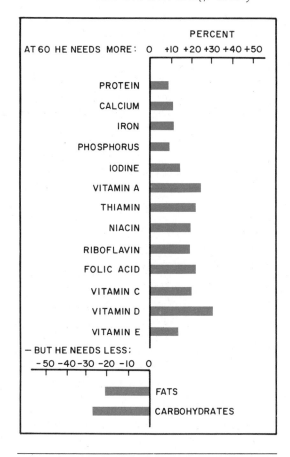

Chart 15–3. *Dietary Needs of Normal Man of Sixty Compared to Standard Diet at Age Thirty*

PERCENT

AT 60 HE NEEDS MORE: 0 +10 +20 +30 +40 +50

PROTEIN
CALCIUM
IRON
PHOSPHORUS
IODINE
VITAMIN A
THIAMIN
NIACIN
RIBOFLAVIN
FOLIC ACID
VITAMIN C
VITAMIN D
VITAMIN E

– BUT HE NEEDS LESS:
–50 –40 –30 –20 –10 0

FATS
CARBOHYDRATES

Source: C. Ward Crampton, *Live Long and Like It* (New York: Public Affairs Committee, 1948), p. 19.

interested into old age; some actually become more active sexually in later life.[32]

Husbands and wives who have maintained healthful routines through the years fare better in their mutual nurturance of each other as an aging pair than those who have neglected their common health in the earlier stages of life together as a married couple. A good example is found in nutrition, so closely related to the well-being of the older person. The family that has existed for thirty or forty or more years on a meat-and-potato-and-gravy diet may find it difficult to switch to the high-protein, fresh fruit, and vegetable regimes recommended for the aging.

Chart 15–3 outlines the dietary needs of the man at sixty as contrasted with the standard diet at thirty. We note that after age sixty the man or woman needs considerably less fat and carbohydrate, and more of the protective foods: vitamins, minerals, and proteins. Reasons for nutritional differences between age thirty and sixty are (1) the decrease in physical activity between the active thirties and the slowing down of the post-sixty period, and (2) the body building blocks needed more by the aging to keep physically fit than was necessary at the peak of adulthood.

Further preventive regimens, such as healthful balance of rest and activity, regu-

Conjugal coitus continues longer than many couples thought it would. Some continue to have intercourse long after the husband's retirement. Most men who remain in good health continue to be sexually

[32] Eric Pfeiffer, "Geriatric Sex Behavior," *Medical Aspects of Human Sexuality* 3, no. 7 (July 1969): 19–28.

FAMILY DEVELOPMENT

lar medical, dental, and ocular checkups, wholesome acceptance of whatever aids and supplements may be prescribed, a variety of absorbing interests, and good mental hygiene, go a long way toward assuring both husband and wife of maximum well-being during their later years together.

Less tangible but quite as important is the emotional building up that each gives the other through their everyday life together. Too frequent is the embittered couple bent on belittling and tearing each other down in the myriad assaults upon ego and self that only the intimate can inflict. More successful is the support of one another by husbands and wives who have built up patterns of mutual encouragement and appreciation upon which they both can lean as other faculties fail. The wife who can bolster up her husband's sagging ego as he adjusts himself to retirement and a sense of diminished usefulness is often a key fac-

H. ARMSTRONG ROBERTS

Mutual encouragement and appreciation expressed in their relationship through the years give an aging husband and wife emotional support.

tor in his eagerness to start fresh in some other line, or find a place for himself in some single facet of older pursuits that now can pay off in fulfillment and satisfaction. The husband who can make his wife feel his devotion and appreciation for all she has done and all she is helps her feel desired and desirable, more important than ever now in the sunset years. One explicit example of this is given in a report of a man who, on his fifty-fifth wedding anniversary, inserted the following advertisement in his local paper:

To my sweetheart, Sophie Hensel, I wish to thank you publicly for your love and devotion and for fifty-five years of wedded happiness made possible by your unmatched qualities as wife, mother, mother-in-law, grandmother, and great-grandmother. We all revere you. Your husband, Henry Hensel.[33]

Facing Bereavement and Widowhood

Facing the loss of loved ones is a sad task at any time. In the aging family, as dear friends drop off one by one, the sorrow is compounded by the realization, "It might have been I." Then, when inevitably the family undergoes its final break with the death of one of the original partners, the task of facing bereavement may be difficult indeed.

[33] Associated Press release, February 28, 1953.

Bereavement is a compound crisis. It is a painful emotional shock, a sharp change in social status, often an economic catastrophe, and usually a philosophical challenge. It calls for reorganizing the habits and routines and ways of a lifetime of married living. It means the breaking of the identification that has made the marriage a good one through the years. If there have been some problems in the relationship, feelings of guilt and shame over what-I-might-have-done are often as painful as is the acute sense of loss of the familiar beloved companion.

Thomas D. Eliot plotted the immediate effects and the secondary reactions to bereavement and outlined the various patterns found in his studies from total failure to readjust to conspicuous success in the task of facing bereavement, as follows:

Individual Effects of Bereavement

A. Total failure to readjust

1. Suicide
2. Early death
3. Insanity
4. Moral disintegration
5. Obsession

B. Partial failure

1. Eccentricities
2. Physical illness or prostration
3. Aboulia, purposelessness
4. Isolation
5. Embitterment, misanthropy, cynicism

6. Reversion to or recurrence of griefs
7. Self-blame or personal hates
8. Fears
9. Loneliness

C. Partial success

1. Resignation, "God's will," etc.
2. Stoicism
3. Stereotyped formulae of immortality, misery escaped, etc.
4. Sentimental memorials
5. Effective repression of memories
6. Intensification of affections
7. Extension of affections
8. Deliberate absorption in distractions or duties
9. New or fantasied love objects

D. Conspicuous success

1. New love object
2. Thoroughgoing religious rationalization
3. Spontaneous forgetting, relaxation of tensions
4. Devotion to lifework
5. Identification with role of deceased
6. Creation of constructive memorials
7. Transmutation of the experience into a productive reintegration of the personality.[34]

Even before the first shock has been fully felt, there are the funeral arrangements to see to, with all that is involved in balancing the love for the lost one with the economic considerations of the costs to be borne. The funeral usually comes on top of the expenses incurred for the last illness. If that illness has been long, savings have possibly already been spent for doctors and nurses, hospital, and medication costs. If a sudden accident has eventuated in death, then the unexpected bills for ambulance service, hospital, doctors, mortician, and all the other costs come tumbling in simultaneously.

Even if there still is money enough for all these final services rendered the deceased spouse, the choice must be made as to the kind of funeral it shall be, and how much should justifiably be spent for it. Taboos on the discussion of death in our society keep many a husband and wife from discussing these things while they both live, and so the bereaved one is often unprepared for decisions revolving around the choice of a mortician, a casket, the burial place, and funeral service. The softly whispered, "Of course you want the best for your loved one," is too often answered with a numb nod that results in extravagant funeral costs far beyond the family resources or the standard of living represented. Even when a socially sensitive mortician attempts to help the family avoid ostentation, some "adviser" who comes to the aid of the bereaved too often runs the budget into the red in his or her efforts to be helpful.[35]

---

[34] Thomas D. Eliot, "The Bereaved Family," *Annals of the American Academy of Political and Social Science*, March 1932, p. 4.

[35] Ernest Havemann, "Are Funerals Barbaric?" *McCall's*, May 1956, pp. 33, 96–99.

COURTESY OF DANIEL J. RANSOHOFF:
"FAMILY OF MAN"

Even though a widow may be relatively capable of living alone after her husband's death, she very probably will be lonely.

Proportionally more widowers than widows remarry.[36] In one recent year, the remarriage rate (marriages per 1,000 persons) for widowers was 38.4, for widows 10.2, in all age groups; for widows sixty-five and over it was only 2.0.[37] The probability of an aging widow remarrying is thus very small. One reason may be the smaller number of men of her age group and the tendency for men to marry women younger than themselves that holds even for the older age groups. Another reason may be the greater self-sufficiency of the woman to maintain a household alone than is general among men.

Even though the widow may be relatively capable of living alone after her husband's death, she very probably will be lonely. Almost two-thirds of widowed persons report their single life unsatisfactory in the lonesomeness of living without a mate, even ten years after widowhood.[38] The widow may find herself socially marooned in a community organized on a couple basis. Middle-class widows have more friends and more financial resources than do working-class widows,[39] but both face drastic changes, and each must come to terms with death, not only of her loved one(s), but within the foreseeable future for herself.

Most of these readjustments hold for the widower as well as for the widow. The tasks of facing death as a personal reality are urgent whenever they come. At the aging family stage, after years of couple and family living, they require rapid, flexible role changes on the part of both men and women.

The passing of one's life in review at the point of death is widely recognized. This life review accounts in part for the increased interest in former eras of one's life. In no other period is there more effort at self-

[36] Jessie Bernard, *Remarriage: A Study of Marriage* (New York: Dryden Press, 1956), p. 58.

[37] Hugh Carter and Paul C. Glick, *Marriage and Divorce: A Social and Economic Study* (Cambridge, Mass., 1970), p. 46.

[38] E. G. Fried and K. Stern, "The Situation of the Aged within the Family," *American Journal of Orthopsychiatry* 18, no. 1 (January 1948): 31–54.

[39] Zena Smith Blau, "Structural Constraints on Friendship in Old Age," *American Sociological Review* 26, no. 3 (June 1961): 429–439.

awareness. Such personal self-appraisal may contribute to the depression arising from feelings of guilt and inadequacy among some older persons, as well as to the serenity and wisdom that mark the final period of life for others.[40]

Studies of the dynamics of dying suggest that there is a "dying trajectory" that is felt as a person's having lived long enough, not as long as he should, or as lingering too long. Most people sense that there is a time for living and a time for dying, and the process appears to be easier for those who feel their timing is appropriate.[41]

Seminars of professional persons with dying hospital patients discern five sequential steps in the reaction to knowledge of the imminence of death: (1) denial—"No, not me"; (2) anger—"Why me?" (3) bargaining with death to wait; (4) depression as the patient prepares himself to accept the loss of everything and everyone he loves; and (5) acceptance—"I am ready now."[42]

The older family member, left alone after the death of the spouse, seems to surmount widowhood best when he or she has already built some autonomy of personality, some ongoing personal interests, some backlog of economic security, a comforting philosophy of life, and a real investment in friendships. Maintaining active work and avocational interests prolongs interest in life, even after the original family has been irrevocably broken by death. Reintegration of life around remaining values is a real task involving courage and imagination. The task is frequently made easier, especially by women, by success in relationships with grown children and grandchildren.

Caring for Elderly Relatives

As more individuals live out their full lifespan, with greater vigor than in earlier times, it occasionally falls to aging family members to care for elderly relatives. Ruth Albrecht's study of parent-child relationships of people over sixty-five years of age shows that care of aged parents was a responsibility of about 11 percent of those whose parents were in this country, with the task falling to single and widowed women more often than to married ones, and only occasionally to men.

Memories of pleasant and unpleasant experiences with parents that took place in adolescence fifty to seventy years before color the relationships between aging adults and their own parents. While most men and women remember strong attachment

[40] Robert N. Butler, "The Life Review: An Interpretation of Reminiscence in the Aged," chap. 54 in Bernice L. Neugarten, ed., *Middle Age and Aging* (Chicago: University of Chicago Press, 1968), pp. 486–496.

[41] Barney G. Glaser and Anselm L. Strauss, *Time for Dying* (Chicago: Aldine Publishing Company, 1968).

[42] Elisabeth Kubler-Ross, *On Death and Dying* (New York: Macmillan Company, 1969); see also account in "Dying," *Time*, October 10, 1969, p. 60; and Loudon Wainwright, "A Profound Lesson for the Living," *Life* 67, no. 21 (November 21, 1969): 36–42.

to their fathers, and even more to their mothers, somewhat more than one in eight report disliking their parents in adolescence because they felt rejected, or they felt they were made to work too hard, or because they were ashamed of the parent's occupation or behavior.[43]

We would expect relationships between aging family members and their own parents to be related to the amount and the nature of social change that has occurred in the lifetime of the individuals, and how well the various family members had been able to keep up to date as times change both in the social scene and in the shifting scene within the family life cycle. Upwardly mobile family members may be expected to have less in common with their aging parents than more conforming individuals. Persons who marry within their own group usually experience less conflict with their own parents than do those whose marriages have been less homogamous. Some family members love, revere, and welcome a chance to serve aging relatives, even in a culture that calls for individualism and independence of family members. Other families find older parents a burden assumed only reluctantly and as a last resort.

The problem is especially acute when the elderly one is blind, crippled, bedridden, or so senile that he or she needs protective supervision. If the family must provide the constant supervision that such care entails, it can become a severe mental and physical strain unless a companion or nurse is employed to share the load. In cases where institutionalization is indicated, the family has not only to carefully select the most suitable resource and prepare the senile one for it, but also must cope effectively with the feelings of guilt and implied rejection that "putting a loved one away" has meant in our culture.

Fortunately, this dark side of the picture is but a small part of the relationships between aging families and their extended family members. Only a small percentage of older persons are helplessly disabled, as we have already seen. Most families find that the later years are the harvest years in family warmth and closeness. As the older family members get into the latter decades, the differences between parents and children often level out in the sheer fact of all being retired together, able to relax and enjoy life, and to plan together for present and future pleasures.

Maintaining Contact with Children and Grandchildren

In our rapidly changing social scene, each generation adopts attitudes, values, and ways that differ from those of older and younger kinfolk. Some years ago, Dinkel reported conflicts among three generations of the same families. The grandparents in the fifty families that were studied in this research had grown up in and still

---

[43] Ruth Albrecht, "Relationships of Older People to Their Own Parents," *Marriage and Family Living* 15, no. 4 (November 1953): 296–298.

held to rural ways of a pioneer culture, which to the members of the younger generations were irritatingly old-fashioned, dictatorial, and authoritarian.[44] Out of this sample's experience, Dr. Dinkel recommends the practice of mutual avoidance for those families in which there is intergenerational conflict:

When parents and children do not get along, I would not try to promote family harmony, but would rather try to decrease the dependence of one generation on the other and to lessen the number of their contacts. By all means, I would not try to force children to give economic support to their parents. In such cases there are too many potential conflicts that would be brought into being by a common residence, and I assume that support by children most often involves the parent's going to live with a child.[45]

A decade later, another study of older people in a midwestern town of about seven thousand population yielded more hopeful results. In this research only 15 percent of the parents over sixty-five years of age were characterized by dependence and neglect, while 85 percent were seen as relatively independent, as we see in table 15–5, in which the items are ranked from most independent to most dependent and neglectful.

---

[44] Robert M. Dinkel, "Parent-Child Conflict in Minnesota Families," *American Sociological Review*, August 1943, pp. 412–419.

[45] Robert M. Dinkel, "Social and Economic Adjustments of the Aged," *Public Welfare in Indiana*, January 1942, p. 6.

Table 15–5. *Relative Independence of Parents over Sixty-five Years of Age*

Independence		Dependence and neglect	
Parents and children are mutually independent but maintain a close social and affectional relationship	27%	Parents share child's home but are somewhat burdensome	1%
Parents and children are considered as independent adults but may share home or advice with each other	44	Parents live alone but children come in regularly to give care	5
Parents are responsible for children full or part time	1	Children are distant and seldom see parents	8
Parents have some responsibility for children	5	Parents have no interest in the children	1
Parents share home of children and are a help to them	8	Parents are completely neglected by children	0
Total	85%	Total	15%

Source: Ruth Albrecht, "Relationships of Older Parents with Their Children," *Marriage and Family Living* 16, no. 1 (February 1954), excerpts from table 1, p. 33.

Albrecht's study finds that independent parents have certain characteristics in common: they are proud of their children; they brag about their children to strangers; they are realistic about them and treat them as adults; they can accept and give favors and suggestions without feeling threatened. Furthermore, "a basic security in loving and feeling loved removes any threat of authority or dominance of either generation. In fact, they enjoy working and playing with members of the second generation, actually like them as people, and maintain interests and a mode of life that keep some common bonds. But they also have interests outside of the family that help maintain their own self-hood. In addition, they accept the in-laws as members of the family and are not threatened by sharing or by extending parental warmth to include the spouse of the son or daughter."[46]

These qualities are those of developmental parents (chapter 4) who have through the years encouraged their children's autonomy and growth at the same time that they, as members of the older generation, found satisfaction in their own continued development. These are the older persons who find in-law relationships harmonious, with few complaints of meddlesomeness and intrusion, and a large measure of mutual acceptance and respect.[47]

The Cornell Study of Occupational Retirement found that the great majority of the older parents in their sample of 2,300 maintain frequent contact with their children's families. Three out of four see their children often, and 70 percent see their grandchildren often. Other relatives are considerably less often in touch with these older persons. Only one-third see their brothers and sisters often; a fourth see their nieces and nephews often; and but 12 percent are in frequent touch with their cousins.[48]

Most grandparents find significance in their grandparenting roles, along a number of lines (table 15–6).

Finding joy in grandparenthood seems to be something that is learned through the years in incorporating the knowledges, skills, and attitudes that make one an older person who is loving and lovable, interested and interesting. Many older men and women report that they find more satisfaction in their grandchildren and great-grandchildren than they ever did with their own children, when the pressures of young parenthood weighed heavily upon them. Maintaining close and meaningful contact with married children and grandchildren can be a most rewarding task of the later years. It can warm the sunset years with the steady glow of two-way affection and belonging that is well worth achieving. Success in this task is often closely related

[46] Ruth Albrecht, "Relationships of Older Parents with Their Children," *Marriage and Family Living* 16, no. 1 (February 1954), p. 33.

[47] Duvall, *In-Laws: Pro and Con*, chap. 16.

[48] Gordon F. Streib and Wayne E. Thompson, "The Older Person in a Family Context," in Clark Tibbitts, ed., *Handbook of Social Gerontology* (Chicago: University of Chicago Press, 1960), p. 476.

Table 15–6. *Multiple Meanings of the Grandparent Role*

Meanings and significance of being grandparents	Grandmothers (N = 70)	Grandfathers (N = 70)
1. Biological renewal and/or continuity "It's carrying on the family line."	29	16
2. Emotional self-fulfillment "I was too busy with my own children."	13	19
3. Resource person to the child "I set aside money especially for him."	3	8
4. Vicarious achievement through the child "She'll grow up to be a beautiful woman."	3	3
5. Remote: little effect on the self "I don't even feel like a grandfather."	19	20
6. Insufficient data	3	4

Source: Bernice L. Neugarten and Karol K. Weinstein, "The Changing American Grandparent," *Journal of Marriage and the Family* 26, no. 2 (May 1964): 199–204; and also chapter 31 in Bernice L. Neugarten, ed., *Middle Age and Aging* (Chicago: University of Chicago Press, 1968), p. 282.

to effectiveness in the developmental task of keeping alive and interested in the world around in active participation through the years.

Keeping Interests outside the Family

Aging husbands and wives tend to become less active than they may once have been in community activities. Some are not physically able to get about as they used to do. Others lack transportation for getting places. Many have lost interest as time goes by, and spend more and more time by themselves at home.

A study of men and women over sixty-five years of age in rural New York found physical inability, lack of interest, and lack of transportation the three reasons most frequently given by the aging for letting up in organizational participation, as we see in table 15–7.

Table 15–7. *Reasons Given for Less Time Given to Organizations by 143 Men and Women over Sixty-five Years of Age in Rural New York*

Reasons for less organizational participation	Number of times mentioned
Not physically able	51
Lack of interest	41
Lack of transportation	24
Not enough time	17
Can't afford it	14
Moved to a new neighborhood	7
Other	9

Source: Roland L. Warren, "Old Age in a Rural Township," *Age Is No Barrier* (Albany, N.Y.: New York State Joint Legislative Committee on Problems of the Aging, 1952), p. 156.

Over one-half of these rural aged belonged to no organization. It may be that being rural limits the community activities of older persons in that there are fewer recreational and commercial facilities in rural than in urban communities, fewer public and private agencies, and less available transportation than is found in most towns and cities.

The Prairie City study of older persons in a community of seven thousand population describes 37 percent of the men and women over sixty-five whose days are "spotted with wasted hours, during which they merely exist, with more or less feeling of the dreariness of life."[49]

A survey of the leisure-time activities of older persons indicates that the most frequent are solitary, passive, and require no advance planning: radio-listening, reading, and visiting. Gardening falls in fourth place for men and in seventh place for older women, with sewing and crocheting ranking fourth for female family members; both gardening and handiwork are relatively solitary and but slightly more active than the most frequent activities. Next in rank comes taking auto rides, letter writing, movies, and playing cards. Clubs, lodges, and community and church work fall in tenth and eleventh places respectively among men (table 15–8).

Fear of embarrassment keeps many an older person from participating as actively as he otherwise might. Actual or antici-

Table 15–8. *Percentage of Older Men and Women Participating in Leisure-time Activities, Prairie City Study*

Activity	Men (N = 45)	Women (N = 55)
Radio-listening	82	82
Reading	73	71
Visiting	56	73
Gardening	51	40
Sewing, crocheting, etc.	0	60
Taking auto rides	42	45
Letter writing	18	45
Movies	16	31
Playing cards, etc.	20	25
Clubs and lodges	11	33
Community and church work	11	31
Travel	9	14
Golf, other sports	20	4
Woodworking, etc.	13	0

Source: Excerpted from Robert J. Havighurst and Ruth Albrecht, *Older People* (New York: Longmans, Green and Company, 1953), p. 138.

pated embarrassment may be of several types, among which are: (1) inability to reciprocate because of family, economic, or health circumstances; (2) lack of skills at expected levels of competence at his age; and (3) faux pas that expose the individual and his knowledge as being old-fashioned and outdated.[50]

A higher percentage of men and women at the higher social class levels are active in clubs and lodges, community and church

[49] Havighurst and Albrecht, *Older People*, p. 136.

[50] Stephen J. Miller, "The Social Dilemma of the Aging Leisure Participant," chap. 5 in Arnold M. Rose and Warren A. Peterson, eds., *Older People and Their Social World* (Philadelphia: F. A. Davis Company, 1965), pp. 79–92.

work, and travel than is found at the lower social class levels. At every social class level, more women than men are active in the community, and more men engage in golf, woodworking, etc., than do women.

Older people who are active socially tend to be conspicuously happier than more solitary individuals. A study of the older men in a community of retired members of a fraternal order finds that "men with the highest happiness scores participate nine times as much in group recreational activities (cards, shuffleboard, pool, horseshoe pitching, and bingo) than do those with the lowest happiness scores."[51]

There are two theories of successful aging: (1) the activity theory implied in the above discussion, and (2) the disengagement theory, in which life space, quality, and rate of interaction are seen to lessen with age.[52]

Living examples of continued activity into and through the later years make it hard to believe that disengagement is inevitable. For instance, according to a recent United Nations report, a sixty-eight-year-old engineer recruited for the technical assistance program in Turkey was asked, "But are you going way off there and leave your wife, at your age?" "Not a chance," replied the enthusiastic recruit. "My wife is a former nurse, and she's as eager as I am to get over there and see what she can do."

It may be that successful aging is through continued activity for some types of people, and in disengagement for others. "Persons with an active, achieving, and outward-directed life style will be best satisfied with a continuation of this style into old age with only slight diminution. Other persons with a passive, dependent, home-centered life style will be best satisfied with disengagement," suggests Robert Havighurst.[53]

Decrease in social activities may account for the decline in happiness in the later years reported by several researchers.[54] Another study of fathers and mothers of college students concludes that social participation is definitely associated with life satisfaction for both men and women.[55] These trends are in line with other studies at various age and class levels in which

---

[51] Ernest W. Burgess, "Social Relations, Activities, and Personal Adjustment," *American Journal of Sociology* 59, no. 4 (January 1954): 360.

[52] Elaine Cumming, Lois R. Dean, David Newell, and Isabel McCaffrey, "Disengagement—A Tentative Theory of Aging," *Sociometry* 23, no. 1 (March 1960): 23–35.

[53] Robert J. Havighurst, "Successful Aging—Definition and Measurement," paper prepared for the International Research Seminar on the Social and Psychological Aspects of Aging, August 1960, mimeographed, p. 15.

[54] From R. G. Kuhlen, "Age Differences in Personality during Adult Years," *Psychological Bulletin* 42 (1945): 343; and Roland L. Warren, "Old Age in a Rural Township," *Age Is No Barrier* (Albany, N.Y.: New York State Joint Legislative Committee on Problems of the Aging, 1952), p. 157.

[55] Arnold M. Rose, "Factors Associated with the Life Satisfaction of Middle-Class, Middle-Aged Persons," *Marriage and Family Living* 17, no. 1 (February 1955): 19.

social participation and happiness are usually closely associated. Remaining actively related to life outside oneself is a developmental task necessary for the happiness of the aging person.

When men and women over sixty-five are asked what things in life give them the greatest satisfaction, the largest number of them report their children and grandchildren as their greatest satisfaction. Hobbies, pastimes, and housework or employment claim the next largest number, with all others (gardening, visiting, reading, etc.) mentioned much less often.[56] Since these less satisfying activities are those most frequently engaged in, the indications are that many older persons follow the line of least resistance, rather than pursuing their own real interests through the later decades. Here again, as at other stages of the life cycle, satisfactions come from working effectively on the developmental tasks of the period, while dissatisfaction and unhappiness accrue to those who fail the tasks of the period.

The attitudes and the practices developed in childhood are related to the adjustment to aging. One study finds 11 percent of the over-sixty-five population of a midwestern community living from day to day with interests chiefly in the past. These people were hard to live with and gave little or no attention to their appearance. Another 54 percent had little interest beyond their immediate families. Thirty-five percent were altruistic and objective about their problems and tended to project their thoughts into the future. This group of men and women enjoyed social life, met people well, and took pride in their appearance. Some subjects in their eighties were so trim and alert that special questioning had to be done to establish the fact that they were over sixty-five. These were the people who had learned social, job, and recreational skills earlier in life; they had made a good adjustment in life from childhood on; they had good relationships with other people, were able to make decisions and face problems as they came along, and had developed wholesome attitudes toward life and themselves during childhood.[57]

It is never too late to learn. Many individuals who have not previously had a chance to learn special skills and to develop interests find in their later years new joys in new pursuits. A neighbor learned to drive a car at seventy-two, preparatory to a cross-country tour. Grandma Moses learned to paint late in life. Thousands of older men and women in hundreds of towns and cities are playing in community orchestras. One Chicago manufacturer, upon retirement at sixty-five, decided to study the violin. Over seventy now, he plays in a suburban

[56] Warren, "Old Age in a Rural Township," p. 157.

[57] Ruth Albrecht, "Social Roles in the Prevention of Senility," *Journal of Gerontology* 4, no. 4 (October 1951): 380–386.

amateur string quartet. The sixteenth-century flutelike instrument known as the recorder is enjoying a revival, with many older persons actively involved in recorder groups and concerts.[58] A physician over eighty bought a boat and passed the Coast Guard course in navigation. Illustrations are numerous and as varied as older people themselves.

Golden age clubs, senior recreational centers, and other programs for older people are proving their value in helping many men and women to find life full and meaningful during the later years. Professionally trained staff, pleasant surroundings, and a varied program built to challenge and meet many interests of older people yield high dividends in such programs, whose worth has been well established.

Finding Meanings in Life

Working out a philosophy of life is a life-long task. Through the later years its importance is heightened as the aging person reviews his experiences and comes to terms with what life means to him. It is not surprising to find that religion means more to the aging person than it has before. One study of responses that persons over sixty-five make to the question, "Do God and religion hold more, the same, or less

Table 15–9. *Meaning of God and Religion Now as Compared with Formerly by 143 Older Persons*

Aging persons' responses	*Number of persons*
Much more	46
Somewhat more	25
About the same	59
Somewhat less	3
Much less	1
No answer	9
Total	143

Source: Roland L. Warren, "Old Age in a Rural Township," *Age Is No Barrier* (Albany, N.Y.: New York State Joint Legislative Committee on Problems of the Aging, 1952), p. 158.

meaning for you now than formerly?" finds only four who report less meaning in religion now, in contrast to seventy-one who report more meaning in God and religion now, as is summarized in table 15–9.

A study of the religious attitudes and practices of men and women during the later years in a midwestern community similarly shows that favorable attitudes toward religion and certainty of an afterlife tend to increase with age for both men and women. Among the over-ninety-five age group 100 percent of both men and women polled were certain of an afterlife. Some decline in church attendance among the very elderly was more than matched by listening to church services regularly on the radio. Reading the Bible at least once a week increased from 50 percent among

---

[58] Mimeographed release, American Music Conference, Chicago.

women in the sixty- to sixty-four-year-old group to 100 percent among the ninety-five- to ninety-nine-year-olds.[59]

SUMMARY

The aging family stage is rather like a period of fall housecleaning, of putting one's house in order. One reviews one's possessions and weeds out many an object that is no longer useful, with the realization that "you can't take it with you." Things that have been admired by grown children or friends are given to them so that they can get pleasure from their use while the aging ones are still alive to get the satisfaction of giving and sharing. Through the earlier decades of life, all sorts of things are accumulated with the thought that "some day they will come in handy." The aging years are the weighing years when the froth and the frills are discarded and only the really important things are held close.

Some say that the aging years are "second childhood," and in a sense they are. In the years of striving through adolescence and the first decades of full adulthood, the true mystery of life may escape one. Competition and struggle overshadow love and tenderness. A man or woman loses touch with nature in the hustle to get ahead on the job or get a meal on the table. A raise in pay once seemed more important than a sunset. But as one grows older, although the sight is dimmed, one sees more—the glint of dew on the iris, the glory of a storm, the sweet peace of the woods at dusk, as one did as a child.

> The real bond between the generations is the insights they share, the appreciation they have in common, the moments of inner experience in which they meet. . . .
> Old men need a vision, not only recreation.
> Old men need a dream, not only a memory.
> It takes three things to attain a sense of significant being:
>> God
>> A Soul
>> And a Moment.
> And the three are always here.
> Just to be is a blessing. Just to live is holy.[60]

SUGGESTED ACTIVITIES

1. Insurance company statisticians have worked out a simple formula by which any person can estimate his or her life expec-

[59] Ruth S. Cavan, Ernest W. Burgess, and Herbert Goldhamer, *Personal Adjustment in Old Age* (Chicago: Science Research Associates, 1949), p. 58; see also Raymond G. Kuhlen, "Trends in Religious Behavior during the Adult Years," in L. C. Little, ed., *Wider Horizons in Christian Adult Education* (Pittsburgh: University of Pittsburgh Press, 1962), p. 508.

[60] Abraham J. Heschel, "The Older Person and the Family in the Perspective of Jewish Tradition," paper delivered at the White House Conference on Aging, January 9, 1961, pp. 15–16.

tancy. All you do is subtract your present age from eighty and take two-thirds of the difference as the number of years still left to you. According to this scheme, plot your own life expectancy, and write a letter to yourself to be opened in the last decade of your life, outlining the program you recommend for yourself. Include items covering health, family, work, leisure, civic interests, and anything else you feel would be valuable in making your own aging years more meaningful.

2. Write a paper on the topic "More People Rust Out than Wear Out." Document your points with research findings, as well as from your readings generally. Illustrate with cases known to you as fully as you can.

3. Invite a panel of persons over sixty-five in your neighborhood to participate in a group interview in which you and other members of your class question them as to their activities, their work, their personal and family interests, their satisfactions with life now as compared with earlier in life, and their plans for the future. Ask them especially what they feel the community might do to make life better for older persons. Summarize these data, giving rough evaluations of the relative success in the developmental tasks of the various members of the panel of older persons. Tell what you feel might help more of them find their maximum success in the developmental tasks of the period.

4. Produce the play *The Room Upstairs* portraying some of the typical problems arising between older people and their grown children. Ask various members of the class to identify with specific characters during the performance—Mrs. Johnson, her daughter Fran, and her son-in-law Robert—and be prepared to discuss what the various situations portrayed meant to this particular person, as well as to the family as a whole. Order the play from Human Relations Aids, 1790 Broadway, New York, New York 10019.

5. Refute the argument that "you can't teach an old dog new tricks," by quoting research findings on the ability of adults to learn and reviewing the most frequent reasons why persons of any age tend to slow up in their learning (fear of ridicule, fear of failure, laziness, a rigid self-concept, feeling "out of step," or that one doesn't belong). Summarize your findings by outlining a program of adult education for persons over sixty-five years of age.

6. Show the film, *The Steps of Age* (twenty-five minutes, black and white, from International Film Bureau), looking especially for the factors that make life difficult for older persons in the family. Comment on ways in which younger persons so often thoughtlessly ignore or hurt their older relatives, and suggest some of the reasons why the generations sometimes find it difficult to live together.

7. Make a financial plan for a hypothetical married couple whose children are in college that will assure them of security in their later years, without too great sacrifice in the years that lie immediately ahead.

Plot their probable income and expenditures for three decades as a middle-aged and aging couple. Then compute anticipated income from investments, pensions, part-time earnings, annuities, insurance, and/or other potential sources of income that will keep the aging family members free from dependence upon either their children or other assistance in their later years.

8. Review the recommendations being made in the literature for housing for the older person, summarizing your findings in an outline of suggestions for aging families.

9. Review issues of the *Journal of Gerontology* and of *Geriatrics* for the past several years, tabulating the number of articles devoted to the various aspects of aging in our society. Interpret your findings in the light of what you know about the aging family in our society.

10. Write a critical review of one or more of the following novels dealing with situations faced by older persons:

Bennett, Arnold, *Old Wives' Tale* (New York: Harper and Brothers, 1953).

Bromfield, Louis, *Mrs. Parkington* (New York: Harper and Brothers, 1943).

Chase, Mary Ellen, *Mary Peters* (New York: Macmillan Company, 1934).

Lawrence, Josephine, *Web of Time* (New York: Harcourt, Brace and Company, 1953).

11. Discuss the following situation developed as a case excerpt for classroom discussion by Dr. Hazel Ingersoll, Department of Family Relations and Child Development, Oklahoma State University:

Jane's father is old, and she is the youngest and only unmarried child of a large family. Jane feels she must take care of her father. Now that she and Bob are ready to marry, they are concerned about what to do with her father. He has a little savings but he is infirm. He is very forgetful and often childish. They are afraid he cannot live by himself, yet they are reluctant to have him live with them. What are the various alternatives that Jane and Bob face, and what are the difficulties and advantages inherent in each?

READINGS

Adams, Bert N. *Kinship in an Urban Setting.* Chicago: Markham Publishing Company, 1968.

Allport, Gordon W. *Becoming.* New Haven: Yale University Press, 1955.

Anderson, John E., ed. *Psychological Aspects of Aging.* Washington, D.C.: American Psychological Association, 1956.

Birren, James E., ed. *Handbook of Aging and the Individual.* Chicago: University of Chicago Press, 1959.

Blau, Zena Smith. "Structural Constraints on Friendship in Old Age." *American*

Sociological Review 26, no. 3 (June 1961): 429–439.

Burgess, Ernest W., ed. *Aging in Western Societies*. Ann Arbor: University of Michigan, 1961.

Designs for Action for Older Americans. Washington, D.C.: U.S. Government Printing Office, 1969.

Donahue, Wilma, and Clark Tibbitts, eds. *New Frontiers of Aging*. Ann Arbor: University of Michigan, 1957.

Drake, Joseph T. *The Aged in American Society*. New York: Ronald Press Company, 1958.

Duvall, Evelyn Millis. *Faith in Families*. Chicago: Rand McNally and Company, 1970. Chap. 14, "Becoming Older and Wiser."

Fulton, Robert, ed. *Death and Identity*. New York: John Wiley and Sons, 1965.

Glaser, Barney G., and Anselm L. Strauss. *Time for Dying*. Chicago: Aldine Publishing Company, 1968.

Havighurst, Robert J., and Ruth Albrecht. *Older People*. New York: Longmans, Green and Company, 1953.

Hill, Reuben. *Family Development in Three Generations*. Cambridge, Mass.: Schenkman Publishing Company, 1970.

Irwin, Theodore. *Better Health in Later Years*. New York: Public Affairs Committee, 1970.

Jacobs, H. Lee. *Youth Looks at Aging*. Iowa City, Iowa: University of Iowa, 1964.

Kleemeier, Robert W. *Aging and Leisure: A Research Perspective into the Meaningful Use of Time*. Fair Lawn, N.J.: Oxford University Press, 1961.

Kutner, Bernard. *Five Hundred Over Sixty*. New York: Russell Sage Foundation, 1956.

Langer, Marion. *Learning to Live as a Widow*. New York: Julian Messner, 1957.

Lidz, Theodore. *The Person: His Development throughout the Life Cycle*. New York: Basic Books, 1968. Chap. 17, "Old Age," and chap. 18, "Death."

Lopata, Helena Znaniecki. *Widowhood in an American City*. Cambridge, Mass.: Schenkman Publishing Company, in press.

May, Seigmund H. *The Crowning Years: Successful Aging in the Modern World*. Philadelphia: J. B. Lippincott Company, 1968.

Mitford, Jessica. *The American Way of Death*. New York: Simon and Schuster, 1963.

Neugarten, Bernice L., ed. *Middle Age and Aging*. Chicago: University of Chicago Press, 1968.

Neugarten, Bernice L., and associates. *Personality in Middle and Late Life*. New York: Atherton Press, 1964.

Resources for the Aging: An Action Handbook. New York: National Council on the Aging, 1969.

Senior Centers in the United States: A Directory. Washington, D.C.: Superintendent of Documents, U.S. Government Printing Office, 1970.

Start, Clarissa. *When You're a Widow.* St. Louis, Mo.: Concordia Publishing House, 1968.

Stern, Edith M. *A Full Life after 65.* New York: Public Affairs Committee, 1963.

Streib, Gordon F. *The Nature of Retirement.* New York: Macmillan Company, 1959.

The Senior Center: Its Goals, Functions, and Programs. Washington, D.C.: President's Council on Aging, 1964.

Three Budgets for a Retired Couple in Urban Areas of the United States, 1967-1968. Washington, D.C.: Superintendent of Documents, U.S. Government Printing Office, 1970.

Tibbitts, Clark, ed. *Handbook of Social Gerontology.* Chicago: University of Chicago Press, 1960.

Townsend, Peter. *The Family Life of Old People.* New York: Free Press, 1957.

Vickery, Florence. *Aging and Social Functioning.* New York: Association Press, in press.

PART 4

DEVELOPMENTAL
PROGNOSES
AND PROSPECTS

16 WHAT TO EXPECT THROUGH THE FAMILY LIFE CYCLE

All the world's a stage,
And all the men and women merely players:
They have their exits and their entrances,
And one man in his time plays many parts, . . .

William Shakespeare, *As You Like It*

No one can predict with certainty what any given family will go through in the years—or the days—ahead. There are too many unknown factors and far too many contingencies to allow precise prediction in anything as complex as family life. But enough is known about families in general to forecast what to expect through the family life cycle. The stages of the family life cycle differ in length, in activity, in intensity of family interaction, and in relative difficulty of their family development tasks.

During the establishment phase the new husband and wife are building their marriage out of the dreams and realities each brings to their union. Since no two people ever grow up in identical families, each brings to marriage his or her own conceptions of what is appropriate behavior, what should and should not be done, how roles are conceived, and what a family should be like. These differences may be assimilated; they may partially coexist; one may dominate over the others; or they may remain in conflict. The channeling of the forces that bring the two persons together in marriage is powerfully motivated, making this stage not only important but potentially an explosive one in marriage. With the expectant phase of the beginning family comes the realization of imminently becoming a family with the creative thrusts toward preparing for the expected child.

The childbearing family is a busy bustling stage with things strewn about, jobs never quite done, baby's demands, and parents' crises and confusions in becoming father and mother for the first time. When one child follows another in quick succession, this stage may continue to be strenuous for some time, with little of the lull that comes in the one-child family as soon as the youngster trots off to preschool for at least part of the day. In time all of the children are in school; the family enjoys an interval of solidarity and fulfillment; and the parents are plunged into community programs—PTA, scouts, religious school, sports programs, and many etceteras—along with their children.

With the coming of the teen years, the family is atomized, with the teenagers forming peer-group loyalties, establishing their autonomy, and pushing away from their parents in the urgent tasks that must be accomplished if they are to become full-fledged adults. All this makes for emotionally charged relationships at home, with parents concerned about the safety of their adolescents, the good name of the family, and their own peace of mind.

The day comes when even the most active teenager settles down and comes home with stars in eyes to announce that wedding bells are soon to ring. The busy, expensive years of the launching stage, in which young adults leave home for marriage, for work, for military service, or for college, leave middle-class parents financially and emotionally spent, usually quite ready to enjoy the relative peace and quiet that is theirs in the middle and later years.

The latter half of marriage is typically spent as a couple in America today. The grown children come home only at intervals with the grandchildren. The middle-aged and aging husband and wife now are relatively free to come and go as they wish. These are the harvest years of family living, when the big job of raising a family is done and the man and wife can again think of themselves and what they want out of life. If they have developed a variety of satisfying interests, if they have warm friendships and close contact with their grown children and grandchildren, these are indeed the "golden years." When aging family members are impoverished, jobless, useless, iso-lated, homeless, neglected, or incapacitated, these final years can be insufferably bleak and barren, "sans everything," as Shakespeare describes them.

PREDICTABLE VULNERABILITIES THROUGH THE LIFE CYCLE

Life history profiles of today's American families can be seen through the probable difficulties with each family developmental task throughout the family life cycle. At certain stages families feel the pinch of particular pressures more keenly than at others. Through some life cycle stages, families tend to be more vulnerable to problems, disruption, or disenchantment than others. Probabilities apply to a particular family much as growth norms for individuals serve as guidelines of what to expect—not as prescriptions for what has to be. A longitudinal look at the basic tasks of family life through the years highlights points of predictable vulnerability and suggests positive measures for helping families achieve success throughout their development.

Settling Down in a Community

American families typically live in a number of places over the years. Approximately nine out of ten persons in the United States move at least once in their lives. Every year some 20 percent of American families move into a different dwelling. This proportion of one out of five families moving annually has been remarkably constant for years. In the twenty annual surveys conducted by the United States Bureau of the Census since 1948, the percentage of annual movers has ranged between 18.3 and 21.0 percent.[1]

The chance of a family's moving is four times greater, more or less, in the early stages of the life cycle than in the middle and later years (chart 16–1). The coming of the first child brings the desire for more space and for feeling settled as a family. Young husbands have few seniority rights and other advantages to keep them from moving to a different locale when a better opportunity comes along. High mobility in the early years of marriage has been characteristic of families for generations. The latest three-generation family study found

---

[1] U.S. Bureau of the Census, "Mobility of the Population of the United States: March 1966 to March 1967," *Population Characteristics*, Current Population Reports, series P-20, no. 171 (April 30, 1968), p. 1.

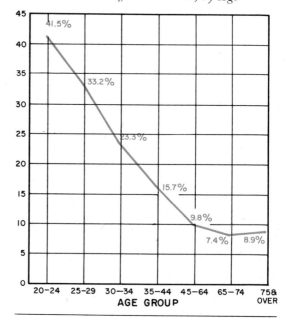

Chart 16–1. *Decreasing Percentages of Persons Moving into a Different House, by Age*

Source: U.S. Bureau of the Census, "Mobility of the Population of the United States: March 1967 to March 1968," *Population Characteristics*, Current Population Reports, series P-20, no. 188 (August 14, 1969), p. 11.

the grandparent, parent, and married child generations all following similar patterns, with a peak in mobility coming at the second year of marriage, and declining rapidly

---

Table 16–1. *High Mobility Comes Early in a Marriage*

| Generation | Percentage of moving by year of marriage | | | |
	1st year of marriage	2nd year of marriage	7th year of marriage	40th year of marriage
Grandparent	12%	42%	14%	4%
Parent	21	48	15	—
Married child	24	50	15	—

Source: Reuben Hill, *Family Development in Three Generations* (Cambridge, Mass.: Schenkman Publishing Company, 1970), chap. 5.

Table 16–2. *School-age Children and Their Families Move Less than Younger or Older Ones*

Age of children	Percentage of the United States population moving	
	1968 data	1969 data
1 to 4 years	27.5%	28.9%
5 to 6 years	20.8	22.3
7 to 13 years	16.2	16.4
14 to 17 years	13.4	14.5
18 to 19 years	23.3	25.3

Source: U.S. Bureau of the Census, "Mobility of the Population of the United States: March 1966 to March 1967," *Population Characteristics*, Current Population Reports, series P-20, no. 171 (April 30, 1968), table 4, p. 12; and U.S. Bureau of the Census, "Mobility of the Population of the United States: March 1967 to March 1968," *Population Characteristics*, Current Population Reports, series P-20, no. 188 (August 14, 1969), p. 11.

thereafter to a low of 4 percent a year in the later years of the grandparent generation.[2]

Larger percentages of children of all ages move now than formerly. See table 16–2 for a recent two-year comparison. Very young children and their families move more than older ones. By the time children are in elementary and secondary schools, their mobility declines; then immediately after high school graduation it rises sharply again with the onset of the launching period. Job shifts and aspirations for a home of their own where children may have play space, good schools, and other advantages combine to push more and more families into the suburban areas that circle our cities.[3]

Until a family gets settled into a new community, they have more visits from their relatives than after they have lived in the new place nine months or more. By that time they typically have joined one or more clubs and know more of their neighbors.[4]

Family members tend to follow their interests out into community activities—often by age groups. Families with young children find other young families congenial in "sitter-swaps," but otherwise are not as active in the community as are those with older children.[5] School-age children

[2] Reuben Hill, *Family Development in Three Generations* (Cambridge, Mass.: Schenkman Publishing Company, 1970), chap. 5.

[3] Factors related to the move to the suburbs are discussed in: Ernest R. Mowrer, "The Family in Suburbia," pp. 147–164; Wendell Bell, "Social Choice, Life Styles, and Suburban Residence," pp. 225–247; and Sylvia F. Fava, "Contrasts in Neighboring: New York City and a Suburban Community," pp. 122–131, in William A. Dobriner, ed., *The Suburban Community* (New York: G. P. Putnam's Sons, 1958). See also such related studies as Peter H. Rossi, *Why Families Move: A Study in the Social Psychology of Urban Mobility* (Glencoe, Ill.: Free Press, 1955), William H. Whyte, Jr., *The Organization Man* (Garden City, N.Y.: Doubleday Anchor Books, 1957), and Gerald R. Leslie and Arthur H. Richardson, "Life-Cycle, Career Pattern, and the Decision to Move," paper presented at the International Conference on the Family, New York City, August 1960.

[4] Eugene Litwak, "Differential Functions of Family and Neighborhood Primary Groups for Social Succor," paper presented at the International Conference on the Family, New York City, August 1960.

[5] Kenneth R. Cunningham and Theodore B. Johannis, Jr., "Research on the Family and Leisure: A Review and Critique of Selected Studies," *Family Life Coordinator* 9, nos. 1–2 (September–December 1960): 25–32.

involve their parents in parent-teacher associations, scout programs, Camp Fire Girls, and a variety of sports, dramatic, and musical activities sponsored by the church, the local "Y," and other agencies. By the time the family reaches the teenage stage, the parents are drawn into various chaperoning, chauffeuring, and sponsoring arrangements which bring them in touch with other families with teenagers and a variety of community activities on their own.

Home Ownership through the Family Cycle

Getting married and raising a family provide powerful incentives for buying a house today. Young couples typically rent their dwelling place until the first baby comes. In a central New York study, 92 percent of the early-married childless couples rent an apartment.[6] With the arrival of children, home ownership increases rapidly and continues to rise throughout most of the rest of the marriage.[7]

---

[6] Harold Feldman, "The Development of Husband-Wife Relationships," paper delivered at the International Conference on the Family, August 1960, mimeographed appendix, table 10, p. 5.

[7] Ibid.; John B. Lansing and Leslie Kish, "Family Life Cycle as an Independent Variable," *American Sociological Review* 22, no. 5 (October 1957): 514; and John B. Lansing and James N. Morgan, "Consumer Finances over the Life Cycle," in Lincoln H. Clark, ed., *Consumer Behavior*, vol. 2, *The Life Cycle and Consumer Behavior* (New York: New York University Press, 1955), p. 42.

Chart 16–2. *Families Owning Own Homes by Stage of the Family Life Cycle*

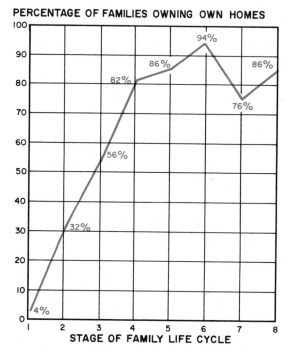

PERCENTAGE OF FAMILIES OWNING OWN HOMES

Source: Harold Feldman, "The Development of Husband-Wife Relationships," paper delivered at the International Conference on the Family, August 1960, p. 5.

Feldman finds (chart 16–2) that only 4 percent of the childless couples in early marriage own their own homes. Practically one-third (32 percent) of the couples with oldest child an infant, more than one-half (56 percent) of the couples with oldest child at preschool age, four out of five (82 percent) of the couples with all children at school age, 86 percent of the couples with oldest child a teenager, and 94 percent of the couples with one or more children at home and one or more out of the home (equivalent to what we are calling the launching stage) own their own homes—a steady rise in home ownership as children come and grow up. Then come the middle years (stage 7), when the children have gone and there is no longer so much need for the house; at that time home ownership drops from a high of 94 percent to 76 percent. By the time the couple is aging (stage 8), the majority own a retirement home (86 percent).

Data from three generations of Minnesota families show the same trends: home ownership rises from 55 percent of the married couples with young children to 93 percent of the middle-aged parents and then drops to 78 percent of the postretirement grandparents.[8]

For most families, buying a home means assuming debts which continue through the years. House payments are closely related to other family indebtedness. In a real sense it is not only the initial cost of the home, but also furnishing, equipping, and keeping it up that are costly.[9] Having a house means filling it with all the necessities and comforts that a modern home seems to require. "Planned obsolescence," whereby an item is designed for a limited life, operates throughout the life cycle in the majority of families.[10]

Even for those who do not own their own homes, there are the ongoing tasks of finding, furnishing, and settling into a place which meets the family requirements at a given life cycle stage within the time and money available. This basic family task is related in many ways to all other developmental tasks—especially to that having to do with paying the bills.

---

[8] Hill, *Family Development in Three Generations*, chap. 2.

[9] "The strongest, most consistent and direct influence on acquisitions of durable goods is residential moving." Ibid., chap. 7.

[10] Ibid.

Table 16–3. *Housing Payments and Indebtedness at Different Stages in the Life Cycle*

		Young married			Older married (45 plus)	
	Young single	Childless	Youngest child under 6	Youngest child 6 or over	With children	No children under 18
Proportion of nonfarm units making any housing payments*	39%	88%	94%	95%	96%	94%
Proportion with debts of any kind†	43	71	88	83	77	49

* Data from John B. Lansing and James N. Morgan, "Consumer Finances over the Life Cycle," in Lincoln H. Clark, ed., *Consumer Behavior*, vol. 2, *The Life Cycle and Consumer Behavior* (New York: New York University Press, 1955), p. 44.

† Ibid., p. 48.

Financial Pressures through the Years

Costs are highest at the times when income is lowest in the family life cycle. During the establishment and childbearing stages, the husband's earnings are lower than they will be until he reaches retirement's reduced income. At both the early and the last years of marriage, costs peak in outlays for health and medical care and for the special housing arrangements families make for both their youngest and their oldest members.

Costs are high during the early years of marriage, partly because durable goods and equipment for the household tend to be regarded as necessities by the newly married.[11] Young couples today start out with as many furnishings and pieces of equipment as their parents and grandparents acquired during their first two decades of marriage.[12]

Financial pressures remain high during the years in which children are being raised. More families with young children buy television sets, for instance, than at any other stage in the family life cycle. Similarly, percentages of families buying new cars are high in the child-rearing stages,

exceeded only by couples in the establishment phase.[13]

A considerable proportion of the young couple's inventory has been given to them. In actual count, percentages of products acquired as gifts by young couples in Minnesota were: coffee makers, 72 percent; electric frypans, 64 percent; sewing machines, 24 percent; vacuum cleaners, 23 percent; sofas, 15 percent; floor carpeting, 12 percent; and washing machines, 12 percent.[14] Gifts of goods and services between relatives in these families accounted for 70 percent of the total 3,781 instances of help exchanges in one year's period. Young married couples with the pressures of children on their limited resources both needed and received the most help from their parents and other kinfolk.[15]

Parents of young married couples are apt to be at the peak of their financial well-being as a family. Their heavy costs of bearing and rearing children and buying, furnishing, and equipping a home have subsided. With each succeeding decade, the workingman's income has probably increased until it reaches its highest levels

---

[11] James N. Morgan, "Consumer Investment Expenditures," *American Economic Review* 48, no. 5 (December 1958): 890.

[12] Hill, *Family Development in Three Generations*, chap. 2.

[13] Lansing and Kish, "Family Life Cycle as an Independent Variable," p. 514; also U.S. Bureau of the Census, "Special Report on Household Ownership and Purchases of Automobiles and Selected Household Durables: 1960 to 1967," *Consumer Buying Indicators*, Current Population Reports, series P-65, no. 18 (August 11, 1967).

[14] Hill, *Family Development in Three Generations*, chap. 7.

[15] Ibid., chap. 3.

in his mid-fifties, a full decade or more before his retirement. So, in the typical American family the middle-aged parents are least in need of help from their relatives and give to them disproportionally more than they get from them.

Disagreements about money lead all others throughout the family life cycle.[16] They rise sharply from 10 percent of honeymooners' squabbles to 28 percent in families with preschool children. From then on they come close to one-fourth of all family disagreements until the children have been launched. High levels of conflict about money coupled with decline in satisfaction with standard of living while children are being raised are paired family problems that must be met. Married couples with high educational and occupational attainments, flexible family organization, and good marital communication are found to do better in their life cycle management, make more choices, and do more preplanning of their actions than less fortunate pairs.[17]

When Wives Work

To fill the gap between her husband's income and her family's needs, today's wife and mother often gets a job. At least nine

[16] Robert O. Blood, Jr., and Donald M. Wolfe, *Husbands and Wives: The Dynamics of Married Living* (Glencoe, Ill.: Free Press, 1960), p. 247.

[17] Hill, *Family Development in Three Generations*, chap. 13.

Chart 16–3. *Percentage of Working Wives by Stage in the Family Life Cycle*

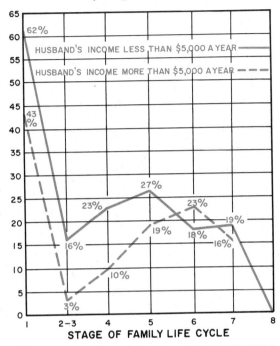

Source: Robert O. Blood, Jr., and Donald M. Wolfe, *Husbands and Wives: The Dynamics of Married Living* (Glencoe, Ill.: Free Press, 1960), p. 105.

out of ten women work outside the home in the course of their lives in the United States.[18] Typically, the young wife works until her first child arrives, when she drops out of the labor force until her children are in school. Then she may return to work to help meet family costs and to assure the children of adequate schooling and the family of the standard of living to which she and her husband aspire.

[18] National Manpower Council, *Womanpower* (New York: Columbia University Press, 1957), p. 10.

Table 16–4. *Percentage of Wives Working, by Age, Age of Children, and Husbands' Income*

Ages of wives and children	Income of husbands				
	Under $3,000	$3,000-$4,999	$5,000-$6,999	$7,000 and over	Average
No children under 18					
Wife 16–34 years	55.4%	63.6%	71.4%	66.6%	64.8%
Children under 6 years	32.0	34.4	31.6	19.5	26.5
Children 6 to 17 years	49.5	52.0	49.9	40.5	45.0
No children under 18					
Wife 35–54 years	55.7	54.7	52.7	46.7	50.8
No children under 18					
Wife 55 years and over	17.6	22.7	30.0	27.5	22.6

Source: U.S. Department of Labor, Bureau of Labor Statistics, *Marital and Family Characteristics of Workers*, Special Labor Force Report, no. 94 (March 1967), table J, p. A-15.

More mothers in low-income families work than in more affluent families, but the pattern of wives' employment through the family life cycle is similar (chart 16–3).

Relevant data from the United States Department of Labor (table 16–4) show clearly that once children arrive in the family, wives' labor force participation drops precipitantly. Percentages of working wives peak again when there are no children under eighteen and the family is going through its launching period stage. Regardless of the size of the husband's income, more thirty-five- to fifty-four-year-old wives work than at any other time since their children were born—possibly to provide a financial cushion for the costs of college education, wardrobes, weddings, and other outlays for suitably launching their young adult children and refurbishing the family home after children have grown and gone.

What "price" does the family pay for the earnings of its wife and mother? It depends on the mother's health, ability, and liking for her job. It depends upon her husband's attitude toward her working, and toward his role in the family. And, it depends upon the age and number of children as well as on their care when their mother is away. A recent analysis of more than fifty studies on the effect of maternal employment on children concludes, "After reading these studies, it looks as if the fact of the mother being employed or staying at home is not such an important factor in determining the behavior of the child as we have been led to think."[19]

There is mounting evidence that a family's satisfaction with its standard of living declines as children come and decreases still

[19] Lois H. Meek Stolz, "Effects of Maternal Employment on Children: Evidence from Research," *Child Development* 31, no. 4 (December 1960): 779.

further as they grow up and need more and more of this world's goods.[20] Low-income families may improve financially as soon as their children are old enough to work. But the teenage and launching periods are a further strain on middle-class families who aspire to do well by their children—support them through college and into homes of their own in the style to which they would like to become accustomed.

Marital Roles as the Marriage Continues

Studies agree that in early marriage husband and wife share jointly many more decisions than they do in the later stages of the family life cycle. There is increasing role differentiation as the marriage continues. By the launching and middle years families tend to assign decisions to one family member or the other rather than to make them jointly. As parents get busier with the many tasks of raising, supporting, and releasing their children, time and energy are depleted, and it becomes easier to divide their responsibilities. Then, as they both become increasingly expert in areas where experience has proven their ability, it is understandable that they agree to allocate to the more competent and available individuals the decisions that are involved in various family tasks. For instance, the Detroit Area Study finds that wives assume an increasing share of household tasks and decisions through the family life cycle. As the wife's responsibilities in the family increase, the husband's decision-making decreases sharply from a peak at the childbearing and preschool stages to a low at the aging family stage.[21]

Although production of goods in the family has decreased rapidly through recent decades, there still are a great many things that have to be done in the home if the family is to live well. While home production levels have decreased, standards of living have appreciably increased. Home production of goods increases sharply through the family life cycle. The newly married wife typically is too busy working outside the home to engage in much home production. The young mother has her hands full in child care activities. By the time children reach the teen and launching years, home production increases sharply, and by the time the children have left home, it reaches a high peak.[22] The homemaker in the middle and later years has the time, the know-how, and a ready market for her homemade clothing and foodstuffs in her children's growing families. So she uses her creative energies in making more things than ever before in the life of her family.

[20] See Blood and Wolfe, *Husbands and Wives,* p. 112; and Lansing and Morgan, "Consumer Finances over the Life Cycle," p. 49.

[21] Blood and Wolfe, *Husbands and Wives.*
[22] Blood and Wolfe, *Husbands and Wives,* p. 85.

Husbands usually make decisions regarding their work and buying a car.[23] Wives generally make the decisions about their work outside the home, as well as within the family, in such areas as food and gardening. Other decisions—medical and dental care, insurance, vacations, and the purchase of such items as radio or television sets—both husband and wife tend to share, in both rural and urban families in various sections of the country in both low and middle income groups.[24]

The amount of time that families spend on various homemaking activities differs greatly from one family to another. Factors determining the allocation of time in a given family include the following:[25]

1. Stage of the family life cycle
2. Number of persons in the home
3. Number and ages of the children
4. Special expectations and interests of the members of the household

5. Responsibilities undertaken by the homemaker in relation to the other members of the family because of their physical, emotional, educational, social, and personal needs
6. Duties undertaken by the homemaker in behalf of the children's school and organizational demands
7. Functions of the homemaker as wife, hostess, companion, partner, and helpmate
8. Out-of-the-home responsibilities of the homemaker in gainful employment, volunteer work, and individual enrichment activities
9. Size and nature of the home that must be maintained
10. Standard of living the family aspires to maintain
11. Levels of competence the homemaker expects of herself in the performance of the various homemaking tasks she undertakes
12. Home management skills and abilities to plan, administer, and run the menage
13. Number and qualifications of other persons helping in the performance of the various household tasks
14. Type of assistance others give the homemaker and with what frequency
15. Availability of emergency resources for special services from time to time
16. Number and efficiency of the various laborsaving devices and equipment available and relative ease of keeping them in good working order

[23] Blood and Wolfe, *Husbands and Wives*, p. 21; and Glenn C. McCann, "Consumer Decisions in the Rural Farm Family in the South," paper read at the American Sociological Association meetings, New York City, August 1960.

[24] Blood and Wolfe, *Husbands and Wives*; McCann, "Consumer Decisions in the Rural Farm Family in the South"; Elizabeth H. Wolgart, "Do Husbands or Wives Make the Purchasing Decisions?" *Journal of Marketing* 23 (October 1958): 151–158.

[25] An elaboration and adaptation of a paper delivered by Helena Znaniecki Lopata, "The Life Cycle of Social Roles of Housewife," Midwest Sociological Society meetings, Spring 1965, mimeographed, p. 7.

17. Location of the household in terms of time and distances required for utilizing needed resources, i.e., shopping areas, medical, dental, and cultural facilities, etc.

18. Flexibility of family and personal routines allowing for simplified methods of care of the household and its members as the situation changes.

Burdens of Guilt and Conflicting Loyalties

Shifting loyalties through the life cycle inevitably bring some anxiety and guilt feelings to various members of the family at different times. During the establishment phase, the young bride often faces conflicting loyalties between her parents and her husband and may feel guilty about neglecting her mother. At the pregnant phase it is the young husband who is apt to feel guilty at having "gotten her that way" especially if she has unpleasant symptoms at the onset of her pregnancy. During the childbearing stage, when the young mother is engrossed in child care procedures that are new and demanding, she may feel guilty, and her husband may be resentful at her neglect of him. As children get into the preschool stage, they normally disobey their parents from time to time with subsequent feelings of guilt, while their parents, departing from their parents' practices in some ways, may experience periods of anxiety, insecurity, and doubt about their parental competence.

As the children go to school and proceed through adolescence, divided loyalties appear as children form close relationships with their peers and pull away from earlier dependence upon their parents. Youthful sex practices, so often hidden from their parents, add further to the burden of guilt school-agers and adolescents carry. The father, engrossed in earning a living for his expanding household, may feel guilty that he does not spend more time with his wife and children. It is when older children reach the launching stage that the mother is most apt to feel "let down," neglected, and misunderstood as she finds herself taken for granted in meeting the many needs and demands of the family. The emancipation of the older teenagers and young adults must be accomplished, but it often is a painful and anxious period for both parents. All this is quite normal, albeit central as storm centers in the emotional climate of the family.

MARITAL COMPANIONSHIP AND SATISFACTION THROUGH THE FAMILY LIFE CYCLE

Husband-wife companionship is at a high point early in marriage and declines through the years of bearing and rearing children. Studying 799 husbands and 799 wives in the eight-stage family life cycle, Harold Feldman and associates at Cornell University have published data that go a step beyond earlier research into marital interaction and satisfaction through the family life cycle. They find four out of ten of the wives (42 percent) and husbands (44 percent) reporting laughing together, calmly discussing something together, having a stimulating exchange of ideas, and working together on a project as often as once a day or more. Both sexes report high frequencies of positive companionship at the beginning of marriage, with substantial declines to the preschool stage and levelling off thereafter. More wives than husbands (41 percent versus 27 percent) report that their marriage was going well "all the time" at the beginning marriage stage. For both partners there was a decline in general marital satisfaction thereafter through childbearing, infancy, preschool, and school-age stages, with some improvement through the latter four family life cycle stages (tables 16–5 and 16–6).

Table 16–5. *Marital Satisfaction by Stage of the Family Life Cycle—Wives*

Measure and level of marital satisfaction	Stage of family life cycle									Statistical evaluation
	1 N = 51	2 N = 51	3 N = 82	4 N = 244	5 N = 227	6 N = 64	7 N = 30	8 N = 50	Total N = 799	
General marital satisfaction										
All the time	41%	31%	22%	11%	14%	20%	17%	38%	20%	$\chi^2 = 55.8$
Most of the time	47	51	58	63	55	56	43	50	56	df = 14
Less often	12	18	20	26	31	24	40	12	24	p < .001
										C = .31
Negative feelings										
Never	10%	4%	4%	8%	12%	25%	13%	28%	11%	$\chi^2 = 61.9$
Once-twice a year	41	37	40	36	49	42	54	44	42	df = 21
Once-twice a month	35	41	45	39	26	20	30	18	33	p < .001
More often	14	18	11	17	13	13	3	10	14	C = .31
Positive companionship										
More than once a day	16%	10%	7%	5%	5%	5%	10%	12%	7%	$\chi^2 = 46.0$
About once a day	55	39	29	31	36	38	27	24	35	df = 21
Once-twice a week	25	39	49	46	34	45	40	44	50	p < .001
Less often	4	12	25	18	25	12	23	20	18	C = .27
Present family life cycle stage										
Very satisfying	74%	76%	50%	35%	17%	8%	17%	82%	45%	$\chi^2 = 242.2$
Quite satisfying	22	18	33	44	38	16	13	14	33	df = 14
Less satisfying	4	6	17	21	15	76	70	4	22	p < .001
										C = .59

Source: Boyd C. Rollins and Harold Feldman, "Marital Satisfaction over the Family Life Cycle," *Journal of Marriage and the Family* 32, no. 1 (February 1970): 24.

Most husbands (81 percent) and wives (78 percent) in this study find their present stage in the family life cycle either "very satisfying" or "quite satisfying." Both husbands and wives rate highly the beginning marriage, childbearing, and child-rearing stages, and are at a low point in satisfaction with their present stage while launching their children from the home. After the last child has grown and gone, satisfaction of both partners with their present stage in the family life cycle rapidly increases to about the levels reported when the first child was expected.

Wives and husbands rate their marital satisfaction differently at critical points in their lives. These data suggest that bearing and rearing children are accompanied by declines in marital satisfaction on the part of wives, while the most difficult period of marriage for husbands is when they are anticipating retirement. The researchers suggest that a developmental theory of marital satisfaction focus on parenting roles for

Table 16–6. *Marital Satisfaction by Stage of the Family Life Cycle—Husbands*

Measure and level of marital satisfaction	Stage of family life cycle									Statistical evaluation
	1 $N=51$	2 $N=51$	3 $N=82$	4 $N=244$	5 $N=227$	6 $N=64$	7 $N=30$	8 $N=50$	Total $N=799$	
General marital satisfaction										
All the time	27%	22%	17%	14%	18%	27%	27%	42%	20%	$\chi^2 = 32.5$
Most of the time	61	62	59	63	60	55	40	52	60	df = 14
Less often	12	16	24	23	22	18	33	6	20	p < .01
										C = .24
Negative feelings										
Never	10%	10%	7%	15%	19%	12%	10%	32%	15%	$\chi^2 = 32.4$
Once-twice a year	41	47	54	50	44	63	43	40	48	df = 21
Once-twice a month	31	31	28	25	28	17	37	22	27	p > .05
More often	18	12	11	10	9	8	10	6	10	C = .23
Positive companionship										
More than once a day	22%	8%	4%	6%	8%	10%	10%	6%	8%	$\chi^2 = 42.2$
About once a day	49	43	34	35	34	31	40	26	36	df = 21
Once-twice a week	27	37	38	41	39	45	33	60	40	p < .01
Less often	2	12	24	18	19	14	17	8	16	C = .26
Present family life cycle stage										
Very satisfying	55%	69%	61%	39%	44%	9%	24%	66%	44%	$\chi^2 = 184.7$
Quite satisfying	39	23	31	45	41	25	13	30	37	df = 14
Less satisfying	6	8	8	16	15	66	63	4	19	p < .001
										C = .53

Source: Boyd C. Rollins and Harold Feldman, "Marital Satisfaction over the Family Life Cycle," *Journal of Marriage and the Family* 32, no. 1 (February 1970): 24.

wives, while for husbands the contingent occupational role may be more relevant.[26]

Other studies suggest that during the child-rearing years, husbands and wives tend to be absorbed in their separate roles as fathers and mothers. They stop doing things together and grow apart. Then when the children have grown and the couple might enjoy each other's company, they have become strangers under a common roof, with little to share with one another. This is not inevitable. Among older wives, one in four is still enthusiastic about her husband's companionship, and another one in four is quite satisfied. But fully half eventually become so dissatisfied that they either look elsewhere for companionship, or they become resigned to loneliness.[27]

It makes a woman feel better to tell her husband about her day. But the percentage

[26] Boyd C. Rollins and Harold Feldman, "Marital Satisfaction over the Family Life Cycle," *Journal of Marriage and the Family* 32, no. 1 (February 1970): 27.

[27] Blood and Wolfe, *Husbands and Wives,* chap. 6.

MAGNUM—PHOTO BY DAVID HURN

Hobbies, community activities, and projects help the mature man meet the challenge of social isolation in the middle and later years.

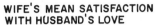

Chart 16–4. *Wives' Decreasing Satisfaction with Love through the Family Life Cycle*

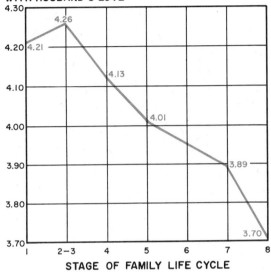

WIFE'S MEAN SATISFACTION WITH HUSBAND'S LOVE

STAGE OF FAMILY LIFE CYCLE

Source: Robert O. Blood, Jr., and Donald M. Wolfe, *Husbands and Wives: The Dynamics of Married Living* (Glencoe, Ill.: Free Press, 1960), p. 232. Stage 6 has been omitted after consultation with Dr. Blood.

A wife's satisfaction with her husband's love declines steadily from a peak when the babies are small to a low at the later stages of the marriage, as is seen in chart 16–4. Studies agree that there tends to be disenchantment, disillusionment, and unhappiness in the later years of marriage. Reporting a follow-up study of the Burgess-Wallin couples married up to twenty years, Pineo finds a general drop in marital satisfaction. "There is a loss of a certain intimacy. Confiding, kissing, and reciprocal settlement of disagreements become less frequent; more individuals report loneliness. This loss of intimacy appears to be an aspect of disenchantment."[29]

During engagement, adjustment scores of men and women are about the same. Men become disenchanted earlier in the marriage, but the drop in adjustment scores between the early and middle years of marriage is greater for women than for men, so that by the middle years the marital adjustment scores of both husbands and wives are again about equal. There is some evidence that men are premaritally more romantic than women, and so become disillusioned earlier in marriage than do their wives.[30] There are indications too that wives tend to be most unhappy in their late

of wives reporting this satisfaction declines with the coming of children—from 40 percent of those without children to 25 percent with school-agers to a low of 17 percent at the launching stage, recovering only slightly to 20 percent of those whose children have been launched.[28] It is as though many a mother learns to cope with her problems alone during the bustling years when there are children in the home, and never fully regains the intimate sharing with her husband she once found satisfying.

[28] Ibid., p. 202.

[29] Peter C. Pineo, "Disenchantment in the Later Years of Marriage," *Marriage and Family Living* 23, no. 1 (February 1961): 3–11.

[30] Charles W. Hobart, "Disillusionment in Marriage and Romanticism," *Marriage and Family Living* 20, no. 2 (May 1958): 156–162.

forties and early fifties, when their children no longer need them, their husbands are less adequate as mates than previously, and they have not yet found a second career for themselves.[31]

Further light is shown on the decline in marital communication with age by the nationwide interview study conducted by the Joint Commission on Mental Illness and Health. They find that although marital happiness and adjustment tend to decrease with age, the percentages of husbands and wives who say they feel inadequate and have marital problems decline even more sharply as men and women grow older. The suggestion is that maturity and age bring increasing acceptance of one's lot rather than increasing positive gratifications.[32]

Sex through the Life of the Family

Both husbands and wives agree that sex relationships are important throughout a

31 James H. S. Bossard and Eleanor S. Boll, "Marital Unhappiness in the Life Cycle," *Marriage and Family Living* 17, no. 1 (February 1955): 10–14; and Arnold M. Rose, "Factors Associated with the Life Satisfaction of Middle-Class, Middle-Aged Persons," *Marriage and Family Living* 17, no. 1 (February 1955): 15–19.

32 Gerald Gurin, Joseph Veroff, and Sheila Feld, *Americans View Their Mental Health: A Nationwide Interview Study* (New York: Basic Books, 1960), pp. 103–104.

Table 16–7. *Mean Weekly Frequency of Marital Coitus Reported by Wives and Husbands*

Age group	Wives	Husbands
16–20	3.7	3.7
21–25	3.0	3.2
26–30	2.6	2.7
31–35	2.3	2.2
36–40	2.0	2.0
41–45	1.7	1.6
46–50	1.4	1.4
51–55	1.2	1.2
56–60	0.8	0.8

Source: Alfred C. Kinsey, Wardell B. Pomeroy, Clyde E. Martin, and Paul H. Gebhard, *Sexual Behavior in the Human Female* (Philadelphia: W. B. Saunders Company, 1953), p. 77.

satisfying marriage. However, sex expression declines in importance through the life cycle from a peak in the preschool stage, when both spouses rate it somewhere between "very important" and "quite important," to the aging family period, when it still is rated midway between "quite important" and "somewhat important."[33]

The frequency of coitus in marriage declines gradually from three to four times a week for husbands and wives under twenty years of age to something less than once a week for both men and women approaching sixty, as is seen in table 16–7.

Men and women who have not graduated from high school report more frequent marital coitus in each age group than do the

33 Feldman, "The Development of Husband-Wife Relationships," p. 11.

college-educated.[34] This suggests that better-educated couples have other avenues of mutual interest and sharing besides that of physical union. As the couple proceeds through the family life cycle, both husband and wife become immersed in various other responsibilities. Fatigue takes a toll in decreasing interest in or vitality for sexual activity. The first pregnancy has unfavorable effects on the marital sexual adjustment of one out of four husbands (23 percent) and wives (25 percent).[35] Most couples are advised to discontinue intercourse for a number of weeks before and after childbirth—the exact period dependent upon the individual case. Although many women report they lose most of their sexual urge while pregnant, others maintain their desire for their husbands at the usual level.[36]

After menopause, women often have a greater sexual appetite than do their husbands.[37] This may be due to the feeling of freedom that comes when the former possibility of pregnancy is gone, to the vitality modern women in their middle years enjoy, and to the fact that the husband is usually older and ages more rapidly than his wife.

Orgasm ability in the wife increases with the duration of the marriage. One out of four wives (25 percent) fails to achieve orgasm by the end of the first year of marriage. With duration of marriage, the percentage of wives yet to experience orgasm drops to 17 percent in the fifth year, to 14 percent the tenth year, 12 percent the fifteenth year, and 11 percent in the twentieth year of marriage. By the thirtieth year of marriage nine out of ten wives are fully sexually responsive.[38] For most married couples, the frequency of sexual expression decreases through the life cycle, while the level of satisfaction continues to increase up through the middle years.

The sex interests of children, teenagers, and young adults add their dimension to the family task of channeling sex expression through the family life cycle. In early childhood, sex play, masturbation, the erotic implications of soiling, messing, and oedipal attachments, as well as sex questions challenge parental understanding and management. With school days comes an increase in "dirty" stories, "naughty" words, and the rash of "little sweethearts" whose kissing, note-passing, and "understandings" are recognized by classmates and parents of both families.[39] Teenagers coping with their maturing bodies, deepening interests in the other sex, and emancipating themselves

[34] Alfred C. Kinsey, Wardell B. Pomeroy, Clyde E. Martin, and Paul H. Gebhard, *Sexual Behavior in the Human Female* (Philadelphia: W. B. Saunders Company, 1953), p. 77.

[35] Judson T. Landis, Thomas Poffenberger, and Shirley Poffenberger, "The Effects of First Pregnancy upon the Sexual Adjustment of 212 Couples," *American Sociological Review* 15, no. 6 (December 1950): 767–772.

[36] Bernard R. Greenblat, *A Doctor's Marital Guide for Patients* (Chicago: Budlong Press, 1959), p. 48.

[37] Ibid., p. 46.

[38] Kinsey, Pomeroy, Martin, and Gebhard, *Sexual Behavior in the Human Female*, p. 408.

[39] Carlfred B. Broderick and Stanley E. Fowler, "New Patterns of Relationships between the Sexes among Preadolescents," *Marriage and Family Living* 23, no. 1 (February 1961): 27–30.

from their families may confide less in their parents, ask fewer questions, and avoid family discussions of the very areas that most concern both themselves and their parents—sex, petting, and marriage.[40] By the time the launching stage arrives, parents may make a last-ditch effort to make sure that their daughters know what to expect in marriage, but their sons more usually are expected to work things out for themselves in the sexual areas of life.[41]

Some families are more comfortable than others in dealing with sex throughout the life cycle. These parents tend to have wholesome, accepting attitudes about the sex side of life. They answer their children's questions easily. They don't get too excited about youngsters' sex play or language. They accept their teenagers' developing interests with understanding and respect. They provide helpful materials for their children's sex education. They release their young adults into full maturity without too much of a personal sense of loss.

Their reward is in more mutually meaningful relationships with their children and with each other throughout the entire life cycle.

Bearing, Rearing, and Relating to Children through the Years

There is a new tendency toward starting childbearing at an older age. Now, when men and women are better educated and marry at somewhat later ages, they tend to have fewer children and to space them farther apart. The median interval is twenty-six months between the first and second child and about six months longer between the second and third births in white families.[42] Negro families have more children and bear them earlier (table 16–8). Furthermore, 67 percent of Negro children under eighteen years old, compared with 92 percent of white children, were living with both parents in 1969.[43]

[40] Marvin C. Dubbé, "What Young People Can't Talk over with Their Parents," *National Parent-Teacher* 52, no. 2 (October 1957): 18–20.
[41] Irving Tebor, "Male Virgins: Conflicts and Group Support in American Culture," *Family Life Coordinator* 9, nos. 3–4 (March–June 1961): 40–42.

[42] U.S. Bureau of the Census, "Marriage, Fertility, and Childspacing: June 1965," *Population Characteristics*, Current Population Reports, series P-20, no. 186 (August 6, 1969), p. 1.
[43] Ibid., p. 12.

Table 16–8. *The Trend of More Children Living in Negro Families Continues*

Average number of children under 18	1967		1968		1969	
	White	Negro	White	Negro	White	Negro
All families	1.30	1.76	1.29	1.78	1.27	1.80
Fatherless families	0.98	1.93	1.01	1.98	1.03	1.95

Source: U.S. Bureau of the Census, "Selected Characteristics of Persons and Families: March 1969," *Population Characteristics,* Current Population Reports, series P-20, no. 189 (August 18, 1969), p. 12.

Some families find themselves burdened with more children than they can care for, even in areas where family planning help is available. According to one exploratory study, "The lack of effective contraception so common in this group is not due simply to ignorance or misunderstanding; it is embodied in particular personalities, world views, and ways of life which have consistency and stability and which do not readily admit such foreign elements as conscious planning and emotion-laden contraceptive practices."[44]

Married college students often find themselves with their first baby before they had planned to have it.[45] Even though the first baby has been planned and very much wanted, its arrival is apt to be a crisis for a number of reasons: (1) inadequate preparation—as one mother put it, "We knew where babies came from, but we didn't know *what they were like*"; (2) fatigue resulting from loss of sleep; (3) confinement in home-based child care; (4) curtailment of social life; (5) loss of income and satisfactions of wife's employment; (6) guilt in not being a better parent; (7) decline in house-keeping standards; (8) neglect of the young mother's appearance; (9) decline in wife's sexual response; (10) increased costs in having a child at time when wife's income is cut off; (11) worry about a second pregnancy in the near future; and (12) a general disenchantment with the parental role.[46] Not all pregnancies come to term. About one in ten spontaneously miscarries, and there are at least 200 to 250 induced abortions for each 1,000 pregnancies in this country—bringing another kind of crisis with possible emotional and physical toll.[47]

Problems of raising and relating to children change from stage to stage of their development. Longitudinal studies show that wetting, soiling, thumb-sucking, and speech problems tend to be general in the first two years. Temper tantrums, fears, and negativism reach their peaks among preschool children. Disturbing dreams and mood swings appear often among both boys and girls of ten and eleven.[48]

One of the first signs of the onset of adolescence is the young teenager's critical attitude toward the physical features of his

---

[44] Lee Rainwater and Karol K. Weinstein, *And the Poor Get Children: Sex, Contraception, and Family Planning in the Working Class* (Chicago: Quadrangle Books, 1960), pp. 167–168.

[45] Kate Hevner Mueller, in Opal D. David, ed., *The Education of Women* (Washington, D.C.: American Council on Education, 1959), p. 78, reports, "Many of these wives are able and talented, with one or two college years to their credit, but now they are dropping out of school to do typing, to have a child—either intentionally (33 percent) or inadvertently (67 percent). . . ."

[46] E. E. LeMasters, "Parenthood as Crisis," *Marriage and Family Living* 19, no. 4 (November 1957): 352–355.

[47] Alan F. Guttmacher, "Abortions—Medical and Social Review," in Evelyn M. Duvall and Sylvanus M. Duvall, eds., *Sex Ways—in Fact and Faith: Bases for Christian Family Policy* (New York: Association Press, 1961), pp. 211–226.

[48] Jean W. Macfarlane, Lucille Allen, and Marjorie P. Honzik, *A Developmental Study of the Behavior Problems of Normal Children between Twenty-one Months and Fourteen Years* (Berkeley: University of California Press, 1954), pp. 147–160.

home. By middle adolescence, teenage girls criticize their mothers as homemakers, and boys challenge their fathers in disturbing ways. As a Harvard longitudinal study reports, "Adolescents in this phase criticize every aspect of their parents' personalities but it would appear that the criticisms most difficult for the parents to bear are those directed toward personal traits, mannerisms, or idiosyncrasies about which the parents have long been sensitive."[49] Parental disagreement about child-rearing reaches a high point in the second decade of marriage, during the children's teen years, when so many family squabbles occur.[50] The launching stage brings problems of love affairs, mate selection, marriage, educational and vocational choices that often disturb parents who are emotionally involved in, yet possibly have little voice in, their youngsters' plans.

With the marriage of a family's sons and daughters comes the challenge (especially for the mother) of working out new relationships with daughters- and sons-in-law. By the time a woman has begun to find out what it means to be a mother-in-law, the grandchildren arrive, and she becomes a grandmother. Fortunately, feelings of inadequacy as parents drop through the years.

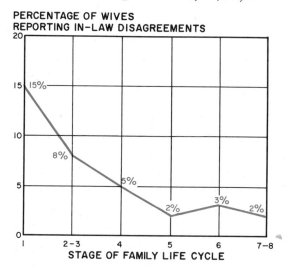

Chart 16–5. *Decline in In-law Disagreements through the Family Life Cycle*

PERCENTAGE OF WIVES
REPORTING IN-LAW DISAGREEMENTS

STAGE OF FAMILY LIFE CYCLE

Source: Robert O. Blood, Jr., and Donald M. Wolfe, *Husbands and Wives: The Dynamics of Married Living* (Glencoe, Ill.: Free Press, 1960), p. 247.

By the time mothers and fathers reach fifty-five, and presumably have launched their children, fewer ever feel inadequate (41 percent) than at any previous time as parents.[51]

In-law Problems

Difficulties with relatives decline through the family life cycle. In the early years of marriage husband and wife are getting used to their roles as members of each other's families. Then they are leaving their par-

---

[49] Ruth M. Butler, "Mothers' Attitudes toward the Social Development of Their Adolescents," *Social Casework*, May–June 1956.

[50] Charles Bowerman, "Adjustment in Marriage: Over-all and in Specific Areas," *Sociology and Social Research* 41, no. 4 (March–April 1957): 257–263; and Blood and Wolfe, *Husbands and Wives*, p. 247.

[51] Gurin, Veroff, and Feld, *Americans View Their Mental Health*, p. 137.

FAMILY DEVELOPMENT

ents in favor of their mates as first loyalties. In-law problems loom larger in the first stage than they ever will again in the family life cycle (chart 16–5).

Several reasons are advanced for the rapid decline of in-law problems after the first stage of the family life cycle. One is the softening effect that becoming a grand-mother has on the mother-in-law relation-ship, which is found to be the most difficult, in families with in-law problems.[52] A closely related second factor is the maturing of hus-band and wife, so that their parents-in-law are more esteemed as they themselves be-come parents. A third is the wearing off of the stereotype of trouble with in-laws; and fourth, growing appreciation for the help that the older families give the younger.[53] Fifth is the gradual acceptance of the marriage by parents who have pre-viously disapproved. This may be particu-larly true of the mixed marriage.[54]

Difficulties with relatives are best worked out early in the marriage, or before.[55] Some couples continue to cope with in-law trou-bles through the years. One study of sup-posedly successful marriages found nearly one in ten (9.6 percent) of the husbands and wives agreeing that they never had made a satisfactory adjustment in their in-law relationships. A similar percentage (10.9 percent) disagreed on whether they had worked out a satisfactory adjustment from the beginning, and another 7 percent said that it had taken them from one to twenty years of marriage to make satisfac-tory adjustments to their relatives.[56]

Analysis of what husbands and wives say is effective in working out harmonious rela-tionships with their in-laws finds two sig-nificant factors: (1) acceptance ("They accept me, they are friendly, close, under-standing . . ."), and (2) mutual respect ("We respect each other's personalities"). Out of 748 reasons why their in-law relationships had worked out harmoniously, items involv-ing either acceptance or mutual respect were mentioned spontaneously 563 times, or in 75.2 percent of the cases, involving 345 married persons.[57] Acceptance and mutual respect call for emotional maturity on the part of all the family members.

[52] Evelyn Millis Duvall, *In-Laws: Pro and Con* (New York: Association Press, 1954), pp. 141–160, 187–220.

[53] Ibid., pp. 37–51; and Marvin B. Sussman, "The Help Pattern in the Middle Class Family," *American Sociological Review* 18, no. 1 (February 1953): 22–28.

[54] Duvall, *In-Laws: Pro and Con,* pp. 70–88; M. L. Barron, *People Who Intermarry* (Syracuse, N.Y.: Syracuse University Press, 1946); Judson T. Landis, "Marriages of Mixed and Non-Mixed Religious Faith," *American Sociological Review* 14, no. 3 (June 1949): 401–407; Murray Lieffer, as reported in *Time*, January 31, 1949; Raban Hathorn, William H. Genné, and Mordecai Brill, eds., *Marriage: An Interfaith Guide for All Couples* (New York: Asso-ciation Press; St. Meinrad, Ind.: Abbey Press, 1970).

[55] John L. Thomas, *The American Catholic Fam-ily* (Englewood Cliffs, N.J.: Prentice-Hall, 1956), p. 234.

[56] Judson T. Landis, "Length of Time Required to Achieve Adjustment in Marriage," *American Sociological Review* 11, no. 6 (December 1946): 668.

[57] Duvall, *In-Laws: Pro and Con,* pp. 331–336.

Chart 16–6. *Probabilities of Divorce per 1,000 White Males by Age at First Marriage and Duration of First Marriage: 1960–1966*

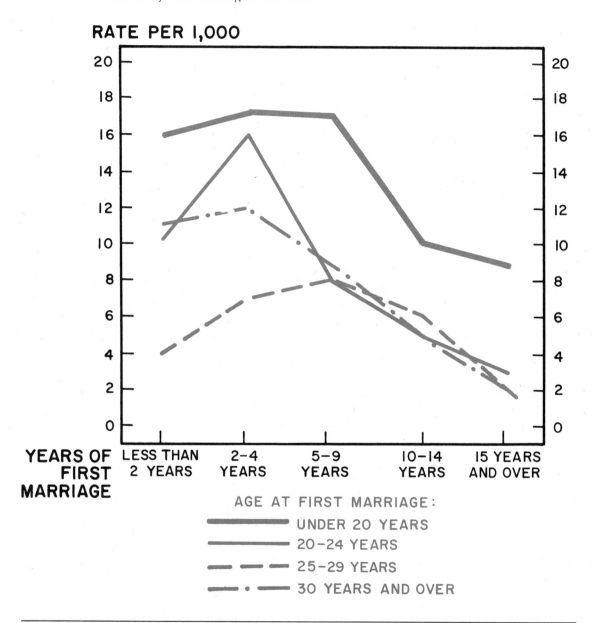

RATE PER 1,000

YEARS OF FIRST MARRIAGE

AGE AT FIRST MARRIAGE:
UNDER 20 YEARS
20–24 YEARS
25–29 YEARS
30 YEARS AND OVER

Source: U.S. Bureau of the Census, unpublished data from the 1967 Survey of Economic Opportunity, presented by Paul C. Glick and Arthur J. Norton, "Probabilities of Marriage, Divorce, Widowhood, and Remarriage," at the annual meeting of the Population Association of America, Atlanta, Ga., April 16–18, 1970, mimeographed, fig. 3.

They further indicate the successful accomplishment of the family developmental task of relating to relatives on both sides of the family.

Divorce-prone Marriages

Divorce is more frequent during the early years of marriage than at any other time in the family life cycle. The probability of divorce rises rapidly in the first few years of marriage and declines thereafter through the years, as is seen in chart 16–6, based upon data from a 1967 nationwide survey conducted by the United States Bureau of the Census. Men who marry in their teens are more divorce-prone than all others throughout their marriages, as indicated by the line at the top of the chart that shows their probability of divorce four times that of men who marry in their middle to late twenties, both at the beginning of marriage and after fifteen or more years of marriage.

Several decades of research into what makes for success or failure in marriage find a score of factors: social-cultural, familial, and personal that make some marriages more vulnerable than others. These are as follows:

Social and cultural factors:

1. Race—more divorces among Negroes than whites
2. Social status—more divorces at lower socioeconomic strata
3. Education—more divorces among less educated
4. Occupation—more divorces among unskilled workers
5. Religion—more divorces among persons with few religious roots
6. Faith—more divorces in interfaith combinations
7. Urbanization—more divorces in couples with urban backgrounds
8. Region—more divorces in West and South
9. Prosperity—more divorces in wartime prosperity than depressions

Family factors:

10. Family history—more divorces among children of divorced parents
11. Parents' marriage—more divorces among children of unhappy parents
12. Parent-child conflict—more divorces among those in conflict with parents
13. Childbearing—more divorces in childless marriages
14. Premarital pregnancy—more divorces among pregnant brides

Personal factors:

15. Age—more divorces among those marrying before twenty
16. Maturity—more divorces among emotionally immature
17. Responsibility—more divorces among irresponsible persons
18. Preparation—more divorces among persons poorly prepared for marriage
19. Motive for marriage—more divorces among those who married to escape
20. Concurrence—more divorces among couples intolerant of difference

Chart 16–7. *Percentage of Ever-married Women Fourteen Years Old and Over Who Were Separated or Divorced, by Age and Color, for the United States: March 1968*

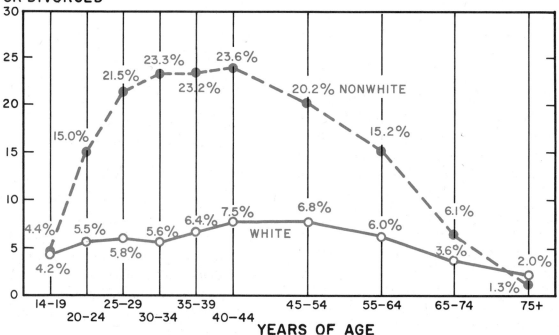

Source: U.S. Bureau of the Census, "Marital Status and Family Status: March 1968," *Population Characteristics,* Current Population Reports, series P-20, no. 187 (August 11, 1969), p. 3; see also Hugh Carter and Paul C. Glick, *Marriage and Divorce: A Social and Economic Study* (Cambridge, Mass.: Harvard University Press, 1970).

Table 16–9. *Proportion of Ever-married Women Fourteen Years Old and Over Who Were Separated or Divorced, by Age and Color, for the United States: March 1968 (Numbers in Thousands)*

| | White | | | Nonwhite | | |
| | Women ever married | Percent with disrupted marriage | | Women ever married | Percent with disrupted marriage | |
Age		Separated	Divorced		Separated	Divorced
Total	52,294	1.8	3.9	6,020	11.9	5.8
14 to 24 years	5,242	2.4	2.9	674	10.5	2.4
25 to 39 years	14,516	2.1	3.8	1,938	16.3	6.4
40 to 54 years	15,364	2.1	4.9	1,802	12.9	8.5
55 and over	17,174	1.0	3.4	1,603	6.2	3.6

Source: U.S. Bureau of the Census, "Marital Status and Family Status: March, 1968," *Population Characteristics,* Current Population Reports, series P-20, no. 187 (August 11, 1969), p. 3; see also Hugh Carter and Paul C. Glick, *Marriage and Divorce: A Social and Economic Study* (Cambridge, Mass.: Harvard University Press, 1970).

21. Personality—more divorces among ego-centric, rigid, neurotic personalities.[58]

Rarely is but one factor responsible for the breakup of a marriage. Nor are the legally required "grounds for divorce" the actual cause of the dissolution in many cases. Rather a complex of interrelated factors—rational and irrational, personal and social—usually brings about the marital break.

Some factors are more powerful than others in divorce-proneness, as is evident in chart 16–7 comparing white and non-white percentages of divorced women at various ages in the United States. Such statistical disparities do not guarantee white women of never divorcing, nor nonwhite women of probable divorce, any more than an actuarial table forecasts the length of life of any one person. They are statistical probabilities that pertain to given groups of individuals of which a given factor is characteristic. Determination to succeed, personal and family strengths, and the willingness to work on one's marriage can reverse the forecast of marital instability, much as health and safety precautions may help an individual outlive his statistical probabilities.

Family Crises

A family crisis may be defined as any situation for which the usual patterns of family living are inadequate. Family crises may be classified as those resulting from loss of a member (dismemberment), those resulting from loss of status and of face (demoralization), those resulting from the addition of a member (accession), and those resulting from a combination of demoralization and dismemberment or accession (table 16–10).

Family crises range from the birth of the first child,[59] or the reunion of war-separated fathers and families,[60] to such final disruptions as death, desertion, or divorce.[61]

[58] Jessie Bernard, "Divorce and Remarriage—Research Related to Policy," in Duvall and Duvall, eds., *Sex Ways—in Fact and Faith*, p. 95; Ernest W. Burgess and Leonard S. Cottrell, Jr., *Predicting Success or Failure in Marriage* (New York: Prentice-Hall, 1939); Ernest W. Burgess and Paul Wallin, *Engagement and Marriage* (Chicago: J. B. Lippincott Company, 1953); Harold T. Christensen, ed., *Handbook of Marriage and the Family* (Chicago: Rand McNally and Company, 1964); William J. Goode, *After Divorce* (Glencoe, Ill.: Free Press, 1956); William J. Goode, *The Family* (Englewood Cliffs, N.J.: Prentice-Hall, 1964); Judson T. Landis, "Religiousness, Family Relationships, and Family Values in Protestant, Catholic, and Jewish Families," *Marriage and Family Living* 22, no. 4 (November 1960): 342; Harvey J. Locke, *Predicting Adjustment in Marriage: A Comparison of a Divorced and a Happily Married Group* (New York: Henry Holt and Company, 1951); and various data from U.S. Bureau of the Census.

[59] LeMasters, "Parenthood as Crisis," pp. 352–355.

[60] Reuben Hill, *Families under Stress* (New York: Harper and Brothers, 1949).

[61] William J. Goode, *After Divorce* (Glencoe, Ill.: Free Press, 1956); Earl Lomon Koos, *Families in Trouble* (New York: King's Crown Press, 1946); and Thomas D. Eliot, "Handling Family Strains and Shocks," in Howard Becker and Reuben Hill, eds., *Family, Marriage, and Parenthood* (Boston: D. C. Heath and Company, 1948), pp. 616–668.

Table 16–10. *Types of Family Crises*

Dismemberment
  Hospitalization
  Loss of child
  Loss of spouse
  Orphanhood
  Separation (military service, work, etc.)

Demoralization
  Disgrace (alcoholism, crime, delinquency, drug
    addiction, etc.)
  Infidelity
  Nonsupport
  Progressive dissension

Accession
  Adoption
  Birth (and possibly pregnancy)
  Deserter returns
  Relative moves in
  Reunion after separation
  Stepmother, stepfather marries in

Demoralization plus dismemberment or accession
  Annulment
  Desertion
  Divorce
  Illegitimacy
  Imprisonment
  Institutionalization
  Runaway
  Suicide or homicide

Source: Adapted from Evelyn Millis Duvall and Reuben
Hill, *Being Married* (New York: Association Press; Boston:
D. C. Heath and Company, 1960), pp. 298–299, from a classi-
fication originally suggested by T. D. Eliot.

Families who have but incompletely
achieved their previous developmental tasks
are more susceptible to trouble in those
areas at later stages of the life cycle. Thus,
a first pregnancy that comes before the
young husband and wife have soundly

established their relationship as a married
couple may be a real crisis, whereas pregnancy and the birth of the first child to a
mature couple whose marriage is already
soundly based and ready for its childbearing functions is taken more in stride.

Usually, there is no one inadequacy.
There is an initial cause which tends to
create tension in other areas of family life,
which in turn may become critical in themselves. For example, cultural disparity may
cause a lack of sexual satisfaction because

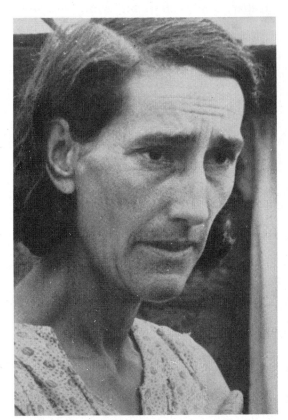

COURTESY OF BEN SHAHN: "FAMILY OF MAN"

*It is the unexpected quality of much in family liv-
ing that makes it hazardous.*

FAMILY DEVELOPMENT

of differing ideas and standards of sex behavior, which in turn may lead to suspicion of the mate and lack of cooperation as breadwinner or homemaker, which in turn may create crises in reciprocal roles in the family and draw some family members into new positions of power and responsibility at the expense of other members. All this may so weaken the affectional relationships and integration of the family as to render it unable to meet even a simple departure from its ordinary life patterns. The result, when an out-of-the-ordinary event occurs, is a crisis.

Every family is, to a greater or lesser extent, harassed, anxious or guilty, beset with complexities, and burdened with conflicts, both within the family and within its larger relationships. Modern families are under the growing pressure of various agencies, industries, professions, and programs to modify, change, and reorganize one or more of their living habits in accordance with new knowledges, norms, and values. Traditional patterns of family living and child-rearing, derived from an earlier way of life now largely passed, no longer are adequate today.

The breakdown of traditional definitions of masculine and feminine roles, by which men and women were guided in the performance of their obligations and the enjoyment of their privileges, has brought confusion and conflict within the family. Men and women are coming to marriage today with divergent expectations and needs, which frequently clash with those of the spouse. These conflicting beliefs and conceptions hamper and often frustrate both men and women in achieving their developmental tasks as husband and wife and as father and mother.

Children today grow up in a social situation in which changes in beliefs, expectations, and conduct are taking place so rapidly that parents often are unable to understand, let alone accept, what their adolescents think and do. Thus the more or less normal cleavages between the generations have been enlarged and accentuated, sometimes becoming bitter conflicts and resentful rivalries at the time when both parents and children are acutely in need of reassurance and support.

Overshadowing these family-focused difficulties are the larger social, economic, and political situations in which the needs and interests of families are not only ignored but frequently are sacrificed to the varied objectives of business and numerous vested interests within the modern world.

Family developmental tasks are difficult under the most favorable circumstances. Meeting the demanding requirements of a growing family and encouraging the development of family members of differing ages, sexes, interests, and personalities are ongoing responsibilities of exacting magnitude. Yet the strength and fate of the entire society depend, in large measure, upon how well families fulfill their central task of raising creative men and women able to solve their personal and family problems.

Solving Personal-Family Problems

Interviews with 2,460 representative Americans over the age of twenty-one living at home provide a picture of what relatively normal, stable adults are concerned about today. That most of their problems are family-connected is obvious from table 16–11.

Table 16–11. *Types of Personal Problems for Which People Sought Professional Help*

Problem area	Percentage
Spouse, marriage	42%
Child, relationship with child	12
Other family relationships—parents, in-laws, etc.	5
Other relationship problems, type of relationship problem unspecified	4
Job or school problems, vocational choice	6
Nonjob adjustment problems in the self (general adjustment, specific symptoms)	18
Situational problems involving other people (e.g., death or illness of a loved one) causing extreme psychological reaction	6
Nonpsychological situational problems	8
Nothing specific, a lot of little things, can't remember	2
Not ascertained	1

(Percentages total more than 100 percent because some respondents gave more than one response.)

Source: Gerald Gurin, Joseph Veroff, and Sheila Feld, *Americans View Their Mental Health: A Nationwide Interview Study* (New York: Basic Books, 1960), p. 305.

This nationwide survey of the ways in which Americans are facing their problems finds:

First, they have more chance for dealing with their troubles when they approach them subjectively, when they see them in internal-psychological, rather than external-physical terms, and at the same time wrestle with them actively instead of accepting them with apathy.

Second, their ability to adopt this attitude of "healthful worry" is more than any other factor dependent upon education. The higher their education, the greater their self-awareness, the greater their knowledge of channels for help, and, as a corollary to education, the more they can afford to spend on expert, effective help.

Third, most people have to rely on their own inner resources as they face their problems. When they do obtain help, it is usually informal, expedient, and temporary.

Fourth, the problem of obtaining adequate professional help is particularly important in the lower status groups of the population.[62]

Some families weather their crises better than do others. A study of families subjected to the stresses of living in a rapidly urbanizing southern community found good family adjustment associated highly

[62] Joint Commission on Mental Illness and Health, *Action for Mental Health* (New York: Basic Books, 1961), p. 107.

with family philosophy and outlook, family policies and practices, and with the personal resources of individual family members. Of high statistical significance in accounting for good family adjustment were these factors:

1. Nonmaterialistic philosophy of life
2. Family orientation to trouble
3. Developmental conceptions of parenthood
4. Number of tasks shared by husband and wife
5. Family adaptability
6. Accuracy of family perception of problems
7. Perception of emotional problems as family concern
8. Diffusion of leadership in family problem-solving
9. Problem-solving skill of wife
10. Personal adjustment of husband and wife.[63]

Married couples who continue to assume responsibility for achieving their developmental tasks at each stage of the family life cycle avoid many of the difficulties, hazards, and crises that threaten many another family. A sound philosophy of life makes family members less vulnerable to crisis than are those less well established within a value system.

---

[63] Reuben Hill, Joel Moss, and Claudine Wirths, "Eddyville's Families," mimeographed (Chapel Hill, N.C.: Institute for Research in Social Science, University of North Carolina, 1953).

The good family is not a family without problems; it is rather one that uses its resources to weather the storms of life that strike from time to time. Even the most successful family faces certain inevitable crises. Knowing what to expect and preparing for what lies ahead are part of the challenge of effective family living.

SUMMARY

There are predictable vulnerabilities through the family life cycle that enable the family-helping professions and individual families to know what to expect, in general. Families change their residences more in their early stages than later. Home ownership increases through the years of the family life cycle. Marriage starts and ends with financial pressures, when costs are high and income is relatively low. Wives work when their families need their income in most cases. The roles of husband and wife diverge as their marriage continues. Feelings of guilt arising out of conflicting loyalties appear from time to time in various intrafamily relationships. Satisfaction with marital love and frequency of sexual intercourse decrease over the years. Some families burden themselves with more children than they can care for, but for all families the bearing, rearing, and releasing of children is an ever-changing responsibility. In-law problems taper off as a marriage continues, for understandable reasons. Some marriages are more divorce-prone than others in various combinations of more than a score of significant factors. All families go through crises and have problems at times. Some families weather their crises better than others in ways that point to family policies making for good adjustment. Strong families are not without their problems, but use their resources to weather the storms that strike every family from time to time.

SUGGESTED ACTIVITIES

1. Prepare a case history of a family crisis, including the precipitating factor(s), the elements contributing to its buildup, and the developmental tasks of each family member involved and of the family as a whole which were halted or blocked during the critical period. List the resources that were available, both within the family and in the larger community. Indicate which resources the family found most helpful, and give a documented appraisal of how the family weathered the crisis. Footnote your material with references to recent research and clinical findings, using some of the sources cited in this chapter as guides.

2. Prepare a paper on the relative vulnerability of the various life cycle stages of present-day American families to (a) disruption, (b) energy depletion, (c) economic strains, (d) disillusionment, and (e) disengagement. Document your material with relevant data from recent research.

3. Using one of the studies with family life cycle data (such as Blood and Wolfe, *Husbands and Wives;* Harold Feldman's contemporary research; Gurin and others, *Americans View Their Mental Health;* or various studies from one or more volumes of *Consumer Behavior*, and similar research reports listed in your readings and elsewhere), plot on graph paper the curves for various variables through the family life cycle. Discuss, interpret, and document the trends that are apparent as families move from stage to stage through their life cycles.

4. Choose one stage of the family life cycle and elaborate its challenges, hazards, and services needed. Document with data from research reports, and with illustrations from one or more families at this stage of development known to you.

5. Make a directory of services for families at various stages of the family life cycle and in several areas (i.e., economic, educational, religious, social work, etc.) of life in your community at the present time. Interview the key personnel in as many as possible in an effort to get information on how many families use their services in a given year, which families in the community make most use of them, how effective their work with family members is, and what elaborations of the type of service rendered they recommend.

6. Invite one or more members of the board of education of a nearby school system to discuss with you current attitudes and practices in family life education

FAMILY DEVELOPMENT

within both public and private schools in your area. Interview him on the extent of community support for or criticism of courses for boys and girls in family living in the schools. Write up the interview with documentation from nationwide reports.

7. Collect a variety of catalogues of college and university curricula and review their offerings in the field of marriage and family life for (a) functional courses related to students' personal needs and interests, and (b) professional and preprofessional courses and courses in the various specialties. Prepare a report on your investigation.

READINGS

Blood, Robert O., Jr., and Donald M. Wolfe. *Husbands and Wives: The Dynamics of Married Living.* Glencoe, Ill.: Free Press, 1960.

Carter, Hugh, and Paul C. Glick. *Marriage and Divorce: A Social and Economic Study.* Cambridge, Mass.: Harvard University Press, 1970.

Chilman, Catherine S. *Growing Up Poor.* Welfare Administration Publication, no. 13. Washington, D.C., 1966.

Christensen, Harold T., ed. *Handbook of Marriage and the Family.* Chicago: Rand McNally and Company, 1964.

Clark, Lincoln H., ed. *Consumer Behavior,* vol. 2, *The Life Cycle and Consumer Behavior.* New York: New York University Press, 1955.

Duvall, Evelyn Millis. "Implications for Education through the Family Life Cycle." *Marriage and Family Living* 20, no. 4 (November 1958): 334–342.

Duvall, Evelyn Millis, and Reuben Hill. *Being Married.* New York: Association Press; Boston: D. C. Heath and Company, 1960. Chaps. 15–17.

Fairchild, Roy W., and John Charles Wynn. *Families in the Church: A Protestant Survey.* New York: Association Press, 1961.

Feldman, Harold. *Development of the Husband-Wife Relationship: A Research Report.* Ithaca, N.Y.: Cornell University, 1965.

Gurin, Gerald, Joseph Veroff, and Sheila Feld. *Americans View Their Mental Health: A Nationwide Interview Study.* New York: Basic Books, 1960.

Herzog, Elizabeth, and Catharine Richards, eds. *The Nation's Youth.* Children's Bureau Publication, no. 460. Washington, D.C., 1968.

Hill, Reuben. *Family Development in Three Generations.* Cambridge, Mass.: Schenkman Publishing Company, 1970.

Jacobson, Paul H. *American Marriage and Divorce.* New York: Rinehart and Company, 1959.

Joint Commission on Mental Illness and Health. *Action for Mental Health.* New York: Basic Books, 1961.

Koos, Earl Lomon. *Families in Trouble.* New York: King's Crown Press, 1946.

Lansing, John B., and Leslie Kish. "Family Life Cycle as an Independent Variable." *American Sociological Review* 22, no. 5 (October 1957): 512–519.

Mayer, John E. *The Disclosure of Marital Problems: An Exploratory Study of Lower and Middle Class Wives.* New York: Community Service Society of New York, 1966.

Rollins, Boyd C., and Harold Feldman. "Marital Satisfaction over the Family Life Cycle." *Journal of Marriage and the Family* 32, no. 1 (February 1970): 20–28.

Steinzor, Bernard. *When Parents Divorce: A New Approach to New Relationships.* New York: Random House Pantheon Books, 1969.

Stolz, Lois H. Meek. "Effects of Maternal Employment on Children: Evidence from Research." *Child Development* 31, no. 4 (December 1960): 749–782.

United States Bureau of the Census, current reports.

17 POLICIES AND PROGRAMS FOR FAMILY DEVELOPMENT

We are marching along the endless pathway
of unrealized possibilities of human growth.   Francis W. Parker

The nation looks to its families for the kinds of persons and participation needed to keep the society alive and growing in all aspects of its corporate life. Government counts on the leadership, manpower, taxes, and civic concern of citizens who grow up in families. Political parties depend upon family members' loyalty in backing candidates, interpreting issues, raising money, getting out the votes, and providing the concerned citizenry that makes for vitality. Schools expect families to send their children clean, well fed, bright, and ready for the educational process, in which parents are expected to play their part. Churches continue because their member families come to religious services, support the various projects, raise the money and give their continuing commitment to programs, buildings, staff, and goals of the faith. Cultural institutions look to families for the inculcation of the tastes that keep alive the art galleries, theaters, ballet troupes, orchestras, libraries, and the rest, generation after generation. Medical, health, and safety professionals channel their services through family implementation. Businesses depend upon family purchases to keep them solvent. Industry uses family member workers at all levels of competence. But few of these institutions are actively engaged in encouraging the development of strong families capable of producing creative, effective human beings.

Welfare programs, crisis intervention efforts, and other family services are made available for families too weak or ineffective to continue on their own. Massive rehabilitation programs costing hundreds of millions of dollars try to reclaim the human defectives coming from inadequate families—the mentally ill, the retarded (intellectually, educationally, socially, and occupationally), the unmarried mothers and unwanted babies, the juvenile delinquent and adult criminal, the alienated tuned out, and the many turned on. Relatively little is being done to help families become more adequate in the years when a little outside help would go a long way.

A vision of positive family development

is being discussed among behavioral scientists today in ways that offer hope for the future of American families.

The day of taking the family for granted should be drawn to a close in America. Family specialists must consider what concerted effort they can make to help *all families* in a program of *family development,* which in a democratic society can be seen as a progressive upgrading of families comparable to urban development, and community development. . . .

The capacity of families to take up the slack in the social order has limits which should not be tested by continued negligence. The tremendous resilience and recuperative strengths of families must be fostered and developed. The formulation of national policies which deal with America's millions of families as a precious national resource in social organization should be undertaken by this generation. This task will have the support of findings from hundreds of research studies and the approval of the great majority of families rearing children today.[1]

The concept of prevention only recently has begun to be considered as applicable to positive family development. Research findings, implications, and recommendations point to the stage-critical potentials through-

out the family life cycle. These may well serve as valid guidelines for policies and programs designed to encourage full, positive, healthy family development.

CRITICAL PERIODS IN FAMILY DEVELOPMENT WITH STAGE-SPECIFIC IMPLICATIONS

Families develop through a series of stages that can be seen as critical periods, each of which has its family developmental tasks with their specific challenges, problems, and promises. It is toward these stage-critical tasks that policies and programs can be focused for greatest effectiveness. Plans established on the basis of the developmental potentials of families at any given stage of the family life cycle have possibilities for positive outcomes beyond random efforts to "strengthen family life," however well-meaning the latter may be. It is the sharp focus upon what is most needed at each stage of the family life cycle that permits a clear vision of paths to be taken to enhance family development at times of greatest change and potential growth. In the eight-stage treatment that follows may be found summaries of the stage-critical tasks of families, favorable factors suggested by research, and the implications for policies and programs inherent therein.

---

[1] Reuben Hill, "The American Family of the Future," *Journal of Marriage and the Family* 26, no. 1 (February 1964): 28.

Stage 1—Newly Married Couples

The first critical period in family development comes at the time of the marriage. It is then that the couple is making the decisions and initiating the behaviors that determine many of the elements of their lives for years to come. Through the months that precede and follow their marriage, a couple is either contemplating or commencing every one of their *basic family tasks* (chapter 6):

1. Physical maintenance—deciding on and settling into their first home, furnishing it according to their joint tastes and available resources, and adapting their individual patterns for eating, sleeping, clothing, and caring for the health of the newly established family unit

2. Allocation of resources—deciding priorities and distribution of financial and other material goods, facilities, space, authority, respect, affection, and all other resources a newly married couple have going for it

3. Division of labor—deciding who will do what in the new family unit, assigning responsibilities for work both in and out of the home, establishing patterns of supervision and accountability between the members of the pair, and possibly with other interested family members

4. Socialization of family members—minimal at this stage, except in discussing how a couple feels about bringing up their children when they arrive; and often critical in marriages of previously married spouses whose children are a part of the new family unit from the time of the marriage

5. Reproduction and release of family members—releasing themselves from their families of orientation, and maintaining intergenerational contacts with in-laws and other kinfolk in appropriate ways; deciding when they will be ready to have children and undertaking the necessary planning procedures to implement their decision

6. Maintenance of order—establishing patterns of effective communication, interaction, affection, and sexual practices

7. Placement of members in the larger society—fitting into community life as a pair, participating in religious, political, and civic life as a married couple

8. Maintenance of motivation and morale—satisfying each other's needs for acceptance, appreciation, encouragement, and affection as a couple and in their relationships with both sets of parents and other relatives.

During the courtship, mate selection, engagement, and early married phases of a couple's life together, their personal and family developmental tasks are being undertaken with little or no effective guidance. Popular advice-to-the-lovelorn columns and commercial wedding consultation services leave much to be desired. A young pair is expected to "fall in love," to choose life partners at a time when rational appraisal is minimal, and to "get married and live happily ever after," with few opportunities for learning what is expected or what makes for success in marriage. Research and clinical evidence offer a wealth of recommendations as to the factors that augur for success that only a fortunate few learn in any reliable way.[2]

Training programs for newly married couples are being proposed, covering specific help in decision-making processes, marital communication competence, intergenerational involvement in plans for the continued education of one or both members of the young couple, and establishment of the first home base, entailing the major investments toward which both sets of parents may be expected to make some contribution, as many do today. This proposal grew out of the three-generation study that found clear evidence of the "striking advantages in later economic achievements which couples have in postponing marriage until higher education has been completed, the advantages of having had some professional experience before marriage for both spouses, and the advantages of timing and spacing of children. . . . Such couples tend to have a headstart not only in income and economic bargaining power of a good education but also tend to develop the equalitarian form of family organization and a favorable marital climate for making good decisions . . . (that) distinguishes the successful from the unsuccessful in life cycle management."[3]

There is a well-recognized tendency for persons to repeat and reproduce in their further experiences those patterns that have proven satisfying in the past, and to avoid or to repudiate those conditions or experiences that have been unsatisfying in the past.[4] Yet, the dynamics of the reproduction or repudiation of early family experience is not widely recognized at the times when a young couple is most vulnerable to their effects. Premarital counseling and education for marriage help many a young person understand enough of his or her urgency for rebelling from parental ties to consider the nature of the marriage relationship being considered as an escape. Premarital and marital counseling and

[2] Evelyn Millis Duvall, "How Effective Are Marriage Courses?" *Journal of Marriage and the Family* 27, no. 2 (May 1965): 176–184.

[3] Reuben Hill, *Family Development in Three Generations* (Cambridge, Mass.: Schenkman Publishing Company, 1970), chap. 14.

[4] Clifford Kirkpatrick, "Familial Development, Selective Needs, and Predictive Theory," *Journal of Marriage and the Family* 29, no. 2 (May 1967): 229–236; Carlfred B. Broderick, "Reaction to 'Familial Development, Selective Needs, and Predictive Theory,'" *Journal of Marriage and the Family* 29, no. 2 (May 1967): 237–240; and Walter Toman, *Family Constellation* (New York: Springer Publishing Company, 1961).

education help many a young pair reappraise their earlier behaviors in terms of their goals for a life together. Premarital examinations and consultations that go beyond legally required blood tests to provide opportunities for both members of the pair to work through their sexual anxieties and questions, enough so that the burden of past mistakes is not too heavy upon the new marriage, have much to offer both the uninitiated and the sexually experienced. Family planning policies and procedures are most effective in anticipation of marriage, before unplanned pregnancy dashes hopes for years ahead. Prenatal programs have proven merit in maternal health and family formation. Intergenerational decision-making between the young pair and their parents is indicated to assure mutually satisfactory in-law relationships and the establishment of a workable kin network that has been found to be a viable source of strength in families today.

Stage 2—Childbearing Families

The early months and years of a baby's life are the critical ones for the establishment of his personality with its full complement of uniquely human characteristics. It is then that the child's environment, including especially his intimate interaction with his mother and other members of his family, has most profound and permanent effect upon his development. There is a sevenfold reason for the crucial importance of the individual's early experiences: (1) it is then that the child grows faster and changes more than he ever will again as long as he lives; (2) most human development is sequential, in that each new step of progress is based upon what has gone before, thus the earliest experiences serve literally as the foundation for what comes later; (3) learning taking place before language development is especially powerful because it is not readily accessible to conscious memory; (4) the repeated performance of a given behavior and the reinforcement through overlearning that characterizes earliest learning becomes stabilized; (5) the psychology of learning indicates clearly that it is much easier to learn something correctly the first time than to have to erase and replace later on;[5] (6) warm, nurturing care during infancy establishes the sense of trust in oneself, in others, and in life that provides the dynamic for continuing learning and development; and (7) positive early responses and patterns tend to be repeated in later development, providing healthy pathways for development in the many facets of the personality. Upon reviewing many hundreds of research studies on the development of a variety of human characteristics and qualities that bring satisfaction to a person and make a positive contribu-

---

[5] Benjamin S. Bloom, *Stability and Change in Human Characteristics* (New York: John Wiley and Sons, 1964), p. 215; also, Benjamin S. Bloom, "Early Learning in the Home," first B. J. Paley lecture, University of California at Los Angeles, July 18, 1965, mimeographed.

tion to society, Bloom concludes, "certain types of interaction between the child and others and between the child and the world of things, ideas, and events are more likely to lead to the development of the desired characteristics, whereas other types of interaction are likely to retard or even block the development of these characteristics."[6]

Up until very recently it was assumed that the early development of the little child was of little importance for his further development. Babies were kept in darkened rooms where they could sleep undisturbed by the normal activities and interaction of their families before it was known that an infant thrives on a great deal of stimulation of all his senses, with multifaceted opportunities to explore, investigate, and intimately interact with his world and its people. Millions of toddlers and infants have grown older in stultifying, impoverished settings that left them intellectually and culturally stunted, until it was realized that what a child learns in the first five or six years of his life either opens his mind for further learning or dampens his interest and slows his development. As Urie Bronfenbrenner, eminent specialist in child development, sees it:

A short two decades ago, most students of childhood believed that the early experiences of an infant and young child were of minor importance for his future development. Psychological growth was seen as a process of natural unfolding, predetermined by inexorable genetic forces. Today we know that early experiences can be decisive not only for the child's mental health, but also for his ability to learn. Scientific evidence both from laboratory and field studies demonstrates that mental development occurs primarily through interaction with adults in an encouraging atmosphere.[7]

The coming of the first baby is a critical period for the parents. Their motivation for learning how best to care for their child and assume their parental roles is at a high level, now more than ever again. When they get off to a good start, they feel good about themselves, secure as parents, and accepting of their children in ways that establish positive patterns for future family living. Policies and programs geared to upgrading the competence of new mothers and fathers come at a highly teachable moment for parent education and child-rearing guidance. Otherwise, old resentments, feelings of deprivation, and uncertainty coming out of the parents' childhood experiences may have an exaggerated effect on the way they relate to their children. Or, quite as harmfully, the conflicts in learned patterns of parenting that come from having been reared in two different

---

[6] Bloom, *Stability and Change in Human Characteristics,* p. 229.

[7] Urie Bronfenbrenner, "Damping the Unemployability Explosion," *Saturday Review,* January 4, 1969, p. 108.

homes are fought out with the child as a battlefield in ways that damage the nuclear family's structure and function.[8]

Fatigue and energy depletion are recurrent problems for young parents. Twenty-four-hour-a-day care of infants and small children disrupts parents' normal rest and relaxation. The young father works harder at his job in an effort to assume the responsibilities that his growing family puts upon him. The young mother, left alone at home with her babies hour after hour, often longs for a break in pace and for people her own age to talk to at times. The marriage relationship needs more privacy and uninterrupted periods of union than may be available unless some special provisions can be made.

A number of recommendations can be made to meet the pressure points in the childbearing family: counseling that gives reassurance that personal and pair well-being are crucial values, occasional respites for the parents when their children are cared for by their grandparents, cooperative parenting in which young parents team up with others in caring for their children for an evening out on a scheduled basis, and child care facets of community life in which young parents may participate.

Proposals for effective policies at the childbearing stage include such established and experimental programs as: (1) cooperative nursery schools in which mothers and fathers as well as their very little children are enrolled as active participants in a living laboratory of child and parent development; (2) day care services that go way beyond custodial care for children of mothers who work to become training centers for entire families in the essentials of optimal child care;[9] (3) formal and informal counseling and education for young parents in a variety of settings, in accessible and acceptable forms to meet the critical needs of members of childbearing families; (4) grandparent refresher courses that facilitate the eager assistance of members of the older generation in the healthy nurture of their grandchildren; and (5) most comprehensive is the proposal for the establishment of an Office for Family and Children's Services in the federal government, with responsibility for coordinating all existing programs relating to children and encouraging in every community at least one commission for children, as a quasi-public corporation. These, in turn, would establish, staff, and maintain centers for parents and children in every neighborhood, where parents and children, enrolled together, would participate in a full complement of services and activities designed to enrich the devel-

---

[8] Studies at Cornell University conclude that differences in child-rearing attitudes appear to have marked effect on marital happiness. Harold Feldman, "Parent and Marriage: Myths and Realities," address presented at the Merrill-Palmer Institute Conference on the Family, November 21, 1969, mimeographed, p. 22.

[9] Catherine S. Chilman, *Growing Up Poor*, Welfare Administration Publication, no. 13 (Washington, D.C., 1966), pp. 88–89.

opment of children and families.[10] Such proposals are bold and demanding, but possibly no more expensive than existing programs functioning on a mop-up basis after human problems have spawned and spiraled to frightening proportions that defy effective treatment.

Stage 3—Preschool Families

The possibilities of the childbearing period continue on throughout the preschool years. Parents still struggle with problems of fatigue and lack of privacy in maintaining their morale as persons, as a married couple, and as mother and father involved in continuing care of their infants and small children. As children come, the chances are that the family has moved to larger accommodations, with all that is involved in finding, financing, and outfitting the new home. This quite possibly has put a strain on the family budget, involving careful planning and many interlocking decisions that will affect the family for years to come.

Preschool children are still at a fast-growing, rapid-learning period of their lives in which they have urgent needs for experiences that encourage their development. Objectives of programs for preschool children can be listed as:

1. Stimulation of children to perceive aspects of the world about them and to fix these aspects by the use of language

2. Development of more extended and accurate language

3. Development of a sense of mastery over aspects of the immediate environment and an enthusiasm for learning for its own sake

4. Development of thinking and reasoning and the ability to make new discoveries for oneself

5. Development of purposive learning activity and ability to attend for longer periods of time.[11]

While many of these objectives are met in the best families, it is clear that preschool children generally can be further stimulated to optimal social, personality, and intellectual development in good preschool situations. Children growing up in deprived areas, with overburdened parents, working mothers, and disadvantaged homes, have especial needs for environmental enrichment. The "Project Head Start" begun in 1965 under the auspices of the Office of Economic Opportunity has been a national effort to decrease the cognitive deficits of children in low-income families. Many other strategies for upgrading preschool children's learning are being explored along the lines of reading readiness

---

[10] Bronfenbrenner, "Damping the Unemployability Explosion," pp. 109–110.

[11] Bloom, "Early Learning in the Home."

programs, day care enrichment projects, utilization of college resources and personnel to meet the needs of preschool children and their families, and efforts to encourage and enrich the lives of disadvantaged parents. Parent education, counseling for parents of young children, role-playing and learning-by-doing efforts at various levels of family therapy, guidance in impulse-control for parents, and other types of community action are promising possibilities.[12]

Continuation of the various policies and programs recommended for earlier stages of the family life cycle is indicated through the preschool period. Research findings especially suggest: (1) effective safety and health education; (2) accessible mental hygiene programs including child guidance clinics and spotter services for detecting exceptional problems; (3) preventive and therapeutic counseling facilities that are both acceptable and accessible; (4) parent education, group and individual counseling for parents, books and discussion guides in child development; (5) specific helps for parents in answering preschool children's questions in areas usually considered "sex education"; (6) family life orientation in the training of physicians, clergymen, community workers, and all others dealing with family members in the family-helping professions.[13]

Stage 4—School-age Families

By the time a family gets its first child in school, it enters into a fairly stable period in its history, for which there are relatively few critical needs. Family patterns for accomplishing its basic family tasks have already been established in one way or another. Foundations for child development and learning have already been laid by the time the child goes into the first grade. The attitudes he has toward school and the habits he establishes early in his school experience are of great importance for his continuing education. For instance, arithmetic achievement at the sixth grade level can be predicted before a child is six years old, with a correlation of $+.68$, and by the end of his first year in school, it can be predicted with correlations of $+.85$ and higher.[14] Along the same line, reading comprehension at the eighth grade can be predicted by second grade with a correlation of $+.73$.[15] Family policies that encourage close cooperation between parents and their children's teachers give a schoolchild the united backing of the significant adults in his life at the time when he is beginning his

---

[12] Chilman, *Growing Up Poor*, pp. 75–108.

[13] Evelyn Millis Duvall, "Implications for Education through the Family Life Cycle," *Marriage and Family Living* 20, no. 4 (November 1958): 338–339.

[14] Arlene Payne, "The Selection and Treatment of Data for Certain Curriculum Decision Problems: A Methodological Study" (Ph.D. dissertation, University of Chicago, 1963).

[15] M. Alexander, "The Relation of Environment to Intelligence and Achievement: A Longitudinal Study" (Master's thesis, University of Chicago, 1961).

formal education, and they help the entire family move into the school-age stage of its family life cycle with all that is involved in home-school, parent-teacher association, and family-community interaction. School guidance facilities, mental health programs, and environmental enrichment efforts for both children and their parents can be especially effective in the early school years before defenses build up and problems become either chronic or critical.

Stage 5—Teenagers' Families

Family policies established earlier in the home either ease or exaggerate the problems of bridging the generation gap during the children's teen years. At the time of life when young people are establishing their autonomy and stretching away from too-close parental control, effective communication between the generations is a decided advantage. Parents who have learned to listen to their sons and daughters, to enlist their participation in family decisions, and to encourage their assumption of responsibilities commensurate with the new freedoms they demand encounter less turbulence during adolescence than do more traditionally-oriented fathers and mothers (chapter 12 and its research references). Established policies in the family for making decisions cooperatively and resolving conflicts as they arise ease the tensions that are characteristic of this period of the family life cycle.

During the high school years, when discouragement with academic life may lead to dropping out of school, remedial programs, tutoring procedures, vocational guidance, and other helps for marginal students may make the difference between going on or dropping out of school. It is at this time that financial assistance to low-income families may enable many a student to continue his education rather than have to stop as soon as the law allows and get a job to support himself and help out at home. Upward Bound, the federally funded teenage program, has helped tens of thousands of high school students, whose grades had fallen behind their potentials, to upgrade their scholastic work so that many have been enabled to take advantage of higher education. Widened horizons and broader social experiences have served in many cases to improve teenagers' social competence for associations beyond their homes. Social enrichment programs are effective not only with youth from deprived backgrounds, but also for middle-class teenagers, who have been involved in group travel, broad-based camping experiences, work and service projects both abroad and in depressed areas at home, creative writing and drama projects, and traveling folk music groups.

Formal and informal education for family living is indicated for most teenagers to provide what help they want and need in appraising their feelings adequately, finding and maintaining friendships on the basis of personal goals, setting personal standards of conduct that reflect their potentials, and determining when and whom to marry from the security of a thought-through sense of personal identity. It is during the teen years, too, that preparation for parenthood is urgently needed, as Dr. O. Spurgeon English and others have found.[16] Then when teenagers are pulling away from close ties to their own parents, they are ready for study of child development and methods of child-rearing that they may follow when they have children of their own. This gives a positive direction to youth's emancipatory thrusts, and new insights into their own personality development, in ways that are measurably effective.[17]

Family therapy, counseling, and other procedures designed to help parents let their adolescent children go and grow in wholesome ways are recommended for the release of pressure upon the young person, for the emotional stability of younger children coming along in the family, and for the further maturing of the parents for the launching tasks that lie immediately ahead.

Stage 6—Launching-center Families

Three-generation family studies indicate that the launching-center stage of the family life cycle begins at about the twentieth year of marriage and is completed for the majority of families at approximately the twenty-seventh year of the marriage.[18] During these six or seven years of a family's life, the children, one by one, leave home for marriage, for military service, for further education, or for work. The young adults being released as well as their families face many developmental tasks toward which specific programs may be beamed:

1. Adequate scholarship systems for young people on the basis of ability and need
2. Vocational guidance from an early age
3. Counseling and specific preparation for military service or its alternative
4. Effective preparation-for-marriage courses and premarital counseling in home, school, church, and college, including the acquisition of the knowledges and skills and development of the attitudes and values conducive to competence in the processes that lead to marriage
5. New-citizen programs for induction and training of young people for capable roles as citizens
6. Education and guidance to help parents release their young people and find other sources of satisfaction and usefulness beyond their children
7. General interpretation of the meanings of marriage and the values to

---

[16] O. Spurgeon English, Max Katz, Albert E. Scheflen, Elliot R. Dansig, and Jeanne B. Speiser, "Preparedness of High School and College Seniors for Parenthood," *A.M.A. Archives of Neurology and Psychiatry* 81, no. 4 (April 1959): 469–479.

[17] Duvall, "How Effective Are Marriage Courses?" pp. 176–184.

[18] Hill, *Family Development in Three Generations,* chap. 14.

be achieved in the wedding (beyond the concentration on the wedding gown and other symbols)

8. Consumer guidance in wedding costs and choices

9. Discussions, panels, mass media treatment, and general consideration given to the variety and flexibility of modern sex roles with public encouragement of creative innovations

10. Open discussion of viable life-styles available to today's young adults in a context of encouraging healthy, satisfying values and appropriate decisions supporting them

11. Intergenerational consultation and consideration of choices that will affect both parents' families as well as the new family being established.[19]

Stage 7—Middle-aged Parents in the "Empty Nest"

At the time the last child is launched, a couple has half its marriage still ahead. Financially they may be depleted; emotionally they may be spent from their years of parenting, now over. If the last of life is to be full and satisfying, the marriage must be restructured so that prime attention and effort go to the pair relationship, without the dilution and distraction that parenthood entails. Few families are prepared for the middle and later years. In the present youth culture in which all Americans live, being middle-aged is kept quiet and not talked about any more than is necessary. There are pressures for staying young, even when one's declining strength and thickening silhouette say otherwise. If the transition into the middle years of marriage is to be smooth, a number of programs and policies are indicated:

1. Marriage education and group and individual counseling for middle-aged husbands and wives

2. Retraining programs for middle-aged women, whose children have grown, designed to develop and sharpen salable skills and fit the mature woman for several decades of constructively creative satisfactions

3. Special programs of skill- and interest-building among middle-aged couples that bring a variety of satisfying activities into the range of their capacities now and for the years ahead

4. Education for financial well-being that will build up a couple's resources in wise planning for retirement and later years

5. Availability of special service projects for middle-aged adults whose children have grown, in ways that channel their nurturing interests and make significant contributions to those who

---

[19] Adapted and enlarged from Duvall, "Implications for Education through the Family Life Cycle," p. 340.

need such attention—fatherless children, emotionally neglected children, disadvantaged families, overworked parents of small children, VISTA-type projects at home and abroad, tutoring, etc.

6. Intergenerational consideration of the mutual needs for acceptance and respect of married children, their spouses, and their parental families in ways that promise two-way satisfaction in newly established in-law relationships

7. Wider recognition of the contributions each generation has for the others and open discussion of how help patterns are best worked out in the larger family

8. Preparation of grandparents for competence with their grandchildren through updating their knowledge and skills in child-rearing procedures

9. Wide selection of resources for care of aging great-grandparents, for whom the middle-aged couple usually has responsibility.[20]

There is a two-way stretch in the middle years that is felt in ties and responsibilities both for their own children and grandchildren and for their own aging parents who now look to them for help in the many decisions that have to be made in the later years of life. It is fortunate that the middle years find most present-day men and women physically and financially flexible enough to serve adequately as the generation between, without unduly taxing their own resources. Programs for the elderly today relieve the more extreme pressures on younger generations in the family in ways that were previously unknown.

Stage 8—Aging Family Members

With the husband's retirement, the couple enter the final stage of their family life cycle. In the years that remain they will face the inevitability of failing strength, vitality, and capabilities. One of them will suffer the loss of a life partner with whom most if not all of adulthood has been shared. Before, during, and after the final illness of the first to go, choices must be made about the kind of medical, nursing, and finally funeral services needed within the available resources. Long before that the couple usually has active years in which to travel, pursue interests of their choice, and reap the rewards of lives well lived. Some disengagement is inevitable, but the healthy older person keeps as vitally alive and as vigorously interested in life as is feasible, as long as it is possible. In maintaining a high quality of life through the later years, there is a variety of programs and policies that have much to offer.

Physical strength fails in time, but emotional, social, intellectual, and spiritual interests continue as long as personal

---

[20] Expanded and adapted from Duvall, "Implications for Education through the Family Life Cycle," pp. 340–341.

motivation and opportunities are present. Programs that encourage continued involvement in educational, civic, social, and religious life all through the retirement years have proven their effectiveness. Senior centers, under paid professional leadership, provide recreation, adult education, health services, counseling and other social services, information and referral assistance, and a variety of other projects in well over a thousand communities across the country.[21]

A variety of retirement facilities offer residential accommodations of many types for aging family members of all income levels and degrees of fitness. Some of these are publicly supported; others are under the sponsorship of religious, fraternal, and other associations. Many are well run from physical, social, psychological, and financial standpoints. They often provide aging family members with a degree of independence that living with a married child or in the traditional "old people's home" could not approximate.

Inadequate income is probably the most difficult problem for aging family members. They may have counted upon social security, pensions, annuities, insurance, and other postretirement benefits, only to find that spiraling costs of living, high medical expenses, and their own increased longevity eat up their resources at alarming rates.

H. ARMSTRONG ROBERTS

The aging couple pursue interests of their choice.

Those whose incomes have always been marginal may be up against extreme hardship as they grow older. These are some of the reasons why government programs are being reviewed for possible broader bases for old age assistance and other supports for aging citizens. Private resources in the form of church-supported facilities for the aging, industrial pension plans, community programs for senior citizens, and intergenerational responsibility within a given family supplement what the various levels of government can do in most instances.

---

[21] *The Senior Center: Its Goals, Functions, and Programs* (Washington, D.C.: President's Council on Aging, 1964); see also Florence E. Vickery, *Aging and Social Functioning*, in press.

FAMILY POLICIES AND SOCIAL POLICIES

Family policies are those procedures a family works out for guiding decisions it makes in pursuit of its goals. A dozen illustrative family policies were found in. the three-generation study of the consumer practices of three hundred families in the Minneapolis–St. Paul area. These were policies for the:

1. use of credit
2. saving for holidays and vacations
3. saving for children's education
4. financial planning for retirement
5. buying at discount stores
6. shopping for weekend specials in the local neighborhood
7. insuring the breadwinner
8. investing in travel, education, and books
9. selecting modern housing and furnishings
10. family activities with children
11. gift-giving to relatives and friends
12. borrowing for family needs.[22]

Other families would have different policies for the ways they spend or save their money, of course. In addition, a family has policies for the ways it plans for and rears its children; divides its resources among the many interests and needs of family members from time to time; relates to groups, organizations, and activities outside the home; and encourages the continuing development and education of its members, to mention but a few.

Most families find that there are certain ways of managing their time, talents, abilities, money, and possessions (no matter how much or how little of these they have) so as to provide more of the things they want most out of life. Research into how families actually perform in pursuit of their policies suggests strongly that when families decide how they will handle the changes they foresee in some area of life, they increase their chances of having their plans work out as they wish. Even unexpected emergencies can better be met when a family has established a general policy for such contingencies in advance.[23]

Policies differ widely among individuals, families, social classes, ethnic and nationality groups, and by particular life-styles that are part of the cultural heritage in a given subculture. Such differences have been widely studied and are discussed in chapters 2, 3, and 4, as well as in chapters 7 through 15, in which the eight life cycle stages are considered in some detail. In general, the evidence is clear that some family policies

[22] Hill, *Family Development in Three Generations*, chap. 14.

[23] Ibid., chap. 14.

are more effective than others in (1) economic and vocational attainment, (2) marital adjustment, and (3) producing children of good character, to mention but three aspects of family success.

1. Economic and vocational attainments of a family are related to such policies as postponing marriage until higher education has been completed and some professional experience has been acquired, timing the number and spacing of children, and planning ahead in consultation with parents on major decisions in which help from other family members may be needed. "Such couples have a headstart not only in income and economic bargaining power of a good education but also tend to develop an equalitarian form of family organization and a favorable marital climate for making good decisions. Making prudent decisions about these matters of timing, taking into account long-term consequences as well as short-term satisfactions, distinguishes the successful from the unsuccessful in life cycle management."[24]

2. Not all the evidence is in on what makes for success in marriage, but a considerable body of accumulating research points clearly to a number of factors related significantly to the attainment of good marital adjustment. These are summarized as follows:

Legacies from families of orientation of the married couple:

a. Happiness of parents' marriage

b. Lack of divorce in families of orientation

c. Mild, firm discipline during childhood

d. Adequate, wholesome sex education from accepting parents

e. Parental respect for and acceptance of both members of the pair

f. Communication between the generations frequently and mutually sought.

Policies and practices of the married pair:

a. Education at least through high school; more is an advantage

b. Adequate time for courtship and engagement

c. Responsible sex standards and low levels of premarital pregnancy

d. Marriage in the early or middle twenties or later

e. Open expression of affection

f. Mutual enjoyment of sexual intercourse

g. Trust in one another based upon open, free communication

h. Equalitarian, flexible interaction

i. Responsible behavior in performance of personal, family, and marital roles

j. Adequate financial base

k. Stable, single-family home

l. Joint participation in outside interests; friends in common.[25]

---

[24] Ibid., chap. 14.

3. Producing children who become worthy members of society with contributions to make that bring them satisfaction is a goal of many families. In a real sense it is what families are for in the modern world. Factors related to the development of many human characteristics in children have been discussed in earlier chapters.

Child-rearing patterns of families who produce children who are honest, responsible, dependable, and able to resist temptation, considered as being of "good character," have been found to cluster around a number of family policies: democratic methods in rearing children; mild, reasonable, consistent discipline; viewing the child's capacity for making moral judgments as a developing ability; open discussions and clarification for moral values; parents who set a good example in their own conduct.[26]

Family policies are present in all areas of family decision-making and functioning. The three aspects summarized above are but illustrative of the research evidence available in many dimensions of family life that point toward more effective family policies.

---

[25] Charles Bowerman, "Adjustment in Marriage: Over-all and in Specific Areas," *Sociology and Social Research* 41, no. 4 (March-April 1957): 257–263; Ernest W. Burgess and Leonard S. Cottrell, Jr., *Predicting Success or Failure in Marriage* (New York: Prentice-Hall, 1939), pp. 58–74; Chilman, *Growing Up Poor*, pp. 72–73; Evelyn Millis Duvall, *In-Laws: Pro and Con* (New York: Association Press, 1954); Evelyn Millis Duvall, *Why Wait Till Marriage?* (New York: Association Press, 1965); Charles E. King, "The Burgess-Cottrell Method of Measuring Marital Adjustment Applied to a Non-White Southern Urban Population," *Marriage and Family Living* 14 (1952): 284; Clifford Kirkpatrick, *The Family as Process and Institution*, 2d ed. (New York: Ronald Press Company, 1963), pp. 375–407; Harvey J. Locke, *Predicting Adjustment in Marriage: A Comparison of a Divorced and a Happily Married Group* (New York: Henry Holt and Company, 1951); Harvey J. Locke and Karl M. Wallace, "Short Marital-Adjustment and Prediction Tests: Their Reliability and Validity," *Marriage and Family Living* 21 (1959): 251–255; Harvey J. Locke and Robert C. Williamson, "Marital Adjustment: A Factor Analysis Study," *American Sociological Review* 23 (1958): 562–569; F. Ivan Nye and Evelyn MacDougall, "The Dependent Variable in Marriage Research," *Pacific Sociological Review* 2 (1949): 67–70; Atlee L. Stroup, "Predicting Marital Success or Failure in an Urban Population," *American Sociological Review* 28 (1953): 560; Lewis M. Terman, assisted by Paul Buttenwieser, Leonard W. Ferguson, Winifred Bent Johnson, and Donald P. Wilson, *Psychological Factors in Marital Happiness* (New York: McGraw-Hill Book Company, 1938).

[26] Summarized in Chilman, *Growing Up Poor*, p. 63, from primary sources: Hugh Hartshorne and Mark A. May, *Studies in the Nature of Character* (New York: Macmillan Company, 1928–1930); Martin L. Hoffman, "Early Processes in Moral Development," mimeographed (New York: Social Science Research Council, Conference on Character Development, 1963); Lawrence Kohlberg, "Development of Moral Character and Moral Ideology," chap. 5 of Martin L. Hoffman and Lois W. Hoffman, eds., *Review of Child Development Research* (New York: Russell Sage Foundation, 1964); Lawrence Kohlberg, "The Development of Children's Orientations toward a Moral Order: Sequence in the Development of Moral Thought," *Vita Humana* 6, no. 1–2 (1963): 11–33; Robert F. Peck and Robert J. Havighurst, *The Psychology of Character Development* (New York: John Wiley and Sons, 1960); Ralph K. White and Ronald O. Lippitt, *Autocracy and Democracy* (New York: Harper and Brothers, 1960).

Social Policies Affecting Families

There is hardly a social policy emanating from the larger society that does not have some effect on families and their functioning. Those of immediate and direct influence are fiscal and economic policies affecting relative prosperity, employment rates, standards of living, availability of adequate housing at various income levels and for the several types of family need, freedom to move and to live where a family wishes, public education for all children and for those adults who wish it, availability of health and medical services at costs that families can carry, social security benefits for those unable to work for whatever reason, availability of family planning services and supplies so that children are born into families who want them and are prepared to care for them adequately, military and defense programs that protect family life and that have the support of the people, number of avenues of recourse for citizens to make their wishes known to officials at local, state, and national levels, and responsiveness of government that is capable of legislating and administering programs that safeguard the welfare of families in all possible respects. These are complex expectations that are not always met in an industrial society manned by millions of people. That so many are met so often is a tribute to the system of checks and balances of an open republic like the United States of America. That some families fare much better than do others is a source of general concern today.

Strengthening Families of the Culturally Deprived

When a family lives on a marginal economic base, it is apt to be seriously deprived in many of the qualities that make for strong family life. When a family lives in an urban ghetto or in a rural slum, it is likely to lack many of the opportunities and motivations for development more readily available in more comfortable areas. Disadvantage in one area of life is often coupled with deprivation in other areas as well, so that a subculture of poverty tends to be self-perpetuating for families cut off from the mainstream of American life.

For reasons that lie deep in the alienation of families caught in the cycle of poverty, these are the hard-to-reach in many a community. They not only lack what others have; they do not avail themselves of those resources that are present. Educators observe that the children and adults most in need of education are those least interested in it. Social work agencies find that families most in need of their services are least cooperative in participating in programs set up for them. Family planning clinics do well in medium-sized, middle-class neighborhoods, but have to take the initiative in going after clients whose family size is a

Social policies call for bringing families into full participation in the American economy.

chronic burden. Health and medical services readily sought by the well are sometimes actively rejected or avoided by those who function at low levels of health and well-being. So it goes in many other efforts to strengthen the nation's weakest families; they are hard to reach and outside the competence of many lay and professional workers. The evidence is strong that methods and approaches emanating from middle-class values and personnel are often ineffective with lower-class families. Reaching the hard-to-reach calls for social policies beamed upon their needs and situations. Working with the culturally deprived involves sharply focusing on their interests,

goals, and feelings as the point of contact.

Recent recommendations for breaking into the cycle of poverty effectively have been many. Three focal points of family need amply documented by current research imply social policies for (1) bringing minority group families into full participation in the American economy, (2) safeguarding families at the point of their formation, and (3) enriching the lives of little children in ways conducive to stimulating their optimal development.

1. As the conclusion of his study of the plight of the Negro family in America, Dr. Daniel P. Moynihan specifies the direction national efforts should take: "The policy of the United States is to bring the Negro American to full and equal sharing in the responsibilities and rewards of citizenship. To this end, the programs of the Federal government bearing on this objective shall be designed to have the effect, directly or indirectly, of enhancing the stability and resources of the Negro American family."[27]

2. Joan Aldous, Reuben Hill, and others interpret the vast amount of research on limited family functioning as calling for massive thrusts at the point when youth are emerging from their parental homes into lives of their own. They point to the need for social policies and programs that would enable families to keep their teenage chil-

---

[27] *The Negro Family: The Case for National Action* (Washington, D.C.: Office of Policy Planning and Research, U.S. Department of Labor, 1965), p. 48.

dren in school through educational allowances and other basic sources of support. This should be accompanied, they feel, by effective programs in sex and marriage education by schools and community agencies. Hopefully, these would delay marriage and discourage premature parenthood until the young of both sexes had the requisite education, training, and vocational experience to make a good start in marriage.[28]

3. Extensive work in differential child development progress results in a variety of proposals and experimental programs designed to enrich the lives of infants and small children with the stimulation and broad-based environmental upgrading that would give them a reasonably good chance to develop their potentials. Some of these social policies would be beamed at whole-family enrichment, others at the little child as a developing personality either in or outside his home setting.[29]

---

[28] Joan Aldous and Reuben Hill, "Strategies for Breaking the Poverty Cycle," *Social Work*, July 1969.

[29] See, for instance, the major section, "Children under Three—Finding Ways to Stimulate Development," including articles by Lois Barclay Murphy, "Issues in Research"; Sally Provence, "A Three-Pronged Project"; Francis H. Palmer, "Learning at Two"; Ira J. Gordon, "Stimulation via Parent Education"; Earl S. Schaefer, "A Home Tutoring Program"; Halbert B. Robinson, "From Infancy through School"; and Alice V. Keliher, "Parent and Child Centers—Where They Are, Where They Are Going," *Children* 16, no. 2 (March-April 1969). Review also Chilman, *Growing Up Poor*, pp. 75–100.

There are a number of dilemmas in designing and implementing broad social welfare programs that should be recognized. (1) In trying to protect children in fatherless families, there may be financial incentives for parents to separate and for fathers to leave their families. (2) In a guaranteed annual wage or family support system there is encouragement for many people who can and should work to escape their responsibilities to support themselves and their families. (3) Many a welfare program keeps families from moving to places where they might improve their condition and lower their costs, simultaneously maintaining high concentrations of poor families in rural and urban slums. (4) Some social policies encourage either lying and cheating among recipients or attempted supervision by such rigid controls that the process of getting help is unnecessarily embarrassing, time-consuming, and uncertain. (5) Making work obligatory for those who are able puts undue weight on the judgment of often-untrained social workers for making the decision of who is and is not eligible for support. (6) Upgrading the status, functioning, and income of one or more family members may break the cohesion of the family as a whole. (7) Too-generous social welfare programs threaten to put such a burden on the taxpayer that massive citizen revolts are possible, while inadequate social policies threaten the well-being of millions of American families that might be helped to function effectively. (8) Providing ample child support for poor families perpetuates the problems stemming from their bearing more children than they can care for adequately. (9) Complete social welfare states can so undermine incentive that chronic underdevelopment can result—industrially, educationally, culturally, economically, and personally. When everyone is assured of cradle-to-the-grave security against any problem that befalls, many elect to go surfing rather than to school.[30]

Difficult as social planning for families may be, it must be done. The human, family, and national costs of delaying effective action are too great and too far-reaching to be ignored. The bottleneck is in those policies that fail to put high priority on individual and family development. The problem today is more in a lack of public consensus on what is most important than in professional know-how and know-when.

If school dropouts, delinquent behavior, and frustration with the educational requirements of a society can be predicted long in advance, can we sit idly by and watch the prophecies come true? If remedial actions and therapy are less effective at later stages in the individual's development, can we satisfy a social conscience by indulging in such activities when it is far too late? When the school environment is at variance with the home and peer group environment, can we find ways of reconciling these different environments?

Put briefly, the increased ability to predict long-term consequences of environmental forces and developmental characteristics places new responsibilities on the home, the school, and on society. If these responsibilities are not adequately met, society will suffer in the long run.[31]

EDUCATION FOR FAMILY LIVING THROUGH THE LIFE CYCLE

There is no stage of the family life cycle when family members do not need some explicit education in what to expect and how to wholesomely satisfy their needs, fill their roles, and achieve their developmental tasks, both as individuals and as whole families. Education for family living throughout the family life cycle has been

---

[30] *The New Zealand Yearbook* (Wellington, New Zealand: Government Publication, 1969); Edward C. Banfield, "Welfare Reform: Choose Your Evil," National Affairs, Inc., 1969, digested in *Wall Street Journal*, August 14, 1969; and Gertrude Zemon Gass, William C. Nichols, Jr., and Aaron L. Rutledge, "Family Problems in Upgrading the Hardcore," *Family Coordinator* 18, no. 2 (April 1969): 99–106.

[31] Bloom, *Stability and Change in Human Characteristics*, p. 231.

recommended by many people in recent years.[32]

Family life education has made great progress in the twentieth century, but it still faces real problems which greatly limit its present-day effectiveness in equipping families to carry on their multifold tasks. Some of the more common difficulties family life education confronts are: (1) Knowledge about interpersonal and intrafamily relationships is not definite, explicit, or tangible. There are no pat answers in the back of the book as in mathematics, no recipes as in cooking, nothing tangible to carry home as from a sewing class. (2) Sound principles of child guidance, marriage, and family relationships compete with multimillion-dollar mass media, which tend to repeat outmoded superstitions, taboos, stereotypes, and old wives' tales and to exploit the love-hungry needs of individuals and of families. (3) Relatively few well-trained professional persons are as yet available to fill the rapidly growing number of posts for teachers, supervisors, counselors, and con-

sultants in family life education. (4) Curricula are already so overcrowded that it is administratively difficult to add anything as all-pervasive as family life education to existing programs. (5) Highly articulate critics speak for small minorities who resist elements of family life education and overrule the vast majority of American men and women, boys and girls, who favor such programs. (6) Progress in the knowledge, skills, attitudes, and values acquired in family life education is difficult to appraise, to grade, and to evaluate.

No one of the challenges family life education faces in the United States at present is overwhelming. Each one is effectively being met in many programs, too numerous to list, too varied to catalogue completely. Where once school administrators hesitated to consider family life education emphases in their schools, now those who are not making some efforts in this direction are on the defensive at national, regional, and state meetings of their profession. At one time very few schools, colleges, and universities offered courses of a functional or preprofessional nature in family life education. Now most institutions of higher learning offer something which may range from a single course or two to an entire curriculum in the field of marriage and family life. Churches and youth-serving agencies, such as the YMCA, have greatly expanded their offerings in recent years. Books, pamphlets, films, skits, and teaching aids of all kinds have been developed in greater quantity and quality. Basic research is being carried

---

[32] Review, for instance, *Education for Personal and Family Living: A Working Guide for Colleges* (New York: American Social Health Association, 1955), pp. 20–46; 1960 White House Conference on Children and Youth, *Recommendations: Composite Report of Forum Findings* (Washington, D.C.: U.S. Government Printing Office, 1960), esp. pp. 12–13; Roy W. Fairchild and John Charles Wynn, *Families in the Church: A Protestant Survey* (New York: Association Press, 1961), esp. pp. 241–247; John L. Thomas, *The American Catholic Family* (Englewood Cliffs, N.J.: Prentice-Hall, 1956), chap. 15; and Joint Commission on Mental Illness and Health, *Action for Mental Health*.

on in every area of family life throughout the life cycle with findings that challenge the educator at every level.

Medical school students are beginning to get professional training in family-centered medical practice. Theological students increasingly are exposed to basic materials on the nature of family life and the processes of courtship, marriage, childbearing, and living as a family member, as well as in the skills of group interviewing, marriage and family counseling, and family life education for family members of all ages in their parishes. So too, lawyers, home economists, social workers, nurses, guidance personnel, science educators, human development students, teachers of humanities, religious educators, health and physical educators, mental health specialists, and human relations experts, as well as marriage counselors and family life specialists, are devoting more and more time and attention to the family aspects of their work.

PREDICTABLY VULNERABLE FAMILIES

Some families are more vulnerable to stress and strains than are others. Numerous studies indicate clearly that lower-class, less well-educated, newcomers in a community, and racial and ethnic minorities have more severe family crises and weather them less well than do more comfortably situated families with financial and educational supports and status to help cushion the shocks that come their way.

To the low-income family, living up to and beyond its income, there is a quality of desperation that is less frequent in the middle-class family, with reserves upon which it can draw. Conversely, the low-status family has less to lose in prestige and therefore sees as critical fewer problem situations than does a middle-class family whose position and pride are at stake.[33] One family may have a rigid family organization, with a firm adherence to a certain pattern of action in all family situations, while another may have more flexible family ways, with quite different attitudes toward what constitutes a crisis and what to do about it.

National interview surveys of mental health find differences of symptoms and of ways of handling unhappy periods by levels of income:

> High income is associated with greater happiness, fewer worries, more frequent anticipation of future happiness, fewer physical symptoms, and more symptoms of energy immobilization. Low income implies current unhappiness and worries, a lack of confidence in the future, and the expression of anxiety through physical symptoms. Middle-income groups, who worry the most about money mat-

[33] Earl L. Koos, "Class Differences in Family Reactions to Crisis," *Marriage and Family Living* 12, no. 3 (Summer 1950): 77–78, 99; and Carson McGuire, "Family Backgrounds and Community Patterns," *Marriage and Family Living* 13, no. 4 (November 1951): 160–164.

ters, are least likely to show symptoms of psychological anxiety and are most optimistic about the future.[34]

Fewer low-income families seek help with their problems or cope with them directly than do family members with more adequate incomes.[35] Low-status groups have least access to professional help because they are less able to recognize their problems, because they do not known where to look for help, and because help is not so readily available to them.[36]

---

[34] Gerald Gurin, Joseph Veroff, and Sheila Feld, *Americans View Their Mental Health: A Nationwide Interview Study* (New York: Basic Books, 1960), p. 218.

[35] Ibid., pp. 374–376.

[36] A. B. Hollingshead and F. C. Redlich, *Social Class and Mental Illness* (New York: John Wiley and Sons, 1958).

Surveys reveal a high concentration of problems of dependency, ill health, and maladjustment in relatively small numbers of families. In one city, 1 percent of the city's families were responsible for 75 percent of its juvenile delinquency in 1956. In all areas studied to date, a small percentage of hard-core families account for the great majority of family problems and crises requiring attention.[37]

Studies of multi-problem families have established criteria for adequacy of family functioning as a guide for community intervention at critical points (table 17–1).

Three serious problems confronting community organizations are (1) locating vul-

---

[37] 1960 White House Conference on Children and Youth, *Children in a Changing World* (New York: Columbia University Press, 1960), p. 23.

Table 17–1. *Criteria for Levels of Social Functioning of Families*

Inadequate—Community Has a Right to Intervene	Marginal—Behavior Not Sufficiently Harmful to Justify Intervention	Adequate—Behavior Is in Line with Community Expectations
Laws and/or mores are clearly violated. Behavior of family members is a threat to the community.	No violation of major laws, although behavior of family members is contrary to what is accepted for status group.	Laws obeyed and mores are observed. Behavior is acceptable to status group.
Children in clear and present danger because of extreme conflict or imminent disruption of family life, serious neglect of children, or other types of behavior inimical to their welfare.	Children in no immediate danger, but family life marked by conflict or apathy which is a potential threat to the welfare of children.	Children are being raised in an atmosphere conducive to healthy physical and emotional development. Socialization process carried out affirmatively. Adequate training in social skills.

Source: L. L. Geismar and Beverly Ayres, *Measuring Family Functioning* (St. Paul, Minn.: Family Centered Project, Greater St. Paul Community Chest and Councils, 1960), p. 19.

nerable families, (2) developing suitable institutional aids for families, and (3) finding ways of getting families in need of help to use these aids where they do exist. The relative "aloneness" of the American family presents both a serious problem and a distinct challenge to the family-helping professions. Effective ways of making institutional aids more acceptable and usable to families are needed. New approaches must be planned and put into effect if our families are to function at levels that insure the well-being of the nation's children.

RELATIVELY STRONG AND SUCCESSFUL FAMILIES

Strength and success in family living are at best relative. There are few absolutes or ideal situations in family development. Families are pulsing, dynamic units of interpersonal interaction with great potentials for change, growth, and development. Strengths that can be identified and channeled at strategic points in a family's development can somewhat offset the effects of inherent weaknesses that any human family has. Family members aware of their potential strengths and weaknesses can sometimes be helped to accomplish their developmental tasks effectively, thereby enhancing their further personal and family development.

One measure of success in family living is in the extent to which basic family tasks are being accomplished. The major tasks of modern American families are bearing, rearing, socializing, and educating children; assuring the physical, mental, economic, and spiritual nurture of each family member; allocating responsibilities, opportunities, and resources according to the needs, readinesses, and potentialities of every member of the family; and maintaining family morale and motivation for carrying out its family functions, tasks, and goals.[38]

Families' success in finding happiness and satisfaction in any one of the stages of life is dependent primarily upon how well they achieve the developmental tasks of the period. Failure tends to predispose future frustration, while success is built upon previous success. Every individual, every family, is doing well or not so well in the developmental tasks of the moment. Doing well, the person or the family as a whole is happy, well adjusted, competent, and relatively self-assured. The challenge to families, and to those who care about them, is to increase the incidence of success and diminish the frequencies of failure in the developmental tasks of life, throughout the entire family life cycle.

Family interaction in a dynamic world calls for good relationships between family members and with other aspects of the

---

[38] Emily H. Mudd and Reuben Hill, "Memorandum on Strengthening Family Life in the United States," prepared for Commissioners Charles I. Schottland and William L. Mitchell of the U.S. Department of Health, Education, and Welfare, the Social Security Administration, 1956, mimeographed.

entire culture. Throughout the entire life cycle, families face certain inevitable, urgent developmental tasks necessary for their survival, continuation, and development. At every stage of the life cycle, there are challenges and hazards that call for the extension of programs of proven worth and for creative innovations that will assist families to carry more effectively the burdens of twentieth-century living. Family development as a frame of reference may provide a tool which can explore the human frontiers of interpersonal and family interrelationships with the research, education, counseling, and community services urgently needed. Today we push our way through the wilderness of family confusion, but tomorrow our children's children may experience smooth, established ways of family life. Road-building is strenuous work, but the dream of a nation of vital, happy families producing generation after generation of strong, creative persons is a worthy one, and a goal worth the struggle.

A basic statement jointly written by lay and professional workers in the largest family service agency in the world concludes with these words that express the sentiments of many an individual caught up in the day-to-day experience of family development:

Family life is never completely easy, but . . . the rewards can be great; although it is a serious enterprise, it ought not be a burdensome one. A sense of excitement

H. ARMSTRONG ROBERTS

Family life is never easy, but the rewards are great.

and adventure is inherent in family life and so, too, is a feeling of security and of belonging, a sense of awe and humility, of hope and pride. A family is a loving, growing organism, composed of different and changing individuals. It is compounded of love, laughter, joy and work, of agreement and conflict, of disappointment, pain, sorrow and tears. It is, in short, a microcosm of the physical, emotional and social experiences to which the individual is subject in the course of his journey through life.[39]

---

[39] *What Makes for Strong Family Life* (New York: Family Service Association of America, 1958), p. 14.

SUGGESTED ACTIVITIES

1. Prepare a rationale for policies and programs in family development, including a review of modern families' contributions to the larger society that merit prime consideration to family welfare, definitions and illustrations of your understanding of both family policies and social policies affecting families, and concluding with recommendations as to when and how such policies should be planned and put into effect. Document your generalizations with primary sources, research-based where possible.

2. Select the stage of the family life cycle which you feel is the most strategic for effecting lasting changes in family attitudes and behavior. Support your choice with documented arguments from available research, detailing interpretations and implications of the substantive findings. When your case is complete, find a member of your class who has chosen a different stage of the family life cycle as most strategic from his or her point of view. Plan to present your materials jointly as a basis for class discussion.

3. On the bases of your reading and your personal family experience, prepare a listing of twenty family policies that modern families are known to adopt in the pursuit of their goals. Illustrate in detail, and document in full.

4. Your text points to the fact that some family policies are more effective than others. It discusses three areas of family life in which certain family policies are superior to others. Select a fourth quality of family life in which you can find recommended policies suggested by valid research. Footnote the recommendations for specific family policies in detail.

5. Do a neighborhood study of the area in which you now live with particular attention to the various social policies affecting families in one or more ways. Consider the many laws, regulations, ordinances, and restrictions that curtail and/or protect families. Get the help of your precinct captain, alderman, or other local official in making as complete a listing as possible of all the social policies that possibly influence family life, and indicate in what ways their impact is felt.

6. Review the current national social welfare structure by getting materials directly from the United States Department of Health, Education, and Welfare, Washington, D.C. Point up the highlights of the federal social welfare program in terms of family benefits and assistance to family members in specific ways. From what you know of family development, attempt an appraisal of the positive and negative aspects of various facets of the current social welfare program.

7. Visit a local child care center, nursery school, cooperative play school, or other facility that claims to give more than cus-

todial care to its young charges. Look for ways in which the children are being stimulated to explore their world and to develop their potentials. Interview a member of the staff or a board member as to evaluative methods being used to measure the development of specific characteristics of their children over stated periods of time. Find out how involved the children's parents are in the program and what evidence there is of carry-over of the learning environment into the families of the children. Write up your observations, using verbatim anecdotal material to illustrate the points you make, tying into what is known about the foundations of personality development and the learning process in very young children.

8. Write a letter to a hypothetical younger brother who is talking of dropping out of school, giving him reasons why completing his education might be advisable in terms of long-term goals and career planning.

READINGS

Bloom, Benjamin S. *Stability and Change in Human Characteristics.* New York: John Wiley and Sons, 1964.

Broderick, Carlfred B. "Reaction to 'Familial Development, Selective Needs, and Predictive Theory.'" *Journal of Marriage and the Family* 29, no. 2 (May 1967): 237–240.

Bronfenbrenner, Urie. "Damping the Unemployability Explosion." *Saturday Review,* January 4, 1969, pp. 108–110.

Children: An Interdisciplinary Journal for the Professions Serving Children 16, no. 2 (March-April 1969): entire issue.

Chilman, Catherine S. *Growing Up Poor.* Welfare Administration Publication, no. 13. Washington, D.C., 1966.

Drucker, Peter F. *The Age of Discontinuity: Guidelines to Our Changing Society.* New York: Harper and Row, 1969.

Duvall, Evelyn Millis. *Faith in Families.* Chicago: Rand McNally and Company, 1970.

Etziono, Amitai. *The Active Society.* New York: Free Press, 1969.

Family Coordinator: Journal of Education, Counseling, and Services 19, no. 4 (October 1970): entire issue.

Gass, Gertrude Zemon, William C. Nichols, Jr., and Aaron L. Rutledge. "Family Problems in Upgrading the Hardcore." *Family Coordinator* 18, no. 2 (April 1969): 99–106.

Hill, Reuben. *Family Development in Three Generations.* Cambridge, Mass.: Schenkman Publishing Company, 1970. Esp. chap. 14, "Applying the Research Findings for Families."

Hill, Reuben. "The American Family of the Future." *Journal of Marriage and the Family* 26, no. 1 (February 1964): 20–28.

Kirkpatrick, Clifford. "Familial Development, Selective Needs, and Predictive Theory." *Journal of Marriage and the Family* 29, no. 2 (May 1967): 229–236.

Otto, Herbert A. "What Is a Strong Family?" *Marriage and Family Living* 24, no. 1 (February 1962): 77–80.

Pohlman, Edward W. *The Psychology of Birth Planning*. Cambridge, Mass.: Schenkman Publishing Company, 1969.

Rainwater, Lee, and William L. Yancey. *The Moynihan Report and the Politics of Controversy* (including the text of Daniel P. Moynihan's *The Negro Family: The Case for National Action*). Cambridge, Mass.: M.I.T. Press, 1967.

Stewart, Maxwell S. *A Chance for Every Child*. New York: Public Affairs Committee, 1970.

Toman, Walter. *Family Constellation*. New York: Springer Publishing Company, 1961.

Turner, Francis J., ed. *Differential Diagnosis and Treatment in Social Work*. New York: Free Press, 1968.

What Makes for Strong Family Life. New York: Family Service Association of America, 1958.

GLOSSARY OF TERMS
AND CONCEPTS*

Adaptability: ability of a person to modify his roles, attitudes, and behavior

Adaptation: process of adjusting to new and different conditions

Affect: emotional feeling tone; emotion

Affluence: wealth; a state of plenty; comfortable living

Age and sex grades (categories, sets): ways of classifying the members of a society by age and sex

Alienation: being estranged and cut off from others

Ambivalence: simultaneous presence of opposite feelings (e.g., love and hate) toward the same person, thing, or possibility

Annulment: legally rescinding a marriage and returning the husband and wife to the same legal status they had before they married

Autonomy: ability of a person to be self-governing

Basic needs: those things felt to be essential for the individual, family, or society

Birth cohorts: group of persons who were born in a specified calendar period

Birth order: sequence of children born alive by the mother (first, second, etc.)

Career: set of role clusters in sequence; a position in the family consisting of role clusters in sequence over time; see positional career

Child-rearing: ways in which a child is brought up; patterns of discipline in the home

Commitment: intent to follow a given course of action; unreserved devotion to a person or a cause

Communication: network for transmitting information, ideas, and feelings between members of a group; exchange of meaningful symbols (words and gestures)

Community: group of people sharing in common activities

Companionship: association of two or more persons based upon common interests and mutual acceptance

* Selected and adapted from sources representing various disciplines, including: U.S. Bureau of the Census; *A Psychiatric Glossary* (Washington, D.C.: American Psychiatric Association, 1969); Harold T. Christensen, ed., *Handbook of Marriage and the Family* (Chicago: Rand McNally and Company, 1964); F. Ivan Nye and Felix M. Berardo, eds., *Emerging Conceptual Frameworks in Family Analysis* (New York: Macmillan Company, 1966); American Home Economics Association, "Report of a National Project," in *Concepts and Generalizations* (Washington, D.C.: American Home Economics Association, 1967); and a number of sources of terms in child, adolescent, and adult human development. Omitted are many terms and concepts dealt with in detail in the various chapters of this text, as well as those to be found in any standard dictionary that provides general rather than technical definitions.

Compatibility: condition of getting along well together

Complementarity: meeting one another's needs in an intimate relationship

Compulsion: insistent, repetitive, irrational urge to perform an act or ritual

Condonation: action that erases the grounds for divorce in most states

Conflict: opposing interests, ideas, drives, or impulses within an individual or between two or more persons

Conjugal family: family unit in which the husband-wife relationship is given preponderant importance

Consanguineal family: family unit in which blood relatives take precedence over marriage partners

Consumption: use of economic resources by the ultimate consumer

Copes: behaves in a purposeful, problem-solving manner

Coverture: legal rights of and status of a wife

Creativity: ability to invent or improvise new roles or alternative lines of action in problematic situations

Crisis: any decisive change that creates a condition for which habitual patterns of behavior are inadequate

Cultural conflict: inconsistencies arising out of incompatible elements in a culture or between cultures

Cultural inconsistency: discrepancy or contradiction existing between various aspects of a culture

Cultural lag: discrepancy in a culture resulting from some aspects changing more slowly than others

Cultural patterns: standardized behavioral forms, practices, rules, and sentiments in a society

Cultural variation: cross-cultural or historical differences in institutional behavioral patterns in societies resulting from different cultures and values

Culture: way of life; the patterned behaviors, knowledge, and attitudes which members of a society learn and teach to their children

Culture of poverty: distinguishing folkways of the very poor

Customs: standardized ways of doing, knowing, thinking, and feeling valued in a given group at a given time

Cycle of poverty: poverty extending from generation to generation

Definition of the situation: interpreting, making judgments, and representing the elements in a situation to oneself and others

Deprivation: inadequate standard of living; lacking essential or needed care and attention

Development: process leading toward fulfillment and realization of potential of an individual, family, or group over time

Developmental task: growth responsibility that arises at or about a certain time in the life of an individual, successful accomplishment of which leads to success in later tasks

Differential change: condition in which

one mate outgrows the other, emotionally, intellectually, or socially

Disenchantment: decline in satisfaction and adjustment

Disengagement: decline in the number and quality of relationships between a person and other individuals, groups, and associations

Disorganization: loss of common objectives and of functioning roles and tasks

Dissolution: dissolving of marriage by death, divorce, or separation

Divorce: legally dissolving the marriage

Dyadic relation: interaction between two partners

Dysfunction: negative consequences of an activity

Economic stratification: levels in society ordered by differences in income and wealth

Efficiency: effective use of resources to obtain goals

Electra complex: girl's attachment to her father, accompanied by aggressive feelings toward her mother

Empathy: subtle interpersonal sensitivity in which a person can step into another's experience and think and feel as he does

Erogenous zones: areas of the body susceptible to sexual stimulation

Evaluation: appraising actions, decisions, and results in relation to goals

Expressed culture: that part of the cultural content that operates on the surface, with activities and words taken at their face value

Expressive feelings: emotions that reveal personal feeling states

Family: two or more persons related by marriage, blood, birth, or adoption; structurally a family is a set of positions each of which is composed of roles, which in turn are composed of norms; dynamically a family is a system of role complexes played sequentially to form a set of related careers

Family developmental tasks: growth responsibilities that arise at certain stages in the life of a family, achievement of which leads to success with later tasks; sequential functional prerequisites

Family functions: what a family does to meet the needs of its members, to survive, and to make a contribution to the larger society

Family integration: bonds of unity including affection, common interests, and economic interdependence within a family

Family life cycle: sequence of characteristic stages beginning with family formation and continuing through the life of the family to its dissolution

Family life education: systematic study or guidance in the development of those knowledges, skills, attitudes, and values conducive to effective functioning as a family member of any age or status

Family life-style: unique patterning of an individual family seen in its goals and how it goes about achieving them

Family of orientation: family into which one is born and from which he gets his most basic socialization

Family of procreation: family one establishes through marriage and reproduction

Family ritual: established procedure in a family, involving patterned behavior that is valued for itself

Family structure: regular, routinized characteristics of the family as a whole, in style, pattern of interaction, and power hierarchy, established as properties of the group

Family subculture: complex of family habits, attitudes, and relationships that aid family members in selecting, interpreting, and evaluating the various cultural patterns to which they are exposed

Family types: classification of families by descent, location of residence, authority, and life-style

Family values: what a family appreciates, considers desirable and of worth

Fidelity: faithful devotion to one's vows; loyalty to one's spouse; exclusiveness in sexual behavior of monogamous mates

Firm discipline: child-rearing that allows freedom within limits, allowing the child to know clearly what is expected of him without undue harshness

Fixation: intense attachment to an object; arrest of psychosexual maturation

Functional prerequisites: conditions necessary for the survival and continuation of a family, group, or society; social imperatives

Generation spiral: continuous overlapping of family life cycles in one generation after another in a family

Genetic: determined by heredity

Goals: the ends toward which an individual, family, group, or society directs its efforts in the pursuit of values

Growth: change in amount, degree, or function of bodily structure, or personality feature, or of a group as a whole, like a family, over time

Growth and development: increasing amount or complexity or both in living things

Habit: acquired disposition to act in a certain way when in a given situation

Health: positive realization of physical and emotional potentialities

Heredity: characteristics and potentialities attributable to the genes

Home management: making decisions and utilizing resources to obtain goals in the family

Homogamy: tendency of courting and married couples to resemble each other; choosing a marriage partner like oneself in many respects

Household: all persons living in the same residence

Human development: sum total of processes of change in a person from conception through old age

Idealization: consciously or unconsciously overestimating an admired attribute of another person; a mental mechanism

Ideal mate: preconceived combination of characteristics embodied in one's image of the kind of person he or she would like to marry

Identification: unconscious endeavor to pattern oneself after another; defense mechanism playing a major role in personality development

Identity confusion: uncertainty as to what one wants to do with his life

Identity crisis: loss of the sense of continuity in oneself and inability to accept or adopt the role expected of oneself

Income management: use of financial resources

Individual: sum total of qualities that make each person unique among all others

Insight: self-understanding; a person's awareness of the origins, nature, and dynamics of his attitudes and behavior

Instinct: a natural, inborn drive, such as self-preservation

Institution: reasonably enduring complex pattern of behavior by which social control is exerted and through which social needs can be met

Integration: effective incorporation of new experience, knowledge, and emotional capacities into the personality or into a relationship; i.e., marital integration is the unity between husband and wife that brings mutual satisfaction

Intelligence: capacity to learn and to use appropriately what one has learned

Interaction: mutual stimulation and response between persons, or between individuals and groups, or between families and other institutions in the society

Interpersonal competence: skills making for effective social interaction

Interpersonal relationship: system of interaction betwen two or more persons

Intimacy: quality of a personal relationship that satisfies desires for love, affection, understanding, appreciation, and security

Judgment: capacity to evaluate a number of alternatives in a given situation

Kinship: relationships within the larger family to which all the members belong; kinship may be traced through the father's line (patrilineal), through the mother's line (matrilineal), or through both family lines (bilineal) in "lineage tracing"

Libido: psychic drive or energy stemming from the life instinct, or the sexual drive, broadly defined

Limited divorce: legal dissolution of a marriage similar to separation with no right to remarry

Love: strong attachment, affection, or devotion to a person or object; active concern for the life and growth of the beloved

Manifest function: recognized and intended consequences of an activity (in contrast to *latent* function which is unrecognized and unintended)

Marital adjustment: relation between husband and wife on the major issues of their marriage

Marital status: condition of being single, married, widowed, or divorced

Marriage: socially sanctioned union of husband and wife with the expectation that they will assume the responsibilities and play the roles of married partners

Marriageability: readiness for marriage based on such factors as adaptability, interpersonal competence, preparation for marital roles, and maturity

Marriage cohorts: a group of persons first married in a specified calendar period

Mate selection: process of choosing and being chosen by one's future marriage partner

Maturation: coming to full growth and development

Median: a value that divides a distribution into two equal parts (the midpoint)

Mental health: having relatively good personal integration so that one can love and work and play with satisfaction; emotional health and well-being

Mental hygiene: prevention and early treatment of mental disorders

Minimum standard of living: material resources in the least amounts consistent with health and decency

Mobility: moving; changing status (upward or downward)

Modeling: process by which an individual incorporates into his behavior the perceived behavior of another with whom he identifies intentionally or unintentionally

Needs: conditions essential for healthy growth and development; wants, lacks, requirements, or demands that a person, family, or group attempts to satisfy

Norm: a patterned or commonly held behavior expectation; a learned response held in common by members of a group; i.e., ways in which a family member is expected to play one of his roles

Normality: usual, healthy, conforming to expected standards

Nuclear family: husband, wife, and their immediate children

Nurturance: ministering to the vital processes and emotional needs of another person

Obsession: persistent, unwanted impulse or idea that cannot be eliminated by reasoning

Oedipus complex: attachment of the child for the parent of the opposite sex, accompanied by aggressive and envious feelings toward the parent of the same sex

Orgasm: sexual climax that relieves physical and emotional tension

Parental responsibility: producing, rearing, and caring for one's children

Parsimony: saving rather than spending money on consumable items; the "law of parsimony" is choosing the simplest of several interpretations of a phenomenon

Personality: the whole person embodying all his physiological, psychological, and social characteristics; distinctive individual qualities of a person seen collectively; composite of inborn capacities molded and expressed through cultural conditioning

Personification: images a person holds of himself or of another person

Pleasure principle: tendency to seek gratification independent of all other considerations; striving for pleasure

Position: location in a social structure which is associated with a set of social norms; socially recognized category; the location of a family member in the family structure, i.e., husband-father, wife-mother, son-brother, daughter-sister

Positional career: longitudinal history of an individual family position composed of an ever-changing cluster of roles

Power: actions which control, initiate, change, or modify the behavior of others

Primary group: face-to-face relationships involving a high degree of intimacy and communication; e.g., the family is a primary group

Psychic states: various levels of awareness—conscious, preconscious, unconscious

Readiness: physical, emotional, and intellectual capacity to learn a particular thing at a particular time

Reality principle: tendency to do what is required in a situation rather than pursuing one's own wishes alone

Recreation: activities voluntarily engaged in during leisure primarily motivated by the pleasure they bring or the satisfaction inherent in them

Recrimination: action which nullifies the ground for divorce in most states; both partners have committed acts which would be grounds for divorce, thus nullifying the original suit

Residence rules: a society's regulations for the residence of newly married couples: the husband leaves his parental home to live with his bride's family (matrilocal); the bride leaves her parental home to live with or near her husband's family (patrilocal); the young couple live with or near either parental homes (bilocal); the newly married couple establish their own independent home (neolocal)

Resources: means available for meeting needs and wishes toward desired goals

Role: part of a social position consisting of a more or less integrated or related set of social norms which is distinguishable from other sets of norms forming the same position; i.e., father plays many roles: breadwinner, companion, disciplinarian, etc.; generally institutionalized social expectations, obligations, and rights imposed upon an individual and arising from the status accorded to him (status roles)

Role behavior: actual behavior of the occupant of a position with reference to a particular role, i.e., how father performs in the role of breadwinner

Role cluster: set of roles being played by an occupant of a position at any one time; concurrent roles of a family member

Role complex: two or more sets of role clusters

Role differentiation: differences between individuals that affect the role distribution in a family or other group

Role-making: creation and modification of existing roles

Role-playing: acting out assigned roles; living up to obligations because of one's commitments

Role reversal: swapping roles; e.g., the wife works and the husband cares for the children

Role sequence: series of roles an occupant of a position plays throughout the life cycle; longitudinal expression of roles

Role-taking: modification of one's behavior in anticipation of the responses of others; imagining how one looks from another person's viewpoint

Sanctions: institutionalized ways of constraining individuals or groups to conform to accepted norms; role behavior having reward or punishment implications

Self: way one describes his relationships with others; consciously recognized pattern of perceptions pertaining to an individual; composite of the individual's thoughts, feelings, values, and perceptions of his roles

Self-concept: who a person thinks he is; how an individual perceives himself

Self-consciousness: ability to call out in ourselves a set of definite responses which belong to the others of the group; awareness of inner reality

Self-system: part of the personality of the individual serving as an anti-anxiety system; the inner protector of the person by which he guards himself from criticism, embarrassment, and loss of self-esteem

Sentiments: complex combination of feelings and opinions as a basis for action or judgment

Separation agreement: disposition of marriage rights in which a married couple can legally separate but cannot give each other the right to remarry

Sequence of action: ordering of the parts of a task or of several tasks in management

Sequential roles: series of roles an occupant of a position (e.g., family member) plays over time

Sex education: guiding individuals of any age or status in wholesome awareness of what it means to be a male or female person, of the process of individual development and the responsible use of sexuality for personal fulfillment and social well-being; the knowledge, skills, attitudes, and values that have to do with healthy, effective relationships with persons of the same and opposite sex

Sibling rivalry: competition between brothers and sisters for their parents' love, attention, and favors

Significant others: persons of especial importance in the life of an individual

Situation content: attitudes, ideas, words, and gestures thought of as culture

Situation process: interaction of the elements of a situation; a moving picture of a situation

Situation structure: form and organization of a situation; a still life of a situation

Social act: any behavior in which the appropriate object is another person; a social act implicates at least two individuals, each of whom takes the other into account in the processes of satisfying impulses and achieving goals

Social context: complex of interpersonal relationships which help shape the personality for life

Social control: ways in which a society or group maintains its integrity, through folkways, mores, customs, sanctions, etc., either coercive or persuasive

Social functions: ways in which individuals and groups serve society's purposes and serve given ends

Social imperatives: functional prerequisites; the things that must be done in any society if it is to continue

Social interest: concern for the welfare of a group

Socialization: process by which the individual is taught the ways of a given culture, the cultural expectations related to his age, sex, and other roles, and by which he seeks to conform to those expectations

Socialized person: one who has learned to participate effectively in social groups

Social patterns: attitudes, values, and behavior ascribed by a society to its members through various roles and statuses

Social process: operation of the social life; the multitude of actions and interactions of human beings, acting as individuals or in groups

Social relations: ties by which persons and groups are bound to one another in the activities of social life

Social relationship: interaction occurring between two or more partners in a relationship

Social status: place in a particular system a given individual occupies at a given time

Social structure: division of society into social groups, based upon conventionally standardized social relations between individuals; social organization

Society: organized set of individuals in a given way of life; an aggregate of social relations; a social system which survives its original members and replaces them through biological reproduction and is relatively self-sufficient

Solidarity: mutual affection, value consensus, and interdependence of roles, as in a family

Standard: measure of quality and/or quantity which reflects reconciliation of resources with demands

Standard of living: an ideal or desired norm of consumption, usually defined in terms of quantity and quality of goods and services

Status: social position defined by society; the position a person or a group (family) maintains in society because of the way one (or it) is evaluated

Stimulus: any action or agent which causes or changes an activity in an organism or group

Symptom: specific manifestation of an unhealthy physical or mental state

Syndrome: combination of symptoms that constitutes a recognizable condition

Task behavior: interaction directed toward

the completion of group or individual tasks

Thinking: internalized manipulation of symbols by which solutions are found

Two-way communication: process of understanding each others' thoughts and feelings as well as the implications involved in such thoughts and feelings

Utility: the want-satisfying power of goods; i.e., time, place, form, or possession utility

Value: the power of one good to command other goods (or money) in exchange; that which is cherished, appreciated, and sought after

Volition: the process of selecting among alternatives symbolically present in the experiences of the individual

INDEX

(Figures in italics indicate pages on which there are charts or tables.)